CONFORMITY & CONFLICT

READINGS IN CULTURAL ANTHROPOLOGY

SEVENTH
EDITION

CONFORMITY & CONFLICT

READINGS IN CULTURAL ANTHROPOLOGY

James P. Spradley

David W. McCurdy
Macalester College

 HarperCollins*Publishers*

To Barbara Spradley and Carolyn McCurdy

Photo Credits
Cover photos: (left) © Silvester/Rapho Amazonie-Bresil/Photo Researchers.
(right) © Loren McIntyre.
2 — "Family Group" bronze by Henry Moore, 1948–49, cast 1950. The Museum of Modern Art, New York. A. Conger Goodyear Fund; 14 — Beryl Goldberg Photo; 60 — © Richard Stromberg; 118 — © Robert Frerck, Odyssey Productions, Inc.; 172 — From "China: Empire of the 700 Million" by Harry Hamm, translated by Victor Anderson. Copyright © 1966 by Harry Hamm. Reproduced by permission of Doubleday & Co., Inc.; 216 — Lawrence Manning/Black Star; 256 — Photo Researchers, Inc.; 310 — © Diane Rawson/Photo Researchers, Inc.; 358 — © Mickey Pfleger; 404 — Bernadine Bailey

Library of Congress Cataloging-in-Publication Data
Conformity and conflict : readings in cultural anthropology / edited
  by James P. Spradley, David W. McCurdy. — 7th ed.
     p. cm.
    ISBN 0-673-52073-0
    1. Ethnology. I. Spradley, James P. II. McCurdy, David W.
GN325.C69   1990
306 — dc20   89-24063
                                                                        CIP

Artwork, illustrations, and other materials supplied by the publisher. Copyright © 1990
HarperCollins*Publishers* Inc.

5 6-EBL-94 93 92

Preface

Cultural anthropology has a twofold mission: to understand other cultures and to communicate that understanding. Twenty years ago, in preparing the first edition of this book, we sought to make communication easier and more enjoyable for teachers and students alike. We focused on the twin themes stated in the title — conformity, or order, and conflict, or change — while organizing selections into sections based on traditional topics. We balanced the coverage of cultures between non-Western and Western (including American) so students could make their own cultural comparisons and see the relation between anthropology and their lives. We searched extensively for scholarly articles written with insight and clarity. Students and instructors in hundreds of colleges and universities responded enthusiastically to our efforts, and a pattern was set that carried through five subsequent editions.

This seventh edition retains the features of earlier editions: the focus on stability and change, the coverage of a broad range of societies, and the combination of professionalism and readability in the selections. As in previous editions, we have revamped topics and added or subtracted selections in response to the suggestions of instructors and students across the country. There are major revisions of the sections on culture and fieldwork, language and communication, and kinship and family. We expanded the section on ecology to include subsistence strategies, and moved it in front of the section on kinship and family, following the practice of most popular textbooks. In all, there are 14 new articles and three others brought back from earlier editions. Every section has at least one new selection.

We have also continued to expand the special features in the text. We completely rewrote section introductions in the sixth edition to include many basic anthropological terms. We continued that expansion by updating three section introductions for this new edition. We added lists of key terms and review questions after each article for the sixth edition. This edition adds a glossary, subject index, and map locations for the societies discussed in the selections. An expanded complementary instructor's manual, which offers abstracts of each selection along with true or false and multiple choice questions, is also available from the publisher.

It has always been our aim to provide a book that meets the needs of students and instructors. To help us with this goal we encourage you to send us your comments and ideas for improving *Conformity and Conflict.*

Many people have made suggestions that guided this revision of *Conformity and Conflict.* We are especially grateful to Myrdene Anderson, Joan Barber, Peter Bertocci, Fred Blake, Gerald Broce, Richard Curles, Charles Ellenbaum, Gerald Erchak, William Fisher, Juliana Flinn, Richard Glaser, Joan Greenway, Laura Klein, Patrick McKim, David Minderhout, David Murray, Michael Whiteford, Walter Zenner, and Larry Zimmerman for their advice. We would also like to thank Harriett Prentiss and Nancy Benjamin for their invaluable editorial support, and Sherri West, Susan Dege, Sherry Gauldin, Charlotte Olsen, Anna Priedhorsky, Meetal Bharat Raj, Eric Thompson, and Kristen Warrior for their help in production. Finally, we are grateful to our students at Macalester College for their advice and inspiration.

D. W. M.

Contents

prestige, and women in marriage — an economic system that broke down when the British introduced general-purpose money.

VIII *Law and Politics* 310

World Map and Geographical Placement of Readings

The numbers on this map correspond to the reading numbers and indicate the places on which the articles focus. Screened maps also accompany readings themselves, and white areas on these maps highlight the subject locations. Readings labeled as *world* on this global map do not include white areas.

18

7, 20, 23, 30, 36
United States

18

31

22,28

1, 5, 8, 15, 34
World

24

4

25

35

10

17

3

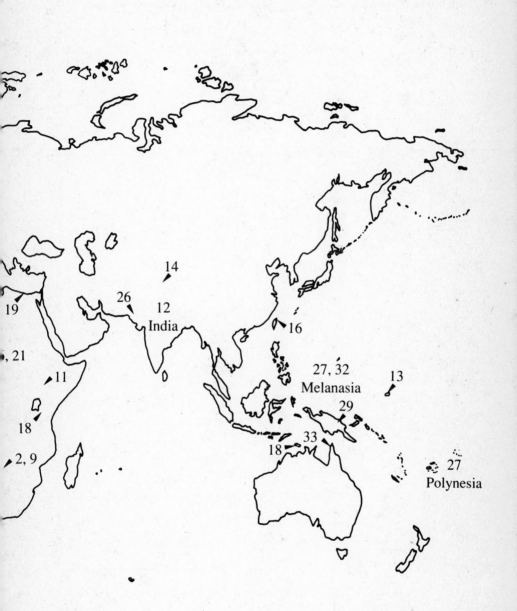

14

26

12
India

19

, 21

11

18

2, 9

16

27, 32
Melanasia

29

13

33

18

27
Polynesia

CONFORMITY & CONFLICT

READINGS IN CULTURAL
ANTHROPOLOGY

I

Culture and the Contemporary World

$\mathbf{M}$any students associate cultural anthropology with the study of primitive peoples. They picture the anthropologist as that slightly peculiar person who, dressed in khaki shorts and pith helmet, lives among some exotic tribe in order to record the group's bizarre and not altogether pleasant customs. Like most stereotypes, this one is not completely true but it does reflect anthropology's traditional interest in describing the culture of less complex societies. In the last century, when anthropology became a recognized discipline, its members collected and analyzed the growing numbers of reports on non-Western peoples by missionaries, travelers, and colonial administrators. This tradition continued into the twentieth century, although the collection of data was refined by actual fieldwork. Impressed by the variety of human behavior, anthropologists sought to record these cultures that were vanishing before the onslaught of Western civilization. Such studies continue among remote groups, and reports of this research are regularly found in professional journals.

3

During recent decades, however, anthropologists have developed wider interests. As primitive groups have been obliterated or assimilated, anthropologists have increasingly studied subcultures within more complex societies. Certainly World War II and the Cold War stimulated this trend. The United States government employed anthropologists to describe societies in whose territories we fought. The Cold War years, marked by competition with the Russians for influence in developing nations, led to studies of peasant life-styles and culture change.

Today, however, our position in the world has changed. Americans are less welcome in developing nations. Concurrently, problems in our own country have multiplied and taken the center stage of national concern. It is not surprising that anthropologists have extended their attention to subcultures within our own society.

But what can anthropology contribute to an understanding of American life? After all, other social scientists have been doing research in this country for years. Is there anything special about anthropology? In many ways the answer to this question is no. The various social sciences often share the same interests. Yet, as a result of their intensive cross-cultural experience, anthropologists have developed a unique perspective on the nature and the significance of *culture*. This view has emerged from over a century of fieldwork among populations whose behavior was dramatically different from the anthropologists' own. Why, for example, did Iroquois women participate with apparent relish in the gruesome torture of prisoners? How could Bhil tribesmen put chili powder in the eyes of witches, blindfold them, and swing them over a smoky fire by their feet? What possessed Kwakiutl chiefs to destroy their wealth publicly at potlatch ceremonies? Why did Rajput widows cast themselves upon their husbands' funeral pyres? Why did Nagas engage in raids to acquire human heads? In every case, anthropologists were impressed by the fact that this "bizarre" behavior was intentional and meaningful to the participants. Bhils wanted to swing witches; to them it was appropriate. Kwakiutl chiefs made careful investments to increase the wealth they destroyed. These acts were planned; people had a notion of what they were going to do before they did it, and others shared their expectations.

CULTURE

The acquired knowledge that people use to interpret their world and generate social behavior is called *culture*. Culture is not behavior itself, but the knowledge used to construct and understand behavior. It is learned as children grow up in society and discover how their parents, and others around them, interpret the world. In our society we learn to distinguish objects such as cars, windows, houses, children, and food; to recognize attributes like sharp, hot, beautiful, and humid; to classify and perform different kinds of acts; to evaluate what is good and bad and to judge when an unusual action is appropriate or inappropriate. How often have you heard parents explain something about life to a child? Why do you think children are forever asking why? During socialization children learn a culture, and because they learn it from others, they share it with others, a fact that makes human social existence possible.

Culture is thus the system of knowledge by which people design their own actions and interpret the behavior of others. It tells an American that eating with one's mouth closed is proper, while an Indian knows that to be polite one must chew with one's mouth open. There is nothing preordained about culture categories; they are arbitrary. The same act can have different meanings in various cultures. For example, when adolescent Hindu boys walk holding hands, it signifies friendship, while to Americans the same act may suggest homosexuality. This arbitrariness is particularly important to remember if we are to understand our own complex society. We tend to think that the norms we follow represent the "natural" way human beings do things. Those who behave otherwise are judged morally wrong. This viewpoint is *ethnocentric*, which means that people think their own culture represents the best, or at least the most appropriate, way for human beings to live.

Although in our complex society we share many cultural norms with everyone, each of us belongs to a number of groups possessing exclusive cultural knowledge. We share some categories and plans with family members alone. And our occupational group, ethnic group, voluntary society, and age group each has its distinctive culture. Instead of assuming that another's behavior is reasonable to him, that it is motivated by a different set of cultural norms, we frequently assume that he has intentionally violated accepted conventions. In their attempt to build bridges of understanding across cultural barriers, anthropologists identified the universality of ethnocentrism many years ago. The study of subcultures in our own society is another attempt to further mutual understanding, as some of the selections in this volume indicate.

How do anthropologists discover and map another culture? Are their methods applicable in the United States? Typically, anthropologists live among the people of the society that interests them. They learn the culture by observing, asking questions, and participating in daily activities — a process resembling childhood socialization or enculturation. Obviously, the anthroplogist cannot become a child, and must try to learn the norms in a strange group despite his or her foreign appearance and advanced age. Those who study in the United States have followed a similar procedure.

More than anything else, the study of culture separates anthropologists from other social scientists. Other scholars do not ignore culture; they assume their subjects have it, but their main interest is to account for human behavior by plotting correlations among variables. Some social scientists have explained the rise in the American divorce rate as a function of industrialization; this hypothesis can be tested by seeing if higher divorce rates are associated with industrialization and mobility. Anthropologists share a concern for this kind of explanation; for example, many have employed the Human Relations Area Files, a collection of ethnographies describing several hundred societies, as data for testing more general hypotheses. Almost every anthropologist starts with an *ethnography*, the description of a particular culture, and such studies are required to understand the complexity within American society.

As anthropologists have encountered, studied, and compared the world's societies, they have learned more about the concept of culture itself. As we have seen, culture is the knowledge people use to generate behavior, not behavior itself; it is arbitrary, learned, and shared. In addition, culture is adaptive. Human beings cope with their natural and social environment by means of their traditional knowledge. Culture allows for rapid adaptation because it is flexible and permits the invention of new strategies — although change often appears to be painfully slow to those who are in a hurry for it. By the same token, the adaptive nature of culture accounts for the enormous variety of the world's distinct societies.

Culture is a system of interrelated parts. If Americans were to give up automobiles, then other modes of travel, places for courtship, marks of status, and sources of income would have to be found. Culture meets personal needs; through it, people seek security and a sense of control over experience. Indeed, every tradition includes ways to cure the sick, to prepare for the unexpected, and to support the individual. In a complex society with many ways of life in contact with each other, change is persistent. It may be illusion to think that people can control the course of change, or can modify the resulting culture conflict. But if we can understand human cultures — including our own — the illusion may become reality.

CULTURE AND VALUES

It is easy for people to feel that their own way of life is natural and God-given. One's culture is not like a suit of clothing that can be discarded easily or exchanged for each new life-style that comes along. It is rather like a security blanket, and though to some it may appear worn and tattered, outmoded and ridiculous, it has great meaning to its owner. Although there are many reasons for this fact, one of the most important is the value-laden nature of what we learn as members of society. Whether it is acquired in a tribal band, a peasant village, or an urban neighborhood, each culture is like a giant iceberg. Beneath the surface of rules, norms, and behavior patterns there is a system of values. Some of these premises are easily stated by members of a society, while others are outside their awareness. Because many difficulties in the modern world involve values, we must examine this concept in some detail.

A value is an arbitrary conception of what is *desirable* in human experience. During socialization all children are exposed to a constant barrage of evaluations — the arbitrary "rating system" of their culture. Nearly everything they learn is labeled in terms of its desirability. The value attached to each bit of information may result from the pain of a hot stove, the look of disapproval from a parent, the smile of appreciation from a teacher, or some specific verbal instruction. When parents tell a child, "You should go to college and get a good education," they are expressing a value. Those who do not conform to society's rating system are identified with derogatory labels or are punished in a more severe way. When a Tlingit Indian says to his nephew, "You should marry your father's sister," he is expressing one of the core values of his culture. When a young couple saves income for future emergencies, they are conforming to the American value that the future is more important than the present. When a tramp urinates in an alley, he is violating the value attached to privacy. All these concepts of what is desirable combine cognitive and affective meanings. Individuals internalize their ideas about right and wrong, good and bad, and invest them with strong feelings.

Why do values constitute an inevitable part of all human experience? That human potential is at odds with the requirements of social life is well known. Behavior within the realm of possibility is often outside the realm of necessity. There are numerous ways to resolve the conflict between what people *can do* by themselves, and what they *must do* as members of society. It is a popular notion that prisons and other correctional institutions are the primary means by which our society enforces conformity, but this is not the case. Socialization may be ineffective for a few who require such drastic action, but for the vast majority in any society, conformity results from the internalization of values. As we learn through imitation, identification, and instruction, values are internalized. They provide security and contribute to a sense of personal and social identity. For this reason, individuals in every society cling tenaciously to the values they have acquired and feel threatened when confronted with others who live according to different conceptions of what is desirable.

CULTURAL RELATIVISM

A misconception about values has been spawned by science and, in particular, by the anthropological doctrine of cultural relativism. Some have maintained that it is possible to separate values from facts, and since science is limited to facts, it is possible to do "value-free" research. By an exercise in mental gymnastics, the very scholars who admit the influence of values in the behavior of others sometimes deny it for themselves. Preferences operate whenever an individual must *select* one action from a multitude of possible courses. Anyone who decides to observe one thing and not another is making that decision on the basis of an implicit or explicit conception of desirability. Science is an activity that makes many value judgments — including which approaches to information gathering are the best. When biologists decide to examine the structure of the DNA molecule using an empirical approach, rather than a mystical, intuitive, or religious one, they are doing so with reference to their sense of what is desirable. Even the decision to study DNA rather than some other substance involves an exercise of values. When doing research on human behavior, the influence of one's values is undeniable. The "objective observer" who is detached from the subject matter, who refrains from allowing values to influence observations, is a myth. This fact does not suggest a retreat from the *quest for objectivity*. It does not mean that social scientists are free to disparage the customs encountered in other societies, or to impose their morals on those being studied. Skilled anthropologists are aware of their own values and then approach other cultures with tolerance and respect. They *identify* rather than *deny* the influence of their own viewpoints. They strive to achieve the ideal of value-free research but realize that it would be naive to assume such a goal possible.

Cultural relativism rests on the premise that it is possible to remain aloof and free from making value judgments. Put simply, this doctrine is based on four interrelated propositions.

1. Each person's value system is a result of his or her experience, that is, it is learned.

2. The values that individuals learn differ from one society to another because of different learning experiences.

3. Values, therefore, are relative to the society in which they occur.

4. There are no universal values, but we should respect the values of each of the world's cultures.

Cultural relativism has enabled the uninformed to understand what appears to be strange and immoral behavior. Although we may not believe it is good to kill infants, for example, we have found it intelligible in the context of a native Australian band. Although Americans generally believe in the desirability of monogamous marriage (or at least serial monogamy), we have found the practice of polygamy in other societies to be comprehensible when related to their cultures. This view presents numerous difficulties. Does one respect a society that believes it best to murder six million of its members who happen to be Jewish? How do anthropologists respect the values of a head-hunting tribe when their own heads are at stake?

Moreover, all the statements in this doctrine of relativism are either based on implicit values (that is, empiricism), or they are outright statements of desirability. The belief that it is good to *respect* the ideals of each of the world's cultures is itself a "relative" value. An extreme relativism is based on the philosophy that it is best to "let everyone do his or her own thing." Given unlimited resources and space this might have been possible, but in the modern world this philosophy represents a retreat from the realities facing us. It absolves the believer from the responsibility of finding some way to resolve conflicts among the world's different value systems. What is needed today is not a "live and let live" policy but a commitment to a higher, more inclusive value system, and this requires changes that are extremely difficult to achieve.

CONFORMITY AND CONFLICT

Every social system is a moral order; shared values act as the mortar binding together the structure of each human community. Rewards and punishments are based on commonly held values; those persons achieving high status do so in terms of cultural rating systems. These values are expressed in symbolic ways — through food, clothing, wealth, language, behavior—all of which carry implicit messages about good and bad. The pervasiveness of values gives each person a sense of belonging, a sense of being a member of a community, the feeling of joining other human beings who share a commitment to the good life. But the moral nature of every culture has two sides—it facilitates adaptation and survival on the one hand, but it often generates conflict and destruction on the other. Let us examine each of these possibilities.

For almost a million years, people have successfully adapted to a variety of terrestrial environments. From the frozen tundra to the steaming jungle, people have built their homes, reared their children, performed their rituals, and buried their dead. In recent years we have escaped the thin layer of atmosphere surrounding the earth to live, if only for a few days, in outer space and beneath the ocean. All these achievements have been possible because of a unique endowment, our capacity for culture. Wherever people wandered, they developed patterns for organizing behavior, using natural resources, relating to others, and creating a meaningful life. A genetic inheritance did not channel behavior into specialized responses but instead provided a reservoir of plasticity that was shaped by values into one of the many ways to be human. Children in every society do not learn the entire range of potential human behavior—they are taught to *conform* to a very limited number of behavior patterns that are appropriate to a particular society. Human survival depends on cultural conformity, which requires that every individual become a specialist, be committed to a few values, and acquire knowledge and skills of a single society.

This very specialization has led to diversity, resulting in a myriad of contrasting cultures. This volume contains only a small sample of the different symbolic worlds created by people in their attempt to cope with the common problems of human existence. We will see how the generosity of the American Christmas spirit stands in contrast to the daily sharing among the !Kung. Chicago suburbanites and natives of the Brazilian jungle both adorn their bodies with paint, clothing, and rings, but neither can comprehend how the other defines these symbols. All elements of human experience—kinship, marriage, age, race, sexuality, food, warfare—are socially defined and valued. The difficulty of moving from one cultural world to another is immense.

Cultural diversity has fascinated people for centuries. The study of strange and exotic peoples has attracted the curious for many generations. In the isolation of a remote jungle village or South Sea island, anthropologists found a natural laboratory for carrying out research. Their research reports often seemed more like novels than scientific studies and were read by both professionals and laymen;

seldom did any reader feel threatened by the strange behavior of far-off "savages."

But isolation rapidly disappeared, sometimes by virtue of the anthropologists' intrusion! Exploration gave way to colonization, trade, and the massive troop movements of modern warfare. Today it is impossible to find groups of people who are isolated from the remainder of the world. Instead we have a conglomeration of cultures within a single nation, and often within a single city. Anthropologists need only walk down the street from the university to encounter those who have learned a culture unlike their own. Individuals with different language styles, sexual practices, religious rituals, and a host of other strange behavior patterns sit in their classrooms or play with their children on the urban playgrounds. Anthropology today is a science concerned with understanding how people can survive in a world where village, hamlet, city, and nation are all *multicultural*. In isolation, each value system is interesting. Crowded into close and intimate contact, these distinct culture patterns often lead to conflict, oppression, and warfare. Barbara Ward has eloquently summed up our situation:

> In the last few decades, mankind has been overcome by the most change in its entire history. Modern science and technology have created so close a network of communication, transport, economic interdependence — and potential nuclear destruction — that planet Earth, on its journey through infinity, has acquired the intimacy, the fellowship and the vulnerability of a spaceship.[1]

In a sense, our greatest resource for adapting to different environments — the capacity to create different cultures — has become the source of greatest danger. Diversity is required for survival in the ecological niches of earth, but it can be destructive when all people suddenly find themselves in the same niche. Numerous species have become extinct because of their inability to adapt to a changing *natural* environment. Culture was the survival kit that enabled us to meet fluctuating natural conditions with flexibility, but now we are faced with a radically altered *human* environment. Successful adaptation will require changes that fly in the face of thousands of years of cultural specialization. Our ingenuity has been used to develop unique cultures,

---

[1] Barbara Ward, *Spaceship Earth* (New York: Columbia University Press, 1966), vii.

but thus far we have failed to develop satisfactory patterns and rules for articulating these differences. Can we survive in a world where our neighbors and even our children have different cultures? Can we adapt to the close, intimate fellowship of a spaceship when each group of passengers lives by different values?

TOWARD A MULTICULTURAL SOCIETY

What is required? In the first place, instead of suppressing cultural diversity by stressing assimilation into the mainstream of American life, we must recognize the extent to which our culture is pluralistic. We must accept the fact that groups within our society are committed to disparate and sometimes conflicting values. The second requirement for a truly multicultural society is that we continuously examine the *consequences* of each value system. What is the long-range effect of our commitment to a "gospel of growth"? What are the results of a belief in male superiority? How do our values of privacy affect those without homes? What is the consequence for minority groups when all students are taught to use "standard English"? As we study American culture we must discover the effect of our dominant values on every sector of life. The ideals that have made this country what it is have also been destructive to some citizens. In our efforts to assimilate ethnic groups, we have destroyed their pride and self-identity. In our attempt to offer the advantages of education to American Indians, we have induced them to become failures because our schools are not able to educate for diversity. In order to demonstrate the tolerance built into American values, we have created the "culturally deprived," but the sophistication of labels does not conceal our prejudice. The absence of men in the families of the urban poor is a logical consequence of welfare institutions created from a single value system. The consumer suffers from dangerous products because in our culture productive enterprise is more important than consumer protection. We have only begun to understand some of the consequences of our values, and during the next few decades our survival will demand that the study of values be given top priority.

Finally, the most difficult task for the contemporary world is to induce people to relinquish those values with destructive consequences. This will not be simple, and it probably will not occur without a better understanding of the nature and the function of the world's many value systems. People's capacity to learn has not yet reached its full potential. In every society, children learn to shift from *egocentric* behavior to *ethnocentric* behavior. In deference to desirable community standards, individuals give up those things they desire, and life in a particular society becomes secure and meaningful, with conventional values acting as warp and woof of social interaction.

Can we now learn to shift from *ethnocentric* to *homocentric* behavior? Can we relinquish values desirable from the standpoint of a single community but destructive to the wider world? This change will require a system of ideals greater than the conventions of any localized culture. The change will necessitate a morality that can articulate conflicting value systems and create a climate of tolerance, respect, and cooperation. Only then can we begin to create a culture that will be truly adaptive in today's world.

II

IN
SHICA

Culture and Ethnography

Culture, as its name suggests, lies at the heart of cultural anthropology. And the concept of culture, along with ethnography, sets anthropology apart from other social and behavioral sciences. Let us look more closely at these concepts.

To understand what anthropologists mean by culture, imagine yourself in a foreign setting, such as a market town in India, forgetting what you might already know about that country. You step off a bus onto a dusty street where you are immediately confronted by strange sights, sounds, and smells. Men dress in Western clothes, but of a different style. Women drape themselves in long shawls that entirely cover their bodies. They peer at you through a small gap in this garment as they walk by. Buildings are one- or two-story affairs, open at the front so you can see inside. Near you some people sit on wicker chairs eating strange foods. Most unusual is how people talk. They utter vocalizations unlike any you have ever heard, and you wonder how they can possibly understand each other. But obviously they do since their behavior seems organized and purposeful.

Scenes such as this confronted early explorers, missionaries, and anthropologists, and from their observations an obvious point emerged. People living in various parts of the world looked and behaved in dramatically different ways. And these differences correlated with groups. The people of India had customs different from those of the Papuans; the British did not act and dress like the Iroquois.

Two possible explanations for group differences came to mind. Some argued that group behavior was inherited. Dahomeans of the African Gold Coast, for example, were characterized as particularly "clever and adaptive" by one British colonial official, while, according to the same authority, another African group was "happy-go-lucky and improvident." Usually implied in such statements was the idea that group members were born that way. Such thinking persists to the present and in its least discriminating guise takes the form of racism.

But a second explanation also emerged. Perhaps, rather than a product of inheritance, the behavior characteristic of a group was learned. The way people dressed, what they ate, how they talked — all these could more easily be explained as acquisitions. Thus, a baby born on the African Gold Coast would, if immediately transported to China and raised like other children there, grow up to dress, eat, and talk like a Chinese. Cultural anthropologists focus on the explanation of learned behavior.

The idea of learning, and a need to label the life-styles associated with particular groups, led to the definition of culture. In 1871, British anthropologist Sir Edward Burnet Tylor argued that "Culture . . . is that complex whole which includes knowledge, belief, art, law, morals, custom, and any other capabilities and habits acquired by man as a member of society."[1]

The definition we present here places more emphasis on the importance of knowledge than does Tylor's. We will say that *culture is the acquired knowledge that people use to generate behavior and interpret experience.*

Important to this definition is the idea that culture is a kind of knowledge, not behavior. It is in people's heads. It reflects the mental categories they learn from others as they grow up. It helps them *generate* behavior and *interpret* what they experience. At the moment of birth, we lack a culture. We don't yet have a system of beliefs, knowledge, and patterns of customary behavior. But from that moment until we die, each of us participates in a kind of universal schooling that teaches us our native culture. Laughing and smiling are genetic responses, but as infants we soon learn when to smile, when to laugh, and even how to laugh. We also inherit the potential to cry, but we must learn our cultural rules for when it is appropriate.

As we learn our culture, we acquire a way to interpret experience. For example, we Americans learn that dogs are like little people in furry suits. Dogs live in our houses, eat our food, share our beds. They hold a place in our hearts; their loss causes us to grieve. Villagers in India, on the other hand, view dogs as pests that admittedly are useful for hunting in those few parts of the country where one still can hunt, and as watchdogs. Quiet days in Indian villages are often punc-

---

[1] Edward Burnet Tylor, *Primitive Culture* (New York: Harper Torchbooks, Harper and Row, 1958; originally published by John Murray, London, 1871), 1.

tuated by the yelp of a dog that has been threatened or actually hurt by its master or a bystander.

Clearly, it is not the dogs that are different in these two societies. Rather, it is the meaning that dogs have for people that varies. And such meaning is cultural; it is learned as part of growing up in each group.

Ethnography is the process of discovering and describing a particular culture. It involves anthropologists in an intimate and personal activity as they attempt to learn how the members of a particular group see their worlds.

But which groups qualify as culture-bearing units? How does the anthropologist identify the existence of a culture to study? This was not a difficult question when anthropology was a new science. As Tylor's definition notes, culture was the whole way of life of a people. To find it, one sought out distinctive ethnic units, such as Bhil tribals in India or Apaches in the American Southwest. Anything one learned from such people would be part of their culture.

But discrete cultures of this sort are becoming more difficult to find. The world is increasingly divided into large national societies, each subdivided into a myriad of subgroups. Anthropologists are finding it increasingly attractive to study such subgroups, because they form the arena for most of life in complex society. And this is where the concept of the microculture enters the scene.

Microcultures are systems of cultural knowledge characteristic of subgroups within larger societies. Members of a microculture will usually share much of what they know with everyone in the greater society, but will possess a special cultural knowledge that is unique to the subgroup. For example, a college fraternity has a microculture within the context of a university and nation. Its members have special daily routines, jokes, and meanings for events. It is this shared knowledge that makes up their microculture and that can serve as the basis for ethnographic study. More and more, anthropologists are turning to the study of microcultures, using the same ethnographic techniques they employ when they investigate the broader culture of an ethnic or national group.

More than anything else, it is ethnography that is anthropology's unique contribution to social science. Most scientists, including many who view people in social context, approach their research as *detached observers*. As social scientists, they observe the human subjects of their study, categorize what they see, and generate theory to account for their findings. They work from the outside, creating a system of knowledge to account for other people's behavior. Although this is a legitimate and often useful way to conduct research, it is not the main task of ethnography.

Ethnographers seek out the insider's viewpoint. Because culture is the knowledge people use to generate behavior and interpret experience, the ethnographer seeks to understand group members' behavior from the inside, or cultural, perspective. Instead of looking for a *subject* to observe, ethnographers look for an *informant* to teach them the culture. Just as a child learns its native culture from parents and other people in its social environment, the ethnographer learns another culture by inferring folk categories from the observation of behavior and by asking informants what things mean.

Anthropologists employ many strategies during field research to understand another culture better. But all strategies and all research ultimately rest on the cooperation of *informants*. An informant is neither a subject in a scientific experiment nor a respondent who answers the investigator's questions. An informant is a teacher who has a special kind of pupil — a professional anthropologist. In this unique relationship a transformation occurs in the anthropologist's understanding of an alien culture. It is the informant who transforms the anthropologist from a tourist into an ethnographer. The informant may be a child who explains how to play hopscotch, a cocktail waitress who teaches the anthropologist to serve drinks and to encourage customers to leave tips, an elderly man who teaches the anthropologist to build an igloo, or a grandmother who explains the intricacies of Zapotec kinship. Almost any individual who has acquired a repertoire of cultural behavior can become an informant.

Ethnography is not as easy to do as we might think. For one thing, Americans are not taught to be good listeners. We prefer to observe and draw our own conclusions. We like a sense of control in social contexts; passive listening is a sign of weakness in our culture. But listening and learning from others is at the heart of ethnography, and we must put aside our discomfort with the student role.

It is also not easy for informants to teach us about their cultures. Culture is often *tacit*; it is so regular and routine that it lies below a conscious level. A major ethnographic task is to help informants remember their culture, to make their knowledge part of their *explicit culture*.

But, in some cases, it is necessary to infer cultural knowledge by observing an informant's behavior because the cultural rules governing it cannot be expressed in language. Speaking distances, which vary from one culture to the next, and language sound categories, called phonemes, are good examples of this kind of tacit culture.

Naive realism may also impede ethnography. *Naive realism* is the belief that people everywhere see the world in the same way. It may, for example, lead the unwary ethnographer to assume that beauty is the same for all people everywhere, or, to use our previous example, dogs should mean the same thing in India as they do in the United States. If an ethnographer fails to control his or her own naive realism, inside cultural meanings will surely be overlooked.

Culture shock and ethnocentrism may also stand in the way of ethnographers. *Culture shock* is a state of anxiety that results from cross-cultural misunderstanding. Immersed alone in another society, the ethnographer understands few of the culturally defined rules for behavior and interpretation used by his or her hosts. The result is anxiety about proper action and an inability to interact appropriately in the new context.

Ethnocentrism can be just as much of a liability. *Ethnocentrism* is the belief and feeling that one's own culture is best. It reflects our tendency to judge other people's beliefs and behavior using values of our own native culture. Thus, if we come from a society that abhors painful treatment of animals, we are likely to react with anger when an Indian villager hits a dog with a rock. Our feeling is ethnocentric.

It is impossible to rid ourselves entirely of the cultural values that make us ethnocentric when we do ethnography. But it is important to control our ethnocentric feeling in the field if we are to learn from informants. Informants resent negative judgment.

Finally, the role assigned to ethnographers by informants affects the quality of what can be learned. Ethnography is a personal enterprise, as all the articles in this section illustrate. Unlike survey research using questionnaires or short interviews, ethnography requires prolonged social contact. Informants will assign the ethnographer some kind of role and what that turns out to be will affect research.

The selections in Part II illustrate several points about culture and ethnography discussed in the preceding section. The first piece, written by James Spradley, takes a close look at the concept of culture and its role in ethnographic research. The second, by Richard Lee, illustrates how a simple act of giving can have dramatically different cultural meaning in two societies, leading to cross-cultural misunderstanding. Elizabeth Eames's article illustrates the importance of understanding cross-cultural difference in order to do fieldwork at all: she had to learn a special set of cultural rules before she could receive necessary authorizations from the Nigerian government to conduct research. Finally, the fourth article, by Mary Ellen Conaway, shows the intimate and personal nature of ethnography: although the anthropologist may believe she can remain neutral and objective, informants may apply their own cultural meanings to her presence and activity.

KEY TERMS

culture	subject
ethnography	respondent
microculture	naive realism
tacit culture	enthnocentrism
explicit culture	culture shock
informant	detached observer

Readings in this Section

1   Ethnography and Culture

JAMES P. SPRADLEY

Most Americans associate science with detached observation; we learn to observe whatever we wish to understand, introduce our own classification of what is going on, and explain what we see in our own terms. In this selection, James Spradley argues that cultural anthropologists work differently. Ethnography is the work of discovering and describing a particular culture; culture is the learned, shared knowledge that people use to generate behavior and interpret experience. To get at culture, ethnographers must learn the meanings of action and experience from the insider's or informant's point of view. Many of the examples used by Spradley also show the relevance of anthropology to the study of culture in this country.

Ethnographic fieldwork is the hallmark of cultural anthropology. Whether in a jungle village in Peru or on the streets of New York, the anthropologist goes to where people live and "does fieldwork." This means participating in activities, asking questions, eating strange foods, learning a new language, watching ceremonies, taking field-notes, washing clothes, writing letters home, tracing out genealogies, observing play, interviewing informants, and hundreds of other things.

This vast range of activities often obscures the nature of the most fundamental task of all fieldwork — doing ethnography.

Ethnography is the work of describing a culture. The central aim of ethnography is to understand another way of life from the native point of view. The goal of ethnography, as Malinowski put it, is "to grasp the native's point of view, his relation to life, to realize *his* vision of *his* world."[1] Fieldwork, then, involves the disciplined study of what the world is like to people who have learned to see, hear, speak, think, and act in ways that are different. Rather than *studying people*, ethnography means *learning from people*. Consider the following illustration.

George Hicks set out, in 1965, to learn about another way of life, that of the mountain people in an Appalachian valley.[2] His goal was to discover their culture, to learn to see the world from their perspective. With his family he moved into Little Laurel Valley, his daughter attended the local school, and his wife became one of the local Girl Scout leaders. Hicks soon discovered that stores and storekeepers were at the center of the valley's communication system, providing the most important social arena for the entire valley. He learned this by watching what other people did, by following their example, and slowly becoming part of the groups that congregated daily in the stores. He writes:

> At least once each day I would visit several stores in the valley, and sit in on the groups of gossiping men or, if the storekeeper happened to be alone, perhaps attempt to clear up puzzling points about kinship obligations. I found these hours, particularly those spent in the presence of the two or three excellent storytellers in the Little Laurel, thoroughly enjoyable. . . . At other times, I helped a number of local men gather corn or hay, build sheds, cut trees, pull and pack galax, and search for rich stands of huckleberries. When I needed aid in, for example, repairing frozen water pipes, it was readily and cheerfully provided.[3]

In order to discover the hidden principles of another way of life, the researcher must become a *student*. Storekeepers and storytellers and local farmers become *teachers*. Instead of studying the "climate," the "flora," and the "fauna" that made up the environment of this Appalachian valley, Hicks tried to discover how these mountain people defined and evaluated trees and galax and huckleberries. He did not attempt to describe social life in terms of what most Americans know about "marriage," "family," and "friendship"; instead he sought to

---

[1] Bronislaw Malinowski, *Argonauts of the Western Pacific* (London: Routledge, 1922), 22.

[2] George Hicks, *Appalachian Valley* (New York: Holt, Rinehart, and Winston, 1976).

[3] Hicks, 3.

discover how these mountain people identified relatives and friends. He tried to learn the obligations they felt toward kinsmen and discover how they felt about friends. Discovering the *insider's view* is a different species of knowledge from one that rests mainly on the outsider's view, even when the outsider is a trained social scientist.

Consider another example, this time from the perspective of a non-Western ethnographer. Imagine an Eskimo woman setting out to learn the culture of Macalester College. What would she, so well schooled in the rich heritage of Eskimo culture, have to do in order to understand the culture of Macalester College students, faculty, and staff? How would she discover the patterns that made up their lives? How would she avoid imposing Eskimo ideas, categories, and values on everything she saw?

First, and perhaps most difficult, she would have to set aside her belief in *naive realism*, the almost universal belief that all people define the *real* world of objects, events, and living creatures in pretty much the same way. Human languages may differ from one society to the next, but behind the strange words and sentences, all people are talking about the same things. The naive realist assumes that love, snow, marriage, worship, animals, death, food, and hundreds of other things have essentially the same meaning to all human beings. Although few of us would admit to such ethnocentrism, the assumption may unconsciously influence our research. Ethnography starts with a conscious attitude of almost complete ignorance. "I don't know how the people at Macalester College understand their world. That remains to be discovered."

This Eskimo woman would have to begin by learning the language spoken by students, faculty, and staff. She could stroll the campus paths, sit in classes, and attend special events, but only if she consciously tried to see things from the native point of view would she grasp their perspective. She would need to observe and listen to first-year students during their week-long orientation program. She would have to stand in line during registration, listen to students discuss the classes they hoped to get, and visit departments to watch faculty advising students on course selection. She would want to observe secretaries typing, janitors sweeping, and maintenance personnel plowing snow from walks. She would watch the more than 1600 students crowd into the post office area to open their tiny mailboxes, and she would listen to their comments about junk mail and letters from home and no mail at all. She would attend faculty meetings to watch what went on, recording what professors and administrators said and how they behaved. She would sample various courses, attend "keggers" on weekends, read the *Mac Weekly*, and listen by the hour to students discussing things like their "relationships," the "football team," and "work study." She would want to learn the *meanings* of all these things. She would have to listen to the members of this college community, watch what they did, and participate in their activities to learn such meanings.

The essential core of ethnography is this concern with the meaning of actions and events to the people we seek to understand. Some of these meanings are directly expressed in language; many are taken for granted and communicated only indirectly through word and action. But in every society people make constant use of these complex meaning systems to organize their behavior, to understand themselves and others, and to make sense out of the world in which they live. These systems of meaning constitute their culture; ethnography always implies a theory of culture.

CULTURE

When ethnographers study other cultures, they must deal with three fundamental aspects of human experience: what people do, what people know, and the things people make and use. When each of these is learned and shared by members of some group, we speak of them as *cultural behavior, cultural knowledge*, and *cultural artifacts*. Whenever you do ethnographic fieldwork, you will want to distinguish among these three, although in most situations they are usually mixed together. Let's try to unravel them.

Recently I took a commuter train from a western suburb to downtown Chicago. It was late in the day, and when I boarded the train only a handful of people were scattered about the car. Each was engaged in a common form of *cultural behavior: reading*. Across the aisle a man held the *Chicago Tribune* out in front of him, looking intently at the small print and every now and then turning the pages noisily. In front of him a young woman held a paperback book about twelve inches from her face. I could see her head shift slightly as her eyes moved from the bottom of one page to the top of the next. Near the front of the car a student was reading a large textbook and using a pen to underline words and sentences. Directly in front of me I noticed a man looking at the ticket he had purchased and reading it. It took me an instant to survey this scene and then I settled back, looked out the window, and read a billboard advertisement for a plumbing service proclaiming it would open any plugged drains. All of us were engaged in the same kind of cultural behavior: reading.

This common activity depended on a great many *cultural artifacts*, the things people shape or make from natural resources. I could see artifacts like books and tickets and newspapers and billboards, all of which contained tiny black marks arranged into intricate patterns called "letters." And these tiny artifacts were arranged into larger patterns of words, sentences, and paragraphs. Those of us on that commuter train could read, in part, because of still other artifacts: the bark of trees made into paper; steel made into printing presses; dyes of various colors made into ink; glue used to hold book pages together; large wooden frames to hold billboards. If an ethnographer wanted to understand the full cultural meaning in our society, it would involve a careful study of these and many other cultural artifacts.

Although we can easily see behavior and artifacts, they represent only the thin surface of a deep lake. Beneath the surface, hidden from view, lies a vast reservoir of *cultural knowledge*. Think for a moment what the people on that train needed to know in order to read. First, they had to know the grammatical rules for at least one language. Then they had to learn what the little marks on paper represented. They also had to know the meaning of space and lines and pages. They had learned cultural rules like "move your eyes from left to right, from the top of the page to the bottom." They had to know that a sentence at the bottom of a page continues on the top of the next page. The man reading a newspaper had to know a great deal about columns and the spaces between columns and what headlines mean. All of us needed to know what kinds of messages were intended by whoever wrote what we read. If a person cannot distinguish the importance of a message on a billboard from one that comes in a letter from a spouse or child, problems would develop. I knew how to recognize when other people were reading. We all knew it was impolite to read aloud on a train. We all knew how to feel when reading things like jokes or calamitous news in the paper. Our culture has a large body of shared knowledge that people learn and use to engage in this behavior called *reading* and make proper use of the artifacts connected with it.

Although cultural knowledge is hidden from view, it is of fundamental importance because we all use it constantly to generate behavior and interpret our experience. Cultural knowledge is so important that I will frequently use the broader term *culture* when speaking about it. Indeed, I will define culture as *the acquired knowledge people use to interpret experience and generate behavior*. Let's consider another example to see how people use their culture to interpret experience and do things.

One afternoon in 1973 I came across the following news item in the *Minneapolis Tribune*:

CROWD MISTAKES RESCUE ATTEMPT, ATTACKS POLICE

Nov. 23, 1973. Hartford, Connecticut. Three policemen giving a heart massage and oxygen to a heart attack victim Friday were attacked by a crowd of 75 to 100 persons who apparently did not realize what the policemen were doing.

Other policemen fended off the crowd of mostly Spanish-speaking residents until an ambulance arrived. Police said they tried to explain to the crowd what they were doing, but the crowd apparently thought they were beating the woman.

Despite the policemen's efforts the victim, Evangelica Echevacria, 59, died.

Here we see people using their culture. Members of two different groups observed the same event, but their *interpretations* were drastically different. The crowd used their cultural knowledge (a) to interpret the behavior of the policemen as cruel and (b) to act on the woman's behalf to put a stop to what they perceived as brutality. They had acquired the cultural principles for acting and interpreting things in this way through a particular shared experience.

The policemen, on the other hand, used their cultural knowledge (a) to interpret the woman's condition as heart failure and their own behavior as a life-saving effort and (b) to give her cardiac massage and oxygen. They used artifacts like an oxygen mask and an ambulance. Furthermore, they interpreted the actions of the crowd in an entirely different manner from how the crowd saw their own behavior. The two groups of people each had elaborate cultural rules for interpreting their experience and for acting in emergency situations, and the conflict arose, at least in part, because these cultural rules were so different.

We can now diagram this definition of culture and see more clearly the relationships among knowledge, behavior, and artifacts (Figure 1). By identifying cultural knowledge as fundamental, we have merely shifted the emphasis from behavior and artifacts to their *meaning*. The ethnographer observes behavior but goes beyond it to inquire about the meaning of that behavior. The ethnographer sees artifacts and natural objects but goes beyond them to discover what meanings people assign to these objects. The ethnographer observes and records emotional states but goes beyond them to discover the meaning of fear, anxiety, anger, and other feelings.

As represented in Figure 1, cultural knowledge exists at two levels of consciousness. *Explicit culture* makes up part of what we know, a level of knowledge people can communicate about with relative ease. When George Hicks asked storekeepers and others in Little Laurel Valley about their relatives, he discovered that any adult over fifty could tell him the genealogical connections among large numbers of people. They knew how to trace kin relationships and the cultural rules for appropriate behavior among kins. All of us have acquired large areas of cultural knowledge such as this which we can talk about and make explicit.

At the same time, a large portion of our cultural knowledge remains *tacit*, outside our awareness. Edward Hall has done much to

FIGURE I
The Two Levels of Cultural Knowledge

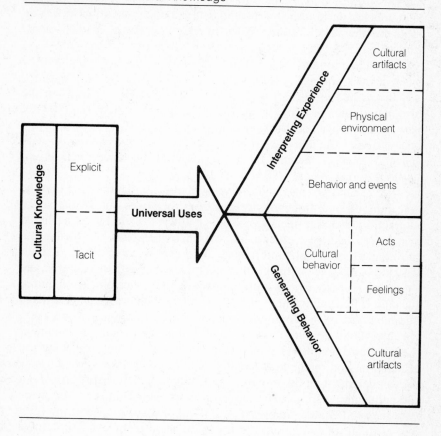

elucidate the nature of tacit cultural knowledge in his books *The Silent Language* and *The Hidden Dimension*.[4] The way each culture defines space often occurs at the level of tacit knowledge. Hall points out that all of us have acquired thousands of spatial cues about how close to stand to others, how to arrange furniture, when to touch others, and when to feel cramped inside a room. Without realizing that our tacit culture is operating, we begin to feel uneasy when someone from another culture stands too close, breathes on us when talking, touches us, or when we find furniture arranged in the center of the room rather than around the edges. Ethnography is the study of both explicit and tacit cultural knowledge; the research strategies discussed in this book are designed to reveal both levels.

---

[4] Edward T. Hall, *The Silent Language* (Garden City, NY: Doubleday, 1959); *The Hidden Dimension* (Garden City, NY: Doubleday, 1966).

The concept of culture as acquired knowledge has much in common with symbolic interactionism, a theory that seeks to explain human behavior in terms of meanings. Symbolic interactionism has its roots in the work of sociologists like Cooley, Mead, and Thomas. Blumer has identified three premises on which this theory rests.

The first premise is that "human beings act toward things on the basis of the meanings that the things have for them."[5] The policemen and the crowd in our earlier example interacted on the basis of the meanings things had for them. The geographic location, the types of people, the police car, the policemen's movements, the sick woman's behavior, and the activities of the onlookers — all were *symbols* with special meanings. People did not act toward the things themselves, but to their meanings.

The second premise underlying symbolic interactionism is that the "meaning of such things is derived from, or arises out of, the social interaction that one has with one's fellows."[6] Culture, as a shared system of meanings, is learned, revised, maintained, and defined in the context of people interacting. The crowd came to share their definitions of police behavior through interacting with one another and through past associations with the police. The police officers acquired the cultural meanings they used through interacting with other officers and members of the community. The culture of each group was inextricably bound up with the social life of their particular communities.

The third premise of symbolic interactionism is that "meanings are handled in, and modified through, an interpretive process used by the person dealing with the things he encounters."[7] Neither the crowd nor the policemen were automatons, driven by their culture to act in the way they did. Rather, they used their cultural knowledge to interpret and evaluate the situation. At any moment, a member of the crowd might have interpreted the behavior of the policemen in a slightly different way, leading to a different reaction.

We may see this interpretive aspect more clearly if we think of culture as a cognitive map. In the recurrent activities that make up everyday life, we refer to this map. It serves as a guide for acting and for interpreting our experience; it does not compel us to follow a particular course. Like this brief drama between the policemen, a dying woman, and the crowd, much of life is a series of unanticipated social occasions. Although our culture may not include a detailed map for such occasions, it does provide principles for interpreting and

---

[5] Herbert Blumer, *Symbolic Interactionism* (Englewood Cliffs, NJ: Prentice-Hall, 1969), 2.

[6] Blumer, 2.

[7] Blumer, 2.

responding to them. Rather than a rigid map that people must follow, culture is best thought of as

> a set of principles for creating dramas, for writing script, and of course, for recruiting players and audiences. . . . Culture is not simply a cognitive map that people acquire, in whole or in part, more or less accurately, and then learn to read. People are not just map-readers; they are map-makers. People are cast out into imperfectly charted, continually revised sketch maps. Culture does not provide a cognitive map, but rather a set of principles for map making and navigation. Different cultures are like different schools of navigation to cope with different terrains and seas.[8]

If we take *meaning* seriously, as symbolic interactionists argue we must, it becomes necessary to study meaning carefully. We need a theory of meaning and a specific methodology designed for the investigation of it. This book presents such a theory and methodology.

REVIEW QUESTIONS

1. What is the definition of culture? How is this definition related to the way anthropologists do ethnographic fieldwork?
2. What is the relationship among cultural behavior, cultural artifacts, and cultural knowledge?
3. What is the difference between tacit and explicit culture? How can anthropologists discover these two kinds of culture?
4. What are some examples of naive realism in the way Americans think about people in other societies?

---

[8] Charles O. Frake, "Plying Frames Can Be Dangerous: Some Reflections on Methodology in Cognitive Anthropology," *Quarterly Newsletter of the Institute for Comparative Human Development* 3 (1977): 6–7.

2   *Eating Christmas in the Kalahari*

RICHARD BORSHAY LEE

*What happens when an anthropologist living among the !Kung of
Africa decides to be generous and to share a large animal with
everyone at Christmastime? This compelling account of the misunderstanding and confusion that resulted takes the reader deeper
into the nature of culture. Richard Lee carefully traces how the
natives perceived his generosity and taught the anthropologist
something about his own culture.*

The !Kung Bushmen's knowledge of Christmas is thirdhand. The London Missionary Society brought the holiday to the southern Tswana
tribes in the early nineteenth century. Later, native catechists spread
the idea far and wide among the Bantu-speaking pastoralists, even in
the remotest corners of the Kalahari Desert. The Bushmen's idea of
the Christmas story, stripped to its essentials, is "praise the birth of
white man's god-chief"; what keeps their interest in the holiday high
is the Tswana-Herero custom of slaughtering an ox for his Bushmen
neighbors as an annual goodwill gesture. Since the 1930s, part of the
Bushmen's annual round of activities has included a December congregation at the cattle posts for trading, marriage brokering, and several days of trance dance feasting at which the local Tswana headman
is host.

Originally published as "A Naturalist at Large: Eating Christmas in the Kalahari." With
permission from *Natural History*, December 1969; Copyright the American Museum of
Natural History, 1969.

As a social anthropologist working with !Kung Bushmen, I found that the Christmas ox custom suited my purposes. I had come to the Kalahari to study the hunting and gathering subsistence economy of the !Kung, and to accomplish this it was essential not to provide them with food, share my own food, or interfere in any way with their food-gathering activities. While liberal handouts of tobacco and medical supplies were appreciated, they were scarcely adequate to erase the glaring disparity in wealth between the anthropologist, who maintained a two-month inventory of canned goods, and the Bushmen, who rarely had a day's supply of food on hand. My approach, while paying off in terms of data, left me open to frequent accusations of stinginess and hardheartedness. By their lights, I was a miser.

The Christmas ox was to be my way of saying thank you for the cooperation of the past year; and since it was to be our last Christmas in the field, I determined to slaughter the largest, meatiest ox that money could buy, insuring that the feast and trance dance would be a success.

Through December I kept my eyes open at the wells as the cattle were brought down for watering. Several animals were offered, but none had quite the grossness that I had in mind. Then, ten days before the holiday, a Herero friend led an ox of astonishing size and mass up to our camp. It was solid black, stood five feet high at the shoulder, had a five-foot span of horns, and must have weighed 1,200 pounds on the hoof. Food consumption calculations are my specialty, and I quickly figured that bones and viscera aside, there was enough meat —at least four pounds—for every man, woman, and child of the 150 Bushmen in the vicinity of /ai/ai who were expected at the feast.

Having found the right animal at last, I paid the Herero £20 ($56) and asked him to keep the beast with his herd until Christmas day. The next morning word spread among the people that the big solid black one was the ox chosen by /ontah (my Bushman name; it means, roughly, "whitey") for the Christmas feast. That afternoon I received the first delegation. Ben!a, an outspoken sixty-year-old mother of five, came to the point slowly.

"Where were you planning to eat Christmas?"

"Right here at /ai/ai," I replied.

"Alone or with others?"

"I expect to invite all the people to eat Christmas with me."

"Eat what?"

"I have purchased Yehave's black ox, and I am going to slaughter and cook it."

"That's what we were told at the well but refused to believe it until we heard it from yourself."

"Well, it's the black one," I replied expansively, although wondering what she was driving at.

"Oh, no!" Ben!a groaned, turning to her group. "They were right." Turning back to me she asked, "Do you expect us to eat that bag of bones?"

"Bag of bones! It's the biggest ox at /ai/ai."

"Big, yes, but old. And thin. Everybody knows there's no meat on that old ox. What did you expect us to eat off it, the horns?"

Everybody chuckled at Ben!a's one-liner as they walked away, but all I could manage was a weak grin.

That evening it was the turn of the young men. They came to sit at our evening fire. /gaugo, about my age, spoke to me man-to-man.

"/ontah, you have always been square with us," he lied. "What has happened to change your heart? That sack of guts and bones of Yehave's will hardly feed one camp, let alone all the Bushmen around /ai/ai." And he proceeded to enumerate the seven camps in the /ai/ai vicinity, family by family. "Perhaps you have forgotten that we are not few, but many. Or are you too blind to tell the difference between a proper cow and an old wreck? That ox is thin to the point of death."

"Look, you guys," I retorted, "that is a beautiful animal, and I'm sure you will eat it with pleasure at Christmas."

"Of course we will eat it; it's food. But it won't fill us up to the point where we will have enough strength to dance. We will eat and go home to bed with stomachs rumbling."

That night as we turned in, I asked my wife, Nancy, "What did you think of the black ox?"

"It looked enormous to me. Why?"

"Well, about eight different people have told me I got gypped; that the ox is nothing but bones."

"What's the angle?" Nancy asked. "Did they have a better one to sell?"

"No, they just said that it was going to be a grim Christmas because there won't be enough meat to go around. Maybe I'll get an independent judge to look at the beast in the morning."

Bright and early, Halingisi, a Tswana cattle owner, appeared at our camp. But before I could ask him to give me his opinion on Yehave's black ox, he gave me the eye signal that indicated a confidential chat. We left the camp and sat down.

"/ontah, I'm surprised at you; you've lived here for three years and still haven't learned anything about cattle."

"But what else can a person do but choose the biggest, strongest animal one can find?" I retorted.

"Look, just because an animal is big doesn't mean that it has plenty of meat on it. The black one was a beauty when it was younger, but now it is thin to the point of death."

"Well I've already bought it. What can I do at this stage?"

"Bought it already? I thought you were just considering it. Well, you'll have to kill it and serve it, I suppose. But don't expect much of a dance to follow."

My spirits dropped rapidly. I could believe that Ben!a and /gaugo just might be putting me on about the black ox, but Halingisi seemed to be an impartial critic. I went around that day feeling as though I had bought a lemon of a used car.

In the afternoon it was Tomazo's turn. Tomazo is a fine hunter, a top trance performer . . . and one of my most reliable informants. He approached the subject of the Christmas cow as part of my continuing Bushman education.

"My friend, the way it is with us Bushmen," he began, "is that we love meat. And even more than that, we love fat. When we hunt we always search for the fat ones, the ones dripping with layers of white fat: fat that turns into a clear, thick oil in the cooking pot, fat that slides down your gullet, fills your stomach and gives you a roaring diarrhea," he rhapsodized.

"So, feeling as we do," he continued, "it gives us pain to be served such a scrawny thing as Yehave's black ox. It is big, yes, and no doubt its giant bones are good for soup, but fat is what we really crave and so we will eat Christmas this year with a heavy heart."

The prospect of a gloomy Christmas now had me worried, so I asked Tomazo what I could do about it.

"Look for a fat one, a young one . . . smaller, but fat. Fat enough to make us //gom (evacuate the bowels), then we will be happy."

My suspicions were aroused when Tomazo said that he happened to know a young, fat, barren cow that the owner was willing to part with. Was Tomazo working on commission, I wondered? But I dispelled this unworthy thought when we approached the Herero owner of the cow in question and found that he had decided not to sell.

The scrawny wreck of a Christmas ox now became the talk of the /ai/ai water hole and was the first news told to the outlying groups as they began to come in from the bush for the feast. What finally convinced me that real trouble might be brewing was the visit from u!au, an old conservative with a reputation for fierceness. His nickname meant spear and referred to an incident thirty years ago in which he had speared a man to death. He had an intense manner; fixing me with his eyes, he said in clipped tones:

"I have only just heard about the black ox today, or else I would have come here earlier. /ontah, do you honestly think you can serve meat like that to people and avoid a fight?" He paused, letting the implications sink in. "I don't mean fight you, /ontah; you are a white man. I mean a fight between Bushmen. There are many fierce ones here, and with such a small quantity of meat to distribute, how can you give everybody a fair share? Someone is sure to accuse another of taking too much or hogging all the choice pieces. Then you will see what happens when some go hungry while others eat."

The possibility of at least a serious argument struck me as all too real. I had witnessed the tension that surrounds the distribution of meat from a kudu or gemsbok kill, and had documented many arguments that sprang up from a real or imagined slight in meat distribution. The owners of a kill may spend up to two hours arranging and rearranging the piles of meat under the gaze of a circle of recipients before handing them out. And I knew that the Christmas feast at /ai/ai would be bringing together groups that had feuded in the past.

Convinced now of the gravity of the situation, I went in earnest to search for a second cow; but all my inquiries failed to turn one up.

The Christmas feast was evidently going to be a disaster, and the incessant complaints about the meagerness of the ox had already taken the fun out of it for me. Moreover, I was getting bored with the wisecracks, and after losing my temper a few times, I resolved to serve the beast anyway. If the meat fell short, the hell with it. In the Bushmen idiom, I announced to all who would listen:

"I am a poor man and blind. If I have chosen one that is too old and too thin, we will eat it anyway and see if there is enough meat there to quiet the rumbling of our stomachs."

On hearing this speech, Ben!a offered me a rare word of comfort. "It's thin," she said philosophically, "but the bones will make a good soup."

At dawn Christmas morning, instinct told me to turn over the butchering and cooking to a friend and take off with Nancy to spend Christmas alone in the bush. But curiosity kept me from retreating. I wanted to see what such a scrawny ox looked like on butchering, and if there *was* going to be a fight, I wanted to catch every word of it. Anthropologists are incurable that way.

The great beast was driven up to our dancing ground, and a shot in the forehead dropped it in its tracks. Then, freshly cut branches were heaped around the fallen carcass to receive the meat. Ten men volunteered to help with the cutting, I asked /gaugo to make the breast bone cut. This cut, which begins the butchering process for most large game, offers easy access for removal of the viscera. But it also allows the hunter to spot-check the amount of fat on an animal. A fat game animal carries a white layer up to an inch thick on the chest, while in a thin one, the knife will quickly cut to bone. All eyes fixed on his hand as /gaugo, dwarfed by the great carcass, knelt to the breast. The first cut opened a pool of solid white in the black skin. The second and third cut widened and deepened the creamy white. Still no bone. It was pure fat; it must have been two inches thick.

"Hey /gau," I burst out, "that ox is loaded with fat. What's this about the ox being too thin to bother eating? Are you out of your mind?"

"Fat?" /gau shot back. "You call that fat? This wreck is thin, sick, dead!" And he broke out laughing. So did everyone else. They rolled on the ground, paralyzed with laughter. Everybody laughed except me; I was thinking.

I ran back to the tent and burst in just as Nancy was getting up. "Hey, the black ox. It's fat as hell! They were kidding about it being too thin to eat. It was a joke or something. A put-on. Everyone is really delighted with it."

"Some joke," my wife replied. "It was so funny that you were ready to pack up and leave /ai/ai."

If it had indeed been a joke, it had been an extraordinarily convincing one, and tinged, I thought, with more than a touch of malice as many jokes are. Nevertheless, that it was a joke lifted my spirits considerably, and I returned to the butchering site where the shape of the ox was rapidly disappearing under the axes and knives of the butchers. The atmosphere had become festive. Grinning broadly, their arms covered with blood well past the elbow, men packed chunks of meat into the big cast-iron cooking pots, fifty pounds to the load, and muttered and chuckled all the while about the thinness and worthlessness of the animal and /ontah's poor judgment.

We danced and ate that ox two days and two nights; we cooked and distributed fourteen potfuls of meat and no one went home hungry and no fights broke out.

But the "joke" stayed in my mind. I had a growing feeling that something important had happened in my relationship with the Bushmen and that the clue lay in the meaning of the joke. Several days later, when most of the people had dispersed back to the bush camps, I raised the question with Hakekgose, a Tswana man who had grown up among the !Kung, married a !Kung girl, and who probably knew their culture better than any other non-Bushman.

"With us whites," I began, "Christmas is supposed to be the day of friendship and brotherly love. What I can't figure out is why the Bushmen went to such lengths to criticize and belittle the ox I had bought for the feast. The animal was perfectly good and their jokes and wisecracks practically ruined the holiday for me."

"So it really did bother you," said Hakekgose. "Well, that's the way they always talk. When I take my rifle and go hunting with them, if I miss, they laugh at me for the rest of the day. But even if I hit and bring one down, it's no better. To them, the kill is always too small or too old or too thin; and as we sit down on the kill site to cook and eat the liver, they keep grumbling, even with their mouths full of meat. They say things like, 'Oh, this is awful! What a worthless animal! Whatever made me think that this Tswana rascal could hunt!'"

"Is this the way outsiders are treated?" I asked.

"No, it is their custom; they talk that way to each other too. Go and ask them."

/gaugo had been one of the most enthusiastic in making me feel bad about the merit of the Christmas ox. I sought him out first.

"Why did you tell me the black ox was worthless, when you could see that it was loaded with fat and meat?"

"It is our way," he said, smiling. "We always like to fool people about that. Say there is a Bushman who has been hunting. He must not come home and announce like a braggart, 'I have killed a big one in the bush!' He must first sit down in silence until I or someone else comes up to his fire and asks, 'What did you see today?' He replies quietly, 'Ah, I'm no good for hunting. I saw nothing at all [pause] just a little tiny one.' Then I smile to myself," /gaugo continued, "because I know he has killed something big.

"In the morning we make up a party of four or five people to cut up and carry the meat back to the camp. When we arrive at the kill we examine it and cry out, 'You mean to say you have dragged us all the way out here in order to make us cart home your pile of bones? Oh, if I had known it was this thin I wouldn't have come.' Another one pipes up, 'People, to think I gave up a nice day in the shade for this. At home we may be hungry but at least we have nice cool water to drink.' If the horns are big, someone says, 'Did you think that somehow you were going to boil down the horns for soup?'

"To all this you must respond in kind. 'I agree,' you say, 'this one is not worth the effort; let's just cook the liver for strength and leave the rest for the hyenas. It is not too late to hunt today and even a duiker or a steenbok would be better than this mess.'

"Then you set to work nevertheless; butcher the animal, carry the meat back to the camp and everyone eats," /gaugo concluded.

Things were beginning to make sense. Next, I went to Tomazo. He corroborated /gaugo's story of the obligatory insults over a kill and added a few details of his own.

"But," I asked, "why insult a man after he has gone to all that trouble to track and kill an animal and when he is going to share the meat with you so that your children will have something to eat?"

"Arrogance," was his cryptic answer.

"Arrogance?"

"Yes, when a young man kills much meat he comes to think of himself as a chief or a big man, and he thinks of the rest of us as his servants or inferiors. We can't accept this. We refuse one who boasts, for someday his pride will make him kill somebody. So we always speak of his meat as worthless. This way we cool his heart and make him gentle."

"But why didn't you tell me this before?" I asked Tomazo with some heat.

"Because you never asked me," said Tomazo, echoing the refrain that has come to haunt every field ethnographer.

The pieces now fell into place. I had known for a long time that in situations of social conflict with Bushmen I held all the cards. I was the only source of tobacco in a thousand square miles, and I was not incapable of cutting an individual off for noncooperation. Though my boycott never lasted longer than a few days, it was an indication of my strength. People resented my presence at the water hole, yet simultaneously dreaded my leaving. In short I was a perfect target for the charge of arrogance and for the Bushmen tactic of enforcing humility.

I had been taught an object lesson by the Bushmen; it had come from an unexpected corner and had hurt me in a vulnerable area. For the big black ox was to be the one totally generous, unstinting act of my year at /ai/ai and I was quite unprepared for the reaction I received.

As I read it, their message was this: There are no totally generous acts. All "acts" have an element of calculation. One black ox slaughtered at Christmas does not wipe out a year of careful manipulation of gifts given to serve your own ends. After all, to kill an animal and share the meat with people is really no more than the Bushmen do for each other every day and with far less fanfare.

In the end, I had to admire how the Bushmen had played out the farce — collectively straight-faced to the end. Curiously, the episode reminded me of the *Good Soldier Schweik* and his marvelous encounters with authority. Like Schweik, the Bushmen had retained a thoroughgoing skepticism of good intentions. Was it this independence of spirit, I wondered, that had kept them culturally viable in the face of generations of contact with more powerful societies, both black and white? The thought that the Bushmen were alive and well in the Kalahari was strangely comforting. Perhaps, armed with that independence and with their superb knowledge of their environment, they might yet survive the future.

REVIEW QUESTIONS

1. What was the basis of the misunderstanding experienced by Lee when he gave an ox for the Christmas feast held by the !Kung?
2. Construct a model of cross-cultural misunderstanding, using the information presented by Lee in this article.
3. Why do you think the !Kung ridicule and denigrate people who have been successful hunters or who have provided them with a Christmas ox? Why do Americans expect people to be grateful to receive gifts?

3   Navigating Nigerian Bureaucracies

ELIZABETH A. EAMES

*All of us use the cultural knowledge acquired as members of our
own society to organize perception and behavior. Most of us are
also naive realists; we tend to believe our culture mirrors a reality
shared by everyone. But cultures are different, and other people
rarely behave according to our cultural plan. In this article, Elizabeth Eames describes such a difference as she portrays her initial
frustration with Nigerian bureaucrats. Nigerian bureaucracies work
on* patrimonial domination, *where transactions depend on establishing and cultivating social relations; this differs from the American
system of* legal domination *organized by formal rules and imper-
sonality. When Eames understood this, the door to successful interaction with bureaucrats opened.*

Americans have a saying: "It's not *what* you know, it's *who* you
know." This aphorism captures the usually subtle use of old-boy networks for personal advancement in the United States. But what happens when this principle becomes the primary dynamic of an entire
social system? The period of three years I spent pursuing anthropological field research in a small Nigerian city was one of continual
adjustment and re-ordering of expectations. This paper discusses a

From Elizabeth A. Eames, "Navigating Nigerian Bureaucracies, or 'Why Can't You
Beg?' She Demanded," in *Work in Modern Society: A Sociology Reader.* Edited by
Lauri Perman (Dubuque, IA: Kendall/Hunt, 1986). Copyright © 1985 by Elizabeth A.
Eames. Reprinted by permission of the author.

single case — how I discovered the importance personal ties have for Nigerian bureaucrats — but also illustrates the *general process* by which any open-minded visitor to a foreign land might decipher the rules of proper behavior. I was already familiar with Max Weber's work on bureaucracy and patrimony, yet its tremendous significance and explanatory power only became clear to me following the incidents discussed below. Accordingly, the paper concludes with a discussion of Weber's concept of *patrimonial authority*.

I heard the same comment from every expatriate I met in Nigeria — U.S. foreign service officers, U.N. "experts," and visiting business consultants alike: "If you survive a stint in Nigeria, you can survive *anywhere*." The negative implications of this statement stem from outsiders' futile attempts to apply, in a new social setting, home-grown notions of how bureaucratic organizations function. This is indeed a natural inclination and all the more tempting where organizational structure *appears* bureaucratic. Yet in Nigeria, the office-holders behaved according to different rules; their attitudes and sentiments reflected a different moral code. A bureaucratic organizational structure coexisted with an incompatible set of moral imperatives. The resulting unwieldy, inflexible structure may be singled out as one of the British Colonialism's most devastating legacies.[1]

Please bear in mind, the problem of understanding another culture works both ways. Any Nigerian student reading for the first time the following passage by a prominent American sociologist would probably howl with laughter:

> The chief merit of a bureaucracy is its technical efficiency, with a premium placed on precision, speed, expert control, continuity, discretion and optimal returns on input. The structure is one which approaches the complete elimination of personalized relationships and nonrational considerations (hostility, anxiety, affectual involvements, etc.)[2]

Even those well-educated administrative officers who had once been required to incorporate such notions into their papers and exams do not *live* by them.

To many foreigners who have spent time in Nigeria, "the system" remains a mystery. What motivating principles explain the behavior of Nigerian administrative officers? How do local people understand

---

[1] One common misunderstanding must be clarified: *bureaucratic organization is not a recent Western invention*. Even during the Han Dynasty (3rd century B.C.), China had developed an efficient bureaucracy based on a system of official examinations. This was the start of a "modern" type of civil service system based on merit. It was almost two thousand years before the West adopted such a system, partly inspired by the Chinese example.

[2] Robert K. Merton, *Social Theory and Social Structure* (New York: Free Press, 1969), 250.

the behavior of their fellow workers? Why do some people successfully maneuver their way through the system while others founder?

Recently I attended a party. As often happens at a gathering of anthropologists, we started swapping fieldwork stories, and meandered onto a topic of our most unpleasant sensation or unsettling experience. That night, I heard tales of surviving strange diseases, eating repulsive foods, losing one's way in the rain forest, being caught between hostile rebel factions or kidnapped by guerrilla fighters. As for me? All that came to mind were exasperating encounters with intransigent clerks and secretaries. I began to ponder why these interactions had proved so unsettling.

My discipline — social anthropology — hinges on the practice of "participant observation." To a fledgling anthropologist, the "fieldwork" research experience takes on all the connotations of initiation into full membership. For some, a vision-quest; for others, perhaps, a trial-by-ordeal: the goal is to experience another way of life from the inside and to internalize, as does a growing child, the accumulating lessons of daily life. But the anthropologist is not a child; therefore, he or she experiences not conversion, but self-revelation.

I came to understand my American-ness during the period spent coming to terms with Nigerian-ness. I found that I believed in my right to fair treatment and justice simply because I was a human being. I believed in equal protection under the law. But my Nigerian friends did not. What I found was a social system where status, relationships, and rights were fundamentally negotiable, and justice was *never* impartial. In the United States, impersonalized bureaucracies are the norm: we do not question them; our behavior automatically adjusts to them. But just imagine spending a year working in a corporation where none of these rules applied.

You see, a Nigerian immigration officer will only sign your form *if* doing so will perpetuate some mutually beneficial relationship or *if* he wishes to initiate a relationship by putting you in his debt. For those unlucky enough to be without connections (this must necessarily include most foreigners), the only other option is bribery — where the supplicant initiates a personal relationship of sorts and the ensuing favor evens matters up.[3]

Hence, Nigeria becomes labeled "inefficient," "tribalistic," and "corrupt." And so it is.[4] Yet this system exists and persists for a

---

[3] Bribery exists for several reasons: it initiates a personal relationship, unlike a tip, which terminates all intimacy; if not dedicated to "duty," a worker must be given added incentive to perform a service; the poor salary scale aggravated by the unpredictable nature of extended kin obligations means everyone is desperately in search of extra cash.

[4] Corruption is condemned only in the abstract, when far removed and on a grand scale. But anyone and everyone knows someone "well-placed," and that person is now

profound reason: Whereas in Europe and Asia, power and authority always derived from ownership of landed property, in West Africa the key ingredient was a large number of loyal dependents. Because land was plentiful and agriculture of the extensive slash-and-burn variety,[5] discontented subordinates could simply move on. The trick was to maintain power over subordinates through ostentatious displays of generosity. This meant more than simply putting on a lavish feast — you must demonstrate a willingness to use your influence to support others in times of need. Even now, all Nigerians participate in such patron-client relationships. In fact, *all legitimate authority derives from being in a position to grant favors and not the other way around.*

Actually, only a minuscule portion of my time in the field was spent dealing with Nigeria's "formal sector." My research entailed living within an extended family household (approximately a dozen adults and two dozen children), chatting with friends, visiting women in their market stalls, even at times conducting formal or informal interviews. And during the years spent researching women's economic resources and domestic responsibilities, I came to understand — indeed to deeply *admire* — their sense of moral responsibility to a wide-ranging network of kin, colleagues, neighbors, friends, and acquaintances. Even now, I often take the time to recall someone's overwhelming hospitality, a friendly greeting, the sharing and eating together. Such warm interpersonal relations more than made up for the lack of amenities.

The longer I stayed, however, the clearer it became that what I loved most and what I found most distressing about life in Nigeria were two sides of the same coin, inextricably related.

The first few months in a new place can be instructive for those with an open mind:

LESSON ONE: THE STRENGTH OF WEAK TIES

My first exposure to Nigerian civil servants occurred when, after waiting several months, I realized my visa application was stalled somewhere in the New York consulate. Letter-writing and telephoning proved futile, and as my departure date approached, panic made me plan a personal visit.

---

powerful precisely because he or she has been generous. Moreover, one is more likely to be condemned for going by the book than for corruption. If, for instance, the brother of the man married to one of my cousins (my mother's father's sister's daughter's husband's brother) did not see to it that his colleague signed my tax form with the minimum of fuss, life could be made quite miserable for him indeed!

[5] Also known as shifting cultivation or swidden agriculture: small pieces of land are cultivated for a few years, until the natural fertility of the soil diminishes. When crop yields decline, the field must be abandoned. This has obvious implications for the concepts of private property, ownership, and monopoly.

The waiting room was populated with sullen, miserable people — a roomful of hostile eyes fixed on the uniformed man guarding the office door. They had been waiting for hours on end. Any passing official was simultaneously accosted by half a dozen supplicants — much as a political celebrity is accosted by the news media. Everyone's immediate goal was to enter through that door to the inner sanctum — so far, they had failed. But I was lucky — I had the name of an acquaintance's wife's schoolmate currently employed at the consulate. After some discussion, the guard allowed me to telephone her.

Mrs. Ojo greeted me cordially, then — quickly, quietly — she coaxed my application forms through the maze of cubicles. It was a miracle!

"What a wonderful woman," I thought to myself. "She understands." I thought she had taken pity on me and acted out of disgust for her colleagues' mishandling of my application. I now realize that by helping me, she was reinforcing a relationship with her schoolmate. Needless to say, my gratitude extended to her schoolmate's husband, my acquaintance. As I later came to understand it, this natural emotional reaction — gratitude for favors granted — is the currency fueling the system. Even we Americans have an appropriate saying: "What goes around comes around." But at this point, I had merely learned that, here as elsewhere, connections open doors.

LESSON TWO: NO IMPERSONAL TRANSACTIONS ALLOWED

Once on Nigerian soil I confronted the mayhem of Muritala Muhammad airport. Joining the crowd surrounding one officer's station, jostled slowly forward, I finally confronted her face-to-face. Apparently I was missing the requisite currency form. No, sorry, there were none available that day. "Stand back," she declared: "You can't pass here today." I waited squeamishly. If I could only catch her eye once more! But then what? After some time a fellow passenger asked me what was the problem. At this point, the officer, stealing a glance at me while processing someone else, inquired: "Why can't you beg?" The person being processed proclaimed: "She doesn't know how to beg![6] Please, O! Let her go." And I was waved on.

A young post office clerk soon reinforced my conclusion that being employed in a given capacity did not in and of itself mean one performed it. Additional incentive was required. Again, I was confronted with a mass of people crowded round a window. Everyone was trying to catch the clerk's attention, but the young man was adept at avoiding eye contact. Clients were calling him by name, invoking the name of mutual friends, and so on. After some time, he noticed me, and I grabbed the opportunity to ask for stamps. In a voice full of recrimination yet tinged

---

[6] It turns out that "begging" means throwing yourself on someone's mercy, rubbing one's hands together, eyes downcast, even kneeling or prostrating if necessary, and literally begging for a favor.

with regret, he announced more to the crowd than to me: "Why can't you greet?" and proceeded to ignore me. This proved my tip-off to the elaborate and complex cultural code of greetings so central to Nigerian social life.[7] In other words, a personal relationship is like a "jump-start" for business transactions.

LESSON THREE: EVERY CASE IS UNIQUE

Mrs. Ojo had succeeded in obtaining for me a three-month visa, but I planned to stay for over two years. Prerequisite for a "regularized" visa was university affiliation. This sounded deceptively simple. The following two months spent registering as an "occasional postgraduate student" took a terrible toll on my nervous stomach.[8] The worst feeling was of an ever-receding target, an ever-thickening tangle of convoluted mazeways. No one could tell me what it took to register, for in fact, no one could possibly predict what I would confront farther down the road. Nothing was routinized, everything personalized, no two cases could possibly be alike.

LESSON FOUR: "DASH" OR "LONG-LEG" GETS RESULTS

This very unpredictability of the process forms a cybernetic system with the strength of personal ties, however initiated. *Dash* and *Long-Leg* are the locally recognized means for cutting through red tape or confronting noncooperative personnel. *Dash* is local parlance for gift or bribe. *Long-Leg* (sometimes called *L-L* or *L-squared*) refers to petitioning a powerful person to help hack your way through the tangled overgrowth. To me, it evokes the image of something swooping down from on high to stomp on the petty bureaucrat causing the problem.

LESSON FIVE: EXERCISE KEEPS TIES LIMBER

During my drawn-out tussle with the registrar's office, I recounted my problem to anyone who would listen. A friend's grown son, upon hearing of my difficulties, wrote a note on his business card to a Mr. Ade in the Exams Section. Amused by his attempt to act important, I thanked Ayo politely. When I next saw him at his mother's home, he took the offensive, and accused me of shunning him. It came out that I had not seen Mr. Ade. But, I protested, I did not know the man. Moreover, he worked in

---

[7] Nigerians coming to the United States are always taken aback by our positively inhuman greeting behavior.

[8] A few years later, I timed my registration as a graduate student at Harvard. The result: three offices in twelve minutes! Even a foreign graduate student could probably register in less than a day.

exams not the registry. That, I learned, was not the point. I was supposed to assume that Mr. Ade would have known someone at the registry. Not only had I denied Ayo the chance to further his link to Mr. Ade, but ignoring his help was tantamount to denying any connection to him or — more important for me — his mother.

This revelation was reinforced when I ran into a colleague. He accused me of not greeting him very well. I had greeted him adequately, but apologized nonetheless. As the conversation progressed, he told me that he had heard I had had "some difficulty." He lamented the fact that I had not called on him, since as Assistant Dean of Social Science he could have helped me. His feelings were truly hurt, provoking his accusation of a lackluster greeting. Indeed, things were never the same between us again, for I had betrayed — or denied — our relationship.

LESSON SIX: YOUR FRIENDS HAVE ENEMIES

Well, I did eventually obtain a regularized visa, and it came through *Long-Leg*.[9] But the problems inherent in its use derive from the highly politicized and factionalized nature of Nigerian organizations, where personal loyalty is everything:

Early on, I became friendly with a certain sociologist and his family. Thereby, I had unwittingly become his ally in a long, drawn-out war between himself and his female colleagues. The disagreement had its origins ten years before in accusations of sex discrimination, but had long since spilled over into every aspect of departmental functioning. Even the office workers had chosen sides, and would perform only for members of the proper faction. More significant, though, was the fact that my friend's chief antagonist and I had similar theoretical interests. Though in retrospect I regret the missed opportunity, I realize that I was in the thick of things before I could have known what was happening. Given the original complaint, my sympathies should have been with the other camp. But ambiguous loyalty is equivalent to none.

Early in the century, Max Weber, the great pioneering sociologist, articulated the difference between systems of *legal* and *patrimonial domination*. Within systems of legal domination, organized bureaucratically, authority is the property of a given office or position (not an attribute of the person) and is validated by general rules applying to the whole structure of offices. Assignment to an office is based on merit: rights and duties are properties of the office not its incumbent. The system functions according to routine and is therefore predictable and efficient. Great stress is placed on making relationships impersonal.

---

[9] I never paid *dash* in Nigeria.

In contrast, patrimonial authority (from the Latin term for personal estate) pertains to the form of government organized as a more or less direct extension of the noble household, where officials originate as household servants and remain personal dependents of the ruler. Note how the following passage summarizing Weber's characterization of patrimonial administration fits with my own observations of Nigerian life:

> *First*, whether or not the patrimonial ruler and his officials conduct administrative business is usually a matter of discretion; normally they do so only when they are paid for their troubles. *Second*, a patrimonial ruler resists the delimitation of his authority by the stipulation of rules. He may observe traditional or customary limitations, but these are un-written: indeed, tradition endorses the principled arbitrariness of the ruler. *Third*, this combination of tradition and arbitrariness is reflected in the delegation and supervision of authority. Within the limits of sacred tra-dition the ruler decides whether or not to delegate authority, and his entirely personal recruitment of "officials" makes the supervision of their work a matter of personal preference and loyalty. *Fourth* and *fifth*, all administrative "offices" under patrimonial rule are a part of the ruler's personal household and private property: his "officials" are servants, and the costs of administration are met out of his treasury. *Sixth*, official business is transacted in personal encounter and by oral communication, not on the basis of impersonal documents.[10]

Weber himself believed that bureaucracy would supplant patri-monial authority. He believed that the world was becoming progres-sively more rationalized and bureaucratized. But there are several different dimensions along which I dispute this contention:

> Bureaucracy has been invented, declined, and re-invented, several times over the millenia.
>
> We have seen how patrimonial ties persisted within a bureaucratic structure of offices in Nigeria. This is also true in America. Within certain organizational structures, personal loyalty remains important, favoritism prevails, connections count, and nepotism or corruption abounds. For instance, urban "political machines" function according to a patrimonial logic. Bureaucracy and patrimonialism may be opposite poles on a con-tinuum (Weber called them "ideal types"), but they are *not* mutually exclusive. Most institutions combine both types of authority structures, with a greater emphasis on one or the other. Personal connections can help in either society, but in America, their use is widely perceived as *illegitimate*.

---

[10] Max Weber quoted from Reinhard Bendix, *Max Weber: An Intellectual Portrait* (Berkeley: University of California Press, 1960), 245; emphasis added.

The system I have outlined is not irrational by any means — but rational actions are based on a different set of assumptions.

Ties of kinship and clientship have an ally in human nature.

By the latter, I mean Weber's ideal types cannot be mutually exclusive for emotional/cognitive reasons: an individual's cognitive understanding of hierarchy is necessarily patterned on the relationship between infant and caretaker. Whatever the form of the earliest pattern (and child-rearing practices vary tremendously between and within cultures), it leaves a residual tendency for personal attachment to develop between authority figures and dependents. Clients in the Unemployment Office naturally wish to be considered individuals and resent cold, impersonal treatment. Each bureaucrat wages his or her own private struggle with the temptation to treat each case on its merits.

This is why most Nigerians' finely honed interpersonal skills stand them in good stead when they arrive in the United States. They easily make friends with whomever they run across, and naturally friends will grant you the benefit of the doubt *if* there is room to maneuver. The psychological need remains, even in our seemingly formalized, structured world, for a friendly, personable encounter. On the other hand, anyone adept at working this way suffers tremendous pain and anxiety from the impersonal enforcement of seemingly arbitrary rules. For instance, a Nigerian friend took it as a personal affront when his insurance agent refused to pay a claim because a renewal was past due.

Once I learned my lessons well, life became much more pleasant. True, every case was unique and personal relationships were everything. But as my friends and allies multiplied, I could more easily make "the system" work for me. As a result of my Nigerian experience, I am very sensitive to inflexible and impersonal treatment, the flip-side of efficiency.

Leaving Nigeria to return to Boston after 2½ years, I stopped for a week in London. I arrived only to find that my old college friend, with whom I intended to stay, had recently moved. Playing detective, I tried neighbors, the superintendent, directory assistance. Tired and bedraggled, I thought of inquiring whether a forwarding address had been left with the post office. Acknowledging me from inside his cage, the small, graying man reached for his large, gray ledger, peered in, slapped it shut, and answered:

"Yes."

"But . . . what is it?" I asked, caught off guard.

He peered down at me and replied: "I cannot tell you. We are not allowed. We must protect him from creditors."

I was aghast. In no way did I resemble a creditor. Noticing my reaction, he conceded:

"But, if you send him a letter, I will forward it."

Bursting into tears of frustration, in my thickest American accent, displaying my luggage and my air ticket, I begged and cajoled him, to no avail. I spent my entire London week in a Bed 'n Breakfast, cursing petty bureaucrats as my bill piled up. "THAT," I thought, "COULD NEVER HAPPEN IN NIGERIA!"

REVIEW QUESTIONS

1. What is naive realism and how is this concept illustrated by Eames's experience with Nigerian bureaucrats?

2. What is the difference between American and Nigerian bureaucracies? How does this difference relate to Weber's concepts of "legal" and "patrimonial" domination?

3. What experiences did Eames use to discover the cultural rules that govern bureaucratic transactions among Nigerians? What does this reveal about how anthropologists do fieldwork?

4. What are six features of patrimonial domination suggested by Weber as his views are represented by Eames? Do all six apply to the Nigerian case?

4 The Pretense of the Neutral Researcher

MARY ELLEN CONAWAY

Americans like to believe that scientific research is objective, that scientists remain apart from the things they study. Complete objectivity is impossible to achieve, however, especially for anthropologists as they conduct ethnographic field research. In this article, Mary Ellen Conaway illustrates this point. She shows how fieldwork among the Guahibo and criollos living in the Venezuelan town of Puerto Ayacucho was affected by local expectations about women and sex. These expectations and the reputation of a female Peace Corps worker combined to give her a sexual image that complicated research. Eventually, she discovered that acting businesslike and unavailable diffused the sexual expectations of local men more effectively than hiding her femininity.

Indifferent about gender, without judgment on cultural content, free of prejudice, the ideal, the neutral researcher — there used to be such a person in our mind's eye, in our ethnographies and our seminars. As an undergraduate in the early 1960s, I was fascinated with the prospect of study in another culture. Both women and men studied for and practiced fieldwork, and these exercises seemed to carry them outside the common categories of gender- and sex-defined behavior. Whereas men became doctors, dentists, and lawyers, and women were nurses, hygienists, and legal secretaries, anyone could be, potentially, an anthropologist. Well-known women, Margaret Mead in particular, had done field research just as men had. To travel to a far-off, "exotic" place, live with the "natives," endure local housing and food customs, and collect data were but a test of the power of knowledge and scientific method over cultural norms, over personal preference or prejudice. Social scientists were above or outside the usual cultural constraints when they did research. The image of the neutral researcher included the nuclear scientists and engineers who argued their right to create, develop, and go in any research direction without moralizing about the probable result of their work. They were also outside the bounds of the usual cultural conventions. Just because they created something like a nuclear bomb was no reason to make them morally responsible for how politicians might use it.

Anthropologists were no different. Courses in field methods focused on unbiased data collection, on neutrality in the cultural laboratory, as field sites were often called. Two means anthropologists have used for establishing an image of neutralization — or more precisely, a nonthreatening role — are adoption into an indigenous kin unit and pretending to have no gender, or at least no gender constraints. How many dozens of ethnographies tell us of the life cycle — birth to death — of a certain people? And from how many of these can we determine, for certain, that the ethnographer saw a birth, observed rites of passage, mourned with a widow? We've all pretended that the influences of our sex and our gender can be substituted for by talking to the right informant.

Thus entranced by anthropology, and desirous of being a good student, I had no felt need to reconcile the ideal image of the neutral researcher with personal experience and logical deductions. When I began graduate studies in the late 1960s, I read dozens of books and articles on field methods, ethics, and general field experiences. Some women anthropologists indicated that gender boundaries have directed aspects of their work, but how they handled these restrictions was given only the slightest description. Older women on college faculties who had done field research in anthropology continued to tell me that being female makes no difference when doing fieldwork. In seminars, faculty men sometimes mentioned peripherally the presence of their spouses at their research sites or boastfully, or with nervous laughter, a sexual interaction or confrontation. Yet I never heard in any course, in any seminar, an acknowledgment that who we are sexually and what our gender norms are have definite impacts on data collection. That I should reconcile the "scientific" approach — the pretense of the neutral researcher — with my own data-collection experiences was a postponed exercise.

By the time of my departure for a year in Venezuela, I felt prepared for difficult field conditions, research orientation, note taking in an alien language, and all the other realities that graduate studies are said to prepare one for. Still uneasy that something was missing in my training, I asked several advisors on the university staff about interpersonal relations with local people. "Don't marry one" and "take birth control pills" were their responses. We were to maintain the pretense.

FIELD SITE

Prior to arriving in Venezuela, I established contact with a Venezuelan anthropologist who extended herself in a collegial manner beyond my expectations. With her guidance I was able to meet government requirements for fieldwork and establish field site living quarters within two weeks of my arrival.

The field site, Puerto Ayacucho, capital of the Federal Amazon Territory, has the environmental characteristics of both a savannah and a tropical forest. The surrounding region is geographically marginal because it is on the lower edges of the *llanos* and the upper edges of the tropical forest in an economically unproductive and sparsely populated area. The term *marginality* also describes the sociocultural system with limited integration of groups, individuals, and places into the national scene. Puerto Ayacucho is peripheral to national events, a genuine frontier town that depends on the sustaining influx of government monies rather than on local production and export; on indigenous-produced foods rather than factory-prepared ones; and on the lure of frontier challenges. Its residents, nearly all recent migrants (all but the very young and the Native Americans), experience the limitations and languidness, the excitement and opportunities that life on a frontier evinces. The town population was around ten thousand in 1974, composed of native American groups, criollos,[1] Lebanese, Syrians, Brazilians, Colombians, North Americans, and others. The major language is Spanish.

I lived in a brick house with internal plumbing in the older, main section of town. The indigenous group I chose to work with, the Guahibo, were recent circular migrants living on the outskirts of the town. Only three of the more than eighty indigenous settlements had water spigots in or near their dwellings; two of those also had outhouses, and one had a concrete floor. Thus, my daily activities found me interacting in the cultural environments of both a town criollo setting and a peripheral indigenous one.

---

[1] In Venezuela, *criollo* originally referred to the descendants of European settlers, but it since has come to signify all that is original, typical, or folk, as opposed to that coming from abroad.

CRIOLLO AND INDIGENOUS GENDER ROLES

The criollo view of gender roles is tempered by the frontier circumstances, including a standard of living that requires women to contribute substantially to the household income. A double standard for women and men is the accepted ideal, however, Criollo women are appropriately escorted at night or travel in twosomes. Young women and men should not be familiar in public, but men may shout obscene comments at women and make invitations. Men pay for entertainment and food. To be appropriately feminine, women wear a lot of makeup, very tight pants and blouses, and protect themselves from the sun. Associations between nonrelated adults are discussed as possible sexual liaisons. Town gossip usually includes the latest tryst, the participants' eventual (and appropriate) repentance, and reconciliation with a spouse. Both women and men drink publicly, though more men than women are found in sidewalk taverns during daylight hours. Women maintain the household by cleaning, cooking, taking care of the children, and engaging in small-scale economic activities such as making meat-vegetable pies for sale at the market and during holidays, or taking in laundry. When men are not employed, which is rather frequently, they sit around town in front of the shops and in the plazas, talking and resting.

The indigenous view of gender roles shares some similarities with the criollo view — that is, economic circumstances dictate cooperation between women and men. The Guahibo, who number over 4,000 on the Venezuelan side of the Orinoco River, practice some hunting, gathering, and fishing. They are also horticulturalists, and some of them have recently adopted Western agricultural methods and crops. Both women and men travel freely. The families I knew best held discussions and reached a consensus about their economic and social plans. Women have the primary responsibility for child care and food preparation, but I saw men care for children by seeing to their toilet needs and by feeding them and playing with them. Men have primary responsibility for constructing shelters and for heavy garden work. Guahibo enjoy hearing about sexual liaisons, especially among young people, as long as particular kinship and religious beliefs are respected. Above all, they feel that a person should not be alone and that a variety of male and female relationships are to be expected.

The Guahibo have a delightful sense of humor which extends to gender roles and more than once saved me from awkward situations. In one such instance, early in my field research, I was mapping and identifying house types and had discovered specific areas of indigenous concentration. In the course of this work I met a Guahibo man, around sixty years of age, who delighted in sharing with me his life story and the history of the region. His wife had died a year earlier and he had resolved to live in town permanently. He offered to introduce me to "all the Guahibo" in town. I departed ebullient — my first informant! After our third session, when I rose to depart, he extended his slight, four-foot-ten-inch frame and, quick as lightning, rubbed his nose across my clavicle. I left disturbed. Future quick movement on my part prevented repetition of his affectionate behavior, but he tried other tactics. My distress was alleviated by the Guahibo who were entertained by the man's behavior. They laughed, teased, and joked about him, and thought me tolerant, if not overly so, of his hopes for a new wife.

I found gender role expectations among the criollo more confining because they take them more seriously than the Guahibo do. Refusing to accept a ride from a male criollo would be taken both as an affront to maleness, to his perceived male power and control, and a denial of female weakness, namely, the need for protection from the sun and from undue stress. Some of these criollo boundaries of appropriate behavior impinged on my definition of self as an independent person willing to work to support my goals. For example, during the entire year of my town residence I was asked repeatedly where my male guardian was. Since I was unmarried and my father and brothers were in the United States, the criollo wondered who was looking after me. How could I survive without being cared for? As a result, I received sympathetic marriage proposals from men who desired to "look after me."

After a few weeks of coping with this situation, I found such inquiries and expectations routine. With criollo and indigenous gender roles and my own cultural baggage in tow, I developed a behavior pattern I thought was ambiguously feminine, almost like a mytholog-ical-style powerful person, a testimony to neutrality. I looked like a female but did not behave like local females. Since my research design did not require me to become an *integral* part of either the criollo or Guahibo social structures, I developed and maintained my fieldwork self-image. This behavior, however, evolved and became pronounced not only in the context of the townspeople and surrounding inhabit-ants, but also because of the living arrangements I had made.

THE GLITCH

Prior to selecting a living site in their research area, anthropologists have been advised to consider political circumstances, including kin-ship ties and power structure, location, and condition. Yet the over-riding influence is often the availability of housing. According to Wax, "the scarcity of housing is one of the most difficult (and least discussed) practical problems in participant observation," and once living quar-ters are established, attempts to change them require delicate handling.[2] She argued that "most field experiences that involve living with or close to the host people fall into three stages." The first is one of "initiation or resocialization, when the fieldworker tries to involve himself in the kinds of relationships which will enable him to do his fieldwork — the period during which he and his hosts work out or develop the kinds and varieties of roles which he and they will play."[3]

Such cautions rang in my head as I agreed to share a house with a woman in the Peace Corps who had been in Puerto Ayacucho for a month. Se assured me that she had rented the last vacant house, and indeed she had. She also had obtained a small table and three plastic chairs, a refrigerator, a small wash basin, and a window screen; and she even had the shower nozzle moved from over the toilet to over the floor, a costly project. The house had two small rooms, two larger rooms, and small bath and kitchen areas — big enough, I thought to myself. My roommate, whom I shall call Virginia, had requested to work with indigenous people as her Peace Corps assignment. A Venezuelan anthropologist welcomed the possibility of research assistance and assigned a series of readings to Virginia during the first few months of her service in Caracas.

The impact of my living arrangements with Virginia permeated my personal life and my work. I had never before known anyone like her and was temporarily blind to her character. The acquaintance lasted two and a half months before I admitted to myself that her relationship with the community was unusual and disruptive. I was uncertain about what to do and so continued to share the house for another month.

In truth, I couldn't walk on the street with Virginia without hearing poetic or lewd remarks in reference to her blond hair or bralessness. Groups of men serenaded at our window at 3:00 A.M. and afterward entered our house to drink beer and talk with Virginia. On other days, from 8:00 A.M. on, one man or another would come to the house — Samuel to study English, Antonio to talk about anthropology, José to discuss a plane trip. Often, too, these visitors remained from late evening until early morning. Antonio liked to stay all night and use my toothbrush before bedtime. Often and publicly, Virginia had broken through the boundaries of locally accepted gender and sexual behavior. Her clothing and actions ceased to be seen as cute and appropriate for a young, attractive woman when married men called on her, or when single men brought household goods with the expectation of marrying her, or when she openly slept with a man in a hammock at a local recreational water hole which families frequented.

Although I functioned well within local gender boundaries, doubts

---

[2] Rosalie H. Wax, *Doing Fieldwork: Warnings and Advice* (Chicago: University of Chicago Press, 1971), 7.

[3] Wax, 1971, 16.

about my intentions were evident in the criollo community. After all, I lived with Virginia, many men had entered and left our house at all hours of the day and night, and for the first six weeks of my stay we were frequently seen together. I had to work at establishing an identity distinct from Virginia's. Fortunately, the Guahibo saw little of her, so I worked among them with ease. But when I walked through town on a mapping project or to reach a peripheral town location, some criollo man or another would occasionally shout an obscenity or make a derisive remark. The younger men who sought Virginia's company frequently stopped me in the street to inquire about her.

Since Virginia told everyone she was an anthropologist on a research assignment, I expressed to my Venezuelan colleague, my graduate advisor, and two of the government employees who contributed substantially to my data collection, my concern about the effects of this deception on future anthropological research and also my concern about the image being presented of foreign researchers and American women abroad. United States citizens had not only just lost the war in Vietnam but were increasingly being told that they were not welcome in other countries to conduct research. The two Venezuelan men responded that people in the community did not equate Virginia's behavior with mine, but not all community behavior verified their judgment. My female Venezuelan colleague opined that the young men's behavior with Virginia was unusual for Venezuelan men, atypical in her experience. My graduate advisor (male), said, in essence, "Latin boys will be boys."

My data collection was influenced by the situation in that I delayed interviewing the leading criollo male entrepreneurs who were also the richest and highest-status people in town. I didn't know if I could face them, if they would say "no interview" or else assume that I had come for other than research purposes. However, since they hired more native Americans than other employers in town, information about their enterprises — the number of persons they employed, when they employed indigenous people, what they paid them, and their attitudes toward them — were very pertinent to my study. After several months' delay, I memorized the twelve questions on my two-page interview form and made appointments with these men. I got very specific information but no more; the men's posture, gestures, and tones of voice indicated a nervousness, even an irritation at my presence. I asked the questions as fast as I could before being ushered out, for they were all "busy." The final interview (thank heaven it was the final one or I would have lost my nerve and not continued) was cut short, never to be completed because the informant was "too busy." Although I also needed government statistics and information on development plans and political attitudes, since the territorial government was in a state of flux, my contacts with male government employees were often treated as invitations to a rendezvous, or else my inquiries were considered "cute." More than once I was sent on a wild goose chase for departmental heads or field representatives of some agency who had "just the information" I wanted.

Because of my precarious situation I never collected data at night. Instead I used that time to write up notes, correspond, read, and prepare for the next day's work — anything but face the body grabbing and the belittling comments that flowed from some people's mouths as heavily as the liquor was poured and with meanings as shallow as the Orinoco River waters. The afternoons before holidays and Friday afternoons found criollo and indigenous men alike stumbling the streets, grabbing at me to "sit and listen," to "understand," through the drivel, belches, and farts. Personally I churned inside. I demanded that Virginia put a stop to the early-morning serenading, but the stream of male visitors continued. Attempts were made by Virginia and her male friends to "find a man" for me, under the false assumption that I would prefer daily "diversions" to field research.

After three and a half months Virginia was transferred back to Caracas. Over the next couple of months fewer and fewer of her male coterie dropped by the house or stopped me on the street to inquire if she had returned. My work picked up substantially, and the number of remarks by strangers on the street about my appearance or gender decreased. The effects of Virginia's behavior were long-term, however, as I would soon discover.

Nearly every Saturday morning I went to the market areas where government trucks brought in indigenous people and their products. About 6:30 one morning, after nine months in the field, an assistant to the territorial governor staggered toward me after an all-night drunk. How much did I want, he asked. I replied quietly, so as not to embarrass him, that I was not interested, and then eased into the crowd. The market activities gained momentum and made it relatively easy for me to duck into groups to avoid repeated attempts by the assistant to approach me. Twice I got cornered, however, and the price he was willing to pay for my services went from twenty to forty dollars. Around 9:00 A.M., out in the open market area, the man lurched at me yet again, his reflexes slowed by the liquor he had drunk. I pulled back, protecting my camera from the sticky ice cream he was holding. Loudly he asked, "How much do you want? Eighty dollars?" This time I replied in a regular tone of voice, "I'm not interested. Leave me alone." "You don't understand," he responded. "Virginia understood." I responded in anger, "I'm not Virginia!" Those criollo who heard the exchange smiled. I had made my point well, and publicly. Emotionally drained, I went home and slept for two hours. The event, though most unpleasant, marked a change in community perceptions of me. Communications thereafter seemed to be easier.

RESOLUTION

My response to this entire situation was slow in coming. I feared my research goals might be in jeopardy and that I might be unable to collect sufficient and satisfactory data to complete my project. These fears indicated the tensions and frustration I was experiencing, common in fieldwork but exacerbated in my case. With no real role model and no ready advice on the gender and sex aspects of my field situation from faculty advisors, colleagues, or peers, my strategy became two-fold: to appear less feminine by local standards — and therefore less "available" — and to work endlessly on my research.

Hindsight has made me realize that my less feminine, supposedly more neutral image served as a mask, one that had some, but little, effect. To the populace in the town I was still a female and much too young to be genderless, as old women are considered. I wore odd-looking, loose-fitting clothing, no makeup, and flat-soled shoes. I approached social interaction among criollos with caution, accepting invitations to "diversions" only when they involved several people, but not female-male pairing. I paid for supplies and services rather than accept them as signs of friendship, as invitations, or as exchanges requiring reciprocity. I walked two to five miles a day visiting informants, mapping the town barrios, and observing indigenous behavior rather than accept transportation with men who had known Virginia. I refrained from the pleasure of a late afternoon beer in a tavern and did not permit my indigenous informants to visit me at my house, although several asked repeatedly to see how I lived.

With such a contrived image I felt better, as if I had stemmed the tide of public discussion about my motives and had begun to establish a semblance of professional research activity. Actually, my persistent work pattern, businesslike relationships, and affiliation with the Organization of American States[4] as a grant recipient served well to separate my behavior from Virginia's. The mask of genderlessness probably was unnecessary, but I only realized that after months of trying to pretend I was beyond gender classification.

Carrying out research in an ethical and scientific manner was of great importance to me. As the living arrangements with Virginia impinged more and more on my daily activities, I had begun to work harder and longer. I mapped the whole town, including house construction types, economic enterprises, and public service areas. I created a file on businesses and used that information to establish rapport and

---

[4] The Organization of American States is highly respected in Venezuela, and to my surprise it is known in Puerto Ayacucho, too. I received a monthly stipend from the Caracas office of the OAS and was required to wire them to indicate receipt prior to depositing the check in the local bank. These transactions were not kept private by those who performed them.

hold informal discussions regarding the employment of indigenous people. I avoided unpleasant encounters with Virginia's acquaintances by knowing every street and walkway, and by observing people's behavior so closely that I could predict it and hence maneuver into positions favorable to me.

The kinds of interruptions brought about by Virginia's actions created in me a need to confirm my research progress. I wrote quarterly evaluations stating what I had accomplished and what I intended to do in the next quarter. I developed systematic recordkeeping on each informant and every aspect of the research problem. As a result, I saw my own progress and knew that I was achieving my research goals. My inability to acquire certain kinds of information or to participate in specific activities due to my early association with Virginia was nearly inconsequential in view of the intensity of effort and level of organization the situation led me to develop. I had overcompensated, but I learned something in the process.

Conclusions

My intense experience in Venezuela, and the analysis undertaken for this account, helped me to understand and interpret my undergraduate and master's level fieldwork situations in North America as well as in Venezuela. The facade of a gender-neutral researcher role, and the concomitant assumption of a separate status outside the usual cultural parameters, helped me to comprehend a wider range of neutral pretenses assumed by researchers, including apolitical and amoral stances. The agricultural specialist, the computer salesperson, or the physicist is no more immune to culturally defined gender roles than the anthropologist.

In spite of efforts in the late 1960s by Berreman, Hymes, Gough, and others, the concept of acting neutrally is still presented as a viable option, implicitly and explicitly, to graduate students in anthropology (and in other fields). Berreman wrote that "as students of man, we have made a value choice for mankind, and it is inconsistent to their claim of sterile scientism which precludes the realization of the humanistic heritage of social science. As a corollary to this, we believe that neutrality on human issues is simply not an option open to anthropologists."[5] Hymes concurred: "Anthropology is unavoidably a political and ethical discipline, not merely an empirical speciality. It

---

[5] Gerald D. Berreman, "Bringing It All Back Home: Malaise in Anthropology." In Dell Hymes (ed.), *Reinventing Anthropology* (New York: Vintage Books, 1969), 89.

is founded in a personal commitment that has inescapably a reflective philosophical dimension."[6]

Gender neutralization has been but one facet of the overall concept of personal neutrality. It is not a possible, nor even a necessary or desirable, mode for field research, any more than theoretical or ethical neutrality is possible or desirable. Because most of us grow up with specific gender and sex patterns, we tend to consider them as biological-universal givens, which they are not. Sex and gender — sex in particular — have always been major cultural determinants of what we are allowed to do. Past attitudes about the "appropriateness" of discussing these topics prior to cross-cultural work and current laws related to equal rights in the United States should not deter our efforts to understand and clarify the functions of self and cultural definitions on our research and occupational activities.

The study and teaching of cross-cultural sex and gender characteristics should be approached with the same thoroughness and respect for cultural diversity that we are familiar with in other aspects of anthropological studies. The interaction and symbolic interaction studies of Edward T. Hall and Erving Goffman are used widely to introduce business personnel and diplomats to new cultural milieus. If anthropology is to be truly the science of humanity, then the thoroughness that has been devoted to studies of social organization should now be applied to understanding self, sex, and gender cross-cultural experiences.

REVIEW QUESTIONS

1. What is the usual attitude found at graduate schools about neutrality in ethnographic fieldwork, according to Conaway?

2. Why does the field situation described by Conaway affect her neutrality as an anthropological observer?

3. How did Conaway first attempt to present herself to informants in the field? How did informants respond and how did she eventually decide to present herself to them?

---

[6] Dell Hymes, "The Uses of Anthropology: Critical, Political, Personal," in Dell Hymes (ed.), *Reinventing Anthropology* (New York: Vintage Books, 1969), 48.

4. What was the main problem Conaway faced in the early months of her fieldwork in Puerto Ayacucho? How did she eventually overcome it?

5. What advice would you have about gender and sexual conduct for a student anthropologist about to leave for the field?

6. Do you think anthropologists can actually conduct ethnography on a neutral basis?

III

Language and Communication

Culture is a system of symbols that allows us to represent and communicate our experience. We are surrounded by symbols — the flag, a new automobile, a diamond ring, billboard pictures, and, of course, spoken words.

A *symbol* is anything that we can perceive with our senses that stands for something else. Almost anything we experience can come to have symbolic meaning. Every symbol has a referent that it calls to our attention. The term *mother-in-law* refers to a certain kind of relative, the mother of a person's spouse. When we communicate with symbols, we call attention not only to the referent but also to numerous connotations of the symbol. In our culture, *mother-in-law* connotes a stereotype of a person who is difficult to get along with, who meddles in the affairs of her married daughter or son, and who is to be avoided. Human beings have the capacity to assign meaning to anything they experience in an arbitrary fashion. This fact gives rise to limitless possibilities for communication.

Symbols greatly simplify the task of communication. Once we learn that a word like *barn*, for example, stands for a certain type of building, we can communicate about a whole range of specific buildings that fit into the category. And we can communicate about barns in their absence; we can even invent flying barns and dream about barns. Symbols make it possible to communicate the immense variety of human experience, whether past or present, tangible or intangible, good or bad.

Many channels are available to human beings for symbolic communication — sound, sight, touch, and smell. Language, our most highly developed communication system, uses the channel of sound (or for some deaf people, sight). *Language* is a system of cultural knowledge used to generate and interpret speech. It is a feature of every culture and a distinctive characteristic of the human animal. *Speech* refers to the behavior that produces vocal sounds. Our distinction between language and speech is like the one made for culture and behavior. Language is part of culture, the system of knowledge that generates behavior. Speech is the behavior generated and interpreted by language.

Every language is composed of three subsystems for dealing with vocal symbols: phonology, grammar, and semantics. Let's look briefly at each of these.

Phonology consists of the categories and rules for forming vocal symbols. It is concerned not directly with meaning but with the formation and recognition of the vocal sounds to which we assign meaning. For example, if you utter the word *bat*, you have followed a special set of rules for producing and ordering sound categories characteristic of the English language.

A basic element defined by phonological rules for every language is the phoneme. *Phonemes* are the minimal categories of speech sounds that serve to keep utterances apart. For example, speakers of English know that the words *bat, cat, mat, hat, nat,* and *fat* are different utterances because they hear the sounds /b/, /c/, /m/, /h/, /n/, and /f/ as different categories of sounds. In English each of these is a phoneme. Our language contains a limited number of phonemes from which we construct all our vocal symbols.

Phonemes are arbitrarily constructed, however. Each phoneme actually classifies slightly different sounds as though they were the same. Different languages may divide up the same range of speech sounds into different sound categories. For example, speakers of English treat the sound /t/ as a single phoneme. Hindi speakers take the same general range and divide it into four phonemes: /t/, /tʰ/, /T/, and /Tʰ/. (The lowercase *t*'s are made with the tongue against the front teeth, while uppercase *t*'s are made by touching the tongue to the roof of the mouth further back than would be normal for an English speaker. The *h* indicates a puff of air, called aspiration, associated with the *t* sound.) Americans are likely to miss important distinctions among Hindi words because they hear these four different phonemes as a single one. Hindi speakers, on the other hand, tend to hear more than one sound category as they listen to English speakers pronounce *t*'s. The situation is reversed for /w/ and /v/. We treat these as two phonemes, whereas Hindi speakers hear them as one. For them, the English words *wine* and *vine* are the same.

Phonology also includes rules for ordering different sounds. Even when we try to talk nonsense, we usually create words that follow

English phonological rules. It would be unlikely, for example, for us ever to begin a word with the phoneme /ng/ usually written in English as "ing." It must come at the end or in the middle of words.

Grammar is the second subsystem of language. *Grammar* refers to the categories and rules for combining vocal symbols. No grammar contains rules for combining every word or element of meaning in the language. If this were the case, grammars would be so unwieldy that no one could learn all the rules in a lifetime. Every grammar deals with *categories* of symbols, such as the ones we call nouns and verbs. Once you know the rules covering a particular category, you can use it in the appropriate order.

Morphemes are the categories in any language that carry meaning. They are minimal units of meaning that cannot be subdivided. Morphemes occur in more complex patterns than you may think. The term *bats*, for example, is actually two morphemes, /bat/ meaning a flying mammal and /s/ meaning plural. Even more confusing, two different morphemes may have the same sound shape. /Bat/ can refer to a wooden club used in baseball as well as a flying mammal.

The third subsystem of every language is semantics. *Semantics* refers to the categories and rules for relating vocal symbols to their referents. Like the rules of grammar, semantic rules are simple instructions to combine things; they instruct us to combine words with what they refer to. A symbol can be said to *refer* because it focuses our attention and makes us take account of something. For example, /bat/ refers to a family of flying mammals, as we have already noted.

Language regularly occurs in a social context, and to understand its use fully, it is important to recognize its relation to sociolinguistic rules. *Sociolinguistic rules* combine meaningful utterances with social situations into appropriate messages.

Although language is the most important human vehicle for communication, almost anything we can sense may represent a symbol that conveys meaning. The way we sit, how we use our eyes, how we dress, the car we own, the number of bathrooms in our house — all these things carry symbolic meaning. We learn what they mean as we acquire culture. Indeed, a major reason we feel so uncomfortable when we enter a group with a strange culture is our inability to decode our hosts' symbolic world.

The articles in this section illustrate several important aspects of language and communication. In the first selection, "The Sounds of Silence," Edward and Mildred Hall show the significance of nonverbal symbols. They describe how tacit behaviors such as eye contact and speaking distance form powerful channels for communication in human groups. The second selection, Laura Bohannan's "Shakespeare in the Bush," illustrates the misunderstanding that can occur when people do not share each other's cultural categories. When she tells the classic story of Hamlet to African Tiv elders, the plot takes on an entirely different meaning. In the next article, "Race, Culture, and Misunderstanding," Thomas Kochman shows that different *styles* of talking can also cause misunderstanding and conflict, this time in the context of how black and white Americans try to initiate sexual relations. In the final selection, David Thomson decribes the hypothesis generated in the 1930s by a young linguist named Benjamin Lee Whorf. Whorf argued that instead of merely labeling reality, the words and grammatical structure of a language could actually determine the way its speakers perceived the world. Thomson reviews and evaluates this hypothesis and asserts that although language may not create reality, it can *affect* our perceptions, as illustrated by the use of words in American advertising and political doublespeak.

KEY TERMS

symbol	grammar
language	morpheme
speech	semantics
phonology	sociolinguistic rules
phoneme	nonlinguistic symbols

READINGS IN THIS SECTION

5 *The Sounds of Silence*

EDWARD T. HALL and MILDRED REED HALL

*People communicate with more than just words. An important part
of every encounter are the messages we send with our bodies and
faces: the smile, the frown, the slouch of the shoulders, or the
tightly crossed legs are only a few gestures that add another dimension to our verbal statements. These gestures as well as their
social meaning change from one culture to another. In this article,
the Halls describe and explain the function of nonverbal behavior
in social encounters.*

Bob leaves his apartment at 8:15 A.M. and stops at the corner drugstore
for breakfast. Before he can speak, the counterman says, "The usual?"
Bob nods yes. While he savors his Danish, a fat man pushes onto the
adjoining stool and overflows into his space. Bob scowls and the man
pulls himself in as much as he can. Bob has sent two messages without
speaking a syllable.

Henry has an appointment to meet Arthur at 11 o'clock; he arrives
at 11:30. Their conversation is friendly, but Arthur retains a lingering
hostility. Henry has unconsciously communicated that he doesn't think
the appointment is very important or that Arthur is a person who
needs to be treated with respect.

George is talking to Charley's wife at a party. Their conversation is entirely trivial, yet Charley glares at them suspiciously. Their physical proximity and the movements of their eyes reveal that they are powerfully attracted to each other.

José Ybarra and Sir Edmund Jones are at the same party and it is important for them to establish a cordial relationship for business reasons. Each is trying to be warm and friendly, yet they will part with mutual distrust and their business transaction will probably fall through. José, in Latin fashion, moved closer and closer to Sir Edmund as they spoke, and this movement was miscommunicated as pushiness to Sir Edmund, who kept backing away from this intimacy, and this was miscommunicated to José as coldness. The silent languages of Latin and English cultures are more difficult to learn than their spoken languages.

In each of these cases, we see the subtle power of nonverbal communication. The only language used throughout most of the history of humanity (in evolutionary terms, vocal communication is relatively recent), it is the first form of communication you learn. You use this preverbal language, consciously and unconsciously, every day to tell other people how you feel about yourself and them. This language includes your posture, gestures, facial expressions, costume, the way you walk, even your treatment of time and space and material things. All people communicate on several different levels at the same time, but are usually aware of only the verbal dialog and don't realize that they respond to nonverbal messages. But when a person says one thing and really believes something else, the discrepancy between the two can usually be sensed. Nonverbal communication systems are much less subject to the conscious deception that often occurs in verbal systems. When we find ourselves thinking, "I don't know what it is about him, but he doesn't seem sincere," it's usually this lack of congruity between a person's words and his behavior that makes us anxious and uncomfortable.

Few of us realize how much we all depend on body movement in our conversation or are aware of the hidden rules that govern listening behavior. But we know instantly whether or not the person we're talking to is "tuned in" and we're very sensitive to any breach in listening etiquette. In white middle-class American culture, when someone wants to show he is listening to someone else, he looks either at the other person's face or, specifically, at his eyes, shifting his gaze from one eye to the other.

If you observe a person conversing, you'll notice that he indicates he's listening by nodding his head. He also makes little "Hmm" noises. If he agrees with what's being said, he may give a vigorous nod. To show pleasure or affirmation, he smiles; if he has some reservations, he looks skeptical by raising an eyebrow or pulling down the corners of his mouth. If a participant wants to terminate the conversation, he may start shifting his body position, stretching his legs, crossing or uncrossing them, bobbing his foot or diverting his gaze from the speaker. The more he fidgets, the more the speaker becomes aware that he has lost his audience. As a last measure, the listener may look at his watch to indicate the imminent end of the conversation.

Talking and listening are so intricately intertwined that a person cannot do one without the other. Even when one is alone and talking to oneself, there is part of the brain that speaks while another part listens. In all conversations, the listener is positively or negatively reinforcing the speaker all the time. He may even guide the conversation without knowing it, by laughing or frowning or dismissing the argument with a wave of his hand.

The language of the eyes — another age-old way of exchanging feelings — is both subtle and complex. Not only do men and women use their eyes differently but there are class, generation, regional, ethnic, and national cultural differences. Americans often complain about the way foreigners stare at people or hold a glance too long. Most Americans look away from someone who is using his eyes in an unfamiliar way because it makes them self-conscious. If a man looks at another man's wife in a certain way, he's asking for trouble, as indicated earlier. But he might not be ill-mannered or seeking to challenge the husband. He might be a European in this country who hasn't learned our visual mores. Many American women visiting France or Italy are acutely embarrassed because, for the first time in their lives, men really look at them — their eyes, hair, nose, lips, breasts, hips, legs, thighs, knees, ankles, feet, clothes, hairdo, even their walk. These same women, once they have become used to being looked at, often return to the United States and are overcome with the feeling that "No one ever really looks at me anymore."

Analyzing the mass of data on the eyes, it is possible to sort out at least three ways in which the eyes are used to communicate: dominance vs. submission, involvement vs. detachment, and positive vs. negative attitude. In addition, there are three levels of consciousness and control, which can be categorized as follows: (1) conscious use of the eyes to communicate, such as the flirting blink and the intimate nose-wrinkling squint; (2) the very extensive category of unconscious but learned behavior governing where the eyes are directed and when (this unwritten set of rules dictates how and under what circumstances the sexes, as well as people of all status categories, look at each other); and (3) the response of the eye itself, which is completely outside both awareness and control — changes in the cast (the sparkle) of the eye and the pupillary reflex.

The eye is unlike any other organ of the body, for it is an extension of the brain. The unconscious pupillary reflex and the cast of the eye have been known by people of Middle Eastern origin for years—although most are unaware of their knowledge. Depending on the context, Arabs and others look either directly at the eyes or deeply *into* the eyes of their interlocutor. We became aware of this in the Middle East several years ago while looking at jewelry. The merchant suddenly started to push a particular bracelet at a customer and said, "You buy this one." What interested us was that the bracelet was not the one that had been consciously selected by the purchaser. But the merchant, watching the pupils of the eyes, knew what the purchaser really wanted to buy. Whether he specifically knew *how* he knew is debatable.

A psychologist at the University of Chicago, Eckhard Hess, was the first to conduct systematic studies of the pupillary reflex. His wife remarked one evening, while watching him reading in bed, that he must be very interested in the text because his pupils were dilated. Following up on this, Hess slipped some pictures of nudes into a stack of photographs that he gave to his male assistant. Not looking at the photographs but watching his assistant's pupils, Hess was able to tell precisely when the assistant came to the nudes. In further experiments, Hess retouched the eyes in a photograph of a woman. In one print, he made the pupils small, in another, large; nothing else was changed. Subjects who were given the photographs found the woman with the dilated pupils much more attractive. Any man who has had the experience of seeing a woman look at him as her pupils widen with reflex speed knows that she's flashing him a message.

The eye-sparkle phenomenon frequently turns up in our interviews of couples in love. It's apparently one of the first reliable clues in the other person that love is genuine. To date, there is no scientific data to explain eye sparkle; no investigation of the pupil, the cornea, or even the white sclera of the eye shows how the sparkle originates. Yet we all know it when we see it.

One common situation for most people involves the use of the eyes in the street and in public. Although eye behavior follows a definite set of rules, the rules vary according to the place, the needs and feelings of the people, and their ethnic background. For urban whites, once they're within definite recognition distance (16–32 feet for people with average eyesight), there is mutual avoidance of eye contact—unless they want something specific: a pickup, a handout, or information of some kind. In the West and in small towns generally, however, people are much more likely to look at and greet one another, even if they're strangers.

It's permissible to look at people if they're beyond recognition distance; but one inside this sacred zone, you can only steal a glance at strangers. You *must* greet friends, however; to fail to do so is insulting. Yet, to stare too fixedly even at them is considered rude and hostile. Of course, all of these rules are variable.

A great many blacks, for example, greet each other in public even if they don't know each other. To blacks, most eye behavior of whites has the effect of giving the impression that they aren't there, but this is due to white avoidance of eye contact with *anyone* in the street.

Another very basic difference between people of different ethnic backgrounds is their sense of territoriality and how they handle space. This is the silent communication, or miscommunication, that caused friction between Mr. Ybarra and Sir Edmund Jones in our earlier example. We know from research that everyone has around himself an invisible bubble of space that contracts and expands depending on several factors: his emotional state, the activity he's performing at the time and his cultural background. This bubble is a kind of mobile territory that he will defend against intrusion. If he is accustomed to close personal distance between himself and others, his bubble will be smaller than that of someone who's accustomed to greater personal distance. People of North European heritage — English, Scandinavian, Swiss, and German — tend to avoid contact. Those whose heritage is Italian, French, Spanish, Russian, Latin American, or Middle Eastern like close personal contact.

People are very sensitive to any intrusion into their spatial bubble. If someone stands too close to you, your first instinct is to back up. If that's not possible, you lean away and pull yourself in, tensing your muscles. If the intruder doesn't respond to these body signals, you may then try to protect yourself, using a briefcase, umbrella, or raincoat. Women — especially when traveling alone — often plant their pocketbook in such a way that no one can get very close to them. As a last resort, you may move to another spot and position yourself behind a desk or a chair that provides screening. Everyone tries to adjust the space around himself in a way that's comfortable for him; most often, he does this unconsciously.

Emotions also have a direct effect on the size of a person's territory. When you're angry or under stress, your bubble expands and you require more space. New York psychiatrist Augustus Kinzel found a difference in what he calls Body-Buffer Zones between violent and nonviolent prison inmates. Dr. Kinzel conducted experiments in which each prisoner was placed in the center of a small room and then Dr. Kinzel slowly walked toward him. Nonviolent prisoners allowed him to come quite close, while prisoners with a history of violent behavior couldn't tolerate his proximity and reacted with some vehemence.

Apparently, people under stress experience other people as looming larger and closer than they actually are. Studies of schizophrenic patients have indicated that they sometimes have a distorted perception of space, and several psychiatrists have reported patients who experience their body boundaries as filling up an entire room. For these patients, anyone who comes into the room is actually inside their body, and such an intrusion may trigger a violent outburst.

Unfortunately, there is little detailed information about normal people who live in highly congested urban areas. We do know, of course, that the noise, pollution, dirt, crowding, and confusion of our cities induce feelings of stress in most of us, and stress leads to a need for greater space. The man who's packed into a subway, jostled in the street, crowded into an elevator, and forced to work all day in a bull pen or in a small office without auditory or visual privacy is going to be very stressed at the end of his day. He needs places that provide relief from constant overstimulation of his nervous system. Stress from overcrowding is cumulative and people can tolerate more crowding early in the day than later; note the increased bad temper during the evening rush hour as compared with the morning melee. Certainly one factor in people's desire to commute by car is the need for privacy and relief from crowding (except, often, from other cars); it may be the only time of the day when nobody can intrude.

In crowded public places, we tense our muscles and hold ourselves stiff, and thereby communicate to others our desire not to intrude on their space and, above all, not to touch them. We also avoid eye contact, and the total effect is that of someone who has "tuned out." Walking along the street, our bubble expands slightly as we move in a stream of strangers, taking care not to bump into them. In the office, at meetings, in restaurants, our bubble keeps changing as it adjusts to the activity at hand.

Most white middle-class Americans use four main distances in their business and social relations: intimate, personal, social, and public. Each of these distances has a near and a far phase and is accompanied by changes in the volume of the voice. Intimate distance varies from direct physical contact with another person to a distance of six to eighteen inches and is used for our most private activities — caressing another person or making love. At this distance, you are overwhelmed by sensory inputs from the other person — heat from the body, tactile stimulation from the skin, the fragrance of perfume, even the sound of breathing — all of which literally envelop you. Even at the far phase, you're still within easy touching distance. In general, the use of intimate distance in public between adults is frowned on. It's also much too close for strangers, except under conditions of extreme crowding.

In the second zone — personal distance — the close phase is 1½ to 2½ feet; it's at this distance that wives usually stand from their husbands in public. If another woman moves into this zone, the wife will most likely be disturbed. The far phase — 2½ to 4 feet — is the distance used to "keep someone at arm's length" and is the most common spacing used by people in conversation.

The third zone — social distance — is employed during business transactions or exchanges with a clerk or repairman. People who work together tend to use close social distance — 4 to 7 feet. This is also the distance for conversation at social gatherings. To stand at this distance from someone who is seated has a dominating effect (for example, teacher to pupil, boss to secretary). The far phase of the third zone — 7 to 12 feet — is where people stand when someone says, "Stand back so I can look at you." This distance lends a formal tone to business or social discourse. In an executive office, the desk serves to keep people at this distance.

The fourth zone — public distance — is used by teachers in classrooms or speakers at public gatherings. At it farthest phase — 25 feet and beyond — it is used for important public figures. Violations of this distance can lead to serious complications. During his 1970 U.S. visit, the president of France, Georges Pompidou, was harassed by pickets in Chicago, who were permitted to get within touching distance. Since pickets in France are kept behind barricades a block or more away, the president was outraged by this insult to his person, and President Nixon was obliged to communicate his concern as well as offer his personal apologies.

It is interesting to note how American pitchmen and panhandlers exploit the unwritten, unspoken conventions of eye and distance. Both take advantage of the fact that once explicit eye contact is established, it is rude to look away, because to do so means to brusquely dismiss the other person and his needs. Once having caught the eye of his mark, the panhandler then locks on, not letting go until he moves through the public zone, the social zone, and, finally, into the intimate sphere, where people are most vulnerable.

Touch also is an important part of the constant stream of communication that takes place between people. A light touch, a firm touch, a blow, a caress are all communications. In an effort to break down barriers among people, there's been a recent upsurge in group-encounter activities, in which strangers are encouraged to touch one another. In special situations such as these, the rules for not touching are broken with group approval and people gradually lose some of their inhibitions.

Although most people don't realize it, space is perceived and distances are set not by vision alone but with all the senses. Auditory space is perceived with the ears, thermal space with the skin, kinesthetic space with the muscles of the body, and olfactory space with the nose. And, once again, it's our culture that determines how our senses are programmed — which sensory information ranks highest and lowest. The important thing to remember is that culture is very persistent. In this country, we've noted the existence of cultural patterns that determine distance between people in the third and fourth generations of some families, despite their prolonged contact with people of very different cultural heritages.

Whenever there is great cultural distance between two people, there are bound to be problems arising from differences in behavior and expectations. An example is the American couple who consulted a psychiatrist about their marital problems. The husband was from New England and had been brought up by reserved parents who taught him to control his emotions and to respect the need for privacy. His wife was from an Italian family and had been brought up in close contact with all the members of her large family, who were extremely warm, volatile, and demonstrative.

When the husband came home after a hard day at the office, dragging his feet, and longing for peace and quiet, his wife would rush to him and smother him. Clasping his hands, rubbing his brow, crooning over his weary head, she never left him alone. But when his wife was upset or anxious about her day, the husband's response was to withdraw completely and leave her alone. No comforting, no affectionate embrace, no attention — just solitude. The woman became convinced her husband didn't love her and, in desperation, she consulted a psychiatrist. Their problem wasn't basically psychological but cultural.

Why have we developed all these different ways of communicating messages without words? One reason is that people don't like to spell out certain kinds of messages. We prefer to find other ways of showing our feelings. This is especially true in relationships as sensitive as courtship. Men don't like to be rejected and most women don't want to turn a man down bluntly. Instead, we work out subtle ways of encouraging or discouraging each other that save face and avoid confrontations.

How a person handles space in dating others is an obvious and very sensitive indicator of how he or she feels about the other person. On a first date, if a woman sits or stands so close to a man that he is acutely conscious of her physical presence — inside the intimate-distance zone — the man usually construes it to mean that she is encouraging him. However, before the man starts moving in on the woman, he should be sure what message she's really sending; otherwise, he risks bruising his ego. What is close to someone of North European background may be neutral or distant to someone of Italian heritage. Also, women sometimes use space as a way of misleading a man, and there are few things that put men off more than women who communicate contradictory messages — cuddling up and then acting insulted when a man takes the next step.

How does a woman communicate interest in a man? In addition to such familiar gambits as smiling at him, she may glance shyly at him, blush, and then look away. Or she may give him a real come-on look and move in very close when he approaches. She may touch his arm and ask for a light. As she leans forward to light her cigarette, she may brush him lightly, enveloping him in her perfume. She'll probably continue to smile at him and she may use what ethnologists call preening gestures — touching the back of her hair, thrusting her breasts forward, tilting her hips as she stands or crossing her legs if she's seated, perhaps even exposing one thigh or putting a hand on her thigh and stroking it. She may also stroke her wrists as she converses or show the palm of her hand as a way of gaining his attention. Her skin may be unusually flushed or quite pale, her eyes brighter, the pupils larger.

If a man sees a woman whom he wants to attract, he tries to present himself by his posture and stance as someone who is self-assured. He moves briskly and confidently. When he catches the eye of the woman, he may hold her glance a little longer than normal. If he gets an encouraging smile, he'll move in close and engage her in small talk. As they converse, his glance shifts over her face and body. He, too, may make preening gestures — straightening his tie, smoothing his hair, or shooting his cuffs.

How do people learn body language? The same way they learn spoken language — by observing and imitating people around them as they're growing up. Little girls imitate their mothers or an older female. Little boys imitate their fathers or a respected uncle or a character on television. In this way, they learn the gender signals appropriate for their sex. Regional, class, and ethnic patterns of body behavior are also learned in childhood and persist throughout life.

Such patterns of masculine and feminine body behavior vary widely from one culture to another. In America, for example, women stand with their thighs together. Many walk with their pelvis tipped slightly forward and their upper arms close to their body. When they sit, they cross their legs at the knee or, if they are well past middle age, they may cross their ankles. American men hold their arms away from their body, often swinging them as they walk. They stand with their legs apart (an extreme example is the cowboy, with legs apart and thumbs tucked into his belt). When they sit, they put their feet on the floor with legs apart and, in some parts of the country, they cross their legs by putting one ankle on the other knee.

Leg behavior indicates sex, status, and personality. It also indicates whether or not one is at ease or is showing respect or disrespect for the other person. Young Latin-American males avoid crossing their legs. In their world of *machismo*, the preferred position for young males when with one another (if there is no older dominant male present to whom they must show respect) is to sit on the base of their spine with their leg muscles relaxed and their feet wide apart. Their respect position is like our military equivalent; spine straight, heels and ankles together — almost identical to that displayed by properly brought up young women in New England in the early part of this century.

American women who sit with their legs spread apart in the presence of males are *not* normally signaling a come-on — they are simply (and often unconsciously) sitting like men. Middle-class women in the presence of other women to whom they are very close may on occasion throw themselves down on a soft chair or sofa and let themselves go. This is a signal that nothing serious will be taken up. Males, on the other hand, lean back and prop their legs up on the nearest object.

The way we walk, similarly, indicates status, respect, mood, and ethnic or cultural affiliation. The many variants of the female walk are too well known to go into here, except to say that a man would have to be blind not to be turned on by the way some women walk — a fact that made Mae West rich before scientists ever studied these matters. To white Americans, some French middle-class males walk in a way that is both humorous and suspect. There is a bounce and looseness to the French walk, as though the parts of the body were somehow unrelated. Jacques Tati, the French movie actor, walks this way; so does the great mime, Marcel Marceau.

Blacks and whites in America — with the exception of middle- and upper-middle-class professionals of both groups — move and walk very differently from each other. To the blacks, whites often seem incredibly stiff, almost mechanical in their movements. Black males, on the other hand, have a looseness and coordination that frequently makes whites a little uneasy; it's too different, too integrated, too alive, too male. Norman Mailer has said that squares walk from the shoulders, like bears, but blacks and hippies walk from the hips, like cats.

All over the world, people walk not only in their own characteristic way but have walks that communicate the nature of their involvement with whatever it is they're doing. The purposeful walk of North Europeans is an important component of proper behavior on the job. Any male who has been in the military knows how essential it is to walk properly (which makes for a continuing source of tension between blacks and whites in the Service). The quick shuffle of servants in the Far East in the old days was a show of respect. On the island of Truk, when we last visited, the inhabitants even had a name for the respectful walk that one used when in the presence of a chief or when walking past a chief's house. The term was *sufan*, which meant to be humble and respectful.

The notion that people communicate volumes by their gestures, facial expressions, posture, and walk is not new; actors, dancers, writers, and psychiatrists have long been aware of it. Only in recent years, however, have scientists begun to make systematic observations of body motions. Ray L. Birdwhistell of the University of Pennsylvania is one of the pioneers in body-motion research and coined the term *kinesics* to describe this field. He developed an elaborate notation system to record both facial and body movements, using an approach similar to that of the linguist, who studies the basic elements of speech. Birdwhistell and other kinesicists such as Albert Sheflen, Adam Kendon, and William Condon take movies of people interacting. They run the film over and over again, often at reduced speed for frame-by-frame analysis, so that they can observe even the slightest body movements not perceptible at normal interaction speeds. These movements are then recorded in notebooks for later analysis.

To appreciate the importance of nonverbal communication systems, consider the unskilled inner-city black looking for a job. His handling of time and space alone is sufficiently different from the white middle-class pattern to create great misunderstandings on both sides. The black is told to appear for a job interview at a certain time. He arrives late. The white interviewer concludes from his tardy arrival that the black is irresponsible and not really interested in the job. What the interviewer doesn't know is that the black time system (often referred to by blacks as C.P.T. — colored people's time) isn't the same as that of whites. In the words of a black student who had been told to make an appointment to see his professor: "Man, you *must* be putting me on. I never had an appointment in my life."

The black job applicant, having arrived late for his interview, may further antagonize the white interviewer by his posture and his eye behavior. Perhaps he slouches and avoids looking at the interviewer; to him, this is playing it cool. To the interviewer, however, he may well look shifty and sound uninterested. The interviewer has failed to notice the actual signs of interest and eagerness in the black's behavior, such as the subtle shift in the quality of the voice — a gentle and tentative excitement — an almost imperceptible change in the cast of the eyes and a relaxing of the jaw muscles.

Moreover, correct reading of black-white behavior is continually complicated by the fact that both groups are comprised of individuals — some of whom try to accommodate and some of whom make it a point of pride *not* to accommodate. At present, this means that many Americans, when thrown into contact with one another, are in the precarious position of not knowing which pattern applies. Once identified and analyzed, nonverbal communications systems can be taught, like a foreign language. Without this training, we respond to nonverbal communications in terms of our own culture; we read everyone's behavior as if it were our own, and thus we often misunderstand it.

Several years ago in New York City, there was a program for sending children from predominantly black and Puerto Rican low-income neighborhoods to summer school in a white upper-class neighborhood on the East Side. One morning, a group of young black and Puerto Rican boys raced down the street, shouting and screaming and overturning garbage cans on their way to school. A doorman from an apartment building nearby chased them and cornered one of them inside a building. The boy drew a knife and attacked the doorman. This tragedy would not have occurred if the doorman had been familiar with the behavior of boys from low-income neighborhoods, where such antics are routine and socially acceptable and where pursuit would be expected to invite a violent response.

The language of behavior is extremely complex. Most of us are lucky to have under control one subcultural system — the one that reflects our sex, class, generation, and geographic region within the United States. Because of its complexity, efforts to isolate bits of nonverbal communication and generalize from them are in vain; you don't become an instant expert on people's behavior by watching them at cocktail parties. Body language isn't something that's independent of the person, something that can be donned and doffed like a suit of clothes.

Our research and that of our colleagues have shown that, far from being a superficial form of communication that can be consciously manipulated, nonverbal communication systems are interwoven into the fabric of the personality and, as sociologist Erving Goffman has demonstrated, into society itself. They are the warp and woof of daily interactions with others and they influence how one expresses oneself, how one experiences oneself as a man or a woman.

Nonverbal communications signal to members of your own group what kind of person you are, how you feel about others, how you'll fit into and work in a group, whether you're assured or anxious, the degree to which you feel comfortable with the standards of your own culture, as well as deeply significant feelings about the self, including the state of your own psyche. For most of us, it's difficult to accept the reality of another's behavioral system. And, of course, none of us will ever become fully knowledgeable of the importance of every nonverbal signal. But as long as each of us realizes the power of these signals, this society's diversity can be a source of great strength rather than a further — and subtly powerful — source of division.

REVIEW QUESTIONS

1. What are the ways people communicate with each other nonverbally, according to Edward and Mildred Hall?

2. What are the four culturally learned speaking distances used by Americans?

3. How does the nonverbal communication described by the Halls relate to the concept of tacit culture discussed in the last section?

4. Why is nonverbal communication so likely to be a source of cross-cultural misunderstanding?

6   Shakespeare in the Bush

LAURA BOHANNAN

Cultural anthropologists are all concerned with meaning, *with the difficult task of translation from one language to another. In this classic of anthropology, Laura Bohannan shows the difficulty of translating the meaning of* Hamlet *to the Tiv in West Africa. She forcefully demonstrates the way in which different cultures provide distinct and separate worlds of meaning for those who have learned to live by them.*

Just before I left Oxford for the Tiv in West Africa, conversation turned to the season at Stratford. "You Americans," said a friend, "often have difficulty with Shakespeare. He was, after all, a very English poet, and one can easily misinterpret the universal by misunderstanding the particular."

I protested that human nature is pretty much the same the whole world over; at least the general plot and motivation of the greater tragedies would always be clear — everywhere — although some details of custom might have to be explained and difficulties of translation might produce other slight changes. To end an argument we could not conclude, my friend gave me a copy of *Hamlet* to study in the African bush: it would, he hoped, lift my mind above its primitive surround-

Reprinted with permission by the author from *Natural History Magazine*, August/ September 1966. Copyright © 1966 by Laura Bohannan.

ings, and possibly I might, by prolonged meditation, achieve the grace of correct interpretation.

It was my second field trip to that African tribe, and I thought myself ready to live in one of its remote sections — an area difficult to cross even on foot. I eventually settled on the hillock of a very knowledgeable old man, the head of a homestead of some hundred and forty people, all of whom were either his close relatives or their wives and children. Like the other elders of the vicinity, the old man spent most of his time performing ceremonies seldom seen these days in the more accessible parts of the tribe. I was delighted. Soon there would be three months of enforced isolation and leisure, between the harvest that takes place just before the rising of the swamps and the clearing of new farms when the water goes down. Then, I thought, they would have even more time to perform ceremonies and explain them to me.

I was quite mistaken. Most of the ceremonies demanded the presence of elders from several homesteads. As the swamps rose, the old men found it too difficult to walk from one homestead to the next, and the ceremonies gradually ceased. As the swamps rose even higher, all activities but one came to an end. The women brewed beer from maize and millet. Men, women, and children sat on their hillocks and drank it.

People began to drink at dawn. By midmorning the whole homestead was singing, dancing, and drumming. When it rained, people had to sit inside their huts: there they drank and sang or they drank and told stories. In any case, by noon or before, I either had to join the party or retire to my own hut and my books. "One does not discuss serious matters when there is beer. Come, drink with us." Since I lacked their capacity for the thick native beer, I spent more and more time with *Hamlet*. Before the end of the second month, grace descended on me. I was quite sure that *Hamlet* had only one possible interpretation, and that one universally obvious.

Early every morning, in the hope of having some serious talk before the beer party, I used to call on the old man at his reception hut — a circle of posts supporting a thatched roof above a low mud wall to keep out wind and rain. One day I crawled through the low doorway and found most of the men of the homestead sitting huddled in their ragged cloths on stools, low plank beds, and reclining chairs, warming themselves against the chill of the rain around a smoky fire. In the center were three pots of beer. The party had started.

The old man greeted me cordially. "Sit down and drink." I accepted a large calabash full of beer, poured some into a small drinking gourd, and tossed it down. Then I poured some more into the same gourd for the man second in seniority to my host before I handed my calabash over to a young man for further distribution. Important people shouldn't ladle beer themselves.

"It is better like this," the old man said, looking at me approvingly and plucking at the thatch that had caught in my hair. "You should sit and drink with us more often. Your servants tell me that when you are not with us, you sit inside your hut looking at a paper."

· The old man was acquainted with four kinds of "papers": tax receipts, bride price receipts, court fee receipts, and letters. The messenger who brought him letters from the chief used them mainly as a badge of office, for he always knew what was in them and told the old man. Personal letters for the few who had relatives in the government or mission stations were kept until someone went to a large market where there was a letter writer and reader. Since my arrival, letters were brought to me to be read. A few men also brought me bride price receipts, privately, with requests to change the figures to a higher sum. I found moral arguments were of no avail, since in-laws are fair game, and the technical hazards of forgery difficult to explain to an illiterate people. I did not wish them to think me silly enough to look at any such papers for days on end, and I hastily explained that my "paper" was one of the "things of long ago" of my country.

"Ah," said the old men. "Tell us."

I protested that I was not a storyteller. Storytelling is a skilled art among them; their standards are high, and the audiences critical — and vocal in their criticism. I protested in vain. This morning they wanted to hear a story while they drank. They threatened to tell me no more stories until I told them one of mine. Finally, the old man promised that no one would criticize my style "for we know you are struggling with our language." "But," put in one of the elders, "you must explain what we do not understand, as we do when we tell you our stories." Realizing that here was my chance to prove *Hamlet* universally intelligible, I agreed.

The old man handed me some more beer to help me on with my storytelling. Men filled their long wooden pipes and knocked coals from the fire to place in the pipe bowls; then, puffing contentedly, they sat back to listen. I began in the proper style, "Not yesterday, not yesterday, but long ago, a thing occurred. One night three men were keeping watch outside the homestead of the great chief, when suddenly they saw the former chief approach them."

"Why was he no longer their chief?"

"He was dead," I explained. "That is why they were troubled and afraid when they saw him."

"Impossible," began one of the elders, handing his pipe on to his neighbor, who interrupted, "Of course it wasn't the dead chief. It was an omen sent by a witch. Go on."

Slightly shaken, I continued. "One of these three was a man who knew things" — the closest translation for scholar, but unfortunately it also meant witch. The second elder looked triumphantly at the first. "So he spoke to the dead chief, saying, 'Tell us what we must do so you may rest in your grave,' but the dead chief did not answer. He vanished, and they could see him no more. Then the man who knew things — his name was Horatio — said this event was the affair of the dead chief's son, Hamlet."

There was a general shaking of heads around the circle. "Had the dead chief no living brothers? Or was this son the chief?"

"No," I replied. "That is, he had one living brother who became the chief when the elder brother died."

The old men muttered: such omens were matters for chiefs and elders, not for youngsters; no good could come of being behind a chief's back; clearly Horatio was not a man who knew things.

"Yes, he was," I insisted, shooing a chicken away from my beer. "In our country the son is next to the father. The dead chief's younger brother had become the great chief. He had also married his elder brother's widow only about a month after the funeral."

"He did well," the old man beamed and announced to the others, "I told you that if we knew more about Europeans, we would find they really were very like us. In our country also," he added to me, "the younger brother marries the elder brother's widow and becomes the father of his children. Now, if your uncle, who married your widowed mother, is your father's full brother, then he will be a real father to you. Did Hamlet's father and uncle have one mother?"

His question barely penetrated my mind; I was too upset and thrown too far off balance by having one of the most important elements of *Hamlet* knocked straight out of the picture. Rather uncertainly I said that I thought they had the same mother, but I wasn't sure — the story didn't say. The old man told me severely that these genealogical details made all the difference and that when I got home I must ask the elders about it. He shouted out the door to one of his younger wives to bring his goatskin bag.

Determined to save what I could of the mother motif, I took a deep breath and began again. "The son Hamlet was very sad because his mother had married again so quickly. There was no need for her to do so, and it is our custom for a widow not to go to her next husband until she has mourned for two years."

"Two years is too long," objected the wife, who had appeared with the old man's battered goatskin bag. "Who will hoe your farms for you while you have no husband?"

"Hamlet," I retorted without thinking, "was old enough to hoe his mother's farms himself. There was no need for her to remarry." No one looked convinced. I gave up. "His mother and the great chief told Hamlet not to be sad, for the great chief himself would be a father to Hamlet. Furthermore, Hamlet would be the next chief: therefore he must stay to learn the things of a chief. Hamlet agreed to remain, and all the rest went off to drink beer."

While I paused, perplexed at how to render Hamlet's disgusted soliloquy to an audience convinced that Claudius and Gertrude had behaved in the best possible manner, one of the younger men asked me who had married the other wives of the dead chief.

"He had no other wives," I told him.

"But a chief must have many wives! How else can he brew beer and prepare food for all his guests?"

I said firmly that in our country even chiefs had only one wife, that they had servants to do their work, and that they paid them from tax money.

It was better, they returned, for a chief to have many wives and sons who would help him hoe his farms and feed his people; then everyone loved the chief who gave much and took nothing — taxes were a bad thing.

I agreed with the last comment, but for the rest fell back on their favorite way of fobbing off my questions: "That is the way it is done, so that is how we do it."

I decided to skip the soliloquy. Even if Claudius was here thought quite right to marry his brother's widow, there remained the poison motif, and I knew they would disapprove of fratricide. More hopefully I resumed, "That night Hamlet kept watch with the three who had seen his dead father. The dead chief again appeared, and although the others were afraid, Hamlet followed his dead father off to one side. When they were alone, Hamlet's dead father spoke."

"Omens can't talk!" The old man was emphatic.

"Hamlet's dead father wasn't an omen. Seeing him might have been an omen, but he was not." My audience looked as confused as I sounded. "It *was* Hamlet's dead father. It was a thing we call a 'ghost.'" I had to use the English word, for unlike many of the neighboring tribes, these people didn't believe in the survival after death of any individuating part of the personality.

"What is a 'ghost'? An omen?"

"No, a 'ghost' is someone who is dead but who walks around and can talk, and people can hear him and see him but not touch him."

They objected. "One can touch zombis."

"No, no! It was not a dead body the witches had animated to sacrifice and eat. No one else made Hamlet's dead father walk. He did it himself."

"Dead men can't walk," protested my audience as one man.

I was quite willing to compromise. "A 'ghost' is a dead man's shadow."

But again they objected. "Dead men cast no shadows."

"They do in my country," I snapped.

The old man quelled the babble of disbelief that rose immediately and told me with that insincere, but courteous, agreement one extends to the fancies of the young, ignorant, and superstitious, "No doubt in your country the dead can also walk without being zombis." From the depths of his bag he produced a withered fragment of kola nut, bit off one end to show it wasn't poisoned, and handed me the rest as a peace offering.

"Anyhow," I resumed, "Hamlet's dead father said that his own brother, the one who became chief, had poisoned him. He wanted Hamlet to avenge him. Hamlet believed this in his heart, for he did not like his father's brother." I took another swallow of beer. "In the country of the great chief, living in the same homestead, for it was a very large one, was an important elder who was often with the chief to advise and help him. His name was Polonius. Hamlet was courting his daughter, but her father and her brother . . . [I cast hastily about for some tribal analogy] warned her not to let Hamlet visit her when she was alone on her farm, for he would be a great chief and so could not marry her."

"Why not?" asked the wife, who had settled down on the edge of the old man's chair. He frowned at her for asking stupid questions and growled, "They lived in the same homestead."

"That was not the reason," I informed them. "Polonius was a stranger who lived in the homestead because he helped the chief, not because he was a relative."

"Then why couldn't Hamlet marry her?"

"He could have," I explained, "but Polonius didn't think he would. After all, Hamlet was a man of great importance who ought to marry a chief's daughter, for in his country a man could have only one wife. Polonius was afraid that if Hamlet made love to his daughter, then no one else would give a high price for her."

"That might be true," remarked one of the shrewder elders, "but a chief's son would give his mistress's father enough presents and patronage to more than make up the difference. Polonius sounds like a fool to me."

"Many people think he was," I agreed. "Meanwhile Polonius sent his son Laertes off to Paris to learn the things of that country, for it was the homestead of a very great chief indeed. Because he was afraid that Laertes might waste a lot of money on beer and women and gambling, or get into trouble by fighting, he sent one of his servants to Paris secretly, to spy out what Laertes was doing. One day Hamlet came upon Polonius's daughter Ophelia. He behaved so oddly he frightened her. Indeed"—I was fumbling for words to express the dubious quality of Hamlet's madness—"the chief and many others had also noticed that when Hamlet talked one could understand the words but not what they meant. Many people thought that he had become mad." My audience suddenly became much more attentive. "The great chief wanted to know what was wrong with Hamlet, so he sent for two of Hamlet's age mates [school friends would have taken long explanation] to talk to Hamlet and find out what troubled his heart. Hamlet, seeing that they had been bribed by the chief to betray him, told them nothing. Polonius, however, insisted that Hamlet was mad because he had been forbidden to see Ophelia, whom he loved."

"Why," inquired a bewildered voice, "should anyone bewitch Hamlet on that account?"

"Bewitch him?"

"Yes, only witchcraft can make anyone mad, unless, of course, one sees the beings that lurk in the forest."

I stopped being a storyteller, took out my notebook and demanded to be told more about these two causes of madness. Even while they spoke and I jotted notes, I tried to calculate the effect of this new factor on the plot. Hamlet had not been exposed to the beings that lurk in the forest. Only his relatives in the male line could bewitch him. Barring relatives not mentioned by Shakespeare, it had to be Claudius who was attempting to harm him. And, of course, it was.

For the moment I staved off questions by saying that the great chief also refused to believe that Hamlet was mad for the love of Ophelia and nothing else. "He was sure that something much more important was troubling Hamlet's heart."

"Now Hamlet's age mates," I continued, "had brought with them a famous storyteller. Hamlet decided to have this man tell the chief and all his homestead a story about the man who had poisoned his brother because he desired his brother's wife and wished to be chief himself. Hamlet was sure the great chief could not hear the story without making a sign if he was indeed guilty, and then he would discover whether his dead father had told him the truth."

The old man interrupted, with deep cunning. "Why should a father lie to his son?" he asked.

I hedged: "Hamlet wasn't sure that it really was his dead father." It was impossible to say anything, in that language, about devil-inspired visions.

"You mean," he said, "it actually was an omen, and he knew witches sometimes send false ones. Hamlet was a fool not to go to one skilled in reading omens and divining the truth in the first place. A man-who-sees-the-truth could have told him how his father died, if he really had been poisoned, and if there was witchcraft in it; then Hamlet could have called the elders to settle the matter."

The shrewd elder ventured to disagree. "Because his father's brother was a great chief, one-who-sees-the-truth might therefore have been afraid to tell it. I think it was for that reason that a friend of Hamlet's father — a witch and an elder — sent an omen so his friend's son would know. Was the omen true?"

"Yes," I said, abandoning ghosts and the devil; a witch-sent omen it would have to be. "It was true, for when the storyteller was telling his tale before all the homestead, the great chief rose in fear. Afraid that Hamlet knew his secret he planned to have him killed."

The stage set of the next bit presented some difficulties of translation. I began cautiously. "The great chief told Hamlet's mother to find out from her son what he knew. But because a woman's children are always first in her heart, he had the important elder Polonius hide behind a cloth that hung against the wall of Hamlet's mother's sleeping hut. Hamlet started to scold his mother for what she had done."

There was a shocked murmur from everyone. A man should never scold his mother.

"She called out in fear, and Polonius moved behind the cloth. Shouting 'A rat!', Hamlet took his machete and slashed through the cloth." I paused for a dramatic effect. "He had killed Polonius!"

The old men looked at each other in supreme disgust. "That Polonius truly was a fool and a man who knew nothing! What child would not know enough to shout, 'It's me!'" With a pang, I remembered that these people are ardent hunters, always armed with bow, arrow, and machete; at the first rustle in the grass an arrow is aimed and ready, and the hunter shouts "Game!" If no human voice answers immediately, the arrow speeds on its way. Like a good hunter Hamlet had shouted, "A rat!"

I rushed into save Polonius's reputation. "Polonius did speak. Hamlet heard him. But he thought it was the chief and wished to kill him to avenge his father. He had meant to kill him earlier that evening. . . ." I broke down, unable to describe to these pagans, who had no belief in individual afterlife, the difference between dying at one's prayers and dying "unhousell'd, disappointed, unaneled."

This time I had shocked my audience seriously. "For a man to raise his hands against his father's brother and the one who has become his father — that is a terrible thing. The elders ought to let such a man be bewitched."

I nibbled at my kola nut in some perplexity, then pointed out that after all the man had killed Hamlet's father.

"No," pronounced the old man, speaking less to me than to the young men sitting behind the elders. "If your father's brother has killed your father, you must appeal to your father's age mates; *they* may avenge him. No man may use violence against his senior relatives." Another thought struck him. "But if his father's brother had indeed been wicked enough to bewitch Hamlet and make him mad, that would be a good story indeed, for it would be his fault that Hamlet, being mad, no longer had any sense and thus was ready to kill his father's brother."

There was a murmur of applause. *Hamlet* was again a good story to them, but it no longer seemed quite the same story to me. As I thought over the coming complications of plot and motive, I lost courage and decided to skim over dangerous ground quickly.

"The great chief," I went on, "was not sorry that Hamlet had killed Polonius. It gave him a reason to send Hamlet away, with his two treacherous age mates, with letters to a chief of a far country, saying that Hamlet should be killed. But Hamlet changed the writing on their papers, so that the chief killed his age mates instead." I encountered a reproachful glare from one of the men whom I had told undetectable forgery was not merely immoral but beyond human skill. I looked the other way.

"Before Hamlet could return, Laertes came back for his father's funeral. The great chief told him Hamlet had killed Polonius. Laertes swore to kill Hamlet because of this, and because his sister Ophelia, hearing her father had been killed by the man she loved, went mad and drowned in the river."

"Have you already forgotten what we told you?" The old man was reproachful. "One cannot take vengeance on a madman; Hamlet killed Polonius in his madness. As for the girl, she not only went mad, she was drowned. Only witches can make people drown. Water itself can't hurt anything. It is merely something one drinks and bathes in."

I began to get cross. "If you don't like the story, I'll stop."

The old man made soothing noises and himself poured me some more beer. "You tell the story well, and we are listening. But it is clear that the elders of your country have never told you what the story really means. No, don't interrupt! We believe you when you say your marriage customs are different, or your clothes and weapons. But people are the same everywhere; therefore, there are always witches and it is we, the elders, who know how witches work. We told you it was the great chief who wished to kill Hamlet, and now your own words have proved us right. Who were Ophelia's male relatives?"

"There were only her father and her brother." Hamlet was clearly out of my hands.

"There must have been many more; this also you must ask of your elders when you get back to your country. From what you tell us, since Polonius was dead, it must have been Laertes who killed Ophelia, although I do not see the reason for it."

We had emptied one pot of beer, and the old men argued the point with slightly tipsy interest. Finally one of them demanded of me, "What did the servant of Polonius say on his return?"

With difficulty I recollected Reynaldo and his mission. "I don't think he did return before Polonius was killed."

"Listen," said the elder, "and I will tell you how it was and how your story will go, then you may tell me if I am right. Polonius knew his son would get into trouble, and so he did. He had many fines to pay for fighting, and debts from gambling. But he had only two ways of getting money quickly. One was to marry off his sister at once, but it is difficult to find a man who will marry a woman desired by the son of a chief. For if the chief's heir commits adultery with your wife, what can you do? Only a fool calls a case against a man who will someday be his judge. Therefore Laertes had to take the second way: he killed his sister by witchcraft, drowning her so he could secretly sell her body to the witches."

I raised an objection. "They found her body and buried it. Indeed Laertes jumped into the grave to see his sister once more — so, you see, the body was truly there. Hamlet, who had just come back, jumped in after him."

"What did I tell you?" The elder appealed to the others. "Laertes was up to no good with his sister's body. Hamlet prevented him, because the chief's heir, like a chief, does not wish any other man to grow rich and powerful. Laertes would be angry, because he would have killed his sister without benefit to himself. In our country he would try to kill Hamlet for that reason. Is this not what happened?"

"More or less," I admitted. "When the great chief found Hamlet was still alive, he encouraged Laertes to try to kill Hamlet and arranged a fight with machetes between them. In the fight both the young men were wounded to death. Hamlet's mother drank the poisoned beer that the chief meant for Hamlet in case he won the fight. When he saw his mother die of poison, Hamlet, dying, managed to kill his father's brother with his machete."

"You see, I was right!" exclaimed the elder.

"That was a very good story," added the old man, "and you told it with very few mistakes. There was just one more error, at the very end. The poison Hamlet's mother drank was obviously meant for the survivor of the fight, whichever it was. If Laertes had won, the great chief would have poisoned him, for no one would know that he arranged Hamlet's death. Then, too, he need not fear Laertes's witch-craft; it takes a strong heart to kill one's only sister by witchcraft.

"Sometime," concluded the old man, gathering his ragged toga about him, "you must tell us some more stories of your country. We, who are elders, will instruct you in their true meaning, so that when you return to your own land your elders will see that you have not been sitting in the bush, but among those who know things and who have taught you wisdom."

REVIEW QUESTIONS

1. In what ways does Bohannan's attempt to tell the story of *Hamlet* to the Tiv illustrate the concept of naive realism?

2. Using Bohannan's experience of telling the story of *Hamlet* to the Tiv and the response of the Tiv elders to her words, illustrate cross-cultural misunderstanding.

3. What are the most important parts of *Hamlet* that the Tiv found it necessary to reinterpret?

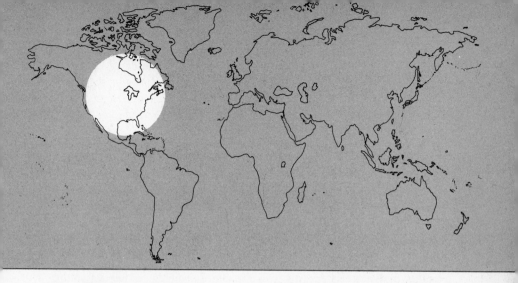

7 Race, Culture, and Misunderstanding

THOMAS KOCHMAN

In the previous article we saw how misunderstanding can occur when members of two different societies do not share each other's cultural concepts. In this article, Thomas Kochman shows how misunderstanding can occur when styles of communication differ between groups. Specifically, he shows that white and black Americans are liable to misunderstand each other's attempts to initiate sexual relations. The black style is direct and competitive; males rap to impress females; females openly encourage or reject the rap. Whites, on the other hand, take an indirect approach based more on displays of continuing interest.

In a recently desegregated high school, a black male student is charged by a white female student with "sexual assault." Upon investigating the charge, the principal learns that during the lunch break, the black student was standing with some of his black male friends when the white female walked by. As she passed him, he said, with obvious reference to her behind, "Shake that thang, baby." The white student continued walking and did not respond. After school another encounter took place. This time, as the white student walked by with a friend, the black student said, "Hey, baby, let me talk to you a minute!" As he said this, he left his group and placed his hand on her

From "Male and Female Interaction: The First Phase," Chapter 5 in *Black and White: Styles in Conflict* (Chicago: University of Chicago Press, 1981). Reprinted by permission of the University of Chicago.

arm to direct her out of hearing range of his friends and hers. He then began to tell her how "fine" she looked, what a great "lover" he was, and how much he could "do" for her. She responded by pleading with him to let her alone, and she turned and walked away. Later the sexual assault charge was filed by the girl and her parents, her father in a rage at his daughter having been "insulted" and having "hands laid upon her." He demanded the black student's suspension from school.

When confronted with the charge, the black student said, "All I said was 'Shake that thang.' Now what the hell is wrong with that?" He also accused the white girl of "*wanting* me to talk to her," saying, "How come she stopped and didn't keep on walking?"

The principal, after listening to both sides, suspended the black student from school for three days, with the warning that he and his friends "had better keep away from white females, either on or off school grounds."

Similar incidents occur frequently in desegregated schools throughout the country. The charge of sexual assault brought by this white student is an unusual and extreme reaction, but the pattern of response is typical, including the disciplining of the black male student. The basis of the response of the white female and her parents — certainly its intensity — is undoubtedly rooted in unresolved conflicts regarding interracial sex in American society.

But it is also important to recognize that the white female's response pattern in this instance was only partially affected by the fact that the male was black, just as the pattern of behavior used by the black male had very little to do with the fact that the female was white. The behavior of the black man would have been much the same if the female had been black, just as the behavior of the white woman would have been much the same if the approach of the black man were used by a white man. This is because in black culture it is customary for black men to approach black women in a manner that openly expresses a sexual interest, while in white culture it is equally customary for "respectable" women to be offended by an approach that presumes sexual interest and availability. The basis of the conflict between the black male and white female, then, is cultural as well as racial. It is this cultural dimension that I wish to develop in this chapter.

CULTURAL NORMS AND PROTOCOLS

Both black and white cultural norms entitle men to express a sexual interest in women. Where the two cultures differ is in their acknowledgment that women are also entitled to express a sexual interest in men. White culture disallows this, or at least operates on the principle that women are not so entitled. Black culture, however, operates on the principle that women are.

Black Cultural Patterns

The black speech event called *rapping* reflects the black perspective. As a cultural mechanism, rapping allows a man to approach a woman, wherever the opportunity presents itself, and start to *rap to* or *hit on* her. An "opportunity" is typically a time and place where a man can talk to a woman without being intruded upon by others. Thus it can occur in a cocktail lounge, on the beach, on the street, in the park, at a party, or on the dance floor. Where talking is not possible, a man may indicate his sexual interest in a woman nonverbally, with what black men call a "silent rap" or "pimp eye." The purpose and motivation of rapping varies little. Men rap to women in the hope of getting sex. Sometimes men rap to exercise their verbal ability: sharpen their line or their wit or, as one black man remarked, to "deposit their image," to try to prove that they could "score" if they wanted to.

The topical content of raps can vary. But it is not unusual for men to declare their sexual interest and desires openly, comment directly on the sexually attractive features of females, or brag about their own sexual ability. The language itself may be explicit and direct or more subtle and metaphorical. But it is invariably sexual. "Street" or "store-front" raps tend to be sexually direct and explicit. Thus in one street rap a young man says to a woman of about twenty, walking in tight shorts:

Male: What's happenin', fox?
Female: Nothing.
Male: You mean with all that you got ain't nothin' happenin'?
Female: Get lost nigger.
Male: Come here you funky bitch.
Female: What the hell do you want?
Male: I want some leg, baby.[1]

In one storefront at a Sunday afternoon "mini-skirt party," a "high gentleman, evidently excited by all the short skirts and legs on parade, announced to the entire gathering: 'Hey, all y'all pretty bitches. I got a numb member and it needs revivin' — right now.'"[2]

---

[1] Leslie Collins, "Rap, Baby, Rap," (Center for Inner City Studies, Northeastern Illinois University, Chicago, 1968, Xerox), 3.

[2] Bertha Young, "Rapping Man to Woman," (Center for Inner City Studies, Northeastern Illinois University, Chicago, 1967, Xerox), 3.

Blues lyrics also reflect this direct and explicit male sexual approach:

> When you see me comin' mama, hang yo' draws on the line,
> When you see me comin' mama, hang yo' draws on the line.
> All I want is yo' behind.

But the use of sexual metaphors in the blues is perhaps more common. Thus, from a male blues singer:

> She's got a sweet jelly, my woman's got a sweet jelly roll,
> Yes she's got a sweet jelly, my woman's got a sweet jelly roll.
> It takes her jelly to satisfy my soul.

And from female blues singer Ida Cox:

> If he didn't like my potatoes, why did he dig so deep?
> If he didn't like my potatoes, why did he dig so deep?
> In his mama's potato patch, five and ten times a week.[3]

The approach of black men in cocktail lounges frequented by more middle-class blacks is less explicit but equally obvious in its sexual reference. One male's opening line was "Say, baby, Give me the keys to your pad. I want to play with your cat." Another said, "Hell baby, don't never give nothin' away. I'm buyin' all of it."[4]

Black women's role and pattern of response to the rapping of black men is active and forceful, for in black culture traits such as independence, aggressiveness, and sexual assertiveness are seen to be common to both males *and* females. Likewise, women are free to express their own sexual interest in men. But of course a woman is not obliged to have such an interest in a man rapping to her simply because he proposes that she should. Collected examples of rapping, with female responses, indicate the variation one would expect. Men are either supported or rejected, in varying ways. In one form of support, the woman may express a reciprocal sexual interest in the man. Thus to one man who said, "Mama, you sure a fine looking woman," the woman responded, "You looking pretty fine yourself!" Another took a similar remark as a simple compliment, which reaction can also indicate an absence of sexual interest while enabling a woman

---

[3] Samuel Charters, *The Poetry of the Blues* (New York: Oak, 1963), 87, 90.
[4] Young, 3.

to avoid rejecting a man directly. In this instance the woman responded, "Why, thank you, you sure made my day," engaged in a few verbal pleasantries, and then left, saying, "I got to run, my kids are waiting, hope to see you again."

Direct rejection by women varies from a simple nonverbal put-down to a more forceful verbal insult. For example, when a group of males were looking at a group of females at the beach, one man said, "Man, they got fine foxes, all up in here." One of the females responded with an "evil" look. The man responded, "Baby, I don't mean no harm. Y'all all know you looking good anyway."[5] But a man who was annoying a woman with his attention gave the following rap: "I may not be the man of yo' dreams on top, but you ain' never had no dream like the one I can give, 'cause I'm a lover." The woman answered, "Fuck you, nigger. You ain' shit, and you know *I* know."[6]

In response to a rap, black women are not only as sexually assertive as black men; they are often equally verbally skilled, frequently *capping* a male rap with an effective retort of their own. In one example, a man coming from the bathroom forgot to zip his pants. An unescorted party of women kept watching him and laughing among themselves. The man's friends "hipped" him to what was going on. He then approached one woman and said, "Hey, baby, did you see that big black Cadillac with full tires — ready for action with nobody but you?" She responded, "No, motherfucker, but I saw a little gray Volkswagen with two flat tires."[7]

Claudia Mitchell-Kernan gives an example of a more extended rap which occurred between her and a black man whom she encountered in a park with his friends while she was doing research:

Male: Mama, you sho is fine.
Mitchell-Kernan: That ain no way to talk to your mother.
Male: You married?
M-K: Um hm.
Male: Is your husband married?
M-K: Very.

At this point the conversation shifts, with Mitchell-Kernan explaining her research project to him. They talk about the project, then the man returns to his original rapping style:

[5] Collins, 2. In this context, "up in here" means excellent; "evil" means inhospitable, cold, and nasty.

[6] Young, 2.

[7] Young, 3.

Male: Baby, you a real scholar, I can tell you want to learn. Now if you'll just cooperate a li'l bit, I'll show you what a good teacher I am. But first we got to get into my area of expertise.

M-K: I may be wrong, but seems to me we already in your area of expertise.

Male: You ain' so bad yourself, girl. I ain't heard you stutter yet. You a li'l fixated on your subject though. I want to help a sweet thang like you all I can. I figure all that book learning you got must mean you been neglecting other areas of your education.

M-K: Why don't you let me point out where I can best use your help?

Male: Are you sho' you in the best position to know?

At this point the rapping exchange ends, with the male saying, "I'mo leave you alone, girl. Ask me what you want to know."[8]

One female response to the black male approach that men typically find unacceptable — especially when the rap is expressed as a compliment — is to ignore it. For a woman to do so often results in her being "loud-talked." Carolyn Jones, a black woman, reported that walking to church with her female friend, she passed a group of men, one of whom said, "Hey, foxes, you all sure do look fine. How you doing?" Jones responded, but her friend looked straight ahead and did not reply. This prompted the man to say, louder and directly to her, "Hey, baby, I said how you doing?" When she still did not respond, he said in an even louder voice, just as she was about to enter the church, "What's the matter? Don't you recognize me with my clothes on?"

Some black women have indicated that they respond to a rap basically to avoid being loud-talked. Others say that their response is based upon the kind of verbal approach used; they react to a more blatant sexual approach with an impatient "rolling of the eyes." Joan McCarty was walking with her young daughter when a man approached. Speaking to the daughter, he said, "I sure would have liked to make you with your mama"; then he looked at McCarty. She remarked on this afterward, "It's obvious by this that the man was not truly interested in me. I'll raise his consciousness!"

Despite the different attitudes that black women express toward what they consider to be an acceptable or unacceptable rap, they agree that they expect black men to rap and to be able to rap well. As

---

[8] Claudia Mitchell-Kernan, *Language Behavior in a Black Urban Community* (Monographs of the Language-Behavior Research Laboratory, No. 2. Berkeley: University of California, 1971), 106–107.

McCarty put it, "The man's inability to come up with a decent rap indicates some kind of ineptness, which is often translated into sexual ineptness by black women."

White Cultural Patterns

The white male's sexual approach is guided by the general cultural view that there are two kinds of women: "good" and "bad." "Good" women are those who deny or conceal their sexual interest. These women are also careful about screening potential male suitors before meeting them. This screening serves two purposes. First, it increases the female's sexual protection by inviting the attention and concern of her family and friends and his. Hence, the man knows that if he makes improper sexual advances, his actions will be called into account. The second purpose of screening is to qualify men with respect to certain social criteria: occupation, education, income, ethnic background, religion, etc., establishing them as suitable or unsuitable marriage material and indicating that the woman is discriminating with regard to males: she is someone who will not go with "just any man." Good women are also assessed with regard to "feminine" character traits. Where men are seen as independent, aggressive, and sexually assertive, good women are seen as dependent, passive, and sexually receptive. Women become "bad" or "less respectable" to the extent that they admit to having a sexual interest, meet men without screening them first, or become "masculine" in character — independent, aggressive, and sexually assertive.

The verbal approach of white men corresponds to the general cultural norms that women are expected to deny or conceal their sexual interest and that any approach that would force a woman to acknowledge such an interest would be rejected, along with the man making it. Thus white men couch messages implying sexual interest in the form of innocent requests or offers. They ask women to have a cup of coffee or offer to give them a lift home. Used in this way, such messages become ambiguous. They are nonsexual on the surface, but the offer and its acceptance have sexual implications, especially if such offers and acceptances increase in frequency and acceptance would lead to a situation where the opportunity to have sex is present.

The interests of white men and women are only partially served by the ambiguity. It allows them to renege at any time before sexual moves actually occur. The sexual implication of a series of offers and acceptances can be repudiated by an insistence that the alleged reason for being together — the lift home, the woman's invitation to a cup of coffee in her place afterward, was the *only* meaning that either of them intended. Publicly, however, the ambiguity often does them a disservice. For example, it may not allow them simply to have a conversation over a drink in a public lounge without outsiders — or one of the couple — attaching sexual significance to it.

Inferring Sexual Outcomes

White male and female encounters acquire their sexual meaning circumstantially. Situational factors, such as how and where a woman allowed herself to be met, whether she agreed to be alone with a man, are significant in establishing the degree of likelihood that a sexual outcome will occur. Equally significant is reference to various male offers and female acceptances that cumulatively signify an investment of time, money, and attentive concern from which the male might hope to gain a sexual return.

Black male and female encounters acquire their sexual meaning through verbal negotiation. The man establishes his sexual interest at the outset by rapping, the woman by her initial agreement to interact with him further. Situational factors play no role in indicating the degree of likelihood of a sexual outcome. Thus a black man who met a black woman on the street or in a cocktail lounge would not feel that he had better prospects for succeeding sexually with her — because of where they met — than with a woman he met through a friend at a party. Nor could he assume that his chances of success were better because she was willing to be alone with him, although he might hope so. Sexual outcomes are transacted among blacks as initial sexual interest is indicated, namely, through open and direct verbal expression and negotiation. One young man who had just started to date a young woman confronted her with "Do you want me as much as I want you?" Upon receiving a nasty look as a response, he asked her half-joking and half-seriously, "Is it no for now or no forever?"[9]

In white culture, women who admit a general sexual interest in men fall into the "less respectable" category and are therefore seen as sexually available. White men are typically less respectful of such women. Consequently they are less patient and restrained, less likely to take no for an answer in moving the course of the transaction to a sexual conclusion. Moreover, white men feel that women who verbally acknowledge a sexual interest as well as those who allow themselves to be "picked up" forfeit some of their prerogative of discrimination with regard to men. White men feel these women will sleep with any man and therefore will not refuse them.

In black culture, it would be wrong to infer female sexual availability simply from an expression of sexual interest or sexual assertiveness, since the culture presumes that *all* women have a general sexual interest in men and are sexually assertive. Black women are

---

[9] Collins, 2.

not viewed as more or less "respectable" on the basis of these criteria. It would also be wrong to infer female sexual availability simply because the black male approach presumes it. As shown in the rapping examples given above, such as the one reported by Mitchell-Kernan, a black woman loses none of her prerogatives of discrimination among men or refusal of a male proposal of a sexual encounter. As the examples above show, black men make their sexually audacious proposals but do not thereby deny females their right of refusal. For while black men may presume all women to be sexually available *generally*, they do not assume that these women will be sexually available to them *specifically*. Male raps are proposals, not non-negotiable commands. Nor are black men necessarily offended when women refuse them, accustomed as they are to hearing many more rejections to their proposals than acceptances. They might be offended by the way they are rejected, if they are degraded or ignored entirely, but not by the rejection itself.

Cross-cultural interpretations and conflicts

Both white and black males and females interpret each other's behavior in accordance with the meaning and value that behavior has within their own culture. In an encounter like the one described at the beginning of this chapter, a white female will correlate the sexual approach of a black male with that of white males in her culture who make "indecent" proposals and try to pick her up. Consequently she will not respond to him, for she feels that to do so would be interpreted as a sign of encouragement and would place her in the "less respectable" female category. She would be subjected to the pressures such women often experience when they respond to sexual proposals in white culture. In this instance, she would regard the explicit sexual content of the black male's rap as even more disconcerting because it would force her to confront the sexual intent behind his remark directly; whereas in white "pick-up" situations, sexual intent is often hidden behind an apparently innocent offer of help such as a lift. Tactically, this allows the female to deny the underlying sexual intent by refusing the offer. It also allows her to deny or conceal any sexual interest on her part in doing so, thereby permitting her to keep her image of respectability intact. But the obvious sexual content of the black male rap, which *presumes* general female sexual interest and availability, defines the situation as one in which the female is given *only* the option of rejecting the individual male — as in black culture

—not the option of denying the presumption of general female availability underlying his approach.

A white female will also be disturbed by what she perceives to be a mismatch in the situation. The black male presents his rap in a verbally skillful, assertive manner, accustomed as he is to interacting with black females who are also verbally skillful and assertive. But the white female has been brought up in a culture that teaches women to be passive and sexually receptive vis-à-vis men and to rely on them, rather than on themselves, for sexual protection. In addition, she does not regard herself as especially skilled in repartee. Consequently, she believes herself unable to manage the kind of self-assertion or verbal skill that she feels is necessary to achieve parity in the situation. She may also be handicapped by norms of politeness that make her reluctant to assert herself when that might also hurt another person's feelings. Thus she will conclude that the only tactics available to her are to ignore the approach or, if that is not possible, to plead with the black man to let her alone.

But the white female's assessment of the potency of the black male's approach is an exaggerated one. So, consequently, is her estimation of the level of self-assertion she would need to create a dynamic balance in the situation. Black men do not draw the same conclusions as white men from the response of women to their sexual approaches. For one thing, because a sexual approach does not violate black cultural norms with regard to female sexual interest, black men do not consider such an approach "indecent," whereas white men do. Where women will lose respect in the eyes of white men by their response, they will not in the eyes of black men. Second, a black man does not infer that a woman is sexually available to him specifically, merely because she admits to having a general sexual interest or allows an approach that presumes that she has. To white men, such an admission would imply sexual promiscuity and immediate sexual availability. Finally, a black man does not infer anything sexual from the circumstances surrounding his meeting with a woman. The term "pick-up" has no special significance for him, because in black culture all women can be met in this fashion. The treatment that a white woman would receive in this situation would be the same as that given to a black woman, which is considerably more respectful and considerate than the way white men treat women whom they regard as falling in the "less respectable" category.

From the black male's perspective, neither of the responses white females typically use to respond to their rap is appropriate. For example, black men consider it rude to snub or ignore a friendly greeting or compliment. Black women who do so are seen as *saditty* or accused of "having an attitude," thinking themselves better than other people. Viewing a lack of response as arrogance, black men often retaliate by "loud-talking" them. However, black men also consider the pleading and helpless posture that a white female might assume entirely inappropriate as a response, for it implies an element of danger in the situation. A black male who raps does not intend sexual assault or rape, as some white women have supposed. Rapping is, after all, a verbal approach, not a physical one: audacious, to be sure, and perhaps offensive to women who do not want their sexual interest or availability presumed. But it is not dangerous. For a white female to suggest the opposite by a pleading response, however, often creates a real risk or danger of some form of punishment for the black man. In the example of the two students, it was a three-day suspension. At other times and places it has led to a man's loss of employment, bodily injury, or even death.

A suitable response for a white woman who did not wish to be bothered would be to interpret the rap as a simple compliment. Since the opening line of a rap often shows sexual approval, it is usually possible to do this. This may also entail having to engage in conversation a little while longer to satisfy the requirements of politeness, but after doing so it would be perfectly appropriate to make an excuse to leave.

Another response would be to consider the rap as a form of verbal play: entertainment, like boasting or bragging. Thus it would be appropriate to comment on the artfulness of the rap itself, or the absence of artfulness, as black women also do. One black male rapped the following to a woman at a party: "Damn, baby, you got what every man dreams of but what few men get." He was met with the reply, "You better tighten up your game cause your sound is sho nuff weak."[10] It may be possible in this way not to respond directly to the sexual intent behind the rap at all. One white woman effectively used the following: "It's a great rap, and I'm sure it'll work on a lot of women, but I've got all the men I can handle right now."

Of course if a white woman were offended by an approach that, as one woman said, "left no doubt at all what that man wanted from me," it is also perfectly acceptable to be direct in saying so, as black women do. As Joan McCarty said, "black women are beginning to just be up front and tell men that if they can't come to them better in the street than in the obviously sexual manner, they can just shut up."

White Males and Black Females
Black women have reported that they often find it difficult to detect when white men are hitting on them or not, even though they suspect on general principles that sex is what men usually have in mind. The reason for this difficulty can be seen from the discussion above. White

---

[10] Collins, 5

men and women communicate sexual intent circumstantially. Black men and women are verbally explicit. Conflict between white men and black women therefore occurs because white men think that the sexual connotation of their encounter has been firmly established by a series of offers and acceptances, whereas black women think the opposite, because the subject itself was never directly brought up.

Invariably, a black woman is later surprised when a white man starts to act on his presumption, asking him what she did that led him to believe that she would be interested in him. He in turn is also surprised by her rejection and her surprise, but he is also chagrined by·being, as he sees it, deliberately deceived. The attitudes of both can be directly traced to different cultural understandings of how male and female encounters can generally be expected to unfold.

A more serious problem for black women is white men's inference of sexual promiscuity, based on their observation of black women who allow themselves to be picked up, who admit having a sexual interest, and who allow a male approach that is obviously sexual and that presumes their sexual availability. This kind of approach and response in white culture invariably leads to a sexual outcome. What whites miss, of course, is that black men do not regard such actions as making a sexual outcome anything more than problematical.

White Males and Black Males

Conflict between white and black males arises as a result of different cultural assumptions about female availability. Thus in one office a white man objected to a black man trying to hit on a white woman in the office not so much because of interracial prejudices but because he had an interest in the woman himself. Moreover, he had let this be known among the other men in the office, and he expected them to keep away from her while he tried to win her over, which the other white men in the office did. The black man, however, did not accept the white man's preemptive claim, since the woman indicated to him that she was not interested in the white man. Until she said otherwise, he felt anyone had the right to hit on her.

The basis of the conflict between the two men is cultural. Both black and white cultures acknowledge that it is ultimately the woman who chooses the man. But in white culture, the man hopes to win the woman by restricting the number of men who have access to her, thus limiting her choice and thereby increasing his own chances of being selected. A rule operating in the group I grew up with said that if one of us indicated that he "liked" a particular female, no one else in the group could say he "liked" her also. The declaration of intent was equivalent to staking a claim, which other males were expected to honor. Without any action on her part, the female became a closed territorial preserve to which only that male could gain access who had a preemptive claim conceded by other males.

Within black culture, the rules of rapping maintain that a woman can be approached and hit on at any time and place. Theoretically this places no restrictions on access to women, and in practice it is not unusual for a woman to be approached by different men during the course of a day, especially if she is attractive. And black men recognize and expect that this will happen. As one man put it with regard to his woman friend, "I can't keep her in a cage, and I know I'm not going to be with her all the time." Thus it is not unusual for a black man to leave the woman he is with for a moment to go to the washroom or to the bar to buy drinks and return to see another man talking to her. This is not to say that some black men might not try to restrict access to their women in some way. However, without the cooperation of other men, this is difficult to accomplish, and the cultural rule that makes women generally accessible works against this possibility. In effect, black culture recognizes that the appropriate person to restrict access to a woman is the woman herself. This is why the black man in the office did not cooperate with the white man who tried to claim the woman preemptively: the woman herself indicated that she was not interested. Of course the black man also viewed the white man's preemptive move as a way to get rid of the competition without having to beat it, which he also considered devious.

Different cultural assumptions also affect the attitudes that men take toward other men trying to hit on their women friends. Because they try to restrict male access to a woman, white men generally see other men talking to their women friends as an immediate threat. A black man does not, rather letting his reaction to the situation depend upon the response that his woman friend makes to the second man. There is another cultural dimension operating here, too. Recognizing that it is women who select men, and that men are granted unrestricted access to women to make their presentations, black men understand that their ultimate success with women depends upon their rap being better than that of other men. For black men this becomes the challenge. The game is not only to win the woman over but to do so by competing with other men. The value of the prize is based in part on the number of others who want it. Thus beautiful women are sought after by black men not only for the value of their beauty but because they are sought after by other men. To succeed in winning such a woman is public proof that a man has beat out the competition. For some men this is not only one of their main satisfactions but one of their principal motivations as well. As Allen Harris points out, some black men become interested only when *other* men become interested. The white male mode that attempts to preclude other male competition works directly against the satisfactions that black men hope to realize in allowing competition and then trying to beat it.

REVIEW QUESTIONS

1. What is the main difference between the way most white and black American males attempt to communicate sexual interest to females? What are the normal cultural ways in which black and white females respond to the sexual advances of males?
2. How does Kochman's material illustrate the process of cross-cultural misunderstanding?
3. Can you think of other contexts in which black and white styles of communication vary? What rules underlie the differences? Do differences lead to misunderstanding?
4. Do you think that black and white styles of communication vary in the classroom? Do these differences lead to differences in grading and evaluation?

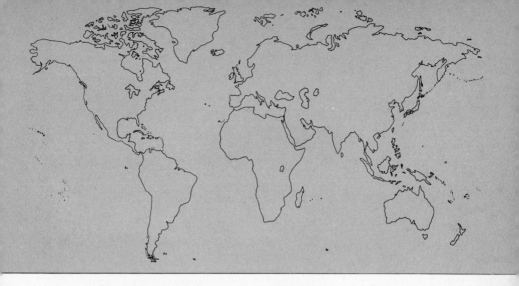

8 Worlds Shaped by Words

DAVID S. THOMSON

For many people, language mirrors reality. Words are labels for what we sense; they record what is already there. This view, which is another manifestation of what we have called naive realism, is clearly challenged by previous selections in this book. We have seen, for example, that members of different societies may not share cultural categories; words from one language often cannot be translated directly into another. In the 1930s, a young linguist named Benjamin Lee Whorf took the objection to the "words label reality" assertion one step further by arguing that words and grammatical structure actually shape reality. This piece by David Thomson describes Whorf's theory, shows how linguists have evaluated it, and applies it in modified form to the use of words, euphemisms, and doublespeak in modern America.

The scene is the storage room at a chemical plant. The time is evening. A night watchman enters the room and notes that it is partially filled with gasoline drums. The drums are in a section of the room where a sign says "Empty Barrels." The watchman lights a cigarette and throws the still-hot match into one of the empty barrels.

The result: an explosion.

The immediate cause of the explosion, of course, was the gasoline

From *Human Behavior: Language* by David S. Thomson and the Editors of Time-Life Books (New York: Time-Life Books, 1975). Copyright © 1975 Time-Life Books, Inc.

fumes that remained in the barrels. But it could be argued that a second cause of the explosion was the English language. The barrels were empty of their original contents and so belonged under the empty sign. Yet they were not empty of everything — the fumes were still present. English has no word — no single term — that can convey such a situation. Containers in English are either empty or they are not; there is no word describing the ambiguous state of being empty and yet not empty. There is no term in the language for "empty but not quite" or "empty of original contents but with something left over." There being no word for such an in-between state, it did not occur to the watchman to think of the explosive fumes.

This incident is hypothetical, but the questions about language it raises are real. The example of the gasoline drums often was cited by Benjamin Lee Whorf to illustrate a revolutionary theory he had about language. Whorf was an unusual man who combined two careers, for he was both a successful insurance executive and a brilliant (and largely self-taught) linguistic scholar. Language, he claimed, may be shaped by the world, but it in turn shapes the world. He reasoned that people can think about only those things that their language can describe or express. Without the words or structures with which to articulate a concept, that concept will not occur. To turn the proposition around, if a language is rich in ways to express certain sorts of ideas, then the speakers of that language will habitually think along those linguistic paths. In short, the language that humans speak govern their view of reality; it determines their perception of the world. The picture of the universe shifts from tongue to tongue.

The originator of this startling notion came from an intellectually active New England family. Whorf's brother John became an artist of note and his brother Richard a consummately professional actor. Benjamin's early bent was not for drawing or acting but photography, especially the chemistry that was involved in developing pictures, and this interest may have influenced his choice of the Massachusetts Institute of Technology, where he majored in chemical engineering. After he was graduated from M.I.T. he became a specialist in fire prevention and in 1919 went to work for the Hartford Fire Insurance Company. His job was to inspect manufacturing plants, particularly chemical plants, that the Hartford insured to determine whether they were safe and thus good insurance risks. He quickly became highly skilled at his work. "In no time at all," wrote C. S. Kremer, then the Hartford's board chairman, "he became in my opinion as thorough and fast a fire prevention inspector as there ever has been."

Whorf was a particularly acute chemical engineer. On one occasion he was refused admittance to inspect a client's building because, a company official maintained, a secret process was in use here. "You are making such-and-such a product?" asked Whorf. "Yes," said the official. Whorf pulled out a pad and scribbled the formula of the supposedly secret process, adding coolly, "You couldn't do it any other way." Needless to say, he was allowed to inspect the building. Whorf rose in the Hartford hierarchy to the post of assistant secretary of the company in 1940. But then in 1941 his health, never strong, gave way, and he died at the early age of forty-four.

While Whorf was becoming a successful insurance executive, he was also doing his revolutionary work in linguistics. He started by studying Hebrew but then switched to Aztec and other related languages of Mexico. Later he deciphered Maya inscriptions, and tried to reconstruct the long-lost language of the ancient Maya people of Mexico and Central America. Finally he tackled the complexities of the still-living language of the Hopi Indians of Arizona. He published his findings in respected anthropological and linguistic journals, earning the praise and respect of scholars in the two fields — all without formal training in linguistic science. As his fame as a linguist spread, the Hartford obligingly afforded him vacations and leaves to travel to the Southwest in pursuit of the structure and lexicon of the Hopi. He also put in countless hours in the Watkinson Library in Connecticut, a rich repository of Mexican and Indian lore.

It was primarily his study of Hopi that impelled Whorf toward his revolutionary ideas. He was encouraged and aided by the great cultural anthropologist and linguist of Yale, Edward Sapir, and the idea that language influences a person's view of the world is generally known as the Sapir-Whorf hypothesis. Whorf formulated it a number of times, but perhaps his clearest statement comes from his 1940 essay "Science and Linguistics": "The background linguistic system (in other words, the grammar) of each language is not merely a reproducing instrument for voicing ideas but rather is itself the shaper of ideas. . . . We dissect nature along lines laid down by our native language. The categories and types that we isolate from the world of phenomena we do not find there because they stare every observer in the face; on the contrary, the world is presented in a kaleidoscopic flux of impressions which has to be organized by our minds — and this means largely by the linguistic systems in our minds."

These ideas developed from Whorf's study of the Hopi language. He discovered that it differs dramatically from languages of the Indo-European family such as English or French, particularly in its expression of the concept of time. English and its related languages have three major tenses — past, present, and future ("it was," "it is," "it will be") — plus the fancier compound tenses such as "it will have been." Having these tenses, Whorf argued, encourages Europeans and Americans to think of time as so many ducks in a row. Time past is made up of uniform units of time — days, weeks, months, years — and the future is similarly measured out. This division of time is essentially artificial, Whorf said, since people can only experience the present. Past and future are only abstractions, but Westerners think of them as real because their language virtually forces them to do so. This view of time has given rise to the fondness in Western cultures for diaries, records, annals, histories, clocks, calendars, wages paid by the hour or day, and elaborate timetables for the use of future time. Time is continually quantified. If Westerners set out to build a house they establish a deadline; the work will be completed at a specified time in the future, such as May 5 or October 15.

Hopis do not behave this way; when they start to weave a mat they are not concerned about when it will be completed. They work on it desultorily, then quit, then begin again; the finished product may take weeks. This casual progress is not laziness but a result of the Hopi's view of time — one symptom of the fact that their language does not have the past, present, and future tenses. Instead it possesses two modes of thought: the objective, that is, things that exist now, and the subjective, things that can be thought about and therefore belong to a state of becoming. Things do not become in terms of a future measured off in days, weeks, months. Each thing that is becoming has its own individual life rhythms, growing or declining or changing in much the same manner as a plant grows, according to its inner nature. The essence of Hopi life, therefore, Whorf said, is preparing in the present so that those things that are capable of becoming can in fact come to pass. Thus weaving a mat is preparing a mat to become a mat; it will reach that state when its nature so ordains — whenever that will be.

This view of the future is understandable, Whorf noted, in an agricultural people whose welfare depends on the proper preparing of earth and seeds and plants for the hoped-for harvest. It also helps explain why the Hopi have such elaborate festivals, rituals, dances, and magic ceremonies: All are intended to aid in the mental preparation that is so necessary if the crops, which the Hopi believe to be influenced by human thought, are to grow properly. This preparing involves "much visible activity," Whorf said, "introductory formalities, preparing of special food . . . intensive sustained muscular activity like running, racing, dancing, which is thought to increase the intensity of development of events (such as growth of crops), mimetic and other magic preparations based on esoteric theory involving perhaps occult instruments like prayer sticks, prayer feathers, and prayer meal, and finally the great cyclic ceremonies and dances, which have the significance of preparing rain and crops." Whorf went on to note that the very noun for *crop* is derived from the verb that means "to prepare." *Crop* therefore is in the Hopi language literally "the prepared." Further, the Hopi prayer pipe, which is smoked as an aid in concentrating good thoughts on the growing fields of corn and wheat, is named *na'twanpi*, "instrument of preparing."

The past to the Hopi, Whorf believed, is also different from the chronological time sense of the speakers of Indo-European languages. The past is not a uniform row of days or weeks to the Hopi. It is rather an undifferentiated stream in which many deeds were done that have accumulated and prepared the present and will continue to prepare the becoming that is ahead. Everything is connected, everything accumulates. The past is not a series of events, separated and completed, but is present in the present.

To Whorf these striking differences in the Hopi language and sense of time implied that the Hopi live almost literally in another world from the speakers of Indo-European languages. The Hopi language grew out of its speakers' peculiar circumstances: As a geographically isolated agricultural people in a land where rainfall was scanty, they did the same things and prayed the same prayers year after year and thus did not need to have past and future tenses. But the language, once it had developed, perpetuated their particular and seemingly very different world view.

Many linguists and anthropologists who have worked with American Indians of the Southwest have been convinced that Whorf's theories are by and large correct. Other linguists are not convinced, however, and through the years since Whorf's death they have attacked his proposals. The controversy is unlikely to be settled soon, if ever. One of the problems is the difficulty of setting up an experiment that would either prove or disprove the existence of correlations between linguistic structure and nonlinguistic behavior. It would be fruitless to go about asking people of various cultures their opinions as to whether the language they spoke had determined the manner in which they thought, had dictated their view of the world. Nobody would be able to answer such a question, for a people's language is so completely embedded in their consciousness that they would be unable to conceive of any other way of interpreting the world.

Despite the near impossibility of proving or disproving Whorf's theory, it will not go away but keeps coming back, intriguing each succeeding generation of linguists. It is certainly one of the most fascinating theories created by the modern mind. It is comparable in some ways to Einstein's theory of relativity. Just as Einstein said that how people saw the phenomena of the universe was relative to their point of observation, so Whorf said that a people's world view was relative to the language they spoke.

And demonstrations of Whorf's ideas are not entirely lacking. They come mainly from studies of color — one of the very few aspects of reality that can be specified by objective scientific methods and also is rather precisely specified by people's naming of colors. In this instance it is possible to compare one person's language, expressing that person's view of the world, with another's language for exactly the same characteristic of the world. The comparison can thus reveal different views that are linked to different descriptions of the same reality. English-speakers view purple as a single relatively uniform color; only if pressed and then only with difficulty will they make any attempt to divide it into such shades as lavender and mauve. But no English-speaker would lump orange with purple; to the users of English, those colors are completely separate, for no single word includes both of them. If other languages made different distinctions in the naming of color — if lavender and mauve were always separate, never encompassed by a word for purple, or if orange and purple were not distinguished but were called by a name that covered both — then it would seem that the users of those languages interpreted those colors differently.

Such differences in color-naming, it turns out, are fairly widespread. Linguist H. A. Gleason compared the color spectrum as described by English-speaking persons to the way it was labeled by speakers of Bassa, a language spoken in Liberia, and by speakers of Shona, spoken in Rhodesia. English-speaking people, when seeing sunlight refracted through a prism, identify by name at least six colors — purple, blue, green, yellow, orange, and red. The speakers of Shona, however, have only three names for the colors of the spectrum. They group orange, red, and purple under one name. They also lump blue and green-blue under one of their other color terms and use their third word to identify yellow and the yellower hues of green. The speakers of Bassa are similarly restricted by a lack of handy terms for color, for they have only two words for the hues of the spectrum.

Gleason's observations prompted psychologists to perform an experiment that also showed the influence words can have on the way colors are handled intellectually and remembered. It was an ingenious and complex experiment with many checks and double checks of the results, but in essence it boiled down to something like this: English-speaking subjects were shown a series of color samples — rather like the little "chips" provided by a paint store to help customers decide what color to paint the living room. The subjects were then asked to pick out the colors they had seen from a far larger array of colors. It turned out that they could more accurately pick out the right colors from the larger selection when the color involved had a handy, ordinary name like "green." The subjects had difficulty with the ambiguous, in-between colors such as off-purples and misty blues. In other words, a person can remember a color better if that person's language offers a handy label for it, but has trouble when the language does not offer such a familiar term. Again the human ability to differentiate reality seemed to be affected by the resources offered by language.

Richness of linguistic resource undoubtedly helps people to cope with subtle gradations in the things they deal with every day. The

Hanunóo people of the Philippine Islands have different names for ninety-two varieties of rice. They can easily distinguish differences in rice that would be all but invisible to English-speaking people, who lump all such grains under the single world *rice*. Of course, English-speakers can make distinctions by resorting to adjectives and perhaps differentiate long-grain, brown rice from small-grain, yellow rice, but surely no European or American would, lacking the terms, have a sufficiently practiced eye to distinguish ninety-two varieties of rice. Language is essentially a code that people use both to think and to communicate. As psychologist Roger Brown sums up the rice question: "Among the Hanunóo, who have names for ninety-two varieties of rice, any one of those varieties is highly codable in the array of ninety-one other varieties. The Hanunóo have a word for it and so can transmit it efficiently and presumably can recognize it easily. Among speakers of English one kind of rice among ninety-one other kinds would have very low codability."

Brown goes on to suppose that the Hanunóo set down in New York would be baffled by the reality around them partly because they would then be the ones lacking the needed words. "If the Hanunóo were to visit the annual Automobile Show in New York City, they would find it difficult to encode distinctively any particular automobile in that array. But an American having such lexical resources as *Chevrolet, Ford, Plymouth, Buick, Corvette, hard-top, convertible, four-door, station wagon*, and the like could easily encode ninety-two varieties."

The very existence of so many different languages, each linked to a disinctive culture, is itself support of a sort for Whorf's hypothesis. At least since the time of the Tower of Babel, no single tongue has been shared by all the people of the world. Many attempts have been made to invent an international language, one so simply structured and easy to learn it would be used by everyone around the globe as a handy adjunct to their native speech. Yet even the most successful of these world languages, Esperanto, has found but limited acceptance.

There are international languages, however, to serve international cultures. The intellectual disciplines of music, dance, and mathematics might be considered specialized cultures; each is shared by people around the world, and each has an international language, used as naturally in Peking as in Paris. English is a world language in certain activities that straddle national boundaries, such as international air travel; it serves for communications between international flights and the ground in every country — a Lufthansa pilot approaching Athens talks with the airport control tower neither in German nor in Greek but in English.

The trouble with most attempts to lend credence to the Sapir-Whorf hypothesis is that, while they indicate connections between culture and language, they do not really prove that a language shaped its users' view of the world. Just because the speakers of Shona have only three main distinctions of color does not mean that their "world view" is all that different from that of the English-speaker who has more convenient color terms. Shona speakers obviously see all the colors in the rainbow that English-speakers see. Their eyes are physiologically the same. Their comparative poverty of words for those colors merely means that it is harder for them to talk about color. Their "code" is not so handy; the colors' codability is lower.

Critics also point out that Whorf may have mistaken what are called dead metaphors for real differences in the Hopi language. All languages are loaded with dead metaphors — figures of speech that have lost all figurative value and are now just familiar words. The word "goodbye" is a dead metaphor. Once it meant "God be with you," but in its contracted form it conjures up no thought or picture of God. If a Whorfian linguist who was a native speaker of Hopi turned the tables and analyzed English he might conclude that English-speakers were perpetually thinking of religion since this everyday word incorporates a reference to God — a ridiculous misreading of a term that has lost all of its original religious significance. In like fashion, perhaps Whorf was reading too much into the Hopi lexicon and grammar, seeing significances where there were none.

The argument about how far Whorf's ideas can be stretched has gone on for several decades and promises to go on for several more. Most psychologists believe that all people see pretty much the same reality; their languages merely have different words and structures to approximate in various idiosyncratic ways a picture of that reality. And yet the experts accept what might be called modified Whorfism — a belief in the power of language to affect, if not to direct, the perception of reality. If a language is rich in terms for certain things or ideas — possesses extensive codability for them — then the people speaking that language can conceive of, and talk about, those things or ideas more conveniently. If different languages do not give their speakers entirely different world views, they certainly influence thinking to some degree.

Even within the Indo-European family of languages, some tongues have words for concepts that other tongues lack. German is especially rich in philosophical terms that have no exact counterparts in English, French, Italian — or any known language. One is *Weltschmerz*, which combines in itself meanings that it takes three English phrases to adequately convey — "weariness of life," "pessimistic outlook," and "romantic discontent." Another German word that has no direct translation is *Weltanschauung*. To approximate its meaning in English requires a number of different terms — "philosophy of life," "world outlook," "ideology" — for all of these elements are included in the

German word. "Weltanschauung" is untranslatable into any single English term. It represents an idea for which only German has a word. Possessing the convenient term, German writers can develop this idea more easily than the users of other languages, and thus explore its ramifications further.

Even when a word from one language may seem to be easily translatable into another, it often is not really equivalent. The French term *distingué* would appear to translate easily enough into the English *distinguished*. But the French use their word in ways that no English-speaker would ever employ for *distinguished*. A Frenchman might reprimand his son by saying that his impolite behavior was not *distingué* or he might tell his wife that a scarf she has worn out to dinner is charmingly *distingué*. The word does not mean "distinguished" as English-speakers employ the term, but something more like "suitable," or "appropriate," or "in keeping with polite standards." It is simply not the same word in the two languages no matter how similar the spelling. It represents a different idea, connoting a subtle difference in mental style.

In some cases the existence of a word leads users of it down tortured logical paths toward dead ends. The common word *nothing* is one example. Since there is a word for the concept, points out philosopher George Pitcher, it tempts people to think that "nothing" is a real entity, that somehow it exists, a palpable realm of not-being. It has in fact led a number of philosophers, including the twentieth-century French thinker Jean-Paul Sartre, to spend a great deal of effort speculating about the nature of "nothing." The difficulty of this philosophic dilemma is indicated by a typical Sartre sentence on the subject: "The Being by which Nothingness arrives in the world must nihilate. Nothingness in its Being, and even so it still runs the risk of establishing Nothingness as a transcendent in the very heart of immanence unless it nihilates Nothingness in its being *in connection with its own being*." Sartre could hardly have gotten himself tangled up in such agonized prose had French lacked a noun for *le neant, nothing*, and the value to human welfare of his attempt to explain is open to question.

The power of language to influence the world can be seen not only in comparisons of one tongue to another, but also within a single language. The way in which people use their native tongue — choosing one term over another to express the same idea or action, varying structures or phrases for different situations — has a strong effect on their attitudes toward those situations. Distasteful ideas can be made to seem acceptable or even desirable by careful choices of words, and language can make actions or beliefs that might otherwise be considered correct appear to be obsolescent or naive. Value judgments of many kinds can be attached to seemingly simple statements. Shakespeare may have believed that "a rose by any other name would smell as sweet," but he was wrong, as other theatrical promoters have proved repeatedly. A young English vaudevillian known as Archibald Leach was a minor comedian until he was given the more romantic name of Cary Grant. The new name did not make him a star, but it did create an atmosphere in which he could demonstrate his talent, suggesting the type of character he came to exemplify.

If the power of a stage name to characterize personality seems of relatively minor consequence in human affairs, consider the effect of a different sort of appellation: "boy." It was — and sometimes still is — the form of address employed by whites in the American South in speaking to black males of any age. This word, many authorities believe, served as an instrument of subjugation. It implied that the black was not a man but a child, someone not mature enough to be entrusted with responsibility for himself, let alone authority over others. His inferior position was thus made to seem natural and justified, and it could be enforced without compunction.

Characterizing people by tagging them with a word label is a worldwide practice. Many peoples use a single word to designate both themselves and the human race. "The Carib Indians, for example, have stated with no equivocation, 'We alone are people,'" reported anthropologist Jack Conrad. "Similarly, the ancient Egyptians used the word *romet* (men) only among themselves and in no case for strangers. The Lapps of Scandinavia reserve the term 'human being' for those of their own kind, while the Cherokee Indians call themselves *Ani-Yunwiya*, which means 'principal people.' The Kiowa Indians of the Southwest are willing to accept other peoples as human, but the very name, *Kiowa*, meaning 'real people,' shows their true feeling." The effect of reserving a term indicating "human" to one group is far-reaching. It alters the perception of anyone from outside that group. He is not called "human," and need not be treated as human. Like an animal, he can be entrapped, beaten, or even killed with more or less impunity. This use of a word to demote whole groups from the human class is often a wartime tactic — the enemy is referred to by a pejorative name to justify killing him.

While language can be twisted to make ordinarily good things seem bad, it can also be twisted in the opposite direction to make bad things seem good or run-of-the-mill things better than they really are. The technique depends on the employment of euphemisms, a term derived from the Greek for "words of good omen." A euphemism is roundabout language that is intended to conceal something embarrassing or unpleasant. Some classes of euphemism — little evasions that people use every day — are inoffensive enough. It is when such cloudy doubletalk invades the vital areas of politics and foreign affairs that it becomes perilous.

A large and commonly used — and relatively harmless — class of euphemism has to do with bodily functions. Many people shy away from frank talk about excretion or sex; in fact, many of the old, vivid terms — the four-letter words — are socially taboo. So people for centuries have skirted the edge of such matters, inventing a rich vocabulary of substitute terms. Americans offered turkey on Thanksgiving commonly say "white meat" or "dark meat" to announce their preference. These terms date back to the nineteenth century when it was considered indelicate to say "breast" or "leg." *Toilet*, itself a euphemism coined from the French *toilette* ("making oneself presentable to the outside world"), long ago became tainted and too graphic for the prudish. The list of euphemistic substitutes is almost endless, ranging from the commonplace *washroom*, *bathroom*, and *restroom* (whoever rests in a restroom?) to *john*, *head*, and *Chic Sale* in the United States, and in England *the loo*. *Loo* may be derived from a mistaken English pronunciation of the French *l'eau*, water. Or it may be a euphemism derived from a euphemism. The French, with Gallic delicacy, once commonly put the number 100 on bathroom doors in hotels. It is easy to see how an English person might have mistaken the number for the word *loo*. Meanwhile, ladies in restaurants have adopted "I'm going to powder my nose" or, in England, where it once cost a penny to use public toilets, "I'm going to spend a penny."

Another generally harmless use of euphemistic language is the practice, especially notable in the United States, of giving prestigious names to more-or-less ordinary trades. As H. L. Mencken pointed out in *The American Language*, his masterly examination of English as spoken in the United States, ratcatchers are fond of calling themselves "exterminating engineers" and hairdressers have long since showed a preference for "beautician." The *-ician* ending, in fact, has proved very popular, doubtless because it echoes "physician" and thus sounds both professional and scientific. In the late nineteenth century undertakers had already begun to call themselves "funeral directors," but starting in 1916 ennobled themselves even further by battening on the newer euphemistic coinage, "mortician." Meanwhile a tree trimmer became a "tree surgeon" (that love of medicine again) and a press agent became a "publicist" or, even more grandly, a "public relations counsel."

Americans (and the English, too) not only chose high-sounding euphemisms for their professions but also gave new and gaudy names to their places of business. Thus pawn shops became "loan offices," saloons became "cocktail rooms," pool halls became "billiard parlors," and barber shops "hair-styling salons."

Purists might say that such shading or blunting of the stark truth leads to moral decay, but it is difficult to see why anybody should be the worse for allowing women to excuse themselves by pleading that they must powder their noses. There are euphemisms, however, that are clearly anything but harmless. These are evasive, beclouding phraseologies that hide truths people must clearly perceive if they are to govern themselves intelligently and keep a check on those in positions of power. Slick phrases, slippery evasions — words deliberately designed to hide unpleasant truth rather than reveal it — can so becloud political processes and so easily hide mistaken policies that the entire health of a nation is imperiled.

The classic treatise on the political misuse of language in modern times is the 1946 essay "Politics and the English Language" by the British writer George Orwell. "In our time, political speech and writing are largely the defence of the indefensible," Orwell said. "Thus political language has to consist largely of euphemism, question-begging and sheer cloudy vagueness." He concluded, "Such phraseology is needed if one wants to name things without calling up mental pictures of them. . . . When there is a gap between one's real and one's declared aims, one turns as it were instinctively to long words and exhausted idioms, like a cuttlefish squirting out ink."

Orwell supplied numerous examples to buttress his charges. "Defenceless villages are bombarded from the air, the inhabitants driven out into the countryside, the cattle machine-gunned, the huts set on fire with incendiary bullets: this is called *pacification*." He went on to observe that in Stalin's Russia people were "imprisoned for years without trial or shot in the back of the neck or sent to die of scurvy in Arctic lumber camps: this is called *elimination of unreliable elements*."

Orwell, who died at the age of forty-six in 1950, did not live to collect even more deplorable distortions of language. The French clothed their brutal war in Algeria with a veil of euphemism; the North Koreans accused the South Koreans of "aggression" when the North invaded the South. The United States invented a whole lexicon of gobbledygook to disguise the horror of the war in Vietnam: "protective reaction strike" (the bombing of a Vietnamese village); "surgical bombing" (the same as protective reaction strike); "free-fire zone" (an area in which troops could shoot anything that moved, including helpless villagers); "new life hamlet" (a refugee camp for survivors of a surgical bombing).

Perhaps the most appalling use of this type of euphemism was the word employed by the Nazis for their program to exterminate all of Europe's Jews. The word is *Endlösung*, which means final solution. Behind that verbal façade the Nazis gassed, burned, shot, or worked to death some six million Jews from Germany, France, Poland, and other conquered parts of Europe. Hitler and Gestapo chief Himmler often employed the euphemism among themselves, and it was always used in official records — but not necessarily to preserve secrecy for purposes of state security. Apparently the euphemism shielded the Nazis from themselves. Openly brutal and murderous as they were, they could not face up to the horrible reality of what they were doing, and they had to hide it in innocuous language.

Such distortion of language can do more than disguise truth. It can turn truth around, so that the idea conveyed is the opposite of actuality. After the USSR savagely crushed the Hungarian rebellion in 1956 the Soviet aggression was made to seem, in the twisted language used by other Communist dictatorships, an expression of friendship. The Peking radio commented after the rebellion was put down: "The Hungarian people can see that Soviet policy toward the people's democracies is truly one of equality, friendship, and mutual assistance, not of conquest, aggression, and plunder."

The possibility that such topsy-turvy language might ultimately make the world topsy-turvy — an ironic demonstration of the fundamental truth of Benjamin Lee Whorf's insights — was raised in a dramatic way by George Orwell. His novel *1984*, a chilling and convincing description of life in a totalitarian society, shows how language might destroy reality. In the imaginary nation of Oceania the official language is Newspeak, which is intended to facilitate "doublethink," the ability to accept simultaneously ideas contradicting each other. The Oceania state apparatus includes a Ministry of Truth, its headquarters building emblazoned with three slogans: "WAR IS PEACE"; "FREEDOM IS SLAVERY"; "IGNORANCE IS STRENGTH." There are also other ministries, Orwell explained: "The Ministry of Peace, which concerned itself with war; the Ministry of Love, which maintained law and order." Anyone who would use language this way, Orwell made clear, denies the meaning of his or her words. He or she has lost touch with reality and substituted for it an emptiness concealed in sounds that once had meaning.

There is another threat to language besides the intentional twisting of words by demagogues and others who would control people's thoughts. It is less obvious, but a danger nevertheless: simple imprecision, slovenliness, mindlessness in the use of the language. It seems a small matter that English-speakers increasingly confuse *uninterested* with *disinterested*, for example. But these words do not mean the same thing. *Disinterested* means impartial, not taking sides. *Uninterested* means lacking in interest, bored. A judge should be *disinterested* but never *uninterested*. Many such changes result from the inevitable evolution of language as it changes over the years, but the change can be a loss. The slow erosion of distinctions, visible in much writing, audible in many conversations, makes language imprecise and thus clumsy and ineffective as communication.

Among the symptoms of such erosion are stock phrases that people mindlessly repeat, substituting noise for thought. Everyone has heard speechmakers use such clichés as "having regard to," "play into the hands of," "in the interest of," "no axe to grind.," Although this brief list is drawn from Orwell's essay of 1946 these exhausted clichés are still heard. Such verbal dead limbs do not distort thought but rather tend to obliterate it in a cloud of meaninglessness. "The slovenliness of our language makes it easier for us to have foolish thoughts," wrote Orwell. And ultimately, as has been pointed out by commentator Edwin Newman in his book *Strictly Speaking*, "Those for whom words have lost their value are likely to find that ideas have also lost their value."

1. According to Thomson, what is the Sapir-Whorf hypothesis? Give some examples.

2. According to Whorf, how can grammar affect people's perceptions? Give examples.

3. The Sapir-Whorf hypothesis has been tested in several ways. What are some of the tests of the hypothesis described by Thomson and how have these modified the theory?

4. What are some of the ways in which language affects or modifies perception in modern America? Can you add examples from your own experience to those presented by Thomson?

IV

Ecology and Subsistence

Ecology is the relationship of an organism to other elements within its environmental sphere. Every species, no matter how simple or complex, fits into a larger complex ecological system; each adapts to its ecological niche unless rapid environmental alterations outstrip the organism's ability and potential to adapt successfully. An important aim of ecological studies is to show how organisms fit within particular environments. Such studies also look at the effect environments have on the shape and behavior of life forms.

Every species has adapted biologically through genetically produced variation and natural selection. For example, the bipedal (two-footed) locomotion characteristic of humans is one possible adaptation to walking on the ground. It also permitted our ancestors to carry food, tools, weapons, and almost anything else they desired, enabling them to range out from a home base and bring things back for others to share. Some anthropologists believe that the social advantages of carrying and sharing may actually account for our bipedalism.

Biological processes have led to another important human characteristic, the development of a large and complex brain. The human brain is capable of holding an enormous inventory of information. With it, we can classify the parts of our environment and retain instructions for complex ways to deal with the things in our world. Because we can communicate our knowledge symbolically through language, we are able to teach one another. Instead of a genetic code that directs behavior automatically, we operate with a learned cultural code. Culture gives us the ability to behave in a much wider variety of ways, and to change rapidly to new situations. With culture, people have been able to live successfully in almost every part of the world.

Cultural ecology is the way people use their culture to adapt to particular environments. All people live in a *physical environment*, the world they can experience through their senses, but they will conceive of it in terms that seem most important to their adaptive needs and cultural perspective. We call this perspective the *cultural environment*.

All human societies must provide for the material needs of their members. People everywhere have to eat, clothe themselves, provide shelter against the elements, and take care of social requirements such as hospitality, gift giving, and proper dress.

Societies employ several different strategies to meet their material needs, strategies that affect their complexity and internal organization as well as relationships to the natural environment and to other human groups. Anthropologists often use these subsistence strategies to classify different groups into five types: hunter/gatherers, horticulturalists, pastoralists, agriculturalists, and industrialists. Let us look briefly at each of these.

Hunter/gatherers depend for subsistence on wild plants and animals. They forage for food, moving to different parts of their territories as supplies of plants, animals, and water grow scarce. They live in small bands of from ten to fifty people and are typically egalitarian, leading a life marked by sharing and cooperation. Because hunter/gatherer bands are so small, they tend to lack formal political, legal, and religious structure, although members have regular ways to make group decisions, settle disputes, and deal ritually with the questions of death, adversity, social value, and world identification.

Hunter/gatherers tend to see themselves as part of the environment, not masters of it. This view shapes a religious ritual aimed at the maintenance and restoration of environmental harmony. All people lived as hunter/gatherers until about ten thousand years ago, when the first human groups began to farm and dwell in more permanent settlements. Today few hunter/gatherers survive. Most have lost their habitats to more powerful groups bent on economic and political exploitation.

Horticulture represents the earliest farming strategy, one that continues on a diminishing basis among many groups today. Horticulturalists garden. They often use a technique called *slash-and-burn agriculture*, which requires them to clear and burn over wild land, and, with the aid of a digging stick, sow seeds in the ashes. When fields lose their fertility after a few years, they are abandoned and new land is cleared. Although horticulturalists farm, they often continue to forage for wild foods and still feel closely related to the natural environment.

Horticulture requires a substantial amount of undeveloped land, so overall population densities must remain fairly low. But the strategy permits higher population densities than hunting and gathering, so horticulturalists tend to live in larger permanent settlements numbering from 50 to 250 individuals. (Some horticultural societies have produced chiefdomships with much larger administrative and religious town centers.) Although they are still small by our standards, horticultural communities are large enough to require more complex organizational strategies. They often display more elaborate kinship systems based on descent, political structures that include headmen or chiefs, political alliances, religions characterized by belief in a variety of supernatural beings, and the beginnings of social inequality. Many of today's so-called tribal peoples are horticulturalists.

Pastoralists follow a subsistence strategy based on the herding of domesticated animals such as cattle, goats, sheep, and camels. Although herding strategies vary from one environment to another, pastoralists share some general attributes. They move on a regular basis during the year to take advantage of fresh sources of water and fodder for their animals. They usually congregate in large encampments for part of the year when food and water are plentiful, then divide into smaller groups when these resources become scarce. Pastoralists often display a strong sense of group identity and pride, a fierce independence, and skill at war and raiding. Despite attempts by modern governments to place them in permanent settlements, many pastoral groups in Africa and Asia continue their nomadic life-style.

Agriculture is still a common subsistence strategy in many parts of the world. Agriculture refers to a kind of farming based on the intensive cultivation of permanent land holdings. Agriculturalists usually use plows and organic fertilizers, and may irrigate their fields under dry conditions.

Agrarian societies are marked by a high degree of social complexity. They are often organized as nation states with armies and bureaucracies, social stratification, markets, extended families and kin groups, and some occupational specialization. Religion takes on a formal structure and is organized as a separate institution.

The term *industrialism* labels the final kind of subsistence strategy. Ours is an industrial society, as is much of the Western, and more recently, the Asian world. Industrial nations are highly complex; they display an extensive variety of subgroups and social statuses. Industrial societies tend to be dominated by market economies in which goods and services are exchanged on the basis of price, supply, and demand. There is a high degree of economic specialization, and mass marketing may lead to a depersonalization of human relations. Religious, legal, political, and economic systems find expression as separate institutions in a way that might look disjointed to hunter/gatherers or others from smaller, more integrated societies.

The selections in Part IV have been chosen to illustrate four of these subsistence strategies. The !Kung discussed by Richard Borshay Lee in the first article are hunter/gatherers. Richard K. Reed describes the subsistence patterns of the Guarani, a rain forest horticultural group living in Paraguay, while J. Terrence McCabe and James E. Ellis look at the adaptive strategies of the pastoral Ngisonyoka of Kenya. Finally, Marvin Harris discusses the importance of cattle to the Indian agricultural system.

A second feature of all four articles relates to the typical ways in which people from Western societies have viewed non-Western modes of subsistence. Impressed by a value on "progress," Westerners often portray people in the rest of the world as "backward," "ignorant," and "underdeveloped." In each case, the authors of the articles in this section point out how the societies they describe are successfully adapted to their natural environments. Industrial techniques, they argue, are either inappropriate for subsistence altogether or fail to achieve a suitable and effective balance with the environment. An excellent summary of this position is presented by Bodley in Part X of this book.

KEY TERMS

ecology
cultural ecology
physical environment
cultural environment
subsistence strategies
hunting and gathering

horticulture
slash-and-burn agriculture
pastoralism
agriculture
industrialism

READINGS IN THIS SECTION

9　The Hunters: Scarce Resources in the Kalahari

RICHARD BORSHAY LEE

Peoples who hunt and gather wild foods experience an intimate relationship with their natural environments. A band's size and structure, the breadth of its territory, and the frequency and pattern of its movement depend on the abundance of vegetable foods, game, and water. For many Western anthropologists, the life of hunter-gatherers seems precarious and fraught with hardship. Yet, according to Richard B. Lee, this picture is largely inaccurate. In this article he points out that the !Kung Bushmen who live in the Kalahari Desert of South Africa survive well in what Westerners would consider a marginal habitat. Depending, like most hunter-gatherers, on vegetable foods for their sustenance, the !Kung actually spend little time at food collecting, yet they live long and fruitful lives in their desert home.

The current anthropological view of hunter-gatherer subsistence rests on two questionable assumptions. First is the notion that these people are primarily dependent on the hunting of game animals, and second is the assumption that their way of life is generally a precarious and arduous struggle for existence.

Recent data on living hunter-gatherers show a radically different picture. We have learned that in many societies, plant and marine

Reprinted by permission from Richard Lee and Irvin Devore, editors, *Man the Hunter* (Hawthorne, NY: Aldine Publishing Company); copyright © 1968 Wenner-Gren Foundation for Anthropological Research, Inc.

resources are far more important than are game animals in the diet. More important, it is becoming clear that, with few conspicuous exceptions, the hunter-gatherer subsistence base is at least routine and reliable and at best surprisingly abundant. Anthropologists have consistently tended to underestimate the viability of even those "marginal isolates" of hunting peoples that have been available to ethnographers.

The purpose of this paper is to analyze the food-getting activities of one such "marginal" people, the !Kung Bushmen of the Kalahari Desert. Three related questions are posed: How do the Bushmen make a living? How easy or difficult is it for them to do this? What kinds of evidence are necessary to measure and evaluate the precariousness or security of a way of life? And after the relevant data are presented, two further questions are asked: What makes this security of life possible? To what extent are the Bushmen typical of hunter-gatherers in general?

BUSHMAN SUBSISTENCE

The !Kung Bushmen of Botswana are an apt case for analysis. They inhabit the semi-arid northwest region of the Kalahari Desert. With only six to nine inches of rainfall per year, this is, by any account, a marginal environment for human habitation. In fact, it is precisely the unattractiveness of their homeland that has kept the !Kung isolated from extensive contact with their agricultural and pastoral neighbors.

Fieldwork was carried out in the Dobe area, a line of eight permanent waterholes near the South-West Africa border and 125 miles south of the Okavango River. The population of the Dobe area consists of 466 Bushmen, including 379 permanent residents living in independent camps or associated with Bantu cattle posts, as well as 87 seasonal visitors. The Bushmen share the area with some 340 Bantu pastoralists largely of the Herero and Tswana tribes. The ethnographic present refers to the period of fieldwork: October 1963 to January 1965.

The Bushmen living in independent camps lack firearms, livestock, and agriculture. Apart from occasional visits to the Herero for milk, these !Kung are entirely dependent upon hunting and gathering for their subsistence. Politically they are under the nominal authority of the Tswana headman, although they pay no taxes and receive very few government services. European presence amounts to one overnight government patrol every six to eight weeks. Although Dobe-area !Kung have had some contact with outsiders since the 1880s, the majority of them continue to hunt and gather because there is no viable alternative locally available to them.

Each of the fourteen independent camps is associated with one of the permanent waterholes. During the dry season (May–October) the entire population is clustered around these wells. Table I shows the numbers at each well at the end of the 1964 dry season. Two wells had no camp resident and one large well supported five camps. The number of camps at each well and the size of each camp changed frequently during the course of the year. The "camp" is an open aggregate of cooperating persons which changes in size and composition from day to day. Therefore, I have avoided the term "band" in describing the !Kung Bushman living groups.

Each waterhole has a hinterland lying within a six-mile radius that is regularly exploited for vegetable and animal foods. These areas are not territories in the zoological sense, since they are not defended against outsiders. Rather, they constitute the resources that lie within a convenient walking distance of a waterhole. The camp is a self-sufficient subsistence unit. The members move out each day to hunt and gather, and return in the evening to pool the collected foods in such a way that every person present receives an equitable share. Trade in foodstuffs between camps is minimal; personnel do move freely from camp to camp, however. The net effect is of a population constantly in motion. On the average, an individual spends a third of his time living only with close relatives, a third visiting other camps, and a third entertaining visitors from other camps.

Because of the strong emphasis on sharing, and the frequency of movement, surplus accumulation of storable plant foods and dried meat is kept to a minimum. There is rarely more than two or three days' supply of food on hand in a camp at any time. The result of this lack of surplus is that a constant subsistence effort must be maintained throughout the year. Unlike agriculturalists, who work hard during the planting and harvesting seasons and undergo "seasonal unemployment" for several months, the Bushmen hunter-gatherers collect food every third or fourth day throughout the year.

TABLE I

Numbers and Distribution of Resident Bushmen and Bantu by Waterhole*

Name of Waterhole	No. of Camps	Population of Camps	Other Bushmen	Total Bushmen	Bantu
Dobe	2	37	—	37	—
!angwa	1	16	23	39	84
Bate	2	30	12	42	21
!ubi	1	19	—	19	65
!gose	3	52	9	61	18
/ai/ai	5	94	13	107	67
!xabe	—	—	8	8	12
Mahopa	—	—	23	23	73
Total	14	248	88	336	340

* Figures do not include 130 Bushmen outside area on the date of census.

Vegetable foods comprise from 60 to 80 percent of the total diet by weight, and collecting involves two or three days of work per woman per week. The men also collect plants and small animals, but their major contribution to the diet is the hunting of medium and large game. The men are conscientious but not particularly successful hunters; although men's and women's work input is roughly equivalent in terms of man-day of effort, the women provide two to three times as much food by weight as the men.

Table II summarizes the seasonal activity cycle observed among the Dobe-area !Kung in 1964. For the greater part of the year, food is locally abundant and easily collected. It is only during the end of the dry season in September and October, when desirable foods have been eaten out in the immediate vicinity of the waterholes, that the people have to plan longer hikes of 10 to 15 miles and carry their own water to those areas where the mongongo nut is still available. The important point is that food is a constant, but distance required to reach food is a variable; it is short in the summer, fall, and early winter, and reaches its maximum in the spring.

This analysis attempts to provide quantitative measures of subsistence status, including data on the following topics: abundance and variety of resources, diet selectivity, range size and population density, the composition of the work force, the ratio of work to leisure time, and the caloric and protein levels in the diet. The value of quantitative data is that they can be used comparatively and also may be useful in archeological reconstruction. In addition, one can avoid the pitfalls of subjective and qualitative impressions; for example, statements about food "anxiety" have proven to be difficult to generalize across cultures.

Abundance and variety of resources. It is impossible to define "abundance" of resources absolutely. However, one index of *relative* abundance is whether or not a population exhausts all the food available from a given area. By this criterion, the habitat of the Dobe-area Bushmen is abundant in naturally occurring foods. By far the most important food is the mongongo (mangetti) nut (*Ricinodendron rautanenii* Schinz). Although tens of thousands of pounds of these nuts are harvested and eaten each year, thousands more rot on the ground each year for want of picking.

The mongongo nut, because of its abundance and reliability, alone accounts for 50 percent of the vegetable diet by weight. In this respect it resembles a cultivated staple crop such as maize or rice. Nutritionally it is even more remarkable, for it contains five times the calories and ten times the proteins per cooked unit of the cereal crops. The average daily per-capita consumption of 300 nuts yields about 1,260 calories and 56 grams of protein. This modest portion, weighing only about 7.5 ounces, contains the caloric equivalent of 2.5 pounds of cooked rice and the protein equivalent of 14 ounces of lean beef.

TABLE II
The Bushman Annual Round

Season	Jan.	Feb. Summer Rains	Mar.	April	May Autumn Dry	June	July Winter Dry	Aug.	Sept.	Oct. Spring Dry	Nov.	Dec. First Rains
Availability of water	Temporary summer pools everywhere			Large summer pools				Permanent waterholes only				Summer pools developing
Group moves	Widely dispersed at summer pools			At large summer pools				All population restricted to permanent waterholes				Moving out to summer pools
Men's subsistence activities	\multicolumn{12}{l}{1. Hunting with bow, arrows, and dogs (year-round)}											
	\multicolumn{2}{l}{2. Running down immatures}					Trapping small game in snares				Running down newborn animals	
	\multicolumn{12}{l}{3. Some gathering (year-round)}											
Women's subsistence activities	\multicolumn{12}{l}{1. Gathering of mongongo nuts (year-round)}											
	\multicolumn{2}{l}{2. Fruits, berries, melons}					Roots, bulbs, resins				Roots, leafy greens	
Ritual activities	\multicolumn{12}{l}{Dancing, trance performances, and ritual curing (year-round)}											
					Boys' initiation*							†
Relative subsistence hardship			Water-food distance minimal					Increasing distance from water to food			Water-food distance minimal	

* Held once every five years; none in 1963–64.

† New Year's: Bushmen join the celebrations of their missionized Bantu neighbors.

Furthermore, the mongongo nut is drought resistant, and it will still be abundant in the dry years when cultivated crops may fail. The extremely hard outer shell protects the inner kernel from rot and allows the nuts to be harvested for up to twelve months after they have fallen to the ground. A diet based on mongongo nuts is in fact more reliable than one based on cultivated foods, and it is not surprising, therefore, that when a Bushman was asked why he hadn't taken to agriculture, he replied: "Why should we plant, when there are so many mongongo nuts in the world?"

Apart from the mongongo, the Bushmen have available eighty-four other species of edible food plants, including twenty-nine species of fruits, berries, and melons and thirty species of roots and bulbs. The existence of this variety allows for a wide range of alternatives in subsistence strategy. During the summer months the Bushmen have no problem other than to choose among the tastiest and most easily collected foods. Many species, which are quite edible but less attractive, are bypassed, so that gathering never exhausts *all* the available plant foods of an area. During the dry season the diet becomes much more eclectic and the many species of roots, bulbs, and edible resins make an important contribution. It is this broad base that provides an essential margin of safety during the end of the dry season, when the mongongo nut forests are difficult to reach. In addition, it is likely that these rarely utilized species provide important nutritional and mineral trace elements that may be lacking in the more popular foods.

Diet selectivity. If the Bushmen were living close to the "starvation" level, then one would expect them to exploit every available source of nutrition. That their life is well above this level is indicated by the data in Table III. Here all the edible plant species are arranged in classes according to the frequency with which they were observed to be eaten. It should be noted that although there are some eighty-five species available, about 90 percent of the vegetable diet by weight is drawn from only twenty-three species. In other words, 75 percent of the listed species provide only 10 percent of the food value.

In their meat-eating habits, the Bushmen show a similar selectivity. Of the 223 local species of animals known and named by the Bushmen, 54 species are classified as edible, and of these only 17 species were hunted on a regular basis. Only a handful of the dozens of edible species of small mammals, birds, reptiles, and insects that occur locally are regarded as food. Such animals as rodents, snakes, lizards, termites, and grasshoppers, which in the literature are included in the Bushman diet, are despised by the Bushmen of the Dobe area.

Range size and population density. The necessity to travel long distances, the high frequency of moves, and the maintenance of populations at low densities are also features commonly associated with

TABLE III
!Kung Bushman Plant Foods

Food Class	Part Eaten								Total Number of Species in Class	Totals (percentages)	
	Fruit and Nut	Bean and Root	Fruit and Stalk	Root, Bulb	Fruit, Berry, Melon	Resin	Leaves	Seed, Bean		Estimated Contribution by Weight to Vegetable Diet	Estimated Contribution of Each Species
I. Primary Eaten daily throughout year (mongongo nut)	1	—	—	—	—	—	—	—	1	c. 50	c. 50*
II. Major Eaten daily in season	1	1	1	1	4	—	—	—	8	c. 25	c. 3
III. Minor Eaten several times per week in season	—	—	—	7	3	2	2	—	14	c.15	c. 1
IV. Supplementary Eaten when classes I–III locally unavailable	—	—	—	9	12	10	1	—	32	c. 7	c. 0.2
V. Rare Eaten several times per year	—	—	—	9	4	—	—	—	13	c. 3	c. 0.1
VI. Problematic Edible but not observed to be eaten	—	—	—	4	6	4	1	2	17	nil	nil
Total Species	2	1	1	30	29	16	4	2	85	100	—

* 1 species constitutes 50 percent of the vegetable diet by weight.
† 23 species constitute 90 percent of the vegetable diet by weight.
‡ 62 species constitute the remaining 10 percent of the diet.

129

the hunting and gathering way of life. Density estimates for hunters in western North America and Australia have ranged from 3 persons/ square mile to as low as 1 person/100 square miles. In 1963–65, the resident and visiting Bushmen were observed to utilize an area of about 1,000 square miles during the course of the annual round for an effective population density of 41 persons/100 square miles. Within this area, however, the amount of ground covered by members of an individual camp was surprisingly small. A day's round-trip of twelve miles serves to define a "core" area six miles in radius surrounding each water point. By fanning out in all directions from their well, the members of a camp can gain access to the food resources of well over 100 square miles of territory within a two-hour hike. Except for a few weeks each year, areas lying beyond this six-mile radius are rarely utilized, even though they are no less rich in plants and game than are the core areas.

Although the Bushmen move their camps frequently (five or six times a year), they do not move them very far. A rainy season camp in the nut forests is rarely more than ten or twelve miles from the home waterhole, and often new campsites are occupied only a few hundred yards away from the previous one. By these criteria, the Bushmen do not lead a free-ranging nomadic way of life. For example, they do not undertake long marches of 30 to 100 miles to get food, since this task can be readily fulfilled within a day's walk of home base. When such long marches do occur they are invariably for visiting, trading, and marriage arrangements, and should not be confused with the normal routine of subsistence.

Demographic factors. Another indicator of the harshness of a way of life is the age at which people die. Ever since Hobbes characterized life in the state of nature as "nasty, brutish and short," the assumption has been that hunting and gathering is so rigorous that members of such societies are rapidly worn out and meet an early death. Silberbauer, for example, says of the Gwi Bushmen of the central Kalahari that "life expectancy . . . is difficult to calculate, but I do not believe that many live beyond 45." And Coon has said of hunters in general:

> The practice of abandoning the hopelessly ill and aged has been observed in many parts of the world. It is always done by people living in poor environments where it is necessary to move about frequently to obtain food, where food is scarce, and transportation difficult. . . . Among peoples who are forced to live in this way the oldest generation, the generation of individuals who have passed their physical peak is reduced in numbers and influence. There is no body of elders to hand on tradition and control the affairs of younger men and women, and no formal system of age grading.

The !Kung Bushmen of the Dobe area flatly contradict this view. In a total population of 466, no fewer than 46 individuals (17 men and 29 women) were determined to be over sixty years of age, a proportion that compares favorably to the percentage of elderly in industrialized populations.

The aged hold a respected position in Bushmen society and are the effective leaders of the camps. Senilicide is extremely rare. Long after their productive years have passed, the old people are fed and cared for by their children and grandchildren. The blind, the senile, and the crippled are respected for the special ritual and technical skills they possess. For instance, the four elders at !gose waterhole were totally or partially blind, but this handicap did not prevent their active participation in decision making and ritual curing.

Another significant feature of the composition of the work force is the late assumption of adult responsibility by the adolescents. Young people are not expected to provide food regularly until they are married. Girls typically marry between the ages of fifteen and twenty, and boys about five years later, so that it is not unusual to find healthy, active teenagers visiting from camp to camp while their older relatives provide food for them.

As a result, the people in the twenty to sixty age group support a surprisingly large percentage of nonproductive young and old people. About 40 percent of the population in camps contributes little to the food supplies. This allocation of work to young and middle-aged adults allows for a relatively carefree childhood and adolescence and a relatively unstrenuous old age.

Leisure and work. Another important index of ease or difficulty of subsistence is the amount of time devoted to the food quest. Hunting has usually been regarded by social scientists as a way of life in which merely keeping alive is so formidable a task that members of such societies lack the leisure time necessary to "build culture." The !Kung Bushmen would appear to conform to the rule, for as Lorna Marshall says:

> It is vividly apparent that among the !Kung Bushmen, ethos, or "the spirit which actuates manners and customs," is survival. Their time and energies are almost wholly given to this task, for life in their environment requires that they spend their days mainly in procuring food.

It is certainly true that getting food is the most important single activity in Bushman life. However, this statement would apply equally well to small-scale agricultural and pastoral societies too. How much time is *actually* devoted to the food quest is fortunately an empirical question. And an analysis of the work effort of the Dobe Bushmen shows some unexpected results. From July 6 to August 2, 1964, I recorded all the daily activities of the Bushmen living at the Dobe waterhole. Because of the coming and going of visitors, the camp population fluctuated in size day by day, from a low of 23 to a high of 40, with a mean of 31.8 persons. Each day some of the adult members of the camp went out to hunt and/or gather while others stayed home or went visiting. The daily recording of all personnel on hand made it possible to calculate the number of man-days of work as a percentage of total number of man-days of consumption.

Although the Bushmen do not organize their activities on the basis of a seven-day week, I have divided the data this way to make them more intelligible. The workweek was calculated to show how many days out of seven each adult spent in subsistence activities (Table IV, Column 7). Week II has been eliminated from the totals since the investigator contributed food. In week I, the people spent an average of 2.3 days in subsistence activities, in week II, 1.9 days, and in week IV, 3.2 days. In all, the adults of the Dobe camp worked about two and a half days a week. Since the average working day was about six hours long, the fact emerges that !Kung Bushmen of Dobe, despite their harsh environment, devote from twelve to nineteen hours a week to getting food. Even the hardest-working individual in the camp, a man named ≠oma who went out hunting on sixteen of the twenty-eight days, spent a maximum of thirty-two hours a week in the food quest.

Because the Bushmen do not amass a surplus of foods, there are no seasons of exceptionally intensive activities such as planting and harvesting, and no seasons of unemployment. The level of work observed is an accurate reflection of the effort required to meet the immediate caloric needs of the group. This work diary covers the midwinter dry season, a period when food is neither at its most plentiful nor at its scarcest levels, and the diary documents the transition from better to worse conditions (see Table II). During the fourth week the gatherers were making overnight trips to camps in the mongongo nut forests seven to ten miles distant from the waterhole. These longer trips account for the rise in the level of work, from twelve or thirteen to nineteen hours per week.

If food getting occupies such a small proportion of a Bushman's waking hours, then how *do* people allocate their time? A woman gathers on one day enough food to feed her family for three days, and spends the rest of her time resting in camp, doing embroidery, visiting other camps, or entertaining visitors from other camps. For each day at home, kitchen routines, such as cooking, nut cracking, collecting firewood, and fetching water, occupy one to three hours of her time. This rhythm of steady work and steady leisure is maintained throughout the year.

TABLE IV
Summary of Dobe Work Diary

Week	(1) Mean Group Size	(2) Adult-Days	(3) Child-Days	(4) Total Man-Days of Consumption	(5) Man-Days of Work	(6) Meat (lbs.)	(7) Average Workweek/Adult	(8) Index of Subsistence Effort
I (July 6–12)	25.6 (23–29)	114	65	179	37	104	2.3	.21
II (July 13–19)	28.3 (23–27)	125	73	198	22	80	1.2	.11
III (July 20–26)	34.3 (29–40)	156	84	240	42	177	1.9	.18
IV (July 27–Aug. 2)	35.6 (32–40)	167	82	249	77	129	3.2	.31
4-wk. total	30.9	562	304	866	178	490	2.2	.21
Adjusted total*	31.8	437	231	668	156	410	2.5	.23

* See text

Key: Column 1: Mean group size = $\dfrac{\text{total man-days of consumption}}{7}$.

Column 7: Workweek = the number of workdays per adult per week.

Column 8: Index of subsistence effort = $\dfrac{\text{man-days of work}}{\text{man-days of consumption}}$ (e.g., in Week I, the value of "S" = 21, i.e.,

21 days of work/100 days of consumption or 1 workday produces food for 5 consumption days).

The hunters tend to work more frequently than the women, but their schedule is uneven. It is not unusual for a man to hunt avidly for a week and then do nothing at all for two or three weeks. Since hunting is an unpredictable business and subject to magical control, hunters sometimes experience a run of bad luck and stop hunting for a month or longer. During these periods, visiting, entertaining, and especially dancing are the primary activities of men. (Unlike the Hadza, gambling is only a minor leisure activity.)

The trance dance is the focus of Bushman ritual life; over 50 percent of the men have trained as trance-performers and regularly enter trance during the course of the all-night dances. At some camps, trance dances occur as frequently as two or three times a week, and those who have entered trances the night before rarely go out hunting the following day. . . . In a camp with five or more hunters, there are usually two or three who are actively hunting and several others who are inactive. The net effect is to phase the hunting and non-hunting so that a fairly steady supply of meat is brought into camp.

Caloric returns. Is the modest work effort of the Bushmen sufficient to provide the calories necessary to maintain the health of the population? Or have the !Kung, in common with some agricultural peoples, adjusted to a permanently substandard nutritional level?

During my fieldwork I did not encounter any cases of kwashiorkor, the most common nutritional disease in the children of African agricultural societies. However, without medical examinations, it is impossible to exclude the possibility that subclinical signs of malnutrition existed.

Another measure of nutritional adequacy is the average consumption of calories and proteins per person per day. The estimate for the Bushmen is based on observations of the weights of foods of known composition that were brought into Dobe camp on each day of the study period. The per-capita figure is obtained by dividing the total weight of foodstuffs by the total number of persons in the camp. These results are set out in detail elsewhere and can only be summarized here. During the study period 410 pounds of meat were brought in by the hunters of the Dobe camp, for a daily share of nine ounces of meat per person. About 700 pounds of vegetables were gathered and consumed during the same period. Table v sets out the calories and proteins available per capita in the !Kung Bushman diet from meat, mongongo nuts, and other vegetable sources.

This output of 2,140 calories and 93.1 grams of protein per person per day may be compared with the Recommended Daily Allowances (RDA) for persons of the small size and stature but vigorous activity regime of the !Kung Bushmen. The RDA for Bushmen can be estimated at 1,975 calories and 60 grams of protein per person per day.

TABLE V

Caloric and Protein Levels in the !Kung Bushman Diet, July–August, 1964

| Class of Food | Percentage Contribution to Diet by Weight | Per-Capita Consumption | | | Percentage Caloric Contribution of Meat and Vegetables |
		Weight in Grams	Protein in Grams	Calories per Person per Day	
Meat	37	230	34.5	690	33
Mongongo nuts	33	210	56.7	1,260	67
Other vegetable foods	30	190	1.9	190	
Total all sources	100	630	93.1	2,140	100

Thus it is apparent that food output exceeds energy requirements by 165 calories and 33 grams of protein. One can tentatively conclude that even a modest subsistence effort of two or three days' work per week is enough to provide an adequate diet for the !Kung Bushmen.

THE SECURITY OF BUSHMAN LIFE

I have attempted to evaluate the subsistence base of one contemporary hunter-gatherer society living in a marginal environment. The !Kung Bushmen have available to them some relatively abundant high-quality foods, and they do not have to walk very far or work very hard to get them. Furthermore, this modest work effort provides sufficient calories to support not only active adults, but also a large number of middle-aged and elderly people. The Bushmen do not have to press their youngsters into the service of the food quest, nor do they have to dispose of the oldsters after they have ceased to be productive.

The evidence presented assumes an added significance because this security of life was observed during the third year of one of the most severe droughts in South Africa's history. Most of the 576,000 people of Botswana are pastoralists and agriculturalists. After the crops had failed three years in succession and over 100,000 head of cattle had died on the range for lack of water, the World Food Program of the United Nations instituted a famine relief program which has grown to include 180,000 people, over 30 percent of the population. This program did not touch the Dobe area in the isolated northwest corner of the country, and the Herero and Tswana women there were able to feed their families only by joining the Bushman women to forage for wild foods. Thus the natural plant resources of the Dobe area were carrying a higher proportion of population than would be the case in years when the Bantu harvested crops. Yet this added pressure on the land did not seem to adversely affect the Bushmen.

In one sense it was unfortunate that the period of my fieldwork happened to coincide with the drought, since I was unable to witness a "typical" annual subsistence cycle. However, in another sense, the coincidence was a lucky one, for the drought put the Bushmen and their subsistence system to the acid test and, in terms of adaptation to scarce resources, they passed with flying colors. One can postulate that their subsistence base would be even more substantial during years of higher rainfall.

What are the crucial factors that make this way of life possible? I suggest that the primary factor is the Bushmen's strong emphasis on vegetable food sources. Although hunting involves a great deal of effort and prestige, plant foods provide from 60 to 80 percent of the annual diet by weight. Meat has come to be regarded as a special treat; when available, it is welcomed as a break from the routine of vegetable foods, but it is never depended upon as a staple. No one ever goes hungry when hunting fails.

The reason for this emphasis is not hard to find. Vegetable foods are abundant, sedentary, and predictable. They grow in the same place year after year, and the gatherer is guaranteed a day's return of food for a day's expenditure of energy. Game animals, by contrast, are scarce, mobile, unpredictable, and difficult to catch. A hunter has no guarantee of success and may in fact go for days or weeks without killing a large mammal. During the study period, there were eleven men in the Dobe camp, of whom four did no hunting at all. The seven active men spent a total of 78 man-days hunting, and this work input yielded eighteen animals killed, or one kill for every four man-days of hunting. The probability of any one hunter making a kill on a given day was 0.23. By contrast, the probability of a woman finding plant food on a given day was 1.00. In other words, hunting and gathering are not equally felicitous subsistence alternatives.

Consider the productivity per man-hour of the two kinds of subsistence activities. One man-hour of hunting produces about 100 edible calories, and of gathering, 240 calories. Gathering is thus seen to be 2.4 times more productive than hunting. In short, hunting is a *high-risk, low-return* subsistence activity, while gathering is a low-risk, high-return subsistence activity.

It is not at all contradictory that the hunting complex holds a central place in the Bushmen ethos and that meat is valued more highly than vegetable foods. Analogously, steak is valued more highly than potatoes in the food preferences of our own society. In both situations the meat is more "costly" than the vegetable food. In the Bushman case, the cost of food can be measured in terms of time and energy expended. By this standard, 1,000 calories of meat "costs" ten man-hours, while the "cost" of 1,000 calories of vegetable foods is only four man-hours. Further, it is to be expected that the less predictable, more expensive food source would have a greater accretion of myth and ritual built up around it than would the routine staples of life, which rarely if ever fail.

CONCLUSIONS

Three points ought to be stressed. First, life in the state of nature is not necessarily nasty, brutish, and short. The Dobe-area Bushmen live well today on wild plants and meat, in spite of the fact that they are confined to the least productive portion of the range in which Bushman peoples were formerly found. It is likely that an even more substantial subsistence would have been characteristic of these hunters and gatherers in the past, when they had the pick of African habitats to choose from.

Second, the basis of Bushman diet is derived from sources other than meat. This emphasis makes good ecological sense to the !Kung Bushmen and appears to be a common feature among hunters and gatherers in general. Since a 30 to 40 percent input of meat is such a consistent target for modern hunters in a variety of habitats, is it not reasonable to postulate a similar percentage for prehistoric hunters? Certainly the absence of plant remains on archeological sites is by itself not sufficient evidence for the absence of gathering. Recently abandoned Bushman campsites show a similar absence of vegetable remains, although this paper has clearly shown that plant foods comprise over 60 percent of the actual diet.

Finally, one gets the impression that hunting societies have been chosen by ethnologists to illustrate a dominant theme, such as the extreme importance of environment in the molding of certain cultures. Such a theme can best be exemplified by cases in which the technology is simple and/or the environment is harsh. This emphasis on the dramatic may have been pedagogically useful, but unfortunately it has led to the assumption that a precarious hunting subsistence base was characteristic of all cultures in the Pleistocene. This view of both modern and ancient hunters ought to be reconsidered. Specifically I am suggesting a shift in focus away from the dramatic and unusual cases, and toward a consideration of hunting and gathering as a persistent and well-adapted way of life.

REVIEW QUESTIONS

1. How does Lee assess the day-to-day quality of !Kung life? How does his view compare with the stereotype of hunter-gatherers?

2. Give the evidence that supports Lee's viewpoint about the !Kung.

3. According to Lee, !Kung children are not expected to work until after they are married; old people are supported and respected. How does this arrangement differ from behavior in our own society, and what might explain the difference?

4. What is the key to successful subsistence for the !Kung and other hunter-gatherers?

10   Cultivating the Tropical Forest
RICHARD K. REED

*To most industrialized peoples, the practice of slash-and-burn agri-
culture seems especially wasteful. The horticulturalists who manifest such practices must often laboriously cut and burn thick forest
cover, then plant in the ashes. Because clearing is difficult and
fields are left fallow for many years to recover from agricultural
use, most land lies dormant. For people used to thinking of agriculture as a source of income, horticultural practices seem to epit-
omize "underdevelopment." In this article, Richard Reed challenges this simplistic notion. Describing the subsistence practices
of the Guarani Indians living in the tropical forests of Paraguay, he
shows that Indian slash-and-burn agriculture combined with foraging for wild game and plants represents the optimal use of the forest and a model for modern forest management programs.*

The world's great tropical forests, which once seemed so forbidding
and impenetrable, are now prime targets for economic exploitation.
Developers and colonists, from Brazil to Indonesia, flock to the jungle
frontiers armed with chain saws and bulldozers. They build roads,
clear-cut timber, and denude the land of foliage, often burning the
trees and brush as they go. The scope of this human invasion staggers
the mind. Development destroys hundreds of square miles of virgin
tropical forest each day. In the Amazon alone, an area the size of

Louisiana is cleared every year. At this rate, authorities predict that the forests will be gone by the year 2000.

Damage to the forest has not gone unnoticed. Publicized by newscasters, environmentalists, rock stars, and a host of others, the plight of rain forests is now familiar to many Americans. Concern has centered most on the consequences of deforestation for the world ecosystem. Forests are the "lungs of the earth," producing crucial oxygen. Burning them not only reduces world oxygen production, it releases large amounts of carbon dioxide, a greenhouse gas, into the atmosphere. A warmer world is the likely result.

Many authorities have also warned about the impact of deforestation on the survival of wildlife. Tropical forests contain the world's richest variety of animals and plants. As the trees disappear, so do countless irreplaceable species.

Curiously, there is less said about the plight of people who are native to the forests. In South America, for example, up to six million Indians once lived scattered across the vast lowland forests. Only a tenth of that population remains today, the rest having fallen victim to the colonial advance over the past 400 years. Each year, these survivors find it increasingly difficult to maintain their populations and communities.

The damage being done to these Indian societies is particularly distressing because they are the only humans who have managed to subsist in the forest without causing permanent harm. By employing a subsistence strategy that combines horticulture, gathering, and hunting, these indigenous peoples have managed to live in harmony with the forest environment for centuries.

We may ask what accounts for this successful adaptation. Is there a special genius to the social organization of indigenous peoples? What subsistence strategies permit them to live amicably with the forest? What happens to them when they are overtaken by settlers and commercial development? Can such people provide a model for successful tropical forest management? Let's look at these questions in the context of one group living in the South American forest, the Guarani of eastern Paraguay.

THE GUARANI

The Guarani Indians provide an excellent example of a group well adapted to the forest environment. Like most horticulturalists, they live in small, widely scattered communities. Because their population densities are low, and because they practice a mixture of slash-and-burn agriculture and foraging, they place a light demand on forest resources. Small size also means a more personal social organization and an emphasis on cooperation and sharing. Although of greater size and complexity than hunter-gatherer bands, Guarani villages contain many of the cultural values found in these nomadic societies.

I have conducted ethnographic fieldwork among the Guarani for the past ten years, mostly in the village of Itanarami, located in eastern Paraguay. The residents of Itanarami are among the last of the Guarani Indians still living in the forests of southern South America. They are the remnants of an ethnic group that once dominated southern Brazil and Paraguay from the Atlantic Ocean to the Andes. The Guarani have suffered as their forests have fallen to development. Today, only 15,500 Guarani remain in Paraguay in isolated settlements where the tropical forest survives.

The forests surrounding Itanarami are characterized by high canopies that shade thick undergrowth and shelter both animal and human populations. From the air, the dense expanse of trees is broken only by streams and rivers that drain westward to the broad, marshy valley of the Parana River. Viewed from the ground, the density of the forest growth is matched only by the diversity of plant species.

Itanarami itself is built along a small stream that gives the settlement its name. To the uninformed observer, it is difficult to recognize the existence of a village at all. Homesteads, which consist of a clearing, a thatched hut, and one or two nearby fields, lie scattered in the forest, often out of sight of one another. Yet a closer look reveals the pathways through the deep forest that connect houses to each other and to a slightly larger homestead, that of the *tamoi* (literally grandfather), the group's religious leader. As in many small societies, households are tied together by kinship; people live only a short distance from close relatives. Kinship networks tie all members of the community together, weaving a tapestry of relations that organize social affairs and link Itanarami to other Guarani communities.

The Guarani emphasize sharing and cooperation. Sisters often share fieldwork and child care. Brothers usually hunt together. Food is distributed among members of the extended family, including cousins, aunts, and uncles. People emphasize the general welfare, not personal wealth.

The *tamoi*, although in no sense a leader with formal authority, commands considerable respect in the community. He settles disputes, chastises errant juniors, and leads the entire community in evening religious ceremonies where people drink *kanguijy* (fermented corn), dance, and sing to the gods.

The people of Itanarami not only live in the forest, they see themselves as part of it. The forest is basic to indigenous cosmology. The people refer to themselves as *ka'aguygua*, or "people of the forest." Villagers often name their children after the numerous varieties of forest song birds, symbolizing their close personal ties to the environment.

SUBSISTENCE

The Guarani have lived in their present locale for centuries and have dwelled throughout the tropical forests of lowland South America for thousands of years. During all this time, they have exploited flora, fauna, and soils of the forests without doing permanent harm. The secret of their success is in their production strategy. The Indians mix agriculture with gathering, hunting, and fishing in a way that permits environmental recovery. They even collect forest products for sale to outsiders, again without causing environmental damage.

Guarani farming is well-suited to forest maintenance. Using a form of shifting agriculture called slash-and-burn farming, the Indians permit the forest to recover from the damage of field clearing. The way Veraju, the *tamoi* of Itanarami, and his wife, Kitu, farm provides a typical example. When the family needs to prepare a new field, it is Veraju who does the heavy work. He cuts the trees and undergrowth to make a half-acre clearing near his house. Then he, Kitu, and some of their five children burn the fallen trees and brush, creating an ash that provides a natural fertilizer on top of the thin forest soils. When the field is prepared, Kitu uses a digging stick fashioned from a sapling to poke small holes in the ground, and plants the three staple Guarani crops, corn, beans, and manioc root (from which tapioca is made). When the crops mature, it is Kitu and her daughters who will harvest them.

The secret to successful slash-and-burn agriculture is field "shifting" or rotation. Crops flourish the first year and are plentiful the next, but the sun and rain soon take their toll on the exposed soil. The thin loam layer, so typical of tropical forests, degenerates rapidly to sand and clay. By the third year, the poor soils are thick with weeds and grow only a sparse corn crop and a few small manioc roots. Rather than replant a fourth time, Veraju and Kitu will clear a new field nearby where soils are naturally more fertile and the forest can be burned for additional ash fertilizer. The surrounding forest quickly reclaims the old field, reconstituting and strengthening the depleted soil. In this way, the forest produces a sustained yield without degrading the natural ecosystem.

The forest recovers sufficiently fast for the same plot to be cleared and planted within ten or fifteen years. This "swidden" agricultural system results in the cyclic use of a large area of forest, with a part under cultivation and a much larger portion lying fallow in various stages of decomposition.

If farming formed the only subsistence base, the Guarani would probably have to clear more land than the forest could rejuvenate. But they also turn to other forest resources — game, fish, and forest products — to meet their needs for food and material items. Guarani men often form small groups to hunt large animals, such as deer, tapir, and peccary, with guns purchased from outsiders or with the more traditional bows and arrows they make themselves. A successful hunt will provide enough meat to share liberally with kin and friends. Men also trap smaller mammals, such as armadillo and paca (a large rodent). They fashion snares and deadfall traps from saplings, tree trunks, and cactus fiber twine. These are set near homesteads, along stream banks, and at the edges of gardens. Traps not only catch small game for meat, they kill animals that would otherwise enter the fields to eat the crops.

Fish also supply protein in the Guarani diet and reduce dependence on agricultural produce. Many rivers and streams flow near Itanarami on flat bottom land. These water courses meander in broad loops that may be cut off when the river or stream changes course during a flood. Meanders, called ox-bow lakes, make ideal fishing spots. In addition to hook and line, men capture the fish by using a poison extracted from the bark of a particular vine. Floated over the surface of the water, the poison stuns the fish and allows the men to catch them by hand.

The forest also supplies a variety of useful products for the Guarani. They make houses from tree trunks and bamboo stalks; rhododendron vines secure the thatched roofs. Villagers collect wild honey and fruit to add sweetness to their diets. Wild tubers replace manioc as a principal food source when crops fail in the gardens. Even several species of insect larva and ants are collected as tasty and nutritious supplements to the daily meal. Finally, the Indians know about a wide variety of medicinal plants. They process several different kinds of roots, leaves, flowers, and seeds to release powerful alkaloids and to make teas and poultices for the sick and injured.

White traders have entered the forests of the Guarani and give the Indians access to manufactured goods. The Guarani continue to produce for most of their needs, but items such as machetes, hooks, soap, and salt are more easily bought than manufactured or collected. As they do with farming and hunting, the Guarani turn to the forest to meet such economic needs. They regularly collect two forest products, *yerba mate* (a caffeinated tea) and oil extract from wild orange trees, used for flavorings and perfumes, to raise the necessary funds.

It is important to note the special Guarani knowledge and values associated with subsistence activities. Because they have lived in the forest for such a long time, and because they would have nowhere to turn if their own resources disappeared, they treat the rain forest with special respect. They can do so, however, only by using a special and complex knowledge of how the forest works and how it can be used.

For example, Guarani, such as Veraju, distinguish among a variety of "ecozones," each with a unique combination of soil, flora, and fauna. They recognize obvious differences, such as those among the high forests that grow on the hills, the deep swamps that cover the flood plains by the rivers, and the grassy savannahs of the high plains. But they make more subtle distinctions within these larger regions. For example, they call the low scrub bordering rivers, *ca'ati*. Flooded each year during the rainy season, this zone supports bamboo groves that harbor small animals for trapping and material for house construction. The forests immediately above the flood plain look like an extension of the *ca'ati*, but to the Guarani they differ in important ways. This ecozone supports varieties of bamboo that are useless for house construction but that attract larger animals, such as peccary and deer, that can be hunted. In all, the Guarani distinguish among nine resource zones, each with distinctive soils, flora, fauna, and uses. These subtle distinctions between ecozones enable the Guarani to use the forest to greatest benefit. By shifting their subsistence efforts from one zone to another, just as they shift their fields from one spot to the next, the Guarani assure that their forest environment, with its rich variety of life, will always be able to renew itself.

THE IMPACT OF DEVELOPMENT

In the last few years, intensive commercial development has come to the region in which Itanarami lies. The spectre of complete ecological destruction stalks the forest. White *colonos* (settlers), armed with chain saws and earth movers, attack the trees. They vandalize the land without concern for the carefully integrated ecozones. As the trees fall, the forest products, such as *yerba mate*, disappear. So do the mammals and fish, the bamboo and the rhododendron vines, the honey and the fruits, and the reconstituting fields. As these resources disappear, so does the economy of the once self-sufficient Guarani. Without their traditional mode of subsistence, their kin-organized society, the influence of the *tamoi*, and the willingness to share, their independence as a people becomes impossible. Indian communities are destroyed by poverty and disease, and the members who remain join the legions of poor laborers who form the lowest class of the national society.

Recent intensive development began near Itanarami in 1974, when *colonos* cut a road into the jungle located within two hours' walk of the village. Through this gash in the forest moved logging trucks, bulldozers, farm equipment, and buses. Accompanying the machinery of development were farmers, ranchers, and speculators, hoping to make a quick profit from the verdant land. They descended from their vehicles onto the muddy streets of a newly built frontier town. They cleared land for general stores and bars, which were soon filled with merchandise and warm beer. By day, the air in the town was fouled by truck noise and exhaust fumes; by night it was infused with the glare of electric lights and the noise of blaring tape players.

Soon the settlers began to fell the forest near the town and road, creating fields for cotton and soybeans, and pasture. Surveying teams demarcated boundaries and drew maps. Lumber companies invaded the forests, clear-cutting vast tracts of trees. Valuable timber was hauled off to newly established lumber mills; remaining brush was piled and burned. Heavy machinery created expanses of sunlight in the previously unbroken forest. Within months, grass, cotton, and soybeans sprouted in the exposed soils. Where once the land had been home for game, it now provided for cattle. Cattle herds often clogged the roads, blocking the path of trucks hauling cotton to market and chewing deep ruts in the soft forest soils. Settlers fenced in the fields and cut lanes through the forest to mark off portions that would be "private property," off-limits to Indians.

Guarani communities nearest the road suffered first from development. The forests they once used for farming and hunting disappeared before the onslaught of chain saws and bulldozers. The paths that previously connected homesteads became sandy jeep tracks across unbroken expanses of open fields. Within a few years, the Guarani of these villages had little left but their homesteads.

Moreover, by destroying the forest resources surrounding Indian villages, the *colonos* set in motion a process that destroyed the native culture and society. Guarani communities became small islands of forest surrounded by a sea of pastures and farm fields. Although the Indians retained some land for agriculture, they lost the forest resources needed to sustain their original mode of subsistence, which depended on hunting, fishing, and gathering in the forest as well as farming. These economic changes forced alterations in the Indian community.

First, without the forest to provide game, fish, and other products, the Guarani became dependent on farming alone for their survival. Without wild foods, they had to clear and farm fields three times larger than original ones. Without the forest production of *yerba mate* leaves to collect for sale, they were forced to plant cash crops, such as cotton and tobacco. These two new crops demanded large, clean fields.

While the loss of the forest for hunting and gathering increased their dependence on agriculture, the fences and land titles of the new settlers reduced the land available to the Indians for cultivation. Families soon cleared the last of the remaining high forests that they controlled. Even the once forested stream banks were denuded.

After they had cleared their communities' remaining forest, Indian farmers were forced to replant fields without allowing sufficient fallow time for the soils to rejuvenate. Crops suffered from lack of nutrients and yields declined despite additional effort devoted to clearing and weeding. As production suffered, the Indians cleared and farmed even larger areas. The resulting spiral of poor harvests and enlarged farms outstripped the soil's capacity to produce and the Guarani's ability to care for the crops. Food in the Indian communities grew scarce. The Indian diet was increasingly restricted to non-nutritious manioc as a dietary staple, because it was the only plant that could survive in the exhausted soils.

The Guarani felt the decline in their subsistence base in other ways. The loss of game and poor crop yields exacerbated health problems. Settlers brought new diseases into the forest, such as colds and flu. The Guarani had no inherited resistance to these illnesses and poor nutrition reduced their defenses even further. Disease not only sapped the adults' energy for farming and child care, it increased death rates at all ages. Tuberculosis, which well-fed Guarani rarely contract, became the major killer in the community.

Deforestation also disrupted social institutions. Without their subsistence base, many Guarani needed additional cash to buy food and goods. Indian men were forced to seek work as farm hands, planting pasture and picking cotton on land where they once hunted. Women stayed at home to tend children and till the deteriorating soils of the family farms.

The search for wage labor eventually forced whole Guarani families to move. Many jobs were available on farms located over a day's walk from their villages. Entire families left home for hovels they constructed on the farms of their employers. From independent farmers and gatherers, they became tenants of *patrones* (landowners). *Patrones* prohibited the Guarani farmhands from planting gardens of their own, so the displaced Indians were forced to buy all their food, usually from the *patrones* themselves. Worse, *patrones* set their own inflated prices on the food and goods sold to Indians. Dependence on the white *patrones* displaced the mutual interdependence of traditional Guarani social organization.

As individuals and families left the Guarani villages in search of work on surrounding farms and ranches, *tamoi* leaders lost influence. It became impossible to gather relatives and friends together from disparate work places for religious ritual. The distances were too great for the elders' nieces and nephews to seek out counsel and medicines. Moreover, the diseases and problems suffered by the people were increasingly caused by people and powers outside the forest. The *tamoi* could neither control nor explain the changing world.

Finally, as the forest disappeared, so did its power to symbolize Guarani identity. No longer did young Indians see themselves as "people of the forest."

Today, many of the Guarani of eastern Paraguay remain in small but impoverished communities in the midst of a frontier society based on soybean farming and cattle ranching. The households that previously were isolated in individual plots are now concentrated in one small area without forest for fallow or privacy. The traditional *tamoi* continue to be the center of the social and religious life of the community, but no longer exert influence over village decisions, which are increasingly dominated by affairs external to the local community.

DEVELOPMENT AND ECOLOGY

Some people might argue that the plight of the Guarani is inevitable and that in the long run, the Indians will be absorbed in a more modern, prosperous society. The forest, they claim, provides a rich, nearly unlimited resource for development. Its exploitation, although painful for a few indigenous Indians, will provide an unequaled opportunity for the poor of Latin America.

Unfortunately, this argument makes forest development appear to be socially responsible. Yet, the long-run implications of forest clearing are disastrous, not simply for the Guarani and other Indians, but for settlers and developers as well. The tropical forest ecosystem is extremely fragile. When the vegetable cover is destroyed, the soil quickly disappears. Erosion clogs rivers with silt, and the soils left behind are baked to a hardpan on which few plants can survive. Rainwater previously captured by foliage and soil is quickly lost to runoff, drying the winds that feed the regional rain systems. Although first harvests in frontier areas seem bountiful, long-term farming and ranching are unprofitable as the soils, deprived of moisture and the rejuvenating forces of the original forest, are reduced to a "red desert." And even worse, leaving the cleared land fallow does not restore it. Once destroyed, the forest cannot reclaim the hardpan left by modern development.

Nor have developers been interested in husbanding the land. The *colonos* who clear the forests are concerned with short-term profit. Entrepreneurs and peasant farmers maximize immediate returns on their labor and investment. When the trees and soils of one area are exhausted, the farmers, ranchers, and loggers move farther into the virgin forest in search of new resources. The process creates a development frontier that moves through fertile forest leaving destruction in its wake. Unlike the Guarani, developers are not forced to contend with the environmental destruction caused by their activities.

CONSERVATION

International agencies and national governments have begun to recognize the damage caused by uncontrolled rain forest development. Although deforestation continues unchecked in many regions of the Amazon Basin, forest conservation programs are being established in some areas, based on the experience of indigenous Indians and often formulated with the help of anthropologists. In one innovative approach, biosphere reserves are being created, which restrict development but permit Indians to practice their traditional subsistence activities.

Such is the case in eastern Paraguay where a program is now being implemented to preserve the remaining tropical forests. Itanarami, so recently threatened by encroaching development, stands to benefit from this plan. The natural forests near the community are the last remaining undisturbed subtropical forest in eastern Paraguay. Although small, this area of 280 square miles is being set aside as a biosphere reserve. The Nature Conservancy, an international conservation agency, is working with the World Bank and the Paraguayan government to preserve the forest.

If the project is successful, Itanarami and its way of life will be preserved. Veraju, Kitu, and their compatriots will be able to continue trapping, hunting, fishing, and gathering on the land. Recognizing that Indian production does not destroy the land, planners are providing the Indians with the right to continue indigenous production, enabling the Guarani to maintain their traditional social organization and ethnic identity.

Furthermore, aided by anthropologists who have made detailed studies of Indian subsistence techniques, planners are integrating the Indian's own models of agro-forestry into an alternative design for tropical forest use. Guarani techniques of commercial extraction have been of special interest, particularly the harvest of *yerba mate* and fragrant oils. Guarani collect these products by trimming the foliage. They allow the trees to regrow so they will produce again. Planners believe that this use of the forest will economically outperform the proceeds gained from destructive farming in the long run, and they have adopted the Guarani model for implementation in other forested areas. Far from being backward and inefficient, the mixed horticultural subsistence strategies of indigenous forest groups have turned out to be the most practical way to manage the fragile tropical forest environment.

REVIEW QUESTIONS

1. Anthropologists claim that subsistence strategies affect a society's social organization and ideology. Evaluate this assertion in light of reading about the way the Guarani live in their rain forest environment.

2. Why is horticulture more environmentally sensible than intensive agricultural and pastoral exploitation of the Amazonian rain forest?

3. Guarani Indians are largely subsistence farmers and foragers. How do they use their forest environment without destroying it?

4. How have *colonos* disrupted the lives of Guarani villagers? What does this tell us about the relationship between subsistence and social structure?

5. How can the Guarani use their rain forest habitat to make money, and what does their experience suggest as a way to integrate forest exploitation into a market economy without environmental destruction?

11 Pastoralism: Beating the Odds in Arid Africa

J. TERRENCE McCABE and JAMES E. ELLIS

In virtually every country where they live, pastoralists are viewed as environmentally destructive. They are accused of causing desertification through overgrazing, and probably because they are difficult to pin down and control, governments have attempted to settle pastoralists in permanent communities, turning them into farmers or at least animal producers within the national economy. In this article, Terrence McCabe and James Ellis argue that attempts by the government of Kenya to permanently settle Turkana pastoralists have only led to starvation and environmental degradation. Using as an example the Ngisonyoka Turkana, a group as yet unaffected by government settlement efforts, the authors show how the traditional pastoral life-style permits survival even in the face of severe drought. By moving regularly to new sources of food and water, the Ngisonyoka manage to subsist without the need of famine relief or by damaging the range on which their animals depend.

Around the brackish waters of Kenya's Lake Turkana, in the Great Rift Valley of East Africa, fossil beds holding evidence of the earliest humans emerge from a desert of sandy wastelands and volcanic rubble. This one-time cradle of humanity is now a harsh and inhospitable environment where drought and famine are all too common. But the pastoralists who live there, raising livestock and tending herds, still successfully lead the nomadic life that has been followed there for thousands of years. And they continue to survive despite concerns that the days of the nomad are numbered.

In the late 1960s, scientists concluded that the large wandering herds of cattle grazing precious grasslands were inherently destructive of the arid environment. So, during the 1970s, administrators from local governments and international relief organizations promoted irrigation agriculture and fish culture as alternatives to pastoralism. But the alternatives failed. After the severe drought of 1979–1981, and another in 1984, many development efforts were scrapped in favor of famine relief. In the early 1980s, almost 80,000 Turkana pastoralists, nearly one-third of the population, occupied famine camps from the shores of Lake Turkana to the border of Uganda supported by the Kenyan government and foreign donors.

With massive relief efforts under way in the northern and central Turkana districts, we, along with a group of colleagues, began investigating the Turkana pastoralists to the south. There, the Ngisonyoka Turkana seemed to be going about their business as usual and surviving despite the devastating drought. While they suffered temporary hunger and losses among their livestock, for the Ngisonyoka there was no famine, no environmental degradation, and no need for outside relief. We set out to find out why.

We began our journey by donkey into the vast region west of Lake Turkana. It was the territory of a people who studiously avoided contact with outsiders, and it took us several months to gain the trust of the few families with whom we eventually traveled.

The Turkana migrated from the southern Sudan into northern Kenya in the mid-eighteenth century. Today, some 200,000 Turkana live in this region. Occasionally warlike and without any clear system of chiefs or officials, the Turkana are divided into nineteen tribal sections, each with its own grazing area.

The Ngisonyoka tribal section, consisting of some 9,600 people, 85,000 sheep and goats, 9,800 cattle, and 5,300 donkeys, occupies 5,500 square miles of land. Within this area families move frequently, seven to fifteen times a year depending on the availability of forage, water, the size of their individual herds, and the degree of hostility among the various tribes. And although each move may cover only five to eight miles, knowing when to move is the key to the self-reliance and survival of the Ngisonyoka.

Through the annual cycle of brief rains followed by a long dry season, the Ngisonyoka and their livestock travel from the low-lying plains of the Rift Valley into the bare lava hills and grass-covered mountains. Along the way, their herds graze on both perennial and annual grasslands, dwarf shrublands, dense bushlands, savannalike grasslands, and true woodlands near the beds of the many ephemeral streams. While near Lake Turkana there are only moonlike volcanic rubble and dunes covered with desert shrubs, doum palms, and acacia trees, the Ngisonyoka's plains are grasslands, with often dense bush and wooded stream beds.

Far to the west the rift escarpment rises steeply and spectacularly, up to 10,000 feet above the valley floor. Between these mountains and the plains are 6,000-foot hills that are crucial to the Ngisonyoka pastoralists. There is more rain and more vegetation. Runoff from seasonal mountain storms feeds the intermittent sand rivers that stripe the sandy plains of the valley floor. Acacia woodlands line these rivers and spread into dry, dwarf shrub grasslands. By knowing when and where to satisfy the forage needs of their herds, then utilizing the livestock to provide milk, meat, and blood for their own needs, the Ngisonyoka continually manage a complex food web. By making the most of the vegetation of one region but moving on before it's overgrazed, the Ngisonyoka also manage a fragile environment.

Wet seasons are the good times for the Turkana. Soon after the vegetation responds to the rains, Ngisonyoka herd owners, together with their wives, children, dependent relatives, and livestock, converge on their home area in an encampment known as an *awi*. The herders return from distant grazing lands with their camels, goats, sheep, and short-horned zebu cows. Soon the plains are dotted with homesteads, hundreds of huts made of skins lashed to acacia branches. Food is abundant and enemies are far away.

Most nights the silence is broken by the calls of young men summoning their neighbors to communal dances that often last until daybreak. Songs are sung without accompaniment and recount the strength and beauty of a favorite ox, the defeat of enemies, the ability of nature to provide the necessities of life — in short, the joys of a pastoral existence. Young men and women share in the excitement of being reunited with friends and lovers. Luckily, labor requirements for both sexes are minimal during this time, and tired dancers return to their own *awi* before dawn to sleep for a few hours before the next workday begins.

Women visit relatives, make clothes, relax, and, in general, revel in the few months of relative ease and safety. Children exhibit a level of energy not seen at other times of the year and often play "hyena and cow" until late into the night.

Most social functions, such as weddings, also occur in the wet season. When herds are healthy, Turkana ceremonies are accompanied by the slaughtering of animals and the eating of meat. All Turkana love to eat meat and will gorge themselves when the opportunity arises. During a large wedding that we recently attended, three camels, three oxen, and ten or more goats and sheep were slaughtered. Hundreds of animals were transferred from the groom's family to the bride's, and more than a hundred and fifty people joined in the singing, dancing, and feasting.

Herd owners, if they have sons or other young men to tend their herds, spend most days sitting under the "tree of the men" (usually the one that provides the most shade), recounting events of the past dry season and discussing the prospects for the upcoming year. Talk centers on pasture conditions, livestock health, herd growth, the timing and location of future moves, and enemy raids. Old relationships are reaffirmed and new ones struck up, each involving some exchange of livestock that may later prove critical to a family's survival. Through this network, a herd owner obtains animals in times of need. Turkana rarely talk about the impending dry season. The rains are too unpredictable. Instead, they talk strategy. For when the rains cease in June or July and the lush grasses the cattle have been feeding on wither and die, the Turkana must move.

Plants are the basis of the pastoral system. Altogether, more than sixty different plants make up significant portions of livestock diets. The energy from these plants translates into livestock milk, meat, and blood, which together make up more than three-quarters of the Ngisonyoka diet. Anthropologist Kathleen Galvin found that during good years and rainy seasons cattle milk may provide 15 to 20 percent of human food energy. But during the dry season, the grasses are among the first resources to disappear and the cattle can only produce enough milk for their calves.

Then the diversity of plants and livestock and the flexibility of the pastoral enterprise become important. Cattle and the young men who herd them leave the *awi* and retreat to mountain and hill pastures. There, perennial grasses will sustain the cattle, though not in a productive state, throughout the long dry season. Herds of goats and camels remain with the family household longer. Goats will eat a variety of plants, and camels feed on the woody shrubs and trees that thrive into the dry season on water stored deep in the sandy soils of the plains. Camels continue to give milk. Galvin found that camels provide 56 percent of the total milk consumed by the Ngisonyoka, or about one-third of all their food energy, year-round.

Eventually, while there will be enough water for the people, there will not be enough for the livestock. The water stored during the wet season dries up. Wells dug by hand into the beds of sand rivers are often 40 feet deep before they prove dry or unsafe and are abandoned. Then the people and animals leave the plains. Many nomads head for the dry-season springs of the lava hills, but forage is scarce on these burned and rocky moonscapes. Others migrate to the more mesic savannas and bushlands to the south but risk raids there by rival Pokot tribesmen.

Camel milk and livestock blood are the dry-season mainstays of the Ngisonyoka diet. A pint or more of blood may be drawn from a camel (less from a goat) and either drunk plain, mixed with milk, or cooked with grain or the grated husk of the palm fruit. Meals may be milk alone or, on occasion, supplemented by wild fruits, goat meat, and bartered or purchased grain. Although grain makes up 10 to 15 percent of food energy annually, it is particularly important during dry periods, when livestock production is lowest.

As food resources dwindle, poorer families travel with wealthier relatives. The size of herds is the measure of wealth among the Ngisonyoka, but since it is not socially acceptable for a wealthy man to deny food to poorer relatives, a man with 100 camels, 500 cattle, and 1,000 goats and sheep may not live much better than a poorer herder since he'll be supporting many more dependents. The extra herds only put more distance between himself and poverty. Herd owners who are down on their luck, without herds or enough workers to attend to them, may strike up deals with relatives or friends. A loan of a milking animal or someone to help with the herds will be repaid to the lender when he himself is in need.

Movement becomes more frequent as the dry season intensifies. Now the goats and camels that are unable to produce milk must be separated from the milking herds and taken to grazing lands often three to six miles from where the rest of the family makes their camp. Water from springs or wells may be even farther away. With herders gone and the grazing land patchy, families become smaller and more isolated. If food is limited, female relatives and their children may be forced to seek food in towns in exchange for work brewing local beer or doing small tasks for the missions or Somali traders. Families try to stay together; herd owners are apprehensive about moving alone because isolated homesteads are far more vulnerable to attack. They move in groups of two to five households, sharing food and herding responsibilities; but the associations, of friends or relatives, are fragile.

People often complain of being lonely and solicit news of friends and relatives whenever they meet someone who is traveling. Under the tree of the men they still avoid speaking of the drought or when it will break. Although the advice of soothsayers may be sought, there is little reliance placed on the supernatural. Most of the talk is about the location of forage and the possibility of enemy raids.

Intertribal raiding has been a feature of pastoral life for thousands of years. The principal enemy for the Ngisonyoka is the Pokot, a tribe of pastoral nomads who live to the south and west of the Ngisonyoka's main dry-season pastures. Although there have been occasional periods of peace between the two tribes when livestock and other goods were exchanged, peace has always been short-lived.

Herd owners try to avoid those places where attacks are most likely to occur. During good dry seasons, Ngisonyoka herders disperse to the northeast lava hills where there is little threat of raiding. In drought years, however, the hills south and west of Ngisonyoka territory may be the only area where livestock forage can be found. In November 1980, two members of our research team witnessed a Pokot raid on an *awi*. Two children were killed and about 350 goats and sheep were stolen. The family was grief-stricken, and the people got little sleep over the next nights, worrying about the possibility of another attack, while the lambs and kids bleated, calling for their lost mothers. Tensions remained high for weeks as rumors circulated wildly among those families pushing south toward the Pokot border. The Ngisonyoka were glad when at last scouts reported that rains had begun in the north and they could begin their return to the open plains.

The Ngisonyoka live a difficult and frequently dangerous existence, but their traditional pastoralism maintains a large population in a severe and unpredictable environment. By tapping a multiplicity of resources in a variety of ways and by sharing the effects of drought stress among families, they have managed to survive severe droughts without assistance. Damage to the environment from large numbers of livestock has not occurred. We estimate Ngisonyoka livestock consume only 7 to 9 percent of the region's annual vegetation production. Their herds of livestock are no greater than the number of native animals grazing African regions with similar rainfall. Overgrazing has not occurred and drought has not brought mass livestock starvation.

The Ngisonyoka have worked out a strategy: they depend most on the most reliable resources in their environment — woody plants and camel milk; they exploit the most productive but ephemeral resources — grasses and cattle milk — when possible; when times are hard, they make use of their precious livestock — drinking its blood, slaughtering it for meat, or trading it for grain. These are never arbitrary decisions. For example, goats are most often slaughtered and traded because goat herds recover most rapidly.

The Ngisonyoka may also be successful because their system has not been disrupted by well-meaning but inappropriate development activities. In some parts of Africa, pastoralists were encouraged to settle and engage in agriculture or to produce beef for markets. These changes might be appropriate in regions of adequate rainfall where there is an established market system, but in places like the Turkana they enhance productivity and living standards in good years while increasing the possibility of famine and destitution during droughts. Irrigation often costs more than the value of what is produced. Raising cattle for market means reducing the size of the herd to increase the size of individual animals. When drought occurs the reduced herd size leaves herders with nothing to fall back on.

In the harsh environment of the Rift Valley, pastoralism has supported humanity for a long time. It would be a serious mistake to assume that such a time-tested strategy can easily be replaced by practices developed in another time and another place. Herds are more than a commodity to the Ngisonyoka. One down-on-his-luck herder told us he was distressed by the possibility that he might have to go to an agricultural settlement where the cost of a bride is paid in sweet potatoes and gourds instead of camels, goats, cattle, and sheep. For the Ngisonyoka, the good life — all life — begins with camels, goats, cattle, and sheep.

REVIEW QUESTIONS

1. How have Ngisonyoka Turkana managed to survive during the most severe drought that Africa has experienced in recent memory?

2. Describe the yearly cycle of movement for the Ngisonyoka Turkana. What determines when and where the Turkana move?

3. On what basis do the authors of this article argue that Ngisonyoka pastoralism is a better solution to life in Northern Kenya than settled agriculture and animal husbandry?

4. What effect does Ngisonyoka pastoral life have on tribal social organization?

12   Mother Cow

MARVIN HARRIS

*How can people permit millions of cattle to roam about eating, but
uneaten, in a land so continuously threatened by food shortages
and starvation? This is a question often asked by American visitors
to India who see the apparently pampered animals in every part of
the country. In this article, Marvin Harris challenges this criticism
by showing that the religious rules designed to protect cattle in
India are ecologically rational. He argues that far from being useless parasites on a starving society, Indian cattle plow and produce
fuel, milk, and hides. Without them agricultural life in India would
be impossible.*

Whenever I get into discussions about the influence of practical and
mundane factors on life-styles, someone is sure to say, "But what
about all those cows the hungry peasants in India refuse to eat?" The
picture of a ragged farmer starving to death alongside a big fat cow
conveys a reassuring sense of mystery to Western observers. In countless learned and popular allusions, it confirms our deepest conviction
about how people with inscrutable Oriental minds ought to act. It is
comforting to know — somewhat like "there will always be an
England" — that in India spiritual values are more precious than life
itself. And at the same time it makes us feel sad. How can we ever
hope to understand people so different from ourselves? Westerners

find the idea that there might be a practical explanation for Hindu love of cow more upsetting than Hindus do. The sacred cow — how else can I say it? — is one of our favorite sacred cows.

Hindus venerate cows because cows are the symbol of everything that is alive. As Mary is to Christians the mother of God, the cow to Hindus is the mother of life. So there is no greater sacrilege for a Hindu than killing a cow. Even the taking of human life lacks the symbolic meaning, the unutterable defilement, that is evoked by cow slaughter.

According to many experts, cow worship is the number one cause of India's hunger and poverty. Some Western-trained agronomists say that the taboo against cow slaughter is keeping one hundred million "useless" animals alive. They claim that cow worship lowers the efficiency of agriculture because the useless animals contribute neither milk nor meat while competing for croplands and foodstuff with useful animals and hungry human beings. A study sponsored by the Ford Foundation in 1959 concluded that possibly half of India's cattle could be regarded as surplus in relation to feed supply. And an economist from the University of Pennsylvania stated in 1971 that India has thirty million unproductive cows.

It does seem that there are enormous numbers of surplus, useless, and uneconomic animals, and that this situation is a direct result of irrational Hindu doctrines. Tourists on their way through Delhi, Calcutta, Madras, Bombay, and other Indian cities are astonished at the liberties enjoyed by stray cattle. The animals wander through the streets, browse off the stalls in the marketplace, break into private gardens, defecate all over the sidewalks, and snarl traffic by pausing to chew their cuds in the middle of busy intersections. In the countryside, the cattle congregate on the shoulders of every highway and spend much of their time taking leisurely walks down the railroad tracks.

Love of cow affects life in many ways. Government agencies maintain old age homes for cows at which owners may board their dry and decrepit animals free of charge. In Madras, the police round up stray cattle that have fallen ill and nurse them back to health by letting them graze on small fields adjacent to the station house. Farmers regard their cows as members of the family, adorn them with garlands and tassels, pray for them when they get sick, and call in their neighbors and a priest to celebrate the birth of a new calf. Throughout India, Hindus hang on their walls calendars that portray beautiful, bejeweled young women who have the bodies of big fat white cows. Milk is shown jetting out of each teat of these half-women, half-zebu goddesses.

Starting with their beautiful human faces, cow pinups bear little resemblance to the typical cow one sees in the flesh. For most of the year their bones are their most prominent feature. Far from having milk gushing from every teat, the gaunt beasts barely manage to nurse a single calf to maturity. The average yield of whole milk from the typical humpbacked breed of zebu cow in India amounts to less than 500 pounds a year. Ordinary American dairy cattle produce over 5,000 pounds, while for champion milkers, 20,000 pounds is not unusual. But this comparison doesn't tell the whole story. In any given year about half of India's zebu cows give no milk at all — not a drop.

To make matters worse, love of cow does not stimulate love of man. Since Moslems spurn pork but eat beef, many Hindus consider them to be cow killers. Before the partition of the Indian subcontinent into India and Pakistan, bloody communal riots aimed at preventing the Moslems from killing cows became annual occurrences. Memories of old cow riots — as, for example, the one in Bihar in 1917 when thirty people died and 170 Moslem villages were looted down to the last doorpost — continue to embitter relations between India and Pakistan.

Although he deplored the rioting, Mohandas K. Gandhi was an ardent advocate of cow love and wanted a total ban on cow slaughter. When the Indian constitution was drawn up, it included a bill of rights for cows which stopped just short of outlawing every form of cow killing. Some states have since banned cow slaughter altogether, but others still permit exceptions. The cow question remains a major cause of rioting and disorders, not only between Hindus and the remnants of the Moslem community, but between the ruling Congress Party and extremist Hindu factions of cow lovers. On November 7, 1966, a mob of 120,000 people, led by a band of chanting, naked holy men draped with garlands of marigolds and smeared with white cow-dung ash, demonstrated against cow slaughter in front of the Indian House of Parliament. Eight persons were killed and forty-eight injured during the ensuing riot. This was followed by a nationwide wave of fasts among holy men, led by Muni Shustril Kumar, president of the All-Party Cow Protection Campaign Committee.

To Western observers familiar with modern industrial techniques of agriculture and stock raising, cow love seems senseless, even suicidal. The efficiency expert yearns to get his hands on all those useless animals and ship them off to a proper fate. And yet one finds certain inconsistencies in the condemnation of cow love. When I began to wonder if there might be a practical explanation for the sacred cow, I came across an intriguing government report. It said that India had too many cows but too few oxen. With so many cows around, how could there be a shortage of oxen? Oxen and male water buffalo are the principal source of traction for plowing India's fields. For each farm of ten acres or less, one pair of oxen or water buffalo is considered adequate. A little arithmetic shows that as far as plowing is concerned, there is indeed a shortage rather than a surplus of animals. India has 60 million farms, but only 80 million traction animals. If each farm had its quota of two oxen or two water buffalo, there ought to be 120 million traction animals — that is, 40 million more than are actually available.

The shortage may not be quite so bad, since some farmers rent or borrow oxen from their neighbors. But the sharing of plow animals often proves impractical. Plowing must be coordinated with the monsoon rains, and by the time one farm has been plowed, the optimum moment for plowing another may already have passed. Also, after plowing is over, a farmer still needs his own pair of oxen to pull his oxcart, the mainstay of bulk transport throughout rural India. Quite possibly private ownership of farms, livestock, plows, and oxcarts lowers the efficiency of Indian agriculture, but this, I soon realized, was not caused by cow love.

The shortage of draft animals is a terrible threat that hangs over most of India's peasant families. When an ox falls sick a poor farmer is in danger of losing his farm. If he has no replacement for it, he will have to borrow money at usurious rates. Millions of rural households have in fact lost all or part of their holdings and have gone into sharecropping or day labor as a result of such debts. Every year hundreds of thousands of destitute farmers end up migrating to the cities, which already teem with unemployed and homeless persons.

The Indian farmer who can't replace his sick or deceased ox is in much the same situation as an American farmer who can neither replace nor repair his broken tractor. But there is an important difference: tractors are made by factories, but oxen are made by cows. A farmer who owns a cow owns a factory for making oxen. With or without cow love, this is a good reason for him not to be too anxious to sell his cow to the slaughterhouse. One also begins to see why Indian farmers might be willing to tolerate cows that give only 500 pounds of milk per year. If the main economic function of the zebu cow is to breed male traction animals, then there's no point in comparing her with specialized American dairy animals, whose main function is to produce milk. Still, the milk produced by zebu cows plays an important role in meeting the nutritional needs of many poor families. Even small amounts of milk products can improve the health of people who are forced to subsist on the edge of starvation.

When Indian farmers want an animal primarily for milking purposes they turn to the female water buffalo, which has longer lactation periods and higher butterfat yields than zebu cattle. Male water buffalo are also superior animals for plowing in flooded rice paddies. But oxen are more versatile and are preferred for dry-field farming and road transport. Above all, zebu breeds are remarkably rugged, and can survive the long droughts that periodically afflict different parts of India.

Agriculture is part of a vast system of human and natural relationships. To judge isolated portions of this "ecosystem" in terms that are relevant to the conduct of American agribusiness leads to some very strange impressions. Cattle figure in the Indian ecosystem in ways that are easily overlooked or demeaned by observers from industrialized high-energy societies. In the United States, chemicals have almost completely replaced animal manure as the principal source of farm fertilizer. American farmers stopped using manure when they began to plow with tractors rather than mules or horses. Since tractors excrete poisons rather than fertilizers, a commitment to large-scale machine farming is almost of necessity a commitment to the use of chemical fertilizers. And around the world today there has in fact grown up a vast integrated petrochemical-tractor-truck industrial complex that produces farm machinery, motorized transport, oil and gasoline, and chemical fertilizers and pesticides upon which new high-yield production techniques depend.

For better or worse, most of India's farmers cannot participate in this complex, not because they worship their cows, but because they can't afford to buy tractors. Like other developing nations, India can't build factories that are competitive with the facilities of the industrialized nations nor pay for large quantities of imported industrial products. To convert from animals and manure to tractors and petrochemicals would require the investment of incredible amounts of capital. Moreover, the inevitable effect of substituting costly machines for cheap animals is to reduce the number of people who can earn their living from agriculture and to force a corresponding increase in the size of the average farm. We know that the development of large-scale agribusiness in the United States has meant the virtual destruction of the small family farm. Less than 5 percent of U.S. families now live on farms, as compared with 60 percent about a hundred years ago. If agribusiness were to develop along similar lines in India, jobs and housing would soon have to be found for a quarter of a billion displaced peasants.

Since the suffering caused by unemployment and homelessness in India's cities is already intolerable, an additional massive buildup of the urban population can only lead to unprecedented upheavals and catastrophes.

With this alternative in view, it becomes easier to understand low-energy, small-scale, animal-based systems. As I have already pointed out, cows and oxen provide low-energy substitutes for tractors and tractor factories. They also should be credited with carrying out the functions of a petrochemical industry. India's cattle annually excrete about 700 million tons of recoverable manure. Approximately half of this is used as fertilizer, while most of the remainder is burned to provide heat for cooking. The annual quantity of heat liberated by this dung, the Indian housewife's main cooking fuel, is the thermal equivalent of 27 million tons of kerosene, 35 million tons of coal, or 68 million tons of wood. Since India has only small reserves of oil and coal and is already the victim of extensive deforestation, none of these fuels can be considered practical substitutes for cow dung. The thought of dung in the kitchen may not appeal to the average American, but Indian women regard it as a superior cooking fuel because it is finely adjusted to their domestic routines. Most Indian dishes are prepared with clarified butter known as *ghee*, for which cow dung is the preferred source of heat since it burns with a clean, slow, long-lasting flame that doesn't scorch the food. This enables the Indian housewife to start cooking her meals and to leave them unattended for several hours while she takes care of the children, helps out in the fields, or performs other chores. American housewives achieve a similar effect through a complex set of electronic controls that come as expensive options on late-model stoves.

Cow dung has at least one other major function. Mixed with water and made into a paste, it is used as a household flooring material. Smeared over a dirt floor and left to harden into a smooth surface, it keeps the dust down and can be swept clean with a broom.

Because cattle droppings have so many useful properties, every bit of dung is carefully collected. Village small fry are given the task of following the family cow around and of bringing home its daily petrochemical output. In the cities, sweeper castes enjoy a monopoly on the dung deposited by strays and earn their living by selling it to housewives.

From an agribusiness point of view, a dry and barren cow is an economic abomination. But from the viewpoint of the peasant farmer, the same dry and barren cow may be a last desperate defense against the moneylenders. There is always the chance that a favorable monsoon may restore the vigor of even the most decrepit specimen and that she will fatten up, calve, and start giving milk again. This is what the farmer prays for; sometimes his prayers are answered. In the meantime, dung-making goes on. And so one gradually begins to understand why a skinny old hag of a cow still looks beautiful in the eyes of her owner.

Zebu cattle have small bodies, energy-storing humps on their backs, and great powers of recuperation. These features are adapted to the specific conditions of Indian agriculture. The native breeds are capable of surviving for long periods with little food or water and are highly resistant to diseases that afflict other breeds in tropical climates. Zebu oxen are worked as long as they continue to breathe. Stuart Odend'hal, a veterinarian formerly associated with Johns Hopkins University, performed field autopsies on Indian cattle that had been working normally a few hours before their deaths but whose vital organs were damaged by massive lesions. Given their enormous recuperative powers, these beasts are never easily written off as completely "useless" while they are still alive.

But sooner or later there must come a time when all hope of an animal's recovery is lost and even dung-making ceases. And still the Hindu farmer refuses to kill it for food or sell it to the slaughterhouse. Isn't this incontrovertible evidence of a harmful economic practice that has no explanation apart from the religious taboos on cow slaughter and beef consumption?

No one can deny that cow love mobilizes people to resist cow slaughter and beef eating. But I don't agree that the anti-slaughter and beef-eating taboos necessarily have an adverse effect on human survival and well-being. By slaughtering or selling his aged and decrepit animals, a farmer might earn a few more rupees or temporarily improve his family's diet. But in the long run, his refusal to sell to the slaughterhouse or kill for his own table may have beneficial consequences. An established principle of ecological analysis states that communities of organisms are adapted not to average but to extreme conditions. The relevant situation in India is the recurrent failure of the monsoon rains. To evaluate the economic significance of the anti-slaughter and anti-beef-eating taboos, we have to consider what these taboos mean in the context of periodic droughts and famine.

The taboo on slaughter and beef eating may be as much a product of natural selection as the small bodies and fantastic recuperative powers of the zebu breeds. During droughts and famines, farmers are severely tempted to kill or sell their livestock. Those who succumb to this temptation seal their doom, even if they survive the drought, for when the rains come, they will be unable to plow their fields. I want to be even more emphatic: Massive slaughter of cattle under the duress of famine constitutes a much greater threat to aggregate welfare than any likely miscalculation by particular farmers concerning the usefulness of their animals during normal times. It seems probable that the sense of unutterable profanity elicited by cow slaughter has its roots in the excruciating contradiction between immediate needs and long-run conditions of survival. Cow love, with its sacred symbols and holy doctrines, protects the farmer against calculations that are "rational" only in the short term. To Western experts it looks as if "the Indian farmer would rather starve to death than eat his cow." The same kinds of experts like to talk about the "inscrutable Oriental mind" and think that "life is not so dear to the Asian masses." They don't realize that the farmer would rather eat his cow than starve, but that he will starve if he does eat it.

Even with the assistance of the holy laws and cow love, the temptation to eat beef under the duress of famine sometimes proves irresistible. During World War II, there was a great famine in Bengal caused by droughts and the Japanese occupation of Burma. Slaughter of cows and draft animals reached such alarming levels in the summer of 1944 that the British had to use troops to enforce the cow-protection laws. In 1967 *The New York Times* reported:

> Hindus facing starvation in the drought-stricken area of Bihar are slaughtering cows and eating the meat even though the animals are sacred to the Hindu religion.

Observers noted that "the misery of the people was beyond imagination."

The survival into old age of a certain number of absolutely useless animals during good times is part of the price that must be paid for protecting useful animals against slaughter during bad times. But I wonder how much is actually lost because of the prohibition on slaughter and the taboo on beef. From a Western agribusiness viewpoint, it seems irrational for India not to have a meat-packing industry. But the actual potential for such an industry in a country like India is very limited. A substantial rise in beef production would strain the entire ecosystem, not because of cow love but because of the laws of thermodynamics. In any food chain, the interposition of additional animal links result in a sharp decrease in the efficiency of food production. The caloric value of what an animal has eaten is always much greater than the caloric value of its body. This means that more calories are available per capita when plant food is eaten directly by a human population than when it is used to feed domesticated animals.

Because of the high level of beef consumption in the United States, three-quarters of all our croplands are used for feeding cattle rather than people. Since the per capita calorie intake in India is already below minimum daily requirements, switching croplands to meat production could only result in higher food prices and a further deterioration in the living standards for poor families. I doubt if more than 10 percent of the Indian people will ever be able to make beef an important part of their diet, regardless of whether they believe in cow love or not.

I also doubt that sending more aged and decrepit animals to existing slaughterhouses would result in nutritional gains for the people who need it most. Most of these animals get eaten anyway, even if they aren't sent to the slaughterhouse, because throughout India there are low-ranking castes whose members have the right to dispose of the bodies of dead cattle. In one way or another, twenty million cattle die every year, and a large portion of their meat is eaten by these carrion-eating "untouchables."

My friend Dr. Joan Mencher, an anthropologist who has worked in India for many years, points out that the existing slaughterhouses cater to urban middle-class non-Hindus. She notes that "the untouchables get their food in other ways. It is good for the untouchable if a cow dies of starvation in a village, but not if it gets sent to an urban slaughterhouse to be sold to Muslims or Christians." Dr. Mencher's informants at first denied that any Hindu would eat beef, but when they learned that "upper-caste" Americans liked steak, they readily confessed their taste for beef curry.

Like everything else I have been discussing, meat eating by untouchables is finely adjusted to practical conditions. The meat-eating castes also tend to be the leather-working castes, since they have the right to dispose of the skin of the fallen cattle. So despite cow love, India manages to have a huge leathercraft industry. Even in death, apparently useless animals continue to be exploited for human purposes.

I could be right about cattle being useful for traction, fuel, fertilizer, milk, floor covering, meat, and leather, and still misjudge the ecological and economic significance of the whole complex. Everything depends on how much all of this costs in natural resources and human labor relative to alternative modes of satisfying the needs of India's huge population. These costs are determined largely by what the cattle eat. Many experts assume that humans and cows are locked in a deadly competition for land and food crops. This might be true if Indian farmers followed the American agribusiness model and fed their animals on food crops. But the shameless truth about the sacred cow is that she is an indefatigable scavenger. Only an insignificant portion of the food consumed by the average cow comes from pastures and food crops set aside for their use.

This ought to have been obvious from all those persistent reports about cows wandering about and snarling traffic. What are those animals doing in the markets, on the lawns, along the highways and railroad tracks, and up on the barren hillsides? What are they doing if not eating every morsel of grass, stubble, and garbage that cannot be directly consumed by human beings and converting it into milk and other useful products! In his study of cattle in West Bengal, Dr. Odend'hal discovered that the major constituent in the cattle's diet is inedible by-products of human food crops, principally rice straw, wheat bran, and rice husks. When the Ford Foundation estimated that half of the cattle were surplus in relation to feed supply, they meant to say that half of the cattle manage to survive even without access to fodder crops. But this is an understatement. Probably less than 20 percent of what the cattle eat consists of humanly edible substances;

most of this is fed to working oxen and water buffalo rather than to dry and barren cows. Odend'hal found that in his study area there was no competition between cattle and humans for land or the food supply: "Basically, the cattle convert items of little direct human value into products of immediate utility."

One reason why cow love is so often misunderstood is that it has different implications for the rich and the poor. Poor farmers use it as a license to scavenge while the wealthy farmers resist it as a rip-off. To the poor farmer, the cow is a holy beggar; to the rich farmer, it's a thief. Occasionally the cows invade someone's pastures or planted fields. The landlords complain, but the poor peasants plead ignorance and depend on cow love to get their animals back. If there is competition, it is between man and man or caste and caste, not between man and beast.

City cows also have owners who let them scrounge by day and call them back at night to be milked. Dr. Mencher recounts that while she lived for a while in a middle-class neighborhood in Madras her neighbors were constantly complaining about "stray" cows breaking into the family compounds. The strays were actually owned by people who lived in a room above a shop and who sold milk door to door in the neighborhood. As for the old-age homes and police cowpounds, they serve very nicely to reduce the risk of maintaining cows in a city environment. If a cow stops producing milk, the owner may decide to let it wander around until the police pick it up and bring it to the precinct house. When the cow has recovered, the owner pays a small fine and returns it to its usual haunts. The old-age homes operate on a similar principle, providing cheap government-subsidized pasture that would otherwise not be available to city cows.

Incidentally, the preferred form of purchasing milk in the cities is to have the cow brought to the house and milked on the spot. This is often the only way that the householder can be sure that he is buying pure milk rather than milk mixed with water or urine.

What seems most incredible about these arrangements is that they have been interpreted as evidence of wasteful, anti-economic Hindu practices, while in fact they reflect a degree of economizing that goes far beyond Western, "Protestant" standards of savings and husbandry. Cow love is perfectly compatible with a merciless determination to get the literal last drop of milk out of the cow. The man who takes the cow door to door brings along a dummy calf made out of stuffed calfskin which he sets down beside the cow to trick it into performing. When this doesn't work, the owner may resort to *phooka*, blowing air into the cow's uterus through a hollow pipe, or *doom dev*, stuffing its tail into the vaginal orifice. Gandhi believed that cows were treated more cruelly in India than anywhere else in the world. "How we bleed her to take the last drop of milk from her," he lamented. "How we starve her to emaciation, how we ill-treat the calves, how we deprive them of their portion of milk, how cruelly we treat the oxen, how we castrate them, how we beat them, how we overload them."

No one understood better than Gandhi that cow love had different implications for rich and poor. For him the cow was a central focus of the struggle to rouse India to authentic nationhood. Cow love went along with small-scale farming, making cotton thread on a hand spinning wheel, sitting cross-legged on the floor, dressing in a loincloth, vegetarianism, reverence for life, and strict nonviolence. To these themes Gandhi owed his vast popular following among the peasant masses, urban poor, and untouchables. It was his way of protecting them against the ravages of industrialization.

The asymmetrical implications of *ahimsa* for rich and poor are ignored by economists who want to make Indian agriculture more efficient by slaughtering "surplus" animals. Professor Alan Heston, for example, accepts the fact that the cattle perform vital functions for which substitutes are not readily available. But he proposes that the same functions could be carried out more efficiently if there were 30 million fewer cows. This figure is based on the assumption that with adequate care only 40 cows per 100 male animals would be needed to replace the present number of oxen. Since there are 72 million adult male cattle, by this formula, 24 million breeding females ought to be sufficient. Actually, there are 54 million cows. Subtracting 24 million from 54 million, Heston arrives at the estimate of 30 million "useless" animals to be slaughtered. The fodder and feed that these "useless" animals have been consuming are to be distributed among the remaining animals, who will become healthier and therefore will be able to keep total milk and dung production at or above previous levels. But whose cows are to be sacrificed? About 43 percent of the total cattle population is found on the poorest 62 percent of the farms. These farms, consisting of five acres or less, have only 5 percent of the pasture and grazing land. In other words, most of the animals that are temporarily dry, barren, and feeble are owned by the people who live on the smallest and poorest farms. So that when the economists talk about getting rid of 30 million cows, they are really talking about getting rid of 30 million cows that belong to poor families, not rich ones. But most poor families own only one cow, so what this economizing boils down to is not so much getting rid of 30 million cows as getting rid of 150 million people — forcing them off the land and into the cities.

Cow-slaughter enthusiasts base their recommendation on an understandable error. They reason that since the farmers refuse to kill their animals, and since there is a religious taboo against doing so, therefore it is the taboo that is mainly responsible for the high ratio of cows to oxen. Their error is hidden in the observed ratio itself: 70

cows to 100 oxen. If cow love prevents farmers from killing cows that are economically useless, how is it there are 30 percent fewer cows than oxen? Since approximately as many female as male animals are born, something must be causing the death of more females than males. The solution to this puzzle is that while no Hindu farmer deliberately slaughters a female calf or decrepit cow with a club or a knife, he can and does get rid of them when they become truly useless from his point of view. Various methods short of direct slaughter are employed. To "kill" unwanted calves, for example, a triangular wooden yoke is placed about their necks so that when they try to nurse they jab the cow's udder and get kicked to death. Older animals are simply tethered on short ropes and allowed to starve — a process that does not take too long if the animal is already weak and diseased. Finally, unknown numbers of decrepit cows are surreptitiously sold through a chain of Moslem and Christian middlemen and end up in the urban slaughter-houses.

If we want to account for the observed proportions of cows to oxen, we must study rain, wind, water, and land-tenure patterns, not cow love. The proof of this is that the proportion of cows to oxen varies with the relative importance of different components of the agricultural system in different regions of India. The most important variable is the amount of irrigation water available for the cultivation of rice. Wherever there are extensive wet rice paddies, the water buffalo tends to be the preferred traction animal, and the female water buffalo is then substituted for the zebu cow as a source of milk. That is why in the vast plains of northern India, where the melting Himalayan snows and monsoons create the Holy River Ganges, the proportion of cows to oxen drops down to 47 to 100. As the distinguished Indian economist K. N. Raj has pointed out, districts in the Ganges Valley, where continuous year-round rice-paddy cultivation is practiced, have cow-to-oxen ratios that approach the theoretical optimum. This is all the more remarkable since the region in question — the Gangetic plain — is the heartland of the Hindu religion and contains its most holy shrines.

The theory that religion is primarily responsible for the high proportion of cows to oxen is also refuted by a comparison between Hindu India and Moslem West Pakistan. Despite the rejection of cow love and the beef-slaughter and beef-eating taboos, West Pakistan as a whole has 60 cows for every 100 male animals, which is considerably higher than the average for the intensely Hindu Indian state of Uttar Pradesh. When districts in Uttar Pradesh are selected for the importance of water buffalo and canal irrigation and compared with ecologically similar districts in West Pakistan, ratios of female to male turn out to be virtually the same.

Do I mean to say that cow love has no effect whatsoever on the cattle sex ratio or on other aspects of the agricultural system? No. What I am saying is that cow love is an active element in a complex, finely articulated material and cultural order. Cow love mobilizes the latent capacity of human beings to persevere in a low-energy ecosystem in which there is little room for waste or indolence. Cow love contributes to the adaptive resilience of the human population by preserving temporarily dry or barren but still useful animals; by discouraging the growth of an energy-expensive beef industry; by protecting cattle that fatten in the public domain or at landlord's expense; and by preserving the recovery potential of the cattle population during droughts and famines. As in any natural or artificial system, there is some slippage, friction, or waste associated with these complex interactions. Half a billion people, animals, land, labor, political economy, soil, and climate are all involved. The slaughter enthusiasts claim that the practice of letting cows breed indiscriminately and then thinning their numbers through neglect and starvation is wasteful and inefficient. I do not doubt that this is correct, but only in a narrow and relatively insignificant sense. The savings that an agricultural engineer might achieve by getting rid of an unknown number of absolutely useless animals must be balanced against catastrophic losses for the marginal peasants, especially during droughts and famines, if cow love ceases to be a holy duty.

Since the effective mobilization of all human action depends upon the acceptance of psychologically compelling creeds and doctrines, we have to expect that economic systems will always oscillate under and over their points of optimum efficiency. But the assumption that the whole system can be made to work better simply by attacking its consciousness is naive and dangerous. Major improvements in the present system can be achieved by stabilizing India's human population, and by making more land, water, oxen, and water buffalo available to more people on a more equitable basis. The alternative is to destroy the present system and replace it with a completely new set of demographic, technological, politico-economic, and ideological relationships — a whole new ecosystem. Hinduism is undoubtedly a conservative force, one that makes it more difficult for the "development" experts and "modernizing" agents to destroy the old system and to replace it with a high-energy industrial and agribusiness complex. But if you think that a high-energy industrial and agribusiness complex will necessarily be more "rational" or "efficient" than the system that now exists, forget it.

Contrary to expectations, studies of energy costs and energy yields show that India makes more efficient use of its cattle than the United States does. In Singur district in West Bengal, Dr. Odend'hal discovered that the cattle's gross energetic efficiency, defined as the total of useful calories produced per year divided by the total calories consumed during the same period, was 17 percent. This compares with a gross energetic efficiency of less than 4 percent for American beef cattle raised on Western range land. As Odend'hal says, the relatively high efficiency of the Indian cattle complex comes about not because the animals are particularly productive, but because of scrupulous product utilization by humans: "The villages are extremely utilitarian and nothing is wasted."

Wastefulness is more a characteristic of modern agribusiness than of traditional peasant economies. Under the new system of automated feed-lot beef production in the United States, for example, cattle manure not only goes unused, but it is allowed to contaminate ground water over wide areas and contributes to the pollution of nearby lakes and streams.

The higher standard of living enjoyed by the industrial nations is not the result of greater productive efficiency, but of an enormously expanded increase in the amount of energy available per person. In 1970 the United States used up the energy equivalent of twelve tons of coal per inhabitant, while the corresponding figure for India was one-fifth ton per inhabitant. The way this energy was expended involved far more energy being wasted per person in the United States than in India. Automobiles and airplanes are faster than oxcarts, but they do not use energy more efficiently. In fact, more calories go up in useless heat and smoke during a single day of traffic jams in the United States than is wasted by all the cows of India during an entire year. The comparison is even less favorable when we consider the fact that the stalled vehicles are burning up irreplaceable reserves of petroleum that it took the earth tens of millions of years to accumulate. If you want to see a real sacred cow, go out and look at the family car.

REVIEW QUESTIONS

1. A friend asks, "Why don't Indians eat the millions of cattle that roam loose over their country?" Based on the information in this article, how would you answer?

2. What are the main uses and products of Indian cattle? What is most important about cattle for continued human material welfare?

3. How does Harris explain the historical rise of cattle protection in India?

4. Clearly Indians need bulls and bullocks to plow, but why can't they limit the number of cows to a level just sufficient for breeding?

5. Some anthropologists argue that the sacredness of Indian cattle evolved as part of the religious system, quite apart from practical considerations. How would Harris respond to this assertion?

V

Kinship and Family

Social life is essential to human existence. We remain in the company of other people from the day we are born to the time of our death. People teach us to speak. They show us how to relate to our surroundings. They give us the help and the support we need to achieve personal security and mental well-being. Alone, we are relatively frail, defenseless primates; in groups we are astonishingly adaptive and powerful. Yet despite these advantages, well-organized human societies are difficult to achieve. Some species manage to produce social organization genetically. But people are not like bees or ants. We lack the genetically coded directions for behavior that make these insects successful social animals. Although we seem to inherit a general need for social approval, we also harbor individual interests and ambitions that can block or destroy close social ties. To overcome these divisive tendencies, human groups organize around several principles designed to foster cooperation and group loyalty. Kinship is among the strongest of these.

We may define *kinship* as the complex system of culturally defined social relationships based on marriage, the principle of *affinity*; and birth, the principle of *consanguinity*. The study of kinship involves consideration of such principles as descent, kinship status and roles, family and other kinship groups, marriage, and residence. In fact, kinship has been such an important organizing factor in many of the societies studied by anthropologists that it is one of the most elaborate areas of the discipline. What are some of the important concepts?

First is descent. *Descent* is based on the notion of common heritage. It is a cultural rule tying together people on the basis of reputed common ancestry. Descent functions to guide inheritance, group loyalty, and, above all, the formation of families and extended kinship groups.

There are three main rules of descent. One is *patrilineal descent*, which links relatives through males only. In patrilineal systems, females are part of their father's line, but their children descend from the husbands. *Matrilineal descent* links relatives through females only. Males belong to their mother's line; the children of males descend from the wives. *Bilateral descent* links a person to kin through both males and females simultaneously. We Americans are said to have bilateral descent, whereas most of the people in India, Japan, and China are patrilineal. Such groups as the Apache and Trobriand Islanders are matrilineal.

Descent often defines groups called, not surprisingly, *descent groups*. One of these is the *lineage*, a localized group that is based on unilineal (patrilineal or matrilineal) descent and that usually has some corporate powers. In the Marshall Islands, for example, the matriline holds rights to land, which, in turn, it allots to its members. Lineages in India sometimes hold rights to land but are a more important arena for other kinds of decisions such as marriage. Lineage mates must be consulted about the advisability, timing, and arrangements for weddings.

Clans are composed of lineages. Clan members believe they are all descended from a common ancestor, but because clans are larger, members cannot trace their genealogical relationships to everyone in the group. In some societies, clans may be linked together in even larger groups called *phratries*. Because phratries are usually large, the feeling of common descent they offer is weaker.

Ramages, or cognatic kin groups, are based on bilateral descent. They often resemble lineages in size and function but provide more recruiting flexibility. An individual can choose membership from among several ramages where he or she has relatives.

Another important kinship group is the family. This unit is more difficult to define than we may think, because people have found so many different ways to organize "family-like" groups. Here we will follow anthropologist George P. Murdock's approach and define the *family* as a kin group consisting of at least one married couple sharing the same residence with their children and performing sexual, reproductive, economic, and educational functions. A *nuclear family* consists of a single married couple and their children. An *extended family* consists of two or more married couples and their children. Extended families have a quality all their own and are often found in societies where family performance and honor are paramount to the reputation of individual family members. Extended families are most commonly based on patrilineal descent. Women marry into such families and must establish themselves among the line members and other women who live there.

Marriage, the socially approved union of a man and woman, is a second major principle of kinship. The regulation of marriage takes elaborate forms from one society to the next. Marriage may be *exogamous*, meaning marriage outside any particular named group, or *endogamous*, indicating the opposite. Bhil tribals of India, for example, are clan and village exogamous (they should marry outside these groups), but tribal endogamous (they should marry other Bhils).

Marriage may also be *monogamous*, where it is preferred that only one woman should be married to one man at a time, or *polygamous*, meaning that one person may be married to more than one person simultaneously. There are two kinds of polygamy, *polygyny*, the marriage of one man with more than one woman simultaneously, and *polyandry*, the marriage of one woman with more than one man.

Many anthropologists view marriage as a system of alliances between families and descent lines. Viewed in these terms, rules such as endogamy and exogamy can be explained as devices to link or internally strengthen various kinship groups. The *incest taboo*, a legal rule that prohibits sexual intercourse or marriage between particular classes of kin, is often explained as a way to extend alliances between kin groups.

Finally, the regulation of marriage falls to the parents and close relatives of eligible young people in many societies. These elders concern themselves with more than wedding preparations; they must also see to it that young people marry appropriately, which means they consider the reputation of prospective spouses and their families' economic strength and social rank.

The selections in Part v illustrate several aspects of kinship systems. In the first article, Michael Rynkiewich illustrates how matrilineal descent organizes a Marshallese group by showing how a young man reestablishes himself in his matrilineage. The second article, by Melvyn Goldstein, looks at a rare form of marriage — polyandry — and shows why, despite other choices, Tibetan brothers often choose to share a single wife among them. Like marriage, divorce is also a part of kinship systems everywhere. In her article on the dissolution of marriage, Helen Fisher takes a general anthropological approach, to explain why divorce rates vary from society to society and from year to year within single societies. Finally, Margery Wolf looks at the structure of the Taiwanese extended family from the point of view of the women who comprise it. It is only by establishing her own uterine family that a woman can gain power within the patrilineal group.

kinship
consanguinity
affinity
descent
patrilineal descent
matrilineal descent
bilateral descent
descent groups
lineage
clan
phratry
ramage

family
nuclear family
extended family
marriage
exogamy
endogamy
monogamy
polygamy
polygyny
polyandry
incest taboo

READINGS IN THIS SECTION

13 Matrilineal Kinship: Coming Home to Bokelab

MICHAEL A. RYNKIEWICH

Matrilineality is a puzzling rule of descent to most of us, who are used to tracing our family name through males and reckoning ancestry through both our parents. But matrilineality is a reasonable way to organize kin relationships and behavior, as Michael Rynkiewich shows in this article about Marshall Islanders. Following the activities of one islander, Benjinij, Rynkiewich shows how matrilineal descent helps to identify kin, generate appropriate behavior, secure rights to land, organize a household, and gain power.

One of the most important ways people all over the world are alike is the fundamental basis on which they organize their social lives. To relate effectively to each other, people must identify themselves and those around them, behave according to roles composed of specific rules for action, and participate in clearly defined groups. Although all of us use information about identity, role, and groups to guide our daily social behavior, the specific knowledge used by different peoples to accomplish this end varies. For example, if you were to live with the people of a Highland New Guinea community, you would quickly discover that their social organization was so different from yours that

This article was written especially for this book. Copyright © 1974 by Little, Brown and Company (Inc.) The research on which it is based was carried out in the Marshall Islands between June 1969 and December 1970. Bojalablab Atoll and the people in the story are fictional, but the account is an accurate recording of form, meaning, and functions of Marshallese kinship.

you would have to learn about a new set of identities, system of roles, and collection of groups. Only after gathering such information would you be able to get along properly with the members of the community in the context of their social system. Even in our own society many small groups have such different organizations that a new language of social behavior must be learned to fit acceptably within them.

Take a football team, for example. Suppose that you were pulled from the stands by a coach at a professional football game, dressed in a uniform, and sent on the field. As you run toward the players whose uniforms are the same color as yours, the coach yells these instructions: "Tell the quarterback to run a sixty series option down, out and down, to the split end." Unless you had played football before, you might not even realize that the term *quarterback* labels a kind of identity for one player. Even if you did understand what a quarterback was, you might not know about any of his identifying attributes — for example, that he wears a number between 10 and 19 on his back. You might also miss the fact that you are the split end (your number is 88, a sign of your position), that you should talk to the quarterback outside the huddle, and that you should line up ten to fifteen yards from the tackle on the line of scrimmage. In addition, you would not understand the instructions for action contained in the phrase "sixty series option," so you would have little idea about what your teammates planned to do or how your opponents might react. Without such information about identities, expectations for behavior, and group composition, you could not begin to play football in a socially organized manner as part of a team. The same principles govern people's behavior in every social situation.

Social organization can be achieved in several basic ways. The structure of the football team, for example, reflects a need to meet particular characteristics inherent in the game itself. As a consequence, the team has a limited and specialized social organization. On the other hand, most societies use a more general approach to achieve systematic social interaction. Instead of the exigencies of a particular game, they face such wider needs as sustenance and defense that must be met if the members of the group are to survive. Thus, their organization is often based on more general human characteristics such as age, sex, and rank. Of these, however, by far the most common and important is kinship.

Kinship provides a way of defining identities, roles, and groups for people everywhere. In many societies kinship is the dominant principle for social organization. The term *kinship* is not as simple as it sounds. Americans tend to think of kin as blood relatives, but in many parts of the world this definition is too limited. In such cases kinship is a complex language of social relationships that includes not only those who are related genealogically through blood and marriage, but also people who share no blood connection but who somehow come to be identified as kin. This extension of the system is possible because individuals determine the identity of kin not only by genealogical linkage, but by behavior as well. Thus, when someone acts like a kin, he or she is often treated as one. Conversely, some people may not be called relatives although they are related by blood ties. They simply do not behave as kin should.

This emphasis on the importance of social organization and the stress on identity, role, and group should not be allowed to obscure the place of the individual in social interaction. People do use kinship rules to structure and interpret behavior, but they also manipulate their knowledge of kinship to serve their own interests. Just as a quarterback uses his knowledge of football and the many plays and options open to him to move his offense and win the game, so individuals use their understanding of their kinship system to meet their own requirements and aspirations. Like every set of cultural rules, kinship is a flexible and ever-changing system.

To better understand the importance and the meaning of kinship, it is useful to look at a society — Bokelab islet of Bojalablab Atoll in the Marshall Islands — in which it plays a dominant role. By taking the perspective of one man, Benjinij, from this society, we can consider some of the problems he solves by the judicious use of his knowledge about kinship. Benjinij is returning to Bojalablab after a long absence. To reestablish himself there among his kin, he must identify and relate to his relatives and demonstrate and manipulate his membership rights in a landholding kinship group.

GOING HOME

Benjinij steadied himself at the bow as the ship left the calm lagoon water and met the jolting ocean waves. His mind was not on the trade goods in the ship's hold nor on the copra the ship would buy. He was a passenger getting off at the first stop, Bokelab islet. He could not see it yet, but it was just over the horizon and his mind dwelt on his situation.

Benjinij's mother had been born on Bojalablab Atoll, the ship's destination. His father was from another atoll, and his mother had gone with her husband to live there. When Benjinij was quite young, the Japanese had sent his father to Palau island for training as a carpenter. Benjinij and his mother went along. However, both of Benjinij's parents were killed in air raids during World War II. When peace returned, the now mature Benjinij became a sailor, and at age thirty, ten years after the conflict had ended, he was coming to live with his mother's people.

Bojalablab Atoll stood against the red of the late afternoon sky, like a pencil line marked on the horizon. As the ship drew nearer, the line differentiated into beach, brush, and coconut trees. Benjinij watched the waves, hypnotized by their motion. As he watched, a wave rose to four feet at the end of the reef, then flattened as it raced over the barrier, its surface reflecting the vivid colors of the coral below. Then the wave's leading edge, white with foam, flung itself on the beach.

The ship slowed and the noise of its small boat being raised from the deck brought Benjinij back from his reverie. When the ship had anchored, Benjinij climbed into the small boat so that he could be first ashore. The steersman caught a wave, then alternately throttled and accelerated the boat's engine to keep just behind the crest. Just as it seemed that it would be smashed on the shore, the boat swerved sharply to the left in response to the steersman's hand and settled down in the lee of the wave, coming gently to rest on the sandy beach. Benjinij walked onto Bokelab islet, home at last.

As he stood on the beach of his mother's home for the first time, Benjinij's thoughts turned to the problems that confronted him. He could see several people coming toward the shore and others standing near bags of dried coconut meat. Many of them were his kin, whom he would eventually have to identify by determining their relationship to him. Only then would he know how to behave toward them and what to expect they would do in return. His parents had taught him what every Marshallese child should know about kin, but he was not very practiced in relating to these particular kin, nor did he know their particular histories or the instances of cooperation and conflict. In addition, he did not know to which groups he or they belonged. He had much to learn to establish himself here, to be socially, economically, and politically successful. His key to the network of relationships on Bokelab islet was something his mother had told him years earlier, that her brother's name was Tibnil and if he ever returned to Bokelab he should depend on him for help.

Benjinij asked for directions to Tibnil's household, and started off down the road that ran parallel to the lagoon. He found Tibnil sitting in his cookhouse talking with two younger men of the household as they waited for the women to finish baking the breadfruit and fish collected that afternoon. They exchanged greetings and Benjinij was enjoined to come into the cookhouse and sit. Though Tibnil would not have recognized him, an old man on the ship had sent word that Benjinij was coming. Consequently, as is the custom, no questions were asked about the other's name. Tibnil did speak at length about his joy at Benjinij's arrival, lamenting the death of his sister and brother-in-law. Benjinij would eat, sleep, and work within this household because he had the kinship right to stay with his mother's brother as long as he liked. Thus, a bond was renewed and through Tibnil,

Benjinij began to find his way into the complex network formed by kin.

KINDS OF KIN

The few basic terms Benjinij used to identify his kin are presented in Figure 1. He calls everyone in his grandfather's generation either *jimau* (male) or *jibu* (female); as he grows old, all kin of his grandchildren's generation he will term *jibu* for either sex. (This differs from our own system in which we mark off grandfather from great-uncle and first cousin twice-removed, and grandson from grand-nephew and first cousin twice-removed.)

In general, Benjinij calls everyone of his father's generation *jinu* (female) or *jema* (male), and everyone in his children's generation *neju* (either sex). Two exceptions are his mother's brothers, only Tibnil in this case, whom he calls *uleba*, and his sister's sons, whom he would call *mangeru*.

In Benjinij's own generation, he refers to anyone born before him as *jeu* (either sex) and everyone born later *jetu* (either sex). Again, this includes kin we would call brother, sister, first cousin, second cousin, and so on. These ten basic terms, though they can be modified somewhat, enable him to identify all his relatives except his brothers-in-law.

All these terms are used to address kin. However, Benjinij must make one other distinction, though it is usually not used in address, but only to refer to a particular group of relatives. In Benjinij's own generation, female parallel cousins and female cross-cousins differ. The children of Benjinij's father's brother and his mother's sister are called parallel cousins because the sex of the two connecting relatives is the same: mother and her sister, father and his brother. Female parallel cousins are classed with Benjinij's own sister and are referred to by a combination of terms; *jeu jinu* if older than Benjinij and *jetu jinu* if younger. On the other hand, cross-cousins, the children of Benjinij's father's sister and his mother's brother, are referred to as *jeu reliku* if older and *jetu reliku* if younger. The significance of this distinction will become clear in the discussion of proper kinship behavior.

Knowing possible classes of kin did not tell Benjinij which kin fit into each category. To make this discovery, he had to depend partly on genealogical information. For example, his mother had told him that Tibnil was her brother, so he was to be called *uleba*. But the genealogical links for many people he met were never entirely clear to him. To place them, he listened to what Tibnil and other known relatives called such kin. For example, when Benjinij arrived at Tibnil's house he was greeted by two pretty girls and some other children.

FIGURE I
Kinship Relationships on Bokelab Islet

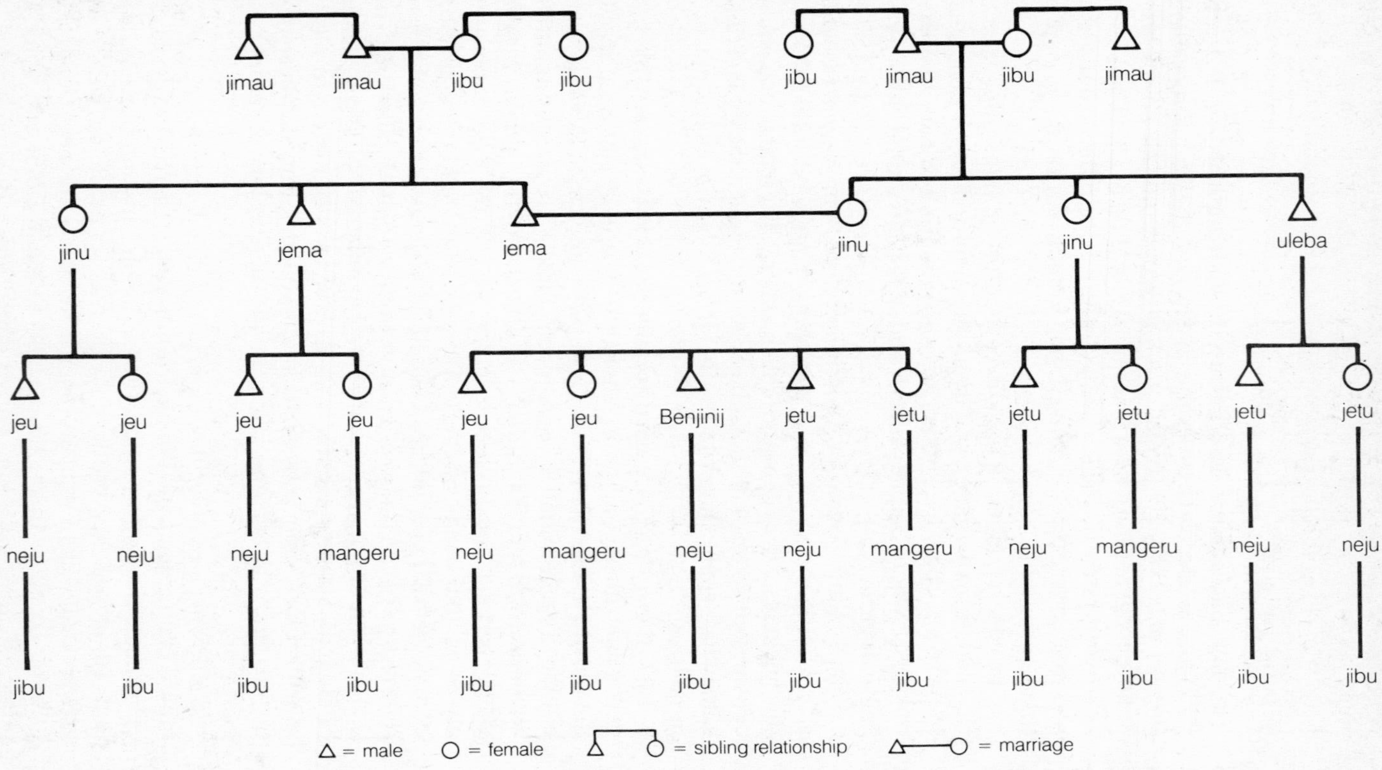

△ = male ○ = female ⊸○ = marriage ⟨ = sibling relationship

Benjinij did not know who they were, but during his first few days there he heard what they called Tibnil. When one of the girls, LiNana, called Tibnil "father," Benjinij knew that she stood in the relationship of younger cross-cousin to him because she was female, younger than him, and a child of his mother's brother.

When the other girl called Tibnil "mother's brother," Benjinij knew that she was an elder sister and parallel cousin. Benjinij quickly figured out the kinship identities of most people on the islet, and from this knowledge he was able to behave in a proper way toward them.

KINSHIP ROLES

To produce such behavior Benjinij needed to know what to call his kin. He would not, for example, act the same way toward Tibnil, his mother's brother, as he would toward a man he called "father." The former relationship involves both authority and some degree of permitted disrespect. Marshallese sayings give the expectation that the mother's brother will be a hard taskmaster while the sister's son is often mischievous. On the other hand, the relationship between father and child has little authority but a lot of respect, so that a child would never be mischievous with his father.

Although each kin requires special forms of behavior, with little exception all may be classified into two groups based on opposite forms of action. One kind of relationship can be called reserved. In the context of Marshallese culture, in the presence of certain kin Benjinij cannot refer to such bodily functions as defecation, urination, bathing, and sexual intercourse. The relationship implies respect and some degree of social distance.

As illustrated in Table I, the most reserved relationship exists between Benjinij and anyone he calls sister and parallel cousin. He is careful never to be alone with such kinswomen for fear of fostering the idea that a sexual interest exists between them. These kinswomen often make requests of Benjinij, and he does all he can to meet such demands. Moreover, he is careful that no one else should behave

TABLE I
Basic Marshallese Kinship Roles

Reserved Behavior	Joking Behavior
Sister (parallel cousin)	Cross-cousin
Mother	Grandmother
Father	Grandfather
Child	Grandchild
Mother's brother or sister's child	

improperly when he is in their presence. Once Benjinij and a "sister," a parallel cousin, sat with a group of young people by the road. A boy began to tell about a fight in which one man was kicked in the groin. Benjinij quickly disappeared. The next day he took the young story-teller aside and told him in annoyed tones to be more careful about ascertaining the relationship of those in his audience before he started talking about such private matters. Relatives called mother, father, and child must also be treated with respect (Table i).

The other major relationship is marked by joking. In many ways, it is the opposite of the reserved relationship because any kind of joking is permitted with no hint of respect or authority. People in these relationships need not hide from each other knowledge of when and where they perform bodily functions. Sexual intercourse between such relatives is permitted, except in the case of genealogical grandparents and grandchildren. The joking relationship provides some of the most interesting and humorous exchanges between kin, often taking the form of a game with one relative trying to outdo another in the gross-ness of his or her references to sexual parts and functions.

For example, Benjinij might be expected to engage in such a discussion of private parts with his cross-cousin, LiNana, if he met her on the road. First, he would likely pretend not to notice her and walk by without a greeting. But she would not allow such a challenge to go unmet, and might open with a comment like, "Your penis!" He could reply, "You have no pubic hair!" to which she might respond, "The hair of your anus!" The conversation would likely escalate with such assertions and retorts as, "Nothing is larger than the lips of your vagina." "Your little penis is half-baked." "Why is there mud in your vagina?" (implying promiscuity in the sense that she will lie anywhere, even in the mud), and the parting and winning shout, "Go masturbate yourself!" Such joking behavior is also enjoyed with kin called grand-father, grandmother, and grandchild. Thus, by knowing kinship terms, Benjinij can identify people and use appropriate behavior with them. In only a few months, Benjinij had become part of an ongoing social system that gave him support for his new life on Bokelab.

DESCENT GROUPS

Although Benjinij had managed to establish himself in the islet's social network of kin, he also wanted a household of his own, a place to work, a family, and the respect of the community. To acquire these things he needed land. The place he had in mind was a plot located near the middle of the islet rising quickly from the lagoon shore to ten feet above high tide, then dropping off to a densely wooded interior with several taro pits before ending on the side facing the ocean. The strip was only three-quarters of a mile long, but like most plots of land, it touched both shores to give the people access to the whole range of the islet's microenvironments. Benjinij suspected that he might have some claim to the land because Tibnil had often sent him there to work. He determined to see if he could get permission to live there.

Benjinij sat with Tibnil one evening, intent on asking him about the land, but he avoided doing so directly. Instead, he asked about Marshallese custom with respect to group membership and inheritance. He knew that both Americans and Japanese placed great importance on their fathers, even taking the paternal name as their own. He also knew from such sayings as "the children of women are most important" that the Marshallese way was different. When he asked about the meaning of that saying, Tibnil replied with this story:

> An old woman, Likatunger, promised the chieftainship to whichever of her sons would win a canoe race. As each of them departed she entreated him to take her along. But when she cried, "*Ekatuke iu!*" each son from the eldest on down replied, "*Kattar wut jetu*" (wait for my younger brother). Only her youngest son, Jabrau, stopped long enough to take her on board. She then gave him the paraphernalia with which to sail and Jabrau easily overtook his brothers. As he broke into the lead his eldest brother asked permission to ride along. Jabrau took him on board, but he knew his brother intended to jump off the canoe first when it reached shore and claim the chieftainship. Therefore, on the last tack, Jabrau allowed to boom to swing, knocking his brother overboard and breaking his back in the process. Jabrau won the chieftainship *kinke e jela kataike ngan jinen* (because he knew how to submit to his mother).

Tibnil stressed that land and authority came through mothers, not fathers. Benjinij had suspected as much and asked Tibnil where the latter got his authority to manage the land. Tibnil said the rights were not his alone, that they were passed down over many generations. Then he began to list all those people who had had a right in the land he controlled, beginning with the name of the oldest woman he could remember, and then her brother. He named her children, both male and female, her daughter's male and female children, and her daughter's daughter's male and female children. On and on he went, naming only the children of women, finally arriving at Benjinij's mother, and then Benjinij himself (their genealogical positions are shown in Figure II).

Benjinij now knew he was on the right track. The group whose members Tibnil had named is called *bwij*, or matrilineage. Matrilineages are formed by the descent ideology that "the children of women are most important," their new members including only the children

FIGURE II
Benjinij's Matrilineage

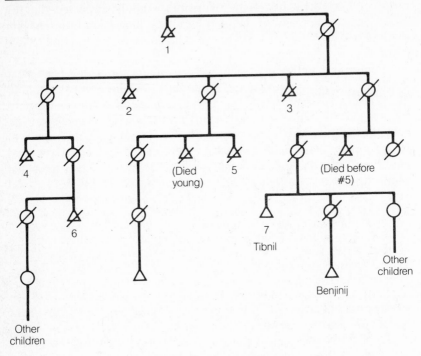

Lineage heads are numbered in succession.
Deceased relatives are shown with a diagonal line through them.

of each group's female members. The matrilineage is the major land-holding unit on Bojalablab atoll and like corporations, no one of its members may dispose of any matrilineage land rights or be denied the use of matrilineage land, except when he has gravely insulted his fellow lineage mates. A matrilineage does have a leader called an *alab*, meaning land manager or lineage head. He handles lineage affairs and represents the kin group in its dealings with other members of the community. He does not own the land; no individual does. Rather, it belongs to the whole group, including the dead and those not yet born. However, the lineage head can allocate specific pieces of land to lineage members and sometimes others, for their own temporary use.

To affirm the source of his rights as lineage head, Tibnil recited the order of succession. He went from the brother of the oldest woman, to his sister's son, and on through brothers and cousins, skipping only those who had died before their chance for succession came (marked on Figure II by numbers). When he had finished, Benjinij knew he had come to the right place. His mother's words, "Go to my brother and he will take care of you," came back to him. He asked for and received permission to build a house on the land he wanted.

ESTABLISHING A HOUSEHOLD

Planning the house and organizing the work was left to Tibnil, who told the women of his own and other households of the lineage to begin collecting pandanus leaves to make thatch and mats. The men of the lineage and other male members of their households cut down pandanus trees and sawed them up to make posts and rafters. Benjinij worked for cash to buy plywood for the walls and, although normally he had to give Tibnil a small percentage of the profits from the sale of any coconut meat derived from lineage land, Tibnil helped Benjinij by not requiring this share. The land was cleared, coral pebbles brought for the floor and yard, walls erected, and roof thatched in about three weeks.

When the house was finished, Benjinij moved in, but not by himself. For several months he had been keeping company in secret with his cross-cousin, LiNana. They had decided to live together for a while, and her father, Tibnil, had agreed. She was pregnant so one of her younger sisters came along to help keep their house. Benjinij had land to work and a household to support.

GAINING POWER

Benjinij had successfully achieved his initial goals because he became adept at manipulating the systems of kinship and descent. However, a year after he moved into his new house, he faced a problem that he could not have envisioned on his arrival. He had to struggle against his kin to protect his position in the matrilineage and the community.

The problem started when Tibnil became ill and died and his sister asserted that she would succeed him as lineage head. Her claim was based on the rule that says the successor should come from the senior generation of the lineage, and she was the only living member of that generation. Benjinij was close to her and knew he would enjoy her favor if she were the leader. However, two others were contending for the position. An old woman of another branch of the lineage claimed that she should become Tibnil's successor, although she was part of the next lower generation. She cited another rule of succession to back her claim, that lineage heads should come from the oldest branch of the lineage, the one to which she belonged. A man from the middle branch of the lineage also claimed Tibnil's position. Although he was in a generation junior to Tibnil's sister and in a lineage branch less old than that of the second claimant, he was a male and entitled to hold power over women. Each contender had a valid claim to leadership, but the rules were contradictory. Naturally, each cited only those rules that demonstrated the priority of his or her claim.

Benjinij vociferously defended the right of Tibnil's sister to succeed. The second woman had the support of her children, and to Benjinij's surprise, the man from the middle branch of the lineage was supported by his sons. True, he was the only living member of the middle branch and had no other supporters, but his sons did not even belong to the lineage, holding membership in their mother's group instead. Benjinij asked Tibnil's sister why these sons would dare argue their father's case. She explained:

> You know that the branches of a matrilineage sometimes split away from each other. Each one takes some of the lineage land and selects its own lineage head. Each branch then becomes a separate matrilineage. Look at our matrilineage. We own three pieces of land, and we have three branches. Many generations have gone by since we were all real siblings. His sons want him to be lineage head in the hope that as the leader he will force our matrilineage to split into three separate ones. If that happened, their father would be the sole member of his matrilineage, and the sole owner of one of the pieces of land. Then, because he is the last of his branch, his sons would inherit his land when he died. That is why we must oppose him, because our land could be stolen away by people who are not in our lineage.

Benjinij had learned a lesson: kin not only cooperate on matters, but they also dispute over the rights they share. If he did not resist the claims of the old man, his plot of land might be taken from the lineage. After this talk, Benjinij argued more earnestly than ever for the succession of Tibnil's sister.

The sons of the old man talked against Benjinij, but their father did not cooperate. Less than a year after the dispute began, he died. A short time later the woman from the oldest branch of the lineage also died and Tibnil's sister was left as undisputed leader of the lineage.

With Tibnil's sister in firm control, Benjinij was assured of control over his own affairs within the framework of the lineage, for he was its oldest living male. Tibnil's sister, embarrassed to go to the islet's council because of her sex, sent Benjinij in her stead. Though she kept the title, he did the work and gained experience representing his lineage to the community. Years later, when Tibnil's sister died, Benjinij's succession as lineage head was not disputed.

THE MEANING OF KINSHIP

When Benjinij stepped ashore on Bokelab islet, he had to establish himself in an ongoing, socially organized community. The cultural knowledge he used to enter the social network is different from the information we would use if we moved to a different town in the United Sates. Although he had to refine this knowledge by attempting to apply it in many new social situations, Benjinij succeeded because he understood the basic features of the Marshallese kinship and descent systems. Because he knew the proper kinship terms and the appropriate ways to behave, he became part of a household and a member of the community. He was able to claim his position as a member of a landholding group and eventually gain an allocation of land because he understood the principles of matrilineal descent. Through the complexities and conflicts of a dispute among lineage members, Benjinij emerged in a strong position because he had backed a winner. In sum, Benjinij's basic needs — food, sex, shelter, power, and meaning — were at least partially satisfied through the Marshallese systems of kinship and descent.

REVIEW QUESTIONS

1. What are some of the distinctive features of matrilineal kinship systems, using the Marshallese system as the source of your data?
2. How did Benjinij use his matrilineal kinship system to obtain land, a wife, a house, and power upon his return to Bokelab?
3. Some people have argued that matrilineality leads to public power for females. Do you think Rynkiewich's account supports this view?
4. What formal kinship relations does Rynkiewich describe in this article? What do you think explains their existence?

14 Polyandry: When Brothers Take a Wife
MELVYN C. GOLDSTEIN

*Many of the world's societies permit polygamy, the marriage of an
individual to more than one spouse. The most common form of
polygamy is polygyny, an arrangement in which a man marries
more than one wife. Polygyny may exist for many reasons, not the
least of which is its relationship to the substantial economic contri-
butions of women. But there is a second kind of polygamy called
polyandry, organized around the marriage of a woman to more
than one husband, and its causes may seem less clear. In this article, Melvyn Goldstein describes the fraternal polyandry practiced
by Tibetans living in Northern Nepal and seeks to explain why,
despite having a choice of marriage forms including monogamy
and polygyny, men and women often choose this rare form of marriage. He argues that by marrying a single wife, a group of brothers can more easily preserve their family resources, whereas monogamous or polygynous marriage usually costs a man his inheritance
and requires him to make a fresh start.*

Eager to reach home, Dorje drives his yaks hard over the seventeen-
thousand-foot mountain pass, stopping only once to rest. He and his
two older brothers, Pema and Sonam, are jointly marrying a woman
from the next village in a few weeks, and he has to help with the
preparations.

Originally published as "When Brothers Take a Wife." With permission from *Natural
History*, March 1987; Copyright the American Museum of Natural History, 1987.

Dorje, Pema, and Sonam are Tibetans living in Limi, a two-hundred-square-mile area in the northwest corner of Nepal, across the border from Tibet. The form of marriage they are about to enter — fraternal polyandry in anthropological parlance — is one of the world's rarest forms of marriage but is not uncommon in Tibetan society, where it has been practiced from time immemorial. For many Tibetan social strata, it traditionally represented the ideal form of marriage and family.

The mechanics of fraternal polyandry are simple. Two, three, four, or more brothers jointly take a wife, who leaves her home to come and live with them. Traditionally, marriage was arranged by parents, with children, particularly females, having little or no say. This is changing somewhat nowadays, but it is still unusual for children to marry without their parents' consent. Marriage ceremonies vary by income and region and range from all the brothers sitting together as grooms to only the eldest one formally doing so. The age of the brothers plays an important role in determining this: very young brothers almost never participate in actual marriage ceremonies, although they typically join the marriage when they reach their midteens.

The eldest brother is normally dominant in terms of authority, that is, in managing the household, but all the brothers share the work and participate as sexual partners. Tibetan males and females do not find the sexual aspect of sharing a spouse the least bit unusual, repulsive, or scandalous, and the norm is for the wife to treat all the brothers the same.

Offspring are treated similarly. There is no attempt to link children biologically to particular brothers, and a brother shows no favoritism toward his child even if he knows he is the real father because, for example, his other brothers were away at the time the wife became pregnant. The children, in turn, consider all of the brothers as their fathers and treat them equally, even if they also know who is their real father. In some regions children use the term "father" for the eldest brother and "father's brother" for the others, while in other areas they call all the brothers by one term, modifying this by the use of "elder" and "younger."

Unlike our own society, where monogamy is the only form of marriage permitted, Tibetan society allows a variety of marriage types, including monogamy, fraternal polyandry, and polygyny. Fraternal polyandry and monogamy are the most common forms of marriage, while polygyny typically occurs in cases where the first wife is barren. The widespread practice of fraternal polyandry, therefore, is not the outcome of a law requiring brothers to marry jointly. There is choice, and in fact, divorce traditionally was relatively simple in Tibetan society. If a brother in a polyandrous marriage became dissatisfied and wanted to separate, he simply left the main house and set up his own household. In such cases, all the children stayed in the main household with the remaining brother(s), even if the departing brother was known to be the real father of one or more of the children.

The Tibetans' own explanation for choosing fraternal polyandry is materialistic. For example, when I asked Dorje why he decided to marry with his two brothers rather than take his own wife, he thought for a moment, then said it prevented the division of his family's farm (and animals) and thus facilitated all of them achieving a higher standard of living. And when I later asked Dorje's bride whether it wasn't difficult for her to cope with three brothers as husbands, she laughed and echoed the rationale of avoiding fragmentation of the family and land, adding that she expected to be better off economically, since she would have three husbands working for her and her children.

Exotic as it may seem to Westerners, Tibetan fraternal polyandry is thus in many ways analogous to the way primogeniture functioned in nineteenth-century England. Primogeniture dictated that the eldest son inherited the family estate, while younger sons had to leave home and seek their own employment — for example, in the military or the clergy. Primogeniture maintained family estates intact over generations by permitting only one heir per generation. Fraternal polyandry also accomplishes this but does so by keeping all the brothers together with just one wife so that there is only one *set* of heirs per generation.

While Tibetans believe that in this way fraternal polyandry reduces the risk of family fission, monogamous marriages among brothers need not necessarily precipitate the division of the family estate: brothers could continue to live together, and the family land could continue to be worked jointly. When I asked Tibetans about this, however, they invariably responded that such joint families are unstable because each wife is primarily oriented to her own children and interested in their success and well-being over that of the children of the other wives. For example, if the youngest brother's wife had three sons while the eldest brother's wife had only one daughter, the wife of the youngest brother might begin to demand more resources for her children since, as males, they represent the future of the family. Thus, the children from different wives in the same generation are competing sets of heirs, and this makes such families inherently unstable. Tibetans perceive that conflict will spread from the wives to their husbands and consider this likely to cause family fission. Consequently, it is almost never done.

Although Tibetans see an economic advantage to fraternal polyandry, they do not value the sharing of a wife as an end in itself. On the contrary, they articulate a number of problems inherent in the practice. For example, because authority is customarily exercised by the eldest brother, his younger male siblings have to subordinate themselves with little hope of changing their status within the family. When these younger brothers are aggressive and individualistic, tensions and difficulties often occur despite there being only one set of heirs.

In addition, tension and conflict may arise in polyandrous families because of sexual favoritism. The bride normally sleeps with the eldest brother, and the two have the responsibility to see to it that the other males have opportunities for sexual access. Since the Tibetan subsistence economy requires males to travel a lot, the temporary absence of one or more brothers facilitates this, but there are also other rotation practices. The cultural ideal unambiguously calls for the wife to show equal affection and sexuality to each of the brothers (and vice versa), but deviations from this ideal occur, especially when there is a sizable difference in age between the partners in the marriage.

Dorje's family represents just such a potential situation. He is fifteen years old and his two older brothers are twenty-five and twenty-two years old. The new bride is twenty-three years old, eight years Dorje's senior. Sometimes such a bride finds the youngest husband immature and adolescent and does not treat him with equal affection; alternatively, she may find his youth attractive and lavish special attention on him. Apart from that consideration, when a younger male like Dorje grows up, he may consider his wife "ancient" and prefer the company of a woman his own age or younger. Consequently, although men and women do not find the idea of sharing a bride or a bridegroom repulsive, individual likes and dislikes can cause familial discord.

Two reasons have commonly been offered for the perpetuation of fraternal polyandry in Tibet: that Tibetans practice female infanticide and therefore have to marry polyandrously, owing to a shortage of females; and that Tibet, lying at extremely high altitudes, is so barren and bleak that Tibetans would starve without resort to this mechanism. A Jesuit who lived in Tibet during the eighteenth century articulated this second view: "One reason for this most odious custom is the sterility of the soil, and the small amount of land that can be cultivated owing to the lack of water. The crops may suffice if the brothers all live together, but if they form separate families they would be reduced to beggary."

Both explanations are wrong, however. Not only has there never been institutionalized female infanticide in Tibet, but Tibetan society gives females considerable rights, including inheriting the family estate in the absence of brothers. In such cases, the woman takes a bridegroom who comes to live in her family and adopts her family's name and identity. Moreover, there is no demographic evidence of a shortage of females. In Limi, for example, there were (in 1974) sixty females and fifty-three males in the fifteen- to thirty-five-year age category, and many adult females were unmarried.

The second reason is also incorrect. The climate in Tibet is extremely harsh, and ecological factors do play a major role in perpetuating polyandry, but polyandry is not a means of preventing starvation. It is characteristic, not of the poorest segments of the society, but rather of the peasant landowning families.

In the old society, the landless poor could not realistically aspire to prosperity, but they did not fear starvation. There was a persistent labor shortage throughout Tibet, and very poor families with little or no land and few animals could subsist through agricultural labor, tenant farming, craft occupations such as carpentry, or by working as servants. Although the per-person family income could increase somewhat if brothers married polyandrously and pooled their wages, in the absence of inheritable land, the advantage of fraternal polyandry was not generally sufficient to prevent them from setting up their own households. A more skilled or energetic younger brother could do as well or better alone, since he would completely control his income and would not have to share it with his siblings. Consequently, while there was and is some polyandry among the poor, it is much less frequent and more prone to result in divorce and family fission.

An alternative reason for the persistence of fraternal polyandry is that it reduces population growth (and thereby reduces the pressure on resources) by relegating some females to lifetime spinsterhood (see Figure 1). Fraternal polyandrous marriages in Limi (in 1974) averaged 2.35 men per woman, and not surprisingly, 31 percent of the females of child-bearing age (twenty to forty-nine) were unmarried. These spinsters either continued to live at home, set up their own households, or worked as servants for other families. They could also become Buddhist nuns. Being unmarried is not synonymous with exclusion from the reproductive pool. Discreet extramarital relationships are tolerated, and actually half of the adult unmarried women in Limi had one or more children. They raised these children as single mothers, working for wages or weaving cloth and blankets for sale. As a group, however, the unmarried women had far fewer offspring than the married women, averaging only 0.7 children per woman, compared with 3.3 for married women, whether polyandrous, monogamous, or polygynous. When polyandry helps regulate population, this function of polyandry is not consciously perceived by Tibetans and is not the reason they consistently choose it.

If neither a shortage of females nor the fear of starvation perpetuates fraternal polyandry, what motivates brothers, particularly younger brothers, to opt for this system of marriage? From the perspective of the younger brother in a landholding family, the main incentive is the attainment or maintenance of the good life. With polyandry, he can expect a more secure and higher standard of living, with access not only to his family's land and animals but also to its inherited collection of clothes, jewelry, rugs, saddles, and horses. In

FIGURE I

Family Planning in Tibet

An economic rationale for fraternal polyandry is outlined in the diagram below, which emphasizes only the male offspring in each generation. If every wife is assumed to bear three sons, a family splitting up into monogamous households would rapidly multiply and fragment the family land. In this case, a rule of inheritance, such as primogeniture, could retain the family land intact, but only at the cost of creating many landless male offspring. In contrast, the family practicing fraternal polyandry maintains a steady ratio of persons to land.

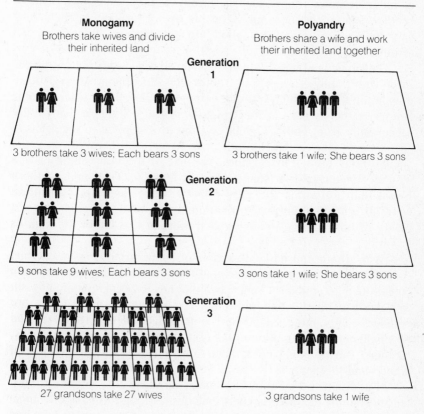

Monogamy	Polyandry
Brothers take wives and divide their inherited land	Brothers share a wife and work their inherited land together

Generation 1

3 brothers take 3 wives; Each bears 3 sons — 3 brothers take 1 wife; She bears 3 sons

Generation 2

9 sons take 9 wives; Each bears 3 sons — 3 sons take 1 wife; She bears 3 sons

Generation 3

27 grandsons take 27 wives — 3 grandsons take 1 wife

addition, he will experience less work pressure and much greater security because all responsibility does not fall on one "father." For Tibetan brothers, the question is whether to trade off the greater personal freedom inherent in monogamy for the real or potential economic security, affluence, and social prestige associated with life in a larger, labor-rich polyandrous family.

A brother thinking of separating from his polyandrous marriage and taking his own wife would face various disadvantages. Although in the majority of Tibetan regions all brothers theoretically have rights to their family's estate, in reality Tibetans are reluctant to divide their land into small fragments. Generally, a younger brother who insists on leaving the family will receive only a small plot of land, if that. Because of its power and wealth, the rest of the family usually can block any attempt of the younger brother to increase his share of land through litigation. Moreover, a younger brother may not even get a house and cannot expect to receive much above the minimum in terms of movable possessions, such as furniture, pots, and pans. Thus, a brother contemplating going it on his own must plan on achieving economic security and the good life not through inheritance but through his own work.

The obvious solution for younger brothers — creating new fields from virgin land — is generally not a feasible option. Most Tibetan populations live at high altitudes (above 12,000 feet), where arable land is extremely scarce. For example, in Dorje's village, agriculture ranges only from about 12,900 feet, the lowest point in the area, to 13,300 feet. Above that altitude, early frost and snow destroy the staple barley crop. Furthermore, because of the low rainfall caused by the Himalayan rain shadow, many areas in Tibet and northern Nepal that are within the appropriate altitude range for agriculture have no reliable sources of irrigation. In the end, although there is plenty of unused land in such areas, most of it is either too high or too arid.

Even where unused land capable of being farmed exists, clearing the land and building the substantial terraces necessary for irrigation constitute a great undertaking. Each plot has to be completely dug out to a depth of two to two and a half feet so that the large rocks and boulders can be removed. At best, a man might be able to bring a few new fields under cultivation in the first years after separating from his brothers, but he could not expect to acquire substantial amounts of arable land this way.

In addition, because of the limited farmland, the Tibetan subsistence economy characteristically includes a strong emphasis on animal husbandry. Tibetan farmers regularly maintain cattle, yaks, goats, and sheep, grazing them in the areas too high for agriculture. These herds produce wool, milk, cheese, butter, meat, and skins. To obtain these resources, however, shepherds must accompany the animals on a daily basis. When first setting up a monogamous household, a younger brother like Dorje would find it difficult to both farm and manage animals.

In traditional Tibetan society, there was an even more critical factor that operated to perpetuate fraternal polyandry — a form of hereditary servitude somewhat analogous to serfdom in Europe. Peasants were tied to large estates held by aristocrats, monasteries, and the Lhasa government. They were allowed the use of some farmland to produce their own subsistence but were required to provide taxes in kind and corvée (free labor) to their lords. The corvée was a substantial hardship, since a peasant household was in many cases required to furnish the lord with one laborer daily for most of the year and more on specific occasions such as the harvest. This enforced labor, along with the lack of new land and the ecological pressure to pursue both agriculture and animal husbandry, made polyandrous families particularly beneficial. The polyandrous family allowed an internal division of adult labor, maximizing economic advantage. For example, while the wife worked the family fields, one brother could perform the lord's corvée, another could look after the animals, and a third could engage in trade.

Although social scientists often discount other people's explanations of why they do things, in the case of Tibetan fraternal polyandry, such explanations are very close to the truth. The custom, however, is very sensitive to changes in its political and economic milieu and, not surprisingly, is in decline in most Tibetan areas. Made less important by the elimination of the traditional serf-based economy, it is disparaged by the dominant non-Tibetan leaders of India, China, and Nepal. New opportunities for economic and social mobility in these countries, such as the tourist trade and government employment, are also eroding the rationale for polyandry, and so it may vanish within the next generation.

REVIEW QUESTIONS

1. What is fraternal polyandry and how does this form of marriage manage potential conflict over sex, children, and inheritance?
2. Why do many Tibetans choose polyandry over monogamous or polygynous marriage?
3. According to Tibetans, what are some of the disadvantages of polyandry?
4. What is wrong with the theory that Tibetan polyandry is caused either by a shortage of women due to infanticide or is a way to prevent famine by limiting population and land pressure?
5. Why might Tibetan polyandry disappear under modern conditions?

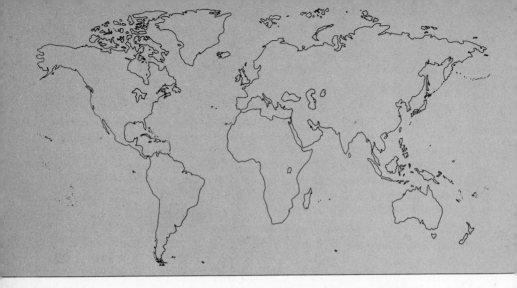

15   Divorce and the Four-Year Itch

HELEN E. FISHER

*Many Americans see divorce as a problem; high rates of divorce
indicate an erosion of morals and an attack on the family. For
most of us, divorce is a sign of moral weakness and personal failure. But a cross-cultural review of divorce rates and timing leads to
a different view, as Helen Fisher shows in this paper. Arguing from
cultural anthropology, she points out that divorce rates correlate
with the economic dependence of spouses. Rates will rise as
spouses each acquire their own economic resources. The timing of
divorce also poses a question. Arguing as a biological anthropologist, Fisher asserts that divorce peaks in four-year cycles in every
society, a period that coincides with biologically determined human
breeding cycles. She concludes that this pattern may have had a
selective advantage for our ancestors.*

Samuel Johnson defined remarriage as the triumph of hope over experience. Anthropologists call this human habit "serial monogamy."
Americans joke about the "seven-year itch." Call it what you will, the
human penchant for divorce and remarriage is worldwide.

Among the !Kung Bushmen of southern Africa's Kalahari Desert,
for example, men and women often marry more than once. Although
the !Kung are rapidly adopting Western values and twentieth-century
technology, divorce is not a new development. The traditional !Kung,

Originally published as "The Four-Year Itch." With permission from *Natural History*,
November, 1987; Copyright the American Museum of Natural History, 1987.

who were studied by anthropologists, lived in semipermanent groups. During the rainy season, ten to thirty individuals — including couples, their children, and other kin — interacted daily. Friends and relatives traveled between communities, connecting a fluid network of several hundred people. Every two or three days some of the women of a band went collecting. They returned from their expeditions with roots, melons, nuts, berries, honey, and, occasionally, small mammals, insects, and birds' eggs. !Kung men went hunting about three days a week. Often they came home with meat: sometimes just a hare; sometimes an antelope large enough to be divided among all community members.

Sixty to 80 percent of the daily staples were provided by women; women shared the rights to waterholes in the desert, too. During their reproductive years, women held high status, and older women had an important say in community affairs. When a woman found herself in a desperate marriage, she often assembled her few belongings and departed for another camp nearby.

Sometimes !Kung couples argued for months before splitting up. Neighbors also got involved. But eventually, many unhappy marriages ended; either the man or the woman walked out. Perhaps they could do so because both partners were relatively self-sufficient. Of the 331 marriages reported by !Kung women to sociologist Nancy Howell, 134 ended in divorce. Some men and women had more than four consecutive spouses.

Divorce is also common in other societies where men and women are relatively economically independent. Among the Yoruba of West Africa, where women traditionally control the complex marketing system, as much as 46 percent of all marriages end in divorce. In highland Nepal, the Tamang give little girls a chicken or other livestock, corn, or a small amount of money and encourage them to increase this wealth. By their late teens, Tamang women often own substantial movable property and the right to distribute it. When she first marries, a young woman rarely transfers all of her livestock or other wealth to her husband's farmland. If the marriage goes poorly, she just walks home. The divorce rate among the Tamang is also high.

The Hadza live in the rocky grasslands of Tanzania. During the dry season, men hunt impala, buffalo, and other large game, but meat is a luxury. Both men and women collect vegetable foods, which are never in short supply. Among the Hadza, marriage is a casual affair; divorce occurs when a couple cease to live together for more than a few days. Anthropologist Ernestine Friedl, reporting on research done in the 1960s, says that divorce rates are "roughly five times as high as in the United States."

Divorce is less common where women and men are economically dependent on one another — most notably in societies that use the plow for agriculture. In such societies, spouses need each other to make ends meet. Examples are India and China and, in the past, preindustrial Europe and America. For example, in 1700 a woman living on a small farm in Massachusetts depended on her husband to move the rocks, fell the trees, and plow the land. He depended on her to sow, weed, pick, prepare, and store the vegetables. Together they worked the farm. More important, whoever elected to leave the marriage left empty-handed; neither spouse could dig up half the land and relocate. Farming women and men were tied to the land, to one another, and to a network of stationary kin. Under these ecological circumstances, divorce was not a practical alternative, and cultural mores made marital separation very difficult.

The Industrial Revolution changed this relationship between the sexes. When factories began to appear beyond the barns of agricultural America, men and women began to leave home for the workplace, bringing back money — movable, divisible property. During much of the 1800s, middle-class women still ran the home. But in the early decades of the twentieth century, American women began to join the labor force in greater numbers. With time, the steady influx of women into the job market began to give them economic autonomy; not coincidentally, the American divorce rate began a slow but steady rise. For an unhappy man will leave a wife who brings home an income long before he will desert a woman he depends on to weed his garden. And a woman with a salary may be less tolerant of marital despair than one dependent on her spouse to provide the evening meal. Since 1960, the number of women in the job market has doubled. The American annual divorce rate has doubled too. Many demographers identify women's employment as a prime factor in this rising frequency of divorce.

The relationship between rising divorce rates and female-male economic autonomy has been seen before in Western culture. Shortly after the Romans conquered Carthage in the third century B.C., an urban upper class emerged. Wealthy Roman patricians were apparently no longer willing to let massive dowries pass into the hands of potentially errant sons-in-law, as was customary under the traditional religious marriage forms. Instead, they married off their daughters in civil unions, and the women themselves were able to control their fortunes. As a class of economically self-sufficient women emerged in ancient Rome, the divorce rate soared.

Since 1947, census takers in places as culturally dissimilar as South Africa, Morocco, Japan, the Soviet Union, Greece, El Salvador, and the United States have periodically asked about divorce. Among their survey questions are: How many years were you married at the time of your divorce? How old were you when you divorced? How many children did you have when you divorced? These data, compiled every decade by the Statistical Office of the United Nations, present a surprisingly consistent global picture.

Most striking, in a sample of fifty-eight populations where data are complete, there are three divorce peaks — among couples married for four years, among people between the ages of twenty-five and twenty-nine, and among couples with no children or one dependent child. Although the data are not sufficient to show the relationship between these three peaks, the relatively high frequency of divorce after about four years of marriage probably accounts in large part for the divorce peak among couples with one or no children. The risk of divorce for men and women in their late twenties is always high, however, regardless of where the divorce peak falls with respect to numbers of years married.

The three-peak pattern appears unrelated to high or low divorce rates. Finland is a typical example. In the 1950s, the divorce rate was relatively low; it has risen steadily since. But the "profile" of divorce has remained almost the same. In 1950, divorces peaked among couples married four years and among women aged twenty-five to twenty-nine and men aged thirty-five to thirty-nine. Seventy-one percent of divorces involved couples with one dependent child. In 1966, divorce peaked after the third year of marriage, then shifted back to the four-year peak in 1974 and 1981; for these years, the peak for men and women was in the twenty-five to twenty-nine age group. The overall pattern remained remarkably similar in all four decades, despite a doubling of divorces. With some variation, this pattern is seen around the world. Across the United Nations sample, an average of 48 percent of the divorces occur within seven years of marriage; they cluster around the four-year peak. So divorce commonly occurs early in marriage, among couples at the height of their reproductive and parenting years.

A comparable statistical breakdown of divorce practices is not available for most so-called primitive cultures. But anthropologist Napoleon Chagnon recently began studying the "decay rate" of the nuclear family in thirteen Yanomamö villages along the upper Orinoco River in Venezuela. He reported that among these hunters and gardeners, nearly all children younger than five lived with their natural mother; the majority had their biological father living with them too. But the cohabitation of biological parents declined sharply among children older than five.

This divorce pattern among the Yanomamö is consistent with the United Nations data on fifty-eight industrial and agricultural peoples. And it is difficult to attribute this pattern to the forces of society. These peoples vary widely in religion, social structure, economy, political views, and per capita income. Why are their divorce profiles similar?

There is a possibility that the common pattern is a result of brain physiology. Psychiatrists divide the love between a man and woman into two fundamental stages: the "attraction phase" and the "attachment phase." During the attraction phase, infatuation engulfs lovers with giddiness, euphoria, optimism, and energy. Michael Liebowitz, a psychiatrist at the New York State Psychiatric Institute, thinks these feelings may be caused by increased activity in the brain of phenylethylamine or other natural brain stimulants. John Money, a sexologist from Johns Hopkins University, suggests that among lovers who see each other regularly, this stage of intense emotion can last only about two or three years — long enough, however, to foster pregnancy.

Liebowitz theorizes that the brain's tolerance for these natural aphrodisiacs grows, eventually dulling the sensation of intense infatuation. Now stage two, the attachment stage, sets in. This is the stage of peaceful, secure, comfortable love that so many couples report. Liebowitz suspects that the attachment stage is associated with a different set of brain chemicals, the endorphins — the opiates of the mind: "Biologically, it appears that we have evolved two distinct chemical systems for romance; one basically serves to bring people together and the other to keep them together." He attributes these systems to our evolutionary heritage:

> For primitive man two aspects of relating to the opposite sex were important for survival as a species. The first was to have males and females become attracted to each other for long enough to have sex and reproduce. The second was for the males to become strongly attached to the females so that they stayed around while the females were raising their young and helped to gather food, find shelter, and teach the kids certain skills.

But Liebowitz cautions that even with this brain circuitry, "if you want a situation where you and your long-term partner can still get very excited about each other — you have to work on it. In some ways you are bucking a biological tide."

Nature seems quite determined that we fall in love; she has dedicated less evolutionary energy to maintaining that state. Anthropologists have, in fact, argued about the essence of the human pair bond for decades. Some think it does not exist. They will tell you that less than one-fifth of human cultures practice monogamy, while more than four-fifths permit men to have several wives simultaneously. But in the vast majority of these polygynous cultures, only about 10 percent of men actually have more than a single wife at one time; moreover, women in polygynous households marry only one man at a time. So monogamy — a mating and marriage system in which an individual forms a social, economic, and sexual union with a single member of the opposite sex at one time — is pretty standard for the human species.

This is not to say that spouses are necessarily faithful to each other; monogamy does not imply fidelity. In the late 1940s and early 1950s, Alfred Kinsey and his colleagues estimated that, based on their sample, about one-third of all American married men and about one-fourth of American married women were sexually unfaithful to their spouses. Since then these statistics have gone up. And American patterns of adultery are not unusual; extramarital affairs are reported in many cultures, even where participants are punished with death. But records taken by the United Nations show that an average of 93 percent of women and 92 percent of men in industrial and agricultural societies marry. The ethnographic literature confirms that marriage is nearly universal in traditional societies.

And in cultures where divorce is common, so too is remarriage. The U.S. National Center for Health Statistics has projected that, if current trends continue, 47.4 percent of all first marriages that were contracted in 1974 will end in divorce. But Andrew Cherlin, a sociologist at Johns Hopkins University, reports that about five out of six men and about three out of four women who divorce remarry, half the time within three years. Statistics on marriage and divorce recorded in other countries, as well as anthropological data on traditional societies, indicate that remarriage among couples of reproductive age occurs regularly.

Monogamy is rare in nonhuman mammals. Less than 3 percent of mammalian species form a pair bond and, as "husband and wife," raise their young. Monogamy is much more common among birds, however. About 90 percent of avian species pair up to raise a brood (in some cases, as among humans, the pair bond does not entail fidelity).

Monogamous species practice this reproductive strategy for several reasons. Gibbons, primate relatives of ours, probably originally evolved monogamy for an ecological reason. In the jungles of Indonesia the resources are so scattered that two females cannot raise their young in the same home range; therefore they must spread out. A male and female pair up shortly after puberty and establish a permanent territory containing fresh water and a few dispersed but continually renewing fruit trees. Here they mate for life, raising their young and defending their small home range. In a fundamental respect, a man and woman living on a small farm in Massachusetts in 1700 displayed the same mating strategy — marrying for life and raising their children on a small plot of land with a continually renewing food supply.

Monogamy is also common in species where more than one parent, the female, may be needed to rear the young successfully. Females of some species bear many infants at once or bear young that are altricial (relatively undeveloped). The female red fox, for example, may deliver too many pups to raise by herself. The male and female form a pair bond in winter and raise a litter together during the spring and summer months. But as autumn leaves pile up around the den, and the young begin to wander, the parents split up to forage independently. The bond only functions to raise the young.

The formation of bonds in association with a breeding season is also common among birds. Most birds bear altricial young and form pair bonds to raise them. Half of this group, like the robin, form a pair bond that lasts only through the breeding season. Some pairs stay together and raise more than one brood in the same season. But after the last fledglings leave the nest, the parents split up. And they do not always mate with the same partner the following year.

Human beings have some things in common with robins and foxes. Human females bear altricial babies and need help in caring for them. Moreover, they do not necessarily mate for life. In societies where men and women are not economically dependent on one another, some bond serially — typically dissolving their marriages after about four years.

Four years may be the length of our ancestral, biological "breeding season." Scientists have observed that among the traditional !Kung Bushmen, women tended to nurse their infants for three or four years. And because !Kung mothers breast-fed regularly throughout the day and night, as well as offered their breasts as pacifiers, ovulation and subsequent pregnancy were postponed; births were about four years apart. Births are spaced about four years apart among groups of Australian aborigines, too. These data have led scientists to suggest that four-year intervals were the natural pattern of birth spacing among our forebears. Human brain physiology for infatuation and attachment also seems to fit this interval. So here is my theory: Perhaps, like serial monogamy in robins, foxes, and other species that mate only for a breeding season, the human pair bond originally evolved to last long enough to raise a single child through infancy. The seven-year itch, recast as a four-year human reproductive cycle, may be a biological phenomenon.

Pair bonding must have evolved when ancestral hominid females first began to deliver helpless young and needed the support of a mate to raise them. Nobody knows when selection for altricial babies occurred. Primates generally bear immature young, but human infants are born much less developed in some respects than are the infants of even our closest relatives, the apes. And human childhood is by far the longest of any primate species. This characteristic may be linked to two critical developments in human history: the evolution of upright walking, about four million years ago, and the expansion of the human brain, about two million years ago.

When our ancestors first began to walk erect, the front-to-back diameter of the pelvic inlet, the bony sides of the birth canal, began to get smaller. Anthropologists Robert Tague and C. Owen Lovejoy conclude that Lucy, the well-known hominid that walked through the woodlands of what is today Ethiopia almost three and a half million years ago, experienced slow, difficult birth. Then, by two million years ago, this obstetric difficulty was complicated by the expanding human brain. Along with others who have studied this question, I believe that at some stage ancestral females must have begun to experience an obstetric crisis — bearing babies that were too large to squeeze through the smaller birth canal. Over time, many must have died in childbirth; but a few, by genetic chance, bore their young earlier — delivering more immature babies that easily slipped through the birth canal. These females and their babies survived more often, passing the critical trait to bear highly immature infants across the eons to women around the world today.

Exactly when this occurred has still to be settled. Recent comparisons of growth patterns in the teeth of modern humans with those of fossil hominids suggest that it was one and a half million years ago or even more recently. But other data on dental growth support the conclusion that females bore babies in the human pattern by two million years ago. In either case, along with this fundamental change in female reproductive physiology must have come modern human mating patterns. Why? Because small groups of these early females, encumbered with infants, were walking through the dangerous grasslands of Africa, from nut grove to berry thicket to fishing pond. They must have begun to need a mate to help feed and protect the helpless babies, and pair bonding between male and female was the solution. The brain physiology of infatuation and attachment — all of the mechanisms that initiate and maintain a bond today — must have evolved with monogamy.

But I see no reason why these early human pair bonds always needed to be permanent. Once a child had been weaned, it could join play groups or become the responsibility of several community members. Why should a couple necessarily remain together unless a second infant was conceived? While there may have been strong evolutionary selection for couples to remain together at least long enough to raise a single baby through infancy, there may have been no stringent selection for permanent monogamy during the reproductive years.

Americans idealize lifelong marriage; they equate divorce with failure. But among our ancestors, there may even have been biological advantages to changing mates during the reproductive years. For instance, a prehistoric male who "divorced" his partner after seeing one offspring through infancy would have had the opportunity to pick a younger "spouse" more capable of bearing and raising babies. A female might leave one mate to "marry" a better provider for her and her forthcoming children. More significant, a male or female who changed mates during his or her reproductive years would have produced genetically more varied young, probably enhancing the likelihood that his or her lineage would survive in fluctuating environments.

There may have been cultural advantages to divorce and remarriage, too. Edward Tylor, one of the founding fathers of anthropology, observed in 1889 that "among tribes of low culture there is but one means known of keeping up alliances, and that means is inter-marriage." More recently, Ernestine Friedl of Duke University noted that in horticultural societies, where men and women garden without the plow, divorce is extremely high, particularly for first marriages arranged by the kin of the married couple. She reports that, nevertheless, there are few permanent negative consequences of divorce for the couple involved or their kin. If this is the case, why not marry more than once and create associations with two or more neighbors?

Similarly, for early human groups, serial monogamy, as opposed to lifelong bonding, would have extended ties. Contemporary observers have commented on the growing role of the "new" extended family, which includes stepparents and other steprelatives. Given the hypothesis that serial pair bonding evolved on the grasslands of Africa two million years ago, these multiconnected households are not new at all.

I am not suggesting that ancestral couples consciously engaged in serial monogamy to further their genetic lines. They probably fell in and out of love for many of the same psychological reasons we do today. But those who did change mates bore genetically more varied children that grew up in environments of extended cultural resources. These young survived disproportionately, passing to modern humankind our nagging restlessness during long relationships, our penchant for divorce, and our perennial optimism about our next relationship.

I also do not wish to suggest that lifelong monogamy was an inferior reproductive strategy. Permanent relationships between compatible partners, in the right ecological circumstances, must have had genetic and cultural payoffs too. Today, about half of American marriages last for life, and about half the spouses are faithful to their partners. Human beings are certainly capable of enduring relationships, particularly as they age. In fact, other things being equal, the statistics bode well for the American family. America is getting older. Our huge baby boom generation is in its late thirties and early forties, past the age of highest divorce risk. As this large group moves beyond its reproductive years, we may experience a few decades of relative family stability.

REVIEW QUESTIONS

1. According to Fisher, what accounts for different rates of divorce among societies?

2. According to Fisher, why has the divorce rate been increasing over the past few years?

3. When are people in any society most likely to divorce? What may account for this timing?

4. What does Fisher's article imply about the usefulness of the broad, general approach in anthropology?

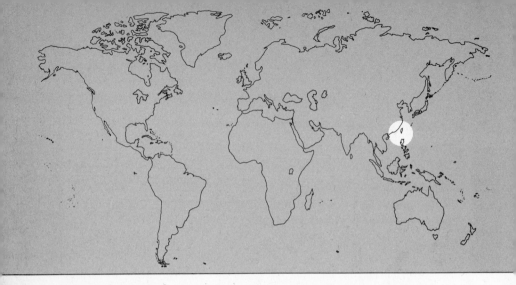

16 Uterine Families and the Women's Community

MARGERY WOLF

The size and organization of extended families vary from one society to the next, but extended families often share some important attributes. They are most often based on a rule of patrilineal descent. For men, the patrilineal family extends in an unbroken line of ancestors and descendants. Membership is permanent; loyalty assured. For women, the patrilineal family is temporary. Born into one family and married into another, women discover that their happiness and interests depend on bearing children to create their own uterine family. This, and the importance of a local women's group, are the subjects of this article by Margery Wolf in her discussion of Taiwanese family life.

Few women in China experience the continuity that is typical of the lives of the menfolk. A woman can and, if she is ever to have any economic security, must provide the links in the male chain of descent, but she will never appear in anyone's genealogy as that all-important name connecting the past to the future. If she dies before she is married, her tablet will not appear on her father's altar; although she was a temporary member of his household, she was not a member of his family. A man is born into his family and remains a member of it throughout his life and even after his death. He is identified with the

Reprinted from *Women and the Family in Rural Taiwan* by Margery Wolf with the permission of the publishers, Stanford University Press. © 1972 by the Board of Trustees of the Leland Stanford Junior University.

family from birth, and every action concerning him, up to and including his death, is in the context of that group. Whatever other uncertainties may trouble his life, his place in the line of ancestors provides a permanent setting. There is no such secure setting for a woman. She will abruptly leave the household into which she is born, either as an infant or as an adult bride, and enter another whose members treat her with suspicion or even hostility.

A man defines his family as a large group that includes the dead, and not-yet-born, and the living members of his household. But how does a woman define her family? This is not a question that China specialists often consider, but from their treatment of the family in general, it would seem that a woman's family is identical with that of the senior male in the household in which she lives. Although I have never asked, I imagine a Taiwanese man would define a woman's family in very much those same terms. Women, I think, would give quite a different answer. They do not have an unchanging place, assigned at birth, in any group, and their view of the family reflects this.

When she is a child, a woman's family is defined for her by her mother and to some extent by her grandmother. No matter how fond of his daughter the father may be, she is only a temporary member of his household and useless to his family — he cannot even marry her to one of his sons as he could an adopted daughter. Her irrelevance to her father's family in turn affects the daughter's attitude toward it. It is of no particular interest to her, and the need to maintain its continuity has little meaning for her beyond the fact that this continuity matters a great deal to some of the people she loves. As a child she probably accepts to some degree her grandmother's orientation toward the family: the household, that is, those people who live together and eat together, including perhaps one or more of her father's married brothers and their children. But the group that has the most meaning for her and with which she will have the most lasting ties is the smaller, more cohesive unit centering on her mother, that is, the uterine family — her mother and her mother's children. Father is important to the group, just as grandmother is important to some of the children, but he is not quite a member of it, and for some uterine families he may even be "the enemy." As the girl grows up and her grandmother dies and a brother or two marries, she discovers that her mother's definition of the family is becoming less exclusive and may even include such outsiders as her brother's new wife. Without knowing precisely when it happened, she finds that her brother's interests and goals have shifted in a direction she cannot follow. Her mother does not push her aside, but when the mother speaks of the future, she speaks in terms of her son's future. Although the mother sees her uterine family as adding new members and another generation, her daughter sees it as dissolving, leaving her with strong particular relationships, but with no group to which she has permanent loyalties and obligations.

When a young woman marries, her formal ties with the household of her father are severed. In one of the rituals of the wedding ceremony the bride's father or brothers symbolically inform her by means of spilt water that she, like the water, may never return, and when her wedding sedan chair passes over the threshold of her father's house, the doors are slammed shut behind her. If she is ill-treated by her husband's family, her father's family may intervene, but unless her parents are willing to bring her home and support her for the rest of her life (and most parents are not), there is little they can do beyond shaming the other family. This is usually enough.

As long as her mother is alive, the daughter will continue her contacts with her father's household by as many visits as her new situation allows. If she lives nearby she may visit every few days, and no matter where she lives she must at least be allowed to return at New Year. After her mother dies her visits may become perfunctory, but her relations with at least one member of her uterine family, the group that centered on her mother, remain strong. Her brother plays an important ritual role throughout her life. She may gradually lose contact with her sisters as she and they become more involved with their own children, but her relations with her brother continue. When her sons marry, he is the guest of honor at the wedding feasts, and when her daughters marry he must give a small banquet in their honor. If her sons wish to divide their father's estate, it is their mother's brother who is called on to supervise. And when she dies, the coffin cannot be closed until her brother determines to his own satisfaction that she died a natural death and that her husband's family did everything possible to prevent it.

With the ritual slam of her father's door on her wedding day, a young woman finds herself quite literally without a family. She enters the household of her husband — a man who in an earlier time, say fifty years ago, she would never have met and who even today, in modern rural Taiwan, she is unlikely to know very well. She is an outsider, and for Chinese an outsider is always an object of deep suspicion. Her husband and her father-in-law do not see her as a member of their family. But they do see her as essential to it; they have gone to great expense to bring her into their household for the purpose of bearing a new generation for their family. Her mother-in-law, who was mainly responsible for negotiating the terms of her entry, may harbor some resentment over the hard bargaining, but she is nonetheless eager to see another generation added to *her* uterine family. A mother-in-law often has the same kind of ambivalence toward her daughter-in-law as she has toward her husband—the younger woman seems a member of her family at times and merely a member of the household at others. The new bride may find that her husband's sister is hostile or at best condescending, both attitudes reflecting the daughter's distress at an outsider who seems to be making her way right into the heart of the family.

Chinese children are taught by proverb, by example, and by experience that the family is the source of their security, and relatives the only people who can be depended on. Ostracism from the family is one of the harshest sanctions that can be imposed on erring youth. One of the reasons mainlanders as individuals are considered so untrustworthy on Taiwan is the fact that they are not subject to the controls of (and therefore have no fear of ostracism from) their families. If a timid new bride is considered an object of suspicion and potentially dangerous because she is a stranger, think how uneasy her own first few months must be surrounded by strangers. Her irrelevance to her father's family may result in her having little reverence for descent lines, but she has warm memories of the security of the family her mother created. If she is ever to return to this certainty and sense of belonging, a woman must create her own uterine family by bearing children, a goal that happily corresponds to the goals of the family into which she has married. She may gradually create a tolerable niche for herself in the household of her mother-in-law, but her family will not be formed until she herself forms it of her own children and grandchildren. In most cases, by the time she adds grandchildren, the uterine family and the household will almost completely overlap, and there will be another daughter-in-law struggling with loneliness and beginning a new uterine family.

The ambiguity of a man's position in relation to the uterine families accounts for much of the hostility between mother-in-law and daughter-in-law. There is no question in the mind of the older woman but that her son *is* her family. The daughter-in-law might be content with this situation once her sons are old enough to represent her interests in the household and in areas strictly under men's control, but until then, she is dependent on her husband. If she were to be completely absorbed into her mother-in-law's family—a rare occurrence unless she is a *simpua*—there would be little or no conflict; but under most circumstances she must rely on her husband, her mother-in-law's son, as her spokesman, and here is where the trouble begins. Since it is usually events within the household that she wishes to affect, and the household more or less overlaps with her mother-in-law's uterine family, even a minor foray by the younger woman suggests to the older one an all-out attack on everything she has worked so hard to build in the years of her own loneliness and insecurity. The birth of grandchildren further complicates their relations, for the one sees them as new members for her family and the other as desperately needed recruits to her own small circle of security.

In summary, my thesis contends . . . that because we have heretofore focused on men when examining the Chinese family — a reasonable approach to a patrilineal system — we have missed not only some of the system's subtleties but also its near-fatal weaknesses. With a male focus we see the Chinese family as a line of descent, bulging to encompass all the members of a man's household and spreading out through his descendants. With a female focus, however, we see the Chinese family not as a continuous line stretching between the vague horizons of past and future, but as a contemporary group that comes into existence out of one woman's need and is held together insofar as she has the strength to do so, or, for that matter, the need to do so. After her death the uterine family survives only in the mind of her son and is symbolized by the special attention he gives her earthly remains and her ancestral tablet. The rites themselves are demanded by the ideology of the patriliny, but the meaning they hold for most sons is formed in the uterine family. The uterine family has no ideology, no formal structure, and no public existence. It is built out of sentiments and loyalties that die with its members, but it is no less real for all that. The descent lines of men are born and nourished in the uterine families of women, and it is here that a male ideology that excludes women makes its accommodations with reality.

Women in rural Taiwan do not live their lives in the walled courtyards of their husbands' households. If they did, they might be as powerless as their stereotype. It is in their relations in the outside world (and for women in rural Taiwan that world consists almost entirely of the village) that women develop sufficient backing to maintain some independence under their powerful mothers-in-law and even occasionally to bring the men's world to terms. A successful venture into the men's world is no small feat when one recalls that the men of a village were born there and are often related to one another, whereas the women are unlikely to have either the ties of childhood or the ties of kinship to unite them. All the same, the needs, shared interests, and common problems of women are reflected in every village in a loosely knit society that can when needed be called on to exercise considerable influence.

Women carry on as many of their activities as possible outside the house. They wash clothes on the riverbank, clean and pare vegetables at a communal pump, mend under a tree that is a known meetingplace, and stop to rest on a bench or group of stones with other women. There is a continual moving back and forth between kitchens, and conversations are carried on from open doorways through the long, hot afternoons of summer. The shy young girl who enters the village as a bride is examined as frankly and suspiciously by the women as an animal that is up for sale. If she is deferential to her elders, does not criticize or compare her new world unfavorably with the one she has left, the older residents will gradually accept her presence on the edge of their conversations and stop changing the topic to general subjects when she brings the family laundry to scrub on the rocks near them. As the young bride meets other girls in her position, she makes allies for the future, but she must also develop relationships with the older women. She learns to use considerable discretion in making and receiving confidences, for a girl who gossips freely about the affairs of her husband's household may find herself labeled a troublemaker. On the other hand, a girl who is too reticent may find herself always on the outside of the group, or worse yet, accused of snobbery. I described in *The House of Lim* the plight of Lim Chui-ieng, who had little village backing in her troubles with her husband and his family as the result of her arrogance toward the women's community. In Peihotien the young wife of the storekeeper's son suffered a similar lack of support. Warned by her husband's parents not to be too "easy" with the other villagers lest they try to buy things on credit, she obeyed to the point of being considered unfriendly by the women of the village. When she began to have serious troubles with her husband and eventually his family, there was no one in the village she could turn to for solace, advice, and, most important, peacemaking.

Once a young bride has established herself as a member of the women's community, she has also established for herself a certain amount of protection. If the members of her husband's family step beyond the limits of propriety in their treatment of her — such as refusing to allow her to return to her natal home for her brother's wedding or beating her without serious justification — she can complain to a woman friend, preferably older, while they are washing vegetables at the communal pump. The story will quickly spread to the other women, and one of them will take it on herself to check the facts with another member of the girl's household. For a few days the matter will be thoroughly discussed whenever a few women gather. In a young wife's first few years in the community, she can expect to have her mother-in-law's side of any disagreement given fuller weight than her own — her mother-in-law has, after all, been a part of the community a lot longer. However, the discussion itself will serve to curb many offenses. Even if the older woman knows that public opinion is falling to her side, she will still be somewhat more judicious about refusing her daughter-in-law's next request. Still, the daughter-in-law who hopes to make use of the village forum to depose her mother-in-law or at least gain herself special privilege will discover just how important the prerogatives of age and length of residence are.

Although the women can serve as a powerful protective force for their defenseless younger members, they are also a very conservative force in the village.

Taiwanese women can and do make use of their collective power to lose face for their menfolk in order to influence decisions that are ostensibly not theirs to make. Although young women may have little or no influence over their husbands and would not dare express an unsolicited opinion (and perhaps not even a solicited one) to their fathers-in-law, older women who have raised their sons properly retain considerable influence over their sons' actions, even in activities exclusive to men. Further, older women who have displayed years of good judgment are regularly consulted by their husbands about major as well as minor economic and social projects. But even men who think themselves free to ignore the opinions of their women are never free of their own concept, face. It is much easier to lose face than to have face. We once asked a male friend in Peihotien just what "having face" amounted to. He replied, "When no one is talking about a family, you can say it has face." This is precisely where women wield their power. When a man behaves in a way that they consider wrong, they talk about him — not only among themselves, but to their sons and husbands. No one "tells him how to mind his own business," but it becomes abundantly clear that he is losing face and by continuing in this manner may bring shame to the family of his ancestors and descendants. Few men will risk that.

The rules that a Taiwanese man must learn and obey to be a successful member of his society are well developed, clear, and relatively easy to stay within. A Taiwanese woman must also learn the rules, but if she is to be a successful woman, she must learn not to stay within them, but to *appear* to stay within them; to manipulate them, but not to appear to be manipulating them; to teach them to her children, but not to depend on her children for her protection. A truly successful Taiwanese woman is a rugged individualist who has learned to depend largely on herself while appearing to lean on her father, her husband, and her son. The contrast between the terrified young bride and the loud, confident, often lewd old woman who has outlived her mother-in-law and her husband reflects the tests met and passed by not strictly following the rules and by making purposeful use of those who must. The Chinese male's conception of women as "narrow-hearted" and socially inept may well be his vague recognition of this facet of women's power and technique.

The women's subculture in rural Taiwan is, I believe, below the level of consciousness. Mothers do not tell their about-to-be-married daughters how to establish themselves in village society so that they may have some protection from an oppressive family situation, nor do they warn them to gather their children into an exclusive circle under their own control. But girls grow up in village society and see their mothers and sisters-in-law settling their differences to keep them from a public airing or presenting them for the women's community to judge. Their mothers have created around them the meaningful unit in their fathers' households, and when they are desperately lonely and unhappy in the households of their husbands, what they long for is what they have lost. . . . [Some] areas in the subculture of women . . . mesh perfectly into the main culture of the society. The two cultures are not symbiotic because they are not sufficiently independent of one another, but neither do they share identical goals or necessarily use the same means to reach the goals they do share. Outside the village the women's subculture seems not to exist. The uterine family also has no public existence, and appears almost as a response to the traditional family organized in terms of a male ideology.

REVIEW QUESTIONS

1. According to Wolf, what is a uterine family and what relatives are likely to be members?

2. Why is the uterine family important to Chinese women who live in their husband's patrilineal extended families?

3. What is the relationship between a woman's uterine family and her power within her husband's family?

4. Why might the existence of the uterine family contribute to the division of extended families into smaller constituent parts?

5. How do you think a Chinese woman's desire to have a uterine family affects attempts to limit the Chinese population?

VI

Roles and Inequality

For most of us, social interaction is unconscious and automatic. We associate with other people from the time we are born. Of course we experience moments when we feel socially awkward and out of place, but generally we learn to act toward others with confidence. Yet our unconscious ease masks an enormously complex process. When we enter a social situation, how do we know what to do? What should we say? How are we supposed to act? Are we dressed appropriately? Are we talking to the right person? Without knowing it, we have learned a complex set of cultural categories for social interaction that enables us to estimate the social situation, identify the people in it, act appropriately, and recognize larger groups of people.

Status and role are basic to social intercourse. *Status* refers to the categories of different kinds of people who interact. The old saying, "You can't tell the players without a program," goes for our daily associations as well. Instead of a program, however, we identify the actors by a range of signs from the way they dress to the claims they make about themselves. Most statuses are named, so we may be heard to say things like, "That's President Gavin," or "She's a lawyer," when we explain social situations to others. This identification of actors is a prerequisite for appropriate social interaction.

Social roles are the rules for action associated with particular statuses. We use them to interpret and generate social behavior. For example, a professor plays a role in the classroom. Although often not conscious of this role, the professor will stand, use the blackboard, look at notes, and speak with a slightly more formal air than usual. The professor does not wear blue jeans and a T-shirt, chew gum, sit cross-legged on the podium, or sing. These actions might be appropriate for this person when assuming the identity of "friend" at a party, but they are out of place in the classroom.

People also always relate to each other in *social situations,* the settings in which social interaction takes place. Social situations consist of a combination of times, places, objects, and events. For example, if we see a stranger carrying a television set across campus at four o'clock in the afternoon, we will probably ignore the activity. Most likely someone is simply moving. But if we see the same person carrying the set at four in the morning, we may suspect a theft. Only the time has changed, but it is a significant marker of the social situation. Similarly, we expect classrooms to be associated with lectures, and stethoscopes to be part of medical exams. Such places and objects mark the social situations of which they are part.

Some degree of inequality is part of most human interaction. One spouse may dominate another; a child may receive more attention than his or her siblings; the boss's friends may be promoted faster than other employees. But inequality becomes most noticeable when it systematically affects whole classes of people. In its most obvious form, inequality emerges as *social stratification,* which is characterized by regularly experienced unequal access to valued economic resources and prestige.

Anthropologists recognize at least two kinds of social stratification, class and caste. *Class* stratification restricts individuals' access to valued resources and prestige within a partially flexible system. Although it is often a difficult process, individuals may change rank in a class system if they manage to acquire the necessary prerequisites.

Many sociologists and anthropologists believe that there is an American class system and use terms such as *lower class, working class, middle class,* and *upper class* to designate the unequal positions within it. Americans born into poverty lack access to goods and prestige in this system, but can change class standing if they acquire wealth and symbols of higher standing on a continuing basis. Upward mobility is difficult to achieve, however, and few people at the bottom of the system manage to change rank significantly. Indeed, many social scientists feel there is now a permanent underclass in the United States.

Caste defines a second kind of social stratification, one based on permanent membership. People are born into castes and cannot change membership, no matter what they do. In India, for example, caste is a pervasive feature of social organization. South Asians are born into castes and remain members for life; intercaste marriage is forbidden. In the past, castes formed the building blocks of rural Indian society. They were governed by strict rules of deference and served to allocate access to jobs, land, wealth, and power. Cash labor and new industrial jobs have eroded the economic aspect of the system today, but caste persists as a form of rank throughout most of the Indian subcontinent.

Several anthropologists and sociologists have argued that American racial groups are the equivalent of Indian castes. Black and white Americans keep their racial identity for life; nothing can change one's race. Racial identity clearly affects chances for the acquisition of prestige and economic success.

Caste identity, whether Indian or American, tends to preserve and create cultural difference. There is noticeable cultural variation among members of castes in most Indian villages, just as cultural variation occurs among black and white people in the United States. (See Kochman's article reprinted earlier in this book for examples of cross-racial cultural differences.)

Using the idea of social stratification, anthropologists have constructed a rough classification of societies into three types: egalitarian, rank, and stratified. *Egalitarian* societies lack formal social stratification. They may display inequality in personal relations based on age, gender, and personal ability, but no category of persons within the same sex or age group has special privilege. Hunter/gatherer societies are most likely to be egalitarian.

Rank societies contain unequal access to prestige, but not to valued economic resources. In such societies there may be chiefs or other persons with authority and prestige, and they may gain access to rank by birth, but their positions give them no substantial economic advantage. Horticultural societies, including some chiefdomships, fit this category.

Stratified societies organize around formal modes of social stratification, as their name suggests. Members of stratified societies are likely to form classes or castes, and inequality affects access to both prestige and economic resources. Most complex societies, including agrarian and industrialized states, fit into this type.

Inequality may also be based on other human attributes, such as age and gender. In many societies, including our own, age and gender affect access to prestige, power, and resources. It is common for men to publicly outrank women along these dimensions, particularly in societies threatened by war or other adversity that requires male intervention.

The articles in this section illustrate the concepts of status, role, and inequality. The first, by Enid Schildkrout, discusses the role of children in Moslem northern Nigeria. Children experience remarkable independence as they market goods produced by their mothers, who must stay out of public view. The second article, by Ernestine Friedl, explores the reasons behind differences in power experienced by women in hunting and gathering societies. Friedl concludes that women's power is governed by access to public resources. Elizabeth and Robert Fernea describe the importance of the veil as a symbol defining the role and rank of women in the Middle East. Finally, Thomas Gladwin explores the problem of low-class mobility in his article on American poverty. Burdened by higher costs and low income, the poor lack the resources to escape their depressed status.

KEY TERMS

role	caste
status	racial inequality
social situation	egalitarian societies
inequality	rank societies
social stratification	stratified societies
class	sexual inequality

READINGS IN THIS SECTION

17   Children's Roles: Young Traders
of Northern Nigeria
ENID SCHILDKROUT

*Age is an important condition of status and role in every society.
For example, anthropologist Jane Goodale identifies ten age
grades (cultural categories that identify stages of biological matur-
ation) in the lives of Tiwi women living on Melville Island, North
Australia. Americans recognize the existence of age grades when
they use such terms as* infant, grade schooler, young marrieds, *and*
retirees. *In both societies, age grade identification shapes expected
behavior. Many societies treat childhood as special, but their visions of this time of life are not necessarily the same. American
children, for example, should work hard at school; they must be
taught independence, yet remain protected from "adult" topics. In
northern Nigeria, however, Hausa children are expected to take on
an active economic role early, as Enid Schildkrout shows in this
article. Because their mothers, who produce goods for sale, are
constrained by* purdah *(see Article 19 in this section), children do
the actual trading and procurement of raw materials in the public
world. This adultlike role may collapse, however, if the Nigerian
government implements a "development program" requiring children to attend school.*

Thirty years ago, Erik Erikson wrote that "the fashionable insistence
on dramatizing the dependence of children on adults often blinds us

to the dependence of the older generation on the younger one." As a psychoanalyst, Erikson was referring mainly to the emotional bonds between parents and children, but his observation is a reminder that in many parts of the world, adults depend on children in quite concrete ways. In northern Nigeria, children with trays balanced on their heads, carrying and selling a variety of goods for their mothers or themselves, are a common sight in villages and towns. Among the Muslim Hausa, aside from being a useful educational experience, this children's trade, as well as children's performance of household chores and errands, complements the activity of adults and is socially and economically significant.

Children's services are especially important to married Hausa women, who, in accordance with Islamic practices, live in *purdah,* or seclusion. In Nigeria, *purdah* is represented not so much by the wearing of the veil but by the mud-brick walls surrounding every house or compound and by the absence of women in the markets and the streets. Women could not carry out their domestic responsibilities, not to mention their many income-earning enterprises, without the help of children, who are free from the rigid sexual segregation that so restricts adults. Except for elderly women, only children can move in and out of their own and other people's houses without violating the rules of *purdah.* Even children under three years of age are sent on short errands, for example, to buy things for their mothers.

Hausa-speaking people are found throughout West Africa and constitute the largest ethnic group in northern Nigeria, where they number over eighteen million. Their adherence to Islam is a legacy of the centuries during which Arabs came from the north to trade goods of North African and European manufacture. The majority of the Hausa are farmers, but markets and large commercial cities have existed in northern Nigeria since long before the period of British colonial rule. The city of Kano, for example, which was a major emporium for the trans-Saharan caravan trade, dates back to the eighth century. Today it has a population of about one million.

Binta is an eleven-year-old girl who lives in Kano, in a mud-brick house that has piped water but no electricity. The household includes her father and mother, her three brothers, her father's second wife and her three children, and a foster child, who is the daughter of one of Binta's cousins. By Kano standards, it is a middle-income family. Binta's father sells shoes, and her mother cooks and sells bean cakes and *tuwo,* the stiff porridge made of guinea corn (*Sorghum vulgare*), which is the Hausa staple. Binta described for me one day's round of activities, which began very early when she arose to start trading.

"After I woke up, I said my prayers and ate breakfast. Then I went outside the house to sell the bean cakes my mother makes every morning. Soon my mother called me in and asked me to take more bean cakes around town to sell; she spoke to me about making an effort to sell as much as I usually do. I sold forty-eight bean cakes at one kobo each [one kobo is worth one and a half cents]. After I returned home, some people came to buy more cakes from me. Then I went out for a second round of trading before setting out for Arabic school. I study the Koran there every morning from eight to nine.

"When school was over, I washed and prepared to sell *tuwo*. First my mother sent me to another neighborhood to gather the customers' empty bowls. I also collected the money from our regular customers. My mother put the *tuwo* in the bowls and told me the amount of money to collect for each. Then I delivered them to the customers.

"On my way home, a man in the street, whom I know, sent me on an errand to buy him fifteen kobo worth of food; he gave me a reward of one kobo. I then sold some more *tuwo* outside our house by standing there and shouting for customers. When the *tuwo* was finished, I was sent to another house to buy some guinea corn, and one of the women there asked me to bring her one of my mother's big pots. The pot was too heavy for me to carry, but finally one of my brothers helped me take it to her.

"When I returned, my mother was busy pounding some grain, and she sent me out to have some locust bean seeds pounded. She then sent me to pick up three bowls of pounded guinea corn, and she gave me money to take to the woman who had pounded it. The woman told me to remind my mother that she still owed money from the day before.

"When I came home I was sent out to trade again, this time with salt, bouillon cubes, and laundry detergent in small packets. Afterward I prepared some pancakes using ingredients I bought myself — ten kobo worth of flour, one kobo worth of salt, five kobo worth of palm oil, and ten kobo worth of firewood. I took this food outside to sell it to children.

"My mother then gave me a calabash of guinea corn to take for grinding; my younger sister also gave me two calabashes of corn to take. The man who ran the grinding machine advised me that I should not carry such a large load, so I made two trips on the way back. He gave me and my younger brothers, who accompanied me, one kobo each.

"I was then told to take a bath, which I did. After that I was sent to visit a sick relative who was in the hospital. On the way I met a friend, and we took the bus together. I also bought some cheese at the market for five kobo. I met another friend on the way home, and she bought some fish near the market for ten kobo and gave me some. I played on the way to the hospital. When I got home, I found the women of the house preparing a meal. One of them was already eating, and I was invited to eat with her.

"After nightfall, I was sent to take some spices for pounding, and I wasted a lot of time there. The other children and I went to a place where some fruits and vegetables are sold along the street. We bought vegetables for soup for fifty kobo, as my mother had asked me to do. By the time I got home it was late, so I went to sleep."

Binta's many responsibilities are typical for a girl her age. Like many women, Binta's mother relies upon her children in carrying out an occupation at home. Although *purdah* implies that a woman will be supported by her husband and need not work, most Hausa women do work, keeping their incomes distinct from the household budget. Women usually cook one main meal a day and purchase their other meals from other women. In this way they are able to use their time earning a living instead of performing only unpaid domestic labor.

Among the Hausa, men and women spend relatively little time together, eating separately and, except in certain ritual contexts, rarely doing the same things. Differences in gender are not as important among children, however. In fact, it is precisely because children's activities are not rigidly defined by sex that they are able to move between the world of women, centered in the inner courtyard of the house, and the world of men, whose activities take place mainly outside the home. Children of both sexes care for younger children, go to the market, and help their mothers cook.

Both boys and girls do trading, although it is more common for girls. From the age of about five until marriage, which is very often at about age twelve for girls, many children like Binta spend part of every day selling such things as fruits, vegetables, and nuts; bouillon cubes, bread, and small packages of detergent, sugar, or salt; and bowls of steaming rice or *tuwo*. If a woman embroiders, children buy the thread and later take the finished product to the client or to an agent who sells it.

Women in *purdah* frequently change their occupations depending on the availability of child helpers. In Kano, women often trade in commodities that can be sold in small quantities, such as various kinds of cooked food. Sewing, embroidery, mat weaving, and other craft activities (including, until recently, spinning) are less remunerative occupations, and women pursue them when they have fewer children around to help. Unlike the situation common in the United States, where children tend to hamper a woman's ability to earn money, the Hausa woman finds it difficult to earn income without children's help. Often, if a woman has no children of her own, a relative's child will come to live with her.

Child care is another service children perform that benefits women. It enables mothers to devote themselves to their young infants, whom they carry on their backs until the age of weaning, between one and two. Even though women are always at home, they specifically delegate the care of young children to older ones. The toddler moves from the mother's back into a group of older children, who take the responsibility very seriously. Until they are old enough, children do not pick up infants or very young children, but by the age of nine, both boys and girls bathe young children, play with them, and take them on errands. The older children do a great deal of direct and indirect teaching of younger ones. As soon as they can walk, younger children accompany their older siblings to Arabic school. There the children sit with their age-mates, and the teacher gives them lessons according to their ability.

Much of a child's activity is directed toward helping his or her parents, but other relatives — grandparents, aunts, uncles, and stepmothers — and adults living in the same house as servants or tenants may call on a child of limited tasks without asking permission of the parents. Like other Muslims, Hausa men may have up to four wives, and these women freely call on each other's children to perform household chores. Even strangers in the street sometimes ask a child to do an errand, such as delivering a message, particularly if the chore requires entering a house to which the adult does not have access. The child will be rewarded with a small amount of money or food.

Adults other than parents also reprimand children, who are taught very early to obey the orders of grownups. Without ever directly refusing to obey a command, however, children do devise numerous strategies of noncompliance, such as claiming that another adult has already co-opted their time or simply leaving the scene and ignoring the command. Given children's greater mobility, there is little an adult can do to enforce compliance.

Besides working on behalf of adults, children also participate in a "children's economy." Children have their own money — from school allowances given to them daily for the purchase of snacks, from gifts, from work they may have done, and even from their own investments. For example, boys make toys for sale, and they rent out valued property, such as slide viewers or bicycles. Just as women distinguish their own enterprises from the labor they do as wives, children regard the work they do for themselves differently from the work they do on behalf of their mothers. When Binta cooks food for sale, using materials she has purchased with her own money, the profits are entirely her own, although she may hand the money over to her mother for safekeeping.

Many girls begin to practice cooking by the age of ten. They do not actually prepare the family meals, for this heavy and tedious work is primarily the wives' responsibility. But they do carry out related chores, such as taking vegetables out for grinding, sifting flour, and washing bowls. Many also cook food for sale on their own. With initial help from their mothers or other adult female relatives, who may give them a cooking pot, charcoal, or a small stove, children purchase small amounts of ingredients and prepare various snacks. Since they sell their products for less than the adult women do, and since the quantities are very small, their customers are mainly children. Child entrepreneurs even extend credit to other children.

Aisha is a ten-year-old girl who was notoriously unsuccessful as a trader. She disliked trading and regularly lost her mother's investment. Disgusted, her mother finally gave her a bit of charcoal, some flour and oil, and a small pot. Aisha set up a little stove outside her house and began making small pancakes, which she sold to very young children. In three months she managed to make enough to buy a new dress, and in a year she bought a pair of shoes. She had clearly chosen her occupation after some unhappy trials at street trading.

In the poorest families, as in Aisha's, the profit from children's work goes toward living expenses. This may occur in households that are headed by divorced or widowed women. It is also true for the *al-majirai*, or Arabic students, who often live with their teachers. The proceeds of most children's economic activity, however, go to the expenses of marriage. The income contributes to a girl's dowry and to a boy's bridewealth, both of which are considered investments.

The girl's dowry includes many brightly painted enamel, brass, and glass bowls, collected years before marriage. These utensils are known as *kayan daki,* or "things of the room." After the wedding they are stacked in a large cupboard beside the girl's bed. Very few of them are used, but they are always proudly displayed, except during the mourning period if the husband dies. *Kayan daki* are not simply for conspicuous display, however. They remain the property of the woman unless she sells them or gives them away. In the case of divorce or financial need, they can provide her most important and immediate source of economic security.

Kayan daki traditionally consisted of brass bowls and beautifully carved calabashes. Today the most common form is painted enamel bowls manufactured in Nigeria or abroad. The styles and designs change frequently, and the cost is continually rising. Among the wealthier urban women and the Western-educated women, other forms of modern household equipment, including electric appliances and china tea sets, are becoming part of the dowry.

The money a young girl earns on her own, as well as the profits she brings home through her trading, are invested by her mother or guardian in *kayan daki* in anticipation of her marriage. Most women put the major part of their income into their daughters' *kayan daki,* as well as helping their sons with marriage expenses. When a woman has many children, the burden can be considerable.

For girls, marriage, which ideally coincides with puberty, marks the transition to adult status. If a girl marries as early as age ten, she does not cook for her husband or have sexual relations with him for some time, but she enters *purdah* and loses the freedom of childhood. Most girls are married by age fifteen, and for many the transition is a difficult one.

Boys usually do not marry until they are over twenty and are able to support a family. They also need to have raised most of the money to cover the cost of getting married. Between the ages of eight and ten, however, they gradually begin to move away from the confines of the house and to regard it as a female domain. They begin taking their food outside and eating it with friends, and they roam much farther than girls in their play activities. By the onset of puberty, boys have begun to observe the rules of *purdah* by refraining from entering the houses of all but their closet relatives. In general, especially if they have sisters, older boys spend less time than girls doing chores and errands and more time playing and, in recent years, going to school. Traditionally, many boys left home to live and study with an Arabic teacher. Today many also pursue Western education, sometimes in boarding school. Although the transition to adulthood is less abrupt for boys, childhood for both sexes ends by age twelve to fourteen.

As each generation assumes the responsibilities of adulthood and the restrictions of sexual separation, it must rely on the younger members of society who can work around the *purdah* system. Recently, however, the introduction of Western education has begun to threaten this traditional arrangement, in part just by altering the pattern of children's lives.

The Nigerian government is now engaged in a massive program to provide Western education to all school-age children. This program has been undertaken for sound economic and political reasons. During the colonial period, which ended in the early 1960s, the British had a "hands-off" policy regarding education in northern Nigeria. They ruled through the Islamic political and judicial hierarchy and supported the many Arabic schools, where the Koran and Islamic law, history, and religion were taught. The British discouraged the introduction of Christian mission schools in the north and spent little on government schools.

The pattern in the rest of Nigeria was very different. In the non-Muslim areas of the country, mission and government schools grew rapidly during the colonial period. The result of this differential policy was the development of vast regional imbalances in the extent and level of Western education in the country. This affected the types of occupational choices open to Nigerians from different regions. Despite a longer tradition of literacy in Arabic in the north, few northerners were eligible for those civil service jobs that required literacy in English, the language of government business. This was one of many issues in the tragic civil war that tore Nigeria apart in the 1960s. The current goal of enrolling all northern children in public schools, which offer training in English and secular subjects, has, therefore, a strong and valid political rationale.

Western education has met a mixed reception in northern Nigeria. While it has been increasingly accepted for boys — as an addition to, not a substitute for, Islamic education — many parents are reluctant to enroll their daughters in primary school. Nevertheless, there are already many more children waiting to get into school than there are classrooms and teachers to accommodate them. If the trend continues, it will almost certainly have important, if unintended, consequences for *purdah* and the system of child enterprise that supports it.

Children who attend Western school continue to attend Arabic school, and thus are removed from the household for much of the day. For many women this causes considerable difficulty in doing daily housework. It means increased isolation and a curtailment of income-producing activity. It creates a new concern about where to obtain the income for children's marriages. As a result of these practical pressures, the institution of *purdah* will inevitably be challenged. Also, the schoolgirl of today may develop new skills and new expectations of her role as a woman that conflict with the traditional ways. As Western education takes hold, today's young traders may witness a dramatic change in Hausa family life — for themselves as adults and for their children.

REVIEW QUESTIONS

1. What roles do children play in the Hausa economy?
2. What is the difference between the women's economy and the children's economy?
3. What part do children play in the maintenance of Muslim-organized Hausa society?
4. The Nigerian government's development plans include schooling for children. What effects will this change have on the traditional social order?

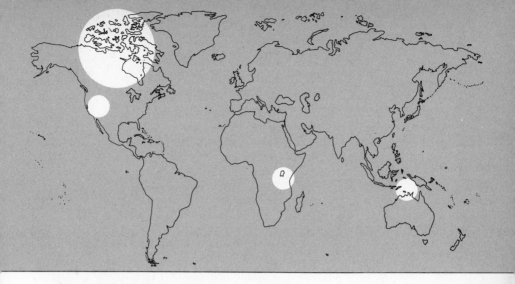

18 Society and Sex Roles

ERNESTINE FRIEDL

Many anthropologists claim that males hold formal authority over females in every society. Although the degree of masculine author-ity may vary from one group to the next, males always have more power. For some researchers, this unequal male-female relation-ship is the result of biological inheritance. As with other primates, they argue, male humans are naturally more aggressive, females more docile. Ernestine Friedl challenges this explanation in this se-lection. Comparing a variety of hunting and gathering groups, she concludes that relations between men and women are shaped by a culturally defined division of labor based on sex, not by inherited predisposition. Given access to resources that circulate publicly, women can attain equal or dominant status in any society, includ-ing our own.

"Women must respond quickly to the demands of their husbands," says anthropolgist Napoleon Chagnon, describing the horticultural Yanomamö Indians of Venezuela. When a man returns from a hunting trip, "the woman, no matter what she is doing, hurries home and quietly but rapidly prepares a meal for her husband. Should the wife be slow in doing this, the husband is within his rights to beat her. Most reprimands . . . take the form of blows with the hand or with a piece of firewood. . . . Some of them chop their wives with the sharp

From *Human Nature,* April 1978. Copyright © 1978 by Human Nature, Inc. Reprinted by permission of the publisher.

edge of a machete or axe, or shoot them with a barbed arrow in some nonvital area, such as the buttocks or leg."

Among the Semai agriculturalists of central Malaya, when one person refuses the request of another, the offended party suffers *punan,* a mixture of emotional pain and frustration. "Enduring *punan* is commonest when a girl has refused the victim her sexual favors," reports Robert Dentan. "The jilted man's 'heart becomes sad.' He loses his energy and his appetite. Much of the time he sleeps, dreaming of his lost love. In this state he is in fact very likely to injure himself 'accidentally.'" The Semai are afraid of violence; a man would never strike a woman.

The social relationship between men and women has emerged as one of the principal disputes occupying the attention of scholars and the public in recent years. Although the discord is sharpest in the United States, the controversy has spread throughout the world. Numerous national and international conferences, including one in Mexico sponsored by the United Nations, have drawn together delegates from all walks of life to discuss such questions as the social and political rights of each sex and even the basic nature of males and females.

Whatever their position, partisans often invoke examples from other cultures to support their ideas about the proper role of each sex. Because women are clearly subservient to men in many societies, like the Yanomamö, some experts conclude that the natural pattern is for men to dominate. But among the Semai no one has the right to command others, and in West Africa women are often chiefs. The place of women in these societies supports the argument of those who believe that sex roles are not fixed, that if there is a natural order, it allows for many different arrangements.

The argument will never be settled as long as the opposing sides toss examples from the world's cultures at each other like intellectual stones. But the effect of biological differences on male and female behavior can be clarified by looking at known examples of the earliest forms of human society and examining the relationship between technology, social organization, environment, and sex roles. The problem is to determine the conditions in which different degrees of male dominance are found, to try to discover the social and cultural arrangements that give rise to equality or inequality between the sexes, and to attempt to apply this knowledge to our understanding of the changes taking place in modern industrial society.

As Western history and the anthropological record have told us, equality between the sexes is rare; in most known societies females are subordinate. Male dominance is so widespread that it is virtually a human universal; societies in which women are consistently dominant do not exist and have never existed.

Evidence of a society in which women control all strategic resources like food and water, and in which women's activities are the most prestigious, has never been found. The Iroquois of North America and the Lovedu of Africa came closest. Among the Iroquois, women raised food, controlled its distribution, and helped to choose male political leaders. Lovedu women ruled as queens, exchanged valuable cattle, led ceremonies, and controlled their own sex lives. But among both the Iroquois and Lovedu, men owned the land and held other positions of power and prestige. Women were equal to men; they did not have ultimate authority over them. Neither culture was a true matriarchy.

Patriarchies are prevalent, and they appear to be strongest in societies in which men control significant goods that are exchanged with people outside the family. Regardless of who produces food, the person who gives it to others creates the obligations and alliances that are at the center of all political relations. The greater the male monopoly on the distribution of scarce items, the stronger their control of women seems to be. This is most obvious in relatively simple hunter-gatherer societies.

Hunter-gatherers, or foragers, subsist on wild plants, small land animals, and small river or sea creatures gathered by hand; large land animals and sea mammals hunted with spears, bows and arrows, and blow guns; and fish caught with hooks and nets. The three hundred thousand hunter-gatherers alive in the world today include the Eskimos, the Australian aborigines, and the Pygmies of Central Africa.

Foraging has endured for two million years and was replaced by farming and animal husbandry only ten thousand years ago; it covers more than 99 percent of human history. Our foraging ancestry is not far behind us and provides a clue to our understanding of the human condition.

Hunter-gatherers are people whose ways of life are technologically simple and socially and politically egalitarian. They live in small groups of 50 to 200 and have neither kings, nor priests, nor social classes. These conditions permit anthropologists to observe the essential bases for inequalities between the sexes without the distortions induced by the complexities of contemporary industrial society.

The source of male power among hunter-gatherers lies in their control of a scarce, hard to acquire, but necessary nutrient — animal protein. When men in a hunter-gatherer society return to camp with game, they divide the meat in some customary way. Among the !Kung San of Africa, certain parts of the animal are given to the owner of the arrow that killed the beast, to the first hunter to sight the game, to the one who threw the first spear, and to all men in the hunting party. After the meat has been divided, each hunter distributes his share to his blood relatives and his in-laws, who in turn share it with others. If an animal is large enough, every member of the band will receive some meat.

Vegetable foods, in contrast, are not distributed beyond the immediate household. Women give food to their children, to their husbands, to other members of the household, and rarely, to the occasional visitor. No one outside the family regularly eats any of the wild fruits and vegetables that are gathered by the women.

The meat distributed by the men is a public gift. Its source is widely known, and the donor expects a reciprocal gift when other men return from a successful hunt. He gains honor as a supplier of a scarce item and simultaneously obligates others to him.

These obligations constitute a form of power or control over others, both men and women. The opinions of hunters play an important part in decisions to move the village; good hunters attract the most desirable women; people in other groups join camps with good hunters; and hunters, because they already participate in an internal system of exchange, control exchange with other groups for flint, salt, and steel axes. The male monopoly on hunting unites men in a system of exchange and gives them power; gathering vegetable food does not give women equal power even among foragers who live in the tropics, where the food collected by women provides more than half the hunter-gatherer diet.

If dominance arises from a monopoly on big-game hunting, why has the male monopoly remained unchallenged? Some women are strong enough to participate in the hunt and their endurance is certainly equal to that of men. Dobe San women of the Kalahari Desert in Africa walk an average of 10 miles a day carrying from 15 to 33 pounds of food plus a baby.

Women do not hunt, I believe, because of four interrelated factors: variability in the supply of game; the different skills required for hunting and gathering; the incompatability between carrying burdens and hunting; and the small size of seminomadic foraging populations.

Because the meat supply is unstable, foragers must make frequent expeditions to provide the band with gathered food. Environmental factors such as seasonal and annual variation in rainfall often affect the size of the wildlife population. Hunters cannot always find game, and when they do encounter animals, they are not always successful in killing their prey. In northern latitudes, where meat is the primary food, periods of starvation are known in every generation. The irregularity of the game supply leads hunter-gatherers in areas where plant foods are available to depend on these predictable foods a good part of the time. Someone must gather the fruits, nuts, and roots and carry them back to camp to feed unsuccessful hunters, children, the elderly, and anyone who might not have gone foraging that day.

Foraging falls to the women because hunting and gathering cannot be combined on the same expedition. Although gatherers sometimes notice signs of game as they work, the skills required to track game are not the same as those required to find edible roots or plants. Hunters scan the horizon and the land for traces of large game; gatherers keep their eyes to the ground, studying the distribution of plants and the texture of the soil for hidden roots and animal holes. Even if a woman who was collecting plants came across the track of an antelope, she could not follow it; it is impossible to carry a load and hunt at the same time. Running with a heavy load is difficult, and should the animal be sighted, the hunter would be off balance and could neither shoot an arrow nor throw a spear accurately.

Pregnancy and child care would also present difficulties for a hunter. An unborn child affects a woman's body balance, as does a child in her arms, on her back, or slung at her side. Until they are two years old, many hunter-gatherer children are carried at all times, and until they are four, they are carried some of the time.

An observer might wonder why young women do not hunt until they become pregnant, or why mature women and men do not hunt and gather on alternate days, with some women staying in camp to act as wet nurses for the young. Apart from the effects hunting might have on a mother's milk production, there are two reasons. First, young girls begin to bear children as soon as they are physically mature and strong enough to hunt, and second, hunter-gatherer bands are so small that there are unlikely to be enough lactating women to serve as wet nurses. No hunter-gatherer group could afford to maintain a specialized female hunting force.

Because game is not always available, because hunting and gathering are specialized skills, because women carrying heavy loads cannot hunt, and because women in hunter-gatherer societies are usually either pregnant or caring for young children, for most of the last two million years of human history men have hunted and women have gathered.

If male dominance depends on controlling the supply of meat, then the degree of male dominance in a society should vary with the amount of meat available and the amount supplied by the men. Some regions, like the East African grasslands and the North American woodlands, abounded with species of large mammals; other zones, like tropical forests and semideserts, are thinly populated with prey. Many elements affect the supply of game, but theoretically, the less meat provided exclusively by the men, the more egalitarian the society.

All known hunter-gatherer societies fit into four basic types: those in which men and women work together in communal hunts and as teams gathering edible plants, as did the Washo Indians of North

America; those in which men and women each collect their own plant foods although the men supply some meat to the group, as do the Hadza of Tanzania; those in which male hunters and female gatherers work apart but return to camp each evening to share their acquisitions, as do the Tiwi of North Australia; and those in which the men provide all the food by hunting large game, as do the Eskimo. In each case the extent of male dominance increases directly with the proportion of meat supplied by individual men and small hunting parties.

Among the most egalitarian of hunter-gatherer societies are the Washo Indians, who inhabited the valleys of the Sierra Nevada in what is now southern California and Nevada. In the spring they moved north to Lake Tahoe for the large fish runs of sucker and native trout. Everyone — men, women, and children — participated in the fishing. Women spent the summer gathering edible berries and seeds while the men continued to fish. In the fall some men hunted deer, but the most important source of animal protein was the jackrabbit, which was captured in communal hunts. Men and women together drove the rabbits into nets tied end to end. To provide food for the winter, husbands and wives worked as teams in the late fall to collect pine nuts.

Since everyone participated in most food-gathering activities, there were no individual distributors of food and relatively little difference in male and female rights. Men and women were not segregated from each other in daily activities; both were free to take lovers after marriage; both had the right to separate whenever they chose; menstruating women were not isolated from the rest of the group; and one of the two major Washo rituals celebrated hunting while the other celebrated gathering. Men were accorded more prestige if they had killed a deer, and men directed decisions about the seasonal movement of the group. But if no male leader stepped forward, women were permitted to lead. The distinctive feature of groups such as the Washo is the relative equality of the sexes.

The sexes are also relatively equal among the Hadza of Tanzania, but this near-equality arises because men and women tend to work alone to feed themselves. They exchange little food. The Hadza lead a leisurely life in the seemingly barren environment of the East African Rift Gorge, which is, in fact, rich in edible berries, roots, and small game. As a result of this abundance, from the time they are ten years old, Hadza men and women gather much of their own food. Women take their young children with them into the bush, eating as they forage, and collect only enough food for a light family meal in the evening. The men eat berries and roots as they hunt for small game, and should they bring down a rabbit or a hyrax, they eat the meat on the spot. Meat is carried back to the camp and shared with the rest of the group only on those rare occasions when a poisoned arrow brings down a large animal — an impala, a zebra, an eland, or a giraffe.

Because Hadza men distribute little meat, their status is only slightly higher than that of the women. People flock to the camp of a good hunter and the camp might take on his name because of his popularity, but he is in no sense a leader of the group. A Hadza man and a woman have an equal right to divorce, and each can repudiate a marriage simply by living apart for a few weeks. Couples tend to live in the same camp as the wife's mother, but they sometimes make long visits to the camp of the husband's mother. Although a man may take more than one wife, most Hadza males cannot afford to indulge in this luxury. In order to maintain a marriage, a man must supply both his wife and his mother-in-law with some meat and trade goods, such as beads and cloth, and the Hadza economy gives few men the wealth to provide for more than one wife and mother-in-law. Washo equality is based on cooperation; Hadza equality is based on independence.

In contrast to both these groups, among the Tiwi of Melville and Bathurst Islands off the northern coast of Australia, male hunters dominate female gatherers. The Tiwi are representative of the most common form of foraging society, in which the men supply large quantities of meat, although less than half the food consumed by the group. Each morning Tiwi women, most with babies on their backs, scatter in different directions in search of vegetables, grubs, worms, and small game such as bandicoots, lizards, and opossums. To track the game, they use hunting dogs. On most days women return to camp with some meat and with baskets full of *korka,* the nut of a native palm, which is soaked and mashed to make a porridge-like dish. The Tiwi men do not hunt small game and do not hunt every day, but when they do they often return with kangaroo, large lizards, fish, and game birds.

The porridge is cooked separately by each household and rarely shared outside the family, but the meat is prepared by a volunteer cook, who can be male or female. After the cook takes one of the parts of the animal traditionally reserved for him or her, the animal's "boss," the one who caught it, distributes the rest to all near kin and then to all others residing with the band. Although the small game supplied by the women is distributed in the same way as the big game supplied by the men, Tiwi men are dominant because the game they kill provides most of the meat.

The power of Tiwi men is clearest in their betrothal practices. Among the Tiwi, a woman must always be married. To ensure this, female infants are betrothed at birth and widows are remarried at the gravesides of their late husbands. Men form alliances by exchanging daughters, sisters, and mothers in marriage, and some collect as many as twenty-five wives. Tiwi men value the quantity and quality of the food many wives can collect and the many children they can produce.

The dominance of the men is offset somewhat by the influence of adult women in selecting their next husbands. Many women are active strategists in the political careers of their male relatives, but to the exasperation of some sons attempting to promote their own futures, widowed mothers sometimes insist on selecting their own partners. Women also influence the marriages of their daughters and grand-daughters, especially when the selected husband dies before the be-stowed child moves to his camp.

Among the Eskimo, representative of the rarest type of forager society, inequality between the sexes is matched by inequality in supplying the group with food. Inland Eskimo men hunt caribou throughout the year to provision the entire society, and maritime Eskimo men depend on whaling, fishing, and some hunting to feed their extended families. The women process the carcasses, cut and sew skins to make clothing, cook, and care for the young; but they collect no food of their own and depend on the men to supply all the raw materials for their work. Since men provide all the meat, they also control the trade in hides, whale oil, seal oil, and other items that move between the maritime and inland Eskimos.

Eskimo women are treated almost exclusively as objects to be used, abused, and traded by men. After puberty all Eskimo girls are fair game for any interested male. A man shows his intentions by grabbing the belt of a woman, and if she protests, he cuts off her trousers and forces himself upon her. These encounters are considered unimportant by the rest of the group. Men offer their wives' sexual services to establish alliances with trading partners and members of hunting and whaling parties.

Despite the consistent pattern of some degree of male dominance among foragers, most of these societies are egalitarian compared with agricultural and industrial societies. No forager has any significant opportunity for political leadership. Foragers, as a rule, do not like to give or take orders, and assume leadership only with reluctance. Sha-mans (those who are thought to be possessed by spirits) may be either male or female. Public rituals conducted by women in order to cele-brate the first menstruation of girls are common, and the symbolism in these rituals is similar to that in the ceremonies that follow a boy's first kill.

In any society, status goes to those who control the distribution of valued goods and services outside the family. Equality arises when both sexes work side by side in food production, as do the Washo, and the products are simply distributed among the workers. In such circumstances, no person or sex has greater access to valued items than do others. But when women make no contribution to the food supply, as in the case of the Eskimo, they are completely subordinate.

When we attempt to apply these generalizations to contemporary industrial society, we can predict that as long as women spend their discretionary income from jobs on domestic needs, they will gain little social recognition and power. To be an effective source of power, money must be exchanged in ways that require returns and create obligations. In other words, it must be invested.

Jobs that do not give women control over valued resources will do little to advance their general status. Only as managers, executives, and professionals are women in a position to trade goods and services, to do others favors, and therefore to obligate others to them. Only as controllers of valued resources can women achieve prestige, power, and equality.

Within the household, women who bring in income from jobs are able to function on a more nearly equal basis with their husbands. Women who contribute services to their husbands and children without pay, as do some middle-class Western housewives, are especially vulnerable to dominance. Like Eskimo women, as long as their services are limited to domestic distribution they have little power relative to their husbands and none with respect to the outside world.

As for the limits imposed on women by their procreative functions in hunter-gatherer societies, childbearing and child care are organized around work as much as work is organized around reproduction. Some foraging groups space their children three to four years apart and have an average of only four to six children, far fewer than many women in other cultures. Hunter-gatherers nurse their infants for extended periods, sometimes for as long as four years. This custom suppresses ovulation and limits the size of their families. Sometimes, although rarely, they practice infanticide. By limiting reproduction, a woman who is gathering food has only one child to carry.

Different societies can and do adjust the frequency of birth and the care of children to accommodate whatever productive activities women customarily engage in. In horticultural societies, where women work long hours in gardens that may be far from home, infants get food to supplement their mothers' milk, older children take care of younger children, and pregnancies are widely spaced. Throughout the world, if a society requires a woman's labor, it finds ways to care for her children.

In the United States, as in some other industrial societies, the accelerated entry of women with preschool children into the labor force has resulted in the development of a variety of child-care arrangements. Individual women have called on friends, relatives, and neighbors. Public and private child-care centers are growing. We should realize that the declining birth rate, the increasing acceptance of childless or single-child families, and de-emphasis on motherhood are adaptations to a sexual division of labor reminiscent of the system of production found in hunter-gatherer societies.

In many countries where women no longer devote most of their productive years to childbearing, they are beginning to demand a change in the social relationship of the sexes. As women gain access to positions that control the exchange of resources, male dominance may become archaic, and industrial societies may one day become as egalitarian as the Washo.

REVIEW QUESTIONS

1. According to Friedl, what factor accounts for the different degrees of dominance and power between males and females found in hunter-gatherer societies?

2. What are the four types of hunter-gatherer societies considered by Friedl in this article, and what is it about the structure of each that relates to the distribution of power and dominance between males and females?

3. Some anthropologists believe that male dominance is inherited. Comment on this assertion in light of Friedl's article.

4. Why does Friedl believe that women will gain equality with men in industrial society?

19   Symbolizing Roles: Behind the Veil

ELIZABETH W. FERNEA and ROBERT A. FERNEA

*Most societies have some things that serve as key symbols. The
flag of the United States, for example, stands not only for the nation, but for a variety of important values that guide American behavior and perception. In this article, Elizabeth and Robert Fernea
trace the meaning of another key symbol, the veil worn by women
in the Middle East. Instead of reference to a national group, the
veil codes many of the values surrounding the role of women.
Often viewed by Westerners as a symbol of female restriction and
inequality, for the women who wear it the veil signals honor, personal protection, the sanctity and privacy of the family, wealth and
high status, and city life.*

Blue jeans have come to mean America all over the world; three-piece
wool suits signal businessmen; and in the 1980s pink or green hair says
"punk." What do we notice, however, in societies other than our own?
Ishi, the last of a "lost" tribe of North American Indians who stumbled
into twentieth-century California in 1911, is reported to have said that
the truly interesting objects in the white culture were pockets and
matches. Rifa'ah Tahtawi, one of the first young Egyptians to be sent
to Europe to study in 1826, wrote an account of French society in
which he noted that Parisians used many unusual objects of dress,
among them something called a belt. Women wore belts, he said,

---

239

apparently to keep their bosoms erect, and to show off the slimness of their waists and the fullness of their hips. Europeans are still fascinated by the Stetson hats worn by American cowboys; an elderly Dutch woman of our acquaintance recently carried six enormous Stetsons back to the Hague as presents for the male members of her family.

Like languages (Inca, French) or food (tacos, hamburgers), clothing has special meaning for people who wear it that strangers may not understand. But some objects become charged with meaning to other cultures. The veil is one article of clothing used in Middle Eastern societies that stirs strong emotions in the West. "The feminine veil has become a symbol: that of the slavery of one portion of humanity," wrote French ethnologist Germaine Tillion in 1966. A hundred years earlier, Sir Richard Burton, British traveler, explorer, and translator of the *Arabian Nights,* recorded a different view. "Europeans inveigh against this article [the face veil] . . . for its hideousness and jealous concealment of charms made to be admired," he wrote in 1855. "It is, on the contrary, the most coquettish article of women's attire . . . it conceals coarse skins, fleshy noses, wide mouths and vanishing chins, whilst it sets off to best advantage what in these lands is most lustrous and liquid — the eye. Who has not remarked this at a masquerade ball?"

In the present generation, the veil has become a focus of attention for Western writers, both popular and academic, who take a measure of Burton's irony and Tillion's anger to equate modernization of the Middle East with the discarding of the veil and to look at its return in Iran and in a number of Arab countries as a sure sign of retrogression. "Iran's 16 million women have come a long way since their floor-length cotton veil officially was abolished in 1935," an article noted in the 1970s, just before the Shah was toppled. Today [1986], with Ayatollah Khomeini in power, those 16 million Iranian women have put their veils back on again, as if to say that the long way they have come is not in the direction of the West.

The thousands of words written about the appearance and disappearance of the veil and of *purdah* (the seclusion of women) do little to help us understand the Middle East or the cultures that grew out of the same Judeo-Christian roots as our own. The veil and the all-enveloping garments that inevitably accompany it (the *milayah* in Egypt, the *abbayah* in Iraq, the *chadoor* in Iran, the *yashmak* in Turkey, the *burga'* in Afghanistan, and the *djellabah* and the *haik* in North Africa) are only the outward manifestations of cultural practices and meanings that are rooted deep in the history of Mediterranean and Southwest Asian society and are now finding expression once again. Today, with the resurgence of Islam, the veil has become a statement of difference between the Middle East and the Western world, a boundary no easier to cross now than it was during the Crusades or during the nineteenth century, when Western colonial powers ruled the area.

In English, the word *veil* has many definitions, and some of them are religious, just as in the Middle East. In addition to a face cover, the term also means "a piece of material worn over the head and shoulders, a part of a nun's head dress." The Arabic word for veiling and secluding comes from the root word *hajaba,* meaning barrier. A *hijab* is an amulet worn to keep away the evil eye; it also means a diaphragm used to prevent conception. The gatekeeper or doorkeeper who guards the entrance to a government minister's office is a *hijab,* and in a casual conversation a person might say, "I want to be more informal with my friend so-and-so, but she always puts a *hijab* [barrier] between us."

In Islam, the Koranic verse that sanctions a barrier between men and women is called the Sura of the *hijab* (curtain): "Prophet, enjoin your wives, your daughters and the wives of true believers to draw their garments close round them. That is more proper, so that they may be recognized and not molested. Allah is forgiving and merciful." Notice, however, that veils of the first true believers did not conceal but rather announced the religious status of the women who wore them, drawing attention to the fact that they were Muslims and therefore to be treated with respect. The special Islamic dress worn by increasing numbers of modern Muslim women has much the same effect; it also says, "treat me with respect."

Certainly some form of seclusion and of veiling was practiced before the time of Muhammad, at least among the urban elites and ruling families, but it was his followers, the first converts to Islam, who used veiling to signal religious faith. According to historic traditions, the *hijab* was established after the wives of the Prophet Muhammad were insulted by people coming to the mosque in search of the Prophet. Muhammad's wives, they said, had been mistaken for slaves. The custom of the *hijab* was thus established, and in the words of historian Nabia Abbott, "Muhammad's women found themselves, on the one hand, deprived of personal liberty, and on the other hand, raised to a position of honor and dignity." It is true, nonetheless, that the forms and uses of veiling and seclusion have varied greatly in practice over the last thousand years since the time of the Prophet, and millions of Muslim women have never been veiled at all. It is a luxury poorer families cannot afford, since any form of arduous activity, such as working in the fields, makes its use impossible. Thus it is likely that the use of the veil was envied by those who could not afford to do so, for it signaled a style of life that was generally admired. Burton, commenting on the Muslims portrayed in the *Arabian Nights,* says, "The women, who delight in restrictions which tend to their honour, accepted it willingly and still affect it, they do not desire a liberty or rather a license which they have learned to regard as inconsistent with their time-honored notions of feminine decorum and delicacy. They would think very meanly of a husband who permitted them to be exposed, like hetairae, to the public gaze."

The veil bears many messages about its wearers and their society, and many men and women in Middle Eastern communities today would quickly denounce nineteenth-century Orientalists like Sir Richard Burton and deny its importance. Nouha al Hejelan, wife of the Saudi Arabian ambassador to London, told Sally Quinn of *The Washington Post,* "If I wanted to take it all off [the *abbayah* and veil], I would have long ago. It wouldn't mean as much to me as it does to you." Basima Bezirgan, a contemporary Iraqi feminist, says, "Compared to the real issues that are involved between men and women in the Middle East today, the veil itself is unimportant." A Moroccan linguist, who buys her clothes in Paris, laughs when asked about the veil. "My mother wears a *djellabah* and a veil. I have never worn them. But so what? I still cannot get divorced as easily as a man, and I am still a member of my family group and responsible to them for everything I do. What is the veil? A piece of cloth." However, early Middle Eastern feminists felt differently. Huda Sharawi, an early Egyptian activist who formed the first Women's Union, removed her veil in public in 1923, a dramatic gesture to demonstrate her dislike of society's attitude toward women and her defiance of the system.

"The seclusion of women had many purposes," states Egyptian anthropologist Nadia Abu Zahra. "It expresses men's status, power, wealth, and manliness. It also helps preserve men's image of virility and masculinity, but men do not admit this; on the contrary they claim that one of the purposes of the veil is to guard women's honor." The veil and *purdah* are symbols of restriction, in men's behavior as well as women's. A respectable woman wearing conservative Islamic dress today on a public street is signaling, "Hands off! Don't touch me or you'll be sorry." Cowboy Jim Sayre of Deadwood, South Dakota, says, "If you deform a cowboy's hat, he'll likely deform you." A man who approaches a veiled woman is asking for similar trouble; not only the woman but also her family is shamed, and serious problems may result. "It is clear," says Egyptian anthropologist Ahmed Abou Zeid, "that honor and shame which are usually attributed to a certain individual or a certain kinship group have in fact a bearing on the total social structure, since most acts involving honor or shame are likely to affect the existing social equilibrium."

Veiling and seclusion almost always can be related to the maintenance of social status. The extreme example of the way the rich could use this practice was found among the wealthy sultans of pre-revolutionary Turkey. Stories of their women, kept in harems and guarded by eunuchs, formed the basis for much of the Western folklore concerning the nature of male-female relationships in Middle Eastern society. The forbidden nature of seclusion inflamed the Western imagination, but the Westerners who created erotic fantasies in films and novels would not have been able to enter the sultans' palaces any more than they could have penetrated their harems! It was eroticism plus opulence and luxury, the signs of wealth, that captured the imagination of the Westerner — and still does, as witnessed by the popularity of "Dallas" and "Dynasty."

The meaning associated with veiling or a lack of veiling changes according to locality. Most village women in the Egyptian delta have not veiled, nor have the Berber women of North Africa, but no one criticizes them for this. "In the village, no one veils, because everyone is considered a member of the same large family," explained Aisha Bint Muhammad, a working-class wife of Marrakesh. "But in the city, veiling is *sunnah,* required by our religion." Veiling has generally been found in towns and cities, among all classes, where families feel that it is necessary to distinguish themselves from strangers. Some women, who must work without the veil in factories and hotels, may put such garments on when they go out on holidays or even walk on the streets after work.

Veiling and *purdah* not only indicate status and wealth; they also have some religious sanction and protect women from the world outside the home. *Purdah* delineates private space and distinguishes between the public and private sectors of society, as does the traditional architecture of the area. Older Middle Eastern houses do not have picture windows facing on the street, nor do they have walks leading invitingly to front doors. Family life is hidden away from strangers; behind blank walls may lie courtyards and gardens, refuges from the heat, cold, and bustle of the outside world, the world of non-kin that is not to be trusted. Outsiders are pointedly excluded.

Even within the household, among her close relatives, a traditional Muslim woman may veil before those kinsmen whom she could legally marry. If her maternal or paternal cousins, her brothers-in-law, or her sons-in-law come to call, she covers her head, or perhaps her whole face. To do otherwise, to neglect such acts of respect and modesty, would be considered shameless.

The veil does more than protect its wearers from known and unknown intruders; it can also conceal identity. Behind the anonymity of the veil, women can go about a city unrecognized and uncriticized. Nadia Abu Zahra reports anecdotes of men donning women's veils in order to visit their lovers undetected; women may do the same. The veil is such an effective disguise that Nouri Al-Sa'id, the late prime minister of Iraq, attempted to escape death from revolutionary forces in 1958 by wearing the *abbayah* and veil of a woman; only his shoes gave him away. When houses of prostitution were closed in Baghdad in the early 1950s, the prostitutes donned the same clothing to cruise the streets. Flashing open their outer garments was an advertisement to potential customers.

Political dissidents in many countries have used the veil for their own ends. The women who marched, veiled, through Cairo during the Nationalist demonstrations against the British after World War I were counting on the strength of Western respect for the veil to protect them against British gunfire. At first they were right. Algerian women also used the protection of the veil to carry bombs through French army checkpoints during the Algerian revolution. But when the French discovered the ruse, Algerian women discarded the veil and dressed like Europeans to move about freely.

The multiple meanings and uses of *purdah* and the veil do not fully explain how such practices came to be so deeply embedded in Mediterranean society. However, their origins lie in the asymmetrical relationship between men and women and the resulting attitudes about men's and women's roles. Women, according to Fatma Mernissi, a Moroccan sociologist, are seen by men in Islamic societies as in need of protection because they are unable to control their sexuality and hence are a danger to the social order. In other words, they need to be restrained and controlled so that men do not give way to the impassioned desire they inspire, and society can thus function in an orderly way.

The notion that women present a danger to the social order is scarcely limited to Muslim society. Anthropologist Julian Pitt-Rivers has pointed out that the supervision and seclusion of women was also found in Christian Europe, even though veiling was not usually practiced there. "The idea that women not subjected to male authority are a danger is a fundamental one in the writings of the moralists from the Archpriest of Talavera to Padre Haro, and it is echoed in the modern Andalusian *pueblo*. It is bound up with the fear of ungoverned female sexuality which had been an integral element of European folklore ever since prudent Odysseus lashed himself to the mast to escape the sirens."

Pitt-Rivers is writing about northern Mediterranean communities, which, like those of the Middle Eastern societies, have been greatly concerned with family honor and shame rather than with individual guilt. The honor of the Middle Eastern extended family, its ancestors and its descendants, is the highest social value. The misdeeds of the grandparents are indeed visited on their grandchildren, but so also grandparents may be disgraced by grandchildren. Men and women always remain members of their natal families. Marriage is a legal contract, but a fragile one that is often broken; the ties between brother and sister, mother and child, father and child are lifelong and enduring. The larger natal family is the group to which the individual man or woman belongs and to which the individual owes responsibility in exchange for the social and economic security that the family group provides. It is the group that is socially honored — or dishonored — by the behavior of the individual.

Both male honor and female honor are involved in the honor of the family, but each is expressed differently. The honor of a man, *sharaf,* is a public matter, involving bravery, hospitality, and piety. It may be lost, but it may also be regained. The honor of a woman, *'ard,* is a private matter involving only one thing, her sexual chastity. Once believed to be lost, it cannot be regained. If the loss of female honor remains only privately known, a rebuke may be all that takes place. But if the loss of female honor becomes public knowledge, the other members of the family may feel bound to cleanse the family name. In extreme cases, the cleansing may require the death of the offending female member. Although such killings are now criminal offenses in the Middle East, suspended sentences are often given, and the newspapers in Cairo and Baghdad frequently carry sad stories of runaway sisters "gone bad" in the city, and the revenge taken upon them in the name of family honor by their brothers or cousins.

This emphasis on female chastity, many say, originated in the patrilineal society's concern with the paternity of the child and the inheritance that follows the male line. How could the husband know that the child in his wife's womb was his son? He could not know unless his wife was a virgin at marriage. Marriages were arranged by parents, and keeping daughters secluded from men was the best way of seeing that a girl remained a virgin until her wedding night.

Middle Eastern women also look upon seclusion as practical protection. In the Iraqi village where we lived from 1956 to 1958, one of us (Elizabeth) wore the *abbayah* and found that it provided a great deal of protection from prying eyes, dust, heat, and flies. Parisian women visiting Istanbul in the sixteenth century were so impressed by the ability of the all-enveloping garment to keep dresses clean of mud and manure and to keep women from being attacked by importuning men that they tried to introduce it into French fashion. Many women have told us that they felt self-conscious, vulnerable, and even naked when they first walked on a public street without the veil and *abbayah* — as if they were making a display of themselves.

The veil, as it has returned in the last decade in a movement away from wearing Western dress, has been called a form of "portable seclusion," allowing women to maintain a modest appearance that indicates respectability and religious piety in the midst of modern Middle Eastern urban life. This new style of dress always includes long skirts, long sleeves, and a head covering (scarf or turban). Some outfits are belted, some are loose, and some include face veils and shapeless robes, as well as gloves so that no skin whatsoever is exposed to the public eye. However, these clothes are seldom black, like the older garments. The women wearing such clothes in Egypt may work in shops or offices or go to college; they are members of the growing middle class.

This new fashion has been described by some scholars as an attempt by men to reassert their Muslim identity and to reestablish their position as heads of families, even though both spouses often must work outside the home. According to this analysis, the presence of the veil is a sign that the males of the household are in control of their women and are more able to assume the responsibilities disturbed or usurped by foreign colonial powers, responsibilities which continue to be threatened by Western politics and materialism. Other scholars argue that it is not men who are choosing the garb today but women themselves, using modest dress as a way of communicating to the rest of the world that though they may work outside their homes, they are nonetheless pious Muslims and respectable women.

The veil is the outward sign of a complex reality. Observers are often deceived by the absence of that sign and fail to see that in Middle Eastern societies (and in many parts of Europe) where the garb no longer exists, basic attitudes are unchanged. Women who have taken off the veil continue to play the old roles within the family, and their chastity remains crucial. A woman's behavior is still the key to the honor and the reputation of her family, no matter what she wears.

In Middle Eastern societies, feminine and masculine continue to be strong poles of identification. This is in marked contrast to Western society, where for more than a generation greater equality between men and women has been reflected in the blurring of distinctions between male and female clothing. Western feminists continue to state that biology is not the basis of behavior and therefore should not be the basis for understanding men's and women's roles. But almost all Middle Eastern reformers, whether upper or middle class, intellectuals or clerics, argue from the assumption of a fundamental, God-given difference, social and psychological as well as physical, between men and women. There are important disagreements among these reformers today about what should be done, however.

Those Muslim reformers still strongly influenced by Western models call for equal access to divorce, child custody, and inheritance; equal opportunities for education and employment; abolition of female circumcision and "crimes of honor"; an end to polygamy; and a law regulating the age of marriage. But of growing importance are reformers of social practice who call for a return to the example set by the Prophet Muhammad and his early followers; they wish to begin by eliminating what they feel to be the licentious practices introduced by Western influence, such as sexual laxity and the consumption of alcohol. To them, change in the laws affecting women should be in strict accord with their view of Islamic law, and women should begin by expressing their modesty and piety by wearing the new forms of veiling in public life. Seclusion may be impossible in modern urban societies, but conservative dress, the new form of veiling, is an option for women that sets the faithful Muslim apart from the corrupt world of the nonbeliever as it was believed to do in the time of the Prophet.

A female English film director, after several months in Morocco, said in an interview, "This business about the veil is nonsense. We all have our veils, between ourselves and other people. The question is what the veils are used for, and by whom." Today the use of the veil continues to trigger Western reaction, for as Islamic dress, it is not only a statement about the honor of the family or the boundary between family and stranger. Just as the changes in the nun's dress in the United States tell us something about the woman who wears it and the society of which she is a part, the various forms of veiling today communicate attitudes and beliefs about politics and religious morality as well as the roles of men and women in the Middle East.

REVIEW QUESTIONS

1. What is the meaning to Westerners of the veil worn by Middle Eastern women? How does this view reflect Western values?

2. List the symbolic meanings of the veil to Middle Eastern women. How do these meanings relate to the Muslim concept of *purdah* and to other important Middle Eastern values?

3. There has been a resurgence of the veil in several Middle Eastern societies over the past few years. How can you explain this change?

4. Using this article as a model, analyze the meaning of some American articles of clothing. How do these relate to core values in the country?

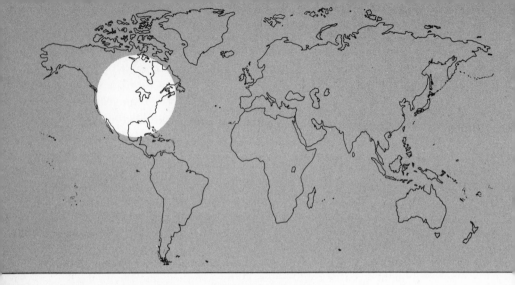

20   Poverty Is Being Poor

THOMAS GLADWIN

*We have argued in the introduction to this section that class is a
form of social stratification that permits mobility. Lower-class people can raise their status; members of the upper class can lose
theirs. Stories about individuals who have made their way out of
poverty abound in American mythology, but the reality of being
poor is less optimistic. Part of the problem lies with what Oscar
Lewis termed a "culture of poverty." Poor people are conditioned
by a culture of failure in a society of plenty. Low self-esteem is
endemic. But above all, it is the economy that locks in low status.
No matter what their motivation, poor people simply lack the economic resources to do anything about their condition. In this classic article, Thomas Gladwin explores the effect of poverty on class
mobility. He argues that because they have so little money to
spend, the poor must make small day-to-day exchanges that increase the cost of doing business for the merchants who serve
them. Higher costs and inferior quality are the result; so is antago-
nism against merchants.*

One of the more extraordinary characteristics not only of the War on
Poverty itself but also of the great amount currently being written
about poverty in general is the relatively minor attention which is
being given to the immediate and direct consequences of simply being

poor. Being poor has a large number of secondary consequences such as powerlessness, inadequate access to resources, lack of education, and a poor diet. However, these follow and are derived from a primary condition of just being poor. Being poor, at least in the United States, consists in a lack of sufficient money to function effectively in the economic system through which everyone is forced to seek the necessities of life. Let us examine what this means for day-to-day living.

Having at any one time at most only a small amount of money, and never being sure that in the immediate future enough will be available to cover even minimum needs, the poor people are forced to spend whatever they have on the most urgent demands which arise each day, and thus to operate constantly through a succession of very small deals. Instead of a weekly trip in the car to a supermarket, food must be bought by walking to a neighborhood store and buying only enough for the next meal or two. The size and the adequacy of the purchase, and therefore of the meal to follow, depends on how much money can be scraped together on that particular day. Improvident, inefficient? Of course. But to do otherwise calls at least for a car, a reserve supply of money, and reliable refrigeration. Louise Richards in a recent article reexamined the standard guidelines which have been customarily recommended ever since Depression days for efficient handling of household finances: spend first for necessities and last for luxuries, buy the best quality of foods for the lowest price, budget carefully and plan purchases in advance, and so on.[1] She then demonstrated that each of these budgeting rules, although rational and sensible, is in fact difficult or impossible to follow when one works with a very small and uncertain income.

In an eloquent and angry article entitled "Keeping the Poor Poor," Paul Jacobs has described the variety of people and of commercial practices which surround poor people and take their money.[2] Although they keep the poor people poor, they also provide the only channels open to them for spending the small sums of money which they can command at any one time. Without a car to get to work it is very hard to obtain a decent job (especially in an area without public transportation such as Watts), but without sufficient funds for a substantial down payment the only cars available are nearly worn out. When they break down the necessary expensive repairs will only be performed for cash. Poor people who need to spend money to meet installments or pay bills cannot sustain a checking account, and if they are lucky enough to be working, cannot get to a bank or a post office for a

[1] Louise G. Richards, "Consumer Practices of the Poor," in *Low Income Life Styles*, Lola M. Irelan, ed. (Washington DC: Welfare Administration, 1966), 67–86.
[2] In *Economic Progress and Social Welfare*, Leonard H. Goodman, ed. (New York: Columbia University Press, 1966), 158–184.

money order. Consequently they must purchase a commercial money order at a rate governed only by what the traffic will bear, and of uncertain reliability. Food and other products are often available in the poverty areas at lower prices in less than standard qualities, but once these products are identified as below standard they often can go very far below without intervention of legal or other controls. The manner in which poor people are gouged and exploited by excessive installment payments and carrying charges has become notorious. Mr. Jacobs describes a variety of other less well-known credit arrangements to which the poor are often forced and which in the long run soak up still more of their meager resources.

Mr. Jacobs is profoundly sympathetic toward poor people and their dilemmas. He has several times joined poor people in their daily lives after deliberately divesting himself of all but a pittance of money. Finding himself and his new friends surrounded by people ready to take every penny they have and give very little in return, he not surprisingly has become angry. He holds those people who are exploiting the poor responsible for what they are doing, and his anger is therefore directed at them. He is also angry with the rest of us who complacently let the exploiters go on about their business. This anger is felt by the poor themselves. It expresses itself, among other things, in the smashing and looting of stores, which is now a standard feature of urban riots. These attacks on local merchants are not merely a means for obtaining otherwise unavailable goods, but also rather clearly reflect a smoldering resentment against people who are seen as coming into the slums to prey upon their inhabitants.

Inherent in the angry resentment directed toward shopkeepers, loan agencies, landlords, and the like is an assumption that the mechanisms they use to extort money from poor people have been deliberately devised as a way to make large profits and grow rich. Put the other way around, it is assumed that if they were willing to make a little less money they could give poor people deals as favorable as those which middle-class people enjoy. As we shall see, this is almost certainly not true.

Not only is exploitation perceived as deliberately contrived to maximize profit, it is also seen by its victims as discriminatory against whatever minority group occupies the slum area involved. It would be surprising if they saw it any other way. Members of minority groups in cities are constantly faced with insulting reminders of their inferior status and therefore inferior rights and privileges. It is thus only natural that they should also interpret the economic policies which they encounter as deliberately designed further to disadvantage them *because* they are black or Puerto Rican or Mexican-American or whatever. In addition, the car dealers and moneylenders and landlords are more often than not English-speaking whites. As a consequence, when there are riots not only are the stores of white merchants the principal targets for vandalism, but business enterprises run by members of the local ethnic group can usually escape damage simply by advertising prominently the ethnic affiliation of the proprietor. This is true even though in many cases the actual business practices of these establishments differ little if at all from those practiced by whites.

Undoubtedly ethnic discrimination contributes to the development of the commercial practices which so disadvantage poor people. It is hard to imagine white middle-class customers putting up with the usurious rates, shabby merchandise, and run-down facilities which poor blacks, Puerto Ricans, and Mexican-Americans usually accept without audible protest.

Beyond this, however, two much broader economic principles are at work, principles which must almost inevitably apply to any really poor people regardless of their color or speech or culture. The first and most crucial of these principles constitutes a central tenet of all commercial transactions in any free economy: the larger the deal the better the terms. At the upper end of the scale stands the man about whom we so often hear who can get it for you wholesale. However, attention is very seldom focused on the other end of the scale where the principle inevitably becomes the converse: *the smaller the deal the worse the terms.* Costs which tend to accrue at a fairly fixed level per deal or unit of business, costs such as handling, packaging, negotiating, carrying inventories, paying rent, and so forth, and the less tangible costs reflected in making judgments and accepting risks, all these costs are proportionately lower when a large number or high value of units are involved in each deal. Conversely, when these factors are all added into the cost of completing a very small deal, this cost necessarily becomes highly inflated. Even riding a bus costs more when tokens must be bought one at a time to conserve cash. A larger markup is needed to pay the rent, the overhead, and the wages of a full-time clerk in a neighborhood store whose daily volume is usually very small. In other kinds of transactions, the size of the deal can become sufficiently small that entirely new bases for making profits must come into play. Despite the very high interest rates which are charged on small loans to poor people, the risks are so high that it is not possible to make a profit from interest payments alone. The profit margin is therefore deliberately planned to come from the equities in repossessed merchandise which a succession of defaulting borrowers are forced to surrender. In other cases dishonest practices, like putting a thumb on the scale, become so widespread among retailers trying to assure their own living that they are almost taken for granted. At least they are accepted by poor people without protest, perhaps because protest would be in vain. But accepted or not, these practices further rob poor people of their rights, their money, and their dignity.

The high cost of doing business through a series of very small deals applies to anyone and is an inherent attribute of the economy of poverty. Unless there is some way to make the deals bigger or else to reduce the risk and high costs involved in transacting business with people who have practically no money, it is hard to see how even the most kindly of businessmen could support themselves in a poor neighborhood without charging exorbitant rates and prices or offering substandard goods or services or both.

A second major principle almost as crippling for a poor person as the first is the need in many kinds of transactions for substantial financial resources before being able to enter into any kind of deal at all. Sometimes this takes the form of a requirement for actual cash, as in the down payment of an automobile or the deposit required for a telephone. Because they are unable to assemble the necessary amounts of cash at one time, persons who could afford the monthly charges for telephone services or the monthly payments on a fairly good car are often denied these facilities, yet these are facilities critical for effective articulation with the larger commercial world. Both a telephone and a car are essential in applying for and obtaining a job, finding out about and capitalizing on sales and other sources of bargains, or obtaining medical and other services without wasting a good part of the day on them. If it were somehow possible to compute the monthly cost in added expenses and lost income of not having a car and telephone, it is probable that this figure would not differ widely from the monthly cost of operating and paying for both.

The resources necessary to get a transaction under way need not take the form of cash. An obvious alternative is to obtain credit at reasonable cost. However, this can usually be achieved only through already having substantial assets that are convertible into cash, or else someone prepared to guarantee repayment of the loan if it is defaulted. Since poor people are very unlikely to have many convertible assets or rich relatives, they cannot obtain these guarantees. There is of course another basis for obtaining credit. This is to have a steady and reliable income at a level high enough to pay for necessities with a little left over. Welfare payments are often fairly steady, but are usually at levels so low they do not really cover necessities, much less leave a little over, so they are no help. The only steady income which can leave some extra cash over is a good job, but this is precisely what the poor person almost by definition does not have and usually cannot get. Therefore, poor people who have to buy something of some size must either do so on credit at very high interest rates and with the constant threat (and cost) of repossession, get it dishonestly, or else do without. When it comes to essentials, doing without usually means that needs have to be met through alternatives, which in the long run are even more costly. Inability to obtain a mortgage frequently results in paying rent at a higher level than mortgage payments, in return for which there is instead of a growing equity only the prospect of a lifetime of shabby accommodations.

Another class of deals which can only be consummated if cash or credit are available in some quantity involves the provision of professional services, especially legal and medical services. Some effort is made to provide both of these for poor people through governmental programs, but they are usually poor in quality, limited in scope, and obtained only through the exercise of patience and persistence. Outside of criminal cases, legal services are virtually unavailable to a poor person who, for example, wishes to sue for damages (except in cases of clear liability with a fairly certain outcome) or to recover something which he believes was taken from him by fraud. With respect to health the miserable and humiliating medical care which poor people must expect is too well known to require comment. Positive and personal medical or legal attention to the problems of a poor person, regardless of his race or language, is usually available only if he is clearly in risk of dying, or is about to go to jail, or has cash.

If, to borrow Paul Jacobs' phrase, the poor are kept poor not simply because of deliberate exploitation and discrimination, but also because being poor is economically so inefficient that people are usually unable to escape from poverty by their own efforts no matter what they do, what does this suggest with respect to planning programs to help poor people? One conclusion which emerges compellingly is that even complete elimination of discrimination against members of any minority group will not substantially improve their life circumstances if they are genuinely poor. Leaving aside questions of personal ability and training, and regardless of the sentimental history of how our Italian or Irish or Jewish ancestors made it from rags to riches, it seems inescapable that if you are born in the mid-twentieth century of really poor parents in an urban slum (or on a sharecropper's farm), the purely economic dice are loaded so heavily against you that the likelihood of your achieving a position of real dignity or security is almost precluded. Put in another way, if only *equal* opportunities are extended to the minority poor and they are therefore subject to the same rules of business which govern middle-class people, their limited cash resources will prevent them from deriving any lasting advantage from this "equality." Thus many of the demands which are currently being made by civil rights leaders in northern as well as southern cities appear impossible of fulfillment within our economic system as it presently operates.

The solution, furthermore, does not seem to lie in trying to coerce businessmen to offer to poor people deals on as favorable terms as they would offer to middle-class customers. The cost both direct and indirect of doing business exclusively in small deals prohibits the offer of terms as good as those which govern large deals without either a subsidy, or else bankruptcy. In other words, regardless of the moral character of businessmen who operate in the slums as bankers or employers or merchants, there is no basis on which they can do business which will simultaneously be fair to them and their customers. At least one has to lose. If this is true, it points unequivocally to the need for some new additional factor in the economic life of poor people through which they can at least have a chance to become self-starting along the road toward improving their circumstances. What this new factor should be is probably already evident, because it consists in an already familiar proposal.

Everything which has been said thus far points strongly in the direction others have been pointing with increasing urgency over the past several years. This is toward the adoption of a policy of guaranteeing for everyone some minimum level of income sufficient to assure at least modest decency and security. A number of different ways have been proposed for accomplishing this, and all have been analyzed for their relative cost and effectiveness from a variety of points of view. Although advantages of one sort or another accrue to each of these proposed plans, for our present purposes their relatively minor differences are far less important than the central principle of guaranteed income maintenance.

Formidable problems of administrative policy, political and moral acceptability, and fiscal feasibility must be resolved before a guaranteed income can become a reality. Yet with increasing unanimity people who are looking at the problems of poverty from almost any point of view, whether they are social scientists or economists or blue ribbon advisory commissions, are arriving at the conclusion that a guaranteed income must be a part of the solution. Without it, people in our society who are disfranchised by poverty and discrimination will never achieve full participation in the way of life which is supposed to be the right of every American to enjoy. Various arguments are advanced to support this position. The one set forth here rests upon the relative efficiency of economic transactions as a function of income. To recapitulate in summary form, below a certain level transactions become so small that their nature changes and sinks into rapidly increasing inefficiency. In addition, at this level of income there can be no surplus, hence no savings, no real control over the future, and therefore no advantage in trying to plan ahead, and no security. Some means must therefore be found to permit people to stabilize their economic activity at a minimal level of efficiency and predictability. The only way to do this is to see that enough money is regularly available to sustain this level of activity. The guaranteed minimum income is the only mechanism thus far proposed which will effectively meet this requirement. . . .

Review questions

1. How does Gladwin explain why most poor Americans remain poor?
2. Why does Gladwin feel that an end to racial discrimination will not end poverty for most poor people? Do you think he is right?
3. Why does Gladwin feel that a guaranteed income is the only answer to poverty in the United States? How do you feel this plan would work?
4. Are there other solutions to the problem of poverty that fit with the market structure of our economy?

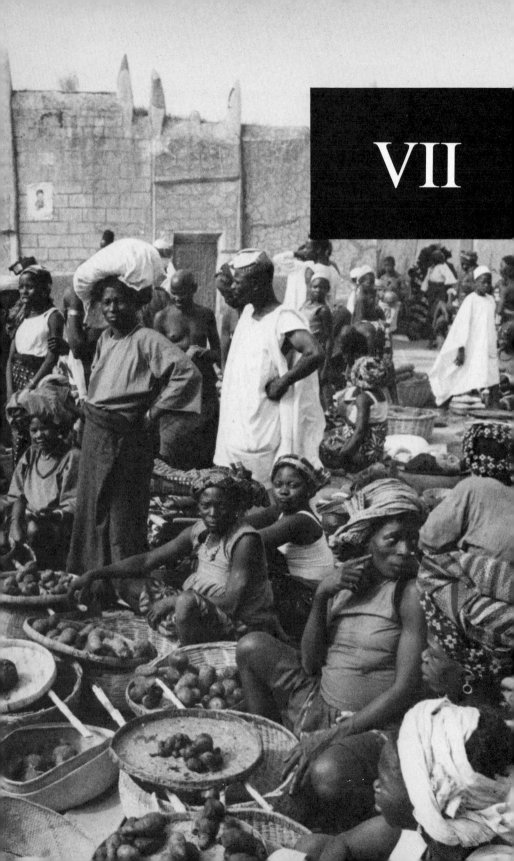

VII

Economic Systems

People everywhere experience wants that can be satisfied only by the acquisition and use of material goods and the services of others. To meet such wants, humans rely on an aspect of their cultural inventory, the *economic system,* which we will define as the provision of goods and services to meet biological and social wants.

The meaning of the term *want* can be confusing. It can refer to what humans *need* for their survival. We must eat, drink, maintain a constant body temperature, defend ourselves, and deal with injury and illness. The economic system meets these needs by providing food, water, clothing, shelter, weapons, medicines, and the cooperative services of others.

But material goods serve more than just our survival needs: they meet our culturally defined *wants* as well. We need clothes to stay warm, but we want garments of a particular style, cut, and fabric to signal our status, rank, or anything else we wish to socially communicate. We need food to sustain life, but we want particular foods prepared in special ways to fill our aesthetic and social desires. Services and goods may also be exchanged to strengthen ties between people or groups. Birthday presents may not always meet physical needs, but they clearly function to strengthen the ties between the parties to the exchange.

Part of the economic system is concerned with *production,* which means rendering material items useful and available for human consumption. Production systems must designate ways to allocate resources. The *allocation of resources* refers to the cultural rules people use to assign rights to ownership and use of resources. Production systems must also include technologies. Americans usually associate technology with the tools and machines used for manufacturing, rather than with the knowledge for doing it. But many anthropologists link the concept directly to culture. Here we will define *technology* as the cultural knowledge for making and using tools and extracting and refining raw materials.

Production systems also include a *division of labor,* which refers to the rules that govern the assignment of jobs to people. In hunting and gathering societies, labor is most often divided along the lines of gender, and sometimes age. In these societies, almost everyone knows how to produce, use, and collect necessary material goods. In industrial society, however, jobs are highly specialized and labor is divided, at least ideally, on the basis of skill and experience. It is rare that we know how to do someone else's job in our complex society.

The *unit of production,* meaning the persons or groups responsible for producing goods, follows a pattern similar to the way labor is divided in various societies. Among hunter-gatherers, there is little specialization; individuals, families, groups of friends, or sometimes bands form the units of production. But in our own complex society, we are surrounded by groups specially organized to manufacture, transport, and sell goods.

Another part of the economic system is *distribution.* There are three basic modes of distribution: market exchange, reciprocal exchange, and redistribution.

We are most conscious of market exchange because it lies at the heart of our capitalist system. *Market exchange* is the transfer of goods and services based on price, supply, and demand. Every time we enter a store and pay for something, we engage in market exchange. The price of an item may change with the supply. For example, a discount store may lower the price of a television set because it has too many of the appliances on hand. Price may go up, however, if everyone wants the sets when there are few to sell. Money is often used in market systems; it enables people to exchange a large variety of items easily. Barter involves the trading of goods, not money, but it, too, is a form of market exchange because the number of items exchanged can also vary with supply and demand. Market exchange appears in human history when societies become larger and more complex. It is well suited for exchange between strangers who make up these larger groups.

Although we are not so aware of it, we also engage in reciprocal exchange. *Reciprocal exchange* involves the transfer of goods and services between two people or groups based on role obligations.

Birthday and holiday gift giving is a fine example of reciprocity. On these occasions we exchange goods not because we necessarily need or want them, but because we are expected to do so as part of our status and role. Parents should give gifts to their children, for example; children should reciprocate. If we fail our reciprocal obligations, we signal an unwillingness to continue the relationship. Small, simply organized societies, such as the !Kung described earlier, base their exchange systems on reciprocity. Complex ones like ours, although largely organized around the market or redistribution, still manifest reciprocity between kin and close friends.

Finally, there is *redistribution,* the transfer of goods and services between a central collecting source and a group of individuals. Like reciprocity, redistribution is based on role obligation. Taxes typify this sort of exchange in the United States. We must pay our taxes because we are citizens, not because we are buying something. We receive goods and services back — education, transportation, roads, defense — but not necessarily in proportion to the amount we contribute. Redistribution may be the predominant mode of exchange in socialist societies.

The selections included in this section illustrate several of the concepts we have just discussed. Paul Bohannan describes a traditional Tiv economy characterized by three spheres of exchange: one that includes the market exchange of subsistence goods; a second involving the reciprocal exchange of prestige goods; and a third consisting of women exchanged between families at marriage. Elliot Liebow's article deals with the division of labor, specifically with the meaning of jobs to poor black men. The third article, by Robert Brain, looks at the importance of reciprocity — of giving gifts and offering hospitality — to business people in pursuit of market deals. Like everyone in the world, we prefer to exchange things with our friends. The last selection, by Bernard Nietschmann, details the impact of the international market system on a local subsistence economy. Motivated by money, Miskito Indians are now dependent on outsiders for food and find themselves unable to meet their traditional reciprocal obligations.

KEY TERMS

economic system	unit of production
production	distribution
allocation of resources	market exchange
technology	reciprocal exchange
division of labor	redistribution

READINGS IN THIS SECTION

21   The Impact of Money on an African Subsistence Economy

PAUL J. BOHANNAN

In this article Paul Bohannan describes the precontact economy of the Tiv of Nigeria and shows that it contained three spheres of exchange. These spheres — subsistence, prestige, and women in marriage — were separated by the rule that goods from one could not be used to purchase goods in another without loss of prestige to one party in the exchange. When general-purpose money was introduced from the West, it became possible to equate the values of each sphere, and radical change took place. The author discusses in detail the changes resulting from the introduction of money.

It has often been claimed that money was to be found in much of the African continent before the impact of the European world and the extension of trade made coinage general. When we examine these claims, however, they tend to evaporate or to emerge as tricks of definition. It is an astounding fact that economists have, for decades, been assigning three or four qualities to money when they discuss it with reference to our own society or to those of the medieval and modern world, yet the moment they have gone to ancient history or to the societies and economies studied by anthropologists they have

From "The Impact of Money on an African Subsistence Economy," *The Journal of Economic History 19* (December 1959): 491–503. Reprinted by permission of the Cambridge University Press and the author. Some footnotes, the bibliographic citations, and the bibliography are omitted.

sought the "real" nature of money by allowing only one of these defining characteristics to dominate their definitions.

All economists learned as students that money serves at least three purposes. It is a means of exchange, it is a mode of payment, it is a standard of value. Depending on the vintage and persuasion of the author of the book one consults, one may find another money use — storage of wealth. In newer books, money is defined as merely the means of unitizing purchasing power, yet behind that definition still lie the standard, the payment, and the exchange uses of money.

It is interesting that on the fairly rare occasions that economists discuss primitive money at all — or at least when they discuss it with any empirical referent — they have discarded one or more of the money uses in framing their definitions. Paul Einzig,[1] to take one example from many, first makes a plea for "elastic definitions," and goes on to point out that different economists have utilized different criteria in their definitions; he then falls into the trap he has been exposing: he excoriates Menger for utilizing only the "medium of exchange" criterion and then himself omits it, utilizing only the standard and payment criteria, thus taking sides in an argument in which there was no real issue.

The answer to these difficulties should be apparent. If we take no more than the three major money uses — payment, standard, and means of exchange — we will find that in many primitive societies as well as some of the ancient empires, one object may serve one money use while quite another object serves another money use. In order to deal with this situation, and to avoid the trap of choosing one of these uses to define "real" money, Karl Polanyi[2] and his associates have labeled as "general-purpose money" any item which serves all three of these primary money uses, while an item which serves only one or two is "special-purpose money." With this distinction in mind, we can see that special-purpose money was very common in pre-contact Africa, but that general-purpose money was rare.

This paper is a brief analysis of the impact of general-purpose money and increase in trade in an African economy which had known only local trade and had used only special-purpose money.

The Tiv are a people, still largely pagan, who live in the Benue Valley in Central Nigeria, among whom I had the good fortune to live and work for well over two years. They are prosperous subsistence farmers and have a highly developed indigenous market in which they exchanged their produce and handicrafts, and through which they

---

[1] Paul Einzig, *Primitive Money in Its Ethnological, Historical and Economic Aspects* (London: Eyre and Spottiswoode, 1949), 319–26.

[2] Karl Polanyi, "The Economy as Instituted Process," in Karl Polanyi, Conrad M. Arensberg, and Harry W. Pearson, eds., *Trade and Market in the Early Empires* (Glencoe, IL: The Free Press and The Falcon's Wing Press, 1957), 264–66.

carried on local trade. The most distinctive feature about the economy of the Tiv — and it is a feature they share with many, perhaps most, of the pre-monetary peoples — is what can be called a multicentric economy. Briefly, a multicentric economy is an economy in which a society's exchangeable goods fall into two or more mutually exclusive spheres, each marked by different institutionalization and different moral values. In some multicentric economies these spheres remain distinct, though in most there are more or less institutionalized means of converting wealth from one into wealth in another.

Indigenously there were three spheres in the multicentric economy of the Tiv. The first of these spheres is that associated with subsistence, which the Tiv called *yiagh*. The commodities in it include all locally produced foodstuffs: the staple yams and cereals, plus all the condiments, vegetable side-dishes, and seasonings, as well as small livestock — chickens, goats, and sheep. It also includes household utensils (mortars, grindstones, calabashes, baskets, and pots), some tools (particularly those used in agriculture), and raw materials for producing any items in the category.

Within this sphere, goods are distributed either by gift giving or through marketing. Traditionally, there was no money of any sort in this sphere — all goods changed hands by barter. There was a highly developed market organization at which people exchanged their produce for their requirements, and in which today traders buy produce in cheap markets and transport it to sell in dearer markets. The morality of this sphere of the economy is the morality of the free and uncontrolled market.

The second sphere of the Tiv economy is one which is in no way associated with markets. The category of goods within this sphere is slaves, cattle, ritual "offices" purchased from the Jukun, that type of large white cloth known as *tugudu,* medicines and magic, and metal rods. One is still entitled to use the present tense in this case, for ideally the category still exists in spite of the fact that metal rods are today very rare, that slavery has been abolished, that European "offices" have replaced Jukun offices and cannot be bought, and that much European medicine has been accepted. Tiv still quote prices of slaves in cows and brass rods, and of cattle in brass rods and *tugudu* cloth. The price of magical rites, as it has been described in the literature, was in terms of *tugudu* cloth or brass rods (though payment might be made in other items); payment for Jukun titles was in cows and slaves, *tugudu* cloths, and metal rods.[3]

None of these goods ever entered the market as it was institutionalized in Tivland, even though it might be possible for an economist

---

[3] B. Akiga Sai, *Akiga's Story* (London: International Institute of African Languages and Cultures, 1939), 382 and passim.

to find the principle of supply and demand at work in the exchanges which characterized it. The actual shifts of goods took place at ceremonies, at more or less ritualized wealth displays, and on occasions when "doctors" performed rites and prescribed medicines. Tiv refer to the items and the activities within this sphere by the word *shagba*, which can be roughly translated as prestige.

Within the prestige sphere there was one item which took on all of the money uses and hence can be called a general-purpose currency, though it must be remembered that it was of only a *very limited range*. Brass rods were used as means of exchange *within the sphere;* they also served as a standard of value within it (though not the only one), and as a means of payment. However, this sphere of the economy was tightly sealed off from the subsistence goods and its market. After European contact, brass rods occasionally entered the market, but they did so only as means of payment, not as medium of exchange or as standard of valuation. Because of the complex institutionalization and morality, no one ever sold a slave for food; no one, save in the depths of extremity, ever paid brass rods for domestic goods.

The supreme and unique sphere of exchangeable values for the Tiv contains a single item: rights in human beings other than slaves, particularly rights in women. Even twenty-five years after official abolition of exchange marriage, it is the category of exchange in which Tiv are emotionally most entangled. All exchanges within this category are exchanges of rights in human beings, usually dependent women and children. Its value is expressed in terms of kinship and marriage.

Tiv marriage is an extremely complex subject. Again, economists might find supply and demand principles at work, but Tiv adamantly separate marriage and market. Before the coming of the Europeans all "real" marriages were exchange marriages. In its simplest form, an exchange marriage involves two men exchanging sisters. Actually, this simple form seldom or never occurred. In order for every man to have a ward (*ingol*) to exchange for a wife, small localized agnatic lineages formed ward-sharing groups ("those who eat one Ingol" — *mbaye ingol i mom*). There was an initial "exchange" — or at least, distribution — of wards among the men of this group, so that each man became the guardian (*tien*) of one or more wards. The guardian, then, saw to the marriage of his ward, exchanging her with outsiders for another woman (her "partner" or *ikyar*) who becomes the bride of the guardian or one of his close agnatic kinsmen, or — in some situations — becomes a ward in the ward-sharing group and is exchanged for yet another woman who becomes a wife.

Tiv are, however, extremely practical and sensible people, and they know that successful marriages cannot be made if women are not consulted and if they are not happy. Elopements occurred, and sometimes a woman in exchange was not forthcoming. Therefore, a debt existed from the ward-sharing group of the husband to that of the guardian.

These debts sometimes lagged two or even three generations behind actual exchanges. The simple way of paying them off was for the eldest daughter of the marriage to return to the ward-sharing group of her mother, as ward, thus cancelling the debt.

Because of its many impracticalities, the system had to be buttressed in several ways in order to work: one way was a provision for "earnest" during the time of the lag, another was to recognize other types of marriage as binding to limited extents. These two elements are somewhat confused with one another, because of the fact that right up until the abolition of exchange marriage in 1927, the inclination was always to treat all non-exchange marriages as if they were "lags" in the completion of exchange marriages.

When lags in exchange occurred, they were usually filled with "earnests" of brass rods, or occasionally, it would seem, of cattle. The brass rods or cattle in such situations were *never* exchange equivalents (*ishe*) for the woman. The only "price" of one woman is another woman.

Although Tiv decline to grant it antiquity, another type of marriage occurred at the time Europeans first met them — it was called "accumulating a woman/wife" (*kem kwase*). It is difficult to tell today just exactly what it consisted in because the terminology of this union has been adapted to describe the bridewealth marriage that was declared by an administrative fiat of 1927 to be the only legal form.

Kem marriage consisted in acquisition of sexual, domestic, and economic rights in a woman — but not the rights to filiate her children to the social group of the husband. Put in another way, in exchange marriage, both rights *in genetricem* (rights to filiate a woman's children) and rights *in uxorem* (sexual, domestic, and economic rights in a woman) automatically were acquired by husbands and their lineages. In *kem* marriage, only rights *in uxorem* were acquired. In order to affiliate the *kem* wife's children, additional payments had to be made to the woman's guardians. These payments were for the children, not for the rights *in genetricem* in their mother, which could be acquired only by exchange of equivalent rights in another woman. *Kem* payments were paid in brass rods. However, rights in women had no equivalent or "price" in brass rods or in any other item — save, of course, identical rights in another woman. *Kem* marriage was similar to but showed important differences from bridewealth marriage as it is known in South and East Africa. There, rights in women and rights in cattle form a single economic sphere, and could be exchanged directly for one another. Among Tiv, however, conveyance of rights in women necessarily involved direct exchange of another woman. The Tiv custom that approached bridewealth was not an exchange of equivalents, but payment in a medium that was specifically not equivalent.

Thus, within the sphere of exchange marriage there was no item that fulfilled any of the uses of money; when second-best types of marriage were made, payment was in an item which was specifically not used as a standard of value.

That Tiv do conceptualize exchange articles as belonging to different categories, and that they rank the categories on a moral basis, and that most but not all exchanges are limited to one sphere, gives rise to the fact that two different kinds of exchanges may be recognized: exchange of items contained within a single category, and exchanges of items belonging to different categories. For Tiv, these two different types of exchange are marked by separate and distinct moral attitudes.

To maintain this distinction between the two types of exchanges which Tiv mark by different behavior and different values, I shall use separate words. I shall call those exchanges of items within a single category "conveyances" and those exchanges of items from one category to another "conversions." Roughly, conveyances are morally neutral; conversions have a strong moral quality in their rationalization.

Exchanges within a category — particularly that of subsistence, the only one intact today — excite no moral judgments. Exchanges between categories, however, do excite a moral reaction: the man who exchanges lower-category goods for higher-category goods does not brag about his market luck but about his "strong heart" and his success in life. The man who exchanges high-category goods for lower rationalizes his action in terms of high-valued motivation (most often the needs of his kin).

The two institutions most intimately connected with conveyance are markets and marriage. Conveyance in the prestige sphere seems (to the latter-day investigator, at least) to have been less highly institutionalized. It centered on slave dealing, on curing, and on the acquisition of status.

Conversion is a much more complex matter. Conversion depends on the fact that some items of every sphere could, on certain occasions, be used in exchanges in which the return was *not* considered equivalent (*ishe*). Obviously, given the moral ranking of the spheres, such a situation leaves one party to the exchange in a good position, and the other in a bad one. Tiv say that it is "good" to trade food for brass rods, but that it is "bad" to trade brass rods for food, that it is good to trade your cows or brass rods for a wife, but very bad to trade your marriage ward for cows or brass rods.

Seen from the individual's point of view, it is profitable and possible to invest one's wealth if one converts it into a morally superior category: to convert subsistence wealth into prestige wealth and both into women is the aim of the economic endeavor of individual Tiv. To put it into economists' terms: conversion is the ultimate type of maximization.

We have already examined the marriage system by which a man can convert his brass rods to a wife: he could get a *kem* wife and *kem* her children as they were born. Her daughters, then, could be used as wards in his exchange marriages. It is the desire of every Tiv to "acquire a woman" (*ngoho kwase*) either as wife or ward in some way other than sharing in the ward-sharing group. A wife whom one acquires in any other way is not the concern of one's marriage-ward sharing group because the woman or other property exchanged for her did not belong to the marriage-ward group. The daughters of such a wife are not divided among the members of a man's marriage-ward group, but only among his sons. Such a wife is not only indicative of a man's ability and success financially and personally, but rights in her are the only form of property which is not ethically subject to the demands of his kin.

Conversion from the prestige sphere to the kinship sphere was, thus, fairly common; it consisted in all the forms of marriage save exchange marriage, usually in terms of brass rods.

Conversion from the subsistence sphere to the prestige sphere was also usually in terms of metal rods. They, on occasion, entered the marketplace as payment. If the owner of the brass rods required an unusually large amount of staples to give a feast, making too heavy a drain on his wives' food supplies, he might buy it with brass rods.

However, brass rods could not possibly have been a general currency. They were not divisible. One could not receive "change" from a brass rod. Moreover, a single rod was worth much more than the usual market purchases for any given day of most Tiv subsistence traders. Although it might be possible to buy chickens with brass rods, one would have to have bought a very large quantity of yams to equal one rod, and to buy an item like pepper with rods would be laughable.

Brass rods, thus, overlapped from the prestige to the subsistence sphere on some occasions, but only on special occasions and for large purchases.

Not only is conversion possible, but it is encouraged — it is, in fact, the behavior which proves a man's worth. Tiv are scornful of a man who is merely rich in subsistence goods (or, today, in money). If, having adequate subsistence, he does not seek prestige in accordance with the old counters, or if he does not strive for more wives, and hence more children, the fault must be personal inadequacy. They also note that they all try to keep a man from making conversions; jealous kinsmen of a rich man will bewitch him and his people by fetishes, in order to make him expend his wealth on sacrifices to repair the fetishes, thus maintaining economic equality. However, once a conversion has been made, demands of kinsmen are not effective — at least, they take a new form.

Therefore, the man who successfully converts his wealth into higher categories is successful — he has a "strong heart." He is both feared and respected.

In this entire process, metal rods hold a pivotal position, and it is not surprising that early administrators considered them money. Originally imported from Europe, they were used as "currency" in some parts of southern Nigeria in the slave trade. They are dowels about a quarter of an inch in diameter and some three feet long; they can be made into jewelry, and were used as a source of metal for castings.

Whatever their use elsewhere, brass rods in Tivland had some but not all of the attributes of money. Within the prestige sphere, they were used as a standard of equivalence, and they were a medium of exchange; they were also a mode for storage of wealth, and were used as payment. In short, brass rods were a general-purpose currency *within the prestige sphere*. However, outside of the prestige sphere — markets and marriage were the most active institutions of exchange outside it — brass rods fulfilled only one of these functions of money: payment. We have examined in detail the reasons why equivalency could not exist between brass rods and rights in women, between brass rods and food.

We have, thus, in Tivland, a multicentric economy of three spheres, and we have a sort of money which was general-purpose money within the limited range of the prestige sphere, and a special-purpose money in the special transactions in which the other spheres overlapped it.

The next question is: What happened to this multicentric economy and to the morality accompanying it when it felt the impact of the expanding European economy in the nineteenth and early twentieth centuries, and when an all-purpose money of very much greater range was introduced?

The Western impact is not, of course, limited to economic institutions. Administrative organizations, missions, and others have been as effective instruments of change as any other.

One of the most startling innovations of the British administration was a general peace. Before the arrival of the British, one did not venture far beyond the area of one's kin or special friends. To do so was to court death or enslavement.

With government police systems and safety, road-building was also begun. Moving about the country has been made both safe and comparatively easy. Peace and the new road network led to both increased trade and a greater number of markets.

Not only has the internal marketing system been perturbed by the introduction of alien institutions, but the economic institutions of the Tiv have in fact been put into touch with world economy. Northern Nigeria, like much of the rest of the colonial world, was originally taken over by trading companies with governing powers. The close linkage of government and trade was evident when taxation was introduced into Tivland. Tax was originally paid in produce, which was transported and sold through Hausa traders, who were government contractors. A few years later, coinage was introduced; taxes were demanded in that medium. It became necessary for Tiv to go into trade or to make their own contract with foreign traders in order to get cash. The trading companies, which had had "canteens" on the Benue for some decades, were quick to cooperate with the government in introducing a "cash crop" which could be bought by the traders in return for cash to pay taxes, and incidentally to buy imported goods. The crop which proved best adapted for this purpose in Tivland was beniseed (*sesamum indicum*), a crop Tiv already grew in small quantities. Acreage need only be increased and facilities for sale established.

There is still another way in which Tiv economy is linked, through the trading companies, to the economy of the outside world. Not only do the companies buy their cash crops, they also "stake" African traders with imported goods. There is, on the part both of the companies and the government, a desire to build up "native entrepreneurial classes." Imported cloth, enamelware, and ironmongery are generally sold through a network of dependent African traders. Thus, African traders are linked to the companies, and hence into international trade.

Probably no single factor has been so important, however, as the introduction of all-purpose money. Neither introduction of cash crops and taxes nor extended trading has affected the basic congruence between Tiv ideas and their institutionalization to the same extent as has money. With the introduction of money the indigenous ideas of maximization — that is, conversion of all forms of wealth into women and children — no longer leads to the result it once did.

General-purpose money provides a common denominator among all the spheres, thus making the commodities within each expressible in terms of a single standard and hence immediately exchangeable. This new money is misunderstood by Tiv. They use it as a standard of value in the subsistence category, even when — as is often the case — the exchange is direct barter. They use it as a means of payment of bridewealth under the new system, but still refuse to admit that a woman has a "price" or can be valued in the same terms as food. At the same time, it has become something formerly lacking in all save the prestige sphere of Tiv economy — a means of exchange. Tiv have tried to categorize money with the other new imported goods and place them all in a fourth economic sphere, to be ranked morally below subsistence. They have, of course, not been successful in so doing.

What in fact happened was that general-purpose money was introduced to Tivland, where formerly only special-purpose money had been known.

It is in the nature of a general-purpose money that it standardizes the exchangeability value of every item to a common scale. It is precisely this function which brass rods, a "limited-purpose money" in the old system, did not perform. As we have seen, brass rods were used as a standard in some situations of conveyance in the intermediate or "prestige" category. They were also used as a means of payment (but specifically not as a standard) in some instances of conversion.

In this situation, the early Administrative officers interpreted brass rods as "money," by which they meant a general-purpose money. It became a fairly easy process, in their view, to establish by fiat an exchange rate between brass rods and a new coinage, "withdraw" the rods, and hence "replace" one currency with another. The actual effect, as we have seen, was to introduce a general-purpose currency in place of a limited-purpose money. Today all conversions and most conveyances are made in terms of coinage. Yet Tiv constantly express their distrust of money. This fact, and another — that a single means of exchange has entered all the economic spheres — has broken down the major distinctions among the spheres. Money has created in Tivland a unicentric economy. Not only is the money a general-purpose money, but it applies to the full range of exchangeable goods.

Thus, when semiprofessional traders, using money, began trading in the foodstuffs marketed by women and formerly solely the province of women, the range of the market was very greatly increased, and hence the price in Tiv markets is determined by supply and demand far distant from the local producer and consumer. Tiv react to this situation by saying that foreign traders "spoil" their markets. The overlap of marketing and men's long-distance trade in staples also results in truckload after truckload of foodstuffs exported from major Tiv markets every day they meet. Tiv say that food is less plentiful today than it was in the past, though more land is being farmed. Tiv elders deplore this situation and know what is happening, but they do not know just where to fix the blame. In attempts to do something about it, they sometimes announce that no women are to sell any food at all. But when their wives disobey them men do not really feel that they were wrong to have done so. Tiv sometimes discriminate against non-Tiv traders in attempts to stop export of food. In their condemnation of the situation which is depriving them of their food faster than they are able to increase production, Tiv elders always curse money itself. It is money which, as the instrument for selling one's life subsistence, is responsible for the worsened situation — money and the Europeans who brought it.

Of even greater concern to Tiv is the influence money has had on marriage institutions. Today every women's guardian, in accepting money as bridewealth, feels that he is converting down. Although attempts are made to spend money which is received in bridewealth to acquire brides for one's self and one's sons, it is in the nature of money, Tiv insist, that it is most difficult to accomplish. The good man still spends his bridewealth receipts for brides — but good men are not so numerous as would be desirable. Tiv deplore the fact that they are required to "sell" (*te*) their daughters and "buy" (*yam*) wives. There is no dignity in it since the possibility of making a bridewealth marriage into an exchange marriage has been removed.

With money, thus, the institutionalization of Tiv economy has become unicentric, even though Tiv still see it with multicentric values. The single sphere takes many of its characteristics from the market, so that the new situation can be considered a spread of the market. But throughout these changes in institutionalization, the basic Tiv value of maximization — converting one's wealth into the highest category, women and children — has remained. And in this discrepancy between values and institutions, Tiv have come upon what is to them a paradox, for all that Westerners understand it and are familiar with it. Today it is easy to sell subsistence goods for money to buy prestige articles and women, thereby aggrandizing oneself at a rapid rate. The food so sold is exported, decreasing the amount of subsistence goods available for consumption. On the other hand, the number of women is limited. The result is that bridewealth gets higher: rights in women have entered the market, and since the supply is fixed, the price of women has become inflated.

The frame of reference given me by the organizer of this symposium asked for comments on the effects of increased monetization on trade, on the distribution of wealth and indebtedness. To sum up the situation in these terms, trade has vastly increased, with the introduction of general-purpose money but also with the other factors brought by a colonial form of government. At the same time, the market has expanded its range of applicability in the society. The Tiv are, indigenously, a people who valued egalitarian distribution of wealth to the extent that they believe they bewitched one another to whittle down the wealth of one man to the size of that of another. With money, the degree and extent of differentiation by wealth has greatly increased and will probably continue to increase. Finally, money has brought a new form of indebtedness — one which we know only too well. In the indigenous system, debt took either the form of owing marriage wards and was hence congruent with the kinship system, or else took the form of decreased prestige. There was no debt in the sphere of subsistence because there was no credit there save among kinsmen and neighbors whose activities were aspects of family status, not acts of moneylenders. The introduction of general-purpose money and the concomitant spread of the market has divorced debt from kinship and status and has created the notion of debt in the subsistence sphere divorced from the activities of kinsmen and neighbors.

In short, because of the spread of the market and the introduction of general-purpose money, Tiv economy has become a part of the world economy. It has brought about profound changes in the institutionalization of Tiv society. Money is one of the shatteringly simplifying ideas of all time, and like any other new and compelling idea, it creates its own revolution. The monetary revolution, at least in this part of Africa, is the turn away from the multicentric economy. Its course may be painful, but there is very little doubt about its outcome.

REVIEW QUESTIONS

1. What is Bohannan's definition of money? What is the difference between general- and special-purpose money?

2. What does Bohannan mean by *economic spheres*? How were these spheres traditionally related in the Tiv economy?

3. What does Bohannan mean by *conveyance* and *conversion*? How could Tiv men use conversion to increase their power and prestige?

4. In what ways are Tiv marriage customs part of the economic system? Do you think American marriage customs also fall within the economic system in some way? How?

5. Explain the effects of European money on the Tiv economic system.

22 Men and Jobs

ELLIOT LIEBOW

*In our complex Western economy, the jobs people have and the
value society places on them determine productive capability and
self-esteem. In this classic work, Elliot Liebow examines the cultural meaning of jobs to men in the black ghetto. Like millions of
today's poor, most black "corner men" have little motivation to
work. Realistic assessment tells them that pay will be too low.
Higher-paying jobs usually require physical stamina, health, training, experience, and personal transportation — all things corner
men may lack. And just as important, corner men place the same
low value on the menial jobs they can get as do the more affluent
members of our society; they are not motivated by current or future
prospects for work.*

A pickup truck drives slowly down the street. The truck stops as it
comes abreast of a man sitting on a cast-iron porch and the white
drive calls out, asking if the man wants a day's work. The man shakes
his head and the truck moves on up the block, stopping again whenever
idling men come within calling distance of the driver. At the Carry-
out corner, five men debate the question briefly and shake their heads
no to the truck. The truck turns the corner and repeats the same
performance up the next street. In the distance, one can see one man,

then another, climb into the back of the truck and sit down. It starts and stops, the truck finally disappears.

What is it we have witnessed here? A labor scavenger rebuffed by his would-be prey? Lazy, irresponsible men turning down an honest day's pay for an honest day's work? Or a more complex phenomenon marking the intersection of economic forces, social values, and individual states of mind and body?

Let us look again at the driver of the truck. He has been able to recruit only two or three men from each twenty or fifty he contacts. To him, it is clear that the others simply do not choose to work. Singly or in groups, belly-empty or belly-full, sullen or gregarious, drunk or sober, they confirm what he has read, heard, and knows from his own experience: these men wouldn't take a job if it were handed to them on a platter.[1]

Quite apart from the question of whether or not this is true of some of the men he sees on the street, it is clearly not true of all of them. If it were, he would not have come here in the first place; or having come, he would have left with an empty truck. It is not even true of most of them, for most of the men he sees on the street this weekday morning do, in fact, have jobs. But since, at the moment, they are neither working nor sleeping, and since they hate the depressing room or apartment they live in, or because there is nothing to do there,[2] or because they want to get away from their wives or anyone else living there, they are out on the street, indistinguishable from those who do not have jobs or do not want them. Some, like Boley, a member of a trash-collection crew in a suburban housing development, work Saturdays and are off on this weekday. Some, like Sweets, work nights cleaning up middle-class trash, dirt, dishes, and garbage, and mopping the floors of the office buildings, hotels, restaurants, toilets, and other public places dirtied during the day. Some men work for retail businesses such as liquor stores, which do not begin the day until ten o'clock. Some laborers, like Tally, have already come back from the job because the ground was too wet for pick and shovel or because the weather was too cold for pouring concrete. Other employed men stayed off the job today for personal reasons: Clarence to go to a funeral at eleven this morning and Sea Cat to answer a subpoena as a witness in a criminal proceeding.

---

[1] By different methods, perhaps, some social scientists have also located the problem in the men themselves, in their unwillingness or lack of desire to work: "To improve the underprivileged worker's performance one must help him to learn to *want* . . . higher social goals for himself and his children. . . . The problem of changing the work habits and motivation of [lower class] people . . . is a problem of changing the goals, the ambitions, and the level of cultural and occupational aspiration of the underprivileged worker." (Emphasis in original.) Allison Davis, "The Motivation of the Underprivileged Worker," 90.

[2] The comparison of sitting at home alone with being in jail is commonplace.

Also on the street, unwitting contributors to the impression taken away by the truck driver, are the halt and the lame. The man on the cast-iron steps strokes one gnarled arthritic hand with the other and says he doesn't know whether or not he'll live long enough to be eligible for Social Security. He pauses, then adds matter-of-factly, "Most times, I don't care whether I do or don't." Stoopy's left leg was polio-withered in childhood. Raymond, who looks as if he could tear out a fire hydrant, coughs up blood if he bends or moves suddenly. The quiet man who hangs out in front of the Saratoga apartments has a steel hook strapped onto his left elbow. And had the man in the truck been able to look into the wine-clouded eyes of the man in the green cap, he would have realized that the man did not even understand he was being offered a day's work.

Others, having had jobs and been laid off, are drawing unemployment compensation (up to $44 per week) and have nothing to gain by accepting work which pays little more than this and frequently less.

Still others, like Bumdoodle the numbers man, are working hard at illegal ways of making money, hustlers who are on the street to turn a dollar any way they can: buying and selling sex, liquor, narcotics, stolen goods, or anything else that turns up.

Only a handful remains unaccounted for. There is Tonk, who cannot bring himself to take a job away from the corner, because, according to the other men, he suspects his wife will be unfaithful if given the opportunity. There is Stanton, who has not reported to work for four days now, not since Bernice disappeared. He bought a brand-new knife against her return. She had done this twice before, he said, but not for so long and not without warning, and he had forgiven her. But this time, "I ain't got it in me to forgive her again." His rage and shame are there for all to see as he paces the Carry-out and the corner, day and night, hoping to catch a glimpse of her.

And finally, there are those like Arthur, able-bodied men who have no visible means of support, legal or illegal, who neither have jobs nor want them. The truck driver, among others, believes the Arthurs to be representative of all the men he sees idling on the street during his own working hours. They are not, but they cannot be dismissed simply because they are a small minority. It is not enough to explain them away as being lazy or irresponsible or both because an able-bodied man with responsibilities who refuses work is, by the truck driver's definition, lazy and irresponsible. Such an answer begs the question. It is descriptive of the facts; it does not explain them.

Moreover, despite their small numbers, the don't-work-and-don't-want-to-work minority is especially significant because they represent the strongest and clearest expression of those values and attitudes associated with making a living which, to varying degrees, are found throughout the streetcorner world. These men differ from the others in degree rather than in kind, the principal difference being that they are carrying out the implications of their values and experiences to their logical, inevitable conclusions. In this sense, the others have yet to come to terms with themselves and the world they live in.

Putting aside, for the moment, what the men say and feel, and looking at what they actually do and the choices they make, getting a job, keeping a job, and doing well at it is clearly of low priority. Arthur will not take a job at all. Leroy is supposed to be on his job at 4:00 P.M. but it is already 4:10 and he still cannot bring himself to leave the free games he has accumulated on the pinball machine in the Carry-out. Tonk started a construction job on Wednesday, worked Thursday and Friday, then didn't go back again. On the same kind of job, Sea Cat quit in the second week. Sweets had been working three months as a busboy in a restaurant, then quit without notice, not sure himself why he did so. A real estate agent, saying he was more interested in getting the job done than in the cost, asked Richard to give him an estimate on repairing and painting the inside of a house, but Richard, after looking over the job, somehow never got around to submitting an estimate. During one period, Tonk would not leave the corner to take a job because his wife might prove unfaithful; Stanton would not take a job because his woman had been unfaithful.

Thus, the man-job relationship is a tenuous one. At any given moment, a job may occupy a relatively low position on the streetcorner scale of real values. Getting a job may be subordinated to relations with women or to other non-job considerations; the commitment to a job one already has is frequently shallow and tentative.

The reasons are many. Some are objective and reside principally in the job; some are subjective and reside principally in the man. The line between them, however, is not a clear one. Behind the man's refusal to take a job or his decision to quit one is not a simple impulse or value choice but a complex combination of assessments of objective reality on the one hand, and values, attitudes, and beliefs drawn from different levels of his experience on the other.

Objective economic considerations are frequently a controlling factor in a man's refusal to take a job. How much the job pays is a crucial question but seldom asked. He knows how much it pays. Working as a stock clerk, a delivery boy, or even behind the counter of liquor stores, drug stores, and other retail businesses pays one dollar an hour. So, too, do most busboy, car-wash, janitorial, and other jobs available to him. Some jobs, such as dishwasher, may dip as low as eighty cents an hour and others, such as elevator operator or work in a junk yard, may offer $1.15 or $1.25. Take-home pay for jobs such as these ranges from $35 to $50 a week, but a take-home pay of over $45 for a five-day week is the exception rather than the rule.

One of the principal advantages of these kinds of jobs is that they offer fairly regular work. Most of them involve essential services and are therefore somewhat less responsive to business conditions than are some higher paying, less menial jobs. Most of them are also inside jobs not dependent on the weather, as are construction jobs and other higher-paying outside work.

Another seemingly important advantage of working in hotels, restaurants, office and apartment buildings, and retail establishments is that they frequently offer an opportunity for stealing on the job. But stealing can be a two-edged sword. Apart from increasing the cost of the goods or services to the general public, a less obvious result is that the practice usually acts as a depressant on the employee's own wage level. Owners of small retail establishments and other employers frequently anticipate employee stealing and adjust the wage rate accordingly. Tonk's employer explained why he was paying Tonk $35 for a fifty-five to sixty hour workweek. These men will all steal, he said. Although he keeps close watch on Tonk, he estimates that Tonk steals from $35 to $40 a week.[3] What he steals, when added to his regular earnings, brings his take-home pay to $70 or $75 per week. The employer said he did not mind this because Tonk is worth that much to the business. But if he were to pay Tonk outright the full value of his labor, Tonk would still be stealing $35–$40 per week and this, he said, the business simply would not support.

This wage arrangement, with stealing built-in, was satisfactory to both parties, with each one independently expressing his satisfaction. Such a wage-theft system, however, is not as balanced and equitable as it appears. Since the wage level rests on the premise that the employee will steal the unpaid value of his labor, the man who does not steal on the job is penalized. And furthermore, even if he does not steal, no one would believe him; the employer and others believe he steals because the system presumes it.

Nor is the man who steals, as he is expected to, as well off as he believes himself to be. The employer may occasionally close his eyes to the worker's stealing but not often and not for long. He is, after all, a businessman and cannot always find it within himself to let a man steal from him, even if the man is stealing his own wages. Moreover, it is only by keeping close watch on the worker that the employer can control how much is stolen and thereby protect himself against the employee's stealing more than he is worth. From this viewpoint, then, the employer is not in wage-theft collusion with the employee. In the case of Tonk, for instance, the employer was not actively

---

[3] Exactly the same estimate as the one made by Tonk himself. On the basis of personal knowledge of the stealing routine employed by Tonk, however, I suspect the actual amount is considerably smaller.

abetting the theft. His estimate of how much Tonk was stealing was based on what he thought Tonk was able to steal despite his own best efforts to prevent him from stealing anything at all. Were he to have caught Tonk in the act of stealing, he would, of course, have fired him from the job and perhaps called the police as well. Thus, in an actual if not in a legal sense, all the elements of entrapment are present. The employer knowingly provides the conditions which entice (force) the employee to steal the unpaid value of his labor, but at the same time he punishes him for theft if he catches him doing so.

Other consequences of the wage-theft system are even more damaging to the employee. Let us, for argument's sake, say that Tonk is in no danger of entrapment; that his employer is willing to wink at the stealing and that Tonk, for his part, is perfectly willing to earn a little, steal a little. Let us say, too, that he is paid $35 a week and allowed to steal $35. His money income — as measured by the goods and services he can purchase with it — is, of course, $70. But not all of his income is available to him for all purposes. He cannot draw on what he steals to build his self-respect or to measure his self-worth. For this, he can draw only on his earnings — the amount given him publicly and voluntarily in exchange for his labor. His "respect" and "self-worth" income remains at $35 — only half that of the man who also receives $70 but all of it in the form of wages. His earnings publicly measure the worth of his labor to his employer, and they are important to others and to himself in taking the measure of his worth as a man.[4]

With or without stealing, and quite apart from any interior processes going on in the man who refuses such a job or quits it casually and without apparent reason, the objective fact is that menial jobs in retailing or in the service trades simply do not pay enough to support a man and his family. This is not to say that the worker is underpaid; this may or may not be true. Whether he is or not, the plain fact is that, in such a job, he cannot make a living. Nor can he take much comfort in the fact that these jobs tend to offer more regular, steadier work. If he cannot live on the $45 or $50 he makes in one week, the longer he works, the longer he cannot live on what he makes.[5]

---

[4] Some public credit may accrue to the clever thief, but not respect.

[5] It might be profitable to compare, as Howard S. Becker suggests, gross aspects of income and housing costs in this particular area with those reported by Herbert Gans for the low-income working class in Boston's West End. In 1958, Gans reports, median income for the West Enders was just under $70 a week, a level considerably higher than that enjoyed by the people in the Carry-out neighborhood five years later. Gans himself rented a six-room apartment in the West End for $46 a month, about $10 more than the going rate for long-time residents. In the Carry-out neighborhood, rooms that could accommodate more than a cot and a miniature dresser — that is, rooms that qualified for family living — rented for $12 to $22 a week. Ignoring differences that really can't be ignored — the privacy and self-contained efficiency of the multi-room apartment as against the fragmented, public living of the rooming-house "apartment," with a public toilet on a floor always different from the one your room is on (no matter,

Construction work, even for unskilled laborers, usually pays better, with the hourly rate ranging from $1.50 to $2.60.[6] Importantly, too, good references, a good driving record, a tenth grade (or any high school) education, previous experience, the ability to "bring police clearance with you" are not normally required of laborers as they frequently are for some of the jobs in retailing or in the service trades.

Construction work, however, has its own objective disadvantages. It is, first of all, seasonal work for the great bulk of the laborers, beginning early in the spring and tapering off as winter weather sets in.[7] And even during the season the work is frequently irregular. Early or late in the season, snow or temperatures too low for concrete frequently sends the laborers back home, and during late spring or summer, a heavy rain on Tuesday or Wednesday, leaving a lot of water and mud behind it, can mean a two- or three-day workweek for the pick-and-shovel men and other unskilled laborers.[8]

The elements are not the only hazard. As the project moves from one construction stage to another, laborers — usually without warning — are laid off, sometimes permanently or sometimes for weeks at a time. The more fortunate or the better workers are told periodically to "take a walk for two, three days."

---

it probably doesn't work, anyway) — and assuming comparable states of disrepair, the West Enders were paying $6 or $7 a month for a room that cost the Carry-outers at least $50 a month, and frequently more. Looking at housing costs as a percentage of income — and again ignoring what cannot be ignored: that what goes by the name of "housing" in the two areas is not at all the same thing — the median income West Ender could get a six-room apartment for about 12 percent of his income, while his 1963 Carry-out counterpart, with a weekly income of $60 (to choose a figure from the upper end of the income range), often paid 20–33 percent of his income for one room. See Herbert J. Gans, *The Urban Villagers,* 10–13.

[6] The higher amount is 1962 union scale for building laborers. According to the Wage Agreement Contract for Heavy Construction Laborers (Washington, DC, and vicinity) covering the period from May 1, 1963 to April 30, 1966, minimum hourly wage for heavy construction laborers was to go from $2.75 (May 1963) by annual increments to $2.92, effective November 1, 1965.

[7] "Open-sky" work, such as building overpasses, highways, etc., in which the workers and materials are directly exposed to the elements, traditionally begins in March and ends around Thanksgiving. The same is true for much of the street repair work and the laying of sewer, electric, gas, and telephone lines by the city and public utilities, all important employers of laborers. Between Thanksgiving and March, they retain only skeleton crews selected from their best, most reliable men.

[8] In a recent year, the crime rate in Washington for the month of August jumped 18 percent over the preceding month. A veteran police officer explained the increase to David L. Bazelon, Chief Judge, U.S. Court of Appeals for the District of Columbia. "It's quite simple. . . . You see, August was a very wet month. . . . These people wait on the streetcorner each morning around 6:00 or 6:30 for a truck to pick them up and take them to a construction site. If it's raining, that truck doesn't come, and the men are going to be idle that day. If the bad weather keeps up for three days . . . we know we are going to have trouble on our hands — and sure enough, there invariably follows a rash of purse-snatchings, house-breakings and the like. . . . These people have to eat like the rest of us, you know." David L. Bazelon, Address to the Federal Bar Association, 3.

Both getting the construction job and getting to it are also relatively more difficult than is the case for the menial jobs in retailing and the service trades. Job competition is always fierce. In the city, the large construction projects are unionized. One has to have ready cash to get into the union to become eligible to work on these projects and, being eligible, one has to find an opening. Unless one "knows somebody," say, a foreman or a laborer who knows the day before that they are going to take on new men in the morning, this can be a difficult and disheartening search.

Many of the nonunion jobs are in suburban Maryland or Virginia. The newspaper ads say, "Report ready to work to the trailer at the intersection of Rte. 11 and Old Bridge Rd., Bunston, Virginia (or Maryland)," but this location may be ten, fifteen, or even twenty-five miles from the Carry-out. Public transportation would require two or more hours to get there, if it services the area at all. Without access to a car or to a car-pool arrangement, it is not worthwhile reading the ad. So the men do not. Jobs such as these are usually filled by word of mouth information, beginning with someone who knows someone or who is himself working there and looking for a paying rider. Furthermore, nonunion jobs in outlying areas tend to be smaller projects of relatively short duration and to pay somewhat less than scale.

Still another objective factor is the work itself. For some men, whether the job be digging, mixing mortar, pushing a wheelbarrow, unloading materials, carrying and placing steel rods for reinforcing concrete, or building or laying concrete forms, the work is simply too hard. Men such as Tally and Wee Tom can make such work look like child's play; some of the older work-hardened men, such as Budder and Stanton, can do it too, although not without showing unmistakable signs of strain and weariness at the end of the workday. But those who lack the robustness of a Tally or the time-inured immunity of a Budder must either forego jobs such as these or pay a heavy toll to keep them. For Leroy, in his early twenties, almost six feet tall but weighing under 140 pounds, it would be as difficult to push a loaded wheelbarrow, or to unload and stack 96-pound bags of cement all day long, as it would be for Stoopy and his withered leg.

Heavy, backbreaking labor of the kind that used to be regularly associated with bull gangs or concrete gangs is no longer characteristic of laboring jobs, especially those with the larger, well-equipped construction companies. Brute strength is still required from time to time, as on smaller jobs where it is not economical to bring in heavy equipment or where the small, undercapitalized contractor has none to bring in. In many cases, however, the conveyor belt has replaced the wheelbarrow or the Georgia buggy, mechanized forklifts have eliminated heavy, manual lifting, and a variety of digging machines have replaced the pick and shovel. The result is fewer jobs for unskilled laborers and, in many cases, a work speed-up for those who do have jobs. Machines now set the pace formerly set by men. Formerly, a laborer pushed a wheelbarrow of wet cement to a particular spot, dumped it, and returned for another load. Another laborer, in hip boots, pushed the wet concrete around with a shovel or a hoe, getting it roughly level in preparation for the skilled finishers. He had relatively small loads to contend with and had only to keep up with the men pushing the wheelbarrows. Now, the job for the man pushing the wheelbarrow is gone and the wet concrete comes rushing down a chute at the man in the hip boots who must "spread it quick or drown."

Men who have been running an elevator, washing dishes, or "pulling trash" cannot easily move into laboring jobs. They lack the basic skills for "unskilled" construction labor, familiarity with tools and materials, and tricks of the trade without which hard jobs are made harder. Previously unused or untrained muscles rebel in pain against the new and insistent demands made upon them, seriously compromising the man's performance and testing his willingness to see the job through.

A healthy, sturdy, active man of good intelligence requires from two to four weeks to break in on a construction job.[9] Even if he is willing somehow to bull his way through the first few weeks, it frequently happens that his foreman or the craftsman he services with materials and general assistance is not willing to wait that long for him to get into condition or to learn at a glance the difference in size between a rough 2″ x 8″ and a finished 2″ x 10″. The foreman and the craftsman are themselves "under the gun" and cannot "carry" the man when other men, who are already used to the work and who know the tools and materials, are lined up to take the job.

Sea Cat was "healthy, sturdy, active, and of good intelligence." When a judge gave him six weeks in which to pay his wife $200 in back child-support payments, he left his grocery-store job in order to take a higher-paying job as a laborer, arranged for him by a foreman friend. During the first week the weather was bad and he worked only Wednesday and Friday, cursing the elements all the while for cheating him out of the money he could have made. The second week, the weather was fair but he quit at the end of the fourth day, saying frankly that the work was too hard for him. He went back to his job at the grocery store and took a second job working nights as a dishwasher in a restaurant,[10] earning little if any more at the two jobs than he

---

[9] Estimate of Mr. Francis Greenfield, President of the International Hod Carriers, Building and Common Laborers' District Council of Washington, DC, and Vicinity. I am indebted to Mr. Greenfield for several points in these paragraphs dealing with construction laborers.

[10] Not a sinecure, even by streetcorner standards.

would have earned as a laborer, and keeping at both of them until he had paid off his debts.

Tonk did not last as long as Sea Cat. No one made any predictions when he got a job in a parking lot, but when the men on the corner learned he was to start on a road construction job, estimates of how long he would last ranged from one to three weeks. Wednesday was his first day. He spent that evening and night at home. He did the same on Thursday. He worked Friday and spent Friday evening and part of Saturday draped over the mailbox on the corner. Sunday afternoon, Tonk decided he was not going to report on the job the next morning. He explained that after working three days, he knew enough about the job to know that it was too hard for him. He knew he wouldn't be able to keep up and he'd just as soon quit now as get fired later.

Logan was a tall, two-hundred-pound man in his late twenties. His back used to hurt him only on the job, he said, but now he can't straighten up for increasingly longer periods of time. He said he had traced this to the awkward walk he was forced to adopt by the loaded wheelbarrows which pull him down into a half-stoop. He's going to quit, he said, as soon as he can find another job. If he can't find one real soon, he guesses he'll quit anyway. It's not worth it, having to walk bent over and leaning to one side.

Sometimes, the strain and effort is greater than the man is willing to admit, even to himself. In the early summer of 1963, Richard was rooming at Nancy's place. His wife and children were "in the country" (his grandmother's home in Carolina), waiting for him to save up enough money so that he could bring them back to Washington and start over again after a disastrous attempt to "make it" in Philadelphia. Richard had gotten a job with a fence company in Virginia. It paid $1.60 an hour. The first few evenings, when he came home from work, he looked ill from exhaustion and the heat. Stanton said Richard would have to quit, "he's too small [thin] for that kind of work." Richard said he was doing O.K. and would stick with the job.

At Nancy's one night, when Richard had been working about two weeks, Nancy and three or four others were sitting around talking, drinking, and listening to music. Someone asked Nancy when was Richard going to bring his wife and children up from the country. Nancy said she didn't know, but it probably depended on how long it would take him to save up enough money. She said she didn't think he could stay with the fence job much longer. This morning, she said, the man Richard rode to work with knocked on the door and Richard didn't answer. She looked in his room. Richard was still asleep. Nancy tried to shake him awake. "No more digging!" Richard cried out. "No more digging! I can't do no more God-damn digging!" When Nancy finally managed to wake him, he dressed quickly and went to work.

Richard stayed on the job two more weeks, then suddenly quit, ostensibly because his pay check was three dollars less than what he thought it should have been.

In summary of objective job considerations, then, the most important fact is that a man who is able and willing to work cannot earn enough money to support himself, his wife, and one or more children. A man's chances for working regularly are good only if he is willing to work for less than he can live on, and sometimes not even then. On some jobs, the wage rate is deceptively higher than on others, but the higher the wage rate, the more difficult it is to get the job, and the less the job security. Higher-paying construction work tends to be seasonal and, during the season, the amount of work available is highly sensitive to business and weather conditions and to the changing requirements of individual projects.[11] Moreover, high-paying construction jobs are frequently beyond the physical capacity of some of the men, and some of the low-paying jobs are scaled down even lower in accordance with the self-fulfilling assumption that the man will steal part of his wages on the job.[12]

Bernard assesses the objective job situation dispassionately over a cup of coffee, sometimes poking at the coffee with his spoon, sometimes staring at it as if, like a crystal ball, it holds tomorrow's secrets. He is twenty-seven years old. He and the woman with whom he lives have a baby son, and she has another child by another man. Bernard does odd jobs — mostly painting — but here it is the end of January, and his last job was with the Post Office during the Christmas mail rush. He would like postal work as a steady job, he says. It pays well (about $2.00 an hour) but he has twice failed the Post Office examination (he graduated from a Washington high school) and has given up the idea as an impractical one. He is supposed to see a man tonight about a job as a parking attendant for a large apartment house. The man told him to bring his birth certificate and driver's license, but his license was suspended because of a backlog of unpaid traffic fines. A friend promised to lend him some money this evening. If he gets it,

---

[11] The overall result is that, in the long run, a black laborer's earnings are not substantially greater — and may be less — than those of the busboy, janitor, or stock clerk. Herman P. Miller, for example, reports that in 1960, 40 percent of all jobs held by black men were as laborers or in the service trades. The average annual wage for nonwhite nonfarm laborers was $2,400. The average earning of nonwhite service workers was $2,500 (*Rich Man, Poor Man*, 90). Francis Greenfield estimates that in the Washington vicinity, the 1965 earnings of the union laborer who works whenever work is available will be about $3,200. Even this figure is high for the man on the streetcorner. Union men in heavy construction are the aristocrats of the laborers. Casual day labor and jobs with small firms in the building and construction trades, or with firms in other industries, pay considerably less.

[12] For an excellent discussion of the self-fulfilling assumption (or prophecy) as a social force, see "The Self-Fulfilling Prophecy," Ch. XI, in Robert K. Merton's *Social Theory and Social Structure*.

he will pay the fines tomorrow morning and have his license reinstated. He hopes the man with the job will wait till tomorrow night.

A "security job" is what he really wants, he said. He would like to save up money for a taxicab. (But having twice failed the postal examination and having a bad driving record as well, it is highly doubtful that he could meet the qualifications or pass the written test.) That would be "a good life." He can always get a job in a restaurant or as a clerk in a drugstore but they don't pay enough, he said. He needs to take home at least $50 to $55 a week. He thinks he can get that much driving a truck somewhere . . . Sometimes he wishes he had stayed in the army . . . A security job, that's what he wants most of all, a real security job . . .

When we look at what the men bring to the job rather than at what the job offers the men, it is essential to keep in mind that we are not looking at men who come to the job fresh, just out of school perhaps, and newly prepared to undertake the task of making a living, or from another job where they earned a living and are prepared to do the same on this job. Each man comes to the job with a long job history characterized by his not being able to support himself and his family. Each man carries this knowledge, born of his experience, with him. He comes to the job flat and stale, wearied by the sameness of it all, convinced of his own incompetence, terrified of responsibility — of being tested still again and found wanting. Possible exceptions are the younger men not yet, or just, married. They suspect all this but have yet to have it confirmed by repeated personal experience over time. But those who are or have been married know it well. It is the experience of the individual and the group; of their fathers and probably their sons. Convinced of their inadequacies, not only do they not seek out those better-paying jobs which test their resources, but they actively avoid them, gravitating in a mass to the menial, routine jobs which offer no challenge — and therefore pose no threat — to the already diminished images they have of themselves.

Thus Richard does not follow through on the real estate agent's offer. He is afraid to do on his own — minor plastering, replacing broken windows, other minor repairs, and painting — exactly what he had been doing for months on a piecework basis under someone else (and which provided him with a solid base from which to derive a cost estimate).

Richard once offered an important clue to what may have gone on in his mind when the job offer was made. We were in the Carry-out, at a time when he was looking for work. He was talking about the kind of jobs available to him.

> I graduated from high school [Baltimore] but I don't know anything. I'm dumb. Most of the time I don't even say I graduated, 'cause then

somebody asks me a question and I can't answer it, and they think I was lying about graduating. . . . They graduated me but I didn't know anything. I had lousy grades but I guess they wanted to get rid of me.

I was at Margaret's house the other night and her little sister asked me to help her with her homework. She showed me some fractions and I knew right away I couldn't do them. I was ashamed so I told her I had to go to the bathroom.

And so it must have been, surely, with the real estate agent's offer. Convinced that "I'm dumb . . . I don't know anything," he "knew right away" he couldn't do it, despite the fact that he had been doing just this sort of work all along.

Thus, the man's low self-esteem generates a fear of being tested and prevents him from accepting a job with responsibilities or, once on a job, from staying with it if responsibilities are thrust on him, even if the wages are commensurately higher. Richard refuses such a job, Leroy leaves one, and another man, given more responsibility and more pay, knows he will fail and proceeds to do so, proving he was right about himself all along. The self-fulfilling prophecy is everywhere at work. In a hallway, Stanton, Tonk, and Boley are passing a bottle around. Stanton recalls the time he was in the service. Everything was fine until he attained the rank of corporal. He worried about everything he did then. Was he doing the right thing? Was he doing it well? When would they discover their mistake and take his stripes (and extra pay) away? When he finally lost his stripes, everything was all right again.

Lethargy, disinterest, and general apathy on the job, so often reported by employers, has its streetcorner counterpart. The men do not ordinarily talk about their jobs or ask one another about them.[13] Although most of the men know who is or is not working at any given time, they may or may not know what particular job an individual man has. There is no overt interest in job specifics as they relate to this or that person, in large part perhaps because the specifics are not especially relevant. To know that a man is working is to know approximately how much he makes and to know as much as one needs or wants to know about how he makes it. After all, how much difference does it make to know whether a man is pushing a mop or pulling trash in an apartment house, a restaurant, or an office building, or delivering groceries, drugs, or liquor, or, if he's a laborer, whether he's pushing a wheelbarrow, mixing mortar, or digging a hole. So much does one

---

[13] This stands in dramatic contrast to the leisure-time conversation of stable, working-class men. For the coal miners (of Ashton, England), for example, "the topic [of conversation] which surpasses all others in frequency is work — the difficulties which have been encountered in the day's shift, the way in which a particular task was accomplished, and so on." Josephine Klein, *Samples from English Cultures*, Vol. I, 88.

job look like every other that there is little to choose between them. In large part, the job market consists of a narrow range of nondescript chores calling for nondistinctive, undifferentiated, unskilled labor. "A job is a job."

A crucial factor in the streetcorner man's lack of job commitment is the overall value he places on the job. *For his part, the streetcorner man puts no lower value on the job than does the larger society around him.* He knows the social value of the job by the amount of money the employer is willing to pay him for doing it. In a real sense, every pay day, he counts in dollars and cents the value placed on the job by society at large. He is no more (and frequently less) ready to quit and look for another job than his employer is ready to fire him and look for another man. Neither the streetcorner man who performs these jobs nor the society which requires him to perform them assess the job as one "worth doing and worth doing well." Both employee and employer are contemptuous of the job. The employee shows his contempt by his reluctance to accept it or keep it, the employer by paying less than is required to support a family.[14] Nor does the low-wage job offer prestige, respect, interesting work, opportunity for learning or advancement, or any other compensation. With few exceptions, jobs filled by the streetcorner men are at the bottom of the employment ladder in every respect, from wage level to prestige. Typically, they are hard, dirty, uninteresting, and underpaid. The rest of society (whatever its ideal values regarding the dignity of labor) holds the job of the dishwasher or janitor or unskilled laborer in low esteem if not outright contempt.[15] So does the streetcorner man. He cannot do otherwise. He cannot draw from a job those social values which other people do not put into it.[16]

Only occasionally does spontaneous conversation touch on these matters directly. Talk about jobs is usually limited to isolated statements of intention, such as "I think I'll get me another gig [job]," "I'm

---

[14] It is important to remember that the employer is not entirely a free agent. Subject to the constraints of the larger society, he acts for the larger society as well as for himself. Child labor laws, safety and sanitation regulations, minimum wage scales in some employment areas, and other constraints are already on the books; other control mechanisms, such as a guaranteed annual wage, are to be had for the voting.

[15] See, for example, the U.S. Bureau of the Census, *Methodology and Scores of Socioeconomic Status.* This assignment of the lowest SES ratings to men who hold such jobs is not peculiar to our own society. A low SES rating for "the shoeshine boy or garbage man . . . seems to be true for all [industrial] countries." Alex Inkeles, "Industrial Man," 8.

[16] That the streetcorner man downgrades manual labor should occasion no surprise. Merton points out that "the American stigmatization of manual labor . . . *has been found to hold rather uniformly in all social classes*" (emphasis in original; *Social Theory and Social Structure,* p. 145). That he finds no satisfaction in such work should also occasion no surprise: "[There is] a clear positive correlation between the over-all status of occupations and the experience of satisfaction in them." Inkeles, "Industrial Man," 12.

going to look for a construction job when the weather breaks," or "I'm going to quit. I can't take no more of his shit." Job assessments typically consist of nothing more than a noncommittal shrug and "It's O.K." or "It's a job."

One reason for the relative absence of talk about one's job is, as suggested earlier, that the sameness of job experience does not bear reiteration. Another and more important reason is the emptiness of the job experience itself. The man sees middle-class occupations as a primary source of prestige, pride, and self-respect; his own job affords him none of these. To think about his job is to see himself as others see him, to remind him of just where he stands in this society.[17] And because society's criteria for placement are generally the same as his own, to talk about his job can trigger a flush of shame and a deep, almost physical ache to change places with someone, almost anyone, else.[18] The desire to be a person in his own right, to be noticed by the world he lives in, is shared by each of the men on the streetcorner. Whether they articulate this desire (as Tally does below) or not, one can see them position themselves to catch the attention of their fellows in much the same way as plants bend or stretch to catch the sunlight.[19]

Tally and I were in the Carry-out. It was summer, Tally's peak earning season as a cement finisher, a semiskilled job a cut or so above that of the unskilled laborer. His take-home pay during these weeks was well over a hundred dollars — "a lot of bread." But for Tally, who no longer had a family to support, bread was not enough.

"You know that boy came in last night? That Black Moozlem? That's what I ought to be doing. I ought to be in his place."
"What do you mean?"
"Dressed nice, going to [night] school, got a good job."
"He's no better off than you, Tally. You make much more than he does."
"It's not the money. [Pause] It's position, I guess. He's got position. When he finish school he gonna be a supervisor. People respect him. . . .

---

[17] "[In our society] a man's work is one of the things by which he is judged, and certainly one of the more significant things by which he judges himself. . . A man's work is one of the more important parts of his social identity, of his self; indeed, of his fate in the one life he has to live." Everett C. Hughes, *Men and Their Work,* 42–43.

[18] Noting that lower-class persons "are constantly exposed to evidence of their own irrelevance," Lee Rainwater spells out still another way in which the poor are poor: "The identity problems of lower class persons make the soul-searching of middle class adolescents and adults seem rather like a kind of conspicuous consumption of psychic riches" ("Work and Identity in the Lower Class," 3).

[19] Sea Cat cuts his pants legs off at the calf and puts a fringe on the raggedy edges. Tonk breaks his "shades" and continues to wear the horn-rimmed frames minus the lenses. Richard cultivates a distinctive manner of speech. Lonny gives himself a birthday party. And so on.

Thinking about people with position and education gives me a feeling right here [pressing his fingers into the pit of his stomach]."

"You're educated, too. You have a skill, a trade. You're a cement finisher. You can make a building, pour a sidewalk."

"That's different. Look, can anybody do what you're doing? Can anybody just come up and do your job? Well, in one week I can teach you cement finishing. You won't be as good as me 'cause you won't have the experience but you'll be a cement finisher. That's what I mean. Anybody can do what I'm doing and that's what gives me this feeling. [Long pause] Suppose I like this girl. I go over to her house and I meet her father. He starts talking about what he done today. He talks about operating on somebody and sewing them up and about surgery. I know he's a doctor 'cause of the way he talks. Then she starts talking about what she did. Maybe she's a boss or a supervisor. Maybe she's a lawyer and her father says to me, 'And what do you do, Mr. Jackson?' [Pause] You remember at the courthouse, Lonny's trial? You and the lawyer was talking in the hall? You remember? I just stood there listening. I didn't say a word. You know why? 'Cause I didn't even know what you was talking about. That's happened to me a lot."

"Hell, you're nothing special. That happens to everybody. Nobody knows everything. One man is a doctor, so he talks about surgery. Another man is a teacher, so he talks about books. But doctors and teachers don't know anything about concrete. You're a cement finisher and that's your specialty."

"Maybe so, but when was the last time you saw anybody standing around talking about concrete?"

The streetcorner man wants to be a person in his own right, to be noticed, to be taken account of, but in this respect, as well as in meeting his money needs, his job fails him. The job and the man are even. The job fails the man and the man fails the job.

Furthermore, the man does not have any reasonable expectation that, however bad it is, his job will lead to better things. Menial jobs are not, by and large, the starting point of a track system which leads to even better jobs for those who are able and willing to do them. The busboy or dishwasher in a restaurant is not on a job track which, if negotiated skillfully, leads to chef or manager of the restaurant. The busboy or dishwasher who works hard becomes, simply, a hard-working busboy or dishwasher. Neither hard work nor perseverance can conceivably carry the janitor to a sitdown job in the office building he cleans up. And it is the apprentice who becomes the journeyman electrician, plumber, steam fitter, or bricklayer, not the common unskilled black laborer.

Thus, the job is not a stepping-stone to something better. It is a dead end. It promises to deliver no more tomorrow, next month, or next year than it does today.

Delivering little, and promising no more, the job is "no big thing." The man appears to treat the job in a cavalier fashion, working and not working as the spirit moves him, as if all that matters is the immediate satisfaction of his present appetites, the surrender to present moods, and the indulgence of whims with no thought for the cost, the consequences, the future. To the middle-class observer, this behavior reflects a "present-time orientation" — an "inability to defer gratification." It is this "present-time" orientation — as against the "future orientation" of the middle-class person — that "explains" to the outsider why Leroy chooses to spend the day at the Carry-out rather than report to work; why Richard, who was paid Friday, was drunk Saturday and Sunday and penniless Monday; why Sweets quit his job today because the boss looked at him "funny" yesterday.

But from the inside looking out, what appears as a "present-time" orientation to the outside observer is, to the man experiencing it, as much a future orientation as that of his middle-class counterpart.[20] The difference between the two men lies not so much in their different orientations to time as in their different orientations to future time or, more specifically, to their different futures.[21]

The future orientation of the middle-class person presumes, among other things, a surplus of resources to be invested in the future and a belief that the future will be sufficiently stable both to justify his investment (money in a bank, time and effort in a job, investment of himself in marriage and family, etc.) and to permit the consumption of his investment at a time, place, and manner of his own choosing and to his greater satisfaction. But the streetcorner man lives in a sea of want. He does not, as a rule, have a surplus of resources, either economic or psychological. Gratification of hunger and the desire for simple creature comforts cannot be long deferred. Neither can support for one's flagging self-esteem. Living on the edge of both economic and psychological subsistence, the streetcorner man is obliged to expend all his resources on maintaining himself from moment to moment.[22]

---

[20] Taking a somewhat different point of view, S. M. Miller and Frank Riessman suggest that "the entire concept of deferred gratification may be inappropriate to understanding the essence of workers' lives" ("The Working Class Subculture: A New View," 87).

[21] This sentence is a paraphrase of a statement made by Marvin Cline at a 1965 colloquium at the Mental Health Study Center, National Institute of Mental Health.

[22] And if, for the moment, he does sometimes have more money than he chooses to spend or more food than he wants to eat, he is pressed to spend the money and eat the food anyway since his friends, neighbors, kin, or acquaintances will beg or borrow whatever surplus he has or, failing this, they may steal it. In one extreme case, one of the men admitted taking the last of a woman's surplus food allotment after she had explained that, with four children, she could not spare any food. The prospect that consumer soft goods not consumed by oneself will be consumed by someone else may

As for the future, the young streetcorner man has a fairly good picture of it. In Richard or Sea Cat or Arthur he can see himself in his middle twenties; he can look at Tally to see himself at thirty, at Wee Tom to see himself in his middle thirties, and at Budder and Stanton to see himself in his forties. It is a future in which everything is uncertain except the ultimate destruction of his hopes and the eventual realization of his fears. The most he can reasonably look forward to is that these things do not come too soon. Thus, when Richard squanders a week's pay in two days it is not because, like an animal or a child, he is "present-time oriented," unaware of or unconcerned with his future. He does so precisely because he is aware of the future and the hopelessness of it all.

Sometimes this kind of response appears as a conscious, explicit choice. Richard had had a violent argument with his wife. He said he was going to leave her and the children, that he had had enough of everything and could not take any more, and he chased her out of the house. His chest still heaving, he leaned back against the wall in the hallway of his basement apartment.

"I've been scuffling for five years," he said. "I've been scuffling for five years from morning till night. And my kids still don't have anything, my wife don't have anything, and I don't have anything.

"There," he said, gesturing down the hall to a bed, a sofa, a couple of chairs, and a television set, all shabby, some broken. "There's everything I have and I'm having trouble holding onto that."

Leroy came in, presumably to petition Richard on behalf of Richard's wife, who was sitting outside on the steps, afraid to come in. Leroy started to say something but Richard cut him short.

"Look, Leroy, don't give me any of that action. You and me are entirely different people. Maybe I look like a boy and maybe I act like a boy sometimes but I got a man's mind. You and me don't want the same things out of life. Maybe some of the same, but you don't care how long you have to wait for yours and *I — want — mine — right — now*."[23]

---

be related to the way in which portable consumer durable goods, such as watches, radios, television sets, or phonographs, are sometimes looked at as a form of savings. When Shirley was on welfare, she regularly took her television set out of pawn when she got her monthly check. Not so much to watch it, she explained, as to have something to fall back on when her money runs out toward the end of the month. For her and others, the television set or the phonograph is her savings, the pawnshop is where she banks her savings, and the pawn ticket is her bankbook.

[23] This was no simple rationalization for irresponsibility. Richard had indeed "been scuffling for five years" trying to keep his family going. Until shortly after this episode, Richard was known and respected as one of the hardest-working men on the street. Richard had said, only a couple of months earlier, "I figure you got to get out there and try. You got to try before you can get anything." His wife, Shirley, confirmed that he had always tried. "If things get tough, with me I'll get all worried. But Richard get worried, he don't want me to see him worried. . . . He *will* get out there. He's shoveled snow, picked beans, and he's done some of everything. . . . He's not ashamed to get

Thus, apparent present-time concerns with consumption and indulgences — material and emotional — reflect a future-time orientation. "I want mine right now" is ultimately a cry of despair, a direct response to the future as he sees it.[24]

In many instances it is precisely the streetcorner man's orientation to the future — but to a future loaded with "trouble" — which not only leads to a greater emphasis on present concerns ("I want mine right now") but also contributes importantly to the instability of employment, family and friend relationships, and to the general transient quality of daily life.

Let me give some concrete examples. One day, after Tally had gotten paid, he gave me four twenty-dollar bills and asked me to keep them for him. Three days later he asked me for the money. I returned it and asked why he did not put his money in a bank. He said that the banks close at two o'clock. I argued that there were four or more banks within a two-block radius of where he was working at the time and that he could easily get to any one of them on his lunch hour. "No, man," he said, "you don't understand. They close at two o'clock and they closed Saturday and Sunday. Suppose I get into trouble and I got to make it [leave]. Me get out of town, and everything I got in the world layin' up in that bank? No good! No good!"

In another instance, Leroy and his girl friend were discussing "trouble." Leroy was trying to decide how best to go about getting his hands on some "long green" (a lot of money), and his girl friend cautioned him about "trouble." Leroy sneered at this, saying he had had "trouble" all his life and wasn't afraid of a little more. "Anyway," he said, "I'm famous for leaving town."[25]

---

out there and get us something to eat." At the time of the episode reported above, Leroy was just starting marriage and raising a family. He and Richard were not, as Richard thought, "entirely different people." Leroy had just not learned, by personal experience over time, what Richard had learned. But within two years Leroy's marriage had broken up and he was talking and acting like Richard. "He just let go completely," said one of the men on the street.

[24] There is no mystically intrinsic connection between "present-time" orientation and lower-class persons. Whenever people of whatever class have been uncertain, skeptical, or downright pessimistic about the future, "I want mine right now" has been one of the characteristic responses, although it is usually couched in more delicate terms: for example, Omar Khayyam's "Take the cash and let the credit go," or Horace's "*Carpe diem.*" In wartime, especially, all classes tend to slough off conventional restraints on sexual and other behavior (that is, become less able or less willing to defer gratification). And when inflation threatens, darkening the fiscal future, persons who formerly husbanded their resources with commendable restraint almost stampede one another rushing to spend their money. Similarly, it seems that future-time orientation tends to collapse toward the present when persons are in pain or under stress. The point here is that, the label notwithstanding, (what passes for) present-time orientation appears to be a situation-specific phenomenon rather than a part of the standard psychic equipment of Cognitive Lower-Class Man.

[25] And proceeded to do just that the following year when "trouble" — in this case,

Thus, the constant awareness of a future loaded with "trouble" results in a constant readiness to leave, to "make it," to "get out of town," and discourages the man from sinking roots into the world he lives in.[26] Just as it discourages him from putting money in the bank, so it discourages him from committing himself to a job, especially one whose payoff lies in the promise of future rewards rather than in the present. In the same way, it discourages him from deep and lasting commitments to family and friends or to any persons, places, or things, since such commitments could hold him hostage, limiting his freedom of movement and thereby compromising his security, which lies in that freedom.

What lies behind the response to the driver of the pickup truck, then, is a complex combination of attitudes and assessments. The streetcorner man is under continuous assault by his job experiences and job fears. His experiences and fears feed on one another. The kind of job he can get — and frequently only after fighting for it, if then — steadily confirms his fears, depresses his self-confidence and self-esteem until finally, terrified of an opportunity even if one presents itself, he stands defeated by his experiences, his belief in his own self-worth destroyed and his fears a confirmed reality.

REVIEW QUESTIONS

1. According to Liebow, how do middle-class Americans view the personal industry of corner men?

2. What are the reasons corner men turn down offers to work by day-labor recruiters?

3. How do corner men assess the work they can get? How does this assessment affect their motivation to work?

4. What values and experiences do corner men bring to their view of work? How do these values and experiences affect their motivation?

5. Recently, some government officials and social scientists have begun to speak of a permanent American underclass. Using the information provided in this article, evaluate this assertion.

---

a grand jury indictment, a pile of debts, and a violent separation from his wife and children — appeared again.

[26] For a discussion of "trouble" as a focal concern of lower-class culture, see Walter Miller, "Lower Class Culture as a Generating Milieu of Gang Delinquency," 7, 8.

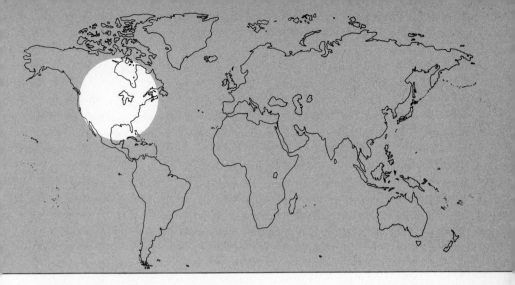

23   *Business Friends*

ROBERT BRAIN

*American economists teach that market exchange requires rational
choice; when given the option, people will pay as little as they can
for as much as they can get. In this article, Robert Brain argues
that despite the pull of standard economic factors — price, supply,
and demand — most business people turn to a reciprocal motive for
exchange — friendship and personal obligation — to ensure that
deals go through. Gifts and hospitality are forms of what anthropologists call reciprocity. They cement relationships on the basis of
mutual obligation, not price, supply, and demand. When business
people take each other out to lunch, send holiday cards and gifts,
or go golfing, they are following the reciprocal exchange strategies
typical of simpler societies such as Australian aborigines and
Trobriand islanders.*

People involved in commerce are "business friends," and the phrase
is not simply a euphemism to disguise cutthroat competitors. Two
strangers about to make a business deal have nothing in common and
every reason to do as much shading and gouging as the situation will
permit. But expense accounts allow them to form friendship bonds
through the exchange of food, a symbolic way of establishing fellowship throughout the world. After ritual meals and drinks, which some-

Reprinted with permission from *Human Nature*, Vol. 1, No. 11, November 1978.
Copyright © 1978 by Human Nature, Inc.

times include the legendary two martinis, they are on first-name terms and begin to exchange jokes and reminiscences.

A group of men in a New York restaurant or a London club would seem to be indulging in a purely convivial routine of gin drinking, storytelling, and backslapping; in fact they are doing business. George Brandt is trying to sell Bill Menotti four thousand pairs of shoes, but before they close the deal, they ceremonially share food and drink. The occasion is no longer purely business: The buyer softens toward the manufacturer, making it easier for George to sell to Bill. The friendship may even continue after the successful deal — a bottle of whiskey at Christmas, an interest in each other's hobbies, a game of golf, dinner with their spouses, and perhaps membership for both men in the local Lions Club.

Recently we have been hearing that competition, particularly in a capitalist economy, gives full rein to aggressive instincts. Some people would argue that the friendship between Menotti and Brandt is not a "real" friendship. Elaborate business deals are said to resemble the games and aggressive tactics of predators, and the firm is likened to a group of hunting primates preying on defenseless game. The popular books of Robert Ardrey have persuaded many people that society is doomed to exist in a state of permanent hostility and that reciprocal relations are limited to competitive and aggressive interactions in which people either defend their territory or intrude on other people's territory.

Yet aggression and defense against aggression are not the hallmarks of animal or human society. The reciprocity of friends, rather than the aggression of enemies, plays the most important role in social activities. Bonding and amity are programmed into human activities. Human bonds derive from a basic trust established in early childhood, usually with the mother. From this trust arises our sociability and our capacity for commitment to people, even our business competitors. *Homo sapiens* may compete for gain and profit, but needs the approval of others.

Even profiteering magnates send Christmas cards to vast networks of friends, and their secretaries bring them sets of birthday greetings to sign every week. Heads of supposedly unfriendly governments, such as Russia and the United States, put on friendly smiles and hug one another in the interests of trade. And experiments have shown that factory workers respond not only to material incentives, such as piecework arrangements, but also to the style and content of managerial behavior. The famous Hawthorne experiment of the late 1920s, which attempted to discover the working conditions that would improve production, showed, among other things, that workers react positively to the attention of their superiors. Amity is essential to all economic relations.

The association of friendship and business has countless examples in history and ethnography. Australian aborigines, scattered in hundreds of independent tribes over the vast continent, were great traders, and the desire for social intercourse was a contributing factor in intertribal trade. Friendly relations with people in many parts of the continent smoothed the way for barter to obtain cosmetics and ornaments. When groups gathered together to haggle over the value of objects, dancing, singing, talking, and romancing were as important to the participants as the acquisition of goods. Special kinds of friendships were based on trading. Among the Yaralde of southern Australia, a sacred and permanent friendship was initiated between two boys belonging to distant communities by the exchange of their umbilical cords. When the boys grew up, they exchanged gifts regularly and their relationship became the commercial tie between the two groups. Friends and traders covered vast distances to meet and barter ceremonial goods. But the effort trading partners put into exchanging ornaments or red ocher seems out of proportion to the usefulness of the objects, and it is difficult to judge whether the friendship or the commercial exchange was more important.

Even in our own society exchange may have a social as well as a commercial justification. This seems to be the lesson learned by those manufacturers who use the relaxed atmosphere of parties to sell their goods. Party selling, a relatively recent phenomenon in America and Europe, encourages the confusion between socializing and marketing. Manufacturers of cosmetics and costume ornaments as well as plastic containers, send out agents to persuade women to become "hostesses" at selling parties. At the party, which is attended by invitation only, the hostess serves refreshments and the demonstrator directs games. Only after a lengthy period of socializing are the guests asked for orders. As in the case of the Australian trading partners, social relations and selling are intertwined. The confusion of business and socializing is so great that when hostesses move to a new neighborhood they sometimes ask the agent to organize a selling party so that they can make new friends.

The interplay of social and economic motives is clearly demonstrated in the complex trading system known as the *kula* of New Guinea. The *kula* was first described by the anthropologist Bronislaw Malinowski. Groups of men from a number of islands take part in an economic and ceremonial exchange involving the circulation of food, stone axes, blades of obsidian, and valuable necklaces and arm bands. Each *kula* member is linked to a number of partners, or business friends, some from the same village or island and others from distant islands where sorcery and witchcraft are to be feared. On arrival at a foreign island, after a long and dangerous voyage, a man's *kula* partner guarantees his safety and provides hospitality and entertainment.

Somewhat like the American businessman who finds friendship and security at a Lions Club wherever he travels, the *kula* partner finds companionship and protection when he arrives on a strange shore.

But mixed with the mutual friendship and concern of *kula* partners there is a profit motive, a search for the most in exchange for the least. When a group leaves in canoes on a trading expedition, a ritual is performed to assure success in the acquisition of valuable ornaments. The magic is meant to make the trading partners "soft," unsteady in mind, and eager to hand over their best *kula* objects. On arrival the men try to make themselves irresistible to their business friends by using spells and cosmetics. They murmur magical formulas, wash in the sea, and rub themselves with medicated leaves and scented coconut oil; they arrange their hair and draw designs on their faces and backs. In one of the Trobriand myths, an ugly old man is magically transformed into a radiant and charming youth who is so beautiful that his *kula* partner simply throws all the best ornaments at him.

Although each *kula* partner tries to use the exchange to maximize profits and increase his status, he is also establishing friendships. Trobriand Islanders recognize competition, but they also recognize the principles of friendship — reciprocity, generosity, and honor. The *kula* symbolizes a human tendency to create social ties by exchanging gifts.

Gift exchange in capitalist societies involves rules of reciprocity that are hardly different from those of the Trobriand Islanders: Christmas presents of equal value, for instance, move back and forth between people of equal status, and the sales of these gifts appear to be independent of ordinary market conditions. Statistics show that the proportion of gifts circulating in British society is roughly equivalent to the proportion of noncommercial goods circulating in simpler societies. In Great Britain the gift economy accounts for roughly 5 percent of all consumer expenditure, and gift sales are about equal to half the money spent on clothes.

The value of the personal element in business relationships was discovered by Dale Carnegie long after the Trobrianders were practicing their mixture of business and pleasure. According to *How to Win Friends and Influence People,* a budding millionaire must look smart, smile continuously, and flatter his business associates. The competitive spirit is there (you "win" friends) but it must be dressed in loving-kindness; and a friendly interest in a man's new tie or his daughter's school report gets you the job, sells shares, and undercuts colleagues more than any amount of intellectual preparation or cutthroat competition. "Fifteen percent of one's financial success," wrote Carnegie, "is due to one's technical knowledge and about eighty-five is due to skill in human engineering." Friendship has helped Dale Carnegie's myriad readers to break strikes, bamboozle chain-store directors, sell insurance, and become likely presidents of the United States. It is of course a self-serving friendship, and even the Trobrianders in their moments of passionate affection for their partners would not deny that the demonstration of amity involves a good deal of self-interest and some pretense. The Carnegie student is told to enter the office of a man he wants to impress in a frame of mind that resembles the attitude of the Melanesian preparing to disembark from his canoe onto the island of his *kula* partner. The student is to tell himself: "I love him, I love him. I must smile and talk about his interests, make him feel important, and above all not argue with him. He is my friend."

What Carnegie did not foresee, as far as I know, was the business value of cosmetics. Since he wrote his book the use of makeup and other artifices has become more and more common in the business world. Scents, skin creams, even hair grafts and plastic surgery can help get jobs and contracts. Older men, afraid of retirement or of being supplanted in the organization, are buying cosmetics in the hope that a bronze tan or the right after-shave will convey an illusion of vital youth. Old *kula* partners are also aware that they may not get the best prizes. In the spells associated with cosmetic preparations before the ceremonial exchange of *kula* goods, the elderly trader prays that he and his partner will become like a pair of lovebirds. "My head is made bright, my face flashes, I have acquired a beautiful shape like that of a chief; I have acquired a shape that is good. I am the only one; my renown stands alone." Like the Melanesian who scents his hair and smooths his wrinkled skin with magical oils, the American business-man must consider his clothes, his hair, his paunch, and his crow's feet. In New Guinea beauty magic makes a man's business friend "hug him and take him to his bosom" whatever his age. In America the demonstration of affection is more reserved, but business firms still spend large amounts of money to send their executives to beauty farms in the interests of successful business.

Love and friendship, along with associated artifices, make the business world go round. Yet, in America, where close emotional relationships between members of the same sex are played down, it seems odd that business partners should be friends and court each other, even to the extent of using cosmetics. The potential conflict with businessmen from more demonstrative societies could be a major obstacle in international trade. In Mediterranean countries a high value is placed on sentimental relationships between men in all spheres of life, and Anglo-Saxons confronted with the public physical expression of affection sometimes have the feeling they are entering a world of wild homoerotic license. A frank and open acceptance of friendship and a delight in the company of members of one's own sex seems possible only in societies where there is no panicky fear of homosexuality. But most businessmen appear to accept friendship for the good of business and to rise above national prejudices in the interests of trade.

Westerners think that friendship should not be "interested" and tend to dismiss business friendships as poor examples of amity. As Dr. Aziz says, in E. M. Forster's *A Passage to India,* "If you are right, there is no point in any friendship; it all comes down to give and take, or give and return, which is disgusting, and we had better all leap over this parapet and kill ourselves." But, as the Melanesians and the Australian tribes have shown us, giving and taking, giving and returning, are not "disgusting." They are essential props to the sentimental business of friendship, just as friendship is an important prop in the unsentimental business of business. Friendship, as much as any other institution, needs its ceremonies and laws and material expectations in order to survive.

REVIEW QUESTIONS

1. What is the difference between reciprocal and market exchange?
2. How are gift giving and friendship used to promote exchange in simpler societies? How are such practices applied in our own?
3. If you are acquainted with Western economic theory, how do you think reciprocity might affect economic models built on the assumptions of market exchange?
4. What is the *kula* and how does it relate to Western systems of exchange?

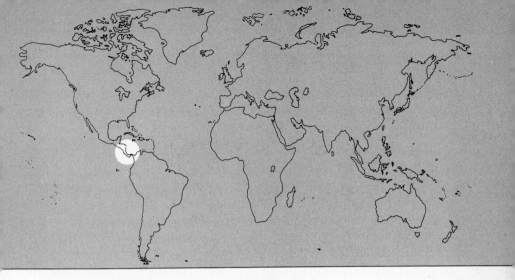

24   Subsistence and Market:
When the Turtle Collapses
BERNARD NIETSCHMANN

*Subsistence economies were once common in the world. People
hunted and gathered or farmed largely for their own needs. But the
world market economy has penetrated even the most remote areas
and has brought with it a change from subsistence economies to
production for money. In this article, Bernard Nietschmann traces
the disturbing effect of the international market for green sea turtles on the Miskito Indians, who once harpooned the large sea reptiles only for food. Trapped in a vicious circle, Indians began to
catch the turtles to sell rather than to eat. With no turtle meat to
eat came a need for money to buy food. Money came only from
catching and selling more turtles. The need for cash also reduced
the Indians' ability to perform reciprocal economic obligations. In
the end, the new economy began to disappear because of a diminished catch of overexploited turtles, leaving the Miskito without
even their original means of subsistence.*

In the half-light of dawn, a sailing canoe approaches a shoal where
nets have been set the day before. A Miskito turtleman stands in the
bow and points to a distant splash that breaks the gray sheen of the
Caribbean waters. Even from a hundred yards, he can tell that a green
turtle has been caught in one of the nets. His two companions quickly

Originally published as "When the Turtle Collapses, the World Ends." With permission
from *Natural History*, June–July 1974; Copyright the American Museum of Natural
History, 1974.

bring the craft alongside the turtle, and as they pull it from the sea, its glistening shell reflects the first rays of the rising sun. As two men work to remove the heavy reptile from the net, the third keeps the canoe headed into the swells and beside the anchored net. After its fins have been pierced and lashed with bark fiber cord, the 250-pound turtle is placed on its back in the bottom of the canoe. The turtlemen are happy. Perhaps their luck will be good today and their other nets will also yield many turtles.

These green turtles, caught by Miskito Indian turtlemen off the eastern coast of Nicaragua, are destined for distant markets. Their butchered bodies will pass through many hands, local and foreign, eventually ending up in tins, bottles, and freezers far away. Their meat, leather, shell, oil, and calipee, a gelatinous substance that is the base for turtle soup, will be used to produce goods consumed in more affluent parts of the world.

The coastal Miskito Indians are very dependent on green turtles. Their culture has long been adapted to utilizing the once vast populations that inhabited the largest sea turtle feeding grounds in the Western Hemisphere. As the most important link between livelihood, social interaction, and environment, green turtles were the pivotal resource around which traditional Miskito Indian society revolved. These large reptiles also provided the major source of protein for Miskito subsistence. Now this priceless and limited resource has become a prized commodity that is being exploited almost entirely for economic reasons.

In the past, turtles fulfilled the nutritional needs as well as the social responsibilities of Miskito society. Today, however, the Miskito depend mainly on the sale of turtles to provide them with the money they need to purchase household goods and other necessities. But turtles are a declining resource; overdependence on them is leading the Miskito into an ecological blind alley. The cultural control mechanisms that once adapted the Miskito to their environment and faunal resources are now circumvented or inoperative, and they are caught up in a system of continued intensification of turtle fishing, which threatens to provide neither cash nor subsistence.

I have been studying this situation for several years, unraveling its historical context and piecing together its past and future effect on Miskito society, economy, and diet, and on the turtle population.

The coastal Miskito Indians are among the world's most adept small-craft seamen and turtlemen. Their traditional subsistence system provided dependable yields from the judicious scheduling of resource procurement activities. Agriculture, hunting, fishing, and gathering were organized in accordance with seasonal fluctuations in weather and resource availability and provided adequate amounts of food and materials without overexploiting any one species or site. Women cultivated the crops while men hunted and fished. Turtle fishing was the backbone of subsistence, providing meat throughout the year.

Miskito society and economy were interdependent. There was no economic activity without a social context and every social act had a reciprocal economic aspect. To the Miskito, meat, especially turtle meat, was the most esteemed and valuable resource, for it was not only a mainstay of subsistence, it was the item most commonly distributed to relatives and friends. Meat shared in this way satisfied mutual obligations and responsibilities and smoothed out daily and seasonal differences in the acquisition of animal protein. In this way, those too young, old, sick, or otherwise unable to secure meat received their share, and a certain balance in the village was achieved: minimal food requirements were met, meat surplus was disposed of to others, and social responsibilities were satisfied.

Today, the older Miskito recall that when meat was scarce in the village, a few turtlemen would put out to sea in their dugout canoes for a day's harpooning on the turtle feeding grounds. In the afternoon, the men would return, sailing before the northeast trade wind, bringing meat for all. Gathered on the beach, the villagers helped drag the canoes into thatched storage sheds. After the turtles were butchered and the meat distributed, everyone returned home to the cooking fires.

Historical circumstances and a series of boom-bust economic cycles disrupted the Miskito's society and environment. In the seventeenth and eighteenth centuries, intermittent trade with English and French buccaneers — based on the exchange of forest and marine resources for metal tools and utensils, rum, and firearms — prompted the Miskito to extend hunting, fishing, and gathering beyond subsistence needs to exploitative enterprises.

During the nineteenth and early twentieth centuries, foreign-owned companies operating in eastern Nicaragua exported rubber, lumber, and gold, and initiated commercial banana production. As alien economic and ecological influences were intensified, contract wage labor replaced seasonal, short-term economic relationships; company commissaries replaced limited trade goods; and large-scale exploitation of natural resources replaced sporadic, selective extraction. During economic boom periods the relationship between resources, subsistence, and environment was drastically altered for the Miskito. Resources became a commodity with a price tag, market exploitation a livelihood, and foreign wages and goods a necessity.

For more than two hundred years, relations between the coastal Miskito and the English were based on sea turtles. It was from the Miskito that the English learned the art of turtling, which they then organized into intensive commercial exploitation of Caribbean turtle grounds and nesting beaches. Sea turtles were among the first resources involved in trade relations and foreign commerce in the Caribbean. Zoologist Archie Carr, an authority on sea turtles, has remarked that "more than any other dietary factor, the green turtle supported the opening up of the Caribbean." The once abundant turtle populations provided sustenance to ships' crews and to the new settlers and plantation laborers.

The Cayman Islands, settled by the English, became in the seventeenth and eighteenth centuries the center of commercial turtle fishing in the Caribbean. By the early nineteenth century, pressure on the Cayman turtle grounds and nesting beaches to supply meat to Caribbean and European markets became so great that the turtle population was decimated. The Cayman Islanders were forced to shift to other turtle areas off Cuba, the Gulf of Honduras, and the coast of eastern Nicaragua. They made annual expeditions, lasting four to seven weeks, to the Miskito turtle grounds to net green turtles, occasionally purchasing live ones, dried calipee, and the shells of hawksbill turtles (*Eretmochelys imbricata*) from the Miskito Indians. Reported catches of green turtles by the Cayman turtlers generally ranged between two thousand and three thousand a year up to the early 1960s, when the Nicaraguan government failed to renew the islanders' fishing privileges.

Intensive resource extraction by foreign companies led to seriously depleted and altered environments. By the 1940s, many of the economic booms had turned to busts. As the resources ran out and operating costs mounted, companies shut down production and moved to other areas in Central America. Thus, the economic mainstays that had helped provide the Miskito with jobs, currency, markets, and foreign goods were gone. The company supply ships and commissaries disappeared, money became scarce, and store-bought items expensive.

In the backwater of the passing golden boom period, the Miskito were left with an ethic of poverty, but they still had the subsistence skills that had maintained their culture for hundreds of years. Their land and water environment was still capable of providing reliable resources for local consumption. As it had been in the past, turtle fishing became a way of life, a provider of life itself. But traditional subsistence culture could no longer integrate Miskito society and environment in a state of equilibrium. Resources were now viewed as having a value and labor a price tag. All that was needed was a market.

Recently, two foreign turtle companies began operations along the east coast of Nicaragua. One was built in Puerto Cabezas in late 1968, and another was completed in Bluefields in 1969. Both companies were capable of processing and shipping large amounts of green turtle meat and by-products to markets in North America and Europe. Turtles were acquired by purchase from the Miskito. Each week company boats visited coastal Miskito communities and offshore island turtle camps to buy green turtles. The "company" was back, money was again available, and the Miskito were expert in securing the desired commodity. Another economic boom period was at hand. But the significant difference between this boom and previous ones was that the Miskito were now selling a subsistence resource.

As a result, the last large surviving green turtle population in the Caribbean was opened to intensive, almost year-round exploitation. Paradoxically, it would be the Miskito Indians, who once caught only what they needed for food, who would conduct the assault on the remaining turtle population. . . .

Green turtles, *Chelonia mydas,* are large, air-breathing, herbivorous marine reptiles. They congregate in large populations and graze on underwater beds of vegetation in relatively clear, shallow, tropical waters. A mature turtle can weigh two hundred fifty pounds or more and when caught, can live indefinitely in a saltwater enclosure or for a couple of weeks if kept in shade on land. Green turtles have at least six behavioral characteristics that are important in their exploitation: they occur in large numbers in localized areas; they are air breathing, so they have to surface; they are mass social nesters; they have an acute location-finding ability; when mature, they migrate seasonally on an overlapping two- or three-year cycle for mating and nesting; and they exhibit predictable local distributional patterns.

The extensive shallow shelf off eastern Nicaragua is dotted with numerous small coral islands, thousands of reefs, and vast underwater pastures of marine vegetation called "turtle banks." During the day, a large group of turtles may be found feeding at one of the many turtle banks, while adjacent marine pastures may have only a few turtles. They graze on the vegetation, rising periodically to the surface for air and to float for a while before diving again. In the late afternoon, groups of turtles will leave the feeding areas and swim to shoals, some up to four or five miles away, to spend the night. By five the next morning, they gather to depart again for the banks. The turtles' precise, commuterlike behavior between sleeping and feeding areas is well known to the Miskito and helps insure good turtling.

Each coastal turtling village exploits an immense sea area, containing many turtle banks and shoals. For example, the Miskito of Tasbapauni utilize a marine area of approximately six hundred square miles, with twenty major turtle banks and almost forty important shoals.

Having rather predictable patterns of movement and habitat preference, green turtles are commonly caught by the Miskito in three ways: on the turtle banks with harpoons; along the shoal-to-feeding area route with harpoons; and on the shoals using nets, which entangle the turtles when they surface for air.

The Miskito's traditional means of taking turtles was by harpoon —an eight- to ten-foot shaft fitted with a detachable short point tied to a strong line. The simple technology pitted two turtlemen in a small, seagoing canoe against the elusive turtles. Successful turtling with harpoons requires an extensive knowledge of turtle behavior and habits and tremendous skill and experience in handling a small canoe in what can be very rough seas. Turtlemen work in partnerships: a "strikerman" in the bow; the "captain" in the stern. Together, they make a single unit engaged in the delicate and almost silent pursuit of a wary prey, their movements coordinated by experience and rewarded by proficiency. Turtlemen have mental maps of all the banks and shoals in their area, each one named and located through a complex system of celestial navigation, distance reckoning, wind and current direction, and the individual surface-swell motion over each site. Traditionally, not all Miskito were sufficiently expert in seamanship and turtle lore to become respected "strikermen," capable of securing turtles even during hazardous sea conditions. Theirs was a very specialized calling. Harpooning restrained possible overexploitation since turtles were taken one at a time by two men directly involved in the chase, and there were only a limited number of really proficient "strikermen" in each village.

Those who still use harpoons must leave early to take advantage of the land breeze and to have enough time to reach the distant offshore turtle grounds by first light. Turtlemen who are going for the day, or for several days, will meet on the beach by 2:00 A.M. They drag the canoes on bamboo rollers from beachfront sheds to the water's edge. There, in the swash of spent breakers, food, water, paddles, lines, harpoons, and sails are loaded and secured. Using a long pole, the standing bowman propels the canoe through the foaming surf while the captain in the stern keeps the craft running straight with a six-foot mahogany paddle. Once past the inside break, the men count the dark rolling seas building outside until there is a momentary pause in the sets; then with paddles digging deep, they drive the narrow, twenty-foot canoe over the cresting swells, rising precipitously on each wave face and then plunging down the far side as the sea and sky seesaw into view. Once past the breakers, they rig the sail and, running with the land breeze, point the canoe toward a star in the eastern sky.

A course is set by star fix and by backsight on a prominent coconut palm on the mainland horizon. Course alterations are made to correct for the direction and intensity of winds and currents. After two or three hours of sailing the men reach a distant spot located between a turtle sleeping shoal and feeding bank. There they intercept and follow the turtles as they leave for specific banks.

On the banks the turtlemen paddle quietly, listening for the sound of a "blowing" turtle. When a turtle surfaces for air it emits a hissing sound audible for fifty yards or more on a calm day. Since a turtle will stay near the surface for only a minute or two before diving to feed, the men must approach quickly and silently, maneuvering the canoe directly in front of or behind the turtle. These are its blind spots. Once harpooned, a turtle explodes into a frenzy of action, pulling the canoe along at high speeds in its hopeless, underwater dash for escape until it tires and can be pulled alongside the canoe.

But turtle harpooning is a dying art. The dominant method of turtling today is the use of nets. Since their introduction, the widespread use of turtle nets has drastically altered turtling strategy and productivity. Originally brought to the Miskito by the Cayman Islanders, nets are now extensively distributed on credit by the turtle companies. This simple technological change, along with a market demand for turtles, has resulted in intensified pressure on green turtle populations.

Buoyed by wooden floats and anchored to the bottom by a single line, the fifty-foot-long by fourteen-foot-wide nets hang from the surface like underwater flags, shifting direction with the current. Nets are set in place during midday when the turtlemen can see the dark shoal areas. Two Miskito will set five to thirty nets from one canoe, often completely saturating a small shoal. In the late afternoon, green turtles return to their shoals to spend the night. There they will sleep beside or beneath a coral outcrop, periodically surfacing for air where a canopy of nets awaits them.

Catching turtles with nets requires little skill; anyone with a canoe can now be a turtleman. The Miskito set thousands of nets daily, providing continuous coverage in densely populated nocturnal habitats. Younger Miskito can become turtlemen almost overnight simply by following more experienced men to the shoal areas, thus circumventing the need for years of accumulated skill and knowledge that once were the domain of the "strikermen." All one has to do is learn where to set the nets, retire for the night, remove the entangled turtles the next morning, and reset the nets. The outcome is predictable: more turtlemen, using more effective methods, catch more turtles.

With an assured market for turtles, the Miskito devote more time to catching turtles, traveling farther and staying at sea longer. Increased dependence on turtles as a source of income and greater time inputs have meant disruption of subsistence agriculture and hunting and fishing. The Miskito no longer produce foodstuffs for themselves; they buy imported foods with money gained from the sale of turtles. Caught between contradictory priorities — their traditional subsistence system and the market economy — the Miskito are opting for cash.

The Miskito are now enveloped in a positive feedback system where change spawns change. Coastal villages rely on turtles for a livelihood. Decline of subsistence provisioning has led to the need to secure food from local shopkeepers on credit to feed the families in the villages and the men during their turtling expeditions. Initial high catches of turtles encouraged more Miskito to participate, and by 1972 the per-person and per-day catch began to decline noticeably.

In late 1972, several months after I had returned to Michigan, I received a letter from an old turtleman, who wrote: "Turtle is getting scarce, Mr. Barney. You said it would happen in five or ten years but it is happening now."

Burdened by an overdependence on an endangered species and with accumulating debts for food and nets, the Miskito are finding it increasingly difficult to break even, much less secure a profit. With few other economic alternatives, the inevitable step is to use more nets and stay out at sea longer.

The turtle companies encourage the Miskito to expand turtling activities by providing them with building materials so that they can construct houses on offshore cays, thereby eliminating the need to return to the mainland during rough weather. On their weekly runs up and down the coast, company boats bring food, turtle gear, and cash for turtles to fishing camps from the Miskito Cays to the Set Net Cays. Frequent visits keep the Miskito from becoming discouraged and returning to their villages with the turtles. On Saturdays, villagers look to sea, watching for returning canoes. A few men will bring turtle for their families; the majority will bring only money. Many return with neither.

Most Miskito prefer to be home on Sunday to visit with friends and for religious reasons. (There are Moravian, Anglican, and Catholic mission churches in many of the villages.) But more and more, turtlemen are staying out for two to four weeks. The church may promise salvation, but only the turtle companies can provide money.

Returning to their villages, turtlemen are confronted with a complex dilemma: how to satisfy both social and economic demands with a limited resource. Traditional Miskito social rules stipulate that turtle meat should be shared among kin, but the new economic system requires that turtles be sold for personal economic gain. Kin expect gifts of meat, and friends expect to be sold meat. Turtlemen are besieged with requests forcing them to decide between who will or will not receive meat. This is contrary to the traditional Miskito ethic, which is based on generosity and mutual concern for the well-being of others. The older Miskito ask why the turtlemen should have to allocate a food that was once abundant and available to all. Turtlemen sell and give to other turtlemen, thereby ensuring reciprocal treatment for themselves, but there simply are not enough turtles to accommodate other economic and social requirements. In order to have enough turtles to sell, fewer are butchered in the villages. This means that less meat is being consumed than before the turtle companies began operations. The Miskito presently sell 70 to 90 percent of the turtles they catch; in the near future they will sell even more and eat less. . . .

Social tension and friction are growing in the villages. Kinship relationships are being strained by what some villagers interpret as preferential and stingy meat distribution. Rather than endure the trauma caused by having to ration a limited item to fellow villagers, many turtlemen prefer to sell all their turtles to the company and return with money, which does not have to be shared. However, if a Miskito sells out to the company, he will probably be unable to acquire meat for himself in the village, regardless of kinship or purchasing power. I overheard an elderly turtleman muttering to himself as he butchered a turtle: "I no going to sell, neither give dem meat. Let dem eat de money."

The situation is bad and getting worse. Individuals too old or sick to provide for themselves often receive little meat or money from relatives. Families without turtlemen are families without money or access to meat. The trend is toward the individualization of nuclear families, operating for their own economic ends. Miskito villages are becoming neighborhoods rather than communities.

The Miskito diet has suffered in quality and quantity. Less protein and fewer diverse vegetables and fruits are consumed. Present dietary staples — rice, white flour, beans, sugar, and coffee — come from the store. In one Miskito village, 65 percent of all food eaten in a year was purchased.

Besides the nutritional significance of what is becoming a largely carbohydrate diet, dependence on purchased foods has also had major economic reverberations. Generated by national and international scarcities, inflationary fallout has hit the Miskito. Most of their purchased foods are imported, much coming from the United States. In the last five years prices for staples have increased 100 to 150 percent. This has had an overwhelming impact on the Miskito, who spend 50 to 75 percent of their income for food. Consequently, their entry into the market by selling a subsistence resource, diverting labor from agriculture, and intensifying exploitation of a vanishing species has resulted in their living off poorer-quality, higher-priced foods.

The Miskito now depend on outside systems to supply them with money and materials that are subject to world market fluctuations. They have lost their autonomy and their adaptive relationship with their environment. Life is no longer socially rewarding, nor is their diet satisfying. The coastal Miskito have become a specialized and highly vulnerable sector of the global market economy.

Loss of turtle market would be a serious economic blow to the Miskito, who have almost no other means of securing cash for what have now become necessities. Nevertheless, continued exploitation will surely reduce the turtle population to a critical level.

National and international legislation is urgently needed. At the very least, commercial turtle fishing must be curtailed for several years until the *Chelonia* population can rebound and exploitation quotas can be set. While turtle fishing for subsistence should be permitted, exportation of sea turtle products used in the gourmet, cosmetic, or jewelry trade should be banned.

Restrictive environmental legislation, however, is not a popular subject in Nicaragua, a country that has recently been torn by earthquakes, volcanic eruption, and hurricanes. A program for sea turtle conservation submitted to the Nicaraguan government for consideration ended up in a pile of rubble during the earthquake that devastated Managua in December 1972, adding a sad footnote to the Miskito–sea turtle situation. With other problems to face, the government has not yet reviewed what is happening on the distant east coast, separated from the capital by more than two hundred miles of rain forest — and years of neglect.

As it is now, the turtles are going down and along with them, the Miskito — seemingly a small problem in terms of the scale of ongoing ecological and cultural change in the world. But each localized situation involves species and societies with long histories and, perhaps, short futures. They are weathervanes in the conflicting winds of economic and environmental priorities. As Bob Dylan sang: "You don't need a weatherman to tell which way the wind blows."

REVIEW QUESTIONS

1. What does Nietschmann mean by *subsistence economy?*
2. How has the Miskito Indians' exploitation of the green sea turtle affected their economy?
3. What does Nietschmann mean when he says that the Miskito Indian economy is "enveloped in a positive feedback system"?
4. How has the world market affected the Miskito economy?

VIII

Law and
Politics

Ideally, culture provides the blueprint for a smoothly oiled social machine whose parts work together under all circumstances. But human society is not like a rigidly constructed machine. It is made of individuals who have their own special needs and desires. Personal interest, competition for scarce resources, and simple accident can cause nonconformity and disputes, resulting in serious disorganization.

One way we manage social disruption is through the socialization of children. As we acquire our culture, we learn the appropriate ways to look at experience, to define our existence, and to feel about life. Each system of cultural knowledge contains implicit values of what is desirable, and we come to share these values with other people. Slowly, with the acquisition of culture, most people find they *want* to do what they *must* do; the requirements of an orderly social life become personal goals.

Enculturation, however, is rarely enough. Disputes among individuals regularly occur in all societies, and how such disagreements are handled defines what anthropologists mean by the legal system. Some disputes are *infralegal;* they never reach a point where they are settled by individuals with special authority. Neighbors, for example, would engage in an infralegal dispute if they argued over who should pay for the damage caused by water that runs off one's land into the other's basement. So long as they don't take the matter to court or resort to violence, the dispute will remain infralegal. This dispute may become *extralegal,* however, if it occurs outside the law and escalates into violence. Had the neighbors come to blows over the waterlogged basement, the dispute would have become extralegal. Feuds and wars are the best examples of this kind of dispute.

Legal disputes, on the other hand, involve socially approved mechanisms for their settlement. *Law* is the cultural knowledge that people use to settle disputes by means of agents who have recognized authority to do so. Thus, if the argument between neighbors cited above ended up in court before a judge or referee, it would have become legal.

Although we Americans often think of courts as synonymous with the legal system, societies have evolved a variety of structures for settling disputes. For example, some disputes may be settled by *self-redress*, meaning that wronged individuals are given the right to settle matters themselves. *Contests* requiring physical or mental combat between disputants may also be used to settle disputes. A trusted third party, or *go-between*, may be asked to negotiate with each side until a settlement is achieved. In some societies, supernatural power or beings may be used. In parts of India, for example, disputants are asked to take an oath in the name of a powerful deity or (at least in the past) to submit to a supernaturally controlled, painful, or physically dangerous test, called an *ordeal*. Disputes may also be taken to a *moot*, an informal community meeting where conflict may be aired. At the moot, talk continues until a settlement is reached. Finally, as we saw above, disputes are often taken to *courts*, which are formally organized and include officials with authority to make and enforce decisions.

Political systems are closely related to legal ones and often involve some of the same offices and actors. The *political system* contains the process for making and carrying out public policy according to cultural categories and rules; *policy* refers to guidelines for action. The *public* are the people affected by the policy. Every society must make decisions that affect all or most of its members. The Mbuti Pygmies of the Ituri Forest described by anthropologist Colin Turnbull, for example, occasionally decide to conduct a communal hunt. Hunters set their nets together and wait for the appearance of forest game. Men, women, and children must work together as beaters to drive the animals toward the nets. When the Mbuti decide to hold a hunt, they make a political decision.

The political process requires that people make and abide by a particular policy, often in the face of competing plans. To do so a policy must have *support*, which is anything that contributes to its adoption and enforcement. Anthropologists recognize two main kinds of support, legitimacy and coercion. *Legitimacy* refers to people's positive evaluation of public officials and public policy. A college faculty, for example, may decide to institute the quarter system because a majority feels that quarters rather than semesters represent the "right length" for courses. Theirs is a positive evaluation of the policy. Some faculty members will oppose the change but will abide by the decision because they value the authority of faculty governance. For them the decision, although unfortunate, is legitimate.

Coercion, on the other hand, is support derived from the threat or use of force or the promise of short-term gain. Had the faculty members adopted the quarter system because they had been threatened with termination by the administration, they would have acted under coercion.

There are also other important aspects of the political process. Some members of a society may be given *authority,* the right to make and enforce public policy. In our country, elected officials are given authority to make certain decisions and exercise particular powers. However, formal political offices with authority do not occur in every society. Most hunting and gathering societies lack such positions, as do many horticulturalists. *Leadership,* which is the ability to influence others to act, must be exercised informally in these societies.

The selections in this section illustrate two important aspects of legal and political systems: the organization of intragroup violence and the acquisition of power within small groups. In the first article, Napoleon Chagnon describes how the Yanomamö of Venezuela and Brazil organize violence into a series of increasingly deadly bouts, ending in lethal raids and the dreaded "trick." The second article, by Lincoln Kaiser, discusses the increasingly prevalent feuds that have broken out among the Kohistani of northern Pakistan. Fueled by efficient modern weapons, a heightened sense of honor, and a failure of traditional controls, feuds put every man's life at risk.

Marshall Sahlins switches the discussion to politics in the third article. Comparing the Polynesians and Melanesians of Oceania, he shows how the chiefdomships of the former create larger political groups than the "big-man" system of the latter. In the final article, Jack Weatherford argues that members of the U.S. Senate acquire power and influence in much the same way as big-men living in New Guinea. Both extend their power by distributing "pork," attracting followers, and obligating others.

KEY TERMS

infralegal	political system
extralegal	policy
law	public
self-redress	support
contest	legitimacy
go-between	coercion
ordeal	authority
moot	leadership
court	

READINGS IN THIS SECTION

25 Yanomamö: The Fierce People
NAPOLEON A. CHAGNON

Every society provides a basis for authority and ways to gain
support for such authority. In this article, Napoleon Chagnon de-
scribes the Yanomamö, a group that bases its authority structure
on a continuum of violence and on claims to fierceness or willing-
ness to do violence.

The Yanomamö Indians are a tribe in Venezuela and Brazil who
practice a slash-and-burn way of horticultural life. Traditionally, they
have been an inland "foot" tribe, avoiding larger rivers and settling
deep in the tropical jungle. Until about 1950 they had no sustained
contact with other peoples except, to a minor extent, with another
tribe, the Carib-speaking Makiritaris to the northeast.

I recently lived with the Yanomamö for more than a year, doing
research sponsored by the U.S. Public Health Service, with the
cooperation of the Venezuela Institute for Scientific Research. My
purpose was to study Yanomamö social organization, language, sex
practices, and forms of violence, ranging from treacherous raids to
chest-pounding duels.

Those Yanomamö who have been encouraged to live on the larger
rivers (Orinoco, Mavaca, Ocamo, and Padamo) are slowly beginning
to realize that they are not the only people in the world; there is also

With permission from *Natural History*, January 1967; Copyright the American Museum
of Natural History, 1966.

a place called Caraca-tedi (Caracas), from whence come foreigners of an entirely new order. These foreigners speak in incomprehensible language, probably a degenerate form of Yanomamö. They bring malaria pills, machetes, axes, cooking pots, and *copetas* (guns), have curious ideas about indecency, and speak of a new "spirit."

However, the Yanomamö remain a people relatively unadulterated by outside contacts. They are also fairly numerous. Their population is roughly ten thousand, the larger portion of them distributed throughout southern Venezuela. Here, in basins of the upper Orinoco and all its tributaries, they dwell in some seventy-five scattered villages, each of which contains from forty to three hundred individuals.

The largest, most all-embracing human reality to these people is humanity itself; *Yanomamö* means true human beings. Their conception of themselves as the only true "domestic" beings (those that dwell in houses) is demonstrated by the contempt with which they treat non-Yanomamö, who, in their language, are "wild." For instance, when referring to themselves, they use an honorific pronoun otherwise reserved for important spirits and headmen; when discussing *nabäs* ("non-Yanomamö"), an ordinary pronoun is enough. Again, in one of the myths about their origin, the first people to be created were the Yanomamö. All others developed by a process of degeneration and are, therefore, not quite on a par with the Yanomamö.

In addition to meaning "people," Yanomamö also refers to the language. Their tribal name does not designate a politically organized entity but is more or less equivalent to our concept of humanity. (This, of course, makes their most outstanding characteristic — chronic warfare, of which I shall speak in detail — seem rather an anomaly.) Sub-Yanomamö groupings are based on language differences, historical separation, and geographical location.

For instance, two distinguishable groups, Waika (from *waikaö* — "to kill off") and Shamatari, speak nearly identical dialects; they are differentiated mostly on the basis of a specific event that led to their separation. The Shamatari, the group I know best, occupy the area south of the Orinoco to, and including portions of, northern Brazil. Their differentiation from the Waika probably occurred in the past seventy-five years.

According to the Indians, there was a large village on a northern tributary of the upper Orinoco River, close to its headwaters. The village had several factions, one of which was led by a man called Kayabawä (big tree). A notably corpulent man, he also had the name Shamatari, derived from *shama*, the tapir, a robust ungulate found throughout tropical South America. As the story goes, Shamatari's faction got into a fight with the rest of the village over the possession of a woman, and the community split into two warring halves. Gradually the fighting involved more villages, and Shamatari led his faction south, crossed the Orinoco, and settled there. He was followed by members of other villages that had taken his part in the fight.

Those who moved to the south side of the Orinoco came to be called Shamataris by those living on the north side, and the term is now applied to any village in this area, whether or not it can trace its origin to the first supporters of Shamatari.

For the Yanomamö, the village is the maximum political unit and the maximum sovereign body, and it is linked to other villages by ephemeral alliances, visiting and trade relationships, and intermarriages. In essence, the village is a building—a continuous, open-roofed lean-to built on a circular plan and surrounded by a protective palisade of split palm logs. The roof starts at or near ground level, ascends at an angle of about 45 degrees, and reaches a height of some 20 to 25 feet. Individual segments under the continuous roof are not partitioned; from a hammock hung anywhere beneath it one can see (and hear, thanks to the band-shell nature of the structure) all that goes on within the village.

The palisade, about three to six feet behind the base of the roof, is some ten feet high and is usually in various stages of disrepair, depending on the current warfare situation. The limited number of entrances are covered with dry palm leaves in the evening; if these are moved even slightly, the sound precipitates the barking of a horde of ill-tempered, underfed dogs, whose bad manners preadapt the stranger to what lies beyond the entrance.

A typical "house" (a segment under the continuous roof) shelters a man, his wife or wives, their children, perhaps one or both of the man's parents, and, farther down, the man's brothers and their families. The roof is alive with cockroaches, scorpions, and spiders, and the ground is littered with the debris of numerous repasts—bird, fish, and animal bones; bits of fur; skulls of monkeys and other animals; banana and plantain peelings; feathers; and the seeds of palm fruits. Bows and arrows stand against housepoles all over the village, baskets hang from roof rafters, and firewood is stacked under the lower part of the roof where it slopes to the ground. Some men will be whittling arrow points with agouti-tooth knives or tying feathers to arrow shafts. Some women will be spinning cotton, weaving baskets, or making hammocks or cotton waistbands. The children, gathered in the center of the village clearing, frequently tie a string to a lizard and entertain themselves by shooting the animal full of tiny arrows. And, of course, many people will be outside the compound, working in their gardens, fishing, or collecting palm fruits in the jungle.

If it is a typical late afternoon, most of the older men are gathered in one part of the village, blowing one of their hallucinatory drugs (ebene) up each other's nostrils by means of a hollow tube and chanting to the forest demons (hekuras) as the drug takes effect. Other men may be curing a sick person by sucking, massaging, and exhorting the evil spirit from him. Everybody in the village is swatting vigorously at the voracious biting gnats, and here and there groups of people delouse each other's heads and eat the vermin.

In composition, the village consists of one or more groups of patrilineally related kin (*mashis*), but it also contains other categories, including people who have come from other villages seeking spouses. All villages try to increase their size and consider it desirable for both the young men and young women to remain at home after marriage. Since one must marry out of his *mashi,* villages with only one patrilineage frequently lose their young men to other villages; they must go to another village to *siohamou* (to "son-in-law") if they want wives. The parents of the bride-to-be, of course, want the young man to remain in their village to help support them in their old age, particularly if they have few or no sons. They will frequently promise a young man one or more of the sisters of his wife in order to make his stay more attractive.

He, on the other hand, would rather return to his home village to be with his own kin, and the tendency is for postmarital residence to be patrilocal (with the father of the groom). If a village is rich in axes and machetes, it can and does coerce its poorer trading partners into permitting their young women to live permanently with the richer village. The latter thus obtains more women, while the poorer village gains some security in the trading network. The poor village then coerces other villages even poorer, or they raid them and steal their women.

The patrilineages that maintain the composition of the villages, rich or poor, include a man and his brothers and sisters, his children and his brothers' children, and the children of his sons and brothers' sons. The ideal marriage pattern is for a group of brothers to exchange sisters with another group of brothers. Furthermore, it is both permissible and desirable for a man to marry his mother's brother's daughter (his matrilateral cross-cousin) and/or his father's sister's daughter (his patrilateral cross-cousin) and, as we have seen earlier, to remain in his parents' village. Hence, the "ideal" village would have at least two patrilineages that exchanged marriageable people.

There is a considerable amount of adherence to these rules, and both brother-sister exchange and cross-cousin marriage are common. However, there are also a substantial number of people in each village who are not related in these ways. For the most part they are women and their children who have been stolen from other villages, segments of lineages that have fled from their own village because of fights, and individuals — mostly young men — who have moved in and attached themselves to the household of one of the lineage (*mashi*) leaders.

Even if the sex ratio is balanced, there is a chronic shortage of women. A pregnant woman or one who is still nursing her children must not have sexual relationships. This means that for as many as three years, even allowing for violations of the taboos, a woman is asexual as far as the men are concerned. Hence, men with pregnant wives, and bachelors too, are potentially disruptive in every village because they constantly seek liaisons with the wives of other men. Eventually such relationships are discovered and violence ensues.

The woman, even if merely suspected of having affairs with other men, is beaten with a club; burned with a glowing brand; shot with a barbed arrow in a nonvital area, such as the buttocks, so that removal of the barb is both difficult and painful; or chopped on the arms or legs with a machete or axe. Most women over thirty carry numerous scars inflicted on them by their enraged husbands. My study of genealogies also indicates that not a few women have been killed outright by their husbands. The women's punishment for infidelity depends on the number of brothers she has in the village, for if her husband is too brutal, her brothers may club him or take her away and give her to someone else.

The guilty man, on the other hand, is challenged to a fight with clubs. This duel is rarely confined to the two parties involved, for their brothers and supporters join the battle. If nobody is seriously injured, the matter may be forgotten. But if the incidents are frequent, the two patrilineages may decide to split while they are still on relatively "peaceable" terms with each other and form two independent villages. They will still be able to reunite when threatened by a raid from a larger village.

This is only one aspect of the chronic warfare of the Yanomamö —warfare that has a basic effect on settlement pattern and demography, intervillage political relationships, leadership, and social organization. The collective aggressive behavior is caused by the desire to accent "sovereignty"—the capacity to initiate fighting and to demonstrate this capacity to others.

Although the Yanomamö are habitually armed with lethal bows and arrows, they have a graded system of violence within which they can express their *waiteri,* or "fierceness." The form of violence is determined by the nature of the affront or wrong to be challenged. The most benign form is a duel between two groups, in which an individual from each group stands (or kneels) with his chest stuck out, head up in the air, and arms held back, and receives a hard blow to the chest. His opponent literally winds up and delivers a close-fist blow from the ground, striking the man on the left pectoral muscle just above the heart. The impact frequently drops the man to his knees, and participants may cough up blood for several days after such a contest. After receiving several such blows, the man then has his turn to strike his opponent, while the respective supporters of each antagonist gather around and frenziedly urge their champion on.

All men in the two villages are obliged to participate as village representatives, and on one occasion I saw some individuals take as many as three or four turns of four blows each. Duels of this type usually result from minor wrongs, such as a village being guilty of spreading bad rumors about another village, questioning its generosity or fierceness, or accusing it of gluttony at a feast. A variant of this form of duel is side slapping, in which an open-handed blow is delivered across the flank just above the pelvis.

More serious are the club fights. Although these almost invariably result from cases in which a wife has been caught in an affair with another man, some fights follow the theft of food within the village. The usual procedure calls for a representative from each belligerent group. One man holds a ten-foot club upright, braces himself by leaning on the club and spreading his feet, then holds his head out for his opponent to strike. Following this comes his turn to do likewise to his adversary. These duels, more often than not, end in a free-for-all in which everybody clubs everybody else on whatever spot he can hit. Such brawls occasionally result in fatalities. However, since headmen of the respective groups stand by with bows drawn, no one dares deliver an intentionally killing blow, for if he does, he will be shot. The scalps of the older men are almost incredible to behold, covered as they are by as many as a dozen ugly welts. Yet, most of them proudly shave the top of their heads to display their scars.

Also precipitated by feuds over women are spear fights, which are even more serious than club fights. Members of a village will warn those of the offending village that they are coming to fight with spears. They specify that they are not planning to shoot arrows unless the others shoot first. On the day of the fight, the attackers enter the other village, armed with five or six sharpened clubs or slender shafts some eight feet long, and attempt to drive the defenders out. If successful, the invaders steal all the valuable possessions — hammocks, cooking pots, and machetes — and retreat. In the spear fight that occurred while I was studying the tribe, the attackers were successful, but they wounded several individuals so badly that one of them died. The fighting then escalated to a raid, the penultimate form of violence.

Such raids may be precipitated by woman-stealing or the killing of a visitor (visitors are sometimes slain because they are suspected of having practiced harmful magic that has led to a death in the host's village). Raids also occur if a man kills his wife in a fit of anger; her natal village is then obliged to avenge the death. Most raids, however, are in revenge for deaths that occurred in previous raids, and once the vendetta gets started, it is not likely to end for a long time. Something else may trigger a raid. Occasionally an ambitious headman wearies of peaceful times — a rarity, certainly — and deliberately creates a situation that will demonstrate his leadership.

A revenge raid is preceded by a feast in which the ground bones of the person to be avenged are mixed in a soup of boiled, ripe plantains (the mainstay of Yanomamö diet) and swallowed. Yanomamö are endocannibals, which means they consume the remains of members of their own group. This ceremony puts the raiders in the appropriate state of frenzy for the business of warfare. A mock raid — rather like a dress rehearsal — is conducted in their own village on the afternoon before the day of the raid, and a life-sized effigy of an enemy, constructed of leaves or a log, is slain. That evening all the participants march, one at a time, to the center of the village clearing, while clacking their bows and arrows and screaming their versions of the calls of carnivorous birds, mammals, and even insects.

When all have lined up facing the direction of the enemy village, they sing their war song, "I am a meat-hungry buzzard," and shout several times in unison until they hear the echo return from the jungle. They then disperse to their individual sections of the village to vomit the symbolic rotten flesh of the enemy that they, as symbolic carnivorous vultures and wasps, partook of in the lineup. The same thing, with the exception of the song, is repeated at dawn the following morning. Then the raiders, covered with black paint made of chewed charcoal, march out of the village in single file and collect the hammocks and plantains that their women have previously set outside the village for them. On each night they spend en route to the enemy they fire arrows at a dummy in a mock raid. They approach the enemy village itself under cover of darkness, ambush the first person they catch, and retreat as rapidly as possible. If they catch a man and his family, they will shoot the man and steal the woman and her children. At a safe distance from her village, each of the raiders rapes the woman, and when they reach their own village, every man in the village may, if he wishes, do likewise before she is given to one of the men as a wife. Ordinarily she attempts to escape, but if caught, she may be killed. So constant is the threat of raids that every woman leaves her village in the knowledge that she may be stolen.

The supreme form of violence is the *nomohoni* — the "trick." During the dry season, the Yanomamö do a great deal of visiting. An entire village will go to another village for a ceremony that involves feasting, dancing, chanting, curing, trading, and just plain gossiping. Shortly after arrival, the visitors are invited to recline in the hammocks of the hosts. By custom they lie motionless to display their fine decorations while the hosts prepare food for them. But now suppose that a village has a grudge to settle with another, such as deaths to avenge.

It enlists the support of a third village to act as accomplice. This third village, which must be on friendly terms with the intended victims, will invite them to a feast. While the guests recline defenseless in the hammocks, the hosts descend on them with axes and sharpened poles, treacherously killing as many as they can. Those that manage to escape the slaughter inside the village are shot outside the palisade by the village that instigated the *nomohoni*. The women and children will be shared between the two accomplices.

Throughout all this ferocity there are two organizational aspects of violence. One concerns leadership: A man must be able to demonstrate his fierceness if he is to be a true leader. It is equally important, however, that he have a large natural following — that is, he must have many male kinsmen to support his position and a quantity of daughters and sisters to distribute to other men. Lineage leaders cannot accurately be described as unilateral initiators of activities; rather, they are the vehicles through which the group's will is expressed. For example, when a certain palm fruit is ripe and is particularly abundant in an area some distance from the village, everybody knows that the whole village will pack its belongings and erect a temporary camp at that spot to collect the fruit. The headman does little more than set the date. When his kinsmen see him packing, they know that the time has come to leave for the collecting trip. True, the headman does have some initiative in raiding, but not even this is completely independent of the attitudes of his followers, which dictate that a death must be avenged. However, when the purpose of a raid is to steal women, the headman does have some freedom to act on his own initiative.

As a general rule, the smaller his natural following, the more he is obliged to demonstrate his personal qualities of fierceness and leadership. Padudiwä, the headman of one of the lineages in Bisaasi-tedi, took pains to demonstrate his personal qualities whenever he could; he had only two living brothers and four living sisters in his group. Most of his demonstrations of ferocity were cruel beatings he administered to his four wives, none of whom had brothers in the village to take their part. Several young men who attached themselves to his household admired him for this.

Padudiwä was also responsible for organizing several raids while I lived with the villagers of Bisaasi-tedi. Every one of them was against Patanowä-tedi, a village that was being raided regularly by some seven or eight other villages, so that the danger of being raided in return was correspondingly reduced. On one occasion, when three young men from Patanowä-tedi arrived as emissaries of peace, Padudiwä wanted to kill them, although he had lived with them at one time and they were fairly close relatives. The murder was prevented by the headman of the other — and larger — lineage in the village, who warned that if an attempt were made on the lives of the visitors he himself would kill Padudiwä.

Obviously, then, Padudiwä's reputation was built largely on calculated acts of fierceness, which carefully reduced the possibility of personal danger to himself and his followers, and on cunning and cruelty. To some extent he was obliged by the smallness of his gathering to behave in such a way, but he was certainly a man to treat with caution.

Despite their extreme aggressiveness, the Yanomamö have at least two qualities I admired. They are kind and indulgent with children and can quickly forget personal angers. (A few even treated me almost as an equal — in their culture this was a considerable concession.) But to portray them as "noble savages" would be misleading. Many of them are delightful and charming people when confronted alone and on a personal basis, but the greater number of them are much like Padudiwä — or strive to be that way. As they frequently told me, "*Yanomamö täbä waiteri!*" — "Yanomamö are fierce!"

REVIEW QUESTIONS

1. What is the most important value for men among the Yanomamö, and how is it acted out in the world of conflict and social control?

2. Describe the Yanomamö social and political organization. What accounts for the proliferation of Yanomamö villages over the past seventy-five years?

3. What are the different kinds of Yanomamö combat? Rank them according to their severity.

4. What are the major causes of disputes that set off physical combat among the Yanomamö?

5. How do men attain positions of leadership among the Yanomamö?

26 *Friend by Day, Enemy by Night*
R. LINCOLN KEISER

*Disputes erupt in every society. Individuals may disagree over
many things, such as the ownership of property, a particular course
of action, or suspected infidelity. People settle many of these disagreements themselves by ignoring them or seeking compromise.
But some disputes grow more serious. Left unsettled, these arguments are potentially disruptive and may drive people to violence.
Most groups have evolved strategies, such as public pressure and
legal action, to contain disputes, but if these mechanisms are absent or cease to work, disagreements may break down into uncon-
trollable, violent feuds. In this article, Lincoln Keiser describes an
outbreak of feuding in Thull, a Kohistani village located in northern Pakistan. Originally controlled by a need to cooperate, disputes
now often break into the open. Forced, on the one hand, to protect
their honor and, on the other, themselves, men must continually be
on guard, forming hasty alliances, stalking antagonists, and watching out for ambush.*

The long bus ride from the Pakistani village of Thull to Dir town is a
torment, made worse by dust and a rutted dirt track that passes for a
road. Passengers who cannot cram into the seats either hang precari-
ously off the back or climb on top, crowding within the intricate metal

---

With permission from *Natural History,* November 1987; Copyright the American Museum of Natural History, 1987.

rack that surrounds the roof. Adorned with garish scenes of speeding streamliners and modern F-15 fighter planes, the bus agonizes over the boulders and ditches in its path. Thus, whenever I made my biweekly grocery run by Jeep to the market in Dir town, friends and acquaintances begged to come along. Through various contortions most of the would-be riders somehow jammed into the back seat.

One trip was particularly memorable. I had agreed to take along Anwar, who was both my good friend and one of my principal sources of ethnographic information. For three years he had sought vengeance for his brother's murder, carefully hoarding his money until he had finally accumulated enough to buy the rifle that would permit him to kill his enemy. In Dir town he planned to catch a bus to Bajour, where local gun shops sold good firearms. I had also promised a place in the Jeep to Mir Said, who each night slept outside my door with his weapons at his side, guarding my safety.

Moments before we left, Mir Said's brother-in-law Hazrat Gul sauntered up to the Jeep to ask for a ride, his Russian-made automatic rifle slung across his shoulder. As he crowded in, tension filled the vehicle: Anwar's close friendship with Gholam Sarwar, one of Hazrat Gul's enemies, caused the problem. Anwar and Hazrat Gul were not themselves feuding, but the potential for violence between them was clear to all in the community. Most of the time the two men avoided each other with studied carelessness.

Much to my surprise the tension quickly dissipated. Throughout the five-hour trip to Dir town, Hazrat Gul and Anwar laughed, joked, and gossiped together. They even swore everlasting friendship, referring to each other as "brothers." Later I asked Anwar if he and Hazrat Gul really were as friendly as they seemed. Anwar thought for a minute and answered, *Doske dos, radke dushman*" (friend by day, enemy by night), a proverb that captures one of the basic realities of life in Thull.

A community of roughly six thousand Moslems, Thull consists of a series of settlements scattered along a six-mile stretch of the upper Panjkora valley, in Pakistan's Northwest Frontier Province. Ethnically these people are Kohistanis, distinct from their better-known neighbors, the Pathans. When I first arrived there in 1984, I was surprised by the intensity of blood feuds (*mar dushmani*, literally "death enmity"). Earlier reports by anthropologists had led me to believe that the Kohistanis generally settled internal disputes without bloodshed. The obsession with *mar dushmani* had in fact developed only in the previous fifteen years. Before then there had been fights, usually expressing opposition between the three major local patrilineal clans or their subdivisions, but they did not involve deadly weapons, since most people in Thull feared death enmity between clans would destroy the community. Today, the majority of conflicts do not involve clans but instead oppose individual male antagonists, alone or supported by various categories of allies. Killing the enemy in retaliation for some personal injury is the goal, and no rules limit the use of weapons.

An enemy (*dushman*) is a person with whom one has bad relations and toward whom one feels enmity (*dushmani*) and distrust. Exchanging bullets and blows (with fist, axe, knife, or club) whenever possible and refusing either to give or to accept food and drink demonstrate *mar dushmani*. In contrast, allies are those with whom one has good relations and toward whom one feels amity and trust. Sharing personal possessions, giving and accepting food and drink, and exchanging labor typify behavior between allies.

The potential for change in relationships of alliance and enmity always exists. Moreover, most men in Thull are neither allies nor enemies although they may unexpectedly become so. Therefore, neither trust nor distrust but guarded suspicion governs behavior between most men in Thull. As my friend Anwar explained, smiling words express normal good manners, but only fools trust those who speak them. The men of Thull are masters of deceit, and except for one's allies, those who give smiles during the day may well give bullets at night.

To make his point clear, Anwar told me how his brother Said Omar was killed. Said Omar lived in an outlying area where houses were scattered among fields and pastures. One day Said Omar heard via village gossip that his neighbor Diliwar Khan had no food. Although Said Omar did not have a close relationship with Diliwar Khan, he gathered together a basket of bread and cheese, went to Diliwar Khan's house, about one hundred yards away, and knocked on the door. When it opened, Diliwar Khan stood in the doorway, his rifle at his shoulder. He fired immediately, the bullet going straight through Said Omar's heart and killing him instantly. To add insult to murder, Diliwar Khan unleashed his attack dogs when Said Omar's young son attempted to retrieve his father's body.

"But why," I asked, "would a man kill a neighbor who was only trying to help him?"

"Who knows?" Anwar shrugged, "The night gave him death. But I will take vengeance."

I heard similar explanations from other men as well. One evening Gholam Sarwar invited his friend Fakir to share a meal at his house. At about nine o'clock, after a pleasant evening of good food and gossip, Fakir left to return home. As far as anyone knew, Fakir had no enemies, yet about ten minutes later an ambush was sprung, and Fakir lay dead, shot in the head. The next morning five men, neighbors of the slain man, left Thull for the high mountain pastures. This was generally interpreted as a sign of their guilt, yet they never publicly admitted the murder or revealed any motive they might have had.

Gholam Sarwar explained it simply: "The night killed him." He too swore vengeance, and soon thereafter purchased a Russian AK-47 assault rifle.

Fakir actually was murdered at night, but to say that "the night killed him" is a metaphor meaning that the real reason is hidden, or secret. No one kills without cause. As a general principle, retaliation is owed whenever a man is wronged by another, but the act of revenge itself should not exceed the original wrong: a blow should answer a blow; a death answer a death. In the first case, antagonists share anger (*roshagat*), and the aggrieved tries to injure his opponent. In the second, foes share death enmity, and the aggrieved tries to kill his enemy. Men prefer to avenge themselves on the actual murderer, but a father, adult brother, or adult son is a permissible substitute. Killing any other kinsman is inappropriate, while killing women and children is unheard of.

Wrongs committed against men through wives, sisters, and daughters are a special case: whatever the transgression, the most appropriate response is to kill the offending person. For example, staring at a man's wife or his daughter or sister (if she is of marriageable age) demands deadly retaliation. Thus, according to some in Thull, Diliwar Khan killed Said Omar because Said Omar had come to Diliwar Khan's door not to bring food, but rather to catch a glimpse of Diliwar Khan's attractive young wife.

Except for attacks through women, taking revenge is not always required. In cases of physical injury and murder, the wronged party can choose to settle the case peacefully by accepting compensation. If a man defending himself against vengeance is desperate enough (usually for fear of being killed), he can try to enter his enemy's house with a piece of white cloth tied to his dagger. If he gets inside without being shot, he will crawl under a string bed and say to his *dushman,* "Kill me! I am at your mercy." The process is a way of formally asking an enemy to accept compensation in lieu of revenge. The enemy cannot kill the supplicant while he is in his house, but he is not obligated to abandon vengeance. He may instead stalk out of his house, find a close relative, and say to him, "A dog is in my house! Make him leave!"

I was told that supplication is common, and that no one criticizes those who ask for mercy. Yet no one settled *mar dushmani* by supplication while I was in Thull. The more normal method seems to be that at a meeting of all men in the community, important individuals unrelated to either side entreat the vengeance seeker to accept compensation. He will most likely acquiesce if those of high standing among his allies pressure him to do so.

Compensation for murder is usually paid in money, normally a sum of four to six thousand dollars. Sometimes land is given; more rarely, women are given in marriage as well. After the opposing sides agree to the compensation, the former enemies sit down to a shared ritual meal of rice and meat. At its conclusion a *mullana* (Moslem priest) intones a special prayer, and the bad relationship between the two *dushman* theoretically ends. The murdered man's father, sons, and brothers usually divide the compensation.

Paying compensation does not always terminate *mar dushmani.* Vengeance often involves the opposition of many people, and not all allies share the compensation. A friend or distant relative who feels aggrieved by a murder sometimes takes it upon himself to seek vengeance in spite of the peaceful settlement. Moreover, vengeance seekers sometimes agree to peace as a ploy to trick enemies into lowering their guard, making them easier to kill. To take revenge by that tactic seriously violates community morality, but those who do so usually find some way to make their deed an open secret, to demonstrate their character.

The rise of *mar dushmani* in Thull can be traced to events since 1965, when the government of Pakistan asserted control over the region and embarked on an ambitious program of social and economic development. The most important external change was the construction of a road and the establishment of regular bus service linking Thull with the rest of Pakistan. As a result, an ever-increasing number of priests from Thull traveled to Mardan and Peshawar to study in centers of Islamic learning with noted scholars and teachers, bringing back an ethnically Pathan vision of Islam that, at the risk of oversimplifying, could be termed fundamentalist.

Whereas saint cults had until then been an important part of Islamic beliefs and practices in Thull, this fundamentalist ideology denied the existence of any humans with special access to God. Priests returned to Thull to campaign against such beliefs, and shrines to saints no longer exist in the community. As part of this Islamic purification movement, the priests also preached against music and dancing (especially at weddings) and for the seclusion of women.

The issue of secluding women was especially important in the development of *mar dushmani,* couched as it was in terms of the Pathan notion of *ghrairat,* or "honor" (in the sense of personal worth, integrity, or character). As men in Thull explain, *ghrairat* is natural, a gift from God (in fact, God's most valuable gift). Every Moslem is born with *ghrairat,* and although the actions of others can pollute it, a man only loses his *ghrairat* by failing to protect it.

Protecting *ghrairat* depends on following a clearly defined code of conduct. A man must provide his wife (or wives) and daughters with appropriate food and clothing to the degree his wealth allows; he must never permit his wife or daughters to speak to men who are not closely related; he must never eat or exchange friendly conversation with the enemy of a close paternal kinsman; and he must always be ready to strike out at those who sully his *ghrairat*. Having sexual relations with a man's wife or unmarried daughter, proposing intimacy with her, or attempting to flee the community with her, sullies the man's *ghrairat*. So does staring at such a woman, reflecting light from a snuff box mirror on her, or looking at her through a camera. The murder of a close paternal kinsman, verbal abuse, theft, and assault also pollute *ghrairat* and similarly demand vengeance.

Because *ghrairat* is rooted in Islam, attacks on a man's identity as a Moslem call forth strong emotions. Men often cast aspersions on their opponents in terms of the distinction between Moslems and kafirs (infidels), each accusing the other of *kafir kar karant* (making kafir work, that is, acting like a kafir). Such accusations are dangerous, however, often leading to violence and even murder. During Ramadan, the Moslem month of fasting, for example, accusations of breaking the fast have led to serious injury and loss of life.

The construction of the road brought about economic changes within Thull that also contributed to the growth of *mar dushmani*. Formerly, subsistence was based on a balance between herding and agriculture. During the winter, herd owners kept their goats and cattle in special quarters in or near permanent settlements, and in the summer they took their herds into the mountains to graze on the rich grass found in high alpine meadows. Men generally did the herding work, while women cultivated maize in the fields near the permanent settlements. Herding also provided the only cash income in the community, the men carrying cheese and butter down from the mountains to sell in surrounding market centers.

The economic importance of herding was instrumental in keeping peace. Summer pastureland was divided into named parcels, each consisting of two clearly demarcated pastures (one for early summer, one for late summer). An annual lottery allocated these pasture parcels to groups, called *lud,* composed of segments from different clans. As a result, the people who herded together, who had common rights to pastures and a common interest in protecting these rights, were often the very people who might oppose one another in political disputes or battles between clans. The crosscutting allegiances encouraged the peaceful settlement of disputes.

The construction of the road changed all this. By allowing relatively rapid and inexpensive trucking of produce to market centers throughout Pakistan, it made potatoes (which grow particularly well at high elevations) a viable cash crop. The road also permitted farmers to bring more land under cultivation. Previously, the number of livestock in the community limited the amount of land that could be cultivated, because manure from animals furnished the sole source of fertilizer. Now farmers could import artificial fertilizer. As a result, the economic base in Thull shifted from a system balanced between herding and cultivation to one weighted in favor of the cultivation of potatoes as a cash crop. As the proportion of men actively involved in herding diminished, cross-clan ties created by the *lud* diminished as well. Although the lottery system of pasture distribution continued virtually unchanged, it no longer had the same moderating influence over disputes.

In addition, the supply of cash in the community increased following the development of large-scale timber operations (for which purpose the government originally constructed the road). Timber contractors hired local men as wage laborers, and the government paid an annual royalty to the community as a whole. In 1984, timber royalties alone came to about $1,000 per family. With increased cash from potatoes and timber came an explosion in the number of firearms owned by members of the community; even poor men could buy rifles. Acting out emotions framed by *ghrairat,* they turned the newly purchased rifles on their neighbors. Bogart's quip in *The Big Sleep,* "Such a lot of guns around town and so few brains," seems appropriate.

The men of Thull are always vigilant in defense of their self-respect. At the same time, they are repeatedly thrown into situations where, unknowingly, they might pollute another's *ghrairat.* Each man is thus in the center of a sea of potential enemies, and tension has become so pervasive in male social relationships that acid indigestion is now a common medical complaint. The rules are such that whole sequences of reciprocal murders may be created. For example, if a man kills another for shining a light on his wife, the killing cleanses his *ghrairat* but just as significantly pollutes the *ghrairat* of the murdered man's close paternal kin, requiring them to kill in return. As a result, relationships of *mar dushmani* develop easily and often, and once developed they are difficult to end.

Organized violence may evolve gradually over a long period of time, changing focus and intensity. One sequence began quite innocently in the summer of 1979. Mamad Said, Ramadin, and Amin were lazing about on one of the high mountain pastures, laughing, gossiping, and in general having a good time. Ramadin joked about Amin's prowess as a hunter, and in playful retaliation Amin shoved Ramadin. Mamad Said, getting into the spirit of things, picked up a stick and swung it at Amin in mock seriousness, fully intending to miss. Unfortunately, at that precise moment Amin turned toward Mamad Said, catching the blow directly across the face. Blood began to flow, and the afternoon turned ugly.

Amin staggered to a lean-to in a nearby pasture where his maternal uncle Shah Hajji Khan and a number of maternal cousins were herding their goats. Shah Hajji Khan and Mamad Said were paternal relatives, thus members of the same clan, while Amin was in a different clan.

Yet the tie between a man and his maternal relatives is particularly strong in Thull; Shah Hajji Khan sided with Amin, his sister's son.

The next day Amin, his uncle, and his cousins attacked Mamad Said's lean-to, hoping to catch him unawares and inflict on him an injury similar to the one Amin had suffered. But Mamad Said cried for help, and a number of his paternal cousins camped nearby rushed to the scene, bringing axes, spades, and fighting clubs. The melee left many seriously wounded, but Amin and his supporters had by far the worst of the fight. Shah Hajji Khan's own son suffered broken bones and an axe blow to the head that almost ended his life. As a result of the two incidents, Shah Hajji Khan and Mamad Said became formal opponents. Because no one had died, anger, rather than death enmity, defined the nature of their opposition.

To gain vengeance for the wounds suffered by his son, Shah Hajji Khan asked for help from Khan Akbar, an uninvolved third person, offering in return to join Khan Akbar's political party. In the spring of 1982 the two finally hatched a plot to ambush Mamad Said. Mamad Said escaped injury, however, by hiding in an irrigation ditch. A few months later he died of tuberculosis. No one blamed his death on the failed ambush — except Mamad Said's brother Hazrat Gul.

Hazrat Gul stands out in a crowd. He had had a bad reputation as a teenager, many in Thull calling him a *badmash* (looter, or outlaw). Although he later outgrew stealing, he remained proud of his notoriety: the swagger in his walk, the hat cocked low over one eye, the twirling of his long luxuriant moustache, the casual but practiced handling of his Kalashnikov assault rifle all convey the image of a dangerous man. Many men in Thull find him abrasive.

In his heart Hazrat Gul never accepted that tuberculosis was the cause of his brother's death. Instead he believed that it was brought about by the cold water of the irrigation ditch in which his brother hid to escape the ambush. His opportunity to avenge Mamad Said's death came the following year when Khan Akbar sent his grown son Sakhi to the high mountain pastures to spend a few days watching over the family's numerous goats and cattle. After dark one evening, while Sakhi hunted for a secluded spot to urinate, a hidden assailant cut him down in a hail of automatic rifle fire. Hazrat Gul dropped from sight for a week. No one actually saw him pull the trigger, but because he did not deny killing Sakhi, and because he disappeared immediately after the murder, people in Thull assumed he was the assassin. Hazrat Gul's actions were more than enough proof for Khan Akbar, who immediately began planning revenge.

Khan Akbar made his move a few months later. Hazrat Gul and his friend Gul Mir secretly planned a trip to the bazaar in a neighboring community. Through his spies, Khan Akbar discovered the plans in time to lay an ambush along the road. When the pair returned to Thull, a volley of bullets cut down Gul Mir; miraculously the real target, Hazrat Gul, walked into the village unscathed.

The murder of Gul Mir ordinarily would have drawn his close relatives into the feud. But Gul Mir's kinsmen were both poor and few in number; they publicly abrogated their responsibility, declaring Hazrat Gul himself should decide whether to seek revenge.

Now both Hazrat Gul and Khan Akbar owed the other murder. Khan Akbar acted first. One morning in the summer of 1984, Hazrat Gul left my house after exchanging gossip and requesting medicine for his wife's illness. When he reached the road, rifle shots rang out from Khan Akbar's property located on the high mesa dominating the road. Although the bullets hit close to his feet, Hazrat Gul sauntered down the road with his usual swagger, not even looking in the direction from which the shots came.

Six days later he was not so lucky. At about 7:15 in the evening rifle bullets struck Hazrat Gul in the arm and stomach as he left his house. Although badly wounded, he somehow managed to crawl back through his front door and return fire with his Kalashnikov machine gun. His close paternal kin who lived nearby quickly opened fire on the attackers. The battle raged for about thirty minutes before third-party elders intervened to stop the fighting. Hazrat Gul was taken to a government hospital in Peshawar where major surgery saved his life.

Serious fighting broke out again two weeks later. A member of Khan Akbar's faction hid in a tree close to Hazrat Gul's house in hopes of gathering some useful intelligence. But one of Hazrat Gul's cousins discovered the intruder's presence and began blazing away with his rifle. The bullets missed, allowing the spy to scramble down the tree and sprint to his uncle's house a few hundred yards away. A furious gun battle then broke out. Khan Akbar heard the shooting in his house two miles away and, gathering his allies, hurried to the scene of battle. In a surprise move Gholam Sarwar and his close paternal kin joined the fighting on the side of Khan Akbar. Later I learned that Gholam Sarwar had met secretly with Khan Akbar a few days earlier and had agreed to become his ally, partly because Khan Akbar promised to help in Gholam Sarwar's *mar dushmani* with the killers of Fakir. Gholam Sarwar had always disliked Hazrat Gul anyway.

The fire fight lasted for about three hours, with tracers lighting the sky until well after dark. Although outnumbered, Hazrat Gul's forces successfully stood off the attack, because they possessed greater fire power. Finally, onlookers had had enough. Several prominent leaders representing powerful groups of allies walked between the warring parties, forcing them to stop fighting. Miraculously no one was killed or wounded, whether by design or poor marksmanship I will never know.

The intensity of the fighting and the number of people involved on each side worried many people in Thull. Hazrat Gul's *mar dushmani* with Khan Akbar appeared to be out of control, threatening many uninvolved members of the community. The same leaders who had intervened to stop the battle called a meeting of all the adult men in the community to cajole the opposing sides into making peace. Hazrat Gul refused to attend, so the attempt fizzled. But the leaders had made their point: for the time being, at least, both sides refrained from further violence. Still, when I left Thull, real peace between Hazrat Gul and Khan Akbar seemed only a distant possibility.

REVIEW QUESTIONS

1. How do Kohistani men conduct feuds? What are the reasons they give for them?

2. How did the villagers of Thull originally control disputes to prevent feuds? What has changed to make feuds so common?

3. What is the role played by the Pakistani government and modern weapons in Kohistani disputes?

4. Are the "wars" between American gangs and drug lords like Kohistani feuds? In what ways are they alike and different?

27   Poor Man, Rich Man, Big-Man, Chief

MARSHALL D. SAHLINS

*Melanesia and Polynesia provide an interesting contrast in political
complexity, as Marshall Sahlins describes in the following article.
The Melanesian "big-man" is the self-made leader of his small localized kinship group, whereas the Polynesian chief is a "born"
leader. The Polynesian system, which depends upon the ascribed
right of its chief to lead, attains far larger proportions than the
Melanesian structure, which depends on the ability of certain individuals to influence others.*

With an eye to their own life goals, the native peoples of Pacific islands
unwittingly present to anthropologists a generous scientific gift: an
extended series of experiments in cultural adaptation and evolutionary
development. They have compressed their institutions within the confines of infertile coral atolls, expanded them on volcanic islands, created with the means history gave them cultures adapted to the deserts
of Australia, the mountains and warm coasts of New Guinea, the rain
forests of the Solomon Islands. From the Australian aborigines, whose
hunting and gathering existence duplicates in outline the cultural life
of the later Paleolithic, to the great chiefdoms of Hawaii, where society

Marshall D. Sahlins, "Poor Man, Big-Man, Rich Man, Chief: Political Types in Melanesia and Polynesia" in *Comparative Studies in Society and History,* Vol. 5, No. 3,
285–303. Copyright by Cambridge University Press. Reprinted with the permission of
Cambridge University Press. Many footnotes, the bibliographic citations, and bibliography are omitted.

approached the formative levels of the old Fertile Crescent civilizations, almost every general phase in the progress of primitive culture is exemplified.

Where culture so experiments, anthropology finds its laboratories — makes its comparisons.

In the southern and eastern Pacific two contrasting cultural provinces have long evoked anthropological interest: *Melanesia,* including New Guinea, the Bismarcks, Solomons, and island groups east to Fiji; and *Polynesia,* consisting in its main portion of the triangular constellation of lands between New Zealand, Easter Island, and the Hawaiian Islands. In and around Fiji, Melanesia and Polynesia intergrade culturally, but west and east of their intersection the two provinces pose broad contrasts in several sectors: in religion, art, kinship groupings, economics, political organization. The differences are the more notable for the underlying similarities from which they emerge. Melanesia and Polynesia are both agricultural regions in which many of the same crops — such as yams, taro, breadfruit, bananas, and coconuts — have long been cultivated by many similar techniques. Some recently presented linguistic and archaeological studies indeed suggest that Polynesian cultures originated from an eastern Melanesian hearth during the first millennium B.C. Yet in anthropological annals the Polynesians were to become famous for elaborate forms of rank and chieftainship, whereas most Melanesian societies broke off advances on this front at more rudimentary levels.

It is obviously imprecise, however, to make out the political contrast in broad culture-area terms. Within Polynesia, certain of the islands, such as Hawaii, the Society Islands, and Tonga, developed unparalleled political momentum. And not all Melanesian polities, on the other side, were constrained and truncated in their evolution. In New Guinea and nearby areas of western Melanesia, small and loosely ordered political groupings are numerous, but in eastern Melanesia, New Caledonia, and Fiji for example, political approximations of the Polynesian condition become common. There is more of an upward west-to-east slope in political development in the southern Pacific than a steplike, quantum progression. It is quite revealing, however, to compare the extremes of this continuum, the western Melanesian underdevelopment against the greater Polynesian chiefdoms. While such comparison does not exhaust the evolutionary variations, it fairly establishes the scope of overall political achievement in this Pacific phylum of cultures.

Measurable along several dimensions, the contrast between developed Polynesian and underdeveloped Melanesian polities is immediately striking for differences in scale. H. Ian Hogbin and Camilla Wedgwood concluded from a survey of Melanesian (most western Melanesian) societies that ordered, independent political bodies in the region typically include seventy to three hundred persons; more recent work in the New Guinea Highlands suggests political groupings of up to a thousand, occasionally a few thousand, people.[1] But in Polynesia sovereignties of two thousand or three thousand are run-of-the-mill, and the most advanced chiefdoms, as in Tonga or Hawaii, might claim ten thousand, even tens of thousands. Varying step by step with such differences in size of the polity are differences in territorial extent: from a few square miles in western Melanesia to tens or even hundreds of square miles in Polynesia.

The Polynesian advance in political scale was supported by advance over Melanesia in political structure. Melanesia presents a great array of social-political forms: here political organization is based upon patrilineal descent groups, there on cognatic groups, or men's clubhouses recruiting neighborhood memberships, on a secret ceremonial society, or perhaps on some combination of these structural principles. Yet a general plan can be discerned. The characteristic western Melanesian "tribe," that is, the ethnic-cultural entity, consists of many autonomous kinship-residential groups. Amounting on the ground to a small village or a local cluster of hamlets, each of these is a copy of the others in organization, each tends to be economically self-governing, and each is the equal of the others in political status. The tribal plan is one of politically unintegrated segments — segmental. But the political geometry in Polynesia is pyramidal. Local groups on the order of self-governing Melanesian communities appear in Polynesia as subdivisions of a more inclusive political body. Smaller units are integrated into larger through a system of intergroup ranking, and the network of representative chiefs of the subdivisions amounts to a coordinating political structure. So instead of the Melanesian scheme of small, separate, and equal political blocs, the Polynesian polity is an extensive pyramid of groups capped by the family and following a paramount chief. (This Polynesian political upshot is often, although not always, facilitated by the development of ranked lineages. Called *conical clan* by Kirchhoff, at one time *ramage* by Firth and *status lineage* by Goldman, the Polynesian ranked lineage is the same in principle as the so-called *obok* system widely distributed in Central Asia, and it is at least analogous to the Scottish clan, the Chinese clan, certain Central African Bantu lineage systems, the housegroups of Northwest Coast Indians, perhaps even the "tribes" of the Israelites. Genealogical ranking is its distinctive feature: members of the same descent unit are ranked by genealogical distance from the common ancestor; lines of the same group become senior and cadet branches

[1] H. Ian Hogbin and Camilla H. Wedgwood, "Local Groupings in Melanesia," *Oceania* 23 (1952–53): 241–276; 24 (1953–54): 58–76.

on this principle; related corporate lineages are relatively ranked, again by genealogical priority.)

Here is another criterion of Polynesian political advance: historical performance. Almost all of the native peoples of the South Pacific were brought up against intense European cultural pressure in the late eighteenth and nineteenth centuries. Yet only the Hawaiians, Tahitians, Tongans, and to a lesser extent the Fijians, successfully defended themselves by evolving countervailing, native-controlled states. Complete with public governments and public law, monarchs and taxes, ministers and minions, these nineteenth-century states are testimony to the native Polynesian political genius, to the level and the potential of indigenous political accomplishments.

Embedded within the grand differences in political scale, structure, and performance is a more personal contrast, one in quality of leadership. An historically particular type of leader-figure, the "big-man" as he is often locally styled, appears in the underdeveloped settings of Melanesia. Another type, a chief properly so-called, is associated with the Polynesian advance. Now these are distinct sociological types; that is to say, differences in the powers, privileges, rights, duties, and obligations of Melanesian big-men and Polynesian chiefs are given by the divergent societal contexts in which they operate. Yet the institutional distinctions cannot help but be manifest also in differences in bearing and character, appearance and manner—in a word, personality. It may be a good way to begin the more rigorous sociological comparison of leadership with a more impressionistic sketch of the contrast in the human dimension. Here I find it useful to apply characterizations—or is it caricature?—from our own history to big-men and chiefs, however much injustice this does to the historically incomparable backgrounds of the Melanesians and Polynesians. The Melanesian big-man seems so thoroughly bourgeois, so reminiscent of the free-enterprising rugged individual of our own heritage. He combines with an ostensible interest in the general welfare a more profound measure of self-interested cunning and economic calculation. His gaze, as Veblen might have put it, is fixed unswervingly to the main chance. His every public action is designed to make a competitive and invidious comparison with others, to show a standing above the masses that is product of his own personal manufacture. The historical caricature of the Polynesian chief, however, is feudal rather than capitalist. His appearance, his bearing is almost regal; very likely he just *is* a big man—"'Can't you see he is a chief? See how big he is?'"[2] In his every public action is a display of the refinements of breeding, in his manner always that *noblesse oblige* of true pedigree

---

[2] Edward Winslow Gifford, *Tongan Society* (Honolulu: Bernice P. Bishop Museum Bulletin 61, 1926).

and an incontestable right of rule. With his standing not so much a personal achievement as a just social due, he can afford to be, and he is, every inch a chief.

In the several Melanesian tribes in which big-men have come under anthropological scrutiny, local cultural differences modify the expression of their personal powers. But the indicative quality of big-man authority is everywhere the same: it is *personal* power. Big-men do not come to office; they do not succeed to, nor are they installed in, existing positions of leadership over political groups. The attainment of big-man status is rather the outcome of a series of acts which elevate a person above the common herd and attract about him a coterie of loyal, lesser men. It is not accurate to speak of "big-man" as a political title, for it is but an acknowledged standing in interpersonal relations — a "prince among men," so to speak, as opposed to "The Prince of Danes." In particular Melanesian tribes the phrase might be "man of importance" or "man of renown," "generous rich-man," or "center-man," as well as "big-man."

A kind of two-sidedness in authority is implied in this series of phrases, a division of the big-man's field of influence into two distinct sectors. "Center-man" particularly connotes a cluster of followers gathered about an influential pivot. It socially implies the division of the tribe into political in-groups dominated by outstanding personalities. To the in-group, the big-man presents this sort of picture:

> The place of the leader in the district group [in northern Malaita] is well summed up by his title, which might be translated as "center-man." . . . He was like a banyan, the natives explain, which, though the biggest and tallest in the forest, is still a tree like the rest. But, just because it exceeds all others, the banyan gives support to more lianas and creepers, provides more food for the birds, and gives better protection against sun and rain.[3]

But "man of renown" connotes a broader tribal field in which a man is not so much a leader as he is some sort of hero. This is the side of the big-man facing outward from his own faction, his status among some or all of the other political clusters of the tribe. The political sphere of the big-man divides itself into a small internal sector composed of his personal satellites — rarely over eighty men — and a much larger external sector, the tribal galaxy consisting of many similar constellations.

As it crosses over from the internal into the external sector, a big-man's power undergoes qualitative change. Within his faction a Melanesian leader has true command ability, outside of it only fame and

---

[3] H. Ian Hogbin, "Native Councils and Courts in the Solomon Islands," *Oceania* 14 (1943–44): 258–283.

indirect influence. It is not that the center-man rules his faction by physical force, but his followers do feel obliged to obey him, and he can usually get what he wants by haranguing them — public verbal suasion is indeed so often employed by center-men that they have been styled "harangueutans." The orbits of outsiders, however, are set by their own center-men. "'Do it yourself. I'm not *your* fool,'" would be the characteristic response to an order issued by a center-man to an outsider among the Siuai.[4] This fragmentation of true authority presents special political difficulties, particularly in organizing large masses of people for the prosecution of such collective ends as warfare or ceremony. Big-men do instigate mass action, but only by establishing both extensive renown and special personal relations of compulsion or reciprocity with other center-men.

Politics is in the main personal politicking in these Melanesian societies, and the size of a leader's faction as well as the extent of his renown are normally set by competition with other ambitious men. Little or no authority is given by social ascription: leadership is a creation — a creation of followership. "Followers," as it is written of the Kapauku of New Guinea, "stand in various relations to the leader. Their obedience to the headman's decisions is caused by motivations which reflect their particular relations to the leader."[5] So a man must be prepared to demonstrate that he possesses the kinds of skills that command respect — magical powers, gardening prowess, mastery of oratorical style, perhaps bravery in war and feud. Typically decisive is the deployment of one's skills and efforts in a certain direction: toward amassing goods, most often pigs, shell monies, and vegetable foods, and distributing them in ways which build a name for cavalier generosity, if not for compassion. A faction is developed by informal private assistance to people of a locale. Tribal rank and renown are developed by great public giveaways sponsored by the rising big-man, often on behalf of his faction as well as himself. In different Melanesian tribes, the renown-making public distribution may appear as one side of a delayed exchange of pigs between corporate kinship groups; a marital consideration given a bride's kinfolk; a set of feasts connected with the erection of a big-man's dwelling, or of a clubhouse for himself and his faction, or with the purchase of higher grades of rank in secret societies; the sponsorship of a religious ceremony; a payment of subsidies and blood compensations to military allies; or perhaps the giveaway is a ceremonial challenge bestowed on another leader in the attempt to outgive and thus outrank him (a potlatch).

---

[4] Douglas Oliver, *A Solomon Islands Society* (Cambridge: Harvard University Press, 1955).

[5] Leopold Pospisil, *Kapauku Papuans and Their Law* (New Haven: Yale University Publications in Anthropology, no. 54, 1958).

The making of the faction, however, is the true making of the Melanesian big-man. It is essential to establish relations of loyalty and obligation on the part of a number of people such that their production can be mobilized for renown-building external distribution. The bigger the faction the greater the renown; once momentum in external distribution has been generated the opposite can also be true. Any ambitious man who can gather a following can launch a societal career. The rising big-man necessarily depends initially on a small core of followers, principally his own household and his closest relatives. Upon these people he can prevail economically: he capitalizes in the first instance on kinship dues and by finessing the relation of reciprocity appropriate among close kinsmen. Often it becomes necessary at an early phase to enlarge one's household. The rising leader goes out of his way to incorporate within his family "strays" of various sorts, people without familial support themselves, such as widows and orphans. Additional wives are especially useful. The more wives a man has the more pigs he has. The relation here is functional, not identical: with more women gardening there will be more food for pigs and more swineherds. A Kiwai Papuan picturesquely put to an anthropologist in pidgin the advantages, economic and political, of polygamy: "'Another woman go garden, another woman go take firewood, another woman go catch fish, another woman cook him — husband he sing out plenty people come kaikai [that is, come to eat].'"[6] Each new marriage, incidentally, creates for the big-man an additional set of in-laws from whom he can exact economic favors. Finally, a leader's career sustains its upward climb when he is able to link other men and their families to his faction, harnessing their production to his ambition. This is done by calculated generosities, by placing others in gratitude and obligation through helping them in some big way. A common technique is payment of bridewealth on behalf of young men seeking wives.

The great Malinowski used a phrase in analyzing primitive political economy that felicitously describes just what the big-man is doing: amassing a "fund of power." A big-man is one who can create and use social relations which give him leverage on others' production and the ability to siphon off an excess product — or sometimes he can cut down their consumption in the interest of the siphon. Now although his attention may be given primarily to short-term personal interests, from an objective standpoint the leader acts to promote long-term societal interests. The fund of power provisions activities that involve other groups of the society at large. In the greater perspective of that society at large, big-men are indispensable means of creating supra-local organization: in tribes normally fragmented into small indepen-

---

[6] Gunnar Landtman, *The Kiwai Papuans of British New Guinea* (London: Macmillan, 1927).

dent groups, big-men at least temporarily widen the sphere of ceremony, recreation and art, economic collaboration, of war too. Yet always this greater societal organization depends on the lesser factional organization, particularly on the ceilings on economic mobilization set by relations between center-men and followers. The limits and the weaknesses of the political order in general are the limits and weaknesses of the factional in-groups.

And the personal quality of subordination to a center-man is a serious weakness in factional structure. A personal loyalty has to be made and continually reinforced; if there is discontent it may well be severed. Merely to create a faction takes time and effort, and to hold it, still more effort. The potential rupture of personal links in the factional chain is at the heart of two broad evolutionary shortcomings of western Melanesian political orders. First, a comparative instability. Shifting dispositions and magnetisms of ambitious men in a region may induce fluctuations in factions, perhaps some overlapping of them, and fluctuations also in the extent of different renowns. The death of a center-man can become a regional political trauma: the death undermines the personally cemented faction, the group dissolves in whole or in part, and the people regroup finally around rising pivotal big-men. Although particular tribal structures in places cushion the disorganization, the big-man political system is generally unstable over short terms: in its superstructure it is a flux of rising and falling leaders, in its substructure of enlarging and contracting factions. Second, the personal political bond contributes to the containment of evolutionary advance. The possibility of their desertion, it is clear, often inhibits a leader's ability to forcibly push up his followers' output, thereby placing constraints on higher political organization, but there is more to it than that. If it is to generate great momentum, a big-man's quest for the summits of renown is likely to bring out a contradiction in his relations to followers, so that he finds himself encouraging defection — or worse, an egalitarian rebellion — by encouraging production.

One side of the Melanesian contradiction is the initial economic reciprocity between a center-man and his followers. For his help they give their help, and for goods going out through his hands other goods (often from outside factions) flow back to his followers by the same path. The other side is that a cumulative buildup of renown forces center-men into economic extortion of the faction. Here it is important that not merely his own status, but the standing and perhaps the military security of his people depend on the big-man's achievements in public distribution. Established at the head of a sizable faction, a center-man comes under increasing pressure to extract goods from his followers, to delay reciprocities owing them, and to deflect incoming goods back into external circulation. Success in competition with other big-men particularly undermines internal-factional reciprocities: such success is precisely measurable by the ability to give outsiders more than they can possibly reciprocate. In well-delineated big-man polities, we find leaders negating the reciprocal obligations upon which their following had been predicated. Substituting extraction for reciprocity, they must compel their people to "eat the leader's renown," as one Solomon Island group puts it, in return for productive efforts. Some center-men appear more able than others to dam the inevitable tide of discontent that mounts within their factions, perhaps because of charismatic personalities, perhaps because of the particular social organizations in which they operate. But paradoxically the ultimate defense of the center-man's position is some slackening of his drive to enlarge the funds of power. The alternative is much worse. In the anthropological record there are not merely instances of big-man chicanery and of material deprivation of the faction in the interests of renown, but some also of overloading of social relations with followers: the generation of antagonisms, defections, and in extreme cases the violent liquidation of the center-man. Developing internal constraints, the Melanesian big-man political order brakes evolutionary advance at a certain level. It sets ceilings on the intensification of political authority, on the intensification of household production by political means, and on the diversion of household outputs in support of wider political organization.

But in Polynesia these constraints were breached, and although Polynesian chiefdoms also found their developmental plateau, it was not before political evolution had been carried above the Melanesian ceilings. The fundamental defects of the Melanesian plan were overcome in Polynesia. The division between small internal and larger external political sectors, upon which all big-man politics hinged, was suppressed in Polynesia by the growth of an enclaving chiefdom-at-large. A chain of command subordinating lesser chiefs and groups to greater, on the basis of inherent societal rank, made local blocs or personal followings (such as were independent in Melanesia) merely dependent parts of the larger Polynesian chiefdom. So the nexus of the Polynesian chiefdom became an extensive set of offices, a pyramid of higher and lower chiefs holding sway over larger and smaller sections of the polity. Indeed, the system of ranked and subdivided lineages (conical clan system), upon which the pyramid was characteristically established, might build up through several orders of inclusion and encompass the whole of an island or group of islands. While the island or the archipelago would normally be divided into several independent chiefdoms, high-order lineage connections between them, as well as kinship ties between their paramount chiefs, provided structural avenues for at least temporary expansion of political scale, for consolidation of great into even greater chiefdoms.

The pivotal paramount chief as well as the chieftains controlling parts of a chiefdom were true office holders and title holders. They were not, like Melanesian big-men, fishers of men: they held positions of authority over permanent groups. The honorifics of Polynesian chiefs likewise did not refer to a standing in interpersonal relations, but to their leadership of political divisions — here "The Prince of Danes," *not* "The prince among men." In western Melanesia the personal superiorities and inferiorities arising in the intercourse of particular men largely defined the political bodies. In Polynesia there emerged suprapersonal structures of leadership and followership, organizations that continued independently of the particular men who occupied positions in them for brief mortal spans.

And these Polynesian chiefs did not make their positions in society — they were installed in societal positions. In several of the islands, men did struggle to office against the will and stratagems of rival aspirants. But then they came *to* power. Power resided in the office; it was not made by the demonstration of personal superiority. In other islands — Tahiti was famous for it — succession to chieftainship was tightly controlled by inherent rank. The chiefly lineage ruled by virtue of its genealogical connections with divinity, and chiefs were succeeded by first sons, who carried "in the blood" the attributes of leadership. The important comparative point is this: the qualities of command that had to reside in men in Melanesia, that had to be personally demonstrated in order to attract loyal followers, were in Polynesia socially assigned to office and rank. In Polynesia, people of high rank and office *ipso facto* were leaders, and by the same token the qualities of leadership were automatically lacking — theirs was not to question why — among the underlying population. Magical powers such as a Melanesian big-man might acquire to sustain his position, a Polynesian high chief inherited by divine descent as the *mana* which sanctified his rule and protected his person against the hands of the commonalty. The productive ability the big-man laboriously had to demonstrate was effortlessly given Polynesian chiefs as religious control over agricultural fertility, and upon the ceremonial implementation of it the rest of the people were conceived dependent. Where a Melanesian leader had to master the compelling oratorical style, Polynesian paramounts often had trained "talking chiefs" whose voice was the chiefly command.

In the Polynesian view, a chiefly personage was in the nature of things powerful. But this merely implies the objective observation that his power was of the group rather than of himself. His authority came from the organization, from an organized acquiescence in his privileges and organized means of sustaining them. A kind of paradox resides in evolutionary developments which detach the exercise of authority from the necessity to demonstrate personal superiority: organizational power actually extends the role of personal decision and conscious planning, gives it greater scope, impact, and effectiveness. The growth of a political system such as the Polynesian constitutes advance over Melanesian orders of interpersonal dominance in the human control of human affairs. Especially significant for society at large were privileges accorded Polynesian chiefs which made them greater architects of funds of power than ever was any Melanesian big-man.

Masters of their people and "owners" in a titular sense of group resources, Polynesian chiefs had rights of call upon the labor and agricultural produce of households within their domains. Economic mobilization did not depend on, as it necessarily had for Melanesian big-men, the *de novo* creation by the leader of personal loyalties and economic obligations. A chief need not stoop to obligate this man or that man, need not by a series of individual acts of generosity induce others to support him, for economic leverage over a group was the inherent chiefly due. Consider the implications for the fund of power of the widespread chiefly privilege, related to titular "ownership" of land, of placing an interdiction, a tabu, on the harvest of some crop by way of reserving its use for a collective project. By means of the tabu the chief directs the course of production in a general way: households of his domain must turn to some other means of subsistence. He delivers a stimulus to household production: in the absence of the tabu further labors would not have been necessary. Most significantly, he has generated a politically utilizable agricultural surplus. A subsequent call on this surplus floats chieftainship as a going concern, capitalizes the fund of power. In certain islands, Polynesian chiefs controlled great storehouses which held the goods congealed by chiefly pressures on the commonalty. David Malo, one of the great native custodians of old Hawaiian lore, felicitously catches the political significance of the chiefly magazine in his well-known *Hawaiian Antiquities:*

> It was the practice for kings [that is, paramount chiefs of individual islands] to build store-houses in which to collect food, fish, tapas [bark cloth], malos [men's loin cloths], pa-us [women's loin skirts], and all sorts of goods. These store-houses were designed by the Kalaimoku [the chief's principal executive] as a means of keeping the people contented, so they would not desert the king. They were like the baskets that were used to entrap the *hinalea* fish. The *hinalea* thought there was something good within the basket, and he hung round the outside of it. In the same way the people thought there was food in the store-houses, and they kept their eyes on the king. As the rat will not desert the pantry . . . where he thinks food is, so the people will not desert the king while they think there is food in his store-house.[7]

_____

[7] David Malo, *Hawaiian Antiquities* (Honolulu: Hawaiian Gazette Co., 1903).

Redistribution of the fund of power was the supreme art of Polynesian politics. By well-planned *noblesse oblige* the large domain of a paramount chief was held together, organized at times for massive projects, protected against other chiefdoms, even further enriched. Uses of the chiefly fund included lavish hospitality and entertainments for outside chiefs and for the chief's own people, and succor of individuals or the underlying population at large in times of scarcities — bread and circuses. Chiefs subsidized craft production, promoting in Polynesia a division of technical labor unparalleled in extent and expertise in most of the Pacific. They supported also great technical construction, as of irrigation complexes, the further returns to which swelled the chiefly fund. They initiated large-scale religious construction too, subsidized the great ceremonies, and organized logistic support for extensive military campaigns. Larger and more easily replenished than their western Melanesian counterparts, Polynesian funds of power permitted greater political regulation of a greater range of social activities on greater scale.

In the most advanced Polynesian chiefdoms, as in Hawaii and Tahiti, a significant part of the chiefly fund was deflected away from general redistribution toward the upkeep of the institution of chieftainship. The fund was siphoned for the support of a permanent administrative establishment. In some measure, goods and services contributed by the people precipitated out as the grand houses, assembly places, and temple platforms of chiefly precincts. In another measure, they were appropriated for the livelihood of circles of retainers, many of them close kinsmen of the chief, who clustered about the powerful paramounts. These were not all useless hangers-on. They were political cadres: supervisors of the stores, talking chiefs, ceremonial attendants, high priests who were intimately involved in political rule, envoys to transmit directives through the chiefdom. There were men in these chiefly retinues — in Tahiti and perhaps Hawaii, specialized warrior corps — whose force could be directed internally as a buttress against fragmenting or rebellious elements of the chiefdom. A Tahitian or Hawaiian high chief had more compelling sanctions than the harangue. He controlled a ready physical force, an armed body of executioners, which gave him mastery particularly over the lesser people of the community. While it looks a lot like the big-man's faction again, the differences in functioning of the great Polynesian chief's retinue are more significant than the superficial similarities in appearance. The chief's coterie, for one thing, is economically dependent upon him rather than he upon them. And in deploying the cadres politically in various sections of the chiefdom, or against the lower orders, the great Polynesian chiefs sustained command where the Melanesian big-man, in his external sector, had at best renown.

This is not to say that the advanced Polynesian chiefdoms were free of internal defect, of potential or actual malfunctioning. The large political-military apparatus indicates something of the opposite. So does the recent work of Irving Goldman[8] on the intensity of "status rivalry" in Polynesia, especially when it is considered that much of the status rivalry in developed chiefdoms, as the Hawaiian, amounted to popular rebellion against chiefly despotism rather than mere contest for position within the ruling stratum. This suggests that Polynesian chiefdoms, just as Melanesian big-man orders, generate along with evolutionary development countervailing anti-authority pressures, and that the weight of the latter may ultimately impede further development.

The Polynesian contradiction seems clear enough. On one side, chieftainship is never detached from kinship moorings and kinship economic ethics. Even the greatest Polynesian chiefs were conceived as superior kinsmen to the masses, fathers of their people, and generosity was morally incumbent upon them. On the other side, the major Polynesian paramounts seemed inclined to "eat the power of the government too much," as the Tahitians put it, to divert an undue proportion of the general wealth toward the chiefly establishment. The diversion could be accomplished by lowering the customary level of general redistribution, lessening the material returns of chieftainship to the community at large — tradition attributes the great rebellion of Mangarevan commoners to such cause. Or the diversion might — and I suspect more commonly did — consist in greater and more forceful exactions from lesser chiefs and people, increasing returns to the chiefly apparatus without necessarily affecting the level of general redistribution. In either case, the well-developed chiefdom creates for itself the dampening paradox of stoking rebellion by funding its authority.

In Hawaii and other islands cycles of political centralization and decentralization may be abstracted from traditional histories. That is, larger chiefdoms periodically fragmented into smaller and then were later reconstituted. Here would be more evidence of a tendency to overtax the political structure. But how to explain the emergence of a developmental stymie, of an inability to sustain political advance beyond a certain level? To point to a chiefly propensity to consume or a Polynesian propensity to rebel is not enough: such propensities are promoted by the very advance of chiefdoms. There is reason to hazard instead that Parkinson's notable law is behind it all: that progressive expansion in political scale entailed more-than-proportionate accretion in the ruling apparatus, unbalancing the flow of wealth in favor of the apparatus. The ensuing unrest then curbs the chiefly impositions,

[8] Irving Goldman, "Status Rivalry and Cultural Evolution in Polynesia," *American Anthropologist* 57 (1957): 680–697; "Variations in Polynesian Social Organization," *Journal of the Polynesian Society* 66 (1957): 374–390.

sometimes by reducing chiefdom scale to the nadir of the periodic cycle. Comparison of the requirements of administration in small and large Polynesian chiefdoms helps make the point.

A lesser chiefdom, confined, say, as in the Marquesas Islands to a narrow valley, could be almost personally ruled by a headman in frequent contact with the relatively small population. Melville's partly romanticized — also for its ethnographic details, partly cribbed — account in *Typee* makes this clear enough. But the great Polynesian chiefs had to rule much larger, spatially dispersed, internally organized populations. Hawaii, an island over four thousand square miles with an aboriginal population approaching one hundred thousand, was at times a single chiefdom, at other times divided into two to six independent chiefdoms, and at all times each chiefdom was composed of large subdivisions under powerful subchiefs. Sometimes a chiefdom in the Hawaiian group extended beyond the confines of one of the islands, incorporating part of another through conquest. Now, such extensive chiefdoms would have to be coordinated; they would have to be centrally tapped for a fund of power, buttressed against internal disruption, sometimes massed for distant, perhaps overseas, military engagements. All of this to be implemented by means of communication still at the level of word-of-mouth, and means of transportation consisting of human bodies and canoes. (The extent of certain larger chieftainships, coupled with the limitations of communication and transportation, incidentally suggests another possible source of political unrest: that the burden of provisioning the governing apparatus would tend to fall disproportionately on groups within easiest access of the paramount.) A tendency for the developed chiefdom to proliferate in executive cadres, to grow top-heavy, seems in these circumstances altogether functional, even though the ensuing drain on wealth proves the chiefdom's undoing. Functional also, and likewise a material drain on the chiefdom at large, would be widening distinctions between chiefs and people in style of life. Palatial housing, ornamentation and luxury, finery and ceremony, in brief, conspicuous consumption, however much it seems mere self-interest always has a more decisive social significance. It creates those invidious distinctions between rulers and ruled so conducive to a passive — hence quite economical! — acceptance of authority. Throughout history, inherently more powerful political organizations than the Polynesian, with more assured logistics of rule, have turned to it — including in our time some ostensibly revolutionary and proletarian governments, despite every prerevolutionary protestation of solidarity with the masses and equality for the classes.

In Polynesia, then, as in Melanesia, political evolution is eventually short-circuited by an overload on the relations between leaders and their people. The Polynesian tragedy, however, was somewhat the opposite of the Melanesian. In Polynesia, the evolutionary ceiling was set by extraction from the population at large in favor of the chiefly faction, in Melanesia by extraction from the big-man's faction in favor of distribution to the population at large. Most important, the Polynesian ceiling was higher. Melanesian big-men and Polynesian chiefs not only reflect different varieties and levels of political evolution, they display in different degrees the capacity to generate and to sustain political progress.

Especially emerging from the juxtaposition is the more decisive impact of Polynesian chiefs on the economy, the chiefs' greater leverage on the output of the several households of society. The success of any primitive political organization is decided here, in the control that can be developed over household economies. For the household is not merely the principal productive unit in primitive societies, it is often quite capable of autonomous direction of its own production, and it is oriented toward production for its own, not societal, consumption. The greater potential of Polynesian chieftainship is precisely the greater pressure it could exert on household output, its capacity both to generate a surplus and to deploy it out of the household toward a broader division of labor, cooperative construction, and massive ceremonial and military action. Polynesian chiefs were the more effective means of societal collaboration on economic, political, indeed all cultural fronts. Perhaps we have been too long accustomed to perceive rank and rule from the standpoint of the individuals involved, rather than from the perspective of the total society, as if the secret of the subordination of man to man lay in the personal satisfactions of power. And then the breakdowns too, or the evolutionary limits, have been searched out in men, in "weak" kings or megalomaniacal dictators—always, "who is the matter?" An excursion into the field of primitive politics suggests the more fruitful conception that the gains of political developments accrue more decisively to society than to individuals, and the failings as well are of structure, not men.

REVIEW QUESTIONS

1. What is the difference between a Melanesian big-man and a Polynesian chief? How does each acquire and maintain power?

2. What are the bases of political integration for the big-man and chiefly political systems?

3. What is the role of kinship in the Melanesian and Polynesian political systems?

4. How does Sahlins support his argument that the chiefly system of Polynesia permits larger political aggregates?

28   Big-Men on Capitol Hill

JACK McIVER WEATHERFORD

*As we saw in the last article, Melanesian big-men gather followers
and power by personal, usually face-to-face, effort. In this article,
Jack Weatherford shows how the road to power is the same for
U.S. senators as it is for New Guinea big-men. Both start with few
supporters and resources. Both must acquire more followers and
valuable items to rise in power. Each must give "pork" to followers
to increase power. For congressmen, the rise to power requires the
acquisition of substantive jurisdictions, staff, and other beholden
senators.*

Ongka, a tribal elder of the Kawelka in Highland New Guinea, knew
that he had finally arrived as a big-man when he was able to give the
biggest *moka* the region had ever witnessed. At this huge feast, Ongka
made speeches to all of his assembled relatives, friends, and allies.
Dressed in his finest feathers and decorations, he distributed the
roasted pigs and yam puddings made by his wives, and to cement his
position as a leader and patron, he presented a great many gifts to the
assembled tribesmen. To some went live pigs or a bird; a few got cows
and cassowaries. In addition to these traditional gifts, Ongka gave
away a motorbike and a Toyota Landcruiser, making his *moka* without

doubt the finest and most modern ever known in New Guinea: as such, it was the culmination of a lifetime of hard work to become a big-man.

In parts of tribal New Guinea and Melanesia where there are no hereditary chiefs, politics are dominated by these successful old warriors known as big-men. The arduous path to become a big-man is one of hard work and careful strategy. It is a path open only to males, but any young man who applies himself to the task can attain this preeminent status. The young politician begins life, as do most of his peers, with a meager patrimony of a small garden plot and a wife to work it. The yam crop from this garden feeds not only the fledgling family but their pigs as well. If the young couple works hard, they can produce an excess of yams, which can be used to raise more pigs. As they become prosperous, the young warrior acquires another wife, who can help to grow even more yams and more pigs. The repetitive acquisition of wives, pigs, and yams lies at the heart of his political power. Through the distribution of pork to other less successful men, he acquires followers, and through his marriages to new wives and the carefully orchestrated marriages of his own children, he acquires allies.

By the time he becomes a senior warrior, he can thereby head a large group of fellow tribesmen bound to him by these pig alliances. He has become a big-man. The great *mokas* crown the process like a combination election and inaugural celebration. Even though the raiding parties that traditionally centered on these big-men have now been outlawed, the practices have never been completely banished from the hinterlands, where big-men are still known by the title "Slayers of Pigs and Men."

The political path to becoming a big-man in the United States Congress resembles the route followed by Ongka and other big-men in New Guinea. As in New Guinea, the role of big-man has been usually reserved for males, but in the United States a few women have broken into these ranks. The baked-chicken dinners and paper hats of American politics may lack some of the color of roasting pigs and cassowary feather headdresses, and American oratory may pale before the eloquent rhetoric of a New Guinea big-man, but underneath the process remains the same. The distribution of pork represents the heart of the organization in both cases, even if the Americans have substituted a metaphorical distribution of grants in aid and water projects for the living, squealing variety. The more pork he distributes, the more followers he attracts, and the more followers he attracts, the more pork he acquires to distribute.

In New Guinea and on Capitol Hill alike, the system rests on a delicately synchronized spiral of growth, in which followers and goods increase each other. Any boost to one part creates a chain reaction that increases all the other parts. By the same set of interrelations, however, a breakdown at any single point in the process can reverse the whole spiral, rapidly depleting power, production, and followers.

A sudden plague that wipes out the pigs, a yam blight, massive budget cuts, or the abolition of a favorite program can destroy a lifetime of careful work and orchestration. Similarly, a rupture in domestic relations and the departure of several wives amid much rumor and gossip or an ethics scandal with public ridicule can deprive a big-man of his reputation, labor force, and thereby his political clout as well.

Few men in New Guinea survive the ravages of jungle disease and war to become senior members of their tribes, much less big-men. In the United States Congress, a few politicians survive the vicissitudes of voter opinion long enough to become senior congressmen. Of those who do survive, fewer still have the combination of ability and luck to become congressional big-men. The key to their success lies in their ability to organize and run a personal political organization within the congress. Most congressmen get some training for this by putting together an electoral organization in the home district, but in contemporary politics an inept politician who is rich can just buy an election campaign staff, public relations firm, and lots of advertising. Once he gets in the Congress, however, he must learn to pit his own organizational skills against other congressmen for control of the resources available. His ability to do this determines whether or not he will ever become a big-man.

Every New Guinea big-man's career originates from his ability to organize his domestic household to produce as many yams and pigs as possible. From this rather undramatic skill develops his opportunity to be a real leader of men in politics, war, and in the big hunt. In parallel fashion, every congressional big-man's career originates from his capacity to organize his personal staff to maximize his political output. This basic skill provides him with the means to be a real political leader within the Congress. The congressman does not begin his legislative career as a leader of other politicians; he begins as the leader of a small staff. Only if he plays the game correctly can he turn his group into one that includes other politicians as well as staff.

The size of each congressman's personal staff is fairly standardized, while those of senators vary according to the population of the state, with only modest room for manipulation. For the freshmen and sophomores, particularly in the House, there is little opportunity for political expansion. Most of their efforts focus on the home district rather than on congressional politics. For senators and representatives who survive the first few terms, playing the insider game of congressional politics begins when they vie for subcommittee jurisdiction and for the accompanying staff. If a member is to expand his following, he must do so in either the committee or the party organization. It is there that both jurisdiction and staff are available.

Until the reforms of the Watergate era, a new senator joining a committee could do nothing but wait until the years passed to chair that committee. Today, however, senators expect and get a small piece of the action from the beginning. How they handle this responsibility will determine how quickly they rise in the power structure. Initial authority comes in the form of a subcommittee chairmanship. The three essentials for a subcommittee are (1) a staff to run it, (2) space in which to operate, and (3) a piece of jurisdiction to manage. These are acquired through a form of "United Fund Drive." The senior senators on the committee, who all chair their own subcommittees, are expected to donate something in one of these three categories to the freshman member. One senator may have a small room he uses for storage in the annex building; he donates that for an office. Another senator has oversight over the census, but since there will not be another census for several years, he hands over that jurisdiction. A third senator is responsible for consumer fraud; since consumer issues generate so much crank mail with very little press attention, he is willing to donate that piece of jurisdiction and the sole accompanying clerical position. The chairman of the committee has been having trouble with the subchairmen and thinks it might be beneficial to win over the freshman as an ally, so in a generous spirit the chairman throws in another clerical position and responsibility for a sewage program that has lost its funding.

If each of the senior senators donates something to this United Fund Drive, bit by bit a subcommittee can be assembled. It may have only one staffer and one secretary, a storage room for an office, and jurisdiction over an area for which there are no bills or pending legislation, but nevertheless it is a start. This miniature chimera is decorated with a title — preferably one that reflects a trendy topic or a relevant campaign issue. The title does not necessarily have to reflect the function of the subcommittee because the subcommittee does not necessarily have to have any function.

By means of a United Fund Drive for each of the two or three committees on which a new member serves, a freshman senator within a few months of election can be chairman of two or three very impressive-sounding subcommittees. Senator Max Baucus of Montana entered the Senate in 1979. From a United Fund Drive in the Senate Finance Committee, he was made chairman of the Subcommittee on Oversight of the Internal Revenue Service. This was a perfect subcommittee. The title sounded important, since every voter knows how important taxes and the Internal Revenue Service are. It was also highly relevant to the big issue of tax cutting. At the same time it was very specific; unlike vague issues such as consumerism, this subcommittee was concerned with one particular government agency — the IRS. The subcommittee was tailored to impress voters. Only a government insider would know that the mention of "oversight" in the title is a code word for powerlessness. In the Congress only "authorizations," which create programs, and "appropriations," which fund them, are a part of the power structure. "Oversight" implies the right to look but not to touch.

Senator Baucus also served on the Judiciary Committee. From the United Fund Drive there, he became chairman of the Limitations of Contracted and Delegated Authority Subcommittee. The name alone is formidable enough to prevent anyone, inside or outside the government, from bothering to ask what it means. If Baucus was to be chairman, however, he needed someone over whom to preside. The Judiciary Committee then assigned the other freshman, Senator Howell Heflin. In the spirit of reciprocity, Baucus joined Heflin's newly created subcommittee on Jurisprudence and Governmental Relations.

Members of the minority party are entitled to their proportion of all committee and subcommittee seats, so Senator Baucus's subcommittee needed a member of the "opposition." Freshman Republican Thad Cochran was assigned to the subcommittee and as the only Republican was made ranking minority member. Baucus and Heflin could then have an opposition faction to represent the minority view of the limitations of contracted and delegated authority, just in case the issue ever came up for discussion. And if they did not do anything, they had a member of the other party on the committee, and they could always blame him for interference.

This modern procedure assures that no one is left out of the power facade. Gone are the days when it took two decades of sitting on one's hands and waiting for the elders to die before a chairmanship became available. In the 96th Congress, the 60 Democrats divided among themselves 105 chairmanships; there were a corresponding 105 ranking minority-member positions for the 40 Republicans. Every man a chairman. With the Republican majority in 1981, the proportions changed, so that Republicans became the chairmen and the Democrats took the ranking minority positions. Nevertheless, each senator can be the *head* of two separate subcommittees, or, as was the case with senator James Abdnor, the freshman may get three subcommittees from the United Fund Campaign.

Be it ever so humble, the first subcommittee chairmanship initiates a senator's political career. Like a young New Guinea man beginning his political career with an older widow as a wife, a poor parcel of a yam field, and a crippled hog, it may not be much, but it is a start. Hard work might turn even that into a family of several young wives, acres of lush fields, and a herd of prize porkers, just as a hardworking senator may eventually build a powerful congressional clan from his meager subcommittee.

Every two years, in January following the November elections, Congress goes through a reorganization. The jurisdictions of departing members are divided up, after which the crumbs are gathered in the United Fund Drive and presented to an entering freshman as a subcommittee. Even though the freshman has to take what is given the first time, in subsequent reorganizations he will be able to increase his meager share of what the departing big-men left behind. He will also use that opportunity to fob off insignificant parts of his jurisdiction on the new cohort of freshmen.

When Donald Riegle of Michigan moved from the House of Representatives to the Senate in the 95th Congress, he joined Senator Proxmire's Committee on Banking, Housing, and Urban Affairs. His United Fund Subcommittee was given the then hot title of Consumer Affairs. When consumer issues gave way in the press to more severe economic problems, Riegle used the reorganization of the 96th Congress to expand his title to Economic Stabilization Subcommittee. The same pressing economic concerns moved Senator Paul Sarbanes from chairman of the Western Hemisphere Affairs Subcommittee of the Foreign Relations Committee to that committee's International Economic Policy Subcommittee. The Foreign Affairs panel tries to keep a stable subcommittee nomenclature (in the interest of better international relations), so Sarbane's old subcommittee title was passed unchanged to committee newcomer Edward Zorinsky of Nebraska.

For the first few organizations in a senator's career, the "gains in jurisdiction" are more apparent than substantial. Reorganization is a public relations exercise of senior members trying to make the juniors look and feel more important. Gradually, however, the senator is able to acquire a bailiwick of real jurisdiction. The process by which he does this is more one of slow accretion and aggrandizement than of dramatic political coups. For the first few terms the gains come as superficial name trades, exchanging words like "application" for "oversight" and "consumer issues" for "economic affairs." Eventually, the senator acquires small bits of the real authorization and appropriations process. Once this begins, the senator loses interest in the subcommittee name. If he has a piece of real power, people will know it, and he does not need to impress them with a fancy name. At this point in his career any old name will suffice, as he abandons word games for power politics.

When a senator captures another staff position, he immediately fires the employee who occupies the job and fills the position with one of his own clients. Every congressional reorganization involves a major shuffle of staff. When control of the Congress changes parties, as the Senate did after the 1980 elections, these staff changes reach monumental proportions. Within hours after the election returns were announced, Senator Strom Thurmond, as the incoming chairman of the Judiciary Committee, the largest employer in the Senate, put all of Senator Ted Kennedy's staff on notice to vacate their jobs. Thurmond was moving in his own people in a quantum jump in power. Over the next three months corresponding chain reactions reverberated through all the committees and subcommittees of the Senate, as Republicans took over each of the chairmanships.

Committee and staff shuffling continues throughout the politician's congressional career. If he is not vigilant in protecting or expanding his staff, he will forfeit it to more aggressive senators. This happened in 1981 when Strom Thurmond successfully abolished the antitrust subcommittee, which Senator Charles Mathias was taking over as chairman. In abolishing it, Thurmond assumed responsibility for the issues and the staff in his capacity as full Judiciary Committee chairman. The same scenario was played out on the Banking and Urban Affairs Committee when Chairman Jake Garn managed to appoint his own staffer to be director over Senator Richard Lugar's subcommittee. Refusing to be chairman in name only, Lugar resigned from the subcommittee. On the House side, Commerce Committee chairman John Dingell managed to abolish the consumer affairs subcommittee, thereby taking away the staff of the second-ranking committee member, James H. Scheuer of New York.

Occasionally, this game of musical chairs forces the politician to transfer jurisdiction from one of his committees, where it is in danger, to another better-fortified one. This is what Senator William Fulbright did when he surrendered the chairmanship of the Banking Committee for Foreign Relations. On the Banking Committee he had spent years acquiring control over the World Bank and the International Monetary Fund. Rather than abandoning them when he gave up the chairmanship of that committee, he simply moved jurisdiction for them to his Foreign Relations Committee. Subsequent banking chairmen, like William Proxmire, have been fighting unsuccessfully ever since to get these programs back in their original committee.

That kind of juggling, however, is less necessary in the wake of recent committee reforms. Subcommittee chairmen can be much more independent today. Were Fulbright around now, he could take over Foreign Relations and still keep his banking interests within a subcommittee. When Fulbright made his move, however, relinquishing the Banking Committee chairmanship meant relinquishing all of the power in it. Today as a subcommittee chairman, he could retain that power within both spheres. The big struggles now are within committees rather than among them. Subcommittee chairmen struggle against each other and against the chairman of the full committee, while committees fight less against each other. In this Congress of rapidly changing jurisdictions, in which some changes are substantive and some are pretense, how is it possible to tell where power actually is? Is the power in the committee or the subcommittee? Is it in the hands of the chairman, or divided among the subchairmen?

The nominal jurisdictions and the titles belong to the facade of Congress. As part of that facade they are rearranged every other year, when new shingles are made and hung out to represent the shifts of public concern and media attention. Behind this variable facade, however, is a simple arrangement that clarifies the location of power. Power is where the staff is.

No matter how grandiose the name and the official jurisdiction, if a subcommittee has only one young counsel and a single secretary, it is obviously not equipped to exercise much power. By the same token, no matter how innocuous the name and how vague the title, if it has a dozen lawyers, three Ph.D.'s, a battery of secretaries, and four interns, it is certain that some real power is being exercised. It may not be immediately apparent what they command, but staff is a sure sign of dominion over something.

A junior senator may fuss over his subcommittee name and supposed territory, but the middle-level senators — the rising comers — go straight to the heart of the matter; they fuss over staff. As Stephen Isaacs of *The Washington Post* described it, senators are "scrambling after staff bodies like hunters in pursuit of prey, hungering for the impact that extra staff person, or two, or three, or even dozens can give to them and their political careers."

Rochelle Jones and Peter Woll call staff "the surrogates of power." As they explain it, "Committees . . . are mere symbols of power, not power itself, unless they are accompanied by adequate staff. A good staff is necessary if a senator wants to wield power through his committees. If he wants to exert influence beyond his committees, a capable staff is essential. Staff and power go together. . . ." Not only is a senator's staff size directly correlated to the amount of public attention he receives in the news media, it is also related to the amount of work he can get done. Having broad jurisdiction and no staff is like a New Guinea tribesman's having a claim to two large yam fields but no wives to tend them. The fields then belong to the jungle, and they will be expropriated by someone who does have wives and children to cultivate them.

Conceptually, the scheme is simple. Like the tribal politicians of New Guinea and the complex of wives, land, and pigs, congressional politicians have to unite the variables of staff, jurisdiction, and pork. The synthesis depends on skill, luck, and hard work. Most important of all, it depends on the strategy devised and pursued by the individual politician. All the politicians know the basic ingredients of power, but each one must conjure up a plan appropriate to his or her own needs, goals, and abilities.

REVIEW QUESTIONS

1. What are the specific steps senators take to acquire power?
2. How are the steps to power taken by U.S. senators like those taken by New Guinea big-men? What are the differences?
3. What part does "pork" play in the acquisition of power by U.S. senators and Melanesian big-men?
4. How is power acquired by people in other kinds of organizations? Use your own experience to answer.

IX

Religion, Magic, and World View

People seem most content when they are confident about themselves and the order of things around them. Uncertainty breeds debilitating anxiety; insecurity saps people's sense of purpose and their willingness to participate in social activity. Most of the time cultural institutions serve as a lens through which to view and interpret the world and respond realistically to its demands. But from time to time the unexpected or contradictory intervenes to shake people's assurance. A farmer may wonder about his skill when a properly planted and tended crop fails to grow. A wife may feel bewildered when the man she has treated with tenderness and justice for many years runs off with another woman. Death, natural disaster, and countless other forms of adversity strike without warning, eating away at the foundations of confidence. At these crucial points in life, many people use religion to help account for the vagaries of their experience.

Religion is the cultural knowledge of the supernatural that people use to cope with the ultimate problems of human existence.[1] In this definition, the term *supernatural* refers to a realm beyond normal experience. Belief in gods, spirits, ghosts, and magical power often defines the supernatural, but the matter is complicated by cultural variation and the lack of a clear distinction in many societies between a natural and supernatural world. *Ultimate problems,* on the other hand, emerge from universal features of human life and include life's meaning, death, evil, and transcendent values. People everywhere

---

[1] This definition draws on the work of Milton Yinger, *Religion, Society, and the Individual: An Introduction to the Sociology of Religion* (New York: Macmillan, 1957).

wonder why they are alive, why they must die, and why evil strikes some individuals and not others. In every society, people's personal desires and goals may conflict with the values of the larger group. Religion often provides a set of *transcendent values* that override differences and unify the group.

An aspect of religion that is more difficult to comprehend is its link to emotion. Ultimate problems "are more appropriately seen as deep-seated emotional needs," not as conscious, rational constructs, according to sociologist Milton Yinger.[2] Anthropologists may describe and analyze religious ritual and belief but find it harder to get at religion's deeper meanings and personal feelings.

Anthropologists have identified two kinds of supernatural power, personified and impersonal. *Personified supernatural force* resides in supernatural beings, in the deities, ghosts, ancestors, and other beings found in the divine world. For the Bhils of India, a *bhut,* or ghost, has the power to cause skin lesions and wasting diseases. *Bhagwan,* the equivalent of the Christian Deity, controls the universe. Both possess and use personified supernatural force.

Impersonal supernatural force is a more difficult concept to grasp. Often called *mana,* the term used in Polynesian and Melanesian belief, it represents a kind of free-floating force lodged in many things and places. The concept is akin to the Western term *luck* and works like an electrical charge that can be introduced into things or discharged from them. Melanesians, for example, might attribute the spectacular growth of yams to some rocks lying in the fields. The rocks possess mana, which is increasing fertility. If yams fail to grow in subsequent years, they may feel that the stones have lost their power.

Supernatural force, both personified and impersonal, may be used by people in many societies. *Magic* refers to the strategies people use to control supernatural power. Magicians have clear ends in mind when they perform magic, and use a set of well-defined procedures to control and manipulate supernatural forces. For example, a Trobriand Island religious specialist will ensure a sunny day for a political event by repeating powerful sayings thought to affect the weather.

Sorcery uses magic to cause harm. For example, some Bhil *bhopas,* who regularly use magic for positive purposes, may also be hired to work revenge. They will recite powerful *mantras* (ritual sayings) over effigies to cause harm to their victims.

Witchcraft is closely related to sorcery because both use supernatural force to cause evil. But many anthropologists use the term to designate envious individuals who are born with or acquire evil power

---

[2] Yinger, p. 9

and who knowingly or unknowingly project it to hurt others. The Azande of Africa believe that most unfortunate events are due to witchcraft, and most Azande witches claim they were unaware of their power and apologize for its use.

Most religions possess ways to influence supernatural power or, if spirits are nearby, to communicate with it directly. For example, people may say *prayers* to petition supernatural beings. They may also give gifts in the form of *sacrifices* and offerings. Direct communication takes different forms. *Spirit possession* occurs when a supernatural being enters and controls the behavior of a human being. With the spirit in possession, others may talk directly with someone from the divine world. *Divination* is a second way to communicate with the supernatural. It usually requires material objects or animals to provide answers to human-directed questions. The Bhils of India, for example, predict the abundance of summer rainfall by watching where a small bird specially caught for the purpose lands when it is released. If it settles on something green, rainfall will be plentiful; if it rests on something brown, the year will be dry.

Almost all religions involve people with special knowledge who either control supernatural power outright or facilitate others in their attempt to influence it. *Shamans* are religious specialists who directly control supernatural power. They may have personal relationships with spiritual beings or know powerful secret medicines and sayings. They are usually associated with curing. *Priests* are religious specialists who mediate between people and supernatural beings. They don't control divine power; instead, they lead congregations in ceremonies and help others to petition the gods.

World view refers to a system of concepts and often unstated assumptions about life. It usually contains a *cosmology* about the way things are and a *mythology* about how things have come to be. World view presents answers to the ultimate questions: life, death, evil, and conflicting values.

The first two articles in this section deal with the use of magic to reduce uncertainty. In Philip Newman's article, it is the anxiety surrounding illness that receives attention; in George Gmelch's article, it is the irregularities of American baseball. The third article, by Donald Sandner, describes the symbolic practices of Navajo medicine men. Like Western psychotherapists, Navajo healers return patients to their symbolic origins, manage or manipulate evil, and bring about symbolic death and rebirth. Finally, Peter Worsley looks at how religion can be used to create new systems of meaning as cultures struggle with the disruptions of acculturation and colonial rule. He specifically describes revitalization movements, called cargo cults, that sprang up over and over again in Melanesia.

religion
supernatural
ultimate problems
transcendent values
personified supernatural force
mana
magic
sorcery
witchcraft

prayer
sacrifice
spirit possession
divination
shaman
priest
world view
cosmology
mythology

READINGS IN THIS SECTION

29   When Technology Fails: Magic and Religion in New Guinea

PHILIP L. NEWMAN

All people experience anxiety when confronted with situations they cannot control, and in many societies natural methods of influencing and predicting events work only part of the time. In such instances, supernatural forces may be invoked to account for such events and our relation to them. In this article, Philip Newman describes the use of magic and witchcraft by a highland New Guinea people and shows that they employ such practices throughout their lives whenever faced with uncertainty. He suggests that magical procedures can be ranked according to their ability to release tension, and that the choice of particular magical practices correlates with the degree of anxiety to be reduced.

Humans have created many forms in their quest for means of dealing with the world around them. Whether these forms be material tools, social groups, or intangible ideas, they are all, in a sense, "instruments": each is a means to some end; each has a purpose that it fulfills. When we think of such things as magical rites, a belief in ghosts, or accusations of sorcery, however, the matter of purpose becomes less obvious. In the descriptions and in the case history that follow, we will try both to show something of the magical and religious beliefs of a New Guinea people and to demonstrate the purposes that these beliefs have for the men who hold them.

Originally published as "Sorcery, Religion, and the Man." With permission from *Natural History,* February 1962; Copyright the American Museum of Natural History, 1962.

In the mountainous interior of Australian New Guinea, the Asaro River has its headwaters some thirty miles to the north of Goroka, a European settlement that serves as the administrative center for the Central Highlands District. Near Goroka, the Asaro flows through a wide valley where the ground cover is mostly grasses and reeds. In its upper reaches, this valley narrows into a gorge where steep, heavily forested ridges reach out toward the river from mountain masses on either side. Some twelve thousand people live on this part of the river, occupying an area of approximately two hundred square miles. While these people are culturally and linguistically similar, they do not form a single political unit. Indeed, before contact with Europeans, the area was characterized by incessant intertribal warfare. Even now, when active warfare is no longer part of their lives, the pattern of alliances and animosities among the tribes is a factor in social intercourse.

Except for the cessation of warfare, life in the valley today is little changed from what it was before the Australian government began active pacification of the area after the end of World War II. Almost daily, the people climb up from the valley floor to enter the dense forest on the mountain slopes. It is here that building wood is gathered; birds and small marsupials are shot for meat, plumage, or fur; plants that provide for many needs are collected.

Below an altitude of some seven thousand feet, the forest has been cut back to make room for gardens that cling to the sides of steep ridges and crowd together in the narrow valley floors. These gardens provide the people's staple foods — sweet potatoes, yams, sugar cane, and a variety of green vegetables. A woman spends most of her time at garden work, preparing new planting areas, weeding the crop, and harvesting the mature plants. In fallow areas nearby she can turn loose the pigs her husband has entrusted to her care. If they wander too far afield by evening, her call will bring them back on the run. They know that a meal awaits them, as well as a snooze by the fire in their "mother's" house.

While each family may have one or more houses near the forest or in their garden, the center of social life is the village. The villages are located on the tops of ridges in spots usually selected with an eye to their defensibility against enemies. The fifteen to twenty houses that compose each village usually march in single file along the narrow ridge. But, if space permits, they are formed into a square. All the houses are much alike — round, about fifteen feet in diameter, made of double rows of five-foot stakes. The space between the stakes is filled with grass and the outside covered with strips of bark. The roof is thatched and topped with a long, tasseled pole.

Two or three houses always stand out. They are larger, they are not in line with the rest, and they may have as many as eight poles protruding through their roofs. These are the men's houses. As a rule, men and women do not live together, for the men fear that too much contact with women is weakening. For this reason, a man builds a house for his wife — or each of them, if he has more than one — and then helps in the construction of the larger house where he and the other men of the village will sleep apart. Ideally, all the men who live together in a single house can trace their descent back to a known, common ancestor. They thus constitute a lineage. Such a lineage is connected to the other village men's houses by descent links, but in many cases the links are so amorphous that no one can actually tell what they are. Similarly, several villages will be linked together into a clan, but genealogical ties may be more imputed than real.

Just as the forest and the garden represent the physical framework within which each individual lives, so too these various orders of grouping — the lineage, the village, the clan, and the tribe — represent the social framework of existence. The members of these groups are the people with whom each individual is in daily contact. They nurture him, teach him, and assist him in times of crisis. It is from these groups that he derives such things as his name, his rights to the land for gardening and hunting, and the financial help that he needs when it is time to purchase a wife. They hail his birth and mourn his death.

In turn, each individual has obligations to the other members of these groups. He acts as a representative of his group when dealing with outsiders. In this way, he enters into a whole series of relationships with individuals and groups outside his own immediate circle. He may visit a neighboring clan to help one of his own clansmen win the admiration of a prospective bride by sitting up all night near the hot fire singing love songs to her. Or a trip may take him to a nearby tribe, where he dances mightily with other men to show that his group is appreciative of the gift of food and valuables they are about to receive. He may walk several days over difficult ground to reach a completely alien group, where he can barter for shells, plumes, or foodstuffs not available in his own group. As in all societies, the groups comprising the society provide for the individual, while the individual, in turn, contributes some of his efforts to the life of the group.

Humans not only have their tools and their society to help cope with the world: they also have their ideas. There are some problems presented by the environment for which the people of the upper Asaro have not yet devised a mechanical or technical solution. There are other problems for which a technical solution seems not enough. Finally, there are problems for which an idea seems to be an inherently better solution than a physical or social tool. It is here that we enter the realm of magic and religion.

A great many of the activities among the upper Asaro people have a magical or religious component. When a child is born, it is cleaned, fed, and covered with grease to help protect it from the cool mountain air. It is also protected, nonphysically, by burying its umbilical cord in some secluded spot — so that sorcerers cannot later use this piece of the newformed being to cause illness or death by magical means. During the first few days of life, the infant is also made to accept, via magic, his first social responsibility — not to cry at night and disturb its mother. A small bundle of sweet-smelling grass is placed on the mother's head and her desire for uninterrupted slumber is blown into the grass by an attendant. The grass is then crushed over the head of the child and its pungent odor released so that the infant will breathe in the command along with the scent of the plant.

Throughout an individual's life there will be magical rites to protect him from various dangers, to overcome difficulties, and to assist his growth. When a young boy kills his first animal, his hand will be magically "locked" in the position that first sent an arrow on a true course. When he reaches puberty and moves out of his mother's house to begin his life in the men's house, he will be ritually cleansed of the contamination he has been subjected to during his years of association with women. If he were not so cleansed, he would never become strong enough to engage in men's activities. During the years when a young man is trying to win the favor of a girl, he not only relies on his prowess in singing love songs and his decorations, but on his knowledge of love magic as well. If all the usual spells and potions fail, he may utilize one especially powerful form that is thought to make him appear to his beloved with an entirely new face — the face of someone he knows she likes.

In his mature years, when a man's attention turns to the growth of pigs and gardens, he will have magical as well as technical skills to help him. Gardens are not difficult to grow in this fertile land, but it is still wise to put a certain series of leaves across one's fences, so that any thief will find his arms and legs paralyzed should he decide to raid the garden. It also behooves one whose gardens are near the main trails and settlements to give them magical assistance, for a slow-growing garden in such a conspicuous place could be an embarrassment.

The raising of pigs is a more difficult matter, and it is here that magical and religious rites become greatly elaborated. Some of these rites are performed by an individual for his own pigs. It may be a simple performance, as when smoke is blown into the ear of a wild pig to tame it. The theory is that the smoke cools and dries the pig's "hot" disposition. On the other hand, these individual rites may attain considerable complexity, as in the propitiation of forest spirits called *nokondisi*. These spirits are capricious in nature — sometimes playing malicious tricks on men and sometimes performing acts of kindness.

Each man, therefore, maintains a small, fenced enclosure in which he builds a miniature earth oven and a tiny house. By placing food in the earth oven he may be able to entice a *nokondisi* to come live near his pigs and watch after them. In return for the food, the spirit will help bring in lost pigs, protect the herd from thieves, and carry the animals safely across flooded streams during the rainy season.

In addition to the magic performed by an individual on behalf of his own pigs, some rather elaborate rites are performed by the lineage and clan for all the pigs belonging to these groups. The largest of these is the *gerua* ceremony, performed at intervals of from five to seven years. In this ritual, hundreds of pigs are killed and used to pay off various kinds of economic obligations to other clans. It is a time for feasting and dancing, for courting and reunion. It is also a time for propitiating the ghosts of the dead in the hope that they will help the living grow their pigs. All the pigs are killed in the name of particular ghosts. The songs are pleas for ghostly assistance. The wooden *gerua* boards, with their colorful geometric designs, are visible symbols to the ghosts that they have not been forgotten. It is not tender sentiment that motivates this display, however. Rather, it is the fear that failure to do so will engender the wrath of the ever-watchful dead.

The magical and religious beliefs that we have so far examined are all used in conjunction with other practices of a nonmagical nature. There are some areas, however, where no purely technical solutions are available, and where magic and religion are the only "tools" available. One such area is sickness. The people of the upper Asaro are not generally aware of modern medical practices, although efforts are being made in that direction. The nonmagical techniques available to them, such as inhaling the steam from fragrant plants to relieve a stopped-up nose, are few. These remedies do not extend to more serious maladies. When serious illness strikes, the only recourse is to magic.

The magical solutions available are many and varied. There are herbs with magical properties that are administered in much the same way as are medicines in our own society. I made a cursory check, however, which seems to show that few of the plants possess any curative value.

Ghosts and forest spirits are frequently thought to be the causes of illness, for they are deemed capable of entering the body and devouring a person's inner organs. Cures for such illnesses usually involve propitiation of the offending supernatural.

Witches and sorcerers are believed to be another major cause of illness, for they are supposedly capable of injecting foreign bodies into a victim, or performing black magic on objects that have been in association with the victim. To cure illness caused in this way involves calling in a magical specialist who can either extract the foreign bodies or retrieve the objects being operated upon.

While the ideas and rites listed here do not exhaust the entire inventory available to the group under discussion, they give some sense of the variety that exists. The notions are interesting in themselves, but the question of how an individual makes use of these notions is even more fascinating. Let us look at a crisis in the life of one of these people, and see how he picks and chooses among the various "tools" at his disposal.

Ombo was a young man in his early thirties. He had been married for about five years, but was childless. Early one April, it was announced in the traditional style that his wife, Magara, was with child. On such an occasion, a food distribution is held in the village and the announcement, along with gifts of food, is sent out to related villages. Ombo was instructed in the food taboos he would have to undergo during the period of his wife's pregnancy to protect himself from her increased contamination.

All went well for the first few weeks, and then Magara became ill. It is doubtful that her illness was associated with her pregnancy, for her symptoms were the classic signs of malaria — a rather rare disease in this part of the highlands. The first attempts to cure her involved a variety of highly regarded pseudomedications.

A potion of sweet-smelling leaves was administered. A command to the effect that the illness should depart was blown into the leaves, and the leaves were eaten. It was thought that the command, thus internalized, would drive out the illness.

At various other times, attempts were made to relieve her headaches and body pains by rubbing the afflicted areas with stinging nettles. It was held that when the welts and the pain caused by the nettles subsided, the pains in her body would also leave. On one occasion her husband blew smoke over her during a period of fever because, as we have seen, smoke is held to have a cooling and drying effect. He also painted various parts of her body with mud in an effort to cause the pain to dry up at the same time the mud dried.

This kind of treatment continued until early May without any noticeable improvement in Magara's condition. After almost a month had passed and it became apparent that the illness was not going away, Ombo began to speculate on a possible cause. During the next few weeks he came up with several solutions. While he had been away from the village, working for Europeans in Goroka, he had acquired some charms to help him win at a card game popular among the sophisticated younger men.

One of these charms was fairly new, and he was worried that he might not have gained sufficient control over it. Since he kept it hidden in his wife's house, his conclusion was that the charm was exerting its influence on her and causing the illness. He therefore removed it from her house and sent it away to a friend in another tribe. There was no improvement in his wife's condition.

Ombo's next action was to destroy his spirit house. He had not kept it in good repair and had not been diligent in feeding the *nokondisi* that lived there. His father suggested that the angered spirit was taking revenge on Magara. By destroying the house of the spirit, Ombo caused it to retreat to the forest, where it could do no harm. Finally, he burned the costly paraphernalia of a potent sorcery technique he had purchased some years before, fearing it affected his wife.

By now it was late in May. Magara had become so ill that she stopped all but the most minimal work in her garden. Concern about her illness began to increase, and people outside the immediate family began to speculate about its cause. Ombo's older brother mentioned one day that a malevolent ghost might be behind it. It was not long after this that a meeting was held in the men's house and Fumai, a member of the lineage, recounted a dream he had had the night before. In it, he had seen the ghost of Ombo's great-grandmother sitting in the forest near the spot where *gerua* boards are displayed for the ancestors. She had covered herself with ashes and, in a fit of self-pity, was wailing loudly because no one had made a *gerua* board in her honor at the last *gerua* ceremony, and no one had killed a pig in her name. Since ashes are put on at the death of a near relative as a sign of mourning, while clay is put on if the deceased is more distantly related, and since ghosts are thought to be capable of causing death, it was concluded that the dream was prophetic. It implied the imminent death of Magara at the great-grandmother's hands unless something were done.

The next day, Ombo and his wife, along with his parents and siblings, set out for the spot where the ghost had been "seen." A pig was killed there in honor of the ghost. It was cooked in an earth oven filled with valued food items — the largest sweet potatoes, the most succulent yams, and the most highly prized varieties of taro. While water was being poured into the oven, a speech was addressed to the ghost. It was pointed out that the food had been prepared and donated in her honor at considerable trouble to those present. The feeling was expressed that she should be satisfied with the amount and the quality of the offering. She was then told to refrain from causing trouble in the future. As the food steamed in the oven, a *gerua* board was made in the ghost's honor and placed among others in a nearby tree. Some of the food was eaten and the rest was later distributed among members of the lineage.

Things seemed to go well for the next few weeks. Magara improved and was able to return to her work in the garden. Discussion of the topic was dropped. Then, late in June, she suddenly became ill again. Ombo was greatly upset. I suggested to him that she might have malaria and should be taken to the medical aid post. But Ombo did not want to do this, for by now he was convinced that his wife was being attacked by a sorcerer. To deal with this threat, a magical specialist had to be called in. It was several days before he arrived, for he lived some distance away in another tribe. As with any good "doctor," his first acts were aimed at relieving his patient's pain and fever. With much physical strain, he literally pulled the pain from her body and cast it into the ground, where it could do no further harm. His next task was to find out what was causing her illness. For over two hours he sat chatting with Ombo and Magara, discussing the history of the illness, the treatments that had been used, and their own life histories. All the while, he puffed on a tobacco pipe made of a bamboo tube. The degree of irritation caused by the smoke in his throat signalized the appearance in the conversation of significant diagnostic events. Finally, he announced his conclusion — illness by black magic.

To eliminate the effects of the imputed black magic, the object being manipulated by the sorcerer had to be recovered. To do this, the magical specialist first had a bundle of long, thin leaves prepared. Into the bundle were put cooked pork and a variety of plants with magical properties. The specialist never directly touched the bundle himself, but directed Ombo in its preparation. When the bundle was completed, it and a specially prepared bamboo tube were both carried into Magara's house. She was given the tube to hold and the bundle was hung in the rafters near the center pole. After a rite to protect her from further sorcery, Ombo and Magara were locked together in the house.

The specialist remained outside. He walked round and round the house, reciting spells and whirling a special plant around his head. He was pulling the unknown object away from the sorcerer and bringing it back home. The ceremony became a real struggle: the object would come tantalizingly close, only to slip away. Then the specialist announced that the object had arrived. Magara was instructed to open the bundle in the rafters. Inside, among the bits of meat, were a small spider and a piece of string of the type used to hang ornaments around the neck.

The spider, Magara and Ombo were told, was an assistant to the specialist. It had taken the string out of the sorcerer's house and into the open where the specialist could reach it with his powers. The sorcerer was thought to be a young man who had once wanted to marry Magara. The existence of a disappointed suitor was one fact that had come out during the specialist's long interview. When Magara had married Ombo, the suitor had become angry and cut a bit of her necklace string to use for sorcery. The specialist placed the recovered string in the bamboo tube that Magara had been holding, and the tube was then hidden away among the thatch.

From that time until late September, when I left the area, Magara did not experience any further attacks of illness, although she was not in the best of health. The community considered her cured. Significantly, her child was born prematurely in September and died two days later, but no one saw any connection between this death and her illness.

What, then, can we say about the purpose of such ideas and behavior patterns? A situation such as Magara's creates a great deal of tension in an individual who experiences it. If magic does nothing more, it allows the bearer of this tension to act. Both the patient and those concerned feel that something is being done. The pioneer anthropologist Bronislaw Malinowski long ago made the point: "Magic expresses the greater value for man of confidence over doubt, of steadfastness over vacillation, of optimism over pessimism."

It is a rare man indeed, however, who can maintain his confidence and optimism in the face of repeated failure. The question then arises, Why is it that magic is not more readily given up? Three answers have traditionally been given to this question, all of them valid. In the first place, for people such as these, there is no alternative. Secondly, for the believer in the efficacy of magic, the occasional chance successes are more significant than repeated failure. Finally, explanations for failures are always at hand. Inadvertent errors in spells or formulas that must be performed precisely, or imagined countermagic, are ready explanations that are necessarily built into the very nature of magic.

The case history we have seen suggests still a fourth answer. This answer becomes apparent, however, only if we examine the way in which an individual makes use of the magical notions available to him. In the progression of the various magical techniques and explanations employed by Ombo, we can see that they call for behavior patterns allowing for increasingly aggressive release of the tension built up in him by the failure of previously selected techniques.

The simple pseudomedicinal rites, such as rubbing with nettles and painting with mud, were enough to reduce the tension of the initial crisis. The treatment was symptomatic and there was no attempt to identify the cause of the illness. When it became apparent that these techniques had failed, we find Ombo resorting to the more drastic measure of destroying valuable property. The frustration was not yet great enough to cause him to seek outlets in other people: that which he destroyed and removed from his use belonged only to him. In the next phase, we find that a ghost is predicated as the causative agent. One need not be nice to ghosts. They, like the living, are thought to be a mercenary lot who do not much care what is said about them as long as they get their just due. The speech made to the great-grand-mother was studded with commands and expressions of anger at the trouble the ghost had caused. This was an excellent mechanism for the release of tension, just as was the physical act of killing the pig.

Finally, we see the most aggressive act of all — accusing a specific individual of sorcery. The accused individual was a member of an enemy tribe and lived some distance away. It was, therefore, unlikely that accuser and accused would often meet. But if the two had come together, a fight would have been inevitable. In former times, this could have led to open warfare. Thus, Ombo not only used magic as a tool against disease, but also selected the magical tools in such an order that his own increasing anxiety was relieved by increasingly aggressive actions. It is thus not only the forms created by humans that enable them to cope with the world they meet, but the very way in which they manipulate those forms that are available to them.

REVIEW QUESTIONS

1. According to Newman, what is the function of magic?
2. Why do the Asaro use magic? What kinds of things do they use it on?
3. Why did the husband depicted in this article use stronger and stronger magic to cure his wife as time went by?
4. How does Newman explain the fact that people continue to use magic even when it fails?

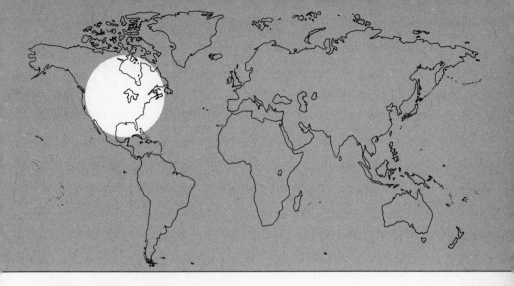

30 Baseball Magic

GEORGE GMELCH

Americans pride themselves on their "scientific" approach to life and problem solving. But as George Gmelch demonstrates in this article, American baseball players, much like the New Guinea highlanders described in the last article by Philip Newman, also depend to a great extent on supernatural forces to ensure success in their athletic endeavors. He demonstrates that the findings of anthropologists in distant cultures shed light on our own cultural practices.

On each pitching day for the first three months of a winning season, Dennis Grossini, a pitcher on a Detroit Tiger farm team, arose from bed at exactly 10:00 A.M. At 1:00 P.M. he went to the nearest restaurant for two glasses of iced tea and a tuna fish sandwich. Although the afternoon was free, he changed into the sweat shirt and supporter he wore during his last winning game, and one hour before the game he chewed a wad of Beech-Nut chewing tobacco. During the game he touched his letters (the team name on his uniform) after each pitch and straightened his cap after each ball. Before the start of each inning he replaced the pitcher's rosin bag next to the spot where it was the inning before. And after every inning in which he gave up a run he would wash his hands.

Reprinted by permission of the author. From *Human Nature*, Volume 1, No. 8, 1978.

I asked him which part of the ritual was most important. He responded, "You can't really tell what's most important so it all becomes important. I'd be afraid to change anything. As long as I'm winning, I do everything the same. Even when I can't wash my hands [this would occur when he had to bat], it scares me going back to the mound. . . . I don't feel quite right."

Trobriand Islanders, according to anthropologist Bronislaw Malinowski, felt the same way about their fishing magic. Among the Trobrianders, fishing took two forms. In the inner lagoon, fish were plentiful and there was little danger; on the open sea, fishing was dangerous and yields varied widely. Malinowski found that magic was not used in lagoon fishing, where men could rely solely on their knowledge and skill. But when fishing on the open sea, Trobrianders used a great deal of magical ritual to ensure safety and increase their catch.

Baseball, the American national sport, is an arena in which the players behave remarkably like Malinowski's Trobriand fishermen. To professional baseball players, baseball is more than a game. It is an occupation. Since their livelihood depends on how well they perform, they use magic to try to control or eliminate the chance and uncertainty built into baseball.

To control uncertainty, ex-San Francisco Giant pitcher Ron Bryant added a new stick of bubble gum to the collection in his bulging back pocket after each game he won. Jim Ohms, my teammate on the Daytona Beach Islanders in 1966, used to put another penny in the pouch of his supporter after each win. Clanging against the hard plastic genital cup, the pennies made an audible sound as the pitcher ran the bases toward the end of a winning season. Fred Caviglia, former Kansas City minor-league pitcher, used to eat the same food before each game he pitched.

Whether they are professional baseball players, Trobriand fishermen, soldiers, or farmers, people resort to magic in situations of chance, when they believe they have limited control over the success of their activities. In technologically advanced societies that pride themselves on a scientific approach to problem solving, as well as in simple societies, rituals of magic are common. Magic is a human attempt to impose order and certainty on a chaotic, uncertain situation. This attempt is irrational in that there is no causal connection between the instruments of magic and the desired consequences of the magical practice. But it is rational in that it creates in the practitioner a sense of confidence, competence, and control, which in turn is important to successfully executing a specific activity and achieving a desired result.

I have long had a close relationship with baseball, first as a participant and then as an observer. I devoted much of my youth to the game and played professionally as a first baseman for five teams in the Detroit Tiger organization over three years. I also spent two years in the Quebec Provincial League. For additional information about baseball magic, I interviewed twenty-eight professional ballplayers and sportswriters.

There are three essential activities in baseball — pitching, hitting, and fielding. The first two, pitching and hitting, involve a great deal of chance and are comparable to the Trobriand fishermen's open sea; in them, players use magic and ritual to increase their chances for success. The third activity, fielding, involves little uncertainty, and is similar to the Trobriander inner lagoon; fielders find it unnecessary to resort to magic.

The pitcher is the player least able to control the outcome of his own efforts. His best pitch may be hit for a home run, and his worst pitch may be hit directly into the hands of a fielder for an out or be swung at and missed for a third strike. He may limit the opposing team to a few hits yet lose the game, or he may give up a dozen hits and win. Frequently pitchers perform well and lose, and perform poorly and win. One has only to look at the frequency with which pitchers end a season with poor won-lost records but good earned run averages (a small number of runs given up per game), or vice versa. For example, in 1977 Jerry Koosman of the Mets had an abysmal won-lost record of 8 and 20, but a competent 3.49 earned run average, while Larry Christenson of the Phillies had an unimpressive earned run average of 4.07 and an excellent won-lost record of 19 and 6. Regardless of how well he performs, the pitcher depends upon the proficiency of his teammates, the inefficiency of the opposition, and caprice.

An incredible example of bad luck in pitching occurred some years ago involving former Giant outfielder Willie Mays. Mays intentionally "dove for the dirt" to avoid being hit in the head by a fastball. While he was falling the ball hit his bat and went shooting down the left-field line. Mays jumped up and ran, turning the play into a double. Players shook their heads in amazement — most players can't hit when they try to, but Mays couldn't avoid hitting even when he tried not to. The pitcher looked on in disgust.

Hitting is also full of risk and uncertainty — Red Sox outfielder and Hall of Famer Ted Williams called it the most difficult single task in the world of sports. Consider the forces and time constraints operating against the batter. A fastball travels from the pitcher's mound to the batter's box, just sixty and one half feet, in three to four tenths of a second. For only 3 feet of the journey, an absurdly short two-hundredths of a second, the ball is in a position where it can be hit. And to be hit well, the ball must be neither too close to the batter's body nor too far from the "meat" of his bat. Any distraction, any slip of a muscle or change in stance can throw a swing off. Once the ball is hit, chance plays a large role in determining where it will go — into a waiting glove, whistling past a fielder's diving stab, or into the wide-open spaces. While the pitcher who threw the fastball to Mays was suffering, Mays was collecting the benefits of luck.

Batters also suffer from the fear of being hit by a pitch — specifically, by a fastball that often travels at speeds exceeding 90 miles per hour. Throughout baseball history the great fastball pitchers — men like Sandy Koufax, Walter Johnson, Bob Gibson, and currently Nolan Ryan of the California Angels — have thrived on this fear and on the level of distraction it causes hitters. The well-armed pitcher inevitably captures the advantage in the psychological war of nerves that characterizes the ongoing tension between pitcher and hitter, and that determines who wins and loses the game. If a hitter is crowding the plate in order to reach balls on the outside corner, or if the batter has been hitting unusually well, pitchers try to regain control of their territory. Indeed, many pitchers intentionally throw at or "dust" a batter in order to instill this sense of fear (what hitters euphemistically call "respect") in him. On one occasion Dock Ellis of the Pittsburgh Pirates, having become convinced that the Cincinnati Reds were dominating his team, intentionally hit the first three Reds batters he faced before his manager removed him from the game.

In fielding, on the other hand, the player has almost complete control over the outcome. Once a ball has been hit in his direction, no one can intervene and ruin his chances of catching it for an out. Infielders have approximately three seconds in which to judge the flight of the ball, field it cleanly, and throw it to first base. Outfielders have almost double that amount of time to track down a fly ball. The average fielding percentage (or success rate) of .975, compared with a .250 success rate for hitters (the average batting percentage), reflects the degree of certainty in fielding. Compared with the pitcher or the hitter, the fielder has little to worry about. He knows that in better than 9.7 times out of 10 he will execute his task flawlessly.

In keeping with Malinowski's hypothesis about the relationship between magic and uncertainty, my research shows that baseball players associate magic with hitting and pitching, but not with fielding. Despite the wide assortment of magic — which includes rituals, taboos, and fetishes — associated with both hitting and pitching, I have never observed any directly connected to fielding. In my experience I have known only one player, a shortstop with fielding problems, who reported any ritual even remotely connected with fielding.

The most common form of magic in professional baseball is personal ritual — a prescribed form of behavior that players scrupulously observe in an effort to ensure that things go their way. These rituals, like those of Malinowski's Trobriand fishermen, are performed in a routine, unemotional manner, much as players do nonmagical things to improve their play: rubbing pine tar on the hands to improve a grip on the bat, or rubbing a new ball to make it more comfortable and responsive to the pitcher's grip. Rituals are infinitely varied since ball players may formalize any activity that they consider important to performing well.

Rituals usually grow out of exceptionally good performances. When a player does well he seldom attributes his success to skill alone. Although his skill remains constant, he may go hitless in one game and in the next get three or four hits. Many players attribute the inconsistencies in their performances to an object, item of food, or form of behavior outside their play. Through ritual, players seek to gain control over their performance. In the 1920s and 1930s sportswriters reported that a player who tripped en route to the field would often retrace his steps and carefully walk over the stumbling block for "insurance."

The word *taboo* comes from a Polynesian term meaning prohibition. Failure to observe a taboo or prohibition leads to undesirable consequences or bad luck. Most players observe a number of taboos. Taboos usually grow out of exceptionally poor performances, which players often attribute to a particular behavior or food. Certain uniforms may become taboo. If a player has a poor spring training season or an unsuccessful year, he may refuse to wear the same number again. During my first season of professional baseball I ate pancakes before a game in which I struck out four times. Several weeks later I had a repeat performance, again after eating pancakes. The result was a pancake taboo—I never ate pancakes during the season from that day on. Another personal taboo, against holding a baseball during the national anthem (the usual practice for the first basemen, who must warm up the other infielders), had a similar origin.

In earlier decades some baseball players believed that it was bad luck to go back and fasten a missed buttonhole after dressing for a game. They simply left missed buttons on shirts or pants undone. This taboo is not practiced by modern ballplayers.

Fetishes or charms are material objects believed to embody supernatural powers that aid or protect the owner. Good-luck fetishes are standard equipment for many ballplayers. They include a wide assortment of objects: horsehide covers from old baseballs, coins, bobby pins (Hall of Fame pitcher Rube Waddell collected these), crucifixes, and old bats. Ordinary objects acquire power by being connected to exceptionally hot batting or pitching streaks, especially ones in which players get all the breaks. The object is often a new possession or something a player finds and holds responsible for his good fortune. A player who is in a slump might find a coin or an odd stone just before he begins a hitting streak, attribute an improvement in his performance to the influence of the new object, and regard it as a fetish.

While playing for Spokane, a Dodger farm team, Alan Foster forgot his baseball shoes on a road trip and borrowed a pair from a teammate. That night he pitched a no-hitter, which he attributed to the borrowed shoes. After he bought them from his teammate, they became a prized possession.

During World War II, American soldiers used fetishes in much the same way. Social psychologist Samuel Stouffer and his colleagues found that in the face of great danger and uncertainty soldiers developed magical practices, particularly the use of protective amulets and good-luck charms (crosses, Bibles, rabbits' feet, medals), and jealously guarded articles of clothing they associated with past experiences of escape from danger. Stouffer also found that prebattle preparations were carried out in a fixed "ritual" order, much as ballplayers prepare for a game.

Because most pitchers play only once every four days, they perform rituals less frequently than hitters. The rituals they do perform, however, are just as important. A pitcher cannot make up for a poor performance the next day, and having to wait three days to redeem oneself can be miserable. Moreover, the team's win or loss depends more on the performance of the pitcher than on any other single player. Considering the pressures to do well, it is not surprising that pitchers' rituals are often more complex than those of hitters.

A seventeen-game winner last year in the Texas Ranger organization, Mike Griffin begins his ritual preparation a full day before he pitches, by washing his hair. The next day, although he does not consider himself superstitious, he eats bacon for lunch. When Griffin dresses for the game he puts on his clothes in the same order, making certain he puts the slightly longer of his two outer, or "stirrup," socks on his right leg. "I just wouldn't feel right mentally if I did it the other way around," he explains. He always wears the same shirt under his uniform on the days he pitches. During the game he takes off his cap after each pitch, and between innings he sits in the same place on the dugout bench.

Steven Hamilton, formerly a relief pitcher for the Yankees, used to motion with his pitching hand as he left the mound after an inning. He would make a fist, holding it at arm's length by his side, and pull it upward, as if he were pulling a chain — which is what the announcers used to call it. Tug McGraw, relief pitcher for the Phillies, slaps his thigh with his glove with each step he takes leaving the mound at the end of an inning. This began as a means of saying hello to his wife in the stands, but has since become a ritual. McGraw now slaps his thigh whether his wife is there or not.

Many of the rituals pitchers engage in — tugging their caps between pitches, touching the rosin bag after each bad pitch, smoothing the dirt on the mound before each new batter or inning (as the Tigers' Mark Fidrych does) — take place on the field. Most baseball fans observe this behavior regularly, never realizing that it may be as important to the pitcher as actually throwing the ball.

Uniform numbers have special significance for some pitchers. Many have a lucky number, which they request. Since the choice is usually limited, pitchers may try to get a number that at least contains their lucky number, such as 14, 24, 34, or 44 for the pitcher whose lucky number is 4. Oddly enough, there is no consensus about the effect of wearing number 13. Some pitchers will not wear it; others, such as Oakland's John "Blue Moon" Odom and Steve Barber, formerly of the Orioles, prefer it. (During a pitching slump, however, Odom asked for a new number. Later he switched back to 13.)

The way in which number preferences emerge varies. Occasionally a pitcher requests the number of a former professional star, hoping that — in a form of imitative magic — it will bring him the same measure of success. Or he may request a favorite number that he has always associated with good luck. Vida Blue, formerly with Oakland and now playing for San Francisco, changed his uniform number from 35 to 14, the number he wore as a high-school quarterback. When the new number did not produce the better pitching performance he was looking for, he switched back to his old number.

One of the sources of his good fortune, Blue believed, was the baseball hat he had worn since 1974. Several American League umpires refused to let him wear the faded and soiled cap last season. When Blue persisted, he was threatened with a fine and suspension from a game. Finally he conceded, but not before he ceremoniously burned the hat on the field before a game.

On the days they are scheduled to appear, many pitchers avoid activities that they believe sap their strength and therefore detract from their effectiveness, or that they otherwise generally link with poor performance. Many pitchers avoid eating certain foods on their pitching days. Some pitchers refuse to walk anywhere on the day of the game in the belief that every little exertion subtracts from their playing strength. One pitcher would never put on his cap until the game started and would not wear it at all on the days he did not pitch. Another had a movie taboo. He refused to watch movies on the day of the game. And until this season Al Hrabosky, recently traded from the St. Louis Cardinals to the Kansas City Royals, had an even more encompassing taboo: Samsonlike, he refused to cut his hair or beard during the entire season — hence part of the reason for his nickname, the "Mad Hungarian."

Many hitters go through a series of preparatory rituals before stepping into the batter's box. These include tugging on their caps, touching their uniform letters or medallions, crossing themselves, tapping or bouncing the bat on the plate, swinging the weighted warmup bat a prescribed number of times, and smoothing the dirt in the batter's box. Rocky Colavito, a colorful home-run hitter active in the 1950s and 1960s, used to stretch his arms behind his back and cross himself when he came to the plate. A player in the Texas Ranger organization draws a triangle in the dirt outside the batter's box, with the peak pointing toward center field. Other players are careful never to step on the chalk lines of the batter's box when standing at the plate.

Clothing, both the choice of clothes and the order in which they are put on, is often ritualized. During a batting streak many players wear the same clothes and uniforms for each game and put them on in exactly the same order. Once I changed sweatshirts midway through the game for seven consecutive games to keep a hitting streak going. During a sixteen-game winning steak in 1954 the New York Giants wore the same clothes in each game and refused to let them be cleaned for fear that their good fortune might be washed away with the dirt. Taking this ritual to the extreme, Leo Durocher, managing the Brooklyn Dodgers to a pennant in 1941, spent three and a half weeks in the same black shoes, gray slacks, blue coat, and knitted blue tie.

The opposite may also occur. Several of the Oakland A's players bought new street clothing last year in an attempt to break a fourteen-game losing streak. Most players, however, single out one or two lucky articles or quirks of dress rather than ritualizing all items of clothing. After hitting two home runs in a game, infielder Jim Davenport of the San Francisco Giants discovered that he had missed a buttonhole while dressing for the game. For the remainder of his career he left the same button undone.

A popular ritual associated with hitting is tagging a base when leaving and returning to the dugout during each inning. Mickey Mantle was in the habit of tagging second base on the way to or from the outfield. During a successful month of the season one player stepped on third base on his way to the dugout after the third, sixth, and ninth innings of each game. Asked if he ever purposely failed to step on the bag he replied, "Never! I wouldn't dare. It would destroy my confidence to hit." A hitter who is playing poorly may try different combinations of tagging and not tagging particular bases in an attempt to find a successful combination.

Another component of a hitter's ritual may be tapping the plate with his bat. A teammate of mine described a variation of this in which he gambled for a certain hit by tapping the plate with his bat a fixed number of times: one tap for a single, two for a double, and so on. He even built in odds that prevented him from asking for a home run each time at bat. The odds of hitting a home run with four taps were 1 in 12.

When their players are not hitting, some managers will rattle the bat bin, the large wooden box containing the team's bats, as if the bats were asleep or in a stupor and could be aroused by a good shaking. Similarly, some hitters rub their hands or their own bats along the handles of the bats protruding from the bin, presumably in hopes of picking up some power or luck from bats that are getting hits for their owners.

There is a taboo against crossing bats, against permitting one bat to rest on top of another. Although this superstition appears to be dying out among professional ballplayers, it was religiously observed by some of my teammates a decade ago. And in some cases it was elaborated even further. One former Detroit minor leaguer became quite annoyed when a teammate tossed a bat from the batting cage and it landed on top of his bat. Later he explained that the top bat might steal hits from the lower one. In his view, bats contained a finite number of hits, a sort of zero-sum game or baseball "image of limited good." For Pirate shortstop Honus Wagner, a charter member of baseball's Hall of Fame, each bat contained only a certain number of hits, and never more than one hundred. Regardless of the quality of the bat, he would discard it after its one hundredth hit.

Hall of Famer Johnny Evers, of the Cub double-play trio Tinker to Evers to Chance, believed in saving his luck. If he was hitting well in practice, he would suddenly stop and retire to the bench to "save" his batting for the game. One player told me that many of his teammates on the Asheville Tourists in the Class A Western Carolinas League would not let pitchers touch or swing their bats, not even to loosen up. The traditionally poor-hitting pitchers were believed to contaminate or weaken the bats.

Food often forms part of a hitter's ritual repertoire. Eating certain foods before a game is supposed to give the ball "eyes," that is, the ability to seek the gaps between fielders after being hit. In hopes of maintaining a batting streak, I once ate chicken every day at 4:00 P.M. until the streak ended. Hitters — like pitchers — also avoid certain foods that are believed to sap their strength during the game.

There are other examples of hitters' ritualized behavior. I once kept my eyes closed during the national anthem in an effort to prolong a batting streak. And a teammate of mine refused to read anything on the day of a game because he believed that reading weakened his eyesight when batting.

These are personal taboos. There are some taboos, however, that all players hold and that do not develop out of individual experiences or misfortunes. These taboos are learned, some as early as Little League. Mentioning a no-hitter while one is in progress is a widely known example. It is believed that if a pitcher hears the words "no-hitter," the spell will be broken and the no-hitter lost. Until recently this taboo was also observed by sports broadcasters, who used various linguistic subterfuges to inform their listeners that the pitcher had not given up a hit, never mentioning "no-hitter."

Most professional baseball coaches or managers will not step on the chalk foul lines when going onto the field to talk to their pitchers. Cincinnati's manager Sparky Anderson jumps over the line. Others follow a different ritual. They intentionally step on the lines when they are going to take a pitcher out of a game.

How do these rituals and taboos get established in the first place? B. F. Skinner's early research with pigeons provides a clue. Like human beings, pigeons quickly learn to associate their behavior with rewards or punishment. By rewarding the birds at the appropriate time, Skinner taught them such elaborate games as table tennis, miniature bowling, or to play simple tunes on a toy piano.

On one occasion he decided to see what would happen if pigeons were rewarded with food pellets every fifteen seconds, regardless of what they did. He found that the birds tended to associate the arrival of food with a particular action — tucking the head under a wing, hopping from side to side, or turning in a clockwise direction. About ten seconds after the arrival of the last pellet, a bird would begin doing whatever it had associated with getting the food and keep it up until the next pellet arrived.

In the same way, baseball players tend to believe there is a causal connection between two events that are linked only temporally. If a superstitious player touches his crucifix and then gets a hit, he may decide the gesture was responsible for his good fortune and follow the same ritual the next time he comes to the plate. If he should get another hit, the chances are good that he will begin touching the crucifix each time he bats and that he will do so whether or not he hits safely each time.

The average batter hits safely approximately one quarter of the time. And, if the behavior of Skinner's pigeons — or of gamblers at a Las Vegas slot machine — is any guide, that is more often than necessary to keep him believing in a ritual. Skinner found that once a pigeon associated one of its actions with the arrival of food or water, sporadic rewards would keep the connection going. One bird, which apparently believed hopping from side to side brought pellets into its feeding cup, hopped ten thousand times without a pellet before it gave up.

Since the batter associates his hits at least in some degree with his ritual touching of a crucifix, each hit he gets reinforces the strength of the ritual. Even if he falls into a batting slump and the hits temporarily stop, he will persist in touching the crucifix in the hope that this will change his luck.

Skinner's and Malinowski's explanations are not contradictory. Skinner focuses on how the individual comes to develop and maintain a particular ritual, taboo, or fetish. Malinowski focuses on why human beings turn to magic in precarious or uncertain situations. In their attempts to gain greater control over their performance, baseball players respond to chance and uncertainty in the same way as do people in simple societies. It is wrong to assume that magical practices are a waste of time for either group. The magic in baseball obviously does not make a pitch travel faster or more accurately, or a batted ball seek the gaps between fielders. Nor does the Trobriand brand of magic make the surrounding seas calmer and more abundant with fish. But both kinds of magic give their practitioners a sense of control — and an important element in any endeavor is confidence.

REVIEW QUESTIONS

1. What is magic and why do people practice it, according to Gmelch?
2. How does Gmelch account for American baseball players practicing magic?
3. In what parts of the game is magic most likely to be used? Why?
4. How are Malinowski's and Skinner's theories of magic alike and different?

31 Navajo Medicine

DONALD F. SANDNER

Religion is a symbolic system concerned with the supernatural and with the basic questions of life — death, evil, meaning, and transcendent values. No wonder, then, that religion finds a place in healing. This selection by Donald Sandner illustrates in detail the role of the Navajo healer as he symbolically treats his patients' ailments. Using a rich array of Navajo myths, prayers, songs, and sand paintings, the healer takes his patients through three important steps: a return to their origins, an identification and cleansing of evil, and a symbolic death and rebirth. This ritual, which shares its structure (although not its cultural symbolism) with Western psychoanalysis, strives to recreate a sense of harmony in the people it touches.

Denet Tsosi was over eighty when I first met him. He was just returning from a grueling all-night sing. Yet, showing no great fatigue, he spent the whole morning talking to me. Denet Tsosi had begun learning Navajo chants in his early teens from his brother, Red Mustache. He followed Red Mustache around for eight years, watching him perform the Male Shooting Chant, and even had the ceremony sung over himself four times, paying for it each time. At last Denet Tsosi felt he

Reprinted with permission from *Human Nature* Magazine, Vol. 1, No. 11, July 1978. Copyright © 1978 by Human Nature, Inc.

could perform the Male Shooting Chant himself and began to treat patients.

But Denet Tsosi, like most other Navajo medicine men, does not reject Western medicine. He understands intuitively that there are at least two kinds of healing: scientific healing based on anatomy and physiology, and symbolic healing that focuses on the cultural being and the symbolic universe that pervades human consciousness. Both types are sometimes necessary for the same patient. "There was a woman from Red Mesa who was in the hospital in Albuquerque," related another medicine man. "She had a gall-bladder operation. After she came home she still wasn't feeling well, but after I did Blessing Way for her she felt all right."

Navajo medicine men generally cooperate with modern medical practitioners and send serious cases of injury or illness to hospitals and clinics. But they insist that their own medicine has a legitimate place in restoring patients to the security of their own society and culture. The aim of symbolic healing, to create a sense of harmony, is in certain respects what I strive for as a psychiatrist, and I became interested in Navajo medicine because it seemed to have many elements in common with contemporary psychiatry. Both the Navajo medicine man and the psychiatrist manipulate cultural symbols to return the patient to his mythic origins, manage the evil within him, and bring about a transformation, a rebirth.

The Navajo are a tribe of well over one hundred thousand Indians living on or around their large reservation in northeastern Arizona and adjoining New Mexico. They migrated into this region during the sixteenth century from western Canada and Alaska. During their southward journey they developed an intense and beautiful religion, which probably reached its highest development in the nineteenth century. They borrowed elements from the Plains tribes to the north as well as the Pueblos to the south and east, but tied these elements together with a value system that is uniquely Navajo.

Harmony with nature, society, and the world of the supernatural are the core and essence of Navajo myth and ritual. "The Navajo religion," writes Gladys Reichard, an anthropologist who made a life-long study of Navajo religion, "must be considered as a design in harmony, a striving for rapport between man and every phase of nature, the earth and the waters under the earth, and the sky and the 'land beyond the sky,' and of course, the earth and everything on and in it." When this harmony is threatened by illness, misfortune, or despair, the Navajo calls in a medicine man who performs the religious ceremony — called a chant, a sing, or a way — appropriate to restoring equilibrium.

Chants are performed by men like Denet Tsosi who provide the services of both priest and doctor. Many of those I interviewed in six summers of fieldwork were quite old, but still in active practice. Most had acquired their knowledge during a close apprenticeship to an older chanter, often a relative or clan member, but sometimes only a friend or an acquaintance. Natani Tso did not start learning the chants until he was in middle life. "First I learned a blackening ceremony," he told me, "then Chiricahua Wind Way, then some special prayers. Then I started learning Blessing Way, which included prayers concerning Mother Earth and other supernatural beings. After that I learned Big Star Way, a five-night ceremony."

One medicine man supported his instructor for the three years it took him to learn the Night Chant. "If I happened to have some money," he said, "I gave it to him. When he was leaving to go home I would butcher a sheep or two for him to take. In this way I paid him for what he did." Before the apprentice was ready to use the chant on patients, he had to have the long form of the ceremony performed over him.

All the medicine men agree that a prospective medicine man must have perseverance, an intense interest, and the willingness to learn. "He must not be lazy. He's got to have patience," said Natani Tso; "If he gets easily discouraged there's no use starting. When they are drunk, young men often ask me what a particular song or prayer means, but there is no use telling them. Their minds are not clear." No special vision, dream, or mystical experience is necessary for one to become a chant practitioner. Like the physician, the Navajo medicine man relies on knowledge, patiently learned and remembered, to practice his art.

Most of the learning takes place at sings where the young apprentice can watch his teacher administer the chant. This observation is often supplemented by private instruction. Sometimes the apprentice uses mnemonic devices or diagrams to help him remember the order of events in a given chant. There is usually a close bond between student and teacher, but should the teachings break off before the medicine man believes his student is ready, he may withhold his approval from his pupil. Without the endorsement of his teacher, a young man cannot be in good standing as a healer in the community.

Medicine men seem to have great confidence in their work. They often recount times when the chants brought about a great cure. One said: "This boy that I'm talking about, he was still in the womb of his mother when his father passed away. She cleaned and touched the body and took part in the burial. So naturally this affected the child. That was why he was sick and needed the ceremony. When I did this treatment I know I restored him back to normal. It gave me a happy feeling. The family was also happy with my ceremony."

Medicine men are friendly toward Christian churches on the reservation, but they regard the Native American Church, the pan-Indian religious movement based on Christianity that uses peyote in rituals, with ambivalence. "When I learned my chant, that was the only thing used by the Navajo people," one medicine man explained. "There was no such thing as peyote. The chants were the treatment for any illness. . . . On one occasion someone said to me, 'My friend, if you add peyote to your ceremony, it would make it stronger.' I was not interested. I told him, 'You always come to me when you want a ceremony. You come because you think it does some good. I don't want to mix the two.'" Some consider peyote useful, but most medicine men emphasize that it is not part of classical Navajo religion. They fear that it hinders the clarity of knowledge needed for the chants.

When a patient first comes to a medicine man, the chanter interviews him to determine the problem, often calling on the help of a diagnostician. Diagnosticians, unlike medicine men, place themselves in a trance state to locate the source of a patient's problem. Many of them practice "hand trembling." As the diagnostician stands or kneels over the patient his hand begins to tremble in a slow shaking motion. Then it begins pointing at various parts of the patient's body. By observing his hand, the diagnostician can tell what is wrong with the patient and what chant will correct it. Some diagnosticians are crystal-gazers and stargazers. Crystal-gazers surround themselves with crystals and church candles. They claim that just by looking at the crystals, they can see the cause of the patient's trouble. Stargazers diagnose an ailment by studying the night sky.

Most diagnoses lay the blame for illness on some mythic force. For instance, powerful animals like the coyote, eagle, bear, or snake may cause illness, even by remote contact. It is a kind of "infection" by animal power. Natural phenomena such as strong winds, lightning, hailstorms, and winter thunder may be the cause of disharmony. One of the practitioners of Navajo Wind Way said, "Anything that injures you by way of cyclones, tornadoes, whirlwinds, or even ordinary strong winds may run over you and twist your mind. Then you must have Navajo Wind Way." Perhaps the patient's illness has come from contact with outsiders, ghosts of dead people, malicious witchcraft, violation of rules surrounding the chants, or failure to observe strict burial procedures.

Dreams are important to diagnosis, but they are not part of the healing ritual. In Navajo culture there is no quest for vision or search for personal power through dreams. But some dreams, like those in which dead people or ghosts appear, indicate that the patient has had contact with an evil force and requires purification. One medicine man who specialized in Blessing Way said, "We go to sleep and then we dream about something. That dream is a warning telling you what you will encounter in the future. You should think about your dreams and what they mean. You should believe in your dreams and use Blessing Way as a remedy for them."

Not all dreams are bad. Dreams of the Holy People or of good fortune or abundant crops are welcome. But even good dreams are double-edged. If you dream that you are going to get rich and know this will not come true, it is a bad dream. In this situation, one medicine man claimed, you should have a prayer sung over you.

Once the problem has been diagnosed, the patient and his family hire a medicine man to perform the proper ritual, set a date for the ceremony, and sometimes invite friends, neighbors, and relatives to participate as spectators and assistants. Medicine men expect a reasonable fee for their efforts. For short ceremonies this could be as little as $10 to $20, but a long ceremony might cost well over $1,000. Without payment the chant cannot be expected to work. The Navajo believe that a chant is a reciprocal exchange between the medicine man and the patient and unless the patient gives something to the chanter, the chanter can give nothing in return. Fees are usually established in advance, generally on a sliding scale according to the patient's means. Medicine men seldom fail to respond to urgent requests.

The proper chant is chosen from among the ten in common use today. Fifty years ago there were about thirty-five principal chants, each with several variations. But most have been forgotten. Often the chant a patient needs is determined by comparing the symptoms with those suffered by the heroes or heroines of the chants. A patient with swollen or painful joints, for instance, would be advised to have a Beauty Way because the heroine of Beauty Way suffers from similar difficulties. Thus from the beginning of the healing process the patient strongly identifies with the main character in the chant. The chant consists of a complex of songs, prayers, rites, and sand paintings that relate the tale of a hero's journey to the land of the supernatural to acquire the special knowledge and healing power of the chant. Many chants have forms of several lengths that begin at sundown, last for two, five, or nine nights, and end with an all-night sing.

Blessing Way is the shortest (two nights), least expensive, and most popular ceremony. The chanters described it as "the main beam in the chant-way house." It is given to correct mistakes in ceremonial errors, dispel fear from bad dreams and omens, protect flocks and herds, promote good mental health, and ensure a harmonious life. From it derive the girls' puberty ceremony, the ceremony preceding childbirth, the marriage ceremony, the house-blessing rite, and other social rituals.

The three major groups of chant ways — Holy Way, Evil Way, and Life Way — are also based on Blessing Way. Holy Way promotes goodness and harmony, summons the Holy People, and cures illness; Evil Way exorcises evil spirits, ghosts, witches, and aliens; and Life Way heals injuries from accidents, such as sprains, fractures, swelling, cuts, and burns. Although the structure of chants varies, all include the same five stages — purification, evocation, identification, transformation, and release. These stages blend into one another and more than one may take place at the same time, but usually they are sequential and cumulative.

First the patient and the medicine man are cleansed of evil influences. This begins with the consecration of the hogan, the traditional six-sided Navajo dwelling made of logs or stone. The chanter, moving sunwise (clockwise), places sacred cornmeal and oak sprigs on the main beams of the hogan. During the first four nights of long ceremonies the patient is purified and released from his illness. In one such ritual, the medicine man applies a bundle of feathers and herbs tied with a wool string to various parts of the patient's body and pulls the spirits out of the victim's body. In another, the curer places a garment of spruce branches about the patient's body. The chanter or his assistants, impersonating the Navajo gods, then quickly cuts the garment away. In Big Star Way the standing chanter shoots arrows over the seated patient, who then passes through a series of specially constructed hoops. All these rites are designed to dispel evil and purify the patient.

Another part of the purification ceremony is the sweating and emetic rite held on each of the first four mornings. The chanter kindles a fire in the ceremonial hogan or the sweat house, and the patient and (at times) other participants remove their outer clothes, sweating intensely for as long as half an hour. The patient then drinks a special concoction that induces vomiting. Afterward, the chanter may use eagle feathers to sprinkle cooling lotion on the patient or to brush away any remaining evil.

Many herbal ingredients are also used for purification. A bull-roarer, a wooden slat attached to a string that makes a roaring sound when it is whirled, also helps to drive away evil influences. Each ritual act ends with the sprinkling of an herbal liquid on glowing coals; after the fourth day, the purifying rites are nearly complete.

During purification rituals, lengthy songs are chanted to evoke the gods. These songs, accompanied by drum or rattle, describe what the gods look like, what they do, and what the chanter is doing to draw them into the chant. One Night Way song goes:

A little one now is prepared.
A little one now is prepared.

For Calling God, it now is prepared.
A little message now is prepared.
Toward the trail of the he-rain, now is prepared.
As the rain will hang down, now it is prepared.

On each of the first four mornings the chanter makes different sets
of prayer sticks, painted wood and feather images used to invite the
gods to the ceremony, and blesses them with song and prayer. He also
fills painted reeds (appropriately called cigarettes) with native tobacco,
seals them with moistened pollen, and lights them with sunlight passed
through a piece of rock crystal. He places these sacred objects in the
patient's hands and sanctifies them with long prayers calling the gods'
attention to the offerings and describing what is expected of them in
return. Then he sets the sacred objects out and sings songs that imply
the gods have heard and are on the way. On the fourth night of the
Night Chant, a special evocation rite is held in which the masks of the
gods are "brought to life" by feeding them sacred gruel and shaking
them. If the chanter performs all the songs and rites correctly, the
gods must respond.

Once the gods have been summoned the third stage begins. With
long prayers and songs the patient must be identified with the gods,
thus allowing him to be cured. One such prayer intoned by the patient
on his way to the sweat house goes in part:

This I walk with, this I walk with.
Now Talking God I walk with.
These are his feet I walk with.
These are his limbs I walk with.
This is his body I walk with.
This is his mind I walk with.
This is his voice I walk with.
These are his twelve plumes I walk with.

But the sand paintings, which are the main components of the last
four days, are the strongest source of identification. Sand paintings
are large, complex symbolic pictures made by spreading pulverized
red, yellow, and white sandstone and ground minerals on smooth sand
on the hogan floor. While the patient remains outside, the medicine
man carefully prepares the painting by trickling the finely ground
pigments between his thumb and forefinger onto the desired spot.

Paintings vary from one to twenty feet in diameter and generally
take three to four hours to complete. The skill is difficult to master
and produces delicate designs that depict the supernatural animals,

heroes, and gods of the myth, as well as powerful natural forces, such as mountains, winds, thunders, and stars. When the picture is completed the prayer sticks are set up around it. Then the patient enters, sprinkles cornmeal on the painting, and under the direction of the medicine man, recites a long prayer. The patient then sits on one of the supernatural figures in the painting while the medicine man or one of his assistants transfers the figure's power by pressing his moistened hands against the colored sands and then onto the patient's body. After the ritual is finished the patient leaves and the sand, with its residue of power, is dispersed.

One of the most famous paintings from the Night Chant is the Whirling Logs sand painting. It commemorates the hero's visit to the Lake of Whirling Logs, where he saw a vision that embodied the secret of the chant. The painting is in the form of a great cross made of spruce logs. Two gods sit on each arm of the cross, and outside the area of the logs stand four gods. They seem to cause the cross to whirl with their magic wands. The entire figure forms a huge swastika that seems to be whirling sunwise. This sand painting is associated with fertility and healing.

After the power has been transferred from the painting and the patient is identified with the gods, the fourth stage, transformation, takes place. This consists mainly of long prayers recited by the medicine man and the patient, such as this one from the Night Chant:

Happily I recover.
Happily my interior becomes cool.
Happily my eyes regain their power.
Happily my head becomes cool.
Happily my limbs regain their power.
Happily I hear again.
Happily for me the spell is taken off.
Happily I may walk.
Impervious to pain, I walk.
Feeling light within, I walk.
With lively feeling, I walk.

In the final stage, release, the power so carefully built up must be diffused. An all-night sing on the final night summarizes and recapitulates the myth and rituals of the chant. In some of the longer chants, trained groups perform special dances and other magical acts on the last night. At dawn the closing songs are sung, the patient breathes in the rising sun, and the chant is over.

But for four more days the patient must observe special restrictions such as not washing or combing his hair, not eating certain foods, and not mingling closely with others. The patient has, after all, been one with the gods for a brief period of time, and the excess power must be gradually dispersed.

Navajo ceremonies cure the patient on several levels. There are physiological effects from the medications, sweat houses, heat treatments, and wound applications used in the chant, but the effect of these has not been adequately investigated. There is also a powerful psychosocial factor. The gathering of so many people to exert their best efforts for the well-being of one patient is bound to have a positive effect. But the main curative agents, the focus of most of the chant activity, and the objects of main interest to the medicine men are the chant symbols. The chanter uses prayers, rites, sand paintings, songs, and myths to present the symbols to the patient, to evoke their presence in the patient's psyche, and then to identify the patient with their power. This is an entirely different mode of healing from the kind we are accustomed to dealing with in our own culture: it is intuitive and symbolic.

Scientific healing, in contrast, is rational. It deals with physiological and anatomical facts and has the great advantage of being cross-cultural in its effects. Antibiotics or antimalarial drugs work in any part of the world, regardless of culture. But the great disadvantage of scientific healing is that it ignores the subtle integrations of mind and body. Although it heals an organ system, it does not integrate health and well-being or pain and suffering into a meaningful human experience. That is properly the work of the culturally alive symbol.

Symbolic healing, as practiced by the Navajo and other preliterate cultures, deals only incidentally with anatomy and physiology. It focuses on meaningful symbols, and practitioners — medicine men, shamans, or priests — are trained in the manipulation of those symbols. Unless the patient and the practitioner are part of the same culture, the cure cannot work. Symbolic healing strives to bring the patient into harmony with his own social and cultural environment, and because symbols vary from one society to the next it cannot be transferred from one culture to another.

But each culture, including our own, has some form of symbolic healing, and certain basic features are common to all such systems. Among the best-developed types of symbolic curing in Western society are the forms of psychotherapy, such as Jungian therapy, that make extensive use of dreams and fantasies. All forms of symbolic healing, regardless of the society in which they exist, attempt to return the patient to his symbolic origins, manage or manipulate evil, and bring about a symbolic death and rebirth of the patient. In Navajo healing ceremonies, by means of prayers, rituals, and sand paintings, the patient returns to the mythic place where outpouring energy gave rise to the universe. One sand painting that illustrates the creation myth shows the four underworlds arranged in the form of a lotus around the central hole from which the Navajo emerged into the present world. Around this figure is a square of blue symbolizing the great flood that drove the Navajo upward to higher worlds. Talking God and Calling God, two gentle tutelary deities, stand near the center, and the four sacred mountains that stand at the edges of the Navajo territory border the painting.

The myths in the chants relate similar tales. The Upward-reaching Way myth tells of the progress of primordial beings through the lower worlds upward to greater light and clarity. Blessing Way tells the story of Changing Woman, her birth, her gifts to the Navajo of corn and life renewal, and the birth of her two sons, Monster Slayer and the Child of the Waters. In Monster Way and the Two Who Came to Their Father, the story of these two heroes continues. They tell of the journey of Monster Slayer and Child of the Waters to visit Sun Father, their terrible ordeals in order to win a paternal blessing, the weapons given to them by him to kill the monsters of the earth, and how they established Navajo culture. With sand paintings, songs, and myths, the patient is drawn into the cosmic network and back to the earliest beginnings of life and consciousness.

In Western industrial society the return to origin finds expression in the psychotherapeutic search for the origins of neurotic illness in childhood, at birth, or even before birth. Through mediated regression under the control of the psychotherapist, a patient can experience once more the influx of the original creative energy.

The second basic theme found in symbolic medicine is the management of evil. Among the Navajo, evil takes the form of ghosts and witches, and many exorcistic rites are used to rid the patient of their influence. The medicine man blackens the body of the patient, for instance, to frighten away ghosts. Sometimes the evil power is deliberately invoked, brought under the power of the medicine man, and then banished to a distant place. In certain prayers the medicine man actually announces that he has become the evil in order to be in greater control of it. This is regarded as a dangerous procedure and must be performed with great caution and impeccable technique.

The management of evil is perhaps the most prevalent pattern in symbolic healing. In Western society this occurs in all forms of psychotherapy. The evil may take the form of aggressive or sadistic fantasies or unacceptable sexual impulses. Together the patient and the therapist must attempt to integrate or neutralize the evil, or if that fails, to exorcise it. The process of giving evil a reality and inviting the patient to confront it in the presence of a supportive person may be more fundamental to therapy than the actual content of the evil. The content must be in accord with the patient's and the therapist's cultural expectations, but it may be of only symbolic value.

Even in the use of strong medications or surgical procedures the symbolic element is not far away. Western patients often feel better after the physician has "named" their ailment. Whatever the actual physiological and anatomical effects of these therapies, the symbolic neutralization of "evil" by medicines or surgical methods is a significant force.

The third and possibly most important pattern common to all forms of symbolic healing is the theme of death and rebirth. In many of the chant myths, the hero is abducted by enemies of the Navajo or snatched up by the gods to be taken to other worlds and is regarded as dead by his relatives. The tale of the Night Chant describes the abduction of the hero by the Yei gods, who appear in the form of mountain sheep. The hero is taken to the upper world, where he stays for four years to learn the Night Chant. In other myths the hero is literally torn apart or physically deformed by his bold encounters and has to undergo a long and difficult process of rebirth. The patient goes through the same process. In prayers of liberation, for instance, the twin Navajo heroes, Monster Slayer and Child of the Waters, descend into the land of the dead where a spirit facsimile of the patient's body is lying. They must go down from the earth's surface through the hole of emergence and through layers of clouds, mists, and guarded doorways to overcome ferocious animals and neutralize the power of the woman chieftain in the land of the dead. After revitalizing the patient's spirit body, they accompany him back to the surface of this world. The end always includes the restoration of the universe to ritual control with everything in its proper place and operating in harmony and balance.

The theme of death and rebirth is found in Western society wherever a psychic threshold is reached and crossed. It may be expressed in the imagery of a long dream sequence or as a profound regressive experience in psychoanalytic therapy. It may also be felt in any serious illness that brings the patient into intimate contact with his own mortality. As unsuccessful suicides have found, once the experience has been survived, the patient often feels an upsurge of vitality, a renewed will to live.

Symbolic patterns are inherent in all therapeutic acts. They are sometimes referred to as suggestion, persuasion, or placebo effects, but they are unexpectedly powerful. All this suggests that the effectiveness of therapy depends on the basic symbolic elements in what we do above and beyond the physiological effectiveness of our acts. By studying the operation of these symbols in traditional cultures, such as the Navajo, we can begin to discern in ancient healing systems a strength and value we have only begun to appreciate.

REVIEW QUESTIONS

1. What is the major goal of Navajo religion? How is this goal reflected in the curing ritual?

2. What are the main steps in a Navajo curing ritual? What are they intended to accomplish?

3. How do Navajo healers culturally symbolize the return of patients to their origins, the identification of evil, and death and rebirth?

4. Why is Navajo healing like psychiatric treatment?

5. What movements in American medicine today resemble Navajo healing techniques?

6. Why does Sandner think that Navajo medicine works? What can it do for people that standard medicine cannot?

32   Cargo Cults

PETER M. WORSLEY

*When one cultural group becomes dominated by another, its origi-
nal meaning system may seem thin, ineffective, and contradictory.
The resulting state of deprivation often causes members to rebuild
their culture along more satisfying lines. In this article Peter Worsley describes a religious movement among the peoples of New
Guinea and adjacent islands, an area where Western influence has
caused cultural disorientation and where cargo cults have provided
the basis for reorganization.*

Patrols of the Australian government venturing into the "uncontrolled"
central highlands of New Guinea in 1946 found the primitive people
there swept up in a wave of religious excitement. Prophecy was being
fulfilled: The arrival of the whites was the sign that the end of the
world was at hand. The natives proceeded to butcher all of their pigs
—animals that were not only a principal source of subsistence but
also symbols of social status and ritual preeminence in their culture.
They killed these valued animals in expression of the belief that after
three days of darkness "Great Pigs" would appear from the sky. Food,
firewood, and other necessities had to be stockpiled to see the people
through to the arrival of the Great Pigs. Mock wireless antennae of
bamboo and rope had been erected to receive in advance the news of

From "Cargo Cults," by Peter M. Worsley, *Scientific American* 200 (May 1959): 117–
128. Reprinted with permission. Copyright © 1959 by Scientific American, Inc. All
rights reserved. Illustrations are omitted.

the millennium. Many believed that with the great event they would exchange their black skins for white ones.

This bizarre episode is by no means the single event of its kind in the murky history of the collision of European civilization with the indigenous cultures of the southwest Pacific. For more than one hundred years traders and missionaries have been reporting similar disturbances among the people of Melanesia, the group of Negro-inhabited islands (including New Guinea, Fiji, the Solomons, and the New Hebrides) lying between Australia and the open Pacific Ocean. Though their technologies were based largely upon stone and wood, these peoples had highly developed cultures, as measured by the standards of maritime and agricultural ingenuity, the complexity of their varied social organizations, and the elaboration of religious belief and ritual. They were nonetheless ill prepared for the shock of the encounter with the whites, a people so radically different from themselves and so infinitely more powerful. The sudden transition from the society of the ceremonial stone axe to the society of sailing ships and now of airplanes has not been easy to make.

After four centuries of Western expansion, the densely populated central highlands of New Guinea remain one of the few regions where the people still carry on their primitive existence in complete independence of the world outside. Yet as the agents of the Australian government penetrate into ever more remote mountain valleys, they find these backwaters of antiquity already deeply disturbed by contact with the ideas and artifacts of European civilization. For "cargo" — Pidgin English for trade goods — has long flowed along the indigenous channels of communication from the seacoast into the wilderness. With it has traveled the frightening knowledge of the white man's magical power. No small element in the white man's magic is the hopeful message sent abroad by his missionaries: the news that a Messiah will come and that the present order of Creation will end.

The people of the central highlands of New Guinea are only the latest to be gripped in the recurrent religious frenzy of the "cargo cults." However variously embellished with details from native myth and Christian belief, these cults all advance the same central theme: the world is about to end in a terrible cataclysm. Thereafter God, the ancestors, or some local culture hero will appear and inaugurate a blissful paradise on earth. Death, old age, illness, and evil will be unknown. The riches of the white man will accrue to the Melanesians.

Although the news of such a movement in one area has doubtless often inspired similar movements in other areas, the evidence indicates that these cults have arisen independently in many places as parallel responses to the same enormous social stress and strain. Among the movements best known to students of Melanesia are the "Taro Cult" of New Guinea, the "Vailala Madness" of Papua, the "Naked Cult" of Espiritu Santo, the "John Frum Movement" of the New Hebrides, and the "Tuka Cult" of the Fiji Islands.

At times the cults have been so well organized and fanatically persistent that they have brought the work of government to a standstill. The outbreaks have often taken the authorities completely by surprise and have confronted them with mass opposition of an alarming kind. In the 1930s, for example, villagers in the vicinity of Wewak, New Guinea, were stirred by a succession of "Black King" movements. The prophets announced that the Europeans would soon leave the island, abandoning their property to the natives, and urged their followers to cease paying taxes, since the government station was about to disappear into the sea in a great earthquake. To the tiny community of whites in charge of the region, such talk was dangerous. The authorities jailed four of the prophets and exiled three others. In yet another movement, which sprang up in declared opposition to the local Christian mission, the cult leader took Satan as his god.

Troops on both sides in World War II found their arrival in Melanesia heralded as a sign of the Apocalypse. The G.I.'s who landed in the New Hebrides, moving up for the bloody fighting on Guadalcanal, found the natives furiously at work preparing airfields, roads, and docks for the magic ships and planes that they believed were coming from "Rusefel" (Roosevelt), the friendly king of America.

The Japanese also encountered millenarian visionaries during their southward march to Guadalcanal. Indeed, one of the strangest minor military actions of World War II occurred in Dutch New Guinea, when Japanese forces had to be turned against the local Papuan inhabitants of the Geelvink Bay region. The Japanese had at first been received with great joy, not because their "Greater East Asia Co-Prosperity Sphere" propaganda had made any great impact upon the Papuans, but because the natives regarded them as harbingers of the new world that was dawning, the flight of the Dutch having already given the first sign. Mansren, creator of the islands and their peoples, would now return, bringing with him the ancestral dead. All this had been known, the cult leaders declared, to the crafty Dutch, who had torn out the first page of the Bible where these truths were inscribed. When Mansren returned, the existing world order would be entirely overturned. White men would turn black like Papuans, Papuans would become whites; root crops would grow in trees, and coconuts and fruits would grow like tubers. Some of the islanders now began to draw together into large "towns"; others took biblical names such as "Jericho" and "Galilee" for their villages. Soon they adopted military uniforms and began drilling. The Japanese, by now highly unpopular, tried to disarm and disperse the Papuans; resistance inevitably developed. The climax of this tragedy came when several canoe-loads of fanatics sailed out to attack Japanese warships, believing themselves to be invulnerable by virtue of the holy water with which they had sprinkled themselves. But the bullets of the Japanese did not turn to water, and the attackers were mowed down by machine-gun fire.

Behind this incident lay a long history. As long ago as 1857 missionaries in the Geelvink Bay region had made note of the story of Mansren. It is typical of many Melanesian myths that became confounded with Christian doctrine to form the ideological basis of the movements. The legend tells how long ago there lived an old man named Manamakeri ("he who itches"), whose body was covered with sores. Manamakeri was extremely fond of palm wine, and used to climb a huge tree every day to tap the liquid from the flowers. He soon found that someone was getting there before him and removing the liquid. Eventually he trapped the thief, who turned out to be none other than the Morning Star. In return for his freedom, the Star gave the old man a wand that would produce as much fish as he liked, a magic tree, and a magic staff. If he drew in the sand and stamped his foot, the drawing would become real. Manamakeri, aged as he was, now magically impregnated a young maiden; the child of this union was a miracle-child who spoke as soon as he was born. But the maiden's parents were horrified, and banished her, the child, and the old man. The trio sailed off in a canoe created by Mansren ("The Lord"), as the old man now became known. On this journey Mansren rejuvenated himself by stepping into a fire and flaking off his scaly skin, which changed into valuables. He then sailed around Geelvink Bay, creating islands where he stopped, and peopling them with the ancestors of the present-day Papuans.

The Mansren myth is plainly a creation myth full of symbolic ideas relating to fertility and rebirth. Comparative evidence — especially the shedding of his scaly skin — confirms the suspicion that the old man is, in fact, the Snake in another guise. Psychoanalytic writers argue that the snake occupies such a prominent part in mythology the world over because it stands for the penis, another fertility symbol. This may be so, but its symbolic significance is surely more complex than this. It is the "rebirth" of the hero, whether Mansren or the Snake, that exercises such universal fascination over men's minds.

The nineteenth-century missionaries thought that the Mansren story would make the introduction of Christianity easier, since the concept of "resurrection," not to mention that of the "virgin birth" and the "second coming," was already there. By 1867, however, the first cult organized around the Mansren legend was reported.

Though such myths were widespread in Melanesia, and may have sparked occasional movements even in the pre-white era, they took on a new significance in the late nineteenth century, once the European powers had finished parceling out the Melanesian region among themselves. In many coastal areas the long history of "blackbirding" — the seizure of islanders for work on the plantations of Australia and Fiji — had built up a reservoir of hostility to Europeans. In other areas, however, the arrival of the whites was accepted, even welcomed, for it meant access to bully beef and cigarettes, shirts and paraffin lamps, whisky and bicycles. It also meant access to the knowledge behind these material goods, for the Europeans brought missions and schools as well as cargo.

Practically the only teaching the natives received about European life came from the missions, which emphasized the central significance of religion in European society. The Melanesians already believed that human activities — whether gardening, sailing canoes, or bearing children — needed magical assistance. Ritual without human effort was not enough. But neither was human effort on its own. This outlook was reinforced by mission teaching.

The initial enthusiasm for European rule, however, was speedily dispelled. The rapid growth of the plantation economy removed the bulk of the able-bodied men from the villages, leaving women, children, and old men to carry on as best they could. The splendid vision of the equality of all Christians began to seem a pious deception in face of the realities of the color bar, the multiplicity of rival Christian missions, and the open irreligion of many whites.

For a long time the natives accepted the European mission as the means by which the "cargo" would eventually be made available to them. But they found that acceptance of Christianity did not bring the cargo any nearer. They grew disillusioned. The story now began to be put about that it was not the whites who made the cargo, but the dead ancestors. To people completely ignorant of factory production, this made good sense. White men did not work; they merely wrote secret signs on scraps of paper, for which they were given shiploads of goods. On the other hand, the Melanesians labored week after week for pitiful wages. Plainly the goods must be made for Melanesians somewhere, perhaps in the Land of the Dead. The whites, who possessed the secret of the cargo, were intercepting it and keeping it from the hands of the islanders, to whom it was really consigned. In the Madang district of New Guinea, after some forty years' experience of the missions, the natives went in a body one day with a petition demanding that the cargo secret should now be revealed to them, for they had been very patient.

So strong is this belief in the existence of a "secret" that the cargo cults generally contain some ritual in imitation of the mysterious European customs which are held to be the clue to the white man's extraordinary power over goods and men. The believers sit around tables with bottles of flowers in front of them, dressed in European clothes, waiting for the cargo ship or airplane to materialize; other cultists feature magic pieces of paper and cabalistic writing. Many of them deliberately turn their backs on the past by destroying secret ritual objects, or exposing them to the gaze of uninitiated youths and women, for whom formerly even a glimpse of the sacred objects would have meant the severest penalties, even death. The belief that they were the chosen people is further reinforced by their reading of the Bible, for the lives and customs of the people in the Old Testament resemble their own lives rather than those of the Europeans. In the New Testament they find the Apocalypse, with its prophecies of destruction and resurrection, particularly attractive.

Missions that stress the imminence of the Second Coming, like those of the Seventh Day Adventists, are often accused of stimulating millenarian cults among the islanders. In reality, however, the Melanesians themselves rework the doctrines the missionaries teach them, selecting from the Bible what they themselves find particularly congenial in it. Such movements have occurred in areas where missions of quite different types have been dominant, from Roman Catholic to Seventh Day Adventists. The reasons for the emergence of these cults, of course, lie far deeper in the life experience of the people.

The economy of most of the islands is very backward. Native agriculture produces little for the world market, and even the European plantations and mines export only a few primary products and raw materials: copra, rubber, gold. Melanesians are quite unable to understand why copra, for example, fetches thirty pounds sterling per ton one month and but five pounds a few months later. With no notion of the workings of world-commodity markets, the natives see only the sudden closing of plantations, reduced wages, and unemployment, and are inclined to attribute their insecurity to the whim or evil in the nature of individual planters.

Such shocks have not been confined to the economic order. Governments, too, have come and gone, especially during the two world wars: German, Dutch, British, and French administrations melted overnight. Then came the Japanese, only to be ousted in turn largely by the previously unknown Americans. And among these Americans the Melanesians saw Negroes like themselves, living lives of luxury on equal terms with white G.I.'s. The sight of these Negroes seemed like a fulfillment of the old prophecies to many cargo cult leaders. Nor must we forget the sheer scale of this invasion. Around a million U.S. troops passed through the Admiralty Islands, completely swamping the inhabitants. It was a world of meaningless and chaotic changes, in which anything was possible. New ideas were imported and given local twists. Thus in the Loyalty Islands people expected the French Communist Party to bring the millennium. There is no real evidence, however, of any Communist influence in these movements, despite the rather hysterical belief among Solomon Island planters that the name of the local "Masinga Rule" movement was derived from the word "Marxian"! In reality the name comes from a Solomon Island tongue, and means "brotherhood."

Europeans who have witnessed outbreaks inspired by the cargo cults are usually at a loss to understand what they behold. The islanders throw away their money, break their most sacred taboos, abandon their gardens, and destroy their precious livestock; they indulge in sexual license or, alternatively, rigidly separate men from women in huge communal establishments. Sometimes they spend days sitting gazing at the horizon for a glimpse of the long-awaited ship or airplane; sometimes they dance, pray, and sing in mass congregations, becoming possessed and "speaking with tongues."

Observers have not hesitated to use such words as "madness," "mania," and "irrationality" to characterize the cults. But the cults reflect quite logical and rational attempts to make sense out of a social order that appears senseless and chaotic. Given the ignorance of the Melanesians about the wider European society, its economic organization and its highly developed technology, their reactions form a consistent and understandable pattern. They wrap up all their yearning and hope in an amalgam that combines the best counsel they can find in Christianity and their native belief. If the world is soon to end, gardening or fishing is unnecessary; everything will be provided. If the Melanesians are to be part of a much wider order, the taboos that prescribe their social conduct must now be lifted or broken in a newly prescribed way.

Of course the cargo never comes. The cults nonetheless live on. If the millennium does not arrive on schedule, then perhaps there is some failure in the magic, some error in the ritual. New breakaway groups organize around "purer" faith and ritual. The cult rarely disappears, so long as the social situation which brings it into being persists.

At this point it should be observed that cults of this general kind are not peculiar to Melanesia. People who feel themselves oppressed and deceived have always been ready to pour their hopes and fears, their aspirations and frustrations, into dreams of a millennium to come or of a golden age to return. All parts of the world have had their counterparts of the cargo cults, from the American Indian ghost dance to the Communist-millenarist "reign of the saints" in Münster during the Reformation, from medieval European apocalyptic cults to African "witch-finding" movements and Chinese Buddhist heresies. In some situations men have been content to wait and pray; in others they have sought to hasten the day by using their strong right arms to do the Lord's work. And always the cults serve to bring together scattered groups, notably the peasants and urban plebians of agrarian societies and peoples of "stateless" societies where the cult unites separate (and often hostile) villages, clans, and tribes into a wider religio-political unity.

Once the people begin to develop secular political organizations, however, the sects tend to lose their importance as vehicles of protest. They begin to relegate the Second Coming to the distant future or to the next world. In Melanesia ordinary political bodies, trade unions, and native councils are becoming the normal media through which the islanders express their aspirations. In recent years continued economic prosperity and political stability have taken some of the edge off their despair. It now seems unlikely that any major movement along cargo-cult lines will recur in areas where the transition to secular politics has been made, even if the insecurity of prewar times returned. I would predict that the embryonic nationalism represented by cargo cults is likely in future to take forms familiar in the history of other countries that have moved from subsistence agriculture to participation in the world economy.

REVIEW QUESTIONS

1. What do the Melanesians mean by cargo, and why is it so important to them?
2. What are the main features of cargo cults? What is their purpose?
3. Why have so many cargo cults, each remarkably similar to the others, appeared in so many different places in Melanesia?
4. How do cargo cults contribute to culture change in Melanesia?

X

Culture Change and Applied Anthropology

Nowhere in the world do human affairs remain precisely constant from year to year. New ways of doing things mark the history of even the most stable groups. Change occurs when an Australian aboriginal dreams about a new myth and teaches it to the members of his band; when a loader in a restaurant kitchen invents a way to stack plates more quickly in the dishwasher; or when a New Guinea big-man cites the traditional beliefs about ghosts to justify the existence of a new political office devised by a colonial government. Wherever people interpret their natural and social worlds in a new way, cultural change has occurred. Broad or narrow, leisurely or rapid, such change is part of life in every society.

Culture change can originate from two sources, innovation and borrowing. *Innovation* is the invention of qualitatively new forms. It involves the recombination of what people already know into something different. For example, Canadian Joseph-Armand Bombardier became an innovator when he mated tracks, designed to propel earth-moving equipment, to a small bus that originally ran on tires, producing the first snowmobile in the 1950s. Later the Skolt Lapps of Finland joined him as innovators when they adapted his now smaller, more refined, snowmobile for herding reindeer in 1961. The Lapp innovation was not the vehicle itself. That was borrowed. What was new was the use of the vehicle in herding, something usually done by men on skis.

Innovations are more likely to occur and be adopted during stressful times when traditional culture no longer works well. Bombardier, for example, began work on his snowmobile after he was unable to reach medical help in time to save the life of his critically ill son during a Canadian winter storm. Frustrated by the slowness of his horse and sleigh, he set out to create a faster vehicle.

The other basis of culture change is *borrowing*. Borrowing, or *diffusion* as it is sometimes called, refers to the adoption of something new from another group. Tobacco, for example, was first domesticated and grown in the New World but quickly diffused to Europe and Asia after 1492. Such items as the umbrella, pajamas, Arabic numerals, and perhaps even the technology to make steel came to Europe from India. Ideologies and religions may diffuse from one society to another.

An extreme diffusionist view has been used to explain most human achievements. For example, author Erik Von Däniken argues that features of ancient New World civilizations were brought by space invaders. Englishman G. Elliot Smith claimed that Mayan and Aztec culture diffused from Egypt. Thor Heyerdahl sailed a reed boat, the Ra II, from Africa to South America to prove that an Egyptian cultural origin was possible for New World civilization.

Whether something is an innovation or borrowed, it must pass through a process of *social acceptance* before it can become part of a culture. Indeed many, if not most, novel ideas and things remain unattractive and relegated to obscurity. To achieve social acceptance, an innovation must become known to members of a society, be accepted as valid, and fit into a system of cultural knowledge revised to accept it.

Several principles facilitate social acceptance. If a change wins the support of a person in authority, it may gain the approval of others. Timing is also important. It would make little sense for a Lapp to attempt the introduction of snowmobiles when there was no snow or when the men who do the reindeer herding were scattered over their vast grazing territory. Other factors also affect social acceptance. Changes have a greater chance of acceptance if they meet a felt need, if they appeal to people's prestige (in societies where prestige is important), and if they provide some continuity with traditional customs.

Change may take place under a variety of conditions, from the apparently dull day-to-day routine of a stable society to the frantic climate of a revolution. One situation that has occupied many anthropologists interested in change is *cultural contact*, particularly situations of contact where one society politically dominates another. World history is replete with examples of such domination, which vary in outcome from annihilation, in the case of the Tasmanians and hundreds of tribes in North and South America, Africa, Asia, and even ancient Europe, to the political rule that indentured countless millions of people to colonial powers.

The study of change caused by these conditions is called acculturation. *Acculturation* is the process of change that results from cultural contact. Acculturative change may affect dominant societies as well as subordinate ones. After their ascendance in India, for example, the British came to wear *khaki* clothes, live in *bungalows*, and trek through *jungles* — all Indian concepts.

But those who are subordinated experience the most far-reaching changes in their way of life. From politically independent, self-sufficient people, they usually become subordinate and dependent. Sweeping changes in social structure and values may occur with resultant social disorganization.

Although the age of colonial empires is largely over, the destruction of tribal culture continues at a rapid pace today. As we saw in Reed's article in Part IV of this book, hundreds of thousands of Amazonian Indians have already perished in the last few years because of an intrusive frontier and development programs. Following almost exactly in the footsteps of past colonial exploitation, modern governments bent on "progress" displace and often kill off indigenous tribal populations. The frequent failure of development, coupled with its damaging impact on native peoples, has caused many anthropologists to reassess their role. As a result, more and more anthropologists have become part of native resistance to outside intrusion.

A less dramatic but in many ways no less important agent of change is the world economy. No longer can most people live in self-sufficient isolation. Their future is inevitably tied in with an overall system of market exchange. Take the Marshall Islanders described by Rynkiewich in Part V, for example. Although they cultivate to meet their own subsistence needs, they also raise coconuts for sale on the world market. Receipts from the coconut crop go to pay for outboard motors and gasoline, cooking utensils, and a variety of other goods they don't manufacture themselves but have come to depend on. Recently several major American food companies eliminated coconut oil from their products because of its high level of saturated fat. This loss has created lower demand for copra (dried coconut meat), from which the oil is pressed. Reduced demand, in turn, may cause substantial losses to Marshall Islanders. A people who once could subsist independently have now become prisoners of the world economic system.

Anthropologists may themselves become agents of change, applying their work to practical problems. *Applied anthropology,* as opposed to *academic anthropology*, includes any use of anthropological knowledge to influence social interaction, to maintain or change social institutions, or to direct the course of cultural change. There are four basic uses of anthropology contained within the applied field: adjustment anthropology, administrative anthropology, advocate anthropology, and action anthropology.

Adjustment anthropology uses anthropological knowledge to make social interaction more predictable among people who operate with different cultural codes. For example, take the anthropologists who consult with companies and government agencies about intercultural communication. It is often their job to train Americans to interpret the cultural rules that govern interaction in another society. For a business person who will work in Latin America, the anthropologist may point out the appropriate culturally defined speaking distances, ways to sit, definitions of time, topics of conversation, times for business talk, and so on. All of these activities would be classified as adjustment anthropology.

Administrative anthropology uses anthropological knowledge for planned change by those who are external to the local cultural group. It is the use of anthropological knowledge by a person with the power to make decisions. If an anthropologist provides knowledge about the culture of constituents to a mayor, he or she is engaged in administrative anthropology. So would advisers to chief administrators of U.S. trust territories such as once existed in places like the Marshall Islands.

Action anthropology uses anthropological knowledge for planned change by the local cultural group. The anthropologist acts as a catalyst, providing information but avoiding decision making, which remains in the hands of the people affected by decisions.

Advocate anthropology uses anthropological knowledge by the anthropologist to increase the power of self-determination for a particular cultural group. Instead of focusing on the process of innovation, the anthropologist centers attention on discovering the sources of power and how a group can gain access to them. James Spradley took such action when he studied tramps. He discovered that police and courts systematically deprived tramps of their power to control their lives and of the rights accorded normal citizens. By releasing his findings to the Seattle newspapers, he helped tramps gain additional power and weakened the control of Seattle authorities.

Whether they are doing administrative, advocate, adjustment, or action anthropology, anthropologists will take, at least in part, a qualitative approach. They will do ethnography, discover the cultural knowledge of informants, and apply this information in the ways discussed previously. In contrast to the quantitative data so often prized by other social scientists, they will use the insider's viewpoint to discover problems, advise, and generate policy.

The articles in this section illustrate several aspects of culture change and applied anthropology. The first, by Lauriston Sharp, reveals how the introduction of a tool as simple as a hatchet-sized steel axe can destroy a functionally integrated society. John Bodley's piece describes the process of tribal destruction as it has happened over and over again at the hands of more powerful governments. Bodley, a pioneer spokesperson for tribal rights, argues that progress means the destruction of indigenous culture and society. Jack Weatherford deals with the world economy in the next article. He shows that the Western demand for cocaine has devastating consequences for the indigenous peoples of Peru, Bolivia, and Columbia who grow coca and prepare the drug for market. Finally, David McCurdy discusses the modern uses of anthropology. From studies of General Motors workers, to program assessment for people with AIDS, to participation in government health projects, to international counseling, professional anthropologists put their discipline to work. But just as important, the discipline can be used in everyday life by anyone who has become acquainted with it.

KEY TERMS

innovation

borrowing

diffusion

social acceptance

cultural contact

acculturation

applied anthropology

adjustment anthropology

administrative anthropology

action anthropology

advocate anthropology

READINGS IN THIS SECTION

33   Steel Axes for Stone-Age Australians
LAURISTON SHARP

*Technology and social structure are closely linked in every society.
In this article, Lauriston Sharp shows how the introduction of an
apparently insignificant, hatchet-sized steel axe to Australian aborigines can alter the relationship among family members, change
patterns of economic exchange, and threaten the very meaning of
life itself.*

I.

Like other Australian aboriginals, the Yir Yoront group which lives at
the mouth of the Coleman River on the west coast of Cape York
Peninsula originally had no knowledge of metals. Technologically their
culture was of the old Stone Age or paleolithic type. They supported
themselves by hunting and fishing, and obtained vegetables and other
materials from the bush by simple gathering techniques. Their only
domesticated animal was the dog; they had no cultivated plants of any
kind. Unlike some other aboriginal groups, however, the Yir Yoront
did have polished stone axes hafted in short handles which were most
important in their economy.

Toward the end of the nineteenth century metal tools and other
European artifacts began to filter into the Yir Yoront territory. The
flow increased with the gradual expansion of the white frontier outward

---

Reproduced by permission of the Society for Applied Anthropology from *Human Organization* 11 (2): 17–22, 1952.

from southern and eastern Queensland. Of all the items of Western technology thus made available, the hatchet, or short-handled steel axe, was the most acceptable to and the most highly valued by all aboriginals.

In the mid-1930s an American anthropologist lived alone in the bush among the Yir Yoront for thirteen months without seeing another white man. The Yir Yoront were thus still relatively isolated and continued to live an essentially independent economic existence, supporting themselves entirely by means of their old Stone Age techniques. Yet their polished stone axes were disappearing fast and being replaced by steel axes which came to them in considerable numbers, directly or indirectly, from various European sources to the south.

What changes in the life of the Yir Yoront still living under aboriginal conditions in the Australian bush could be expected as a result of their increasing possession and use of the steel axe?

II. THE COURSE OF EVENTS

Events leading up to the introduction of the steel axe among the Yir Yoront begin with the advent of the second known group of Europeans to reach the shores of the Australian continent. In 1623 a Dutch expedition landed on the coast where the Yir Yoront now live.[1] In 1935 the Yir Yoront were still using the few cultural items recorded in the Dutch log for the aboriginals they encountered. To this cultural inventory the Dutch added beads and pieces of iron which they offered in an effort to attract the frightened "Indians." Among these natives metal and beads have disappeared, together with any memory of this first encounter with whites.

The next recorded contact in this area was in 1864. Here there is more positive assurance that the natives concerned were the immediate ancestors of the Yir Yoront community. These aboriginals had the temerity to attack a party of cattlemen who were driving a small herd from southern Queensland through the length of the then unknown Cape York Peninsula to a newly established government station at the northern tip.[2] Known as the "Battle of the Mitchell River," this was one of the rare instances in which Australian aboriginals stood up to European gunfire for any length of time. A diary kept by the cattlemen records that:

> . . . 10 carbines poured volley after volley into them from all directions, killing and wounding with every shot with very little return, nearly all

---

[1] An account of this expedition from Amboina is given in R. Logan Jack, *Northmost Australia* (2 vols.), London, 1921, vol. 1, 18–57.

[2] R. Logan Jack, *op. cit.*, 298–335.

their spears having already been expended. . . . About 30 being killed, the leader thought it prudent to hold his hand, and let the rest escape. Many more must have been wounded and probably drowned, for 59 rounds were counted as discharged.

The European party was in the Yir Yoront area for three days; they then disappeared over the horizon to the north and never returned. In the almost three-year-long anthropological investigation conducted some seventy years later — in all the material of hundreds of free association interviews, in texts of hundreds of dreams and myths, in genealogies, and eventually in hundreds of answers to direct and indirect questioning on just this particular matter — there was nothing that could be interpreted as a reference to this shocking contact with Europeans.

The aboriginal accounts of their first remembered contact with whites begin in about 1900 with references to persons known to have had sporadic but lethal encounters with them. From that time on whites continued to remain on the southern periphery of Yir Yoront territory. With the establishment of cattle stations (ranches) to the south, cattlemen made occasional excursions among the "wild black-fellows" in order to inspect the country and abduct natives to be trained as cattle boys and "house girls." At least one such expedition reached the Coleman River, where a number of Yir Yoront men and women were shot for no apparent reason.

About this time the government was persuaded to sponsor the establishment of three mission stations along the seven-hundred-mile western coast of the Peninsula in an attempt to help regulate the treatment of natives. To further this purpose a strip of coastal territory was set aside as an aboriginal reserve and closed to further white settlement.

In 1915, an Anglican mission station was established near the mouth of the Mitchell River, about a three-day march from the heart of the Yir Yoront country. Some Yir Yoront refused to have anything to do with the mission, others visited it occasionally while only a few eventually settled more or less permanently in one of the three "villages" established at the mission.

Thus the majority of the Yir Yoront continued to live their old self-supporting life in the bush, protected until 1942 by the government reserve and the intervening mission from the cruder realities of the encroaching new order from the south. To the east was poor, uninhabited country. To the north were other bush tribes extending on along the coast to the distant Archer River Presbyterian mission with which the Yir Yoront had no contact. Westward was the shallow Gulf of Carpentaria, on which the natives saw only a mission lugger making its infrequent dry season trips to the Mitchell River. In this protected environment for over a generation the Yir Yoront were able to recuperate from shocks received at the hands of civilized society. During the 1930s their raiding and fighting, their trading and stealing of women, their evisceration and two- or three-year care of their dead, and their totemic ceremonies continued, apparently uninhibited by Western influence. In 1931 they killed a European who wandered into their territory from the east, but the investigating police never approached the group whose members were responsible for the act.

As a direct result of the work of the Mitchell River mission, all Yir Yoront received a great many more Western artifacts of all kinds than ever before. As part of their plan for raising native living standards, the missionaries made it possible for aboriginals living at the mission to earn some Western goods, many of which were then given or traded to natives still living under bush conditions; they also handed out certain useful articles gratis to both mission and bush aboriginals. They prevented guns, liquor, and damaging narcotics, as well as decimating diseases, from reaching the tribes of this area, while encouraging the introduction of goods they considered "improving." As has been noted, no item of Western technology available, with the possible exception of trade tobacco, was in greater demand among all groups of aboriginals than the short-handled steel axe. The mission always kept a good supply of these axes in stock; at Christmas parties or other mission festivals they were given away to mission or visiting aboriginals indiscriminately and in considerable numbers. In addition, some steel axes as well as other European goods were still traded in to the Yir Yoront by natives in contact with cattle stations in the south. Indeed, steel axes had probably come to the Yir Yoront through established lines of aboriginal trade long before any regular contact with whites had occurred.

III. RELEVANT FACTORS

If we concentrate our attention on Yir Yoront behavior centering about the original stone axe (rather than on the axe — the object — itself) as a cultural trait or item of cultural equipment, we should get some conception of the role this implement played in aboriginal culture. This, in turn, should enable us to foresee with considerable accuracy some of the results stemming from the displacement of the Stone Age by the steel axe.

The production of a stone axe required a number of simple technological skills. With the various details of the axe well in mind, adult men could set about producing it (a task not considered appropriate for women or children). First of all, a man had to know the location and properties of several natural resources found in his immediate environment: pliable wood for a handle, which could be doubled or bent over the axe head and bound tightly; bark, which could be rolled into cord for the binding; and gum, to fix the stone head in the haft. These materials had to be correctly gathered, stored, prepared, cut to size, and applied or manipulated. They were in plentiful supply, and could be taken from anyone's property without special permission. Postponing consideration of the stone head, the axe could be made by any normal man who had a simple knowledge of nature and of the technological skills involved, together with fire (for heating the gum), and a few simple cutting tools — perhaps the sharp shells of plentiful bivalves.

The use of the stone axe as a piece of capital equipment used in producing other goods indicates its very great importance to the subsistence economy of the aboriginal. Anyone — man, woman, or child — could use the axe; indeed, it was used primarily by women, for theirs was the task of obtaining sufficient wood to keep the family campfire burning all day, for cooking, or other purposes, and all night against mosquitoes and cold (for in July, winter temperature might drop below 40 degrees). In a normal lifetime a woman would use the axe to cut or knock down literally tons of firewood. The axe was also used to make other tools or weapons, and a variety of material equipment required by the aboriginal in his daily life. The stone axe was essential in the construction of the wet season domed huts which keep out some rain and some insects; of platforms which provide dry storage; or shelters which give shade in the dry summer when days are bright and hot. In hunting and fishing and in gathering vegetable or animal food the axe was also a necessary tool, and in this tropical culture, where preservatives or other means of storage are lacking, the natives spend more time obtaining food than in any other occupation — except sleeping. In only two instances was the use of the stone axe strictly limited to adult men: for gathering wild honey, the most prized food known to the Yir Yoront; and for making the secret paraphernalia for ceremonies. From this brief listing of some of the activities involving the use of the axe, it is easy to understand why there was at least one stone axe in every camp, in every hunting or fighting party, and in every group out on a "walkabout" in the bush.

The stone axe was also prominent in interpersonal relations. Yir Yoront men were dependent upon interpersonal relations for their stone axe heads, since the flat, geologically recent alluvial country over which they range provides no suitable stone for this purpose. The stone they used came from quarries four hundred miles to the south, reaching the Yir Yoront through long lines of male trading partners. Some of these chains terminated with the Yir Yoront men, others extended on farther north to other groups, using Yir Yoront men as links. Almost every older adult man had one or more regular trading partners, some to the north and some to the south. He provided his partner or partners in the south with surplus spears, particularly fighting spears tipped with the barbed spines of stingray which snap into vicious fragments when they penetrate human flesh. For a dozen such spears, some of which he may have obtained from a partner to the north, he would receive one stone axe head. Studies have shown that the stingray barb spears increased in value as they moved south and farther from the sea. One hundred and fifty miles south of the Yir Yoront one such spear may be exchanged for one stone axe head. Although actual investigations could not be made, it was presumed that farther south, nearer the quarries, one stingray barb spear would bring several stone axe heads. Apparently people who acted as links in the middle of the chain and who made neither spears nor axe heads would receive a certain number of each as a middleman's profit.

Thus trading relations, which may extend the individual's personal relationships beyond that of his own group, were associated with spears and axes, two of the most important items in a man's equipment. Finally, most of the exchanges took place during the dry season, at the time of the great aboriginal celebrations centering about initiation rites or other totemic ceremonials which attracted hundreds and were the occasion for much exciting activity in addition to trading.

Returning to the Yir Yoront, we find that adult men kept their axes in camp with their other equipment, or carried them when traveling. Thus a woman or child who wanted to use an axe — as might frequently happen during the day — had to get one from a man, use it promptly, and return it in good condition. While a man might speak of "my axe," a woman or child could not.

This necessary and constant borrowing of axes from older men by women and children was in accordance with regular patterns of kinship behavior. A woman would expect to use her husband's axe unless he himself was using it; if unmarried, or if her husband was absent, a woman would go first to her older brother or to her father. Only in extraordinary circumstances would she seek a stone axe from other male kin. A girl, a boy, or a young man would look to a father or an older brother to provide an axe for their use. Older men, too, would follow similar rules if they had to borrow an axe.

It will be noted that all these social relationships in which the stone axe had a place are pair relationships and that the use of the axe helped to define and maintain their character and the roles of the two individual participants. Every active relationship among the Yir Yoront involved a definite and accepted status of superordination or subordination. A person could have no dealings with another on exactly equal terms. The nearest approach to equality was between brothers, although the older was always superordinate to the younger. Since the exchange of goods in a trading relationship involved a mutual reciprocity, trading partners usually stood in a brotherly type of relationship, although one was always classified as older than the other and would have some advantage in case of dispute. It can be seen that repeated and widespread conduct centering around the use of the axe helped to generalize and standardize these sex, age, and kinship roles both in their normal benevolent and exceptional malevolent aspects.

The status of any individual Yir Yoront was determined not only by sex, age, and extended kin relationships, but also by membership in one of two dozen patrilineal totemic clans into which the entire community was divided.[3] Each clan had literally hundreds of totems, from one or two of which the clan derived its name, and the clan members their personal names. These totems included natural species or phenomena such as the sun, stars, and daybreak, as well as cultural "species": imagined ghosts, rainbow serpents, heroic ancestors; such eternal cultural verities as fires, spears, huts; and such human activities, conditions, or attributes as eating, vomiting, swimming, fighting, babies and corpses, milk and blood, lips and loins. While individual members of such totemic classes or species might disappear or be destroyed, the class itself was obviously ever-present and indestructible. The totems, therefore, lent permanence and stability to the clans, to the groupings of human individuals who generation after generation were each associated with a set of totems which distinguished one clan from another.

The stone axe was one of the most important of the many totems of the Sunlit Cloud Iguana clan. The names of many members of this clan referred to the axe itself, to activities in which the axe played a vital part, or to the clan's mythical ancestors, with whom the axe was prominently associated. When it was necesssary to represent the stone axe in totemic ceremonies, only men of this clan exhibited it or pantomimed its use. In secular life, the axe could be made by any man and used by all; but in the sacred realm of the totems it belonged exclusively to the Sunlit Cloud Iguana people.

Supporting those aspects of cultural behavior which we have called technology and conduct is a third area of culture, which includes ideas, sentiments, and values. These are most difficult to deal with, for they are latent and covert, and even unconscious, and must be deduced from overt actions and language or other communicating behavior. In this aspect of the culture lies the significance of the stone axe to the Yir Yoront and to their cultural way of life.

The stone axe was an important symbol of masculinity among the Yir Yoront (just as pants or pipes are to us). By a complicated set of

---

[3] The best, although highly concentrated, summaries of totemism among the Yir Yoront and the other tribes of north Queensland will be found in R. Lauriston Sharp, "Tribes and Totemism in Northeast Australia," *Oceania*, Vol. 8, 1939, pp. 254–275 and 439–461 (especially pp. 268–275); also "Notes on Northeast Australian Totemism," in *Papers of the Peabody Museum of American Archaeology and Ethnology*, Vol. 20, *Studies in the Anthropology of Oceania and Asia*, Cambridge, 1943, 66–71.

ideas the axe was defined as "belonging" to males, and everyone in the society (except untrained infants) accepted these ideas. Similarly spears, spear throwers, and fire-making sticks were owned only by men and were also symbols of masculinity. But the masculine values represented by the stone axe were constantly being impressed on all members of society by the fact that females borrowed axes but not other masculine artifacts. Thus the axe stood for an important theme of Yir Yoront culture: the superiority and rightful dominance of the male, and the greater value of his concerns and of all things associated with him. As the axe also had to be borrowed by the younger people it represented the prestige of age, another important theme running through Yir Yoront behavior.

To understand the Yir Yoront culture it is necessary to be aware of a system of ideas which may be called their totemic ideology. A fundamental belief of the aboriginal divided time into two great epochs: (1) a distant and sacred period at the beginning of the world when the earth was peopled by mildly marvelous ancestral beings or culture heroes who are in a special sense the forebears of the clans; and (2) a period when the old was succeeded by a new order, which includes the present. Originally there was no anticipation of another era supplanting the present. The future would simply be an eternal continuation and reproduction of the present, which itself had remained unchanged since the epochal revolution of ancestral times.

The important thing to note is that the aboriginal believed that the present world, as a natural and cultural environment, was and should be simply a detailed reproduction of the world of the ancestors. He believed that the entire universe "is now as it was in the beginning," when it was established and left by the ancestors. The ordinary cultural life of the ancestors became the daily life of the Yir Yoront camps, and the extraordinary life of the ancestors remained extant in the recurring symbolic pantomimes and paraphernalia found only in the most sacred atmosphere of the totemic rites.

Such beliefs, accordingly, opened the way for ideas of what *should be* (because it supposedly *was*) to influence or help determine what actually *is*. A man called Dog-chases-iguana-up-a-tree-and-barks-at-him-all-night had that and other names because he believed his ancestral alter ego had also had them; he was a member of the Sunlit Cloud Iguana clan because his ancestor was; he was associated with particular countries and totems of this same ancestor; during an initiation he played the role of a dog and symbolically attacked and killed certain members of other clans because his ancestor (conveniently either anthropomorphic or kynomorphic) really did the same to the ancestral alter egos of these men; and he would avoid his mother-in-law, joke with a mother's distant brother, and make spears in a certain way because his and other people's ancestors did these things. His behavior in these specific ways was outlined, and to that extent determined for him, by a set of ideas concerning the past and the relation of the present to the past.

But when we are informed that Dog-chases-etc. had two wives from the Spear Black Duck clan and one from the Native Companion clan, one of them being blind, that he had four children with such and such names, that he had a broken wrist and was left-handed, all because his ancestor had exactly these same attributes, then we know (though he apparently didn't) that the present has influenced the past, that the mythical world has been somewhat adjusted to meet the exigencies and accidents of the inescapably real present.

There was thus in Yir Yoront ideology a nice balance in which the mythical was adjusted in part to the real world, the real world in part to the ideal preexisting mythical world, the adjustments occurring to maintain a fundamental tenet of native faith that the present must be a mirror of the past. Thus the stone axe, in all its aspects, uses, and associations, was integrated into the context of Yir Yoront technology and conduct because a myth, a set of ideas, had put it there.

IV. THE OUTCOME

The introduction of the steel axe indiscriminately and in large numbers into the Yir Yoront technology occurred simultaneously with many other changes. It is therefore impossible to separate all the results of this single innovation. Nevertheless, a number of specific effects of the change from stone to steel axes may be noted, and the steel axe may be used as an epitome of the increasing quantity of European goods and implements received by the aboriginals and of their general influence on the native culture. The use of the steel axe to illustrate such influences would seem to be justified. It was one of the first European artifacts to be adopted for regular use by the Yir Yoront, and whether made of stone or steel, the axe was clearly one of the most important items of cultural equipment they possessed.

The shift from stone to steel axes provided no major technological difficulties. While the aboriginals themselves could not manufacture steel axe heads, a steady supply from outside continued; broken wooden handles could easily be replaced from bush timbers with aboriginal tools. Among the Yir Yoront the new axe was never used to the extent it was on mission or cattle stations (for carpentry work, pounding tent pegs, as a hammer, and so on); indeed, it had so few more uses than the stone axe that its practical effect on the native standard of living was negligible. It did some jobs better, and could be used longer without breakage. These factors were sufficient to make it of value to the native. The white man believed that a shift from steel to stone axe on his part would be a definite regression. He was convinced that his axe was much more efficient, that its use would save time, and that it therefore represented technical "progress" toward goals which he had set up for the native. But this assumption was hardly borne out in aboriginal practice. Any leisure time the Yir Yoront might gain by using steel axes or other Western tools was not invested in "improving the conditions of life," nor, certainly, in developing aesthetic activities, but in sleep — an art they had mastered thoroughly.

Previously, a man in need of an axe would acquire a stone axe head through regular trading partners from whom he knew what to expect, and was then dependent solely upon a known and adequate natural environment, and his own skills or easily acquired techniques. A man wanting a steel axe, however, was in no such self-reliant position. If he attended a mission festival when steel axes were handed out as gifts, he might receive one either by chance or by happening to impress upon the mission staff that he was one of the "better" bush aboriginals (the missionaries' definition of "better" being quite different from that of his bush fellows). Or, again, almost by pure chance, he might get some brief job in connection with the mission which would enable him to earn a steel axe. In either case, for older men a preference for the steel axe helped change the situation from one of self-reliance to one of dependence, and a shift in behavior from well-structured or defined situations in technology or conduct to ill-defined situations in conduct alone. Among the men, the older ones whose earlier experience or knowledge of the white man's harshness made them suspicious were particularly careful to avoid having relations with the mission, and thus excluded themselves from acquiring steel axes from that source.

In other aspects of conduct or social relations, the steel axe was even more significantly at the root of psychological stress among the Yir Yoront. This was the result of new factors which the missionary considered beneficial: the simple numerical increase in axes per capita as a result of mission distribution, and distribution directly to younger men, women, and even children. By winning the favor of the mission staff, a woman might be given a steel axe which was clearly intended to be hers, thus creating a situation quite different from the previous custom which necessitated her borrowing an axe from a male relative. As a result a woman would refer to the axe as "mine," a possessive form she was never able to use of the stone axe. In the same fashion, young men or even boys also obtained steel axes directly from the mission, with the result that older men no longer had a complete monopoly of all the axes in the bush community. All this led to a revolutionary confusion of sex, age, and kinship roles, with a major gain in independence and loss of subordination on the part of those who now owned steel axes when they had previously been unable to possess stone axes.

The trading partner relationship was also affected by the new situation. A Yir Yoront might have a trading partner in a tribe to the south whom he defined as a younger brother and over whom he would therefore have some authority. But if the partner were in contact with the mission or had other access to steel axes, his subordination obviously decreased. Among other things, this took some of the excitement away from the dry season fiesta-like tribal gatherings centering around initiations. These had traditionally been the climactic annual occasions for exchanges between trading partners, when a man might seek to acquire a whole year's supply of stone axe heads. Now he might find himself prostituting his wife to almost total strangers in return for steel axes or other white man's goods. With trading partnerships weakened, there was less reason to attend the ceremonies, and less fun for those who did.

Not only did an increase in steel axes and their distribution to women change the character of the relations between individuals (the paired relationships that have been noted), but a previously rare type of relationship was created in the Yir Yoront's conduct toward whites. In the aboriginal society there were few occasions outside of the immediate family when an individual would initiate action to several other people at once. In any average group, in accordance with the kinship system, while a person might be superordinate to several people to whom he could suggest or command action, he was also subordinate to several others with whom such behavior would be taboo. There was thus no overall chieftainship or authoritarian leadership of any kind. Such complicated operations as grass-burning animal drives or totemic ceremonies could be carried out smoothly because each person was aware of his role.

On both mission and cattle stations, however, the whites imposed their conception of leadership roles upon the aboriginals, consisting of one person in a controlling relationship with a subordinate group. Aboriginals called together to receive gifts, including axes, at a mission Christmas party found themselves facing one or two whites who sought to control their behavior for the occasion, who disregarded the age, sex, and kinship variables of which the aboriginals were so conscious, and who considered them all at one subordinate level. The white also sought to impose similar patterns on work parties. (However, if he placed an aboriginal in charge of a mixed group of post-hole diggers, for example, half of the group, those subordinate to the "boss," would work while the other half, who were superordinate to him, would sleep.) For the aboriginal, the steel axe and other European goods came to symbolize this new and uncomfortable form of social organization, the leader-group relationship.

The most disturbing effects of the steel axe, operating in conjunction with other elements also being introduced from the white man's several subcultures, developed in the realm of traditional ideas, sentiments, and values. These were undermined at a rapidly mounting rate, with no new conceptions being defined to replace them. The result was the erection of a mental and moral void which foreshadowed the collapse and destruction of all Yir Yoront culture, if not, indeed, the extinction of the biological group itself.

From what has been said it should be clear how changes in overt behavior, in technology and conduct, weakened the values inherent in a reliance on nature, in the prestige of masculinity and of age, and in the various kinship relations. A scene was set in which a wife, or a young son whose initiation may not yet have been completed, need no longer defer to the husband or father who, in turn, became confused and insecure as he was forced to borrow a steel axe from them. For the woman and boy the steel axe helped establish a new degree of freedom which they accepted readily as an escape from the unconscious stress of the old patterns — but they, too, were left confused and insecure. Ownership became less well defined with the result that stealing and trespassing were introduced into technology and conduct. Some of the excitement surrounding the great ceremonies evaporated and they lost their previous gaiety and interest. Indeed, life itself became less interesting, although this did not lead the Yir Yoront to discover suicide, a concept foreign to them.

The whole process may be most specifically illustrated in terms of totemic system, which also illustrates the significant role played by a system of ideas, in this case a totemic ideology, in the breakdown of a culture.

In the first place, under pre-European aboriginal conditions where the native culture has become adjusted to a relatively stable environment, few, if any, unheard of or catastrophic crises can occur. It is clear, therefore, that the totemic system serves very effectively in inhibiting radical cultural changes. The closed system of totemic ideas, explaining and categorizing a well-known universe as it was fixed at the beginning of time, presents a considerable obstacle to the adoption of new or the dropping of old culture traits. The obstacle is not insurmountable and the system allows for the minor variations which occur in the norms of daily life. But the inception of major changes cannot easily take place.

Among the bush Yir Yoront, the only means of water transport is a light wood log to which they cling in their constant swimming of rivers, salt creeks, and tidal inlets. These natives know that tribes forty-five miles further north have a bark canoe. They know these northern tribes can thus fish from midstream or out at sea, instead of clinging to the river banks and beaches, that they can cross coastal waters infested with crocodiles, sharks, stingrays, and Portuguese men-of-war without danger. They know the materials of which the canoe is made exist in their own environment. But they also know, as they say, that they do not have canoes because their own mythical ancestors did not have them. They assume that the canoe was part of the ancestral universe of the northern tribes. For them, then, the adoption of the canoe would not be simply a matter of learning a number of new behavioral skills for its manufacture and use. The adoption would require a much more difficult procedure; the acceptance by the entire society of a myth, either locally developed or borrowed, to explain the presence of the canoe, to associate it with some one or more of the several hundred mythical ancestors (and how decide which?), and thus establish it as an accepted totem of one of the clans ready to be used by the whole community. The Yir Yoront have not made this adjustment, and in this case we can only say that for the time being at least, ideas have won out over very real pressures for technological change. In the elaborateness and explicitness of the totemic ideologies we seem to have one explanation for the notorious stability of Australian cultures under aboriginal conditions, an explanation which gives due weight to the importance of ideas in determining human behavior.

At a later stage of the contact situation, as has been indicated, phenomena unaccounted for by the totemic ideological system begin to appear with regularity and frequency and remain within the range of native experience. Accordingly, they cannot be ignored (as the "Battle of the Mitchell" was apparently ignored), and there is an attempt to assimilate them and account for them along the lines of principles inherent in the ideology. The bush Yir Yoront of the mid-thirties represent this stage of the acculturation process. Still trying to maintain their aboriginal definition of the situation, they accept European artifacts and behavior patterns, but fit them into their totemic system, assigning them to various clans on a par with original totems. There is an attempt to have the myth-making process keep up with these cultural changes so that the idea system can continue to support the rest of the culture. But analysis of overt behavior, of dreams, and of some of the new myths indicates that this arrangement is not entirely satisfactory, that the native clings to his totemic system with intellectual loyalty (lacking any substitute ideology), but that associated sentiments and values are weakened. His attitude toward his own and toward European culture is found to be highly ambivalent.

All ghosts are totems of the Head-to-the-East Corpse clan, are thought of as white, and are of course closely associated with death. The white man, too, is closely associated with death, and he and all things pertaining to him are naturally assigned to the Corpse clan as totems. The steel axe, as a totem, was thus associated with the Corpse clan. But as an "axe," clearly linked with the stone axe, it is a totem of the Sunlit Cloud Iguana clan. Moreover, the steel axe, like most European goods, has no distinctive origin myth, nor are mythical ancestors associated with it. Can anyone, sitting in the shade of a *ti* tree one afternoon, create a myth to resolve this confusion? No one has, and the horrid suspicion arises as to the authenticity of the origin myths, which failed to take into account this vast new universe of the white man. The steel axe, shifting hopelessly between one clan and the other, is not only replacing the stone axe physically, but is hacking at the supports of the entire cultural system.

The aboriginals to the south of the Yir Yoront have clearly passed beyond this stage. They are engulfed by European culture, either by the mission or cattle station subcultures or, for some natives, by a baffling, paradoxical combination of both incongruent varieties. The totemic ideology can no longer support the inrushing mass of foreign culture traits, and the myth-making process in its native form breaks down completely. Both intellectually and emotionally a saturation point is reached so that the myriad new traits which can neither be ignored nor any longer assimilated simply force the aboriginal to abandon his totemic system. With the collapse of this system of ideas, which is so closely related to so many other aspects of the native culture, there follows an appallingly sudden and complete cultural disintegration, and a demoralization of the individual such as has seldom been recorded elsewhere. Without the support of a system of ideas well devised to provide cultural stability in a stable environment, but admittedly too rigid for the new realities pressing in from outside, native behavior and native sentiments and values are simply dead. Apathy reigns. The aboriginal has passed beyond the realm of any outsider who might wish to do him well or ill.

Returning from the broken natives huddled on cattle stations or on the fringes of frontier towns to the ambivalent but still lively aboriginals settled on the Mitchell River mission, we note one further devious result of the introduction of European artifacts. During a wet season stay at the mission, the anthropologist discovered that his supply of toothpaste was being depleted at an alarming rate. Investigation showed that it was being taken by old men for use in a new toothpaste cult. Old materials of magic having failed, new materials were being tried out in a malevolent magic directed toward the mission staff and some of the younger aboriginal men. Old males, largely ignored by the missionaries, were seeking to regain some of their lost power and prestige. This mild aggression proved hardly effective, but perhaps only because confidence in any kind of magic on the mission was by this time at a low ebb.

For the Yir Yoront still in the bush, a time could be predicted when personal deprivation and frustration in a confused culture would produce an overload of anxiety. The mythical past of the totemic ancestors would disappear as a guarantee of a present of which the future was supposed to be a stable continuation. Without the past, the present could be meaningless and the future unstructured and uncertain. Insecurities would be inevitable. Reaction to this stress might be some form of symbolic aggression, or withdrawal and apathy, or some more realistic approach. In such a situation the missionary with understanding of the processes going on about him would find his opportunity to introduce his forms of religion and to help create a new cultural universe.

REVIEW QUESTIONS

1. What part did traditional stone axes play in the social integration of Yir Yoront society?
2. How could a simple tool such as a small steel axe disrupt Yir Yoront social organization?
3. How did the way the missionaries gave out steel axes contribute to Yir Yoront social disorganization?
4. Can the model of change be applied to other cases? What are some examples?

34   Progress and Tribal Peoples
JOHN H. BODLEY

As John Bodley points out in this selection, tribal peoples have been virtually wiped out in the last two hundred years. Until that time, several million tribals, usually hunter-gatherers and horticulturalists, inhabited a large area of the world. But the onset of industrialization meant a run on local resources for many nations and the need to exploit untapped territory. Tribals paid the price. Bodley discusses the process of world detribalization, looking at everything from the ethnocentrism of nation-states to the question of tribal self-determination.

Tribal peoples are being drastically affected by civilization, and their cultural patterns and, in many cases, the peoples themselves are disappearing as civilization advances. For many years anthropologists have made this topic a special field of study, but many seem to have missed its larger significance by failing to stress that the ecological irresponsibility of modern industrial nations and the reckless pursuit of progress are the basic causes of the continuing destruction of tribal peoples. . . .

At the outset the problem must be viewed in long-term perspective as a struggle between two incompatible cultural systems — tribes and states. For the purpose of understanding the interaction between these two systems, the most critical features of tribal groups are their polit-

From *Victims of Progress*, 3rd edition, by John H. Bodley by permission of Mayfield Publishing Company. Copyright © 1990, 1982 by Mayfield Publishing Company.

ical independence, reliance on local natural resources, and relative internal social equality. Tribes are small-scale sovereign nations that tend to manage local ecosystems for long-term sustained use. In comparison with states, and especially industrial states, tribal systems tend to expand more slowly and have been environmentally less destructive. Maintaining a greater internal social equality translates into less incentive for tribes to elevate economic production and consumption beyond local subsistence demands and more uniformly satisfies basic human needs. These differences explain why territories still controlled by tribal groups are so attractive to "developing nations"—because tribal territories contain "underutilized" resources.

The struggle between tribes and states has been over conflicting systems of resource management and internal social organization. Tribes represent small-scale, classless societies, with decentralized, communal, long-term resource management strategies, whereas states are class-based societies, with centralized management systems that extract resources for the short-term profit of special interest groups. Understandably, then, the political conquest of tribal areas often brings rapid environmental deterioration and may impoverish tribal peoples.

I am speaking here in global terms about a generalized tribal system for the purpose of understanding the causes and consequences of the incorporation and conquest of tribes by states. There are many exceptions to this ideal tribal model, and any specific culture exists at some point along a continuum between tribal and state organization. I am not assuming that tribes were ever isolated or completely self-sufficient, or existed in perfect equality, harmony, and absolute "balance" with nature. Nor would I argue that tribes are inherently good and states inherently evil. Both systems have advantages and disadvantages. However, given this disclaimer, significant qualitative differences between tribes and states remain, and these differences illuminate the recent fate of tribals along the frontiers of national expansion. The most advantageous unique qualities of tribal systems will need to be acknowledged and safeguarded by national governments if the future of indigenous peoples is to be secured.

People have led a tribal existence for at least the past half million years, and only for the past ten thousand years or so have any people lived in cities or states. Since the first appearance of urban life and state organization, the earlier tribal cultures were gradually displaced from the world's most productive agricultural lands and were relegated to marginal areas. Tribal peoples persisted for thousands of years in a dynamic equilibrium or symbiotic relationship with civilizations that had reached and remained within their ecological boundaries. But this situation shifted abruptly a mere five hundred years ago as Europeans began to expand beyond the long-established frontiers separating tribal peoples from states. However, by 1750, after two hundred and fifty years of preindustrial European expansion, tribal peoples still seemed secure and successfully adapted to their economically "marginal" refuges — but industrialization suddenly reduced the possibilities for the continued existence of politically independent tribal groups.

PROGRESS: THE INDUSTRIAL EXPLOSION

In the mid-eighteenth century the industrial revolution launched the developing Western nations on an explosive growth in population and consumption called "progress," which led to an unprecedented assault on the world's tribal peoples and their resources. Within the two hundred and fifty years since then the world has been totally transformed, many self-sufficient tribal cultures have disappeared, and dramatic resource shortages and environmental disasters have materialized. Now that many researchers are struggling to explain why industrial civilization seems to be floundering in its own success, anthropologists are beginning to realize that the first and most ominous victims of industrial progress were the several million tribal people who still controlled over half the globe in 1820 and who shared a relatively stable, satisfying, and proven cultural adaptation. It is highly significant and somewhat unsettling to realize that the cultural systems of these first victims of progress present a striking contrast to the characteristics of industrial civilization.

The industrial revolution is nothing less than an *explosion* because of the unparalleled scope and the catastrophic nature of the transformations that it has initiated. Phenomenal increases in both population and per-capita consumption rates were the two most critical correlates of industrialization because they quickly led to overwhelming pressure on natural resources.

The acceleration in world population growth rates and their relationship to industrial progress have been well documented. Immediately prior to the industrial revolution, for example, the doubling time of the world's population was approximately two hundred and fifty years. However, after industrialization was under way, the European population of 1850 doubled in just over eighty years, and the European populations of the United States, Canada, Australia, and Argentina tripled between 1851 and 1900. The doubling time of the world's population reached its lowest point of about thirty-three years (an annual growth rate of over 2 percent) during the period 1965–1973. By 1986 the global rate of population growth had declined only slightly to 1.8 percent a year. In contrast, clear anthropological evidence shows that tribal populations grow slowly and use their natural resources conservatively. The relative stability of tribal populations is due only partly to higher mortality rates; it is also attributed to social, economic, and religious controls on fertility, the significance of which is still not fully understood. Although tribal populations have the capacity for growth, and may expand rapidly into empty lands, they are politically and economically designed to operate most effectively at low densities and low absolute size.

THE CULTURE OF CONSUMPTION

The increased rates of resource consumption accompanying industrialization have been even more critical than mere population increase. Above all else, industrial civilization is a culture of *consumption*, and in this respect it differs most strikingly from tribal cultures. Industrial economies are founded on the principle that consumption must be ever expanded, and complex systems of mass marketing and advertising have been developed for that specific purpose. Social stratification in industrial societies is based primarily on inequalities in material wealth and is both supported and reflected by differential access to resources. Industrial ideological systems stress belief in continual economic growth and progress and characteristically measure "standard of living" in terms of levels of material consumption.

Tribal cultures contrast strikingly in all of these aspects. Their economies are geared to the satisfaction of basic subsistence needs, which are assumed to be fixed, while a variety of cultural mechanisms serve to limit material acquisitiveness and to redistribute wealth. Wealth itself is rarely the basis of social stratification, and there is generally free access to natural resources for all. These contrasts are the basis for the incompatibility between tribal and industrial cultures, and are the traits that are the sources of particular problems during the modernization process.

The most obvious consequences of tribal consumption patterns are that these cultures tend to be highly stable, make light demands on their environments, and can easily support themselves within their own boundaries. The opposite situation prevails for the culture of consumption. Almost overnight the industrialized nations quite literally ate up their own local resources and outgrew their boundaries. This was dramatically apparent in England, where local resources comfortably supported tribal cultures for thousands of years, but after a hundred years of industrial progress the area was unable to meet its basic needs for grain, wood, fibers, and hides. Between 1851 and 1900 Europe was forced to export 35 million people because it could no longer support them. In the United States, where industrial progress has gone the furthest, since 1970 Americans have been consuming per capita some fifteen times more energy than neolithic agriculturalists and seven times the world average in nonrenewable resources. They were also importing vast tonnages of food, fuels, and other resources to support themselves.

Indeed few, if any, industrial nations can now supply from within their own boundaries the resources needed to support further growth or even to maintain current consumption levels. It should not be surprising, then, that the "underdeveloped" resources controlled by the world's self-sufficient tribal peoples were quickly appropriated by outsiders to support their own industrial progress.

RESOURCE APPROPRIATION AND ACCULTURATION

In case after case, government programs for the progress of tribal peoples directly or indirectly force culture change, and these programs in turn are linked invariably to the extraction of tribal resources to benefit the national economy. From the strength of this relationship between tribal "progress" and the exploitation of tribal resources, we might even infer that tribal peoples would not be asked to surrender their resources and independence if industrial societies learned to control their own culture of consumption. This point must be made explicit, because considerable confusion exists in the enormous culture change literature regarding the basic question of why tribal cultures seem inevitably to be acculturated or modernized by industrial civilization. The consensus, at least among economic development writers (and the view often expressed in introductory textbooks), is the ethnocentric view that contact with superior industrial culture causes tribal peoples to voluntarily reject their own cultures in order to obtain a better life. Other writers, however, have seemed curiously mystified by the entire process. An example of this latter position can be seen in Julian Steward's summary of a monumental study of change in traditional cultures in eleven countries. Steward concluded that while many startling parallels could be identified, the causal factors involved in the modernization process were still "not well conceptualized."

This inability to conceptualize the causes of the transformation process in simple, nonethnocentric terms — or indeed the inability to conceptualize the causes at all — may be due to the fact that the analysts are members of the culture of consumption that today is the dominant world culture type. The most powerful cultures have always assumed a natural right to exploit the world's resources wherever they find them, regardless of the prior claims of indigenous populations. Arguing for efficiency and survival of the fittest, early colonialists elevated this "right" to the level of an ethical and legal principle that could be invoked to justify the elimination of any cultures that were not making "effective" use of their resources.

Members of the expanding culture rationalized as "natural" evolutionary processes that eliminated groups considered to be either culturally or racially inferior. They thought this "selection" process was so natural and "inevitable" that nothing could prevent it. For example, in 1915 Paul Popenoe told the scientists assembled in Washington, D.C., for the 19th International Congress of Americanists that the mass destruction of native Americans following the European invasion was "a process of racial purification of weak stocks." The Indian was "killed off by natural selection." Popenoe declared: "The native succumbed to the process of evolution, and no conceivable kindnesses from their conquerors could have prevented this elimination." Certainly, disease was a major factor in New World depopulation, but it was accompanied by conquest and colonization, which were political processes for which people were responsible. Treating ethnocide and genocide as scientific law is to mask their underlying political causes.

These old attitudes of social darwinism are deeply embedded in our ideological system and still occur in the professional literature on culture change. In fact, one development writer recently declared: "Perhaps entire societies will lack survival value and vanish before the onslaught of industrialization."[1] This viewpoint also appears in modern theories of cultural evolution, where it is expressed as the "Law of Cultural Dominance":

> That cultural system which more effectively exploits the energy resources of a given environment will tend to spread in that environment at the expense of less effective systems.[2]

Apart from the obvious ethical implications involved here, upon close inspection all of these theories expounding the greater adaptability, efficiency, and survival value of the dominant industrial culture prove to be misleading. Of course, as a culture of consumption, industrial civilization is uniquely capable of consuming resources at tremendous rates, but this does not make it a more *effective* culture than low-energy tribal cultures, if stability or long-run ecological success is taken as the criterion for "effectiveness." Likewise, the assumption that a given environment is not being exploited effectively by a traditional culture may merely reflect the unwillingness of national political authorities to allow local tribal groups to manage their own resources for their own interests. We should expect, then, that members of the culture of consumption would probably consider another culture's resources to be underexploited and to use this as a justification for appropriating them.

---

[1] Dennis Goulet, *The Cruel Choice: A New Concept in the Theory of Development* (New York: Atheneum, 1971), 266.

[2] David Kaplan, "The Law of Cultural Dominance" in *Evolution and Culture*, edited by Marshall D. Sahlins and Elman R. Service (Ann Arbor: University of Michigan Press, 1960), 75.

"Optimum" Land Use for Hill Tribes

The experience of the Chittagong Hills peoples of East Pakistan (Bangladesh since 1972) provides an excellent example of the process by which industrialization leads to a shortage of resources at the national level and ultimately results in political conquest and dispossession of tribal peoples who have preserved their resources more effectively. Along with other parts of the world — thanks to the intervention of the industrial nations — East Pakistan had such a severe population explosion that by 1965 population densities reached an average of four hundred and seventy people per square kilometer and the soil resources of the country were being pushed to the limits. As the crunch on resources worsened, the government made dramatic efforts to emulate the industrialization-economic development route of the developed nations, and soon directed special attention to the still largely self-sufficient Chittagong Hills tribal areas, which had managed to remain outside of the cash economy and had avoided major disruptions due to industrial intrusion. The French anthropologist Claude Levi-Strauss, who visited the area in 1950, found the hill tribes flourishing and observed that the Chittagong Hills "form a kind of anthropological sanctuary." Although the twelve ethnic groups making up the hill tribes were not totally isolated, they had enjoyed considerable political autonomy, especially under British control. However, the tribal areas were beginning to show population growth and subsequent pressure on their own resources due to shortening swidden cycles. But with only thirty-five people per square kilometer, they remained an island of low population density and "underdeveloped" resources in what had suddenly become an impoverished and overpopulated country.

External exploitation of tribal resources in the interests of the national economy initially focused on the forests of the Chittagong Hills. Twenty-two percent of the district was declared a forest "reserve," a "Forest Industries Development Corporation" was organized by the provincial government, and in 1953 lumber and paper mills were in operation to facilitate the modern commercial utilization of the region's bamboo and tropical hardwoods. In 1962 the largest river in the tribal area was dammed to supply hydroelectric power to help feed the rising energy demands of East Pakistan's urban affluent. In the process, however, 673 square kilometers of the best tribal agricultural land were converted into a lake, thus further aggravating the land scarcity that was already developing because of earlier disruptions of the population-resources balance and requiring the resettlement and "rehabilitation" of many hill people.

Still dissatisfied with the level of resource exploitation in the Chittagong Hills, in 1964 the Pakistani government enlisted an eleven-member international team of geologists, soil scientists, biologists, foresters, economists, and agricultural engineers to devise a master plan for the integrated development of the area based on what they considered to be optimum land-use possibilities. The team worked for two years with helicopters, aerial photographs, and computers. They concluded that regardless of how well the traditional economic system of shifting cultivation and subsistence production may have been attuned to its environment in the past, today it "can no longer be tolerated."[3] The research team decided that the hill tribes should allow their land to be used primarily for the production of forest products for the benefit of the national economy because it was not well suited for large-scale cash cropping. The report left no alternative to the tribal peoples, as a member of the research team observes:

> More of the Hills tribesmen will have to become wage earners in the forest or other developing industries, and purchase their food from farmers practicing permanent agriculture on an intensive basis on the limited better land classes. It is realized that a whole system of culture and an age-old way of life cannot be changed overnight, but change it must, and quickly. The time is opportune. The maps and the basic data have been collected for an integrated development toward optimum land use.[4]

The government policy of "optimum" land use brought immediate disaster for the hill tribes. The USAID-funded Kaptai Dam inundated 253 square miles of tribal land, including much of the best cultivable land, and displaced 100,000 tribal people. At the same time, the government allowed large-scale entry by Bengali settlers, who practiced plow agriculture and began to further displace the tribals. In 1977 the Bangladeshi military initiated a genocidal extermination policy against the hill tribes. By 1982 some 400,000 Bengali settlers held tribal lands and were supported by 30,000 government troops. Two years later international organizations reported that 185,000 tribals had been killed. The Shanti Bahini, a guerrilla organization formed to defend tribal interests, proved unable to prevent the slaughter.

THE ROLE OF ETHNOCENTRISM

Although resource exploitation is clearly the basic cause of the destruction of tribal peoples and cultures, it is important to identify the underlying ethnocentric attitudes that are often used to justify what are actually exploitative policies. *Ethnocentrism*, the belief in the superiority of one's own culture, is vital to the integrity of any culture, but it can be a threat to the well-being of other peoples when it

---

[3] W. E. Webb, "Land Capacity Classification and Land Use in the Chittagong Hills Tracts of East Pakistan" (*Proceedings of the Sixth World Forestry Congress* 3: 3229–3232, 1966), 3232.

[4] Webb, 3232.

becomes the basis for forcing irrelevant standards upon tribal cultures. Anthropologists may justifiably take credit for exposing the ethnocentrism of nineteenth-century writers who described tribal peoples as badly in need of improvement, but they often overlook the ethnocentrism that occurs in the modern professional literature on economic development. This is ironic because ethnocentrism threatens tribal peoples even today by its support of culturally insentive government policies.

Ethnocentrism and Ethnocide

Anthropologists have been quick to stress the presumed deficiencies of tribal cultures as a justification for externally imposed change or a rejection of proposals that tribals be granted political autonomy. For example, in 1940 British anthropologist Lord Fitzroy Raglan, who later became president of the Royal Anthropological Institute, declared that tribal beliefs in magic were a chief cause of "folly and unhappiness" and the "worst evils of the day." He argued that, as long as tribals persist in such beliefs, the rest of the world cannot be considered civilized. In his view, existing tribes constituted "plague spots" that threatened to reinfect civilized areas, and the rapid imposition of civilization was the only solution. He declared:

> We should bring to them our justice, our education, and our science. Few will deny that these are better than anything which savages have got.[5]

More recently, American anthropologist Arthur Hippler echoed Raglan's remarks. In a debate with Gerald Weiss over the merits of tribal autonomy, Hippler argued that national religions are superior to the "terrors of shamanism." He found "our own culture" more exciting, interesting, and varied, and better at promoting human potential than are "backward" tribal cultures, and he assumed that all tribals would inevitably be drawn to it. Hippler suggested that only internal oppression from tribal elders prevents tribals from improving their culture. Not surprisingly, Hippler specifically opposed autonomy proposals for the defense of tribal groups because autonomy would keep people "backward" against their will. Furthermore, he argued that "culture" is an abstraction, not something that can be defended or "saved" from extinction. Thus, ethnocide, the destruction of a cultural or an ethnic group, could not occur. In his response, Weiss exposed the ethnocentrism of Hippler's position point by point.

---

[5] Lord Fitzroy R. S. Raglan, "The Future of the Savage Races," *Man* 40: 62.

Crude Customs and Traditions

Ethnocentrism by culture change professionals, as illustrated in the following example from India, has often been a powerful support for coercive government policies directed against tribal peoples. A group of Indian scholars and administrators presented an unsympathetic view of tribal culture in a series of papers and speeches at a seminar on new policy directions for the hill tribes of North East India, which was held at Calcutta in 1966. Some participants in the seminar complained that prior British administrators had committed the fundamental error of placing tribal culture above the "basic need for human progress,"[6] because for a time they had attempted to prevent the economic exploitation of the region by nontribal peoples. Throughout the seminar the participants attacked the entire range of traditional culture on ethnocentric grounds. They called the tribal economic system backward, wasteful, and obviously in need of "scientific permanent farming"[7]; an Indian professor complained of "crude customs and traditions" and characterized the tribal Garo peoples as being steeped in "primitive ignorance," "tradition-bound," and "static." Participants called for more thorough research to determine whether or not Garo society could be lifted out of its "morass of backwardness, traditionalism and pseudo-modernism."[8]

In one paper curiously entitled "An Outlook for a Better Understanding of Tribal People,"[9] an enlightened tribal member characterized his tribal kin as backward, lacking in culture, and living in darkness. Not only were these people described as cultureless, but according to an educated official they also lacked language:

> You see, unfortunately here they do not have a language, what they speak is an illiterate dialect, lacking grammar and orthography.[10]

A few years earlier, an Indian sociologist supported the conclusion that tribal languages were "merely corruptions of good speech and

---

[6] P. Moasosang, "The Naga Search for Self-Identity" in *A Common Perspective for North-East India*, edited by Rathin Mittra and Barun Das Gupta (Calcutta: Pannalal Das Gupta, 1967), 51.

[7] Admit Kumar Nag, "The Society in Transition in the Mizo District" in *A Common Perspective for North-East India*, edited by Rathin Mittra and Barun Das Gupta (Calcutta: Pannalal Das Gupta, 1967), 90.

[8] Parimal Chandra Kar, "A Point of View on the Garos in Transition" in *A Common Perspective for North-East India*, edited by Rathin Mittra and Barun Das Gupta (Calcutta: Pannalal Das Gupta, 1967), 80–90.

[9] Hrilrokhum Thiek, "An Outlook for a Better Understanding of the Tribal People" in *A Common Perspective for North-East India*, edited by Rathin Mittra and Barun Das Gupta (Calcutta: Pannalal Das Gupta, 1967), 103–109.

[10] Suhas Chatterjee, "Language and Literacy in the North-Eastern Regions" in *A Common Perspective for North-East India*, edited by Rathin Mittra and Barun Das Gupta (Calcutta: Pannalal Das Gupta, 1967), 20.

unworthy of survival." He wanted to see these people adopt the "more highly evolved" Indo-Aryan languages, because he considered the tribal peoples to be nothing more than backward Hindus.[11]

Technological Ethnocentrism
Development writers with tractors and chemicals to sell have expressed more ethnocentrism in their treatment of traditional economic systems than for any other aspect of tribal culture. These writers automatically assume that tribal economies must be unproductive and technologically inadequate and therefore consistently disregard the abundant evidence to the contrary. It has long been fashionable to attack the supposed inefficiency of shifting cultivation and pastoral nomadism and the precariousness of subsistence economies in general. But it could be argued that it is industrial subsistence techniques that are inefficient and precarious. Mono-crop agriculture, with its hybrid gains and dependence on chemical fertilizers, pesticides, and costly machinery, is extremely expensive in terms of energy demands and is highly unstable because of its susceptibility to disease, insects, and the depletion of critical minerals and fuels. The complexity of the food distribution system in industrial society also makes it highly vulnerable to collapse because of the breakdowns in the long chain from producer to consumer. In contrast, tribal systems are highly productive in terms of energy flow and are ecologically much stabler, while they enjoy efficient and reliable distribution systems.

Cultural reformers almost unanimously agree that all people share our desire for what we define as material wealth, prosperity, and progress and that others have different cultures only because they have not yet been exposed to the superior technological alternatives offered by industrial civilization. Supporters of this view seem to minimize the difficulties of creating new wants in a culture and at the same time make the following highly questionable and clearly ethnocentric assumptions:

1. The materialistic values of industrial civilization are cultural universals.

2. Tribal cultures are unable to satisfy the material needs of their peoples.

3. Industrial goods are, in fact, always superior to their handcrafted counterparts.

---

[11] G. S. Ghurye, *The Scheduled Tribes*, 3rd ed. (Bombay: G. R. Bhatkal, 1963), 187–190.

Unquestionably, tribal cultures represent a clear rejection of the materialistic values of industrial civilization, yet tribal individuals can be made to reject their traditional values if outside interests create the necessary conditions for this rejection. Far more is involved here than a mere demonstration of the superiority of industrial civilization.

The ethnocentrism of the second assumption is obvious. Clearly, tribal cultures could not have survived for half a million years if they did not do a reasonable job of satisfying basic human needs.

The third assumption — the superiority of industrial goods and techniques — deserves special comment because abundant evidence indicates that many of the material accounterments of industrial civilization may not be worth their real costs regardless of how appealing they may seem initially. To cite a specific example, it could be argued that the bow is superior to a gun in certain cultural and environmental contexts, because it is far more versatile and more efficient to manufacture and maintain. A single bow can be used for both fishing and hunting a variety of animals. Furthermore, bow users are not dependent on an unpredictable external economy, because bows can be constructed of local materials and do not require expensive ammunition. At the same time, use of the bow places some limits on game harvesting and demands a closer relationship between man and animal, which may have great adaptive significance. Hames has shown that Amazon Indians who have adopted shotguns have dramatically increased their hunting yields, but these gains do not entirely offset the extra labor that must go into raising the money to support the new technology. Furthermore, the increased hunting efficiency also means that certain vulnerable species are more likely to be depleted.

Many of the ethnocentric interpretations of tribal cultures are understandable when we realize that development writers often mistakenly attribute to them the conditions of starvation, ill health, and poverty, which are actually related to civilization and industrialization. Self-sufficient tribal peoples do not belong in the underdeveloped category. "Poverty" is an irrelevant concept in tribal societies, and poverty conditions do not result from subsistence economies per se.

Tribal Wards of the State

Writers on international law and colonial experts often called on the *wardship principle* in an effort to justify harsh government programs of culture change directed against tribal peoples. This so-called legal principle reflects the grossest ethnocentrism in that it considers tribal peoples to be incompetent or even retarded children. It defines the relationship between tribal peoples and the state as that of a benevolent parent-guardian and a ward who must be protected from his or her own degrading culture and gradually reformed or corrected. According to the wardship principle, the state is under a moral obligation to make all tribal peoples share in the benefits of civilization — that is, in health, happiness, and prosperity as defined primarily in terms of consumption.

This legal inferiority of tribal peoples has contributed significantly to the speed with which their acculturation or "reform" can occur and has worked marvelously to satisfy both the conscience and the economic needs of modern states.

Placing tribal peoples in the legal category of incompetent children reflects a tendency to view tribal culture as abnormal, sick, and mentally retarded. This obviously ethnocentric theme runs throughout the colonial literature, in which the civilization process is often described as *mental* correction, but this same theme has continued to appear in the modern literature. Some recent economic development writers have lumped tribal peoples indiscriminately with underdeveloped peoples, referred explicitly to economic underdevelopment as a "sickness," spoken of the "medicine of social change," and compared change agents to brain surgeons. It appears that the basic attitudes of some modern cultural reformers were unaffected by the discovery of ethnocentrism.

A Sacred Trust of Civilization

As we have seen, the modern civilizing mission undertaken by governments against tribal peoples was supported by a variety of ethnocentric assumptions, some of which were recognized as principles of international law. Not surprisingly, therefore, prestigious international organizations such as the United Nations also threw their support behind official attempts to bring civilization to all peoples — whether or not they desired it.

During the second half of the nineteenth century the colonizing industrial nations began to justify their scramble for foreign territories as a fulfillment of a sacred duty to spread their form of civilization to the world. When the major imperialist powers met in 1884–1885 at Berlin to set guidelines for the partitioning of Africa, they pledged support for the civilizing crusade and promised to assist missionaries and all institutions "calculated to educate the natives and to teach them to understand and appreciate the benefits of civilization." This position was reiterated and took on a more militant tone in Article Two of the Brussels Act of 1892, which called on the colonial powers to raise African tribal peoples to civilization and to "bring about the extinction of barbarous customs." This constituted an internationally approved mandate for ethnocide in the interests of progress.

Whereas such attitudes are perhaps to be expected from colonial nations at the height of their power, they seem inappropriate when expressed by world organizations dedicated to peace and self-determination of peoples. Nevertheless, the 1919 League of Nations Covenant in Article 22 gave "advanced nations" responsibility for "peoples not yet able to stand by themselves under the strenuous conditions of the modern world," thereby placing many tribal peoples officially under tutelage as "a sacred trust of civilization." In fact, this sacred trust proved to be a profitable colonial booty for the trust powers because it gave them the internationally recognized right to exploit the resources of thousands of square kilometers of formerly nonstate territory while making only token allowance for the wishes of the native peoples involved. Under the 1945 United Nations Charter, many of these same tribal peoples were identified as "peoples who have not yet attained a full measure of self-government," and their continued advancement was to be promoted by their guardians "by constructive measures of development" (Articles 73 and 76, UN Charter). Here again, responsibility for deciding what constitutes a tribal peoples' welfare is effectively taken from them and is legally placed in the hands of outside interests. The carefully worded and seemingly nonderogatory phrases "peoples not yet able to stand by themselves" and "nonself-governing" are glaringly ethnocentric and derogatory because these peoples have governed themselves for thousands of years without the support of civilization. Of course, they were unable to defend themselves against the incursions of militant, resource-hungry states. But many modern nations exist only at the discretion of more powerful nations, and the UN Charter would not advocate making all militarily weak nations surrender their political autonomy to their stronger neighbors.

CIVILIZATION'S UNWILLING CONSCRIPTS

It now seems appropriate to ask the obvious question: How do autonomous tribal peoples themselves feel about becoming participants in the progress of industrial civilization? Because of the power at their disposal, industrial peoples have become so aggressively ethnocentric that they have difficulty even imagining that another life-style — particularly one based on fundamentally different premises — could possibly have value and personal satisfaction for the peoples following it. Happily arrogant in their own supposed cultural superiority, industrial peoples assume that those in other cultures perhaps realize their obsolescence and inferiority and eagerly desire progress toward the better life. This belief persists in the face of abundant evidence that independent tribal peoples are not anxious to scrap their cultures and would rather pursue their own form of the good life undisturbed. Peoples who have already chosen their major cultural patterns and who have spent generations tailoring them to local conditions are probably not even concerned that another culture might be superior to theirs. Indeed, it can perhaps be assumed that people in any autonomous, self-reliant culture would prefer to be left alone. Left to their own devices, tribal peoples are unlikely to volunteer for civilization or acculturation. Instead:

> Acculturation has always been a matter of conquest . . . refugees from the foundering groups may adopt the standards of the more potent society in order to survive as individuals. But these are conscripts of civilization, not volunteers.[12]

Free and Informed Choice

The question of choice is a critical point because many development authorities have stressed that tribal peoples should be allowed to choose progress. This view was obvious at a 1936 conference of administrators, educators, and social scientists concerning education in Pacific colonial dependencies, where it was stated that choices regarding cultural directions "must lie with the indigenous peoples themselves." Anthropologists at a more recent international conference in Tokyo took the same position when they called for "just and scientifically enlightened programs of acculturation which allow the peoples concerned a free and informed basis for choice." Apparently no one noticed the obvious contradiction between a scientific culture change program and free choice, or even the possible conflict between free and informed. The official position of the Australian government on free choice for the aborigine in 1970 indicates the absurdities to which such thinking can lead:

> The Commonwealth and State governments have adopted a common policy of assimilation which seeks that all persons of Aboriginal descent will choose to attain a similar manner and standard of living to that of other Australians and live as members of a single Austalian community.[13]

Those who so glibly demand choice for tribal peoples do not seem to realize the problems of directly instituting such a choice, and at the same time they refuse to acknowledge the numerous indicators that tribal peoples have already chosen their own cultures instead of the progress of civilization. In fact, the question of choice itself is probably ethnocentric and irrelevant to the peoples concerned. Do we choose civilization? is not a question that tribal peoples would ask, because they in effect have already answered it. They might consider the concept of choosing a way of life to be as irrelevant in their own

---

[12] Stanley Diamond, "Introduction: The Uses of the Primitive" in *Primitive Views of the World*, edited by Stanley Diamond (New York: Columbia University Press, 1960), vi.

[13] Australia. Commonwealth Bureau of Census and Statistics, 1970, 976.

cultural context as asking a person if he or she would choose to be a tree.

It is also difficult to ask whether tribal peoples desire civilization or economic development because affirmative responses will undoubtedly be from individuals already alienated from their own cultures by culture modification progams, and their views may not be representative of their still autonomous tribal kin.

Other problems are inherent in the concept of free and informed choice. Even when free to choose, tribal peoples would not generally be in a position to know what they were choosing and would certainly not be given a clear picture of the possible outcomes of their choice, because the present members of industrial cultures do not know what their own futures will be. Even if tribal peoples could be given a full and unbiased picture of what they were choosing, obtaining that information could destroy their freedom to choose, because participation in such an "educational" program might destroy their self-reliance and effectively deny them their right to choose their own tribal culture. An obvious contradiction exists in calling for culture change in order to allow people to choose or not to choose culture change. The authorities at the 1936 conference referred to earlier were caught in just such Alice-in-Wonderland doubletalk when they recommended the promotion of formal education programs (which would disrupt native culture) so that the people could freely decide whether they wanted their cultures disrupted:

> It is the responsibility of the governing people, through schools and other means, to make available to the native an adequate understanding of non-native systems of life so that these can be ranged alongside his own in order that his choices may be made.[14]

Such a program of education might sound like a sort of "cultural smorgasbord," but in fact there is really only one correct choice allowed — tribal peoples must choose progress.

One further problem overlooked in the "free choice" approach is that of the appropriateness of industrial progress or of any foreign cultural system in a given cultural and environmental context — even if freely chosen. Should Eskimos be encouraged to become nomadic camel herders or to develop a taste for bananas? Does the American "car complex" belong on a Micronesian coral atoll of four square kilometers? What will be the long-term effects of a shift from a self-reliant subsistence economy to a cash economy based on the sale of a single product on the uncertain world market? There are inescapable

---

[14] Cited in Felix M. Keesing, *The South Seas in the Modern World* (Institute of Pacific Relations International Research Series. New York: John Day, 1941), 84.

limits to what can constitute a successful human adaptation in a given cultural and environmental setting.

We Ask To Be Left Alone

At this point we will again ask the question posed earlier regarding whether tribal peoples freely choose progress. This question has actually been answered many times by independent tribal peoples who, in confrontations with industrial civilization, have (1) ignored it, (2) avoided it, or (3) responded with defiant arrogance. Any one of these responses could be interpreted as a rejection of further involvement with progress.

Many of the Australian aborigines reportedly chose the first response in their early contacts with members of Western civilization. According to Captain Cook's account of his first landing on the Australian mainland, aborigines on the beach ignored both his ship and his men until they became obnoxious. Elkin confirms that this complete lack of interest in white people's habits, material possessions, and beliefs was characteristic of aborigines in a variety of contact settings. In many cases, tribal peoples have shown little interest in initial contacts with civilized visitors because they simply assumed that the visitors would soon leave and they would again be free to pursue their own way of life undisturbed.

Among contemporary tribal peoples who still retain their cultural autonomy, rejection of outside interference is a general phenomenon that cannot be ignored. The Pygmies of the Congo represent a classic case of determined resistance to the incursions of civilization. Turnbull, who studied the Pygmies intensively in their forest environment, was impressed with the fact that in spite of long contact with outsiders they had successfully rejected foreign cultural domination for hundreds of years. Attempts of Belgian colonial authorities to settle them on plantations ended in complete failure, basically because the Pygmies were unwilling to sacrifice their way of life for one patterned for them by outsiders whose values were irrelevant to their environment and culture. According to Turnbull, the Pygmies deliberated over the changes proposed by the government and opted to remain within their traditional territory and pursue their own way of life. Their decision was clear:

> So for the Pygmies, in a sense, there is no problem. They have seen enough of the outside world to feel able to make their choice, and their choice is to preserve the sanctity of their own world up to the very end. Being what they are, they will doubtless play a masterful game of hide-and-seek, but they will not easily sacrifice their integrity.[15]

---

[15] Colin M. Turnbull, "The Lessons of the Pygmies," *Scientific American*, 1963, 208.

Anthropologist Cavalli-Sforza, who coordinated a long-term series of multidisciplinary field studies of Pygmies throughout Africa beginning in 1966, confirmed Turnbull's basic conclusion about the Pygmy rejection of directed change. He attributes the remarkable two-thousand-year persistence of Pygmies as a distinct people to the attractiveness of their way of life and the effectiveness of their enculturation practices. But like Turnbull, he also cites the importance of the forest itself and the Pygmies' successful symbiosis with their village-farmer neighbors. The most critical threat to Pygmies is now deforestation and disruption of their exchange relationships caused by the invasion of new colonists and the development of large-scale coffee plantations. As the forest shrinks, there simply will be no place for Pygmies as forest peoples. Bailey warns, "Unless sufficient areas of forest are set aside, a unique subsistence culture based on hunting and gathering forest resources will be lost in the Ituri [rain forest] and throughout central Africa forever."[16]

Avoiding Progress: Those Who Run Away
Direct avoidance of progress represents what is a widespread, long-established pattern of cultural survival whose implications should not be ignored by those who promote culture change.

Throughout South America and many other parts of the world, many nonhostile tribal peoples have made their attitudes toward progress clear by choosing to follow the Pygmies' game of hide-and-seek and actively avoiding all contact with outsiders. In the Philippines, a special term meaning "those who run away" has been applied to tribal peoples who have chosen to flee in order to preserve their cultures from government influence.

Many little-known tribal peoples scattered in isolated areas around the world have, in fact, managed to retain their cultural integrity and autonomy until recently by quietly retreating farther and farther into more isolated refuge areas. As the exploitative frontier has gradually engulfed these stubborn tribes, the outside world periodically has been surprised by the discovery of small pockets of unknown "Stone-Age" peoples who have clung tenaciously to their cultures up to the last possible moment. The extent and significance of this phenomenon have seldom been recognized by the public at large and certainly not by professional agents of culture change. In South America throughout this century, many different groups, including the Xeta, the Kreen-a-Kove in Brazil, various Panoan speakers such as the Amarakaeri and Amahuaka in headwater areas of the Peruvian Amazon, and the Akuriyo of Surinam, have been found using stone tools and deliber-

---

[16] Robert Bailey, "Development in the Ituri Forest of Zaire," *Cultural Survival Quarterly*, 6(2): 23–25.

ately avoiding contact with outsiders. These determined people are generally peaceful, except when harassed too severely. To avoid contact they prefer to desert their homes and gardens and thrust arrows point-up in their paths, rather than resort to violence. All that even the most persistent civilized visitors usually find — if they do manage to locate the natives' well-hidden villages — are empty houses and perhaps smoldering cooking fires. If a village is disturbed too often, the people abandon the site and relocate in a more isolated place. When, after continuous encroachment, their resource base shrinks to the point that it will no longer support their population and there is no place to retreat to, or when violent attacks by civilized raiders and introduced illnesses reduce their numbers to the point that they are no longer a viable society, then they must surrender to progress.

How successfully some of these groups have managed to avoid contact can be seen in the case of the Akuriyo Indians of Surinam. These foraging people were first seen by outsiders in 1937, when a Dutch expedition discovered them while surveying the Surinam-Brazil border. After this brief encounter the Akuriyo remained out of sight for nearly thirty years until American missionaries began to find traces of their camps. The missionaries were determined to make contact with them in order to win them for Christianity, but it was three years before they finally succeeded with the assistance of ten missionized Indians, shortwave radios, and airplanes. They tracked the Akuriyo along their concealed trails through a succession of hastily abandoned camps until they caught up with a few women and children and an old man who, with obvious displeasure, asked the first man who greeted them, "Are you a tiger that you smelled me out?" This small group had been left behind by others who had gone in search of arrow canes to defend themselves against the intruders. The Indians allowed the missionary party to remain with them only one night. Refusing to reveal either their tribal or their personal identities, they fed and traded with the intruders, and then insisted that they leave. The mission Indians sang hymns and tried to tell them about God, but the Akuriyo were unimpressed. According to the missionaries:

> The old chief commented that God must really be good. He said he knew nothing about Him, and that he had to leave now to get arrow cane.[17]

Obviously these people were expressing their desire to be left alone in the most dignified and elegant terms. But the missionaries proceeded to make plans for placing Christianized Indian workers

---

[17] Ivan L. Schoen, "Contact with the Stone Age," *Natural History*, Vol. 78, No. 1, January 1969.

among them and requested "for the sake of this tribe" that the Surinam government grant their mission exclusive permission to supervise further contacts with the Akuriyo. Within a short time contact was reestablished and the mission was able to encourage about fifty Akuriyo to settle in mission villages. Tragically, in barely two years 25 percent of the group had died and only about a dozen people still remained in the forest.

Whereas the Akuriyo are an example of a group avoiding contact in a remote area, many other examples can be cited of small tribes that have survived successfully on the fringes of civilized areas. One of the most outstanding of such cases was the discovery in 1970 that unknown bands of Indians were secretly living within the boundaries of the Iguazú Falls national park in Argentina.

Some observers argue that these cases do not represent real rejections of civilization and progress, because these people were given no choice by their hostile neighbors, who refused to share the benefits of civilization and so they were forced to pretend that they didn't desire these benefits. Critics point out that such people often eagerly steal or trade for steel tools. This argument misses the real point and represents a misunderstanding of the nature of culture change. Stability and ethnocentrism are fundamental characteristics of all cultures that have established a satisfactory relationship with their environment. Some degree of change, such as adopting steel tools, may well occur to enhance an ongoing adaptation and to prevent greater change from occurring.

CULTURAL PRIDE VERSUS PROGRESS

The pride and defiance of numerous tribal peoples in the face of forced culture change is unmistakable and have often been commented upon by outsiders. The ability of these cultures to withstand external intrusion is related to their degree of ethnocentrism or to the extent to which tribal individuals feel self-reliant and confident that their own culture is best for them. The hallmark of such ethnocentrism is the stubborn unwillingness to feel inferior even in the presence of overwhelming enemy force.

A case of calm but defiant self-assurance of this sort is offered by a warrior-chief of the undefeated Xavante (Shavante) of central Brazil, who had personally participated in the 1941 slaying of seven men of a "pacification" mission sent by the Brazilian government to end the Xavante's bitter fifty-year resistance to civilization. As further evidence of their disdain for intruders, the Xavante shot arrows into an air force plane and burned the gifts it dropped. After one Xavante community finally accepted the government's peace offers in 1953, the air force flew the chief to Rio de Janeiro in order to impress him with the superiority of the Brazilian state and the futility of further resistance. To everyone's amazement, he observed Rio, even from the air, with absolute calm. He was then led into the center of a soccer field to be surrounded by thousands of applauding fans, and it was pointed out to him how powerful the Brazilian state was and how unwise it was for the Xavante to be at war with it. The chief remained unmoved and responded simply: "This is the white man's land, mine is Xavante land." The Xavante have been militant in defense of their lands since "pacification" and have forcibly expelled settlers and occupied government offices to force the authorities to fulfill their promise of legal protections. A Xavante leader, Mario Juruna, carried the struggle further into the political arena by winning election to Brazil's House of Representatives in 1982. Juruna has campaigned effectively for the land rights of Brazilian Indians at both the national and international level.

THE PRINCIPLE OF STABILIZATION

According to theories of cultural evolution, adaptation, and integration, resistance to change is understandable as a natural cultural process. If the technological, social, and ideological systems of a culture gradually specialize to fit the requirements of successful adaptation to a specific environment, other cultural arrangements become increasingly difficult, if not impossible, to accommodate without setting in motion major disruptive changes that have unforeseen consequences. Resistance to change — whether it be direct avoidance of new cultural patterns, overt ethnocentrism, or open hostility to foreigners — may thus be seen to be a significant means of adaptation because it operates as a "cultural isolating mechanism" to protect successfully established cultures from the disruptive effects of foreign cultural elements. The resulting "stability" refers to a relative lack of change in the major cultural patterns and does not imply complete changelessness in all the nuances of culture, because minor changes probably occur constantly in all cultures. Stability is such a fundamental characteristic of cultures that it has been formulated as a general principle: "A culture at rest tends to remain at rest."[18] A corollary of this so-called principle of stabilization states:

> When acted upon by external forces a culture will, if necessary, undergo specific changes only to the extent of and with the effect of *preserving* unchanged its fundamental structure and character.[19]

---

[18] Thomas G. Harding, "Adaptation and Stability" in *Evolution and Culture*, edited by Marshall Sahlins and Elman R. Service (Ann Arbor: University of Michigan Press, 1960), 54.

[19] Harding, 54.

As change agents are well aware, resistance to change is based not only on the natural resistance or inertia of already established cultural patterns, but also on the realization by the people concerned of the risks of experimenting with unproven cultural patterns. Either the rewards of adopting new ways must appear to be worth the risks, or some form of coercion must be applied. However, change agents who are convinced of their own cultural superiority tend to overlook the fact that native fears about the dangers of untested innovations may be justified. Peoples that reject such unproven cultural complexes as miracle grains, pesticides, and chemical fertilizers may prove in the long run to be wiser and better adapted to their natural environments.

For peoples in relatively stable, self-reliant cultures, resistance to change is a positive value. It is only in industrial cultures that such emphasis is placed on change for its own sake, and among those who make a profession of promoting change, that cultural stability is given a negative connotation and is identified as backwardness and stagnation.

REVIEW QUESTIONS

1. What has been the effect of industrialization on the tribal peoples of the world?

2. What is meant by the term *acculturation*? What has acculturation meant for most tribal peoples?

3. What part has ethnocentrism played in the formulation and implementation of development programs? How is ethnocentrism expressed?

4. What should the policy of nation-states be toward tribals, according to Bodley? Do you think there is a realistic answer to the problems of tribes?

5. What should anthropologists do about the plight of tribals? Can they continue ethnographic research among tribals under present circumstances?

35   Cocaine and the Economic
Deterioration of Bolivia

JACK McIVER WEATHERFORD

*The demands of the world market have eroded local subsistence
economies for centuries. Lands, once farmed by individual families
to meet their own needs, now grow sugarcane, cotton, grain, or
vegetables for market. Deprived of their access to land, household-
ers must work as day laborers or migrate to cities to find jobs.
Villages are denuded of the men who have gone elsewhere for
work, leaving women to farm and manage the family. The rhythm
and structure of daily village life are altered dramatically. In this
article, Jack Weatherford describes the impact of a new world market for cocaine on the structure and lives of rural Bolivians. Fed by
an insatiable demand in Europe and the United States, the Bolivian
cocaine trade has drawn males from the countryside, disrupted
communications, destroyed families, unbalanced the local diet, and
upset traditional social organization.*

"They say you Americans can do anything. So, why can't you make
your own cocaine and let our children come home from the coca
plantations in the Chapare?" The Indian woman asked the question
with confused resignation. In the silence that followed, I could hear
only the rats scurrying around in the thatched roof. We continued
shelling corn in the dark. The large house around us had once been
home to an extended clan but was now nearly empty.

447

There was no answer to give her. Yet it was becoming increasingly obvious that the traditional Andean system of production and distribution built over thousands of years was now crumbling. Accompanying the destruction of the economic system was a marked distortion of the social and cultural patterns of the Quechua Indians. Since early in Inca history, the village of Pocona where I was working had been a trading village connecting the highlands, which produced potatoes, with the lowlands, which produced coca, a mildly narcotic plant used by the Incas. Over the past decade, however, new market demands from Europe and the United States have warped this system. Now the commodity is cocaine rather than the coca leaves, and the trade route bypasses the village of Pocona.

Bolivian subsistence patterns range from hunting and gathering in the jungle to intensive farming in the highlands, and since Inca times many parts of the country have depended heavily on mining. In the 1980s all of these patterns have been disrupted by the Western fad for one particular drug. Adoption of cocaine as the "drug of choice" by the urban elite of Europe and America has opened up new jungle lands and brought new Indian groups into Western economic systems. At the same time the cocaine trade has cut off many communities such as Pocona from their traditional role in the national economy. Denied participation in the legal economy, they have been driven back into a world of barter and renewed isolation.

The vagaries of Western consumerism produce extensive and profound effects on Third World countries. It makes little difference whether the demand is for legitimate products such as coffee, tungsten, rubber, and furs marketed through legal corporations, or for illegal commodities such as opium, marijuana, cocaine, and heroin handled through criminal corporations. The same economic principles that govern the open, legal market also govern the clandestine, illegal markets, and the effects of both are frequently brutal.

Before coming to this Bolivian village, I assumed that if Americans and Europeans wanted to waste their money on cocaine, it was probably good that some of the poor countries such as Bolivia profit from it. In Cochabamba, the city in the heart of the cocaine-producing area, I had seen the benefits of this trade among the *narco chic* who lived in a new suburb of houses styled to look like Swiss chalets, Spanish haciendas, and English country homes. All these homes were surrounded by large wrought-iron fences, walls with broken glass set in the tops, and with large dogs that barked loudly and frequently. Such homes cost up to a hundred thousand dollars, an astronomical sum for Bolivia. I had also seen the narco elite of Cochabamba wearing gold chains and the latest Miami fashions and driving Nissans, Audis, Ford Broncos, an occasional BMW, or even a Mercedes through the muddy streets of the city. Some of their children attended the expensive English-speaking school; much of Cochabamba's meager nightlife catered to the elite. But as affluent as they may be in Bolivia, this elite would probably not earn as much as working-class families in such cities as Detroit, Frankfurt, or Tokyo.

Traveling outside of Cochabamba for six hours on the back of a truck, fording the same river three times, and following a rugged path for the last twenty-five kilometers, I reached Pocona and saw a different face of the cocaine trade. Located in a valley a mile and a half above sea level, Pocona is much too high to grow the coca bush. Coca grows best below six thousand feet, in the lush area called the Chapare where the eastern Andes meet the western edge of the Amazon basin and rain forest.

Like the woman with whom I was shelling corn, most of the people of Pocona are older, and community life is dominated by women together with their children who are still too young to leave. This particular woman had already lost both of her sons to the Chapare. She did not know it at the time, but within a few months, she was to lose her husband to the same work as well. With so few men, the women are left alone to plant, work, and harvest the fields of potatoes, corn, and fava beans, but with most of the work force missing, the productivity of Pocona has declined substantially.

In what was once a moderately fertile valley, hunger is now a part of life. The daily diet consists almost exclusively of bread, potato soup, boiled potatoes, corn, and tea. The majority of their daily calories comes from the potatoes and from the sugar that they put in their tea. They have virtually no meat or dairy products and very few fresh vegetables. These products are now sent to the Chapare to feed the workers in the coca fields, and the people of Pocona cannot compete against them. The crops that the people of Pocona produce are now difficult to sell because truck drivers find it much more profitable to take goods in and out of the Chapare rather than face the long and unprofitable trip to reach such remote villages as Pocona.

Despite all the hardships caused by so many people being away from the village, one might assume that more cash should be flowing into Pocona from the Chapare, where young men easily earn three dollars a day — three times the average daily wage of porters or laborers in Cochabamba. But this assumption was contradicted by the evidence of Pocona. As one widowed Indian mother of four explained, the first time her sixteen-year-old son came home, he brought bags of food, presents, and money for her and the younger children. She was very glad that he was working in the Chapare. On the second visit home he brought only a plastic bag of white powder for himself, and instead of bringing food, he took away as much as he could carry on the two-day trip back into the Chapare.

The third time, he told his mother that he could not find enough work in the Chapare. As a way to earn more money he made his mother bake as much bread as she could, and he took Mariana, his ten-year-old sister, with him to sell the bread to the workers in the Chapare. According to the mother, he beat the little girl and abused her repeatedly. Moreover, the money she made disappeared. On one of Mariana's trips home to get more bread, the mother had no more wheat or corn flour to supply her son. So, she sent Mariana away to Cochabamba to work as a maid. The enraged son found where Mariana was working and went to the home to demand that she be returned to him. When the family refused, he tried but failed to have her wages paid to him rather than to his mother. Mariana was separated from her family and community, but at least she was not going to be one more of the prostitutes in the Chapare, and for her mother that was more important.

The standard of living in Pocona was never very high, but with the advent of the cocaine boom in Bolivia, the standard has declined. Ten years ago, Pocona's gasoline-powered generator furnished the homes with a few hours of electric light each night. The electricity also allowed a few families to purchase radios, and occasionally someone brought in a movie projector to show a film in a large adobe building on the main square. For the past two years, the people of Pocona have not been able to buy gasoline for their generator. This has left the village not only without electricity but without entertainment and radio or film contact with the outside world. A few boys have bought portable radios with their earnings from the Chapare, but their families were unable to replace the batteries. Nights in Pocona are now both dark and silent.

In recent years the national economy of Bolivia has been virtually destroyed, and peasants in communities such as Pocona are reverting to barter as the only means of exchange. The value of the peso may rise or fall by as much as 30 percent in a day; the peasants cannot take a chance on trading their crops for money that may be worth nothing in a week. Cocaine alone has not been responsible for the destruction of the Bolivian economy, but it has been a major contributor. It is not mere coincidence that the world's largest producer of coca is also the country with the world's worst inflation.

During part of 1986, inflation in Bolivia varied at a rate between 2,000 and 13,000 percent, if calculated on a yearly basis. Prices in the cities changed by the hour, and on some days the dollar would rise at the rate of more than 1 percent per hour. A piece of bread cost 150,000 pesos, and an American dollar bought between two and three million pesos on the black market. Large items such as airplane tickets were calculated in the billions of pesos, and on one occasion I helped a man carry a large box of money to pay for such a ticket. It took two professional counters half an hour to count the bills. Workers were paid in stacks of bills that were often half a meter high. Because Bolivia is too undeveloped to print its money, the importation of its own bills printed in West Germany and Brazil was one of the leading imports in the mid-1980s.

Ironically, by no longer being able to participate fully in the money economy, the villagers of Pocona who have chewed coca leaves for centuries now find it difficult to afford the leaves. The narcotics industry pays such a high price that the people of Pocona can afford only the rejected trash from the cocaine industry. Whether chewed or made into a tea, the coca produces a mild lift somewhat like a cup of coffee but without the jagged comedown that follows a coffee high. Coca also reduces hunger, thirst, headaches, stomach pains, and the type of altitude sickness known as *sorroche*.

Were this all, coca use might be viewed as merely a bad habit somewhat like drinking coffee, smoking cigarettes, or overindulging in chocolates, but unlike these practices coca actually has a number of marked health benefits. The coca leaf is very high in calcium. In a population with widespread lactose intolerance and in a country without a national system of milk distribution, this calcium source is very important. The calcium also severely reduces cavities in a population with virtually no dental services outside the city. Coca also contains large amounts of vitamins A, C, and D, which are often lacking in the starchy diets of the mountain peasants.

Without coca, and with an excess of corn that they cannot get to market, the people of Pocona now make more *chicha*, a form of home-fermented corn beer that tastes somewhat like the silage that American dairymen feed their cows. It is ironic that as an affluent generation of Americans are decreasing their consumption of alcohol in favor of drugs such as cocaine, the people of Pocona are drinking more alcohol to replace their traditional coca. *Chicha*, like most beers, is more nutritious than other kinds of distilled spirits but lacks the health benefits of the coca leaves. It also produces intoxication, something that no amount of coca leaves can do. Coca chewing is such a slow process and produces such a mild effect that a user would have to chew a bushel of leaves to equal the impact of one mixed drink or one snort of cocaine.

In many ways, the problems and complaints of Pocona echo those of any Third World country with a cash crop, particularly those caught in the boom-and-bust cycle characteristic of capitalist systems. Whether it is the sisal boom of the Yucatan, the banana boom of Central America, the rubber boom of Brazil, or the cocaine boom in Bolivia, the same pattern develops. Rural villages are depleted of their work forces. Family and traditional cultural patterns disintegrate. And the people are no longer able to afford certain local products that suddenly become valued in the West. This is what happened to Pocona.

Frequently, the part of a country that produces the boom crop benefits greatly, while other areas suffer greatly. If this were true in Bolivia, benefits accruing in the coca-producing area of the Chapare would outweigh the adjustment problems of such villages as Pocona. As it turns out, however, the Chapare has been even more adversely affected.

Most of the young men who go to the Chapare do not actually work in the coca fields. The coca bush originated in this area and does not require extensive care. One hectare can easily produce eight hundred kilograms of coca leaves in a year, but not much labor is needed to pick them. After harvesting, the leaves are dried in the sun for three to four days. Most of these tasks can easily be done by the farmer and his family. Wherever one goes in the Chapare one sees coca leaves spread out on large drying cloths. Old people or young children walk up and down these cloths, turning the drying leaves with their whisk brooms.

The need for labor, especially the labor of strong young men, comes in the first stage of cocaine production, in the reduction of large piles of leaves into a small quantity of *pasta*, or coca paste from which the active ingredient, cocaine, can then be refined. Three hundred to five hundred kilograms of leaves must be used to make one kilogram of pure cocaine. The leaves are made into *pasta* by soaking them in vats of kerosene and by applying salt, acetone, and sulfuric acid. To make the chemical reaction occur, someone must trample on the leaves for several days — a process very much like tromping on grapes to make wine, only longer. Because the corrosive mixture dissolves shoes or boots, the young men walk barefooted. These men are called *pisacocas* and usually work in the cool of the night, pounding the green slime with their feet. Each night the chemicals eat away more skin and very quickly open ulcers erupt. Some young men in the Chapare now have feet that are so diseased that they are incapable of standing, much less walking. So, instead, they use their hands to mix the *pasta*, but their hands are eaten away even faster than their feet. Thousands and possibly tens of thousands of young Bolivian men now look like lepers with permanently disfigured hands and feet. It is unlikely that any could return to Pocona and make a decent farmer.

Because this work is painful, the *pisacocas* smoke addictive cigarettes coated with *pasta*. This alleviates their pain and allows them to continue walking the coca throughout the night. The *pasta* is contaminated with chemical residues, and smoking it warps their minds as quickly as the acids eat their hands and feet. Like Mariana's brother, the users become irrational, easily angered, and frequently violent.

Once the boys are no longer able to mix coca because of their mental or their physical condition, they usually become unemployed. If their wounds heal, they may be able to work as loaders or haulers, carrying the cocaine or transporting the controlled chemicals used to process it. By and large, however, women and very small children called *hormigas* (ants), are better at this work. Some of the young men then return home to their villages; others wander to Cochabamba, where they might live on the streets or try to earn money buying and selling dollars on the black market.

The cocaine manufacturers not only supply their workers with food and drugs, they keep them sexually supplied with young girls who serve as prostitutes as well. Bolivian health officials estimate that nearly half of the people living in the Chapare today have venereal disease. As the boys and girls working there return to their villages, they take these diseases with them. Increasing numbers of children born to infected mothers now have bodies covered in syphilitic sores. In 1985, a worse disease hit with the first case of AIDS. Soon after the victim died, a second victim was diagnosed.

In an effort to control its own drug problem, the United States is putting pressure on Bolivia to eradicate coca production in the Andean countries. The army invaded the Chapare during January of 1986, but after nearly three weeks of being surrounded by the workers in the narcotics industry and cut off from their supply bases, the army surrendered. In a nation the size of Texas and California combined, but with a population approximately the size of the city of Chicago, it is difficult for the government to control its own territory. Neither the Incas nor the Spanish conquistadores were ever able to conquer and administer the jungles of Bolivia, where there are still nomadic bands of Indians who have retreated deep into the jungle to escape Western encroachment. The army of the poorest government in South America is no better able to control this country than its predecessors. The government runs the cities, but the countryside and the jungles operate under their own laws.

One of the most significant effects of the coca trade and of the campaigns to eradicate it has come on the most remote Indians of the jungle area. As the campaign against drugs has pushed production into more inaccessible places and as the world demand has promoted greater cultivation of coca, the coca growers are moving into previously unexplored areas. A coca plantation has been opened along the Chimore river less than an hour's walk from one of the few surviving bands of Yuqui Indians. The Yuquis, famous for their eight-foot-long bows and their six-foot arrows, are now hovering on the brink of extinction. In the past year, the three bands of a few hundred Yuquis have lost eleven members in skirmishes with outsiders. In turn, they killed several outsiders this year and even shot the missionary who is their main champion against outside invaders.

According to the reports of missionaries, other Indian bands have been enlisted as workers in cocaine production and trafficking, making virtual slaves out of them. A Bolivian medical doctor explained to me that the Indians are fed the cocaine in their food as a way of keeping them working and preventing their escape. Through cocaine, the drug traffickers may be able to conquer and control these last remnants of the great Indian nations of the Americas. If so, they will accomplish what many have failed to do in the five-hundred-year campaign of Europeans to conquer the free Indians.

The fate of the Indians driven out of their homelands is shown in the case of Juan, a thirteen-year-old Indian boy from the Chimore river where the Yuquis live. I found him one night in a soup kitchen for street children operated in the corner of a potato warehouse by the Maryknoll priests. Juan wore a bright orange undershirt that proclaimed in bold letters Fairfax District Public Schools. I sat with him at the table coated in potato dust while he ate his soup with his fellow street children, some of whom were as young as four years old. He told me what he could remember of his life on the Chimore; he did not know to which tribe he was born or what language he had spoken with his mother. It was difficult for Juan to talk about his Indian past in a country where it is a grave insult to be called an Indian. Rather than talk about the Chimore or the Chapare, he wanted to ask me questions because I was the first American he had ever met. Was I stronger than everyone else, because he had heard that Americans were the strongest people in the world? Did we really have wolves and bears in North America, and was I afraid of them? Had I been to the Chapare? Did I use cocaine?

In between his questions, I found out that Juan had come to Cochabamba several years ago with his mother. The two had fled the Chapare, but he did not know why. Once in the city they lived on the streets for a few years until his mother died, and he had been living alone ever since. He had become a *polilla* (moth), as they call such street boys. To earn money he washed cars and sold cigarettes laced with *pasta*. When he tired of talking about himself and asking about the animals of North America, he and his two friends made plans to go out to one of the nearby *pasta* villages the next day.

Both the Chapare (which supplied the land for growing coca) and highland villages such as Pocona (which supplied the labor) were suffering from the cocaine boom. Where, then, is the profit? The only other sites in Bolivia are the newly developed manufacturing towns where cocaine is refined. Whereas in the past most of this refining took place in Colombia, both the manufacturers and the traffickers find it easier and cheaper to have the work done in Bolivia, closer to the source of coca leaves and closer to much cheaper sources of labor. The strength of the Colombian government and its closeness to the United States also make the drug trafficking more difficult there than in Bolivia, with its weak, unstable government in La Paz.

Toco is one of the villages that has turned into a processing point for cocaine. Located at about the same altitude as Pocona but only a half-day by truck from the Chapare, Toco cannot grow coca, but the village is close enough to the source to become a major producer of the *pasta*. Traffickers bring in large shipments of coca leaves and work them in backyard "kitchens." Not only does Toco still have its young men at home and still have food and electricity, but it has work for a few hundred young men from other villages.

Unlike Pocona, for which there are only a few trucks each week, trucks flow in and out of Toco every day. Emblazoned with names such as Rambo, El Padrino (The Godfather), and Charles Bronson rather than the traditional truck names of San José, Virgen de Copacabana, or Flor de Urkupina, these are the newest and finest trucks found in Bolivia. Going in with a Bolivian physician and another anthropologist from the United States, I easily got a ride, along with a dozen Indians on a truck, which was hauling old car batteries splattered with what appeared to be vomit.

A few kilometers outside of Toco we were stopped by a large crowd of Indian peasants. Several dozen women sat around on the ground and in the road spinning yarn and knitting. Most of the women had babies tied to their shoulders in the brightly colored *awayu* cloth, which the women use to carry everything from potatoes to lambs. Men stood around with farm tools, which they now used to block the roads. The men brandished their machetes and rakes at us, accusing us all of being smugglers and *pisacocas*. Like the Indians on the truck with us, the three of us stood silent and expressionless in the melee.

The hostile peasants were staging an ad hoc strike against the coca trade. They had just had their own fields of potatoes washed away in a flash flood. Now without food and without money to replant, they were demanding that someone help them or they would disrupt all traffic to and from Toco. Shouting at us, several of them climbed on board the truck. Moving among the nervous passengers, they checked for a shipment of coca leaves, kerosene, acid, or anything else that might be a part of the coca trade. Having found nothing, they reluctantly let us pass with stern warnings not to return with cocaine or *pasta*. A few weeks after our encounter with the strikers, their strike ended and most of the men went off to look for work in the Chapare and in Toco; without a crop, the cocaine traffic was their only hope of food for the year.

On our arrival in Toco we found out that the batteries loaded with us in the back of the truck had been hollowed out and filled with acid to be used in making *pasta*. *Chicha* vomit had been smeared around to discourage anyone from checking them. After removal of the acid, the same batteries were then filled with plastic bags of cocaine to be smuggled out of Toco and into the town of Cliza and on to Cochabamba and the outside world.

Toco is an expanding village with new cement-block buildings going up on the edge of town and a variety of large plumbing pipes, tanks, and drains being installed. It also has a large number of motorcycles and cars. By Bolivian standards it is a rich village, but it is still poorer than the average village in Mexico or Brazil. Soon after our arrival in Toco, we were followed by a handful of men wanting to sell us *pasta*, and within a few minutes the few had grown to nearly fifty young men anxious to assist us. Most of them were on foot, but some of them circled us in motorcycles, and many of them were armed with guns and machetes. They became suspicious and then openly hostile when we convinced them that we did not want to buy *pasta*. To escape them we took refuge in the home of an Indian family and waited for the mob to disperse.

When we tried to leave the village a few hours later, we were trapped by a truckload of young men who did not release us until they had checked with everyone we had met with in the village. They wondered why we were there if not to buy *pasta*. We were rescued by the doctor who accompanied us; she happened to be the niece of a popular Quechua writer. Evoking the memory of her uncle who had done so much for the Quechua people, she convinced the villagers of Toco that we were Bolivian doctors who worked with her in Cochabamba, and that we were not foreigners coming to buy *pasta* or to spy on them. An old veteran who claimed that he had served in the Chaco War with her uncle vouched for us, but in return for having saved us he then wanted us to buy *pasta* from him.

The wealth generated by the coca trade from Bolivia is easy to see. It is in the European cars cruising the streets of Cochabamba and Santa Cruz, and in the nice houses in the suburbs. It is in the motorcycles and jeeps in Toco, Cliza, and Trinidad. The poverty is difficult to see because it is in the remote villages like Pocona, among the impoverished miners in the village of Porco, and intertwined in the lives of peasants throughout the highland districts of Potosi and Oruro. But it is in these communities such as Pocona that 70 percent of the population of Bolivia lives. For every modern home built with cocaine money in Cochabamba, a tin mine lies abandoned in Potosi that lost many of its miners when the world price for tin fell and they had to go to the Chapare for food. For every new car in Santa Cruz or every new motorcycle in Toco, a whole village is going hungry in the mountains.

The money for coca does not go to the Bolivians. It goes to the criminal organizations that smuggle the drugs out of the country and into the United States and Europe. A gram of pure cocaine on the streets of Cochabamba costs five dollars; the same gram on the streets of New York, Paris, or Berlin costs over a hundred dollars. The price increase occurs outside Bolivia.

The financial differential is evident in the case of the American housewife and mother sentenced to the Cochabamba prison after being caught with six and a half kilograms of cocaine at the airport. Like all the other women in the prison, she now earns money washing laundry by hand at a cold-water tap in the middle of the prison yard. She receives the equivalent of twenty cents for each pair of pants she washes, dries, and irons. In Bolivian prisons, the prisoner has to furnish his or her own food, clothes, medical attention, and even furniture.

She was paid five thousand dollars to smuggle the cocaine out of Bolivia to the Caribbean. Presumably someone else was then to be paid even more to smuggle it into the United States or Europe. The money that the American housewife received to smuggle the cocaine out of the country would pay the salary of eighty *pisacocas* for a month. It would also pay the monthly wages of two hundred fifty Bolivian schoolteachers, who earn the equivalent of twenty U.S. dollars per month in pay. Even though her price seemed high by Bolivian standards, it is a small part of the final money generated by the drugs. When cut and sold on the streets of the United States, her shipment of cocaine would probably bring in five to seven million dollars. Of that amount, however, only about five hundred dollars goes to the Bolivian farmer.

The peasant in the Chapare growing the coca earns three times as much for a field of coca as he would for a field of papayas. But he is only the first in a long line of people and transactions that brings the final product of cocaine to the streets of the West. At the end of the line, cocaine sells for four to five times its weight in gold.

The United States government made all aid programs and loans to Bolivia dependent on the country's efforts to destroy coca. This produces programs in which Bolivian troops go into the most accessible areas and uproot a few fields of aging or diseased coca plants. Visiting drug-enforcement agents from the United States together with American congressmen applaud, make their reports on the escalating war against drugs, and then retire to a city hotel where they drink hot cups of coca tea and cocktails.

These programs hurt primarily the poor farmer who tries to make a slightly better living by growing coca rather than papayas. The raids on the fields and cocaine factories usually lead to the imprisonment of ulcerated *pisacocas* and women and children *hormigas* from villages throughout Bolivia. Local authorities present the burned fields and full prisons to Washington visitors as proof that the Bolivian government has taken a hard stance against drug trafficking.

International crime figures with bank accounts in New York and Zurich get the money. Bolivia ends up with hunger in its villages, young men with their hands and feet permanently maimed, higher rates of venereal disease, chronic food shortages, less kerosene, higher school dropout rates, increased drug addiction, and a worthless peso.

REVIEW QUESTIONS

1. List and describe the major effects of the cocaine trade on rural Bolivian life.
2. Why has the production of coca and the manufacture of cocaine created a health hazard in Bolivia?
3. Why has the cocaine trade benefited the Bolivian economy so little?
4. How has the cocaine trade disrupted village social organization in Bolivia?

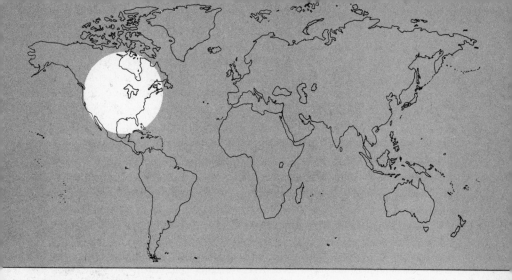

36 Using Anthropology

DAVID W. McCURDY

*Some disciplines, such as economics, have an obvious relationship
to the nonacademic world. Economic theory, although generated as
part of basic research, may often prove useful for understanding
the "real" economy. Anthropology, on the other hand, does not
seem so applicable. In this article, David McCurdy discusses some
of the professional applications of anthropology and argues that
there is a basic anthropological perspective that can help anyone
cope with the everyday world. He uses the case of a company
manager to illustrate this point, asserting that ethnographic "qualitative" research is an important tool for use in the nonacademic
world.*

Recently, a student, whom I had not seen for fifteen years, stopped
by my office. He had returned for his college reunion and thought it
would be interesting to catch up on news about his (and my) major
department, anthropology. The conversation, however, soon shifted
from college events to his own life. Following graduation and a stint
in the Peace Corps, he noted, he had begun to study for his license as
a ship's engineer. He had attended the Maritime Academy, and worked
for years on freighters. He was finally granted his license, he continued, and currently held the engineer's position on a container ship

This article was adapted from "The Shrink-Wrap Solution: Anthropology and Business,"
by David W. McCurdy and Donna F. Carlson in *Conformity and Conflict: Readings in
Cultural Anthropology,* 5th ed. (Boston: Little, Brown and Company, 1983). It was
written especially for this volume. Copyright © 1990 by David W. McCurdy.

that made regular trips between Seattle and Alaska. He soon would be promoted to chief engineer and be at the top of his profession.

As he talked, he made an observation about anthropology that may seem surprising. His background in the discipline, he said, had helped him significantly in his work. He found it useful as he went about his daily tasks, maintaining his ship's complex engines and machinery, his relationships with the crew, and his contacts with land-based management.

And his is not an unusual case. Over the years, several anthropology graduates have made the same observation. One, for example, is a community organizer who feels that the cross-cultural perspective he learned in anthropology helps him mediate disputes and facilitate decision making in a multiethnic neighborhood. Another, who works as an advertising account executive, claims that anthropology helps her discover what products mean to customers. This, in turn, permits her to design more effective ad campaigns. A third says she finds anthropology an invaluable tool as she arranges interviews and writes copy. She is a producer for a metropolitan television news program. I have heard the same opinion expressed by many others, including the executive editor of a magazine for home weavers, the founder of a fencing school, a housewife, a physician, several lawyers, the kitchen manager for a catering firm, and a high school teacher.

The idea that anthropology can be useful is also supported by the experience of many new Ph.Ds. A recent survey has shown, for the first time, that more new doctorates in anthropology find employment in professional settings than in college teaching or scholarly research, and the list of nonacademic work settings revealed by the survey is remarkably broad. There is a biological anthropologist, for example, who conducts research on nutrition for a company that manufactures infant formula. A cultural anthropologist works for a major car manufacturer, researching such questions as how employees adapt to working overseas, and how they relate to conditions on domestic production lines. Others formulate government policy, plan patient care in hospitals, design overseas development projects, run famine relief programs, consult on tropical forest management, and advise on product development, advertising campaigns, and marketing strategy for corporations.

This new-found application of cultural anthropology comes as a surprise to many Americans. Unlike political science, for example, which has a name that logically connects it with practical political and legal professions, there is nothing in the term *anthropology* that tells most Americans how it might be useful.

The research subject of anthropology also makes it more difficult to comprehend. Political scientists investigate political processes, structures, and motivations. Economists look at the production and exchange of goods and services. Psychologists study differences and similarities among individuals. The research of cultural anthropologists, on the other hand, is more difficult to characterize. Instead of a focus on particular human institutions, such as politics, law, and economics, anthropologists are interested in cross-cultural differences and similarities among the world's many groups.

This interest produces a broad view of human behavior that gives anthropology its special cross-cultural flavor. It also produces a unique research strategy, called ethnography, that tends to be qualitative rather than quantitative. Whereas other social sciences moved toward *quantitative* methods of research designed to test theory by using survey questionnaires and structured, repetitive observations, most anthropologists conduct *qualitative* research designed to elicit the cultural knowledge of the people they seek to understand. To do this, anthropologists often live and work with their subjects, called *informants* within the discipline. The result is a highly detailed ethnographic description of the categories and rules people consult when they behave, and the meanings that things and actions have for them.

It is this ethnographic approach, or cultural perspective, that I think makes anthropology useful in such a broad range of everyday settings. I particularly find important the special anthropological understanding of the culture concept, ethnographic field methods, and social analysis. To illustrate these assertions, let us take a single case in detail, that of a manager working for a large corporation who consciously used the ethnographic approach to solve a persistent company problem.

THE PROBLEM

The manager, whom we will name Susan Stanton, works for a large multinational corporation called UTC (not the company's real name). UTC is divided into a number of parts, including divisions, subdivisions, departments, and other units designed to facilitate its highly varied business enterprises. The company is well diversified, engaging in research, manufacturing, and customer services. In addition to serving a wide cross-section of public and private customers, it also works on a variety of government contracts for both military and nonmilitary agencies.

One of its divisions is educational. UTC has established a large number of customer outlets in cities throughout the United States, forming what it calls its "customer outlet network." They are staffed by educational personnel who are trained to offer a variety of special courses and enrichment programs. These courses and programs are marketed mainly to other businesses or to individuals who desire special training or practical information. For example, a small company might have UTC provide its employees with computer training, including instruction on hardware, programming, computer languages, and computer program applications. Another company might ask for instruction on effective management or accounting procedures. The outlets' courses for individuals include such topics as how to get a job, writing a resume, or enlarging your own business.

To organize and manage its customer outlet network, UTC has created a special division. The division office is located at the corporate headquarters and is responsible for developing new courses, improving old ones, training customer outlet personnel, and marketing customer outlet courses, or "products" as they are called inside the company. The division also has departments that develop, produce, and distribute the special learning materials used in customer outlet courses. These include books, pamphlets, video and audio tapes and cassettes, slides, overlays, and films. These materials are stored in a warehouse and are shipped, as they are ordered, to customer outlets around the country.

It is with this division that Susan Stanton first worked as a manager. She had started her career with the company in a small section of the division that designed various program materials. She had worked her way into management, holding a series of increasingly important positions. She was then asked to take over the management of a part of the division that had the manufacture, storage, and shipment of learning materials as one of its responsibilities.

But there was a catch. She was given this new management position with instructions to solve a persistent, although vaguely defined, problem. "Improve the service," they had told her, and "get control of the warehouse inventory." In this case, "service" meant the process of filling orders sent in by customer outlets for various materials stored in the warehouse. The admonition to improve the service seemed to indicate that service was poor, but all she was told about the situation was that customer outlet personnel complained about the service; she did not know exactly why or what "poor" meant.

In addition, inventory was "out of control." Later she was to discover the extent of the difficulty.

> We had a problem with inventory. The computer would say we had two hundred of some kind of book in stock, yet it was back ordered because there was nothing on the shelf. We were supposed to have the book but physically there was nothing there. I'm going, "Uh, we have a small problem. The computer never lies, like your bank statement, so why don't we have the books?"

If inventory was difficult to manage, so were the warehouse employees. They were described by another manager as "a bunch of knuckle draggers. All they care about is getting their money. They are lazy and don't last long at the job." Strangely, the company did not view the actions of the warehouse workers as a major problem. Only later did Susan Stanton tie in poor morale in the warehouse with the other problems she had been given to solve.

MANAGEMENT BY DEFENSE

Although Stanton would take the ethnographic approach to management problems, that was not what many other managers did. They took a defensive stance, a position opposite to the discovery procedures of ethnography. Their major concern — like that of many people in positions of leadership and responsibility — was to protect their authority and their ability to manage and to get things done. Indeed, Stanton also shared this need. But their solution to maintaining their position was different from hers. For them, claiming ignorance and asking questions — the hallmark of the ethnographic approach — is a sign of weakness. Instead of discovering what is going on when they take on a new management assignment, they often impose new work rules and procedures. Employees learn to fear the arrival of new managers because their appearance usually means a host of new, unrealistic demands. They respond by hiding what they actually do, withholding information that would be useful to the manager. Usually, everyone's performance suffers.

Poor performance leads to elaborate excuses as managers attempt to blame the troubles on others. Stanton described this tendency.

> When I came into the new job, this other manager said, "Guess what? You have got a warehouse. You are now the proud owner of a forklift and a bunch of knuckle draggers." And I thought, management's perception of those people is very low. They are treating them as dispensable, that you can't do anything with them. They say the workers don't have any career motives. They don't care if they do a good job. You have to force them to do anything. You can't motivate them. It's only a warehouse, other managers were saying. You can't really do that much about the problems there so why don't you just sort of try to keep it under control.

Other managers diminished the importance of the problem itself. It was not "poor service" that was the trouble. The warehouse was doing the best it could with what it had. It was just the customers — the staff at the customer outlets — were complainers. As Susan Stanton noted:

The people providing the service thought that outlet staff were complainers. They said, "Staff complain about everything. But it can't be that way. We have checked it all out and it isn't that bad."

Making excuses and blaming others leads to low morale and a depressed self-image. Problems essentially are pushed aside in favor of a "let's just get by" philosophy.

ETHNOGRAPHIC MANAGEMENT

By contrast, managers take the offensive when they use ethnographic techniques. That is what Stanton did when she assumed her new managerial assignment over the learning materials manufacturing and distribution system. To understand what the ethnographic approach means, however, we must first look briefly at what anthropologists do when they conduct ethnographic field research. Our discussion necessarily involves a look at the concepts of culture and microculture as well as ethnography. For as we will shortly point out, companies have cultures of their own, a point that has recently received national attention; but more important for the problem we are describing here, companies are normally divided into subgroups, each with its own microculture. It is these cultures and microcultures that anthropologically trained managers can study ethnographically, just as fieldworkers might investigate the culture of a !Kung band living in the Kalahari Desert of West Africa or the Gypsies living in San Francisco.

Ethnography refers to the process of discovering and describing culture, so it is important to discuss this general and often elusive concept. There are numerous definitions of culture, each stressing particular sets of attributes. The definition we employ here is especially appropriate for ethnographic fieldwork. We may define culture as the acquired knowledge that people use to generate behavior and interpret experience. In growing up, one learns a system of cultural knowledge appropriate to the group. For example, an American child learns to chew with a closed mouth because that is the cultural rule. The child's parents interpret open-mouthed chewing as an infraction and tell the child to chew "properly." A person uses such cultural knowledge throughout life to guide actions and to give meaning to surroundings.

Because culture is learned, and because people can easily generate new cultural knowledge as they adapt to other people and things, human behavior and perceptions can vary dramatically from one group to another. In India, for example, children learn to chew "properly" with their mouths open. Their cultural worlds are quite different from the ones found in the United States.

Cultures are associated with groups of people. Traditionally, anthropologists associated culture with relatively distinctive ethnic groups. Culture referred to the whole life-way of a society and particular cultures could be named. Anthropologists talked of German culture, Ibo culture, and Bhil culture. Culture was everything that was distinctive about the group.

Culture is still applied in this manner today, but with the advent of complex societies and a growing interest among anthropologists in understanding them, the culture concept has also been used in a more limited way. Complex societies such as our own are composed of thousands of groups. Members of these groups usually share the national culture, including a language and a huge inventory of knowledge for doing things, but the groups themselves have specific cultures of their own. For example, if you were to walk into the regional office of a stock brokerage firm, you would hear the people there talking an apparently foreign language. You might stand in the "bull pen," listen to brokers make "cold calls," "sell short," "negotiate a waffle," or get ready to go to a "dog and pony show." The fact that events such as this feel strange when you first encounter them is strong evidence to support the notion that you don't yet know the culture that organizes them. We call such specialized groups "microcultures."

We are surrounded by microcultures, participating in a few, encountering many others. Our family has a microculture. So may our neighborhood, our college, and even our dormitory floor. The waitress who serves us lunch at the corner restaurant shares a culture with her coworkers. So do bank tellers at our local savings and loan. Kin, occupational groups, and recreational associations each tend to display special microcultures. Such cultures can be, and now often are, studied by anthropologists interested in understanding life in complex American society.

The concept of microculture is essential to Susan Stanton as she begins to attack management problems at UTC because she assumes that conflict between different microcultural groups is most likely at the bottom of the difficulty. One microculture she could focus on is UTC company culture. She knows, for example, that there are a variety of rules and expectations — written and unwritten — for how things should be done at the company. She must dress in her "corporates," for example, consisting of a neutral-colored suit, bow tie, stockings, and conservative shoes. UTC also espouses values about the way employees should be treated, how people are supposed to feel about company products, and a variety of other things that set that particular organization apart from other businesses.

But the specific problems that afflicted the departments under Stanton's jurisdiction had little to do with UTC's corporate culture. They seemed rather to be the result of misunderstanding and misconnection between two units, the warehouse and the customer outlets. Each had its own microculture. Each could be investigated to discover any information that might lead to a solution of the problems she had been given.

Such investigation would depend on the extent of Stanton's ethnographic training. As an undergraduate in college, she had learned how to conduct ethnographic interviews, observe behavior, and analyze and interpret data. She was not a professional anthropologist, but she felt she was a good enough ethnographer to discover some relevant aspects of microcultures at UTC.

Ethnography is the process of discovering and describing a culture. For example, an anthropologist who travels to India to conduct a study of village culture will use ethnographic techniques. The anthropologist will move into a community, occupy a house, watch people's daily routines, attend rituals, and spend hours interviewing informants. The goal is to discover a detailed picture of what is going on by seeing village culture through the eyes of informants. The anthropologist wants the insider's perspective. Villagers become teachers, patiently explaining different aspects of their culture, praising the anthropologist for acting correctly and appearing to understand, laughing when the anthropologist makes mistakes or seems confused. When the anthropologist knows what to do and can explain in local terms what is going on or what is likely to happen, real progress has been made. The clearest evidence of such progress is when informants say, "You are almost human now," or "You are beginning to talk just like us."

The greatest enemy of good ethnography is the preconceived notion. Anthropologists do not conduct ethnographic research by telling informants what they are like based on earlier views of them. They teach the anthropologist how to see their world: the anthropologist does not tell them what their world should really be like. All too often in business, a new manager will take over a department and begin to impose changes on its personnel to fit a preconceived perception of them. The fact that the manager's efforts are likely to fail makes sense in light of this ignorance. The manager doesn't know their microculture. Nor have they been asked about it.

But can a corporate manager really do ethnography? After all, managers have positions of authority to maintain, as we noted earlier. It is all right for professional anthropologists to enter the field and act ignorant; they don't have a position to maintain and they don't have to continue to live with their informants. The key to the problem appears to be the "grace period." Most managers are given one by their employees when they are new on the job. A new manager cannot be expected to know everything. It is permissible to ask basic questions. The grace period may last only a month or two, but it is usually long enough to find out valuable information.

This is the opportunity that Susan Stanton saw as she assumed direction of the warehouse distribution system. As she described it:

I could use the first month, actually the first six weeks, to find out what was going on, to act dumb and find out what people actually did and why. I talked to end customers. I talked to salespeople, people who were trying to sell things to help customer outlets with their needs. I talked to coordinators at headquarters staff who were trying to help all these customer outlets do their jobs and listened to what kinds of complaints they had heard. I talked to the customer outlet people and the guys in the warehouse. I had this six-week grace period where I could go in and say, "I don't know anything about this. If you were in my position, what would you do, or what would make the biggest difference, and why would it make a difference?" You want to find out what the world they are operating in is like. What do they value. And people were excited because I was asking and listening and, by God, intending to do something about it instead of just disappearing again.

As we shall see shortly, Stanton's approach to the problem worked. But it also resulted in an unexpected bonus. Her ethnographic approach symbolized unexpected interest and concern to her employees. That, combined with realistic management, gave her a position of respect and authority. Their feelings for her were expressed by one warehouse worker when he said:

When she [Susan] was going to be transferred to another job, we gave her a party. We took her to this country-and-western place and we all got to dance with the boss. We told her that she was the first manager who ever tried to understand what it was like to work in the warehouse. We thought she would come in like the other managers and make a lot of changes that didn't make sense. But she didn't. She made it work better for us.

PROBLEMS AND CAUSES

An immediate benefit of her ethnographic inquiry was a much clearer view of what poor service meant to customer outlet personnel. Stanton discovered that learning materials, such as books and cassettes, took too long to arrive after they were ordered. Worse, material did not arrive in the correct quantities. Sometimes there would be too many items, but more often there were too few, a particularly galling discrepancy since customer outlets were charged for what they ordered, not what they received. Books also arrived in poor condition, their covers ripped or scratched, edges frayed, and ends gouged and dented. This, too, bothered customer outlet staff because they were often visited by potential customers who were not impressed by the poor condition of their supplies. Shortages and scruffy books did nothing to retain regular customers either.

The causes of these problems and the difficulties with warehouse inventory also emerged from ethnographic inquiry. Stanton discovered, for example, that most customer outlets operated in large cities, where often they were housed in tall buildings. Materials shipped to their office address often ended up sitting in ground-level lobbies, because few of the buildings had receiving docks or facilities. Books and other items also arrived in large boxes, weighing up to a hundred pounds. Outlet staff, most of whom were women, had to go down to the lobby, open those boxes that were too heavy for them to carry, and haul armloads of supplies up the elevator to the office. Not only was this time-consuming, but customer outlet staff felt it was beneath their dignity to do such work. They were educated specialists, after all.

The poor condition of the books was also readily explained. By packing items loosely in such large boxes, warehouse workers ensured trouble in transit. Books rattled around with ease, smashing into each other and the side of the box, resulting in torn covers and frayed edges. Clearly no one had designed the packing and shipping process with customer outlet staff in mind.

The process, of course, originated in the central warehouse, and here as well, ethnographic data yielded interesting information about the causes of the problem. Stanton learned, for example, how materials were stored in loose stacks on the warehouse shelves. When orders, usually through the mail, arrived at the warehouse, they were placed in a pile and filled in turn (although there were times when special preference was given to some customer outlets). A warehouse employee filled an order by first checking it against the stock recorded by the computer, then by going to the appropriate shelves and picking the items by hand. Items were packed in the large boxes and addressed to customer outlets. With the order complete, the employee was supposed to enter the number of items picked and shipped in the computer so that inventory would be up to date.

But, Stanton discovered, workers in the warehouse were under pressure to work quickly. They often fell behind because materials the computer said were in stock were not there, and because picking by hand took so long. Their solution to the problem of speed resulted in a procedure that even further confused company records.

> Most of the people in the warehouse didn't try to count well. People were looking at the books on the shelves and were going, "Eh, that looks like the right number. You want ten? Gee, that looks like about ten." Most of the time the numbers they shipped were wrong.

The causes of inaccurate amounts in shipping were thus revealed. Later, Stanton discovered that books also disappeared in customer outlet building lobbies. While staff members carried some of the materials upstairs, people passing by the open boxes helped themselves.

Other problems with inventory also became clear. UTC employees, who sometimes walked through the warehouse, would often pick up interesting materials from the loosely stacked shelves. More important, rushed workers often neglected to update records in the computer.

THE SHRINK-WRAP SOLUTION

The detailed discovery of the nature and causes of service and inventory problems suggested a relatively painless solution to Stanton. If she had taken a defensive management position and failed to learn the insider's point of view, she might have resorted to more usual remedies that were impractical and unworkable. Worker retraining is a common answer to corporate difficulties, but it is difficult to accomplish and often fails. Pay incentives, punishments, and motivation enhancements such as prizes and quotas are also frequently tried. But they tend not to work because they don't address fundamental causes.

Shrink-wrapping books and other materials did. Shrink-wrapping is a packaging device that emerged a few years ago. Clear plastic sheeting is placed around items to be packaged, then through a rapid heating and cooling process, shrunk into a tight covering. The plastic molds itself like a tight skin around the things it contains, preventing any internal movement or external contamination. Stanton described her decision.

> I decided to have the books shrink-wrapped. For a few cents more, before the books ever arrived in the warehouse, I had them shrink-wrapped in quantities of five and ten. I made it part of the contract with the people who produced the books for us.

On the first day that shrink-wrapped books arrived at the warehouse, Stanton discovered that they were immediately unwrapped by workers who thought a new impediment had been placed in their way. But the positive effect of shrink-wrapping soon became apparent. For example, most customer outlets ordered books in units of fives and tens. Warehouse personnel could now easily count out orders in fives and tens, instead of having to count each book or estimate numbers in piles. Suddenly, orders filled at the warehouse contained the correct number of items.

Employees were also able to work more quickly, since they no longer had to count each book. Orders were filled faster, pleasing customer outlet staff, and warehouse employees no longer felt the pressure of time so intensely. Shrink-wrapped materials also traveled more securely. Books, protected by their plastic covering, arrived in good condition, again delighting the personnel at customer outlets.

Stanton also changed the way materials were shipped, based on what she had learned from talking to employees. She limited the maximum size of shipments to twenty-five pounds by using smaller boxes. She also had packages marked "inside delivery" so that deliverymen would carry the materials directly to the customer outlet offices. If they failed to do so, boxes were light enough to carry upstairs. No longer would items be lost in skyscraper lobbies.

Inventory control became more effective. Because they could package and ship materials more quickly, the workers in the warehouse had enough time to enter the size and nature of shipments in the computer. Other UTC employees no longer walked off with books from the warehouse, because the shrink-wrapped bundles were larger and more conspicuous, and because taking five or ten books is more like stealing than "borrowing" one.

Finally, the improved service dramatically changed morale in the division. Customer outlet staff members, with their new and improved service, felt that finally someone had cared about them. They were more positive and they let people at corporate headquarters know about their feelings. "What's happening down there?" they asked. "The guys in the warehouse must be taking vitamins."

Morale soared in the warehouse. For the first time, other people liked the service workers there provided. Turnover decreased as pride in their work rose. They began to care more about the job, working faster with greater care. Managers who had previously given up on the "knuckle draggers" now asked openly about what had gotten into them.

Stanton believes the ethnographic approach is the key. She has managers who work for her read anthropology, especially books on ethnography, and she insists that they "find out what is going on."

CONCLUSION

Anthropology is, before all, an academic discipline with a strong emphasis on scholarship and basic research. But, as we have also seen, anthropology is a discipline that contains several intellectual tools — the concept of culture, the ethnographic approach to fieldwork, a cross-cultural perspective, a holistic view of human behavior — that make it useful in a broad range of nonacademic settings. In particular, it is the ability to do qualitative research that makes anthropologists successful in the professional world.

A few years ago an anthropologist consultant was asked by a utility company to answer a puzzling question. Why were its suburban customers, whose questionnaire responses indicated an attempt at conservation, failing to reduce their consumption of natural gas? To answer the question, the anthropologist conducted ethnographic interviews with members of several families, listening as they told him about how warm they liked their houses and how they set the heat throughout the day. He also received permission to install several video cameras aimed at thermostats in private houses. When the results were in, the answer to the question was deceptively simple. Fathers fill out questionnaires and turn down thermostats; wives, children, and cleaning workers, all of whom, in this case, spent time in the houses when fathers were absent, turn them up. Conservation, the anthropologist concluded, would have to involve family decisions, not just admonitions to save gas. The key to this anthropologist's success, and indeed to the application of cultural anthropology by those acquainted with it, is the ethnographic approach. For it is people with experience in the discipline who have the special background needed to, in the words of Susan Stanton, "find out what is going on."

REVIEW QUESTIONS

1. What kinds of jobs do professional anthropologists do?
2. What is special about anthropology that makes it suitable for some jobs?
3. What is meant by qualitative research? Why is such research valuable to business and government?
4. What difficulties did the company manager described in this article face? What solutions did she invent to deal with them? How did her knowledge of anthropology help her with this problem?
5. Why is ethnography useful in everyday life? Can you think of situations in which you could use ethnographic research?

Glossary

A

Acculturation. The process that takes place when groups of individuals having different cultures come into first-hand contact, which results in change to the cultural patterns of both groups.

Action Anthropology. Any use of anthropological knowledge for planned change by the members of a local cultural group.

Adjustment Anthropology. Any use of anthropological knowledge that makes social interaction between persons who operate with different cultural codes more predictable.

Administrative Anthropology. The use of anthropological knowledge for planned change by those who are external to a local cultural group.

Advocate Anthropology. Any use of anthropological knowledge by the anthropologist to increase the power of self-determination for a particular cultural group.

Affinity. A fundamental principle of relationship linking kin through marriage.

Agriculture. A subsistence strategy involving intensive farming of permanent fields through the use of such means as the plow, irrigation, and fertilizer.

Allocation of Resources. The knowledge people use to assign rights to the ownership and use of resources.

Applied Anthropology. Any use of anthropological knowledge to influence social interaction, to maintain or change social institutions, or to direct the course of cultural change.

B

Bilateral (Cognatic) Descent. A rule of descent relating someone to a group of consanguine kin through both males and females.

C

Caste. A form of stratification defined by unequal access to economic resources and prestige, which is acquired at birth and does not permit individuals to alter their rank.

Clan. A kinship group normally comprising several lineages; its members are related by a unilineal descent rule, but it is too large to enable members to trace actual biological links to all other members.

Class. A system of stratification defined by unequal access to economic resources and prestige, but permitting individuals to alter their rank.

Consanguinity. The principle of relationship linking individuals by shared ancestry (blood).

Contest. A method of settling disputes requiring disputants to engage in some kind of mutual challenge such as singing (as among the Inuit).

Cosmology. A set of beliefs that defines the nature of the universe or cosmos.

Court. A formal legal institution in which at least one individual has authority to judge and is backed up by a coercive system to enforce decisions.

Cultural Contact. The situation that occurs when two societies with different cultures somehow come in contact with each other.

Cultural Ecology. The study of the way people use their culture to adapt to particular environments, the effects they have on their natural surroundings, and the impact of the environment on the shape of culture, including its long-term evolution.

Cultural Environment. The categories and rules people use to classify and explain their physical environment.

Culture. The knowledge that is learned, shared, and used by people to interpret experience and generate behavior.

Culture Shock. A form of anxiety that results from an inability to predict the behavior of others or act appropriately in cross-cultural situations.

D

Descent. A rule of relationship that ties people together on the basis of reputed common ancestry.

Descent Groups. Groups based on a rule of descent.

Detached Observation. An approach to scientific inquiry stressing emotional detachment and the construction of categories by the observer in order to classify what is observed.

Diffusion. The passage of a cultural category, culturally defined behavior, or culturally produced artifact from one society to another through borrowing.

Distribution. The strategies for apportioning goods and services among the members of a group.

Divination. The use of supernatural force to provide answers to questions.

Division of Labor. The rules that govern the assignment of jobs to people.

E

Ecology. The study of the way organisms interact with each other within an environment.

Economic System. The provision of goods and services to meet biological and social wants.

Egalitarian Societies. Societies that, with the exception of ranked differences between men and women and adults and children, provide all people an equal chance at economic resources and prestige. Most hunter-gatherer societies are egalitarian by this definition.

Endogamy. Marriage within a designated social unit.

Ethnocentrism. A mixture of belief and feeling that ones own way of life is desirable and actually superior to others'.

Ethnography. The task of discovering and describing a particular culture.

Exogamy. Marriage outside any designated group.

Explicit Culture. The culture that people can talk about and of which they are aware. Opposite of tacit culture.

Extended Family. A family that includes two or more married couples.

Extralegal Dispute. A dispute that remains outside the process of law and develops into repeated acts of violence between groups, such as feuds and wars.

F

Family. A residential group composed of at least one married couple and their children.

G

Go-Between. An individual who arranges agreements and mediates disputes.

Grammar. The categories and rules for combining vocal symbols.

H

Horticulture.   A kind of subsistence strategy involving semi-intensive, usually shifting, agricultural practices. Slash-and-burn farming is a common example of horticulture.

Hunting and Gathering.   A subsistence strategy involving the foraging of wild, naturally occurring foods.

I

Incest Taboo.   The cultural rule that prohibits sexual intercourse and marriage between specified classes of relatives.

Industrialism.   A subsistence strategy marked by intensive, mechanized food production and elaborate distribution networks.

Inequality.   A human relationship marked by differences in power, authority, prestige, and access to valued goods and services, and by the payment of deference.

Informant.   A person who teaches his or her culture to an anthropologist.

Infralegal Dispute.   A dispute that occurs below or outside the legal process without involving regular violence.

Innovation.   A recombination of concepts from two or more mental configurations into a new pattern that is qualitatively different from existing forms.

K

Kinship.   The complex system of social relationships based on marriage (affinity) and birth (consanguinity).

L

Language.   The system of cultural knowledge used to generate and interpret speech.

Law.   The cultural knowledge that people use to settle disputes by means of agents who have recognized authority.

Lineage.   A kinship group based on a unilineal descent rule that is localized, has some corporate powers, and whose members can trace their actual relationships to each other.

M

Magic. Strategies people use to control supernatural power to achieve particular results.

Mana. An impersonal supernatural force inherent in nature and in people. Mana is somewhat like the concept of "luck" in American culture.

Market Exchange. The transfer of goods and services based on price, supply, and demand.

Marriage. The socially recognized union between a man and a woman that accords legitimate birth status rights to their children.

Matrilineal Descent. A rule of descent relating a person to a group of consanguine kin on the basis of descent through females only.

Microculture. The system of knowledge shared by members of a group that is part of a larger national society or ethnic group.

Monogamy. A marriage form in which a person is allowed only one spouse at a time.

Moot. A community meeting held for the informal hearing of a dispute.

Morpheme. The smallest meaningful category in any language.

Mythology. Stories that reveal the religious knowledge of how things have come into being.

N

Naive Realism. The notion that reality is much the same for all people everywhere.

Nonlinguistic Symbols. Any symbols that exist outside the system of language and speech; for example, visual symbols.

Nuclear Family. A family composed of a married couple and their children.

O

Ordeal. A supernaturally controlled, painful, or physically dangerous test, the outcome of which determines a person's guilt or innocence.

P

Pastoralism. A subsistence strategy based on the maintenance and use of large herds of animals.

Patrilineal Descent. A rule of descent relating consanguine kin on the basis of descent through males only.

Personified Supernatural Force. Supernatural force inherent in supernatural beings such as goddesses, gods, spirits, and ghosts.

Phoneme. The minimal category of speech sounds that signals a difference in meaning.

Phonology. The categories and rules for forming vocal symbols.

Phratry. A group composed of two or more clans. Members acknowledge unilineal descent from a common ancestor but recognize that their relationship is distant.

Physical Environment. The world as people experience it with their senses.

Policy. Any guideline that can lead directly to action.

Political System. The organization and process of making and carrying out public policy according to cultural categories and rules.

Polyandry. A form of polygamy in which a woman has two or more husbands at one time.

Polygamy. A marriage form in which a person has two or more spouses at one time. Polygyny and polyandry are both forms of polygamy.

Polygyny. A form of polygamy in which a man is married to two or more wives at one time.

Prayer. A petition directed at a supernatural being or power.

Priest. A full-time religious specialist who intervenes between people and the supernatural, and who often leads a congregation at regular cyclical rites.

Production. The process of making something.

Public. The group of people a policy will affect.

R

Racial Inequality. Inequality based on reputed biological characteristics of the members of different groups.

Ramage. A cognatic (bilateral) descent group that is localized and holds corporate responsibility.

Rank Societies. Societies stratified on the basis of prestige only.

Reciprocal Exchange. The transfer of goods and services between two people or groups based on their role obligations. A form of nonmarket exchange.

Redistribution. The transfer of goods and services between a group of people and a central collecting service based on role obligation. The U.S. income tax is a good example.

Religion. The cultural knowledge of the supernatural that people use to cope with the ultimate problems of human existence.

Respondent. An individual who responds to questions included on questionnaires; the subject of survey research.

Role. The culturally generated behavior associated with particular statuses.

S

Sacrifice. The giving of something of value to supernatural beings or forces.

Self-redress. The actions taken by an individual who has been wronged to settle a dispute.

Semantics. The categories and rules for relating vocal symbols to their referents.

Sexual Inequality. Inequality based on gender.

Shaman. A part-time religious specialist who controls supernatural power, often to cure people or affect the course of life's events.

Slash-and-Burn Agriculture. A form of horticulture in which wild land is cleared and burned over, farmed, then permitted to lie fallow and revert to its wild state.

Social Acceptance. A process that involves learning about an innovation, accepting an innovation as valid, and revising one's cultural knowledge to include the innovation.

Social Situation. The categories and rules for arranging and interpreting the settings in which social interaction occurs.

Sociolinguistic Rules. Rules specifying the nature of the speech community, the particular speech situations within a community, and the speech acts that members use to convey their messages.

Social Stratification. The ranking of people or groups based on their unequal access to valued economic resources and prestige.

Sorcery. The malevolent practice of magic.

Speech. The behavior that produces meaningful vocal sounds.

Spirit Possession. The control of a person by a supernatural being in which the person becomes that being.

Status. A culturally defined position associated with a particular social structure.

Stratified Societies. Societies that are at least partly organized on the principle of social stratification. Contrast with egalitarian and rank societies.

Subject. The person who is observed in a social or psychological experiment.

Subsistence Strategies. Strategies used by groups of people to exploit their environment for material necessities. Hunting and gathering, horticulture, pastoralism, agriculture, and industrialism are subsistence strategies.

Supernatural. Things that are beyond the natural. Anthropologists usually recognize a belief in such things as goddesses, gods, spirits, ghosts, and *mana* to be signs of supernatural belief.

Support. Anything that contributes to the adoption of public policy and its enforcement.

Symbol. Anything that humans can sense that is given an arbitrary relationship to its referent.

T

Tacit Culture. The shared knowledge of which people usually are unaware and do not communicate verbally.

Technology. The part of a culture that involves the knowledge that people use to make and use tools and to extract and refine raw materials.

Transcendent Values. Values that override differences in a society and unify the group.

U

Ultimate Problems. Universal human problems, such as death, the explanation of evil and the meaning of life, and transcendent values that can be answered by religion.

Unit of Production. The group of people responsible for producing something.

W

Witchcraft. The reputed activity of people who inherit supernatural force and use it for evil purposes.

World View. The way people characteristically look out on the universe.

Index

G

Galvin, Kathleen, 153
Gandhi, Mohandas K., 159, 166
Gender. *See* Male dominance; Sex
    roles; Women
Gender neutralization, 58
General-purpose money, 262, 270–72
Genetic code, 119
Ghosts, 367, 369
Gift exchange, 296
Giving, meanings of, 30–37. *See also*
    Reciprocity; Reciprocal ex-
    change
Gleason, H. A., 108
Go-between, 312
Goffman, Erving, 76
Goodale, Jane, 221
Grammar, 63
Grammatical effects on perception,
    105–107
Grazing, effects of, 155
Green sea turtles, 299–300, 303
Group, social, 177–78
Groups, descent, 184–87
Guahibo, 48–58
Guarani, 140–49
Guaranteed minimum income, 254

H

Hadza, 199, 234–35
Hall, Edward, 26–27
Hanunoo, 109
Harmony with nature, 385
Harris, Allen, 101
Hausa, 221–28
Headman, 322
    Guarani, 141, 146
Hekuras (Yanomamö forest spirits),
    317
Herding, 150–56, 329
Herero, 30–31
Hess, Eckhard, 68
Hicks, George, 22, 26
Hill tribes, 431–32
Hindi phonemes, 62
Hogbin, H. Ian, 335

Honor, for men and women, 245
Hopi, 105–107
Horticulture, 120–21
    Guarani example of, 139–49
    and women, 237
Howell, Nancy, 199
Human environment, 11
Human Relations Area Files, 5–6
Hunter/gatherers, 51, 120, 229–38,
    258, 425
    types of, 233–39
Hunter/gatherer value on equality,
    30–37
Hunting and gathering among the
    !Kung, 123–38

I

Illness, 387. *See also* Curing; Magic
Incest taboo, 175
India, 15–17, 218–19, 434–35
    place of cattle in, 157–70
Indians and cocaine production,
    453
Indo-European language family,
    110–11
Industrial explosion, 427–28
Industrial farming, 161
Industrial revolution and divorce,
    200
Industrial societies and women, 237
Industrialism, 121
Industrialization, effects on tribals
    of, 428–29
Inequality, 218–20
Infanticide, female, 193–94
Informant, 18. *See also* Respondent;
    Subject of experiment
Inflation as a result of cocaine pro-
    duction, 448–49
Infralegal dispute, 312
Innovation, 405
International languages, 109
Intimate speaking distance, 70
Iroquois, 4, 231
Islam, 222, 239
    and the seclusion of women, 241–
    42

J

Jacobs, Paul, 249–53
Joking behavior, 183–84
Jurisdiction, acquisition of in U.S.
Congress, 354

K

Kalahari desert, 124
Kanguijy (alcoholic beverage), 141
Kem (type of Tiv marriage), 265–66
Kenya, 150–56
Kin, kinds of, 181–83
Kin groups, 174
Kin terms, 181–83
Kinesics, 75
Kinsey, Alfred, 203
Kinship, 173, 178–79
Kinship roles, 183–84
Kinzel, Augustus, 69
Kohistani, 325
Kula ring, 295–96
!Kung (!Kung San), 30–37, 198–99,
231–32, 259
Kwakiutl, 4

L

Land tenure, among Marshallese,
185–87
Land use, 431–32
Language, 62
affect on perception of, 103–16
imprecision of, 115
international, 109
political, 114–15
subsystems of, 62–63
Law, 312
Leadership, 313, 322
League of Nations, 437
Legal domination, principle of, 38,
44–46
Legitimacy, 312
Legitimate authority, 41
Legs, styles of crossing, 74
Leisure, amount of, 131–32

Liebowitz, Michael, 202
Lineage, 174, 318, 365
Long-leg (influence of a powerful
person in Nigeria), 43
Lovedu, 231
Lovejoy, C. Owen, 205

M

Magic, 360, 365–72
and agriculture, 366
in baseball, 373–83
in life rites, 366
and sense of control, 383
for raising pigs, 366–67
as a way to reduce anxiety, 371–
83
Malaya, 230
Male dominance, 229–30, 233, 319,
417
Male power, 231–32
Malinowski, Bronislaw Kaspar, 221,
340, 371, 374, 383
Malo, David, 344
Mana (impersonal supernatural
force), 360
Management
by defense, 463–64
ethnographic approach to, 461–71
Mansren myth, 399
Mar dushmani (blood feud in Pakistan), 324–33
Market
intrusion of, 301–302
as a kind of exchange, 258
Marriage, 175, 190–97, 226–27
endogamous, 175
as exchange, 264
exogamous, 175
matrilateral cross-cousin, 318
monogamous, 202–204
patrilateral cross-cousin, 318
polyandrous, 175, 190–97
polygamous, 175
polygynous, 175
Marshall Islands, 177–78
Matrilineage, 185–86
Matrilineal descent, 174, 177–89

Want, economic, 257
Ward, Barbara, 10–11
Wards of state, tribal, 436–37
Washo, 233–34
Weber, Max, 39, 45–46
Wedgwood, Camilla, 335
Whorf, Benjamin Lee, 103–107
Witchcraft, 84, 360
Witches, 367–68
Women
  and children, 221–28
  community of, 212–15
  economic activities of, 224, 233
  and family, 208–15
  as foragers, 233
  in patrilineal systems, 208–15
  relative power of, 229–38
  seclusion of, 222, 240–42, 328–29.
    See also Purdah
  and work, among the !Kung, 134–
  35
World languages, 109

Y

Yanomamö, 201, 229–30, 315–23
Yerba mate (caffeinated tea), 143–45
Yir Yoront, 410–24
Yoruba, 199
Yuqui, 453–54

X

Xavante, 442

Z

Zebu cattle, 162–63
Zombie, 82–83